Grand Delusion

Grand Delusion

Stalin and the German Invasion of Russia

Gabriel Gorodetsky

Yale University Press
New Haven and London

Set in Palatino by Best-set Typesetter Ltd., Hong Kong
Printed in Great Britain by Biddles Ltd, Guildford and Kings Lynn

Library of Congress Cataloging in Publication Data

Gorodetsky, Gabriel, 1945–
    Grand delusion: Stalin and the German invasion of Russia / Gabriel Gorodetsky.
    Includes bibliographical references and index.
    ISBN 0–300–07792–0 (cloth: alk. paper)
    1. World War, 1939–1945—Soviet Union.   2. World War, 1939–1945—Diplomatic history.   3. Stalin, Joseph, 1879–1953.
    I. Title. D754.S65G67   1999   99–12728
    940.54′0947—dc21   CIP

A catalogue record for this book is available from the British Library.

10 9 8 7 6 5 4 3 2 1

Contents

Illustrations and Maps

Plates *between pages 208 and 209*

Photographs are from the author's collection unless specified otherwise.

Maps

Preface

Few events of the twentieth century compare in significance with Operation 'Barbarossa'. Its impact on the Second World War and its aftermath was enormous. Yet what springs to mind at the mention of the Ribbentrop–Molotov Pact and the German invasion of Russia is primarily anecdotal: Viacheslav Molotov, the Soviet Commissar for Foreign Affairs, for example, drinking to the success of the Wehrmacht after the German occupation of Poland in 1939; General Guderian and his Soviet counterpart reviewing the joint parade of the Red Army and the Panzer units in Brest-Litovsk held to mark the division of Poland; the passage, on the night of 22 June 1941 and to the sound of German guns, into the German-held territories of the last train loaded with Soviet industrial merchandise.[1] These anecdotes highlight what is known as the 'stab in the back' theory: the pact is still perceived as the most obvious and most immediate cause of the Second World War. It is perhaps one of the ironies of history that, only two years later, Germany and Russia would be locked in a war of unprecedented dimensions, the outcome of which sealed the Allied victory over Nazi Germany.

What prompted me to tread this well-ploughed furrow was the publication in 1985 of a series of articles, later turned into books, by V. Rezun, better known simply as 'Suvorov', a defector from Russian Military Intelligence (GRU). Suvorov depicted Soviet Russia as the aggressor, rather than the victim, in June 1941. He advanced the preposterous and unsubstantiated claim that, throughout 1939–41, Stalin had been meticulously preparing a revolutionary war against Germany. Operation 'Groza' (Thunder) was planned for 6 July 1941 but was pre-empted by Hitler's own invasion of Russia. The implication is breathtaking: in executing his foreign policy Stalin, like Hitler, was pursuing a master plan which sought world domination by transforming the Second World War into a revolutionary war.[2]

I had been crossing swords with Suvorov since the first presentation of his ideas.[3] However, it was the acclaim with which *Icebreaker* was received in Russia, and the reluctance of Russian military and diplomatic historians to respond, which led me to publish, in Moscow and in Russian, a comprehensive rebuttal under the title *The Icebreaker Myth* [in translation].[4] As a former master of disinformation in the GRU, Suvorov exploited the fact that the period in question was rife with myth and conspiracy, most of it deliberately propagated. These inventions were later adopted uncritically by historians, not merely because of the lack of solid information but also because of the political polarization of the Cold War. The popularity of Suvorov's flimsy and fraudulent work in Russia and in many quarters in the West proves that the oldest, stalest conspiracies survive longest. His books engender myths and consistently and deliberately obstruct the search for truth by simplifying a complex situation.

The process of nation-building, particularly through revolutionary means, thrives on myth. The Soviet Union's official cult of the Great Patriotic War created, then promoted, a standard version of the history of the war.[5] For five decades the officially generated account served as the primary cohesive force in the collective social memory of the Soviet people. It concealed Stalin's crimes by glorifying his contribution to victory, and was later exploited by Khrushchev and other communist leaders to galvanize public support. The history of the war thus emerged as a bizarre cocktail of facts, falsifications and, above all, omissions. For obvious reasons what suffered most at the hands of Soviet historians was the era of the Ribbentrop–Molotov Pact and the disastrous opening stages of the war. So sacred was the shrine that it was the last to be demolished after the collapse of the Soviet Union. This, however, was achieved by iconoclasts who, in their eagerness to debunk the myth, have produced an equally distorted and politicized account of the war. The omissions have been filled with historical inventions, of which Suvorov's is the outstanding example.

Suvorov's views would not have warranted serious academic comment had they not coincided with the ongoing *Historikerstreit*, the rancorous debate on the nature and course of German history.[6] Broadly speaking, Suvorov's arguments have been adopted to support Nolte's arguments on the rationality and legitimacy of the politics of Nazi Germany. If Stalin had indeed been intent on 'liberating' Central Europe, then Hitler's decision to fight Russia could no longer be viewed as a fulfilment of the ideological blueprint outlined in *Mein Kampf*, as a strategic folly or crude aggressive act. In Germany *Icebreaker* enabled Professors Nolte, Hoffman, Maser and Post to condone Hitler's move to the East as a pre-emptive strike. The war is vindicated by traditional German geopolitical interests and the threat to Germany and the civilized Western world by the abhorrent Stalinist regime.[7] The Austrian historian Ernst Topitsch went even further, arguing in his book *Stalin's War* that the Second World War 'was essentially a Soviet attack on the Western democracies, in which Germany . . . served only as military surrogate'.[8] Common to this new historiography is a failure to offer any convincing evidence to sustain the allegations. The discourse is essentially confined to a theoretical examination of Soviet foreign policy on the eve of the war, and reveals strong ideological predilections.[9]

While engaged in writing a rebuttal to Suvorov's work I grew increasingly uncomfortable with the vast literature on the Ribbentrop–Molotov Pact and Operation 'Barbarossa'. It became obvious that, by diverting the debate to the issue of the pre-emptive strike, Suvorov had succeeded in deflecting historians from the fundamental issue: a convincing explanation of Hitler's decision to invade Russia. The issue is by no means the focal point of this book, and I make no claim to provide a final judgment. However, by juxtaposing the newly available Soviet archival sources and the German ones, it has been possible to produce a carefully documented sequence of events, exposing the circumstances which led Hitler to issue Directive 21 in December 1940.

The focal point of the present book, however, is the elucidation of Stalin's policies on the eve of the war. After more than half a century of research, Stalin's policies still remain, in the words of Churchill, 'a riddle wrapped in a mystery inside an enigma'. The 'totalitarian model', constructed during the Cold War to deflect hostility from the former enemy on to the new one, makes no real contribution. All it does is suggest an affinity between Marxism and Nazism.[10] The almost total absence of evidence of Stalin's intentions on the eve of the war led historians either to attribute to him a dubious plot or to agree with Churchill in dismissing Stalin and his generals as 'the most completely outwitted bunglers of the Second World War so far as strategy, policy, foresight [and] competence' are concerned.[11] Such scanty evidence as did emerge came from the Soviet army shortly after Stalin's death. After Khrushchev's rise to power the marshals took advantage of their powerful position to dodge responsibility for the disastrous events of 22 June by pinning all the blame on Stalin. But even this abundance of military recollection, in book and article form, examined the events strictly from the military point of view.[12] The emphasis on theoretical foundations and the mental roots of the conflict further deflected the debate from the actual events leading to the war in the East. No serious attempt has been made to explore the intricate political game which Stalin devised and which was linked to his military strategy and political vision. The absence of clear evidence has led historians decisively up a blind alley.[13]

The particular contribution of the present book is a coherent analysis of Stalin's policies which not only challenges the standard interpretations but produces a completely new narrative. Apart from an introductory note, the book does not dwell on the negotiations leading to the Ribbentrop–Molotov Pact or on its immediate repercussions; the ruthless implementation of the secret protocols has been fully surveyed elsewhere. The focus here is the year *preceding* the war. A serious flaw in most military and diplomatic histories is the narrow angle from which the period is examined. It is rarely remembered that, during that year alone, Europe underwent probably the most extensive political transformation of its history. Event after event, ranging from the German invasion of Norway and Denmark in the north through that of the Low Countries and France to the encroachment into the Balkans, had direct repercussions on Soviet policy. The outbreak of war, and the enormity of its consequences, provided a retrospective point of departure for historians, overshadowing the political drama which preceded it.

A second flaw, which this book sets out to rectify, has been the tendency to explore the episode exclusively on the basis of the German–Soviet collaboration of 1939–41. By examining the policies of Stalin in the context of German–Soviet relations alone, historians have avoided the equally complex and significant relationship with Britain, as well as those with Turkey and the Balkan countries.[14] This shortcoming was further exacerbated by a failure to examine the various geographical and thematic aspects sufficiently clearly. Few would deny that the activities of the General Staff, the Comintern, the Central Committee and Narkomindel (the Russian Foreign Ministry) finally converged in the Kremlin. Though a measure of latitude was allowed, the final decision always rested with Stalin, who, formally in charge after assuming the premiership in mid-May 1941, adopted a comprehensive approach to both military and diplomatic affairs. An illuminating example of the complexity of the decision-making process is the evaluation of General Zhukov's proposal for a counter-offensive to forestall the German build-up of May 1941. This was considered by Stalin against the background of rumours of an impending German–Soviet war, Rudolf Hess's mysterious flight to England a few days earlier, the defeats inflicted upon Yugoslavia and the British army in the Balkans and North Africa, and the recently signed Pact of Neutrality with the Japanese, not to mention the puzzling overtures made by Count Werner von Schulenburg (the German ambassador in Moscow) in an attempt to avert the war. By widening the scope and examining the German onslaught on Russia in its broader geographical, military, strategic and political framework, I have been able to detect further clues to Stalin's attitudes on the eve of the war.

The unique feature of the present narrative is that it is substantiated by a wide array of predominantly unpublished and newly published material from a range of national archives. In the last decade, since Glasnost, an endless flow of information has emerged, shedding new light on the approach to war.[15] It seems almost inconceivable that, as late as 1990, the very existence of the secret protocols of the Ribbentrop–Molotov Pact was officially denied by President Gorbachev.[16] So far the majority of analyses of Operation 'Barbarossa' have been based exclusively on German sources. A small number of the most recent works have been based on documentary collections published in Moscow,[17] but none has utilized the growing range of archival resources. Nor have Russian scholars made extensive use of them: new scholarly work tends to be confined in its scope, focusing on selected themes.

Through painstaking efforts, I have succeeded in obtaining access to a vast array of Russian archival sources from the Russian Foreign Ministry and the General Staff, and an extensive selection of documents from both the NKVD (the Internal Affairs Commissariat – later, Ministry – in charge of domestic and foreign intelligence) and the GRU. The files of the Foreign Ministry included those of V. Molotov, his deputy A. Vyshinsky, I. Maisky, the Soviet ambassador in London, and V. G. Dekanozov, the Soviet ambassador in Berlin. I have further consulted the files of the Balkan embassies, the bulkiest in the Ministry for that period.

It is lamentable for the historian that Stalin's terror discouraged his entourage not only from keeping diaries but from expressing themselves in writing at all. Those who could not resist the temptation were fully aware of their vulnerability. It was undoubtedly humiliating for Maisky, for instance, to submit his diary for Stalin's inspection before accompanying Eden to Moscow in December 1941:

> Tomorrow I am setting off to the USSR together with Eden. As travelling by sea is a hazardous affair these days, I address this letter to you.
>   In the enclosed portfolio you will find a diary which I kept, though not very regularly, during the last seven years. . . . from a historical point of view, this diary is undoubtedly of interest. In any case, over the last seven years I have found myself in an ideal position to observe world politics, and have had the opportunity of establishing relations with the leading political figures in England and in other countries. I am sending my diary to you. Do with it as you please.[18]

The human dimension, so vital in Russian political culture, is thus hard to retrieve, compared for instance with the very personal and vivid picture the reader can glean of political life in London. The few glimpses I have been able to capture are drawn from Maisky's detailed and illuminating diary, used extensively in this book for the first time, and an assortment of private papers (such as the encounter between Zhukov, Timoshenko and

Stalin at the Politburo meeting in mid-June 1941). Similarly I have made full use of the more interesting memoirs of military and diplomatic figures which appear in the Bibliography; there is, however, little chance that further such material exists and will emerge. These sources were supplemented by an exhaustive examination of the wide spectrum of printed documentary material. Unfortunately various collections of documents which I was able to consult shortly after 1991 have since been closed. Research in Russian archives is still governed by a mixture of whim and bureaucratic hazard which undermines the process of research. As a matter of principle I have refrained from paying for archival access, apart from legitimate photocopying costs. I succeeded in gaining sight of important material only after endless trips to Moscow, patient haggling and pleading. A typical hurdle is the decision of Russian Military Intelligence to withhold all cipher telegrams for the years 1941–50. Hence, for instance, the recently published second volume of the Russian official publication of documents on Soviet foreign policy (*Dokumenty vneshnei politiki, 1940–22 iunia 1941*) is severely depleted. The ruling included material relating to the six months preceding the war. Fortunately I had already seen most of the key telegrams, and for the remainder I extrapolated from records of meetings within the files of the relevant embassies.

On the military side the material consulted included the entire range of military intelligence placed before Stalin on the eve of the war: the detailed bi-weekly cumulative reports beginning in autumn 1940, the ensuing reports of the head of Military Intelligence and the reports of the military attachés. I also consulted the stenographic minutes of the extraordinary military council of the High Command in December 1940, the proceedings of the war games of January 1941 and the full set of the directives of the General Staff. Similarly an extensive selection of documents dealing with the Red Army's preparations for the war was explored. I further succeeded in gaining access to some key material held in the Presidential Archives, now regrettably closed to research. Most enlightening were the records of the Comintern and particularly the diary of its President, Dimitrov, which I was able to consult in its Bulgarian version. Dimitrov was closely associated with Stalin and left a candid description of some Politburo meetings. I was further able to see many records from the archives of the Russian Security Services which provide remarkable insight into the intelligence scene. Those include, *inter alia*, intercepts of telegrams from Moscow, copies of telegrams from Sir Stafford Cripps (the British ambassador in Moscow on the eve of the war) obtained through members of the 'Cambridge Five' in London, dispatches from various rings in Berlin, as well as the file on Hess, of which J. Costello was able to use only a couple of documents in his *Ten Days to Destiny: The Secret Story of the Hess Peace Initiative and British Efforts to Strike a Deal with Hitler* (New York, 1991).

The book also makes full use of British archives, both of the Foreign Office, the Prime Minister's Papers, the Chiefs of Staff, Military Intelligence and various other branches, as well as a variety of collections of private papers. But the jewel in the crown was undoubtedly the Bulgarian and Yugoslav archives, which have not previously been used by Western scholars and which, juxtaposed with the German and the Soviet documents, give a full picture of the scramble for the Balkans and shed fresh light on Stalin's aims and ambitions. I have further consulted the relevant files dealing with Russia at the Quai d'Orsay. The Swedish ambassador to Moscow, V. Assarasson, was one of the few people in whom the German and the Italian ambassadors confided, and his reports and papers deposited in the Swedish State Archives are a goldmine for the historian.

Acknowledgments

In Russia I was helped by many colleagues. Special gratitude and appreciation is due to the late General Dimitry Volkogonov, who provided unstinting support in my search for new information and material. An invaluable source of information, critical observation and assistance was Dr Lev Bezymensky, the distinguished Russian historian, Zhukov's interpreter during the war and former editor of *Novoe vremiia*. My special thanks to the director, Mr P. Stegny, and staff of the archival department of the Russian Foreign Ministry for their assistance. Major-General V. A. Zolotariov, director of the Institute of Military History, kindly allowed me to consult fragments of its rich collection. Likewise I am grateful to General Yuri Kobaladze of the Russian Security Services for allowing me access to their sources.

Professor John Erickson, an old friend and undisputed expert on the Soviet military on the eve of the war, provided constant assistance: I profited from companionship and eye-opening conversations. I am grateful for the considerable assistance I received from Lieutenant-Colonel David M. Glantz of Fort Leavenworth, Kansas; and I am particularly indebted to Professor Bruce Menning, also of Fort Leavenworth and the foremost expert on Soviet military planning. General Dr Shimon Naveh, an outstanding authority on the Soviet military doctrine, an inspiring original thinker and close friend, guided me with great patience and enthusiasm through the most sophisticated innovations in this field introduced by Generals Triandafilov and Tukhachevsky in the 1930s; he also helped me to master various military issues which called for professional expertise.

An early version of this book was written at St Antony's College, Oxford. I owe special gratitude to my friends Timothy Garton Ash, Anne

Deighton and Harry Shukman for their comments and support, and to Iverach McDonald, the former political editor of *The Times* who shared with me his lively and insightful observations of the period. I thank the Warden and Fellows of the College for their interest in my work and for the congenial atmosphere within which the book was substantially prepared. The late F. H. Hinsley and Dr Zara Steiner, of Cambridge University, read an earlier version of the manuscript and suggested significant improvements. Sir Maurice Shock, former Rector of Lincoln College, Oxford, was kind enough to allow me access to the private papers and diary of Sir Stafford Cripps and to share with me on many occasions his wide knowledge of British politics.

Special warm personal appreciation is due to Dr Boris Morozov, my colleague at the Cummings Center at Tel Aviv University, who went out of his way to assist me in the arduous process of detecting indispensable but often elusive archival material in Moscow. I am equally indebted to Dr Petra Marquand-Bigman, who diligently assisted me in the research of the German aspects of the story. Professor Michael Confino, who first ignited my interest in Russian studies some thirty years ago, and was the first to introduce me to the 'Eastern Question', was kind enough to help me with the translation of various Bulgarian documents. Dr Raphael Vago of the Cummings Center helped me with the translations of the Rumanian sources, and especially the recently released volume of telegrams of G. Gafencu, the Rumanian ambassador in Moscow. My gratitude is due to Dr Ronald Zweig and Professor Dan Diner, my colleagues and friends at Tel Aviv University, who carefully read the final version of the manuscript and made astute observations. A fellowship from the Kennan Institute at the Wilson Center enabled me to consult the rich archival and manuscript resources in Washington. Robert Baldock, my editor at Yale University Press, deserves special gratitude. His unstinted help went well beyond the call of duty.

Finally I am indebted to my wife Sue, who edited the manuscript most meticulously and made valuable comments which profoundly affected the final version of the book.

Gabriel Gorodetsky
The Rubin Chair of Russian and East
European History and Civilization
Tel Aviv University

Introduction: The Premises of Stalin's Foreign Policy

There is little to warrant the suggestion that Stalin's foreign policy followed a blueprint: that a direct line existed between Lenin's militant programme of 'Imperialism as the Highest Form of Capitalism', devised in Switzerland in 1915, and Stalin's supposedly revolutionary war of 1941, which brought this policy to fruition. The first decade after the Russian Revolution was characterized by a dynamic re-evaluation of foreign policy. The Bolsheviks faced a formidable challenge in their attempt to reconcile two contradictory factors, the axiomatic need to spread the revolution beyond Russia's borders and the prosaic need to guarantee survival within them. From its inception, Soviet foreign policy was marked by a gradual but consistent retreat from hostility to the capitalist regimes towards peaceful coexistence based on mutual expediency. This was justified at first as a tactical move, and thus temporary. However, what started as the provisional New Economic Policy (NEP) turned out to be only the first in a series of extended 'breathing spaces', clad in a variety of ideological guises: 'Socialism in One Country', 'United Front', 'Popular Front', 'Grand Alliance', 'Thaw', 'Détente' and, most recently, 'Glasnost'. The prolongation of these 'transitional' periods brought a steady and consistent erosion of the ideological dimension of Soviet foreign policy.

By 1926 officials at the British Foreign Office recognized the rise of the 'strong, stern, silent' Stalin as the unchallenged leader of the Communist Party. 'It is not surprising', they commented, 'that the defeat of the fanatic Bolshevik opposition indicates a foreign policy which utilises "national tools".'[1] The distance between that view and Trotsky's own announcement, on his appointment as the first People's Commissar for Foreign Affairs, that his task would be to 'publish a few revolutionary proclamations and then close shop'[2] reflects the extent to which Soviet foreign policy had changed in its first decade. The initial supposition that foreign relations would be superfluous in a world shattered by revolution was replaced, first in 1921 and particularly after 1924, by a sober evaluation of the need to reach a *modus vivendi* with the outside world. The Comintern (the Communist International Organization run from Moscow), too, bent its ideological line to conform to national interests. By early 1924 its Fifth Congress reluctantly conceded the ascendancy of an 'era of stabilization of capitalism' and advocated a reorientation of the communist parties and the front organizations in defence of Russia.[3] The experience of the first decade of the revolution proved that duality could hardly be maintained without compromising Russian national interests. Stalin's wish to establish the supremacy of moderate diplomacy rather than encourage ideological fervour was reflected by the replacement of G. Chicherin as Commissar for Foreign Affairs by M. Litvinov, the representative of the Western orientation in Narkomindel (the Soviet Foreign Ministry). Despite differences in mentality, temperament and social background, both Litvinov and Stalin shared a prudent and pragmatic approach to foreign affairs.[4]

By the end of the first decade of the Soviet state, a sequence of diplomatic and ideological setbacks dictated an urgent reassessment of priorities. The dream of unconditional support from the world proletariat had been shattered beyond repair. On the face of it the Comintern now resorted to a purely militant line, proclaiming the end of the stabilization of capitalism and the revival of revolutionary opportunities in the West. United-front tactics were abandoned and replaced by militant 'class against class' slogans. However, after thoroughly sovietizing the shaky communist movement in Europe, the Comintern of the 1930s no longer resembled that of the first decade. By 1941 it had lost its grip and was for all practical purposes abandoned, as this book shows, although its formal dissolution came only in 1943.

However, the legacy of imperial rivalry, amplified by the communist experience, intensified the mutual suspicion which marked the early 1920s. Mistrust remained a major factor in the gradual but steady decline into the instability of the 1930s. Rapid industrialization and collectivization were aimed at extracting by brute force economic resources which could not be obtained through normal trading procedures with the West. Given the reality of capitalist encirclement and fears of renewed intervention, defence against the external threat was a prerequisite for the achievement of 'Socialism in One Country'. The search for mutual assistance pacts with Russia's immediate neighbours preceded Hitler's rise to power and gained momentum after 1931.

Historical memory is short. Given the unexpected emergence of the Soviet Union as a superpower after the Second World War, it is perhaps difficult to recall that up to the outbreak of the war the fear of renewed capitalist intervention was widespread. The new Russian military doctrine, devised after 1928, was marked by a recognition of the various threats facing the Soviet Union rather than by an expansionist drive. Rather than anticipating a war among the imperialist states, the fear was of an armed crusade against the Russian Revolution. Up to 1927, due mostly to the weakness of the Red Army and the hope of reaching a *modus vivendi* with the West, it was assumed that the support of the European workers would be effective in deterring the Western governments from embarking on war with the Soviet Union. By 1927, however, revolutionary expectations had subsided and the Red Army was assigned the role of averting the threat.[5] The coherent policy of 'collective security', pursued with only marginal tactical deflections, perceived danger throughout the capitalist camp, whether from fascist Germany or the Western democracies. Adopting balance-of-power policies, so alien to Marxist theory, which rejected siding with one capitalist power against another, Stalin directed his efforts towards safeguarding the revolution from within through collaboration with the West.

The conclusion of the Ribbentrop–Molotov Pact of Neutrality on 23 August 1939 (Molotov had become Commissar for Foreign Affairs three months before) marked a change in the grouping of forces but not in the general aims of Stalin's foreign policy. The same holds for the secret protocols, signed a month later, which established spheres of influence between the Soviet Union and Germany. The motives for signing the pact become clear once we establish the precise timing of Stalin's shift towards Germany. The controversy over the pact's interpretation encompasses two opposing poles and a wide spectrum of opinions between them. At one extreme is the view that the Soviet Union had pursued an indisputably noble policy of erecting a European-wide shield of collective security against Nazi aggression. The collapse of collective security is ascribed not to the lack of Soviet efforts, but rather to 'appeasement', the failure of the Western democracies to combat Hitler's aggression. According to this view, the Russians did not seriously consider the German option until late in August 1939 when they realized that the West was clinging to appeasement, while Hitler was set on occupying Poland.

At the opposite extreme are the allegations that collective security against aggression was never the Kremlin's real objective, but a front from which to woo Hitler into an aggressive alliance. This interpretation underlines the ideological premises of Soviet foreign policy. Historians like Robert Tucker and most recently 'Suvorov' contend that, as far back as 1927, Stalin was determined to drive a wedge between the capitalist states and manoeuvre them into a mutually destructive inter-imperialist war from which the USSR would emerge unscathed and in a strong position to expand territorially from all her borders. To provoke this war, Stalin is purported to have facilitated Hitler's rise to power by meticulously choreographing the policy of the Comintern and the German Communist Party on a suicidal course and undermining a possible alliance with the Social Democrats. The Nazi–Soviet pact was, in this view, always implicit in Stalin's plans, while 'collective security' only concealed his genuine designs on the West. Suvorov is in fact at pains to ascribe to Stalin a continuous aggressive policy in collusion with Germany dating back to the Rapallo Treaty of 1922.[6]

It is most tempting to attribute the Russians' shift to disillusionment with the West after the Munich conference in September 1938. Their exclusion from the conference and the free hand given to Germany in Czechoslovakia confirmed the deep-rooted Soviet suspicion that the British and French Prime Ministers, Chamberlain and Daladier, were determined to fend off the German danger by encouraging Hitler to expand eastwards. However, such an interpretation overlooks the fact that, despite the severe blow to collective security, Munich was not considered by Stalin to be irreversible. Moreover, he had no alternative to pursue as long as Hitler continued to gamble on further Western submission.

A favourite watershed for most historians is Stalin's survey of Soviet foreign policy to the 18th Party Congress on 10 March 1939. Stalin's famous warning to the Western democracies that he did not intend to 'pull the chestnuts out of the fire' is often cited. In retrospect, historians detect here Stalin's decision to collaborate with Nazi Germany. However, even a cursory examination of the entire text of the speech should suffice to show that Stalin in fact dismissed Lenin's ideas of a revolutionary war and warned that a world war posed a threat to Russia. Besides, within a week Hitler abrogated the Munich Agreement and forced Chamberlain to adopt a more bellicose attitude.

The unilateral British guarantees to Poland of 31 March 1939 represent the crucial move towards the Ribbentrop–Molotov Pact and the opening salvoes of the Second World War.[7] They altered the scene at a stroke. In making his declaration Chamberlain barely consulted the Foreign Office or his own advisers; the guarantees were his spontaneous emotional reaction to the personal humiliation he had suffered when Hitler seized Prague on 15 March 1939. Paradoxically, by guaranteeing Poland, Britain in effect challenged Germany, thus effectively abandoning her position as the arbiter of the European balance of power. The guarantees had two possible consequences. The deterrent element was designed to bring Hitler back to the negotiating table. However, were Hitler still to press his territorial claims against Poland, the military axiom inspired by the lessons of earlier wars, of avoiding a war on two fronts, would make it imperative for Hitler to neutralize the Soviet Union. Consequently a German option, hitherto unavailable, opened up for the Soviet Union. Conversely, when it dawned on Chamberlain that the path to a 'second Munich' was not smooth and that war remained a real possibility, he was reluctantly forced to secure at least a measure of Soviet military commitment vital for the implementation of the guarantees. In this manner, and without prior design, the Soviet Union became the pivot of the European balance of power.[8]

The Ribbentrop–Molotov Pact is remembered as a 'shock' and a 'surprise', confirming the perfidious Russian nature. Suvorov recruits this powerful image to question Russian sincerity in the 1939 negotiations for a tripartite agreement with England and France. He argues that 'Stalin did not seek such alliances . . . Stalin could have remained neutral, but chose instead to stab in the back those countries engaged in a struggle with fascism'.[9] This is presented as a corollary to the ideological blueprint drawn up by Stalin in the 1920s. Both myths, the 'stab in the back' and the 'blueprint', were spawned during the Cold War and were sustained by a simplistic reading of events leading up to the pact. In reality the British were quick to recognize the likely impact of the guarantees on Soviet foreign policy. Hardly had the guarantees been given than Sir William Seeds, the British ambassador to Moscow, alerted Whitehall to the consequences: 'Russia had had enough and would henceforth stand aloof free of any commitments.' In mid-April he went on to warn that, if the guarantees to Poland were to remain, Russia could 'quite properly be tempted to stand aloof and in case of war confine its advertised support of the victims of aggression to the profitable business of selling supplies to the latter'. Once Hitler established a common border with Russia, Seeds even expected an agreement on the future of the Baltic States, Poland and Bessarabia. Likewise the British Under-Secretary of State for Foreign Affairs admitted that 'now that HMG have given their guarantees, the Soviet Government will sit back and wash their hands of the whole affair'.[10] On the very day of the signature of the pact, Sir Nevile Henderson, the British ambassador to Berlin, admitted that the British 'policy vis-à-vis Poland would always have made it inevitable in the end'.[11]

In the new circumstances Stalin could theoretically commit himself to the Germans. But, with Czechoslovakia still fresh in his memory, he seemed most concerned that Chamberlain might pursue a policy of appeasement once Germany moved against Poland, and encourage her to continue her progress eastwards. It should be remembered that the lasting feature of Soviet foreign policy in the inter-war period was an intense suspicion that Germany and Britain might close ranks and mount a crusade against communist Russia. Events which had little direct bearing on Russia, such as the Locarno Treaty of 1925, Germany's entry into the League of Nations the following year and, of course, the Munich conference, were seen in this vein. Soviet historians attributed the failure of the negotiations in 1939 to sinister Western attempts to revive German militarism by conspiring with German fascism and diverting the aggressors eastwards. While there is no hard evidence that such a plan was ever contemplated by the British Cabinet, historians have argued that Chamberlain's strategic policy remained deterrent in nature, and actively encouraged efforts to defuse international tension by diplomatic means. Chamberlain remained hostile to binding military agreements, which could be provocative in nature, and to exerting pressure on Poland to accept Soviet assistance.[12] In view of the Germans' constant infringement of treaties signed by them, Russia had no confidence in a written agreement.

From 31 March onwards Stalin faced a severe dilemma which had little to do with ideological predisposition. Essentially cautious and pragmatist in foreign relations, Stalin was haunted by the suspicion that, despite the guarantees, Britain would abandon Poland as she had done Czechoslovakia, thereby fostering German aggression on the eastern front. These apprehensions dictated an alignment with Germany. On the other hand, in the event of a British failure to respond to Germany's invasion of Poland, Germany was likely to violate such an agreement and continue the push eastwards. This prognosis led to desperate Soviet efforts to replace the unilateral guarantees with a contractual military alliance.[13]

However, from the outset such an alliance proved difficult owing to Poland's refusal to permit transit of Soviet troops in the event of war, and to Britain's reluctance to recognize the Soviet Union as her principal ally in Eastern Europe. Collective security continued to be viewed as the more viable and desirable alternative. These negotiations, though they dragged on for a number of months, reached deadlock at the very beginning over the issues which finally drove the Russians into German arms. Soviet and Western historians have often failed to realize that England and the Soviet Union were in fact seeking different agreements. The Russians had consistently pressed, in conformity with their policy of collective security, for a treaty of mutual assistance. The salient features were an unequivocal definition of the military measures to be taken by each of the belligerents once war, which they regarded as inevitable, broke out.[14]

By adhering to deterrent measures the British failed to satisfy Russia's fundamental security needs. There was little room for manoeuvre, and from the outset Britain's Foreign Secretary Lord Halifax had slender expectations. Rather than a commitment, he wished Russia to join one of his endless attempts to discourage Hitler from pursuing his ambitions while cherishing the hope that he might be forced back to the negotiating table. Halifax was therefore careful to advise the Russians to limit their activity to a statement 'on their own initiative', fastidiously restricted with qualifications that 'in the event of any act of aggression against any European neighbour of the Soviet Union *which was resisted by the country concerned*, the assistance of the Soviet Government would be available, *if desired*, and would be afforded in such manner *as would be found most convenient*' (author's italics). Halifax believed that what he termed a 'positive declaration' by the Soviet government 'would have a *steadying effect* upon the international situation'.[15] The 'steadying effect' was tantamount to deterrence. He hardly wavered from this position throughout the arduous summer months of 1939.

The rigid British position led Stalin, out of sheer calculation, to seek an alternative through dialogue with the Germans. But the final decision was practically forced on him on 19 August 1939, when he received remarkable intelligence on Hitler's long- and short-term aims. The report conveyed the Führer's determination to solve the Polish problem at all costs, regardless of the risk of having to fight on two fronts. Hitler further counted on Moscow to 'conduct negotiations with us, as she had no interest whatever in a conflict with Germany, nor was she anxious to be defeated for the sake of England and France'. It is worthwhile noting, for those who adhere to the 'community of fate' model, that although the document advocated 'a new Rapallo stage . . . of rapprochement and economic collaboration with Moscow', it underlined the ephemeral nature of the 'Second Rapallo' which was to be pursued 'for *a limited period*' of approximately two years.[16]

Clearly the dynamic force behind events since the Munich Agreement was Germany. Like the British, Stalin, far from initiating the aggression, had to comply with German demands, which amounted to an ultimatum. Going through the proposal on 19 August, he carefully marked in thick blue pencil Hitler's 'advice' to accept the draft agreement, as Poland's behaviour towards Germany was such that 'a crisis may occur any day'. Hitler further commented that it would be wise for Stalin not 'to lose any time'.[17] The decision was further confirmed by the realization that the Anglo-French military delegation, which reached Moscow in the second week of August, lacked instructions or authority and had constantly to consult London and Paris.[18]

These calculations underpinned the agreement. Soviet policy remained essentially one of level-headed *Realpolitik*.[19] Stalin had wavered for a long time, as was his practice in formulating foreign policy. Under these conditions various opposing factions were able to develop. The principal opponents of Litvinov, and therefore of collective security, were Molotov, chairman of the Soviet Council of Commissars, and Andrei Zhdanov, Stalin's protégé and first secretary of the Leningrad region. Their isolationist view, however, was genuinely aimed at insulating the Soviet Union from imminent war in Europe, rather than at seeking a revolutionary outlet.[20] Stalin always exploited opportunities as they appeared at a given moment. Throughout most of the 1930s he adhered to collective security, in an attempt to protect Russia from a disastrous war, until he despaired of its success at the end of the decade. Given his understandable and ever present suspicion of reconciliation between Britain and Germany, it is doubtful whether Stalin saw the pact as an ironclad guarantee of Russia's western borders. It did not lead to a fraternity of 'blood and steel' with Germany, or to a revival of the long-forgotten dream of relentless expansion.

Neutrality was hardly construed as a prelude to world revolution, as the doctrinaire interpretation of Lenin's 'defeatist' stance in an imperialist war would have required. It served the more mundane Soviet interests of ensuring that Russia would not be involved in the war while creating favourable conditions for the post-war negotiations on the future of Europe. The various communist parties were instructed to prevent the spread of the war into Turkey and South-eastern Europe.[21] The premise underlying Soviet foreign policy was that Russia should be 'content to be confined to its own small Lebensraum'.[22] Stalin's exposition, to none other than Dimitrov, the President of the Comintern, of the reasons which had led him to sign the pact with the Germans was devoid of any ideological considerations. It amounted to a determination not to become the 'mercenary' of Britain and France. True, he did justify the division of Poland in what might be seen as an ideological perspective, suggesting in his typically callous way: 'What harm would have been caused if, as a result of the dismemberment of Poland, we had extended the socialist system to new territories and populations?' However, the thin veneer barely concealed Soviet strategic interests or the need to bring the war to a hasty end before Russia too became involved in the conflict.[23]

When Dimitrov stubbornly adhered to the orthodox ideological paradigm, Stalin personally intervened to ensure that the actions of the Comintern were subordinated to the requirements of Soviet foreign policy. Dimitrov was discouraged by Stalin and Zhdanov from entertaining any illusions about the revolutionary potential of the war. He was led to understand that 'in the First Imperialist War the Bolsheviks overestimated the situation. We all rushed ahead and made mistakes! This can be explained, but not excused, by the conditions prevailing then. Today we must not repeat the position held by the Bolsheviks'.[24] In no time complacency gave way to concern at the setbacks inflicted on the Red Army in the early stages of the war against Finland in autumn 1939. The flamboyant revolutionary slogans were replaced by strange equations such as: 'The activities of the Red Army too are the concern of world revolution.' The Red Army, rather than acting as an icebreaker to advance world revolution, was assigned the role of 'rendering Finland friendly to the Government of the Soviet Union'.[25]

The attention given to Suvorov's interpretation results from current Russian views of the events of 1939. But it is inspired by moral judgments, and focuses on the secret protocols which brought about the division and seizure of Poland and the occupation of the Baltic countries.[26] Stalin was determined to use the opportunities which the war provided to advance what he considered to be the Soviet Union's long-term national interests.

These essentially focused on establishing the Soviet Union's role as a major European country by revising the Versailles Treaty and addressing the grievances inflicted on Russian diplomacy since the Crimean War. Such a moral perspective overlooks the astute observation made by Teddy Uldricks, a leading expert on Soviet foreign policy, that 'the Kremlin pursued a diplomatic course that was neither morally nor ideologically consistent. Moscow's policy, like that of the democracies, was neither pure and noble nor diabolically cunning.'[27]

1

'Potential Enemies': London and Moscow at Loggerheads

'The Truce of the Bear'

The outbreak of war aroused some disguised satisfaction in London at seeing Russia and Germany as partners on the other side of the barricade. The British, as R. A. Butler, the Parliamentary Under-Secretary at the Foreign Office, observed, 'are a proud people, and seem to enjoy the "world at arms"' against them.[1] The self-fulfilling prophecy that Germany and the Soviet Union would join hands in war against Britain fed on two potential rather than real dangers. The first was the damage caused by the Soviet export of war materials to Germany to the fundamental British war effort, which depended on the maintenance of an effective economic blockade. However, regardless of the actual volume of such trade (which is still debated by historians), it should be noted that Whitehall tended to minimize its significance.[2] It was also plainly apparent to the Ministry of Economic Warfare that by imposing an economic boycott on the Soviet Union Britain would curtail the Russians' manoeuvrability while increasing their dependence on trade with Germany. Finally, the Foreign Office conceded that even if the Russians were willing to sacrifice their partnership with Germany, Britain was in no position to offer adequate economic compensation.[3]

The other danger had far-reaching repercussions on future events. The circumstances of the 'Phoney War', when a direct threat to the British Isles seemed remote, highlighted the implications of Soviet relations with Germany on British imperial and strategic assets in the Near and Middle East. The traditional imperialist interests were reinforced by the strong ideological prejudice shared by Chamberlain and his Cabinet. The Chiefs of Staff advocated the protection of areas 'likely to be infected by the

Virus of Bolshevik doctrine'.[4] On the day of the signature of the Ribbentrop–Molotov Pact, Nevile Henderson, the British ambassador in Berlin, expressed it bluntly in a private letter: 'Now H.M.G. is at the crossroads. We have got to help Poland but not to lead her to destruction because we hate & fear the Nazis. After all we have the British Empire to think of . . . it comes before Nazis & the shifting sands of Eastern Europe. The bandits will fall out between themselves there in the end.'[5]

To a degree the British outlook can be explained by the rigid attitude of the French government. In the midst of an acute domestic crisis, the French were eager for a spectacular victory, preferably away from their own borders. Their communications with the Soviet Union had become overtly aggressive at the beginning of 1940, and the Soviet ambassador was even declared *persona non grata*. It was a French initiative which led a reluctant British delegation to expel the Soviet Union from the League of Nations on 14 December 1939 and brought forward the planning of a raid on the Caucasian oilfields.[6]

The poor assessment of Soviet intentions was the result not only of scant information but also the will to reinforce a deep-rooted concept.[7] The pact was conceived as a resurrection of the 'community of fate', following the tradition of Brest-Litovsk and the Rapallo Treaty. It is interesting to note that Count Werner von Schulenburg, the German ambassador in Moscow, made a different analysis, informing his Foreign Ministry in the Wilhelmstrasse in early 1940 that the Soviet Union was genuinely determined 'to cling to neutrality . . . and avoid as much as possible anything that might involve it in a conflict with the Western Powers'.[8]

The concept fed on traditional Russophobia and repugnance towards communism in both the Foreign Office and the armed forces. Since the mid-nineteenth century, when rivalry over Central Asia and Afghanistan had come to dominate Anglo-Russian relations, the metaphor of Russia as the savage bear had been embedded deep in the British consciousness. It comes as no surprise, therefore, that when the Foreign Office considered embarking on negotiations with the Russians, during the German invasion of France, General Ismay, the head of the War Cabinet Secretariat and later Churchill's military adviser, reminded his close friend Sir Orme Sargent, the deputy Under-Secretary and 'ideologist' of the Foreign Office, of Kipling's poem 'The Truce of the Bear'. In this, an old blind beggar who has been mauled by a bear speaks:

> Eyeless, noseless, and lipless – toothless, broken
> of speech, Seeking a dole at the doorway he mumbles his tale
> to each over and over the story, ending as he began:
> 'Make ye no truce with Adam-zad – the Bear that
> walks like a man.'

Horrible, hairy, human, with paws like hands in
prayer, making his supplication rose Adam-zad the Bear!
I looked at the swaying shoulders, at the paunch's
swag and swing, And my heart was touched with pity for the
monstrous, pleading thing.

Touched with pity and wonder, I did not fire then.
I have looked no more on women – I have walked no
more with men. Nearer he tottered and nearer, with paws like hands
that pray – From brow to jaw that steel-shod paw, it ripped my
face away!

But (pay, and I put back the bandage) this is the
time to fear, When he stands up like a tired man, tottering near
and near; When he stands up as pleading, in wavering, man-
brute guise, When he veils the hate and cunning of the little,
swinish eyes;

When he shows as seeking quarter, with paws like
hands in prayer, *That* is the time of peril – the time of the Truce
of the Bear! Over and over the story, ending as he began:
'There is no truce with Adam-zad, the bear that
looks like a man.'[9]

   Shackled by preconceived ideas, the British government overlooked
the intricacy of Soviet policy. Chamberlain adopted a fatalistic attitude
which did not exclude the possibility of hostilities with Russia. The policy
wavered between the wish to pursue the traditional 'reserve' policy of
'sitting tight and avoiding friction as far as possible' and the itch to
encounter Russia in the Balkans or in the north.[10] The concept drew
further support from the obsessive need of the Chamberlain government,
victims of the 'Munich complex', to atone for past mistakes. Acting on
the unverified assumption that Russia was fully allied with Germany, the
Cabinet seized the opportunity of compensating for appeasement
towards Germany by showing stiff resistance to Russia in Finland. Thus
when the Prime Minister reacted favourably to the Soviet request for
mediation in the conflict, he was reproached by the Foreign Office for
attempting 'another appeasement'. No wonder he condemned the
Russians for their 'usual treacherous and cowardly' methods, 'copied
from the Hitler technique in Poland and Czechoslovakia'.[11] Stalin, himself
harbouring deep suspicion towards Britain, could do little but warn her
politicians against 'regarding the Russians as stupid . . . as bears, whose
heads work poorly'.[12]

'He Who Sups with the Devil'

The Ribbentrop–Molotov Pact had thus turned England overnight from a potential ally into a foe. Stalin's overt hostility towards England, conditioned by the British intervention in the Civil War in the wake of the Russian Revolution as well as by the historical legacy of antagonism, was now enhanced by the British mishandling of the 1939 negotiations. In 1941 he would ascribe his hostility to a vivid memory 'of the execution by the British of 26 commissars close to his home region, in Baku' during the intervention.[13] But Stalin was motivated in the first place by pure *Realpolitik*. Vulnerable to the threat posed by the British naval predominance in the Mediterranean and drawing on past historical experience, he expected the blow to be delivered through the Turkish Straits. On the very day of Britain's declaration of war on Germany, Stalin appealed to Turkey to consider Soviet help 'in case the Straits or the Balkans were threatened'.[14]

However, ensuring strict Turkish neutrality was crucial for Germany as well, since most of the Rumanian oil destined for Germany was shipped via the Straits to Italian ports.[15] The Germans spared no effort to inflate Stalin's suspicion that 'Russia's enemy in the Straits is and always will be England' and forestall any agreement between Russia and Turkey which might lead to Soviet participation in the control of the Straits. Saracoglu, the Turkish Foreign Minister, who was well known for his Anglophile leanings, arrived in Moscow on 25 September; but the negotiations, which were drawn out until mid-October, were marred by the second visit of the German Foreign Minister Joachim von Ribbentrop to the Soviet capital, when for ten days Saracoglu was practically ignored by the Russians.

When Saracoglu finally met Stalin the 'heated discussion' revealed that, while the Turks sought an agreement which would cope with a German threat, Stalin viewed the danger as coming from Great Britain. The calculated nature of Stalin's policies is clearly evident. He hardly disputed Turkey's claims in the Dodecanese, which he realized could be fulfilled only through co-operation with England and France. But he tried in vain to persuade Saracoglu that Russia should be Turkey's pivot in the Balkans, where 'Turkey was in a position to aid the British and the French but not the contrary'. 'Events', he went on to explain to him, exposing his pragmatic outlook:

> have their own logic: we speak one way and the events proceed in a different direction. With Germany we divided Poland and England and France did not initiate a war against us, though this may still happen. We do not have an agreement on mutual assistance with the Germans, but if the British and the French start a war against us, we will have to

fight them . . . Who is to be blamed for the fact that events have turned out unfavourably for the conclusion of a pact with Turkey? The circumstantial development of events. The action in Poland contributed. The French, and particularly the British, did not wish to have an agreement with us, believing they could fight without us. If we are to be blamed then it is for not having foreseen it all.

It was fear of Britain, rather than Germany, that overwhelmed Stalin. In the conditions prevailing during the Phoney War, with Chamberlain still the Prime Minister, he still did not exclude the possibility that Germany and England would close ranks after all. Moreover, it became increasingly clear that the embargo strategy employed by England against Germany would be dircected against the Soviet Union as one of the major providers of raw material to Germany. Eager to discourage the Turks from concluding a mutual assistance agreement with Britain, he warned Saracoglu that he 'should bear in mind that these people fulfilled their obligations only when it was convenient for them and did not fulfil their obligations when it was not convenient'. Munich and the guarantees to Poland should serve as a warning. Stalin now demanded an explicit undertaking from the Turks to 'withdraw their forces were France and Great Britain to get involved in a war against Russia' and allow Russia direct control of the passage of warships and the transfer of war material through the Straits. Saracoglu, however, adhered to neutrality. He was finally whisked home in flamboyant style from Sebastopol on board a Soviet warship – an attempted demonstration of Soviet mastery in the Black Sea.[16] Relations with Turkey deteriorated further when upon returning to Ankara Saracoglu finally signed a treaty of mutual assistance with Britain and France.[17]

The Soviet obsession with the Straits cannot be lightly dismissed. It followed on the humiliating Paris Agreement of 1856, the unfavourable arrangements imposed by Bismarck in the Berlin Congress of 1878 and the Montreux Agreement of 1923 which allowed free passage of commercial as well as military ships while the control of the Straits was entrusted to an international commission. The arrangement gave Britain a clear advantage and as such was resisted by both Turkey, who had lost her sovereignty over the Straits, and Russia, who felt directly threatened. The Nazi menace led to a modification of the agreement in 1936. While the passage of merchant vessels and warships to the Black Sea remained free in peacetime, the Straits were closed to warships of belligerent countries as long as Turkey remained neutral. Once Turkey was at war, control of the Straits was fully entrusted to her. From the Russian point of view Turkey's new commitment to England made Turkish neutrality a clear strategic threat. In the new circumstances the Allied contingency plans against Germany, unfolded by Admiral Drax and the other members of the Anglo-French mission in the Kremlin in August, received a sinister twist. The plans aimed to thwart the Germans by closing the Turkish Straits and seizing control of the mouth of the Danube on the Rumanian littoral of the Black Sea. It was now feared by the Kremlin that the Anglo-French navies might indeed carry out this plan, but direct it against the Soviet Union as well as against Germany.[18]

Soviet apprehension was not groundless. The stalemate on the western front during the Phoney War led General Edmund Ironside, the British Chief of the Imperial General Staff, to advocate the invasion of Rumania, thereby seizing the oilfields, diverting Germany to the Balkans and disrupting the transfer of goods from Russia to Germany. The opening of the Turkish Straits to the Royal Navy, which would have rendered Turkey a belligerent, was a prerequisite for the success of the plan. From the Turkish point of view, however, the major threat was an extension of the German–Soviet collusion to the Balkans. President Ismet Inönü, therefore, continued to cling to benevolent neutrality towards Britain, which he still regarded as 'the world's strongest insurance firm'.[19]

Stalin was adequately informed about the Turkish assumption that 'the superiority of the French and British navies' was their most effective shield. The Soviet ambassador in Ankara warned Moscow of a *fait accompli*, as 'the English might even not ask [the Turks] before embarking on some adventure, spreading the fire of war to the Balkans and the districts of the Black Sea'. He depicted in sombre colours the hasty fortification and militarization of the Straits.[20] A flood of reports from various Balkan capitals brought little comfort to Moscow. Suggestions were made that Britain was 'planning a landing in Saloniki [in the western Aegean] to prevent Italian aggression'.[21] The veteran Soviet ambassador in London, Ivan Maisky, fuelled suspicion by revealing that the British had paid tremendous sums for the pact with Turkey, which was their 'trump card against the Soviet Union'. He warned that it 'created for Britain new military opportunities in the Balkans and in the Black Sea, possibilities which in certain conditions she can use against us'.[22]

Chamberlain's failure to formulate a clear-cut strategic plan for the conduct of the war in tune with the changing political realities only contributed to the worsening relations during the Soviet war with Finland in winter 1939. The political perceptions which had prevented an agreement with Russia in the previous summer remained the yardstick for the conduct of foreign policy. Alexander Cadogan, the powerful permanent Under-Secretary at the Foreign Office, confided in his diary that he had been wondering 'more and more lately, whether we need be deterred from any action that we may think advantageous, simply for fear of finding ourselves in a state of war with Russia'.[23] The planners of the Chiefs of Staff were reluctant to become actively involved in the hostilities which from the 'purely military point of view . . . makes it more difficult to achieve our primary object in this war, the defeat of Germany'.[24] However, they were rebuffed by the Northern Department of the Foreign Office, entrusted with Russian affairs, which seriously questioned whether the Red Army 'exercised any restraint upon German military action' and believed it was a propitious opportunity 'to bring about the complete downfall of Russian military power'.[25]

The indirect assistance provided by Britain to Finland during the Winter War seriously alarmed the Kremlin. Stalin was alerted by Maisky to the fact that both the former appeasers and Churchill were 'deeply convinced that a secret military alliance already existed between the USSR and Germany . . . a cast-iron agreement, which was bound to lead Germany and the Soviet Union to an indissoluble alliance'. In Churchill's overtures he saw a 'complex game . . . a manoeuvre to get [the Soviet Union] entangled in war'.[26] It was feared that the belief in an imminent alliance between Russia and Germany would induce the British either to fight Russia or to embroil her in war with Germany. Maisky had already disclosed to Halifax that the 'rapidity' of the German conquest of Poland had come as 'a great surprise' to Russia, who could by no means 'contemplate with pleasure a future in which a powerful and victorious Germany should be her next-door neighbour'.[27] Molotov now urged him to dismiss the 'ludicrous and insulting' assumption that Russia sought a military alliance with Germany; 'even a political simpleton', he stressed, 'would not form such an alliance with a power involved in war, fully aware of the complicity and the risks involved in such an alliance'. Maisky was further provided with the proposed terms for peace with Finland, which had been worked out by the Russian military as 'the absolute minimal and effective guarantees for the security of Leningrad'. Maisky was to reaffirm the Soviet Union's intentions of remaining neutral as long as England and France did not 'take arms against her'.[28] Seeking mediation with Finland through Sir Stafford Cripps, the militant left-wing Member of Parliament, specially flown over from China where he was on a world tour, was yet another manifestation of Russian distress.[29] The Comintern was likewise mobilized to serve Soviet diplomacy by propagating the accusation that Britain and France 'initiated the war against Germany in an attempt to extend the fighting and convert it into a war against the Soviet Union'.[30]

The fear of war with England led the Russians to seek a quick conclusion to the war in Finland and a peace settlement, hopefully through British mediation. The ink was scarcely dry on the agreement when attention reverted to Turkey and the Balkans. In London, the Phoney War seemed to provide an opportunity to tighten the embargo as well as 'to exercise pressure in that part of the world which at present is not open to us'.[31] The British Commander-in-Chief left the Turks in no doubt that the German threat to Rumania and the Russian to Turkey made it 'of vital importance for H.M. Ships to be able to enter the Black Sea without delay'. Istanbul, they were reminded, was only 300 miles away from the Soviet naval base at Sebastopol, while the nearest British base was some 850 miles away. For the moment the Turkish government resisted British pressure, well aware that a commitment in advance might constitute an infringement of the Montreux Convention and render them belligerent.[32]

In the meantime reports reached the Kremlin from various capitals in the Balkans depicting the increased British efforts to direct the 'Little Entente' against Russia rather than against the Central Powers, for which it had been initially designed. The role of Turkey in facilitating the transfer of troops from Syria and Egypt 'through the Dardanelles in preparation of a new Crimean War' became a recurrent theme.[33] Suspicions soared so high that Molotov requested Haydar Aktay, the authoritative and veteran Turkish ambassador in Moscow, to inform him what was happening 'behind the scenes of General Weygand's visit to Turkey and to the strategic regions on the Soviet border'. How could he explain his Prime Minister's enigmatic comment, when denying rumours of the deterioration of relations with Russia, that 'we are living today in an epoch when everyone conceals his intentions'? Before Aktay was able to answer he was recalled to Ankara for consultations, just as the British and French ambassadors were withdrawn from Moscow in protest against the Finnish War.[34] Shortly afterwards the British request for passage of the navy through the Dardanelles was leaked to the press and raised in Parliament.[35] An exaggerated report by the BBC disclosed the joint staff talks in Ankara concerning the implementation of the mutual assistance pact.[36] In Berlin the Germans too continued to play on Soviet apprehensions by inflating the belligerent British intentions in the region.[37]

These apprehensions were magnified with the increasing rumours of Allied plans to bomb the Baku oilfields. The oilfields yielded 80 per cent of the aviation oil, 90 per cent of the kerosene and 96 per cent of the petrol produced by the USSR.[38] Earlier on Schulenburg had disclosed to Molotov that the French troops in Syria were in fact earmarked for operations in Baku and that attempts had been made to reach an understanding with the Shah to allow Allied planes to fly over Iranian territory.[39] Plans were indeed being drawn up in London for a joint Anglo-French raid on the Baku oilfields.[40] Their destruction was expected to 'react decisively on Soviet military efficiency and Soviet national life'.

The possible repercussions of the operation on Russia, and the fact that it 'would almost certainly lead to a definite alliance between Germany and the Soviet Union', were overlooked. In fact it was noted with obvious regret that 'in order to make a direct attack on the Caucasus we should have to pick a quarrel with the Soviet Government unless they were stupid enough to give us a real cause for taking military action against them'.[41] The major reservation concerned the implications for relations with Turkey. While the French wished to force the Turkish government to allow Allied bombers to fly over its territory on their way to Baku, the British regarded Turkey as the ' "lynch-pin" of that part of the world and it wd. be risky to "treat her rough", as we propose treating other neutrals'. Reynaud, the French Prime Minister, was little swayed by such reservations. He persevered in his demand 'to proceed to action in the Black Sea' and even deemed the occupation of Bessarabia to be an essential deterrent against Turkish collusion with Russia.[42]

To overcome Turkish resistance Churchill, as the First Lord of the Admiralty, encouraged Halifax to visit the region. He further hoped that Halifax would persuade the Turks to allow British submarines to operate in the Black Sea against German and Soviet boats; he had been advocating such action since October.[43] Before setting off, Halifax summoned to London the heads of missions from South-eastern Europe for consultations, fully aware that the gathering could not be concealed and would 'give concrete evidence that we are actively interesting ourselves in the Balkans'.[44] While preparations for the consultations were under way, the German invasion of Denmark and Norway led to a reshuffle in Cabinet, strengthening the position of Churchill, who was the moving force behind the Balkan plans.[45]

The Allies ostensibly aimed at consolidating 'a benevolent neutral bloc with the object of preventing the spread of the war to the Balkans'. They realized, however, that their predominance in the Balkans was bound to lead to an armed confrontation with the Soviet Union and hoped that the Turks would 'facilitate possible Allied intervention on their behalf' through control of the Straits and the free transit of troops.[46] Oblivious to the danger lying ahead in Europe, the Chiefs of Staff noted the 'unimpressive' record of the Wehrmacht. Turkey was singled out as England's most important strategic asset, without whose 'active collaboration, it would be difficult, should it be necessary to undertake active hostilities against Russia, to attack the vital sources of oil supply in the Caucasus'.[47]

None of the ambassadors was enthusiastic about the plans to attack Baku. They did not expect the Turks to approve such a scheme unless the Russians advanced beyond the Danube. The new Soviet overtures were correctly attributed to the fear of British action in the Black Sea. Trade negotiations, proposed by the Russians, were therefore to be conducted, as Halifax instructed, 'with a stiff upper lip' in a manner which would not 'prevent us at a later stage from taking action in the Caucasus, should the Turks agree to co-operate with us there'. The significance of the London meeting did not lie in its actual results, which were instantly rendered obsolete by the Wehrmacht action in the West. Rather, the mere convening of the widely publicized meeting enhanced the Russians' suspicion and hastened their own intervention in the Balkans.[48] Chamberlain was far more determined in his opposition to any reconciliatory measures; 'he who sups with the Devil', he warned the Allied Supreme Council, 'needs a long spoon'. Right up to the German invasion of France, Reynaud continued to advocate the bombing of the Caucasus oilfields, hoping it would 'produce chaos in Russia'. However, the implications for relations with Turkey, whose air space would have to be violated, continued to protect Russia.[49]

Cripps's Mission to Moscow

Deep-seated prejudices precluded a significant change in Churchill's policy towards Russia after his assumption of the premiership in May 1940.[50] The one apparent exception was the appointment of Sir Stafford Cripps as ambassador to Moscow. In retrospect Churchill has taken the credit for the decision to appoint Cripps as an ambassador. The idea, however, came from Halifax, who had been the driving force behind Cripps's earlier initiatives, and was much encouraged by the Russians. This is obvious from various entries in Halifax's unpublished diary. On 17 May he wrote, 'After the Cabinet I talked with [Churchill] in the garden for a few minutes, partly about an idea I had had to send Stafford Cripps on an exploratory mission to Moscow, and partly about future prospects of the war,' and three days later he added: 'I had various office engagements, at the end of which I saw Maisky to ask him to see whether the Soviet would concur in my own idea of sending Stafford Cripps on an exploratory mission about trade to Moscow. I should be surprised if they don't, and it may well be that with things going as they are at present the Russians will want to talk a little bit wider.' Finally on the 26th: 'At 6 o'clock I saw Maisky. The Soviet Government agree to Cripps, but want him to be an Ambassador. I told Maisky we meant to send an Ambassador, and hardly supposed the Soviet Government claimed to choose him for us.' As it turned out, that is what indeed transpired.[51] In the light of his subsequent rivalry with Cripps, Churchill would excuse the appointment on the ground that he did not 'realize sufficiently that Soviet Communists hate extreme left wing politicians even more than they do Tories or Liberals'. Churchill explained cynically: 'Moscow is the most expensive Embassy we have. Cripps is the only suitable left-wing man we have who is rolling in money.'[52]

If Cripps's mission ever stood any chance of success, it was dependent on a categorical reconsideration and definition of the Cabinet's policy. Maisky warned him at the outset that the position of an ambassador was like that of a salesman: 'if he is offering goods of high quality he is assured of success even if he is an unremarkable man, but if he is offering

substandard goods he will meet with disaster in spite of the best possible personal qualities'. Later he was sympathetic towards Cripps's frustration, which he attributed to the fact that he had not been 'provided
with quality goods', and his customer did not want to buy 'rotten stuff'.
Maisky was unaware that Orme Sargent, the deputy Under-Secretary at
the Foreign Office, used a similar metaphor: he did not expect Stalin to
respond to Cripps, who 'as a suppliant on his doormat' was holding 'his
pathetic little peace offerings of tin in one hand and rubber in the other'.[53]

At the time of his appointment Cripps, an outcast from his own Labour
Party for having advocated an anti-fascist front with the communists in
1939, was entirely absorbed in the 'formation of the world to be born after
the war'. He foresaw the emergence of the Soviet Union and the United
States as the major powers, with Britain reduced to the position of an
'outpost' in Europe.[54] In that respect he saw eye to eye with Stalin, who
never lost hold of his vision of the post-war order. Cripps, who entertained few illusions about Stalin's ideological outlook, assumed that
the only possibility of drawing Russia away from Germany rested 'on the
basis of recognising a continuing friendship and a partnership in post-
war reconstruction'.[55] Churchill, however, avoided any attempt to discuss
war aims in Cabinet. One should not be distracted by the simplistic presentation of the war aims in his memoirs as the annihilation of Nazism
and a return to the *status quo ante bellum*. This concealed his inherently
imperialist outlook and the opportunity offered by the war for re-
establishing Britain's deteriorating international position. Unlike
Churchill, Cripps regarded the war as a catalyst for social and political
change at home. He rebuked Churchill for his lack of vision and for sub-
ordinating all issues to the winning of the war. To Cripps, Churchill
seemed to be in the 'pre 1914 era and trying desperately hard to keep
there, falsely assuming that it was possible to look behind and take a
permanent position on the safety valve!!'[56] The fundamental political
dispute between Cripps and Churchill, soft-pedalled by Churchill in his
memoirs, is vital for an understanding of the events surrounding the
German invasion and the Grand Alliance at its inception.

Cripps was not alone in spreading his ideas. His political stature
grew after his return to England in 1942, not only because of his association with the heroic resistance of the Red Army, as Churchill wishes us to
believe,[57] but as a result of the experience and reputation he had gained
through his mission in Moscow. Cripps's advocacy of post-war reconstruction seemed to provide a basis for joint efforts not only with Labour
politicians but also with the powerful emerging group of 'progressive
Conservatives'. Sir Walter Monckton, general director of the Ministry
of Information and later Defence Minister, clearly fuelled Cripps's confrontation with Churchill by advising him that from the political point of
view:

I fear that too long a stay in such an unsatisfactory position might injure your prospects of leading us all a little later on. The fact is that there is no satisfactory successor or alternative to Winston. I am pretty clear now that Ernie Bevin will not fill the part. Anthony [Eden] is too conventional a thinker to make a great leader, and one looks in vain among the rest for the right quality of mind and character . . . I have discussed you as a leader with the most diverse people, from Nancy Astor up and down. I find them all attracted by the possibility.[58]

Indeed, when Cripps was recalled to England for consultations at the beginning of June 1941, a leader in *The Times* urged the use of his 'exceptional capacities nearer home . . . in strengthening the quality of Labour Party representation in the supreme councils of the nation'. Churchill was obliged to promise him a seat in the War Cabinet after completion of his mission in Moscow.

An unusual situation emerged whereby Cripps, a member of a minority left-wing faction in Parliament, found himself in an exceptionally crucial role as British ambassador to the sole major power on the Continent still not crushed by Germany, while remaining an outspoken opponent of his own government. The appointment was also motivated by domestic considerations. Rab Butler, the Parliamentary Under-Secretary, warned Halifax of the 'fairly strong urge in this new Govt. both on Right & Left for a rapprochement and you will only be pressed if Cripps doesn't go'.[59] The appointment of Cripps, though originally sanctioned by the Russians, was seen by a desolate government as a last-ditch attempt to drive a wedge between Russia and Germany after the devastating collapse of France. The cornerstone of British policy was a determined attempt to involve Russia in the war.

In essence Cripps obediently followed Churchill's policy of detaching Russia from Germany. However, unlike Churchill and the Foreign Office, he assumed that Stalin was aware of the fragility of the pact and was desperately trying to defer the inevitable clash with Germany. From the outset of his mission, Cripps was under no illusions about Stalin: for him, 'Lenin was the great world reformer whose noble intentions had been botched by Stalin'. Stalin, as he confided to the Swedish ambassador in Moscow, was 'a sly Georgian for whom power was all and who cared little about the millions of beings he ruled with an iron fist, without any sign of improvement in the living condition of the masses being noticeable so far. Power is everything, and in order to stay in power . . . he would be willing to conclude an agreement with the Pope if it were to serve his interests.' Consequently, Cripps did not exclude the possibility that in certain circumstances Stalin might yield to Hitler and make extensive concessions to defer the war which he considered to be a threat to his regime.[60]

In the final analysis, the fall of France and the appointment of Cripps seem to have bolstered the prevailing British attitude towards Russia rather than altering it. True, the loss of their allies on the Continent momentarily inspired the British to close ranks with the Russians. But the measures taken were too little and too late. The Foreign Office was particularly averse to the appointment of Cripps, still a Member of Parliament representing the militant left wing, maintaining that a 'rude duke' was bound to have a better reception in Moscow.

In mid-July Orme Sargent presented an important memorandum for consideration within the Foreign Office which rebutted current speculations that Germany and Russia would inevitably be in opposition. Russia could have a decisive impact on the course of events only if she were to intervene directly in the war on the side of Britain:

> As regards the somewhat drastic step of undertaking a preventive war against Germany at this stage Stalin is likely to be deterred from it by fear of German military might, by the desire to avoid war with a great Power, which, largely for internal reasons, has long been the guiding principle of Soviet foreign policy, and also by the consideration that Germany is unlikely to emerge from her struggle with Great Britain completely unscathed and may well hesitate to undertake the invasion of the Soviet Union this year, especially if the Soviet Government show themselves sufficiently accommodating.

In order to impede Hitler's triumphant progress, Stalin's best course was 'to continue to collaborate with him and thus keep on as good terms with him as possible'.

This realistic and astute analysis was, however, distorted by the Foreign Office's ideological outlook on Russia. Any attempt to disrupt the Ribbentrop–Molotov Pact was deemed by Sargent to be a waste of time, as 'neither dictator *dare* turn away lest the other stab him in the back'. As both Stalin and Hitler considered the British Empire to be 'the ultimate enemy', it was safe to assume that 'their appetites [would] grow with eating'. Consequently, there was little point in attempting to separate Russia from Germany. In short, he expected the two dictators to 'quarrel over the booty, but this is not likely to happen so long as the war continues, and we should not therefore count upon such a quarrel as an element in estimating the difficulties and dangers that Germany may have to face in the immediate future'. In the absence of a coherent policy, this memorandum, highly praised by Halifax, was presented to Churchill and the various intelligence agencies. Its conclusions gradually emerged as the governing concept in the conduct of relations with Moscow until the German invasion of Russia.[61]

2

The Scramble for the Balkans

Soviet–Italian Collusion

In view of the heavy defeats inflicted on the Red Army in the early stages of Operation 'Barbarossa', it is often argued that the stiff resistance of the Finns in the Winter War revealed the weakness of the Red Army, encouraging Hitler to risk war against Russia. However, for contemporaries in Germany and in the countries bordering on the Soviet Union, Red Army engagements rather demonstrated Stalin's resolve to enter war wherever he encountered a threat to Soviet vital interests.[1] As spring 1940 arrived, resting on the laurels of the Ribbentrop–Molotov Pact and final victory against Finland, Stalin was temporarily relaxed. Count Werner von Schulenburg, the German ambassador to Moscow, contributed to that feeling. Though admitting that he knew little of Hitler's inner thoughts, he nonetheless was certain that the British would 'soon find out what is in store for them'. He assured Molotov that the war in Finland had not injured German interests and even congratulated the Red Army on its victory.[2] Both Ribbentrop and Weizsäcker, the director of the German Foreign Ministry, followed suit.[3] In negotiations with Göring, singled out in the Kremlin as the spearhead of the crusade against Russia, the Air Marshal not only promised an early delivery of war material but 'strongly underlined the exceptional friendship between Germany and the Soviet Union'. He even announced the delivery to the Soviet navy of the modern cruiser *Lützow*, from which he was parting 'with a painful heart'. He quoted Hitler as saying that the pact was 'a solid and irreversible act'.[4] Stalin further found out that Hitler had reaffirmed the validity and durability of the division of spheres of interests between Germany and Russia in the talks he had held in Berlin with Sumner Welles, the American Under-Secretary of State.[5]

Stalin in fact felt strong enough to suspend the delivery of raw materials to Germany in retaliation for her failure to provide Russia with coal and military equipment. Recent findings concerning trade between Germany and the Soviet Union cast doubt on the accepted view that the treaty was favourable to Germany. Soviet deliveries, when examined against Soviet production and total German demand, were not very substantial. They provided the Russians with significant advanced German technology. Moreover, to a large extent the Russians were obliged to conduct almost exclusive trade with Germany once the British imposed a tight economic blockade. Out of one million tons of grain promised to Germany, only 150,000 tons had been dispatched, and the supply of oil and coal products fared no better.[6] Perhaps for the last time Mikoyan, the Minister of Foreign Trade, openly cast doubt on German 'honesty', complaining that he could 'no longer afford to make a fool of himself, in practice not conducting a bilateral exchange of goods but unilaterally delivering goods to Germany'.[7] Stalin went one step further in presenting an ultimatum to Germany. He demanded the conclusion of a short-term trade agreement stipulating export of Soviet raw materials of a value of 420–30 million marks in exchange for 'industrial and military deliveries of the same value'.[8] This inflated confidence, however, instantly evaporated after the swift German campaign against Denmark and Norway in early May. The Soviet ultimatum was replaced by an announcement of the decision to resume deliveries, followed by the 'hope' that 'Germany would do the same'.[9] However, the experience of dependence on Stalin's goodwill for deliveries of raw materials undoubtedly weighed heavily on Hitler when Operation 'Barbarossa' was contemplated.[10]

For the moment Stalin was still convinced that fear of Germany and Italy would persuade the Balkan states to 'look more and more to Russia as their natural protector'.[11] Recognizing the ominous implications of a clash over the Balkans, Schulenburg departed for Berlin to pave the road for a visit by Molotov.[12] However, Stalin's satisfaction at having avoided 'becoming Germany's tail' led him to a polite rejection of the idea.[13] Still complacent about a German danger, he continued to be haunted by the threat in the south, where he expected Turkey to serve as a platform for an Allied attack against the Soviet Union. The message accompanying his greetings for Hitler's birthday is an early indication of his concern at the growing reports that the 'fire of war might soon spread' to the Balkans.[14] Ribbentrop played on Stalin's known fears, presenting the German initiatives in the region as a countermeasure to British attempts to force the Turks to open the Straits to the British and French navies.[15] And yet, now that the arrangements concerning Northern and Central Europe had been implemented, the future of South-eastern Europe, ignored by those arrangements, was awaited with apprehension. The French collapse in June 1940 dissolved the Balkan Entente and introduced a dangerous vacuum. The inability of Britain to back her guarantees placed Rumania and Turkey in a perilous state.[16]

Molotov's congratulations to Schulenburg 'on the splendid success of the German Armed Forces' in France stand in contrast to the intense panic which seized Moscow following the 'rapid progress' of the campaign.[17] The accolade was merely a prelude to the feeble excuses presented by Molotov for the hasty occupation of the Baltic States that same morning, to 'undermine the British and French intrigues there'. Equally disconcerting for the Germans was the hasty deployment of the Red Army 'to guard the borders' of Lithuania, without the enemy being named. The explanations were so flimsy that Schulenburg preferred to transmit to Berlin a highly censored version of his conversations.[18]

The need for the Russians to gain a foothold in the Balkans became acute as soon as the ominous information that the battle in the west would be concluded within two months had sunk in; it was clear that the Germans might 'in the not too far future . . . turn against the East'.[19] The shattering defeat of France now drew Russia closer to Italy, with whom relations had been strained since the outbreak of war in September 1939. Mussolini had feared that the Ribbentrop–Molotov Pact might be extended to South-eastern Europe, undermining Italy's ambitions there. It was no secret to Stalin that Mussolini aimed at 'constructing a bridge with England and France, thereby nourishing latent Anti-Soviet constellations'. Hitler was rumoured to have blessed the initiative, hoping to isolate the Russians and make them 'more amenable to comply with their economic obligations'. Count Ciano, the Italian Foreign Minister, even encouraged the Rumanian government to take a 'firm line on Bessarabia', promising lavish assistance in the event of an attack.[20] Still lulled by his pact with Hitler, Stalin hoped to teach the Italians that it was 'hardly advantageous for them to seek the further worsening of relations with the Soviet Union'. Consequently the ambassadors were withdrawn from Rome and Moscow in early January 1940. Relations further deteriorated when the foreign ministers of Italy and Hungary met in Venice to contemplate the future of the Balkans. Though the conference was not ostensibly directed against the Soviet Union, the exclusion of Russia from the negotiations, which dealt with the various claims on Rumania, clearly harmed Soviet interests.[21]

As we have seen,[22] the British were eager to set the Balkans ablaze. Hitler, on the other hand, sought tranquillity while sealing the plans for the campaign in the West. Moreover, Mussolini's attempts to rejuvenate the Balkan Entente jeopardized Ribbentrop's efforts to reconcile the Axis to the Moscow Pact. During a visit to Rome in mid-March Ribbentrop applied pressure to Mussolini to maintain the status quo in relations with Russia. Laying the foundations for his ambitious Continental bloc,[23] Ribbentrop exerted similar pressure on the Russians.[24] Ciano, however,

Annexations by

☰	USSR
⧄	GERMANY
⧄	BULGARIA

TERRITORIAL CHANGES – 1938-40

made only half-hearted moves to accommodate the Russians at the end of April, dissociating Italy from Rumania by revealing that an attempt had been made to use him as a vehicle to carry Rumanian grievances against Russia to Berlin.[25] Reluctantly Mussolini mellowed, vaguely indicating his willingness to return the ambassadors to their posts.[26] For the time being, however, Ciano was perceived in Moscow to be the genuine obstacle to rapprochement, and the impasse remained. Molotov preferred to follow events at his own pace; the Soviet Union, he told Schulenburg, was not 'the right place for being edgy'.[27] 'What a paradoxical condition, is it not?' commented Mascia, the Italian chargé d'affaires in Moscow, during a diplomatic reception, 'that we are enemies with the Soviet Union and friends with Germany and Germany is at the same time bound to Moscow.' He too appeared doubtful whether Mussolini would allow the Russians to 'encroach into this "Italian life centre" '.[28]

It was, however, the dazzling success of the Wehrmacht in France which shuffled all the cards and helped Mussolini and Stalin to overcome their mutual suspicion. The new community of interests rose from the ashes of the former British presence in the region. As soon as the war was unleashed in France, Hans Georg von Mackensen, the German ambassador in Rome, anxious to preserve the peace in the Balkans, promised Gelfand, the Soviet chargé d'affaires, that 'the Balkan problem will be decided together between Germany, Italy and the USSR without war'. The successes on the battlefield, however, brought about a change of heart. Though the Russians continued to regard the statement as a German commitment, Mackensen now described it as a 'figment of Gelfand's imagination'. With his hands relatively free, Hitler had become concerned about an Italian–Soviet collusion which might go beyond his initial plan and challenge German natural dominance in the region. Dizzy with military success, he expected that a settlement of the outstanding issues in the Balkans would be effected 'merely by the exercise of the preponderant power of the victors without striking a blow'. Stalin faced the bleak prospect of being either left out of the arrangements or crushed by German supremacy unless he took the initiative to safeguard Russia's interests.[29]

The fear of an Italian advance into the Balkans from Saloniki after Italy's entry into the war necessitated a new orientation of Soviet policy.[30] Molotov now welcomed the return to Moscow of Rosso, the Italian ambassador, although he arrived empty-handed, having failed to meet Ciano before his departure. Molotov regarded the mere entry of Italy into the war as an asset to the plans to eliminate the British threat to Russia in the Black Sea, and entertained the hope that 'the voice of Germany and Italy and that of the Soviet Union would be listened to more than a year from now'.[31] Mussolini too abandoned his hopes of benefiting from the Allies and appeared genuinely anxious to obtain some assurances from the Russians on the Balkan problem.[32] The Allied guarantees in the Balkans, jeered Ciano, 'could be best compared with a bottle of wine, which has been preserved for many years with the hope of producing strong and good wine, but when the bottle is finally opened, it is found to contain vinegar instead of wine'.[33] In Munich, as Stalin found out, Mussolini had informed Hitler of his intention to 'bring about the ultimate improvement of political and economic relations with the Soviet Union'.[34]

Like Stalin, the Italians expected Hitler to 'inflict a couple of blows on England', break her resilience and draw the more sensible leaders, such as Lloyd George, to the negotiating table where a new European order would be established. This prognosis was confirmed by NKVD agents within Göring's headquarters. The prospect of an imminent peace conference drove both Italy and Russia to consolidate their common interests in the Balkans, the Turkish Straits and the Mediterranean. Once the peace conference convened, Stalin expected Russia to be powerful enough to redress her past and present grievances.[35] The new association clearly served as leverage against the German predominance in Central and Western Europe. In Rome the Soviet ambassador courted Mussolini energetically, admiring Italy's age-old heritage. However, he soon came to the point, suggesting that the end of Anglo-French mastery in Europe made it 'opportune for the voices of the USSR, Italy and Germany to be heard in the international arena'. Mussolini himself, by soft-pedalling ideological differences and dwelling on common interests, instilled in Stalin the false impression that Russia's seat at the peace conference was indeed secure.[36]

The new partnership was consolidated on the day of the Soviet invasion of Bessarabia[37] through the reconfirmation of the 1933 non-aggression pact between Italy and Russia – 'not only in spirit but also to allow it to have teeth to grind with'. Not surprisingly the terms of an agreement with Italy sought by Stalin resembled the essence of the secret Racconigi Agreement between Nicholas II and King Victor Emmanuel III of October 1909. In a complementary move Stalin brought about the establishment of relations with Yugoslavia on 24 June; Yugoslavia had been the only country in South-east Europe to resist recognition of the Soviet Union. The move clearly aimed at curtailing German influence in Yugoslavia while extending Soviet spheres of interest to the region.[38] It gave, warned the German ambassador in Belgrade, 'a strong impetus not only to the Communist, but, above all, to the Russophile tendencies of the country. The general feeling was that the alignment with Russia would provide some protection against the Italian–German danger.'[39]

Italy and Russia now set out to define their respective spheres of influence in the Mediterranean, the Black Sea and the Balkans. Rosso proposed to render the Mediterranean 'a free sea in the interest of Italy and other countries which needed that freedom'. Tacit consent was given to the Soviet claims to Bessarabia, and a place was promised at the peace conference where the outstanding issues between Rumania, Bulgaria and Hungary would be solved by peaceful means. The Russian concern over the Straits was relieved when Rosso renounced any claims on Turkey. The principle governing the new partnership, as Molotov was quick to sum up, was: 'what you want is to establish your legitimate rights in the Mediterranean just as the Soviet Union has the legitimate right to full control of the Black Sea, which must be exclusively Russian. The present regime of the Straits can no longer be maintained and has to be altered.' The prospects for a new order in the Balkans under the aegis of the two powers directly involved in the region seemed bright.

The principles of Soviet policy in the Balkans were therefore hastily worked out. The prize for Italy was a recognition of Hungary's claims on Rumania. As for Bulgaria, Molotov counted on her traditionally close relations with Russia, which he hoped to invigorate through the satisfaction of her territorial claims to Dobrudja from Rumania and Thrace from Greece. Russia was not oblivious to the German interests in Rumania, first and foremost the oilfields, and was prepared to define the spheres of influence there together with Italy and Germany. Finally, Molotov recognized the primary role of Italy in the Mediterranean but in return expected the Italians to concede the Soviet interests in the Black Sea.[40] The Soviet–Italian understanding undoubtedly paved the way for the Russian occupation of Bessarabia. But once the Germans diverted their attention to the Balkans, their overwhelming power was brought to bear on Italy, bringing to an end the stillborn collaboration with the Russians. 'Any further Russian participation', Mussolini was warned, might encourage the Balkan countries 'to pit one great power against another'. The German interest was to keep the Straits in 'as fluid a state as possible' and confront a Turkey that possessed 'only a worthless guarantee from England and was otherwise in sharp opposition to Russia'.[41]

The Soviet Seizure of Bessarabia

The occupation of Bessarabia and Northern Bukovina in the last days of June 1940 resulted from a desire for security arrangements in the Balkans and the Black Sea littoral rather than an insatiable Russian appetite, as is often presented in the literature. It was devoid of any ideological motive for expansion *per se*.[42] As we have seen, Stalin was slow to grasp the threat which the German invasion of the Low Countries posed to Russia by upsetting the delicate equilibrium established between the two countries through the pact.[43] Strangely enough, he expected the invasion to deflect the more imminent threat in the Black Sea and the Balkans. Molotov therefore did not even bother to question the German failure to consult him in advance, as the terms of the Ribbentrop–Molotov Pact required. Unruffled, he accepted the absurd German explanation that the war in the West was 'forced upon Germany by an impending Anglo-French thrust on the Ruhr region through Belgium and Holland', while express-ing the hope that the events would have 'an impact on the next 1,000 years of German history'.[44] He was further mollified by Ribbentrop, who shortly after the conclusion of the war in Norway received the Soviet ambassador in his private lodgings at the Chancellery 'with extreme friendliness'. Ribbentrop skilfully diverted Soviet suspicions by attrib-uting the war in the West to British intrigues, quoting from documents seized in Narvik which described the pressure exerted on Sweden and Norway to allow the transfer of British troops to Finland.[45] Any attempt by the Allies to alert Stalin to the German danger was immediately inter-preted as an attempt to involve Russia in the war.[46]

Rumours of Soviet intentions in Bessarabia had been circulating freely since the outbreak of war.[47] Although Molotov went out of his way to deny the purported Soviet 'foul intentions' to set the Balkans ablaze, he never abandoned the claim to Bessarabia.[48] From the outset he had made it clear that the annexation was tied up with the Soviet need to control the mouth of the Danube. For this reason the Turks were urged as early as October 1939 to condone an invasion of Bessarabia, a com-pliance which would prevent the British and French from rendering assistance to Rumania by sailing their fleet through the Bosphorus.[49] The Turks, however, refused to comply, fearing German–Soviet collusion in the Black Sea. Saracoglu's stand, when he would not exclude the possibility of allowing commercial ships loaded with military equipment to reach the Black Sea if war erupted in the region, gave the Russians pause for thought. Thus the agreement on mutual assistance, signed between Turkey and Britain on the eve of the war, coupled with the British guarantees to Rumania, rendered Allied intervention in the Black Sea likely.[50]

Britain's immediate concern was to prevent the Germans from reach-ing the Black Sea and posing a threat to the Rumanian oilfields. For a while she even toyed with the idea of condoning a Soviet occupation of Bessarabia, as long as it did not lead to a general flare-up in the Balkans.[51] The Rumanians, however, regarded the Soviet threat as the most men-acing. They exploited to the utmost the indignation against Russia over the war with Finland, seeking British military assistance to counter the 'imminent' occupation of Bessarabia, which might lead to 'the Bolshevi-sation of Central and South-eastern Europe'.[52] In the wake of the Winter War Molotov found that the Allies had indeed changed their tune, now appealing to the Rumanians not to surrender Bessarabia and 'spreading slanders and erroneous information to swing the population to assume an anti-Soviet attitude'.[53] Fear of Britain on the one hand and the wish to avert an appearance of a Soviet–British plot on the other prevented Stalin for the moment from implementing his agreement with Ribbentrop on the future of Bessarabia. The unexpected entanglement in Finland further discouraged him from embarking on new military adventures.

The looming British threat in the Black Sea led Stalin to seek a solution of the Bessarabian issue by diplomatic means. In mid-February 1940 he approached the Rumanian government with a proposal for a non-aggression pact. In exchange for territories in Soviet Moldavia Stalin asked for control of the mouth of the Danube, and more specifically the ports of Sulina and Constanza.[54] King Carol of Rumania, however, reacted by making a startling proposal to the British ambassador; he suggested that Britain could overcome the restrictions of the Montreux Agreement by sending a fleet disguised as a Turkish one into the Black Sea. Over a lavish dinner of snails and oysters especially ordered for that purpose from Paris, and fortified by exquisite port, the King further urged the ambassador to exploit the 'great possibilities in the Caucasus'.[55]

Having extended Russia's security arrangements in the Baltic Sea through the peace imposed on Finland, Stalin set out to implement the final stage of the Ribbentrop–Molotov agreement. Bessarabia had been ceded to Russia in 1812 by the Turks. Part of it had been lost to Rumania after the Crimean War but regained after the wars of 1877–8. The Treaty of Neuilly in 1919 entrusted the entire region to Rumania. Although Stalin resorted to ethnic and historical reasonings to justify the Russian claim to Bessarabia, the move continued to be dictated by what he conceived to be the prevalent British threat in the Black Sea. The extension of the Soviet security system to the mouth of the Danube added an indispensable depth of defence for Sebastopol and Odessa, hardly 40 kilometres from the Rumanian border. Even the British ambassador in Bucharest admitted reluctantly that, rather than pursuing territorial claims or contesting the control of the oilfields, the Russians wished to obtain the 'right to garrison certain areas in the north and to have representatives and possibly troops in Rumanian ports'. He adhered to this view, arguing convincingly that:

> From the Russian point of view Bessarabia is not only important on account of ethnographical considerations. It would have been a magnificent *point de départ* for a German attack on the heart of the Ukraine, for a turning movement towards Kiev and the Prypet marshes such as the German High Command has used with such successes in the campaigns in Poland and in Western Europe. The best protection for Russia against such a manoeuvre would be to acquire the line of the Carpathians and the Danube Delta.[56]

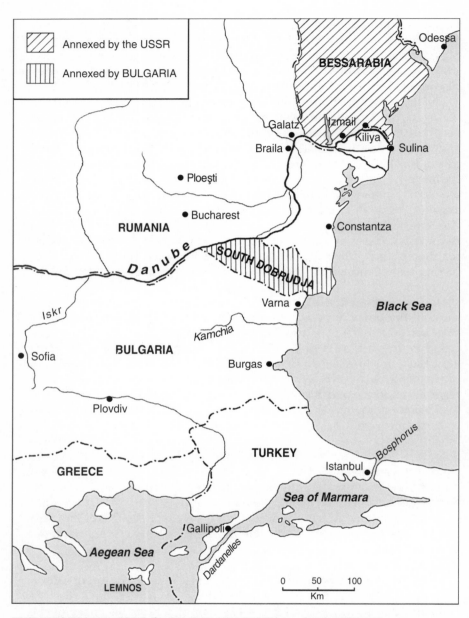

THE WESTERN LITTORAL OF THE BLACK SEA – AUTUMN 1940

That the Russians' attention was focused on the control of the Danube is attested by the fact that they forced the Rumanians to participate in a special mixed commission which was set up in Odessa within days of the occupation to demarcate the border at the mouth of the Danube.[57]

The occupation of Northern Bukovina was also motivated by strategic considerations. It left Stalin with control of the major railway lines between the Ukraine and Bessarabia, via Cernauti and Lvov. Schulenburg made extraordinary efforts to conceal Stalin's strategic considerations from Hitler, presenting the cession of Bukovina as a move forced on the Kremlin by Ukrainian circles close to Stalin. He stressed the fact that Molotov had in fact readily 'waived Russia's claims for Carpathian Ukraine'. The German ambassador preferred to gloss over the real Soviet motives, which implied a potential clash of interests with Germany.[58]

It no longer proved possible for King Carol to hold off the blow through a last-minute improvement of relations. Instead, Molotov started preparing the ground for the annexation by registering complaints about alleged shooting incidents on the border.[59] Stalin carefully timed the annexation to take place while 'the attention of the belligerent states was pinned on the western front', and after securing Mussolini's approval.[60] Swift action was essential in view of the ample evidence he possessed about Germany's intentions to tighten her grip on Rumania, possibly together with the Italians, once the battle against England was over. The resignation of the pro-Western Foreign Minister, Gafencu, on 30 May 1940 confirmed the impression in the Kremlin that Rumania was swinging towards Germany.[61] The propitious time therefore seemed to be the end of June, when, according to intelligence reports put on Stalin's desk, Hitler planned to launch his attack on England.[62] In preparation for his next move Stalin placated the Germans by renewing the raw-material deliveries which had virtually come to a standstill.[63]

On 21 June Lieutenant-General Ernst Köstring, the veteran German military attaché in Moscow, briefed the Russian Ministry of Defence on the harsh terms imposed on the French and the humiliation inflicted on them by the terms of the capitulation in the 'historic wagon' in Compiègne.[64] Within a day Schulenburg was urgently summoned to the Kremlin and informed that the question of Bessarabia 'brooked no further delay'; Molotov was not even prepared to give Schulenburg time to consult his government.[65] The news that Stalin was considering a move into Bessarabia came as an unpleasant surprise to Schulenburg. With Germany triumphant in France, such a belligerent step was unexpected, considering that Hitler could muster sufficient troops 'for a campaign against the Soviet Union and could pretty easily march up to the Ural mountains'.[66] However, for the duration of the Battle of Britain Hitler could do little but abide by the undertakings given by Ribbentrop during his visit to Moscow. At the same time he would exploit the Soviet move to the utmost in order to enhance his hold on South-eastern Europe. To prevent the Bulgarians and the Hungarians from following up with their own claims, which could endanger German vital economic interests in Rumania, Hitler took the initiative, presenting himself both as a mediator and as a saviour of those countries from Bolshevism. King Carol was strongly advised to concede Bessarabia without resistance.[67]

On the night of 26 June Molotov presented the Rumanians with an ultimatum demanding the immediate evacuation of Bessarabia.[68] As a last resort the Rumanians tried to drag the Germans into the conflict. The German ambassador in Bucharest warned that, 'senseless' as it might be from the military point of view, the Rumanians were prepared to set the Balkans on fire. They seemed to be deliberately protracting negotiations with the Russians in the hope that, after the victory in the West, Germany 'might still after all be interested in keeping the Russians out of the Balkans'.[69] Stalin, however, had prepared for all eventualities. The plea of the Rumanian government for an extension of the negotiations, made an hour after the expiry of the ultimatum, was turned down. The Rumanian ambassador was informed by Molotov that it was 'imperative for the Soviet troops to start moving in the next morning and for the Rumanian ones to retreat', completing the evacuation 'in perfect order' within three days.[70] Schulenburg was next informed that the Red Army had already been ordered to cross the Dniester river and that the orders could not be rescinded.[71]

On receipt of the ultimatum King Carol, literally in a tantrum, summoned the German ambassador to the Palace. However, the King's incessant intrigues had robbed him of the respect of any of the major powers. Ribbentrop bluntly blamed him for playing the belligerents off against each other: first by receiving British guarantees and then by seeking Germany's support when her superiority had become obvious.[72] To his great dismay the King found that the Italians were also sympathetic to the Russian claim.[73] He finally tried to enlist British support, painting in bleak colours the Soviet threat to the Straits. Churchill was urged to act like 'Lord Salisbury and Mr. Disraeli, when Bessarabia had changed hands in 1878'. But in London such suggestions were attributed to the 'interest of the Rumanians at the moment to make our flesh creep as regards Russian intentions'.[74]

Eventually the Rumanians received an extra couple of hours to complete the withdrawal and were held responsible for the safety of the railways, bridges, airfields and industrial complexes.[75] The potential claims from Bulgaria and Hungary left King Carol no choice but to place his fate in German hands. Stalin, delighted with his little coup and hopeful about Hitler's co-operation in the Balkans, failed to see how his well-orchestrated move had actually brought Rumania within the German grasp.[76]

British Schemes for the Balkans

Russian historiography since *glasnost* tends to side with the Cold War historians in blaming Stalin personally for the Soviet failure to put up an effective resistance against Germany. They now claim that, by rejecting the British and French overtures for a common struggle in the Balkans, Stalin lost a golden opportunity of averting the war with Germany.[77] This, however, overlooks the context in the Balkans in which the proposals were made. Placing the Balkans on the agenda in close proximity to the collapse of France was ill-timed, as it exposed the genuine Allied intentions of embroiling Russia in war. The long legacy of mutual suspicion and hostility condemned to failure an approach made in such circumstances.

By the summer of 1941, the Balkans had become not only Britain's last outpost in Europe but also the key to the defence of her imperial possessions in the Mediterranean and the Near East. In autumn 1939 Churchill, the First Sea Lord, had belatedly sought to recruit Russia against Germany; attempts to ensnare Russia in the war would become his trademark. The significance he attached to the Balkans had been made public in a famous radio speech shortly after the conclusion of the Ribbentrop–Molotov agreement:

> I cannot forecast to you the action of Russia. It is a riddle wrapped in a mystery inside an enigma. But perhaps there is a key. That key is Russian national interest. It cannot be in accordance with the interest of the safety of Russia that Germany should plant herself upon the shores of the Black Sea, or that she should overrun the Balkan States and subjugate the Slavonic peoples of South-eastern Europe. That would be contrary to the historic life-interests of Russia.[78]

He did not conceal from Maisky his plans for securing access to the Black Sea and preventing German control of the mouth of the Danube; from there he expected Germany to stretch her hands to Asia Minor, Iran and India.[79]

Churchill remained oblivious to the threat which his Balkan policy posed to Russia. Maisky reverted to Stalin's dictum of 1939 that Russia did not intend to 'pull somebody else's chestnuts out of the fire'; it was clear that in the current circumstances he would be just as reluctant 'to fight Germany on [Britain's] behalf'.[80] However, the renewal of German expansionism once again led the Russians to seek ways of defusing the threat of British action in the Straits or in Baku and reaffirming their neutrality. The means chosen was the conclusion of a barter agreement. However, the British insistence on restricting Soviet export of war material to Germany was perceived as 'an attempt to divert the Soviet Union from the policy of neutrality'. Halifax was in fact satisfied merely with having 'opened the ball with Maisky' but did not expect immediate results.[81]

The crumbling of the French defences revived Stalin's fears that Churchill might be tempted to follow in Pétain's footsteps and seek peace with Germany. Drawing on the experience of the Crimean War and the Allied intervention in the Civil War, he could not rule out the possibility that England might exercise her naval supremacy in the Mediterranean and force her way into the Black Sea, thus confronting Russia with a war on two fronts.[82] Alternatively, the Allies might be tempted to relieve the pressure in the West by opening a second front in the Balkans. Reports from Sofia suggested that 'Anglo-French agents' in King Boris's entourage and the military were frenziedly active in that direction.[83] NKVD agents in Istanbul reported the unloading of military equipment and ammunition from French, British and American vessels, while the Dardanelles were being fortified. British tankers were reported to be anchored in the Bosphorus and persistent rumours in Piraeus suggested that a British squadron was heading for the Black Sea, while Turkish troops were deployed on the Bulgarian border.[84] The Turkish suggestion that the presence of the British fleet near the Straits was aimed at Italy was taken with a grain of salt.[85]

This then was the background to the appointment of Cripps as ambassador in Moscow. Ostensibly Cripps arrived, with Soviet blessing, to negotiate a trade agreement. Stalin, however, was well aware even before Cripps's arrival in Moscow that the negotiations 'were apt to flow over into politics' and were aimed at 'encouraging the Russians to double cross the Germans'.[86] The more precise aspiration was that the German, Russian and Italian ambitions in South-eastern Europe might 'cancel each other out, and that it [might] be possible to maintain a kind of precarious vacuum'.[87] Campbell, the veteran ambassador in Belgrade, was quick to warn that in view of the 'welter of Balkan politics' it was 'unprofitable if not unavailing for His Majesty's Government to interfere actively in the relations between the States of the Peninsula . . . An active and above all an open intervention is dangerous and any clear attempt at hustling harmful.'[88] Indeed, Cripps's presence in Moscow and the views he was expressing very shortly gave rise to rumours of a growing split between Germany and Russia.[89] The temptation, however, was near irresistible.

Oblivious to the emerging Italian–Soviet entente, Cripps suggested to Molotov, in their very first meeting, in mid-June, to 'bring the Balkan countries together . . . against German and Italian aggression'.[90] The new French ambassador Labonne, much under the influence of Cripps, made similar approaches but then refused adamantly to discuss the legitimacy of the Russian action in Bessarabia. His own admission that the French army was 'completely blown to pieces' aroused Molotov's suspicion that his sole aim was to provoke a dispute between Germany and Russia; this was not alleviated by the fresh memory of the expulsion of the Soviet ambassador from Paris, and the fact that the French government had been caught red-handed in various plans to attack Russia.[91]

Only after the French collapse did Churchill address Stalin directly. He hoped Cripps would be given an opportunity to discuss in detail the intentions of the Soviet government 'in the face of the sudden overthrow of all military and political equilibrium in Europe'. However, the same circumstances which had led Churchill to approach Stalin made it impossible for Cripps to follow Churchill's instructions to 'be careful not to give [Stalin] the impression that we are running after him in order to ask him to pull the chestnuts out of the fire for us, or dictating to him where Russia's real interests lie in the present crisis'. What turned into a desperate appeal was enhanced by Churchill's sudden willingness to acknowledge that the annexation of the Baltic States 'is dictated by the imminence and magnitude of the German danger now threatening Russia, in which case the Soviet Govt. may well have been justified in taking in self-defence such measures as might in other circumstances have been open to criticism'.[92]

On 1 July Cripps was invited for an almost unprecedented meeting with Stalin which lasted nearly three hours. Cripps was unaware that, on the very day he requested an audience at the Kremlin, Stalin was making what he believed were the final touches to an arrangement with the Italians in the Balkans.[93] As might be expected, Stalin was not impressed by Churchill's personal letter. Later on Cripps, extremely critical of Churchill's policies, would admit that the proposals were made 'upon the basis of getting them to help *us* out of our awkward hole after which we may desert them and even join the enemies who now surround them'.[94] Indeed the British Chiefs of Staff interpreted Cripps's ideas as a way 'to embroil Russia with Germany', but refused to pay the price of relinquishing the right to enter the Black Sea. For them the Soviet strategy was aimed at the 'undermining of British influence in Asia . . . The opportunism of Soviet policy and the worthless character of any Soviet guarantee make it doubtful whether any agreement with the Soviet would have any lasting value.' Attempts to inspire in the Russians 'a fear of Great Britain even greater than their fear of Germany' proved no more successful.[95]

This then was the background to Stalin's apprehension about the British overture, rejecting the proposal which Cripps had made to him to seize the 'hegemony in the Balkans', hegemony which he 'believed to be pretentious and dangerous'. Stalin seemed to attach more significance to a revision of the navigation regulations in the Straits which would bar access to foreign navies at time of war.[96] Molotov confided to the

Bulgarian minister that Moscow 'had no intention of looking for such an advantage but neither did it intend to abandon its interests there'. He hoped to take the lead in the negotiations concerning Turkey, but only as part and parcel of a general arrangement in the Balkans in full co-operation with Germany and Italy.[97]

The impact of Cripps's presence in Moscow and his offers to Stalin on the Balkans cannot be overestimated. Shortly before Cripps's arrival in Moscow General Ivan I. Proskurov, the head of Soviet Military Intelligence, the GRU, had attributed the German hold-up of military deliveries to Russia to Germany's concern that Cripps would be carrying 'some gifts'.[98] However, within days the first report from Russian Military Intelligence on German intentions to invade Russia was put on Stalin's desk, before Hitler had even officially presented the plan to the High Command of the Wehrmacht.[99] The still sporadic information consisted of alleged secret negotiations with Edward, the exiled Duke of Windsor, in Madrid, a redeployment of troops in Poland, increased production at the Skoda armament factories in Czechoslovakia, and the recruitment of Russian-speaking officers and White émigrés in Prague. The military attachés in Berlin unanimously supported the conclusion.[100] It lent force to information, which had been treated with scepticism in June, that Neurath, Germany's former Foreign Minister, had intimated to a group of White emigrants that Hitler 'intended to form two new Russian republics, the Ukrainian and the Kazan' and 'establish a new order' in Russia itself. In more concrete form, Göring's brother had been spotted negotiating arms deals in Sofia and in Rumania.[101]

A week later, Proskurov was purged for his failure to alert Stalin to the German plans in the West.[102] General Filip I. Golikov, who replaced him, provided Stalin with more accurate information about the transfer of troops to the East which indicated that 'The transfer of German troops into Eastern Prussia and the former territories of Poland continues according to various reports of the foreign press and according to the German military attaché in Moscow'.[103] In early July Beria, the head of the NKVD, submitted to Stalin the report of a special mission undertaken by reliable agents in Poland which confirmed that the deployment indicated early preparations for a war against Russia. Information gathered from various frontier districts by NKVD border guards disclosed that high-ranking German officers had been surveying the districts in the summer months. The survey was followed up by the construction of new airfields and the expansion of existing ones, while aircraft transferred from the western front were being overhauled. Finally, the recent arrival of German air force pilots in the border area was registered. This alarmed Military Intelligence, as the information virtually 'corroborated data in our possession and in some cases virtually duplicated it'. By the end of August it was learnt that the Germans contemplated the transfer of 120 divisions to the East.[104]

This intelligence is perhaps the best explanation of Stalin's cautious handling of the mission undertaken by Cripps. 'The choice of this or that person for the post of an ambassador', warned Molotov, 'was the business of the British government'; but he thought it was wrong to assume that 'someone from the "left" wing' would have a preferential attitude. It was far more important that the new ambassador should 'reflect the views of the British government'.[105] To prevent any misrepresentation of the talks, Stalin made sure that the precise content of his conversations with Cripps reached Berlin. But Hitler was unimpressed by Schulenburg's assurances that Stalin was aware of the 'desperate attempts to sow distrust between Germany and the Soviet Union', and that there was 'no reason to doubt the loyal attitude of the Soviet Union'.[106] Hitler remained obsessed with the idea that England's resilience was based on expectations from 'third countries, presumably mainly from the United States, but perhaps also with the secret hope as to Russia'. This argument was not a mere pretext for the contemplation of an early offensive against Russia at the end of July, but reflected the recognition of a genuine potential threat to the sources of Germany's raw material and above all to her European hegemony.[107]

The Vienna Award: The German Encroachment in the Balkans

Throughout the summer and autumn of 1940, Hitler wavered over the future course of the war. The increasing American support to Britain, Churchill's intransigence and the serious logistical challenges to an invasion of Britain threatened to throw German strategy into disarray. He now faced a predicament which he had not anticipated in his plans: that the war in the West might develop into a long war of attrition, which Germany could not afford because of the lack of raw materials and resources. The alternative of isolating Britain through the formation of a Continental bloc, as advocated by Ribbentrop and the 'Easterners' in the Foreign Ministry, required continued co-operation with the Soviet Union. As the summer dragged on, the Battle of Britain failed to achieve its aims, and the implications of Britain's survival sank in. The invasion of Russia, which had first been a tentative scheme, became a viable alternative. Moreover, with England pinned down, the option of launching a successful *Blitzkrieg* against the Soviet Union became more attractive.

Insufficient attention has been paid to the role and impact of the German elites whom Hitler was trying to win over. These included the adherents of the 'Eastern' tradition, now awkwardly represented by Ribbentrop, whose Anglophobia had pushed him to devise the alternative of a Continental bloc, and to a lesser degree sections of the military. The preliminary planning for 'Barbarossa' was barely under way when the High Command of the Armed Forces (OKW) and Ribbentrop induced Hitler to attempt to isolate England by ensuring German control over the Continent. Tight control of South-eastern Europe, they believed, could provide a comfortable hinterland for Germany. Supremacy could be achieved through the construction of a solid coalition from Gibraltar to Japan.[108]

Schulenburg was by far the most ardent proponent of the Continental bloc. He believed that *Mein Kampf* of sixteen years earlier was intended by Hitler mainly as a propagandist tool against Moscow-oriented communism. Having defeated communism at home, Hitler's plans now seemed to be advancing 'in a totally different direction than trying to get at the Soviet regime or expand territorially at their expense'. He was equally dismissive of the suggestion that Germany needed the Ukrainian grain as 'groundless nonsense'. His contacts within the Foreign Ministry reinforced his belief that since the conclusion of the pact Hitler had become convinced that the Soviet Union 'did not constitute an obstacle in the gigantic construction of the European Continent on which he now focused his attention'.[109]

On the face of it, the conditions prevailing after the end of the war in the West seemed favourable for the establishment of a new world order and the extension of the Ribbentrop–Molotov Pact to South-eastern Europe. In Japan, the new Prime Minister Fumimaro Konoe, an ardent advocate of an alliance with Germany, now sanctioned the Japanese expansion southward against the British and the Americans and sought to regulate relations with Russia through German mediation.[110] However, the Soviet advance into Bessarabia, a move precipitated by the dynamism of Hitler's policies, was bound to divert Germany to the Balkans. Schulenburg continued to rebut suggestions that the Soviet annexation of Bessarabia was motivated by a wish to seize the Rumanian oilfields. He rather attributed it to Stalin's wish to participate in the new world order now that the end of war seemed imminent. The important task therefore was to extend the scope of the Ribbentrop–Molotov Pact to prevent a dangerous overlapping of interests in the Balkans.[111] This, he believed, could be realized, as Stalin was not seeking an 'exclusive role' in the region.[112]

Although the contingency plans for a war in Russia had already been activated, both General Franz Halder, Chief of the General Staff, and Field Marshal Walter von Brauchitsch, Commander-in-Chief of the German army, recognized that Russia and Germany could collect the booty and yet 'keep out of one another's way'. The likelihood of reaching an agreement was high as Hitler underestimated the extent of Stalin's interests in the region: 'Even though Moscow is unenthusiastic about Germany's great success, she will nevertheless make no effort to enter the war against Germany of her own accord.'[113]

The occupation of Bessarabia momentarily improved the strategic position of the Soviet Union in the Black Sea region. Securing control of the mouth of the Danube removed the threat to Odessa, while the naval and land routes to Bulgaria and the Bosphorus were safeguarded. To a large extent the arrangements corresponded to those reached with Finland after the conclusion of the Winter War, which protected the maritime approaches to Leningrad. But the move jeopardized what Berlin viewed as an indispensable economic hinterland. Hitler therefore, perhaps reluctantly, turned his gaze to the Balkans, as he could not allow Russia to design a new order in the region with Italian assistance.[114]

A flare-up in the Balkans threatened to undermine Operation 'Sea-Lion', Hitler's plans to invade England, scheduled for mid-August. In mid-July Hitler therefore subjected King Carol to 'impartial' arbitration of the various national claims.[115] The guns had hardly fallen silent in France when Stalin was informed that Bulgaria was seeking Germany's help in gaining Dobrudja and access to the Aegean Sea, as a reward for adhering to strict neutrality. However, Stalin was looking forward to the imminent peace conference rather than to a possible military clash with Germany.[116] At the beginning of July the Soviet ambassador in Berlin, Alexander A. Shkvartsev, warned that the annexation of Bessarabia had increased Hitler's determination to establish German hegemony in the Balkans, and that the German High Command was being summoned to Berlin to devise the military measures to back up such a move.[117] Well-connected sources in Moscow could hardly fail to notice that the Russians had become 'concerned with the German deployment on their borders . . . and irritated and afraid at the same time of the German interference in the Balkans'. Feelers were extended by the Soviet military to find out whether the Rumanian syndrome was being applied to Bulgaria as well.[118] By mid-August the extent of the confrontation with Russia could no longer be concealed. The various intelligence agencies briefed Stalin about Hitler's intention to act as a mediator. More alarming was his alleged declaration that all the territorial adjustments in the Balkans were provisional and that as soon as England collapsed he would launch an attack on the Ukraine.[119] The NKVD resident in Bulgaria reported that German barges were shipping heavy armaments through the Danube to fortify the shores of the Black Sea.[120]

Bulgaria was pivotal in the Soviet security system since she formed the land bridge to the Turkish Straits. Alexandra Kollontai, the Soviet ambassador in Sweden, perhaps the only Soviet ambassador to speak her mind, admitted that the Russians were seriously troubled by the Wehrmacht's deployment on their border and could not allow German troops to advance into the Balkans and pose a direct threat to the Straits.[121] The 'scramble for the Balkans', as the Bulgarian ambassador was quick to inform Sofia, had commenced, reopening the 'Eastern Question'. This development was inevitable since Hitler was no longer observing Europe from Berlin alone but also from Vienna, where he had enthroned himself as the heir of the revived Austro-Hungarian Empire.[122]

Bulgaria drifted into neutrality the moment that war broke out. The tacit British support of Bulgaria's neutrality concealed a genuine wish to use her in the future as a springboard to deny the Rumanian oilfields to Germany. However, King Boris, not unlike Stalin, saw the possibilities which the war provided for satisfying his country's territorial claims. He wasted little time in seeking Hitler's support for Bulgaria's claim to Southern Dobrudja, were the Russians to occupy Bessarabia. The Russians had awarded the northern part of Dobrudja to Rumania after the 1878 war in compensation for Bessarabia, but Rumania annexed the southern part after the second Balkan War of 1913.[123] To forestall a British initiative the Russians had proposed in September 1939 an agreement on mutual assistance, which was tantamount to an alliance.[124]

Antonov, the Bulgarian ambassador in Moscow, who had 'let himself get caught in the Soviet toils', flew in vain to Sofia during the last week of September 1939, to present the proposals personally to the King. 'Had [Antonov] presented only half of the ideas that he had developed for me shortly before his departure,' remarked the Turkish ambassador, 'he would have immediately been shown the door by King Boris.' The King particularly feared the communist threat if the Russians were to gain a foothold in Bulgaria. But he was no less susceptible to the historical and ethnic affinity with Russia of the population at large, sentiments which the Russians 'had not neglected to emphasize'.[125] Ten thousand copies of *Izvestiia*, for instance, were available on the streets in Sofia daily, while some twenty-six Soviet films were shown in cinemas throughout Bulgaria.[126]

The replacement of Antonov by Christov, an experienced diplomat, and the appointment of Professor Bogdan Filov, the former rector of Sofia University, as the Prime Minister in February 1940 were bad omens for the Russians. Filov's Germanophile leanings became more conspicuous after the fall of France.[127] Germany's reliance on Rumanian oil and her association with Italy turned her gaze to the Balkans. Ribbentrop had been pressed by his ambassador in Sofia to wrest the initiative from the Russians in redressing Bulgaria's grievances.[128]

Molotov, in the meantime, had been advising the Bulgarian ambassador to study 'the lessons of what [had] been happening so far to the north and to the west of Germany' and cling to neutrality.[129] As part of the agreement being forged with the Italians, he expected Bulgaria to place her claim for Dobrudja through Moscow. However, Draganov, the Bulgarian ambassador in Berlin who was closely associated with King Boris, had little doubt as to the newly established balance of power. Exploiting the obvious rivalry emerging between Russia and Germany, he placed in the

Wilhelmstrasse a claim to Dobrudja on the very morning that Soviet troops crossed the Dniester into Bessarabia. The Hungarians followed suit.[130] Hitler stole a march on Stalin; Filov was rushed to Salzburg and promised a settlement of Bulgarian claims 'in agreement with Russia and Italy or at least with Italy'. When Filov expressed fears that Bulgaria might be 'swallowed by her great Russian neighbour', Hitler assured him that 'if someone tried to injure German interests the blow would be dreadful'. He still counted, however, on 'the old attraction of the Dardanelles' for Stalin, which he intended to satisfy as long as it did not lead to a division of the Balkans into spheres of influence.[131]

Stalin was walking a tightrope. To observers in Moscow Molotov's survey of Soviet foreign policy in the Supreme Soviet in early August was 'diligent, correct and cautious', yet manifesting 'full independence'. It clearly aimed at vindicating the agreement with Germany while denying rumours accredited to the British about a possible breach in relations. Such rumours were believed to be a blunt attempt to drag Russia into the war. The thorny issues of the Straits and the discontent about the German initiatives in the Balkans were conspicuously absent in Molotov's address. They were, however, amply compensated for by a series of communiqués which reflected the discontent in the Kremlin.[132] In private the arbitration initiative elicited a strong reaction, which Schulenburg preferred to play down in his reports to Berlin. He tried in vain to persuade Molotov that, rather than acting as an arbitrator, Hitler was responding to a plea by King Carol of Rumania; this hardly tallied with the disturbing information that Hitler had in fact coerced the Rumanians into ceding Southern Dobrudja to Bulgaria.[133] The law passed during the Soviet session, annexing the Baltic States, and more significantly Bessarabia, to the Soviet Union, carried a similar message.[134]

In the absence of any tangible leverage on Bulgaria, Stalin continued to rally the reliable popular support there. King Boris was unable to restrain the tumultuous reception given to the Soviet national soccer team.[135] The Soviet pavilion at the Plovdiv book exhibition was the most frequented. A regular maritime line was opened between Odessa and Varna, where a consulate was established. The British consul in Varna commented on the popularity of the open-air showings of Soviet films in the market square every evening. The public, he reported, 'flock to see these films, securing their places (standing) very early. Many come in donkey carts from which to obtain a better view, and not a few peasants drive in from neighbouring villages.'[136]

Schulenburg was, however, prohibited by Ribbentrop from pursuing further consultations with the Russians on Rumania, where Germany claimed exclusive economic interests.[137] The Russians were further reminded that they would not have been able to fulfil their revisionist aims in Bessarabia without 'taking advantage' of the German victories in the West.[138] Hitler now exploited the abortive putsch of the Iron Guard in Rumania to tighten his control over the country. General Antonescu was endowed with dictatorial powers, forming a government 'acceptable' to Germany which would abide by the Vienna arbitration and fulfil Rumania's economic obligations towards the Third Reich. Within a day King Carol was forced to abdicate and go into exile. An agreement with Bulgaria was promptly signed at Craiova on 7 September.[139] The belated Soviet offer of all Dobrudja to Bulgaria was rejected. The Bulgarians perceived their claim for access to the Aegean Sea to be 'of vital interest and fully justified, far more important for [Bulgaria] than the Dobrudja one'.[140]

Clash over the Danube

Most disconcerting for the Russians was their deliberate exclusion from the arrangements for the final borders of Rumania and the control of the Danube. The Danubian International Commission, created at Versailles, dealt with the upper river and was mostly technical. The European Commission, on the other hand, set up in the wake of Russia's defeat in the Crimean War and within the framework of the Paris Treaty of 1856 was highly political. The alterations introduced during the 1878 Berlin Congress enlarged the Danubian interests of Germany and the Austro-Hungarian Empire. After 1918 the river was virtually governed by the Rumanians, though they lost some control over it in the Sinaia Conference of September 1938 when, in the spirit of 'appeasement', Germany was unanimously co-opted as a member. Together with the Montreux regime of the Straits, the European Commission undermined Russia's status as a major European power and constituted a weak point in her defensive arrangements. From the Russians' point of view the mouth of the river could serve alien navies as an outlet to the Black Sea, which they regarded almost as an inland sea. Changes in the Straits regime therefore required a corresponding control over the Danube estuary. The key to Soviet defence lay in the ability to deny the entry of European navies into the Black Sea not only at Istanbul but also in the Sulina arm of the Danube.[141]

Obviously Stalin's great concern about the control of the river followed the traditional policies of imperial Russia. The demand for a seat on the Commission, as Molotov openly admitted, was motivated by a desire not only to redress Russia's grievances of Versailles, but to reverse 'the inferior position . . . imposed on Russia after an unhappy war for her . . . the Crimean!'[142] After joining the League of Nations in 1934, the Russians had continuously pressed for admission to the Commission but had been rebuffed on the ground that they were not a riparian power with direct maritime commercial interests in the region. Having annexed Bessarabia they were now legally entitled to a seat and militarily in a position to force their demand.

The European Commission, with German and British representatives, had met for the last time in a rather surrealistic session in Galatz at the end of May; as if oblivious to the changing fortunes of war, it dwelt on plans for the development of the mouth of the river.[143] A mere fortnight after the Soviet occupation of Bessarabia the Kremlin became privy to ominous information from German sources in Bucharest that 'now that Austria had become part of Germany, the Danube was turning into a German river and the Germans had no intention of allowing the USSR to become a Danubian Power'. The Germans were said to have assured King Carol of Rumania that the occupation of Bessarabia 'was only temporary and would be reversed'.[144]

The arbitration, as Hitler enlightened Schulenburg, was indeed meant to banish the Russians from the Danube region.[145] In Berlin, however, the Russian ambassador firmly objected to the German attempts to belittle the significance of the projected Danubian conference, which was allegedly to be confined to a discussion of the western shores of the Danube and therefore of little or no relevance to Russia. Russia, he asserted, had 'now become a Danubian country and was consequently vitally interested in all Danubian questions'. He proposed to set up a single unified commission from which 'non-river parties, including Italy, would be excluded' and whose jurisdiction would extend from the mouth of the Danube to Bratislava.[146] Stalin did not wait for an answer, taking immediate steps to secure Russia's position as a new Danubian power. He sought to acquire from the British, practically banned from the Commission, their ten tugboats, two tankers and thirty 31,500-ton barges, lying idle in Galatz.[147] The situation became volatile when the Russians issued a communiqué accusing the Rumanians of initiating shooting incidents on the border with Russia.[148]

In Moscow Schulenburg viewed the collision course with growing concern. He believed that the only way to avoid a colossal conflict was a division into spheres of interest of the Danubian region, even though it 'proved to be more favourable to the Russians than to the Germans'.[149] Hitler, heavily engaged in the Battle of Britain and in frenzied diplomatic efforts to form the Continental bloc, temporarily bowed to the pressure and invited the Russians to participate in the Danubian conference. At the back of his mind lay, as always, the possibility of Soviet–British collusion. Still nominally members of the Commission, the British had indeed supported the Soviet application, which they anticipated would 'throw an apple of discord into the proceedings'.[150]

The Danubian conference was a landmark which has been glossed over by historians. To avoid a premature confrontation the Germans acceded to the Russians' wish to form a new Danubian Commission for the area south of Bratislava up to the river's mouth. But they proposed to reduce its significance by delaying its convening and confining its activities to technical matters through interim arrangements.[151] Molotov had different ideas. From the outset he voiced reservations about the inclusion of Italy, which allowed her together with the Germans free access to the Black Sea.[152] To restrict German–Italian manoeuvrability, the Middle Eastern Department of the Russian Foreign Ministry, under the close guidance of the Kremlin, worked out in minute detail a scheme which would entrust the Russians with exclusive control over the mouth of the river. Before their departure for Bucharest Molotov personally briefed the participants about the tactics to be adopted. The high-level mission, headed by Arkady Sobolev, Molotov's deputy, included Major-General V. D. Ivanov, which reflected the military importance attached to the Danube. Instead of flying directly to Bucharest, the mission stopped over in Sofia, where Sobolev pressed King Boris to resist the German demand for Bulgaria to join the Tripartite Pact. Rather significantly, the delegation then chose to proceed to Bucharest by train, first making an on-the-spot inspection of the Bulgarian border region at Ruse, on the Danube.

Severe earthquakes were a bad omen for the conference when it convened on 28 October. The Italian declaration of war on Greece on that very day foreordained deepening German involvement in the Balkan peninsula. The Russian stand at the conference was a precursor of Hitler's confrontation with Molotov in Berlin; it proved beyond any doubt that, despite the pressure exerted by Germany, the Russians refused to accept German dominance in Rumania. Sobolev's initial moderation soon gave way to an obstinate demand for the immediate dissolution of the Four Powers Commission of Rumania, Germany, Italy and Russia and the installation of a mixed Russo-Rumanian administration of the waterways for the whole Danube delta. Such an arrangement would have allowed Soviet warships to navigate freely in the Rumanian Sulina arm and control German access to the Black Sea. Russia also demanded the right for the Soviet fleet to anchor at Galatz and Braila, which would give it *de facto* sovereignty over the gates to the Black Sea. This solution was rejected out of hand by the remaining three participants. In view of the impasse it was decided to allow the German and Soviet delegations to return home for further consultations. While Sobolev travelled to Moscow, General Ivanov and Novikov, head of the Near Eastern Department at the Foreign Ministry, exploited the interregnum to inspect the north-eastern part of Rumania via Ploesti. Inevitably, they were shadowed by the Rumanian security service, an annoying though not unfamiliar experience for the Russian visitors. After shaking off the surveillance, they made an extensive tour along the Danube to Orshuv, the railway bridge over the river, significantly ending with a prolonged stay at the port towns on the Black Sea.[153]

After the failure of the conference, the Russians resorted to unilateral action. In the middle of Molotov's visit to Berlin they seized a dozen small islands in the Kilia arm at the mouth of the Danube and full control of the main stream of Staro Stambul, through which the Kilia waters reach the sea. Soviet warships further violated the Rumanian part of the Danubian delta but were fired on by the Rumanians and withdrew. They made efforts not to alienate the Rumanians, to whom they left control of the arms at Sulina and St George. They clearly wished to establish exclusive control of navigation on the Kilia arm, the only outlet of the river for seagoing ships. Sharing the Musura deviation of the main stream with the Rumanians was of little value, as this was too shallow for any major naval navigation.[154]

No wonder that the German ambassador in Bucharest warned Berlin that the Soviet perseverance proved that they did not 'intend to pursue a policy of reasonable understanding with Germany in the Danube and Black Sea area but at best one of blackmail'. On the eve of Molotov's visit to Berlin it transpired that the Russians were after all creating 'political rather than economic difficulties' for Germany in the Balkans.[155]

3

On a Collision Course

Drang nach Osten: *The Initial Plans*

Hitler's decision to attack Russia is indeed enigmatic. It is hardly possible to detect a direct line leading from his pledge in *Mein Kampf* to 'terminate the endless German drive to the south and west of Europe, and direct our gaze towards the lands in the east' to the actual decision to embark on Operation 'Barbarossa'.[1] The commonly held view bypasses the difficulty by claiming that Hitler had consistently aimed at the destruction of Moscow 'as the headquarters of the "Judaeo-Bolshevist world conspiracy"'.[2] The fact that the crusade against Bolshevism and the extermination of the Jews revolutionized the course of the war in 1941 is not sufficient in itself to prove steadfast adherence to a blueprint. The ideological convictions found open expression only once the decision on 'Barbarossa' had been taken, and to a large extent diverted Hitler from a more rational strategic policy which had characterized his military leadership so far. Perhaps the only explanation lies with those who highlight the symbiosis in Hitler's war policy between calculation and dogma, strategy and ideology, foreign policy and racial policy.[3]

Even if Hitler's decision on 'Barbarossa' was ideologically oriented, it was subjected to fixed geopolitical considerations and altering political circumstances. By unfolding his bitter clash with Stalin in the Balkans it is possible at least to show how the timing of 'Barbarossa' was directly related to the unresolved clash over the spheres of influence in that region. The concrete origins of Operation 'Barbarossa' are still obscure, but the fact that it germinated independently in two or three places seems to indicate a lack of overall guidance. It is clear though that as soon as Marshal Pétain put his signature to the note of surrender in Compiègne, Halder initiated a draft operational study of war in the East.[4] Hitler's initial decision primarily comprised two unforeseen obstacles, which were tied together in his mind and attributed to Soviet policies: Churchill's brazen rejection of his peace offers and Stalin's encroachment into the Balkans. Churchill's refusal to acknowledge the new balance of power appeared incomprehensible, unless he was 'pinning his hopes on Russia and America'. The obvious temptation was therefore to solve the impasse by simply 'crushing' the Soviet Union by force, thus establishing Germany as 'the master of Europe and the Balkans'.[5]

Hitler presented the plan to his Chiefs of Staff in an extraordinary gathering at his Alpine retreat at Berchtesgaden, on 31 July 1940. The timing chosen for the operation is indeed problematic, as it coincided with the planning of the projected invasion of Britain. At first Hitler expected to drive a wedge between England and Russia through the publication of the documents of the Supreme Allied Council, seized by the Germans, which exposed the Allied plans to bomb Batum and Baku.[6] Once informed of Cripps's offer to Stalin to assume hegemony over the Balkans,[7] Hitler rightly became concerned that the Russians might 'establish a connection with Bulgaria' and 'push on to their old historic Byzantium, the Dardanelles, and Constantinople'.[8] This obsessive fear was strengthened when Churchill rejected the peace offer made publicly at the Reichstag on 19 July.[9] Despite Stalin's efforts to belittle the significance of Cripps's proposals, a plethora of reports from various Balkan capitals suggested that Stalin and Cripps had in fact reached an understanding aimed at exerting pressure on Turkey to alter the Straits regime.[10]

It is intriguing that Napoleon reassured his ambassador in Moscow, when rumours of war began to spread in 1811, in the following way: 'You are just like the Russians; you can see nothing but threats, nothing but war, whereas this is just a disposition of forces necessary to make England sue for terms before six months have passed.'[11] Goebbels's diaries show that Hitler also used this sort of argument, when convenient, in the case of France and Greece. It goes without saying that an ideological war with Russia had always appealed to Hitler, and it is indeed possible that by the early summer of 1940 he was under pressure of time to consider such a campaign. But the oral directive at the end of July was still no more than an ephemeral guideline confined to a general definition of objectives rather than operational arrangements.[12]

The rather complex and highly theoretical circumstances leading to the decision resulted from the outset in operational confusion regarding both the war aims and the direction in which the overwhelming strike was to be delivered. The war in Russia was not initially perceived as an end in itself. This explains one of its major pitfalls: the absence of any clear political vision as to the outcome of the campaign not only in Russia but also regarding the status of the Ukraine, Estonia, Latvia, Lithuania and

White Russia once the Soviet Union had collapsed.[13] Hitler's embryonic
plans had envisaged only a swift and limited war in the autumn. There
is no reason to contest the subsequent recollections of Field Marshal
Wilhelm Keitel, the chief commander of the OKW, and his deputy,
General Alfried Jödl, that Hitler's plan was triggered by the increased
Soviet interest in the Balkans. Hitler openly expressed his concern that
further Soviet penetration into Rumania would lead to the seizure of the
oilfields. The centre of gravity lay in the south, thereby also encompass-
ing valuable Soviet economic regions, adding a new dimension and
further confusion to the campaign.[14]

Prior to the meeting in Berchtesgaden the majority of the Supreme
Command had been opposed to a war, following the traditional dogma
that Germany should avoid war on two fronts. When facing Hitler they
dodged the issue, convinced as they were that in the long run the German
claim for hegemony in Europe was indeed endangered by Russia. The
decision was therefore clearly taken within the broad context of the 'new
European order'. As a pragmatic decision it was by no means irreversible.
However, once taken, it had immediate political, military and armament
consequences which set the Wehrmacht in motion.[15] Indeed, hardly had
the decision been taken when Hitler ordered the expansion of the army
to 180 divisions by spring 1941, regardless of the sacrifice inflicted on the
economy.[16] Jödl and Keitel, dizzy with the success in France, did not
exclude the possibility that 80–100 divisions would defeat the Russians
within four to six weeks; but they were still convinced that the operation
could not be executed before spring 1941.[17] The delay therefore seriously
eroded the realization of Hitler's original objective.

The military planning, however, gained momentum while other
political alternatives were being sought during the summer and autumn
of 1940.[18] The planning division worked diligently. Within a few days
Major-General Marcks proposed his 'Operationsentwurf Ost', assuming
that the line Archangel'sk–Gorky–Rostov could be reached within eleven
weeks.[19] By the end of August the embryonic operational plan was
entrusted to General von Paulus; he was assigned the task of preparing
the operational aspects of the campaign such as studies of the terrain, the
availability of forces and ammunition, and the goals of the operation. The
130–40 German divisions earmarked for the operation were intended,
according to Halder, to destroy the Russian troops in west Russia and
establish a line from which the Russian air force could not menace the territories under German control. The Volga–Archangel'sk line was a remote
and vague objective.[20]

The planners pursued their work aware that the war in Russia was
related to the conflicting German and Soviet interests in the Balkans.
Hitler knew that an ill wind would blow on relations with Russia after
the conclusion of the arbitration. On the eve of the meeting in Vienna he

therefore ordered the transfer of two armoured divisions to south Poland to stand ready for a 'quick intervention to protect the Rumanian oil districts'.[21] A military mission under General Hansen was instructed to protect the oilfields. The new deployment seemed already to fit within the plans for war against Russia, as the mission was rather clearly instructed 'to prepare for the possible employment, later, of stronger German forces from Rumania'.[22] That the Balkans and the economic resources of the Ukraine remained the focus of the planners is corroborated by the outcome of the two war games which Paulus conducted in November and which led to the adoption of the more modest plan confining the strike to the Dnieper–Smolensk–Leningrad line. Moreover, the planners became increasingly convinced that, with the passage of time and against the background of developments in the Balkans, the operation which had initially been perceived as a contingency plan was destined to be implemented.[23]

It is totally unwarranted to assume, as is commonly done, that Molotov's negotiations were doomed with the issue of 'Directive 18', on the very day of his arrival in Berlin. It is often forgotten that Russia figured only marginally in the directive, which surveyed the entire course of German strategy and focused primarily on the delivery of the final blow against England in the Mediterranean. In fact the directive predominantly addressed issues concerning the establishment of a Continental-bloc strategy. From our point of view the frequent references to the Balkans are more significant, as they reveal once again that Bulgaria had become the real battlefield between Russia and Germany. When embarking on the negotiations Hitler had already made up his mind about Germany's control of Bulgaria. The Wehrmacht was instructed to make preparations, 'in case of necessity', to occupy Greek territory north of the Aegean, 'entering from Bulgaria'. The justification was the need to forestall a British attack on the Rumanian oilfields from that territory. The directive ordered the execution of Operation 'Felix' (the occupation of Gibraltar), aimed at eliminating the British presence in the Mediterranean. It corresponded to the aims of the Berlin meeting in seeking joint action with Italy in North Africa and the Balkans. The short reference to Russia was made within the context of the Continental bloc, and aimed at clarifying her attitude towards the forthcoming period. As we have seen, there were ominous signs of the Soviet attitude on the eve of the meeting and the planners were therefore instructed that 'regardless of what results these discussions will have, all preparations for the East which already have been orally ordered are to be continued'.[24]

The directive therefore still reflected wavering on Hitler's part. It was closely connected to his expectations in the Balkans, as we shall see later. The door for a political arrangement which might hasten the collapse of the British Empire still remained wide open, while the army was reminded that the planning of a military campaign should not be abandoned.[25] Halder was in fact reassured by Hitler on several occasions that the Russians were displaying a friendly attitude and might still join the Tripartite Pact after the negotiations.[26] Historians who are eager to maintain that Hitler's decision on 'Barbarossa' was entirely ideological overlook the fact that it was by no means an arbitrary and unilateral affair. The final crucial decision was taken only after the Russians had rejected the German terms which were a prerequisite for the creation of the Continental bloc.

Soviet Intelligence and the German Threat

Facing Nazi Germany in 1940–1, Stalin was no less curious than historians are today about Hitler's objectives. While for historians this is a theoretical proposition, it became crucial for Stalin after the fall of France. If Hitler's ideology was an *idée fixe* then the outbreak of war was inevitable. If the seemingly pragmatic line was genuine, and naturally Stalin would tend to project on to Hitler the mirror image of his own outlook, then war could still be averted or at least postponed if the diplomatic cards were astutely played. Reaching a lasting arrangement with Germany or acquiring an adequate breathing space depended on flawless intelligence. Some attention should thus be paid to the state of the security services at this juncture. Most networks of the Military Intelligence had been seriously disrupted by Stalin's purges, when not only operators but also agents in the field had been executed or discharged from the service. All the heads of the Military Directorate and its subsidiary organizations had been removed and their places taken by less experienced and less talented officers.[27] On the whole the organization continued to function and even scored some spectacular successes, such as the recruitment of the 'Cambridge Five' in England, who penetrated both the British security forces and the Foreign Office. The psychological impact of the purges, however, was devastating, draining the security services of any form of independence and free thinking, so vital for successful intelligence.

The GRU office in Berlin was run by the experienced General Tupikov and the NKVD by Amiak Kobulov ('Zakhar'); though a novice, Kobulov enjoyed the full trust of Beria. They cultivated ties with the anti-fascist groups but also recruited professionals into their ranks. Among these was Willy Leman, who under the pseudonym of 'Breitenbach' provided information straight from the Gestapo. When Dekanozov, a former senior NKVD officer, was appointed ambassador in Berlin, in December 1940, he was entrusted with the co-ordination of both the GRU and the NKVD residency. Eventually fear of provocation drove Stalin greatly to decrease the intelligence work in Berlin.[28] The failure to create any fresh nets only enhanced the significance of Harro Schulze-Boysen ('Starshina') and Arvid Harnack ('Corsicanets'),[29] who had been recruited by Kobulov. Both had been active communists in the anti-fascist Rote Kapelle (Red Orchestra) since 1935. By 1941 'Starshina' was well established in the headquarters of the air force with direct access to highly valuable sources. 'Corsicanets', a brilliant economist, was highly placed at the German Economics Ministry, with direct access to most secret documents relating *inter alia* to relations with Russia. Both were uncovered and arrested by the Gestapo in November 1942, court-martialled and executed.

At least one member of that net, 'Litseist' (pseudonym of O. Berlings), was a double agent, and caused considerable damage. His information was regarded by Kobulov as 'most reliable' and frequently found its way straight to Stalin and Molotov. However, after the end of the war he was found to have been provided by the Gestapo with sophisticated disinformation, a hodgepodge of genuine and false information designed to reinforce Stalin's mistaken concepts. Ribbentrop was purported to have said: 'We can pump whatever information we want into this agent.'[30]

The significance of intelligence increased once the military plans had been modified in the autumn of 1940 to accommodate Stalin's conviction that Germany's aspirations were directed towards South-eastern Europe, either against Russia or against British interests in the Near East. And yet one should not overlook his distrust and contempt for all branches of intelligence and the army in general in the 1939–41 period. Stalin's attitude was described by Molotov in retrospect:

I think that one can never trust the intelligence. One has to listen to them but then check on them. The intelligence people can lead to dangerous situations that it is impossible to get out of. There were endless provocateurs on both sides. This is why one cannot count on the intelligence without a thorough and constant checking and double checking. People are so naive and gullible, indulging themselves and quoting memoirs: spies said so and so, defectors crossed the lines . . .[31]

Though he later emerged as a capable officer, General Golikov's earlier career exposed a lack of professionalism which was all too obvious to Stalin. Golikov had reached the top after proving himself to be a tenacious Bolshevik, fighting with the 'Krasnye orly' (Red Eagles) during the Civil War.[32] He subsequently held a number of key political posts in the army, including the directorship of the political department of the Commissariat for Defence. During a deliberately obscured period of his life, Golikov played a decisive role in the suppression of the 'Leningrad Opposition' and most likely in the purges of the Red Army in 1937. His appointment as head of the GRU reflected the havoc prevailing in the armed forces in the wake of the sweeping purges and was a reward for his loyalty.[33] Nonetheless, Stalin kept him at arm's length, just as he would treat his future Chief of Staff, Zhukov. During the party conference in February 1941 he was heard to mutter that he did not rely on Golikov, who 'as a spy was inexperienced, naive. A spy should be like the devil; no one could trust him, not even himself.'[34] Merkulov, head of the Foreign Intelligence of the NKVD, did not fare any better. True, Stalin regarded him as 'brave and dexterous', but complained of him as being 'lacking in principles and weak'; he wished to please all rather than 'adhere strictly to a course regardless of the fact that someone will be offended'.[35]

It is not surprising that such an environment dictated prudence on the part of the intelligence agencies. Consequently, the constant flow of intelligence reflected two contradictory features. The raw data, especially when examined in retrospect, seem to have comprised a steady stream of accurate and detailed information on the German build-up. However, the attempts to accommodate the intelligence with the prevailing political concepts obscured the meaning of the facts. It would be wrong to accept the conspiracy theories which accuse Golikov of deliberate and selective manipulation of the evidence. Indeed, the suggestion that Stalin was oblivious to the dangers because he had been shielded from the truth by Golikov is greatly exaggerated. From the distribution lists it is obvious that copious information did reach Stalin, and he was by no means blind to the danger. Nor was Zhukov, who later claimed to have been deliberately excluded.[36]

By the beginning of 1941 five or more reports (*donesenia*) were received daily from abroad. Every ten to fifteen days a special review of the reports was prepared by the GRU. The reports give a clear idea of the threats facing the country, but there is not always an indication in the archives of the GRU of which evaluations were actually presented to the Kremlin. True, the leadership of the GRU was inclined to avoid passing outright judgment on the inevitability of war on the basis of the hard facts at its disposal. Shortly after the signing of the Ribbentrop–Molotov Pact the intelligence agencies were discouraged from collecting information pointing to German preparations for an attack on Russia. But as the threat intensified the GRU diligently resumed the collection of raw information on German intentions.[37]

Such intelligence was usually sent in up to fourteen copies to Stalin, Molotov, Voroshilov, Timoshenko, Beria, Kuznetsov, the ubiquitous Generals Mekhlis and Kulik, Shaposhnikov and other concerned parties. The intelligence emerged from three major sources: the GRU, the NKGB (which had just been separated from Beria's NKVD, charged with external security and put under Merkulov) and the Foreign Ministry. The diverse data converged on the Politburo and particularly on Stalin's secretariat. All the threads, therefore, led to Stalin. The GRU did not function in a vacuum, as Zhukov rather apologetically suggests in his memoirs. Significant pieces of evidence obtained by the NKGB were transmitted directly to the military. On a number of occasions the NKVD would examine their appreciations in relation to those reached by the GRU and would communicate back to them: 'Your reports on the recent transfer of German forces and military transports to the borders of the USSR are plausible. They corroborate the tendency of our sources.'[38]

Soviet intelligence had been scrutinizing the redeployment of the German troops in France since her capitulation. In September alone a massive transfer of some thirty divisions to the Russian border had been detected. During the last week of the month some seventy trains carrying troops, armaments and equipment were dispatched to the East. The German embassy was further spotted recruiting White Russians, intellectuals and professionals of clear anti-Soviet inclinations, laying the foundations for the 'restoration of national Russia'. The aim of the deployment was predominantly related to future operations in the Balkans, more specifically in Saloniki and the Turkish Straits.[39]

In the autumn of 1940 the Kremlin instructed the NKVD to activate a special operational file, named 'Zateya' (Venture), in which information on German intentions was collated and brought to Stalin's personal attention.[40] In the second part of September, the security services were inundated by top-level reports mapping in detail the German regrouping in the area of former Poland throughout the summer. The reports included precise identification of divisions and the location of their headquarters. Equally significant was the accurate information on the German construction of barracks and infrastructures to facilitate the transfer of troops from the West and accommodate them. Small-scale manoeuvres had been carried out on the theme of 'an attack on a defensive opponent', who, as the report rather laconically mentioned, happened to be located on the Russian borders. The clear conclusion was that the Germans were continuing their concentration of troops in Eastern Prussia, 'and the preparation of a theatre for all possible operative directions'.[41] 'Military preparations' were spotted as well in the eastern regions of Slovakia. Roads were paved and new rail tracks laid; some 30,000 workers were involved in these works. Likewise airfields were constructed and a substantial number of pilots were transferred from the western front to the East.[42]

The collation of intelligence for October, as Stalin became aware, depicted in minute details the increased transfer of both infantry and mechanized divisions to the East. The cautious estimate on the eve of Molotov's meeting with Hitler in Berlin in November was that some '85 infantry divisions, in other words more than two-thirds of the entire German infantry force, were deployed against the USSR'. The evaluation of German aims, however, was affected by the recent developments in the Balkans. A recent slackening of the concentration on the Soviet border marked a German plan 'to occupy Rumania and further to move into the heart of the Balkan peninsula'.[43] It did not conceal, however, the ominous reality that while prior to the occupation of France only twenty-seven infantry divisions were present in Poland, supported by six cavalry formations, seventy infantry divisions could now be specifically identified, in addition to five motorized and seven or eight tank divisions.[44]

On the very eve of Molotov's visit, the Berlin embassy and NKGB residency provided Stalin with contradictory reports on the course of German policy. The embassy, examining the anniversary of the Ribbentrop–Molotov Pact, produced a severe critique of the 'New Europe' devised by Hitler. 'Intoxicated by victory,' it summed up, 'the German Government, together with the Italians and without the consent of the USSR, violated the agreement of 23 August 1939 by deciding the fate of the Balkan peoples.' Rather significantly it ended with a warning that the Germans regarded the Balkans as 'a new bridgehead for a military engagement against the Soviet Union'.[45] Two days before Molotov's departure for Berlin, Golikov informed the Kremlin that the Germans had completed the deployment of fifteen to seventeen divisions in the territory adjacent to the Danube in preparation for the seizure of Saloniki. Partial mobilization was taking place in secret in Bulgaria, where the military academies had been closed to allow the cadets to join their units. Moreover, General von Ingelbart was attached to the Bulgarian Chief of Staff, while fourteen Messerschmitts were transferred to Sofia and kept hidden. Golikov's categorical appreciation left no room for guessing:

1. Germany is continuing to transfer its troops to the Balkans. It cannot be excluded that in the near future Germany will attack Greece, with the aim of crushing the Italian resistance together with Italy, in order to seize the Balkan peninsula and exploit it as a springboard for further actions against Turkey and the English colonies.

2. At the same time Germany is taking measures directed against the Soviet Union (deploying troops in the regions of Cracow and Lodz and recruiting Ukrainian reservists).[46]

The agent 'Meteor' in Berlin corroborated the information, quoting the opinions of Karl Schnurre, head of the Economic Division of the German Foreign Ministry, that Hitler intended 'to solve the issue in the East by military means'.[47]

From the information heaped up on his desk Stalin compiled two scenarios. The first assumed the inevitability of war. The second, which he found preferable, assumed that preliminary negotiations would precede a peace conference. In both cases he attached primary significance to the control of the Straits and a presence in the Balkans. Stalin's state of uncertainty reflected Hitler's own wavering. The ample evidence that the

Russians possessed on the German preparations for war was contradicted by Schulenburg's efforts and by intelligence on Ribbentrop's efforts to form a Continental bloc. The most important and accurate piece of intelligence pointing in this direction was submitted to Stalin by Beria a fortnight before the Berlin conference. Colonel Kleist, a member of Ribbentrop's staff, reported that on 22 October Hitler and Ribbentrop had met in Berchtesgaden and discussed the 'political offensive'. They expected that the conference would isolate England by 'destroying any illusions she might be entertaining about possible help from a third party' and would lead to a compromise peace. France and Spain were expected to adhere to the Axis, and 'pressure was to be exerted on Russia to reach a political agreement with Germany which would demonstrate to the entire world that the Soviet Union is in no way going to remain neutral, and would actively struggle against England in the establishment of a new European order'. At a later stage Germany intended to effect a pact between the Soviet Union and Japan 'to demonstrate to the world the full ties and unity of purpose between the four powers' and thus discourage the USA from assisting Britain.[48]

The Bulgarian Corridor to the Turkish Straits

Thus the Russian approach to the Berlin conference was inspired not by excessive greed but rather by a recognition of the German threat in the Balkans and in the Straits. Rosso, the Italian ambassador in Moscow and confidant of Schulenburg, put it succinctly:

> The Germans have raised a barrier: the march to the south has been stopped, the oil is at the disposal of the Germans, through Constanza the Germans have reached the Black Sea, the Danube is a German river. This is the first diplomatic defeat of Comrade Stalin, who was accustomed to make great gains with small risks, and the defeat is even more humiliating as it hits the dream which throughout the centuries was closest to the Russian soul: the dream of the southern meridian.[49]

It belatedly dawned also on the British Chiefs of Staff that by occupying Rumania Germany had not only succeeded in obtaining the oil resources but had further 'forestalled the possibility of any further Russian move towards the Straits. She is now well on the way to shutting off Russia completely from the oceans of the world in the North, in the Baltic and now in the Black Sea.' Russia was therefore 'likely to take all steps short of war to prevent German penetration into Turkey and the Middle East since this would cause a progressively increasing threat to her interests in the Black Sea and to the Caucasian oilfields'.[50]

Perceiving himself to be a great tactician,[51] Stalin adopted a remarkably realistic approach in safeguarding Russian national interests; these appear to be very much within the historical context of the nineteenth-century struggle for mastery in Europe and the Balkans. The Balkans seemed to be the front line where Hitler had to be stopped and the control of the Turkish Straits had become the key to the preservation of Russia's security. Stalin even identified himself with none other than the historian Miliukov, the Liberal Foreign Minister of the provisional government after the first revolution and an arch-enemy of Lenin, who persevered even after the February Revolution in seeking control over the Bosphorus.[52]

These considerations, rather than insatiable greed and a wish to carry communism to Europe at bayonet point, were what determined Stalin's approach to the Berlin conference. Fortunately, a directive for the talks composed for Molotov in Stalin's dacha, and in his own handwriting, provides a rare insight into the workings of Soviet diplomacy at the time. To start with, the primary aim of the journey was not to seek an agreement but to discover 'the real intentions of Germany's proposal of the New Europe', Russia's role in it, and the German idea of division into 'spheres of interest in Europe and also in the Near and Middle East'. An agreement would be deferred until a future visit by Ribbentrop to Moscow. The leading theme of the directive, besides Finland (where it was assumed that the spheres of interest had already been established), was the intrinsic Soviet security interest in the Balkans. Foremost were the repeated demands for the establishment of Soviet control of the mouth of the Danube, coupled with the expression of 'dissatisfaction with the German guarantees to Rumania'. The directive culminated in an ultimatum for Soviet participation in the decision on the 'fate of Turkey'. Likewise, Molotov was to postulate consultations on issues regarding the future of Hungary, Rumania and Yugoslavia. Though condensed in form, the instructions leave no room for doubt as to Stalin's overwhelming interest: 'Bulgaria – the main topic of the negotiations – must belong by agreement with G. [Germany] and I. [Italy] to the USSR's sphere of interests, *on the same basis* as had been done by Germany and Italy in the case of Rumania, with the right for Soviet troops to enter Bulgaria.' The establishment of Bulgaria as a Soviet sphere of influence, as we will soon see,[53] was a prerequisite for the control of the Straits.

In view of subsequent suggestions that, in Berlin, Germany and Russia had colluded to divide the British Empire, it should be emphasized that the directive made hardly any mention of Soviet interests beyond the Balkans and Europe, and in fact the preservation of the British Empire was advocated. Stalin was much reassured by the poor showings of Germany in the Battle of Britain and of the Italians in the Balkans and North Africa and by the fact that 'the British fleet still dominated the

Middle East'.[54] Maisky's assertion on the eve of Molotov's departure that England could not be written off was cardinal to the objectives sought at the meeting. When the Luftwaffe launched the Blitz on London Churchill had told the Soviet ambassador that 'it was necessary to wait the coming three months, and then to see what happens'. Four months had elapsed and Maisky was prepared to stick his neck out:

> England did not only survive, but was even strengthened when compared with the situation after the defeat of France. The German plans for the invasion of Britain miscarried at least for this year ... In this way in the 'battle for Britain', Hitler, like Napoleon 135 years earlier, suffered a defeat, the first serious defeat in this war; the consequences of it are impossible to foresee through the information available here.

Maisky even went so far as to suggest that through a slow and arduous process Britain might after all emerge victorious.[55] A telegram from Stalin pursued Molotov on the train *en route* to Berlin, reaffirming the instructions not to broach with Germany any issues concerning the British Empire.[56] Later in Berlin Molotov deliberately endorsed Maisky's judgment that Churchill, unlike the French leadership, enjoyed the support of the country and the Empire and therefore that 'it was too early to bury England'. Stalin did not even expect the situation to change dramatically if the Greek islands were to fall into German hands.[57] Moreover Maisky, who seemed to have an inkling of Halifax's decision to bring about a severance of relations with the Soviet Union if the conference were 'to overawe Turkey', intervened with Molotov during his stay in Berlin, warning of the repercussions of a military solution.[58] Soviet military experts in Britain did warn Stalin that England had sustained substantial damage from the German bombardments and that 'industry and high finance were in favour of a compromise peace'. However, they too did not expect the crisis to come to a head in the spring, a further reason for the Russian wish to await events before embarking on negotiations.[59]

Hardening England's resistance, thereby diminishing the likelihood of a compromise peace, remained a constant component in Stalin's elaborate diplomacy.[60] In fact Stalin, as Cripps noted, was trying to play 'both games ... leaving one to Molotov and the other to Vyshinsky [the Deputy Foreign Minister]!' In August 1940 Moscow even proposed a non-aggression pact with Britain, similar in pattern to the Ribbentrop–Molotov Pact. Cripps's counter-proposals a month later were rejected not only because Stalin anticipated that Molotov's talks in Berlin would 'strengthen the bonds between the USSR and Nazi Germany', but because of the imminent threat posed to Russia by the German encroachment in the Balkans.[61]

Thus control of the Straits remained the cornerstone of Soviet strategy. It could both forestall the German incursion into the Black Sea basin and prevent Turkey from becoming a British pawn once hostilities erupted. The closer war approached the Balkans, the more vague Turkish foreign policy became. Eager to avoid the fate of Poland and Rumania, the Turks adhered to a strict neutrality which perpetuated the balance of fear between the major powers. Germany, Russia, Italy and England all tried in vain to sound her out. It was possible to maintain the smokescreen only as long as none of the actors established land and naval predominance in the region. Maintaining the delicate balance demanded considerable diplomatic skills: improvement in the position of one power led to the courting of another by the Turks.

The real danger facing Turkey after the outbreak of war was a possible extension of the Ribbentrop–Molotov Pact to the south. After the Vienna Award, and especially after the Italian declaration of war on Greece and the creeping German encroachment into Bulgaria, the Turkish government attempted to drive a wedge between the Germans and the Russians by overplaying the threat posed to the Straits by each. At the same time the pact with England was waved as a deterrent to a possible Russian pre-emptive strike.

Neither the Turks nor the Russians could watch with equanimity the emergence of Germany as a 'Black Sea power'. Both feared that Germany might seize the Straits and gain a hold on Hungary, Rumania and Bulgaria, while Italy established Great Albania by swallowing Yugoslavia and Greece. For the Russians, that could lead to a siege of the Soviet fleet in the Black Sea.[62] The Germans, however, had expertly fuelled the mutual Turco-Soviet suspicion. The publication in *Izvestiia* of the documents seized by the Germans on the Allied plan to bomb Baku threw Ankara into a state of panic, since the documents implied tacit Turkish support of the plan. Saracoglu sought in vain to impress on Molotov that his government had opposed the operation.[63] Aktay, the ambassador, was observed in Moscow to be 'depressed and nervous'; despite attempts to 'maintain his composure his eyes glowed with worry'.[64] Molotov, whom he met before departing to Ankara for consultations in mid-August, remained convinced of Turkish connivance in the Anglo-French scheme. He kept interrogating Aktay about his alleged inquiries of Laurence Steinhardt, the American ambassador in Moscow, concerning the Soviet fire-fighting facilities in Baku.[65]

The RAF's success in the Battle of Britain temporarily relieved the tension in Ankara; even more so did the German arbitration over Dobrudja, which for the moment blocked the Russian military from making an advance towards the Straits.[66] But the possibility that the Russians might react to the arbitration by making a unilateral change in the Straits regime could not be excluded.[67] On the eve of the Berlin conference the Russians preferred to keep the issue of the Straits open until they had found out what Hitler's intentions were. As a deterrent they certainly wished to give the impression that they would act by force were the Germans to attempt a takeover of the Straits. However, there was an equal chance that, as Schulenburg impressed on Stalin, an agreement on the Straits favouring Russia would be reached in Berlin.

Schulenburg had been an opponent of the Nazi regime and its foreign policy aims. He had been steadily pursuing his own agenda in the Soviet capital which eventually led him into severe conflict with his masters in Berlin.[68] He had reached the conclusion that Stalin had replaced his revolutionary vision by 'national Sovietism . . . trying to grab all he could before it was too late'. In this context he found the claim for a revision of the Straits to be legitimate. Schulenburg hoped that Russia could fulfil her aspirations through co-operation with Germany rather than England. Russia could 'not always remain secluded, as if in a mousetrap'. He dismissed suggestions by his critics that Stalin wished 'to get hold of Constantinople and thus realize the ancient dream of the Russian tsars of conquering Byzantium and planting the Orthodox cross on Haghia Sophia'. All Stalin wished for was 'to obtain free passage for the Soviet Union through the Straits, and make the Black Sea a Russian Sea'. 'The Führer', he insisted, 'was hardly Friedrich Barbarossa' and Stalin stood to gain nothing by reaching Istanbul. He relied on him to seek the preservation of peace in the Balkans. The Turks were in for 'a very unpleasant awakening', as Hitler had been heard to threaten that 'These dirty pigs they will yet have to pay dearly.'[69] Papen, the German ambassador in Ankara and former Chancellor, expected indeed that by the end of October the Soviet and German governments, 'acting in concert, will have brought about demilitarisation of the Straits and internationalised Istanbul'.[70] As the day of the conference drew closer the Turks lost their composure, especially after the Italian invasion of Greece, which brought the war closer to their shores. The war scare prompted various measures, including a blackout of the quarters in Izmir facing the Aegean Sea.[71] At the same time in Moscow Aktay continued to inflate the German threat to the Straits, warning that 'Bulgaria was prepared to become a weapon in the hands of one of the foreign powers.'[72]

Stalin did not count on Turkey's ability to resist the pressure of the powers, even if she wished to do so. With the 'Eastern Question' at the top of the agenda for the Berlin meeting, relations with Turkey were put on hold. The provocative Turkish proposals were rejected on the ground that the impact of the war on Bulgaria was 'the concern of the Bulgarian government itself'.[73] Their approach to the Russians did not prevent the Turks from pressing the Germans for 'a fundamental change' in the relations between the two countries. But, as might be expected, Turkey was not willing to make a commitment to the 'new European order' before the real intentions of the Axis were known.[74]

Throughout October the security services informed Stalin of German and Italian plans to occupy Saloniki, thereby posing a direct threat to the Turkish Straits. Saracoglu too read to Vinogradov, the Russian ambassador in Ankara, telegrams he had received from all over the Balkans pointing to joint German–Italian plans to attack Turkey. The outbreak of war between Italy and Greece on the eve of the Berlin conference only reinforced the Soviet fear that Turkey might be dragged into the war against her will. It was hardly surprising therefore that on the eve of Molotov's visit to Berlin the Turks went out of their way to convince the Russians of their 'friendly and loyal' attitude. They undertook that Turkey would not allow any action which might jeopardize the Soviet Union's interests, 'not even behind its back', a clear reference to Turkish connivance in the plans to bomb Baku six months earlier.[75]

It is intriguing that in formulating his views on Turkey before Molotov's visit to Berlin, Stalin was much influenced by a report of the most trusted agent of the NKVD in Istanbul. Stalin had just been apprised by Beria of the debriefing of 'Omeri' during a recent secret visit to Moscow. The report focused on the dangers which Turkey posed to Russia in the Caucasus. Information from inside the Turkish military confirmed the intentions of the Allies to bomb Baku and Batum in the event of a confrontation with the Soviet Union. Perhaps more significantly, Stalin's antagonism was fanned by the revelation that the Turkish government was allegedly plotting with Trotskyites. Quoting 'Omeri', Beria impressed on Stalin the Turkish government's view that 'whatever Turkey had gained from Russia [a reference to the Agreement of Friendship of 1921], in terms of both armaments and political support, had been given by Trotsky'. Stalin had been opposed to the concessions which Trotsky had granted the Turks in the 1920s, and therefore the Turkish government 'always supported Trotsky and other oppositionists and in the future would continue to support them, as they expected nothing good but only evil from Stalin and his entourage'. The final verdict, therefore, was that 'in the event of war activities between Turkey and the USSR Turkey intended to come out against the Soviet Union with the aim of seizing and annexing the Caucasus which would become "the Caucasian Confederation" '.[76]

The Germans had hoped to pre-empt the Russians by including both Hungary and Bulgaria in the Tripartite Pact prior to Molotov's arrival in Berlin. They were successful only with Hungary, which was of secondary importance for the Russians.[77] Even before the signing of the Vienna Arbitration Stamenov, the Bulgarian ambassador in Moscow, kept his government well abreast of the Soviet concern with German meddling over Dobrudja.[78] King Boris, who now took control of the conduct of foreign affairs, decided to exploit the auspicious circumstances for making a claim on Dobrudja. The temptation was well-nigh irresistible, but by playing the major powers against one another he undermined Bulgaria's neutral status and facilitated the German stranglehold on the country and on Rumania. In early August the King had already lured the Germans into acting by conveying the 'people's opinion' that 'Bulgaria could get the whole of Dobrudja from Russia'.[79] After the settlement of Dobrudja, Draganov in Berlin presented a new set of claims for an outlet to the Aegean. Once again the appeal was accompanied by manipulation of the assumed German–Soviet tension. The occupation of Thrace was presented not only as an anti-British move but also as a way for Germany to overcome the dependence on the Straits, 'where Russia had its interests'.[80]

The key to Soviet security now lay in Bulgaria, where the altering balance of power had been followed with trepidation. The steady drift towards Germany was furthered by rumours emanating from governmental circles about the Russian intention to occupy Burgas and Varna, the key naval ports on the Black Sea.[81] The Germans, resolved to prevent a Soviet move, did not allow Antonescu, the Rumanian Prime Minister, to delay the implementation of the Vienna Award. He was to instruct the Rumanian delegation in Sofia to accept instantly the Bulgarian demand for Dobrudja.[82]

King Boris performed a delicate balancing act, following the approach to Germany with instructions to Stamenov to thank Molotov for the Soviet position on Dobrudja. Molotov was not really fooled, pointing to Filov's speech of a day earlier in which the Bulgarian Prime Minister had thanked Germany and Italy. Stamenov's feeble explanation that this was a recognition of Germany's initiative resulted in the publication of his approach in *Izvestiia* the next morning. Molotov did not abandon the race and now raised the stakes by offering the Bulgarians Northern Dobrudja. He was of course fully aware that Bulgarian expansion would secure territorial continuity between Russia and Bulgaria and eventually the Turkish Straits. Stamenov therefore rejected the idea, using the pretext that Rumania's quest for access to the Black Sea was as justifiable as Bulgaria's to the Aegean, exposing even further Bulgaria's strong leanings towards Germany. Bulgaria was indubitably seeking refuge under the umbrella of the Vienna Award and the guarantees to Rumania. Consequently Russia's ability to transfer troops through Bulgaria if their position in the Straits were to be endangered was seriously curtailed.[83]

The fate of Bulgaria now hung in the balance; her hope of attaining her territorial claims while remaining neutral was fading. The Germans, as we have seen, intended to steal a march on the Russians and present Molotov with a *fait accompli*. Pressure was exerted on King Boris to join the Tripartite Pact prior to Molotov's arrival in Berlin. Judging from his annotations of cipher telegrams, King Boris was inclined to accept the view of his ambassador in Moscow that the Russians were actually frustrated, aware of the German danger but conscious of their military weakness. However, while the Turkish ambassador was of the opinion that the Russians would not fight the Germans even if they reached Istanbul, the Russian military attaché in Sofia persistently warned that Russia might well do so.[84] Facing what he conceived to be a mortal threat from Turkey, England and Russia, the King tried to adhere to his 'quasi neutrality'. His cunning letter to Hitler on 20 October amplified the advantages which Bulgaria's 'cautious policy' carried for Germany: it foiled British attempts to form an anti-German bloc in the heart of the Balkans, while a full commitment to Germany might have driven Turkey straight into Russia's arms. However, when delivering the letter Draganov was warned to bear in mind 'the true considerations which made Germany offer us an act which to her seems to be of a demonstrative and doubtful nature while for us it could be fatal'. The fear of Russia was so overriding that Draganov was specifically instructed to avoid 'creating the impression' that his government was 'inclined to accept the offer'.[85]

It is perhaps impossible to decide how inevitable was Hitler's attack on Russia. However, it is certain that King Boris's determination before, during and after the conference brought home to Hitler the extent to which Soviet influence and interests in the Balkans were impinging on his own. This became the major consideration to the final decision to implement Operation 'Barbarossa'.[86] The alternatives of 'war and peace' now entered the dialogue, though perhaps in a subtle way. Bulgaria's adherence to the pact, Draganov was informed, was vital for German attempts to isolate England. Hitler did not foresee that Russia would be involved in war in the Balkans, nor did she have a good enough reason to draw closer to England 'because Germany could provide her more than England could'. He made allusions to India. He expected that the expansion of the Tripartite Pact would only hasten Stalin's submission. But, if it came to the worst, Germany possessed large 'unemployed armies' which could achieve a military success in the south-eastern flank of Europe at any moment.[87]

King Boris was scarcely reassured. Through Kollontai he learnt that Stalin, who was concerned with events in the Balkans, intended to put his relations with Hitler to the test in Berlin. Moreover, the Russian military attaché in Bucharest continued to express 'open discontent with the occupation of Rumania', reiterating Russia's intentions of 'standing up against anybody who may try to grab the Straits', strongly implying that 'Bulgaria had to enter the Soviet sphere of interest'.[88] Draganov kept pressing the King to join the Axis. However, his attempts to set his mind at rest by quoting Weizsäcker's assurance that relations with Russia 'were very good' were seriously contested by information from Moscow:

Schulenburg, Rosso and Togo, the Japanese ambassador in Moscow, had indicated to the Bulgarian ambassador that they did not expect Russia to be included in the Tripartite Pact in Berlin.[89] Moreover, Timoshenko, the Soviet Minister of Defence, was manifestly alarmed by the deployment of the Wehrmacht on the borders of Rumania and northern Greece, which implied direct intervention in Bulgaria and eventually in Turkey.[90] Having failed to secure Bulgarian entry to the Axis before Molotov's arrival in Berlin, the Germans resorted to their familiar crude methods. Some 200 Wehrmacht officers and men in civilian clothes were infiltrated into Bulgaria to erect an adequate air-warning system, thereby establishing the spearhead for German military presence there.[91]

The Italian attack on Greece on 28 October, made without prior German knowledge a mere fortnight before the Berlin conference, shuffled all the cards. England was now expected to land in Greece, thereby posing a direct threat to Germany and Russia. The Russians feared that Hitler might be tempted to make a dash to Turkey through Bulgaria. The spotlight was once again focused on the Turkish Straits. But in the short term attention was also directed towards Bulgaria, which had so far succeeded in maintaining neutrality and whose next moves were to determine the fate of the Balkans.[92] The unforeseen threat from Italy led the Turks to secure Soviet support in the event of the war reaching their shores. They readily exploited the Bulgarian card, warning the Russians that there were indications that 'Bulgaria was prepared to become a weapon in the hands of one of the foreign powers',[93] a clear allusion to Germany. The Soviet participation in the Berlin conference, however, was governed less by apprehension of German encroachment than by claims on Turkey itself. Stalin, who did not trust Turkey,[94] did not exclude the possibility that she would be willingly dragged into the war by Britain, especially if provided with assistance similar to that given to France and Norway. The attitude of Turkey to the Soviet Union during the Finnish War, as well as the alleged tacit Turkish agreement to allow British bombers to fly over Turkish territory on the way to Baku, left a dark shadow on the relations between the two countries. Stalin was unlikely to entrust Russian security to a paper agreement sustained by Turkish goodwill. In fact, his evasive reply to the Turkish proposals did little to conceal his real intentions of achieving Russia's security through direct Soviet intervention using transit rights in Bulgaria.[95]

Moscow became the scene of frenzied activity. Two days before Molotov's departure he attempted to forestall Germany by giving guarantees to Bulgaria, thus establishing a Soviet presence similar to the German one in Rumania. The proposal was rejected out of hand by Popov, the Bulgarian Foreign Minister, but the Soviet ambassador refused to take no for an answer. He rebutted one by one the Bulgarian reservations and modified some of the proposals to make them more attractive to the

Bulgarians. He even resorted to threats, warning that were Bulgaria to join the Axis it would be tantamount to abandoning her neutrality and could pose a threat to her existence. Finally, to defuse the tension, alleviate Bulgarian fears of the German reaction and prevent a recurrence of the Rumanian syndrome, he made a new proposition which King Boris marked firmly with his thick pencil on the minutes of the talks. Joining the Axis, he argued, would 'not make redundant the Soviet proposal for military assistance but increase the significance of Bulgaria'. So anxious was the Kremlin to reach agreement that Molotov was even prepared to exempt the Bulgarians from any concrete military obligations. The Russians' proposal to Bulgaria of a mutual assistance pact, coupled with their demand for a seat on the Danubian Commission, put Hitler and Stalin on an inevitable collision course.[96]

4

The Road to 'Barbarossa'

Molotov's Visit to Berlin

Historians are still disputing the sincerity of Hitler's negotiations with
Molotov in Berlin in November 1940. Their judgment often corresponds
to their views on the ideological motivation for Hitler's policies. Armed
with hindsight of events yet to come, they are inclined to propose that
at best Hitler used the negotiations as a tactical manoeuvre to demonstrate to Turkey, Spain, Italy, Vichy France and the Balkan States that he
had the full backing of Russia for his plans for mastery of Europe. They
therefore could join the Axis without fearing the reaction in Moscow. It is
argued as well that the negotiations were used by Hitler to demonstrate
to his subordinates that the Russians understood only the language of
force.[1]

The idea of the Berlin meeting, like the Ribbentrop–Molotov Pact and
the subsequent abortive attempts to bring Hitler and Stalin together in
May 1941, originated with Schulenburg during a brief visit to Berlin at
the end of September. Schulenburg had been contemplating a four-power
pact since the collapse of France. The realization that Russia would not
unilaterally retreat from the Balkans prompted him to act. But it was his
general familiarity with the contingency plans 'to bring about a show-
down with Russia' which prompted him to take the initiative. He got an
inkling of the plans from Hans Herwarth, later to be German ambassador
in London, a senior official at the Moscow embassy. A lonely and child-
less figure, Schulenburg seemed to have 'adopted' Herwarth and his wife,
especially after Herwarth joined the army prior to the French campaign.
While on leave in Berlin after the fall of France Herwarth was told in
confidence by his cousin, a colonel on the German General Staff, of

Hitler's plans to attack Russia. On the pretext of visiting his wife, who was still employed at the embassy in Moscow, Herwarth obtained leave from the army (not before promising his commander a full load of caviar). Schulenburg and Köstring, the veteran military attaché, were 'flabbergasted' by the news, but they could not make up their minds whether to take the information at face value or regard it as a contingency plan, aimed at exerting pressure on the Russians to increase their industrial output and deliveries. Some verification, however, was obtained during Köstring's meeting with Halder later on in the month and from visitors from the Ministry. Schulenburg maintained, however, that Hitler and his entourage could still be swayed towards an extension of the agreement with Russia so long as Russian claims were confined to Turkey and Iran.[2]

The harsh Soviet reaction to the Vienna Award throughout September undermined his scheme. Aware of the direction in which the winds of war were blowing in Berlin, Schulenburg continued to send the Wilhelmstrasse highly ambiguous reports of Soviet reactions, concealing Molotov's doubts as to whether Hitler had acted 'in good faith'. Molotov had in fact reverted to the proposals made by Mackensen for a tripartite arrangement in the Balkans. Schulenburg's plea that the absence of prior consultations might have reflected Berlin's failure to perceive Soviet interests was sarcastically dismissed by Molotov; those had been unfolded on the front pages of the entire international press. Ignoring his instructions from Berlin, Schulenburg now initiated a conciliatory move which would lead to the Berlin conference two months later. No longer able to hide his own reservations about the German attitude, he decided on a prompt return to Berlin to iron out the differences.[3]

Schulenburg was given little assistance by a memorandum handed to him by Molotov on the eve of his departure that accused the Germans of breaching the terms of the Ribbentrop–Molotov Pact. Molotov exerted pressure on Berlin by calling for changes in the clauses of the pact which dealt with prior consultations, thereby hinting that Russia wished for a free hand in her dealings with the Turks on the Straits. He blamed the unilateral German action for the widespread rumours that the arbitration was an anti-Soviet move and revealed a growing tension in German–Soviet relations. Schulenburg's record of the conversation shows him forcefully defending the German position, though in reality he was 'strongly in favour of solving the controversies' and was therefore leaving straight away for Berlin 'to liquidate the misunderstandings'.[4]

Schulenburg, however, did not get a chance to discuss the issue with Ribbentrop until 25 September. Ribbentrop was absent in Rome conducting negotiations with Mussolini on the establishment of the Axis, a potentially thorny issue in German–Soviet relations. Schulenburg certainly received encouragement from his colleagues in the Foreign Ministry.

Weizsäcker, himself a convert to the Continental bloc, confided in his diary: 'The public does not expect an early peace, but rather anticipates a conflict with Russia. This is denied officially. However, I personally do believe that the people are right, although I see no sense or necessity of such a new war, unless in spring 1941 conditions force us to take such a step. To beat England in Russia is not a programme.'[5] The Foreign Ministry, however, used trade as the bait for convening the political meeting. By halting deliveries the Russians could inflict a disaster on the German war effort. It had been noticed that the Russians were neglecting long-range projects, concentrating on short-term deliveries in exchange for munitions and armaments which brought them immediate benefits.[6]

Hitler now faced the dilemma of whether to attempt to bring the Ribbentrop–Molotov Pact up to date through arrangements in South-eastern Europe or alternatively to proceed with vigorous preparations for war. Throughout the summer of 1940 he seems to have vacillated. Whether he would have abided by an agreement which excluded Russia from Europe and the Balkans and diverted her to the Near East is obviously a hypothetical question, but there are no indications that the diplomatic measures were not executed in earnest. The first move in an attempt to secure a political solution was the signature on 27 September of the Tripartite Pact. Japan was counted on to engage the United States in the Pacific. It was anticipated that Italy and hopefully Franco's Spain would undermine the British naval dominance in the Mediterranean, while Russia could be diverted against British imperial interests in the Near East. Rumania and Finland were destined to provide Germany's basic raw materials and oil. That his plans concerning Russia did not deflect Hitler from the war against England is obvious from his instructions to unleash the Luftwaffe against Britain, as a preliminary to an invasion, the day after informing his generals about his intention of fighting Russia. Moreover, the plans to increase the size of the army to 180 divisions were prepared in the context of the subsidiary strategy and as an attempt to maintain the combat momentum. While the preliminary general plans for the invasion of Russia were being drawn up, the OKW was zealously engaged in preparing the operations against Gibraltar and Egypt. Hitler hoped to implement a new order through a fresh delimitation of spheres of interest.[7]

Unlike the Russians, Hitler was not guided by any concrete agenda for the meeting. The negotiations were expected to follow his well-known pattern. The presentation of the general idea of the 'new Europe' would gradually develop into a rigid proposal for delimitation which would exclude Russia from Europe and the Balkans and reflect German military supremacy. Ribbentrop was briefed only on secondary issues which might emerge as a result of the discussion of 'high policy' concerning Russia's attitude to the war, the Italo-Greek conflict, Russia's attitude to the Axis and the Straits. The draft agreement on delimitation, prepared by the Moscow embassy, was the sole guideline for the German delegation but was never referred to.[8] It tallied more or less with the views of the Russians: Turkey was to be excluded from the new European order, while Russia received bases on the Asiatic side of the Bosphorus and Germany on the European. An alternative solution was for Russia to control only the Bosphorus while a friendly state, such as Bulgaria, would look after German interests in Istanbul.[9] Shortly after returning from his consultations in Berlin, Schulenburg had composed together with Köstring and Walther, the counsellor at the embassy, a memorandum which elaborated the dangers of a German attack on the Soviet Union. It insisted that the Soviet Union was unlikely to initiate war but that, if war was forced on her, the entire population would stand firmly behind the government. It was possible that Russia would lose the Ukraine, White Russia and the Baltic States, but these would only become a burden for Germany. This document was submitted on 2 November to Halder, who marked it 'received', but it is unknown whether Hitler was made aware of its contents.[10] The views of the Moscow embassy, however, were circulating freely among the higher echelons of the Foreign Ministry, as best reflected by Weizsäcker:

> It is argued that without liquidating Russia there will be no order in Europe. But why should it not stew next to us in its damp Bolshevism? As long as it is ruled by bureaucrats of the present type, this country has to be feared less than in the time of the tsars. I consider it unfavourable to bring war into countries where distances will weaken our forces. The occupation of Russia will not even gain us corn.[11]

The eventual exclusion of Schulenburg, the architect of the meeting, from the talks was a bad omen for the group.[12]

Hitler's general outline for the negotiations was very different from the Russians'. True, he still adhered to Ribbentrop's idea of raising the 'West Wall' to detach England from her potential allies. But the acid test seemed to have become the Russian stand on the Balkans. From the German point of view, as Ribbentrop explained to Mussolini, 'the Vienna Award had plainly indicated to the Russians where the limit for their expansion lay'. The Continental bloc, therefore, was a peaceful and even preferable alternative to 'Barbarossa'. The precondition for it, however, was Soviet acceptance of Germany's dictation, justified by the military superiority she had established through her victories in Northern and Western Europe. It was no secret that the Bosphorus and the Balkans marked 'a dangerous overlapping of interests' which had to be avoided.[13]

Hitler, as he revealed to Mussolini on the eve of the conference, did not intend to accommodate the Russians beyond forcing Turkey to yield 'some' guarantees in the Straits and security arrangements in Baku and Batum. The talks were clearly doomed to failure, as Hitler expected them to put the seal of approval on German supremacy in Europe by diverting the Russians from their 'old goal, the Bosphorus' towards the Indian Ocean. He was resolved to stop Stalin from advancing 'beyond certain definite boundaries', more specifically from 'approaching the Bosphorus via Rumania'. 'One Rumanian bird in the hand', he summed up, was 'worth more than two Russian birds in the bush'. Stalin's obsession with the Danube and Bulgaria rendered Hitler somewhat sceptical about the outcome of the conference. However, he still believed Stalin to be 'shrewd enough' to bow to German predominance and suppress his ambitions. Stalin, he felt, had made the wrong calculation in expecting that Europe would 'bleed white' in a protracted war. With a hundred unscathed divisions deployed on his border, Hitler told his Chief of Staff, Stalin was bound to acquiesce to the German presence in Finland and Rumania, and was unlikely to 'represent any problem for Germany even if worst came to worst'.[14] Within the diplomatic community in Berlin it was believed that after failing to reach an agreement with Britain Hitler was genuinely following in Bismarck's footsteps in seeking an understanding with Russia, regardless of the ideological differences. It was even thought possible that 'the political co-operation might influence Bolshevism towards a national socialist trend . . .'.[15]

Paradoxically, the setting up of the Axis during Schulenburg's stay in Berlin only helped him to further his ideas. The Tripartite Part was clearly a vehicle for the establishment of the Continental bloc and initially assumed the inclusion of the Soviet Union by giving her 'at the proper moment and in a friendly manner . . . a free hand towards the south to fulfil any possible wishes in the direction of the Persian Gulf or India'.[16] The prevailing feeling in the Wilhelmstrasse, best expressed by Weizsäcker, was:

> We annoyed Russia with the guarantees to Romania . . . and yesterday again with the tripartite pact of Germany, Italy, and Japan. It is necessary to compensate these surprises to Russia, if we do not want her to alter her attitude towards us. An attack by Russia is not to be feared because it is not strong enough militarily or as a regime. But Russia could still open its territory to English intrigues and, more importantly, stop the deliveries to us.

Not only were the Russians informed in advance about the setting up of the Axis, but Weizsäcker assured the Soviet ambassador that special efforts would be made to reconcile Russia and Japan.[17] A similar message was conveyed directly to Molotov. His attention was drawn to the clause which clarified that the agreement preserved the special relations with the Soviet Union. To sweeten the pill, Ribbentrop now promised to address

Stalin personally and to extend an invitation for Molotov to discuss in Berlin 'questions relating to the establishment of common political aims for the future'.[18] Ribbentrop belittled the significance of the German activities in Finland and reiterated that all signatories of the Tripartite Pact 'were from the beginning in complete agreement that their accord should in no way affect the Soviet Union'.[19] He promised to elaborate those ideas in his letter to Stalin. The only drawback was the declaration of the irrevocable a German intention of implementing the guarantees to Rumania and establishing a German presence there, a clear though subdued deterrent to Russia. But the German presence in the Balkans was ascribed to the threat which the British posed to the Rumanian oilfields. The German legations in the Balkans were instructed to avoid 'scrupulously' any action which might give an anti-Russian impression.[20]

Ribbentrop's letter, which he wished Schulenburg to submit to Stalin in person, awaited the ambassador's return to Moscow. Schulenburg carefully worked on the translation of the text, which he feared might 'cause serious annoyance to Molotov'. He was finally forced to submit it to Molotov on 17 October, by which time its gist had already been leaked to the press. The letter, though personally endorsed by Hitler, revealed none of the 'fresh ideas' Ribbentrop had promised. Ostensibly the suggestion for bringing the Ribbentrop–Molotov Pact up to date through the 'delimitation of mutual spheres of influence' was prominent, but read carefully it included a caution to the Russians not to collude with the British in the Balkans. The 'friendly advice' was backed up by a concealed warning of the superiority of the Wehrmacht, whose troops 'have routed the British wherever they accepted battle'. Ribbentrop touched a raw nerve in the Kremlin by alluding to the recent British plans to bomb Baku and Batum. The German encroachment in the Balkans was vindicated as a measure to check 'British perfidious activities' and a protection of vital economic needs. It is doubtful whether Stalin was placated by Ribbentrop's account of the 'completely improvised' arbitration in Vienna, which had had to be organized 'within twenty-four hours' because of British machinations, which left 'no time for any negotiations or consultations'. Schulenburg, the Russian report suggests, had to augment the text to respond to Soviet expectations. He stressed that the conference in Berlin would be only a preliminary meeting before the convening of the four powers. He excused the absence of clearer references to the conference by pointing out that Japan and Italy had not yet been consulted about it.[21]

Stalin was nonetheless visibly relieved by the invitation. He was prepared for Molotov to go to Berlin during the first week of November and even made a few gestures of goodwill. Thus he withdrew the objections to Italy's participation in the Danubian Commission, paving the way for its convention in Bucharest at the end of October, and endorsed the agreement on indemnities to German citizens of the former Baltic States.

In his report to Berlin Schulenburg deliberately omitted any mention of Molotov's manifest suspicion about the presence of the German military in Rumania, the transit of German troops through Norway to Finland and the alleged German–Turkish negotiations.[22] And yet it could not have escaped Hitler's attention that Stalin's reply to Ribbentrop's flamboyant letter was succinct, expressing the hope that relations would be improved once 'the permanent basis of a long-range delimitation of mutual interests' was established. Molotov's visit was perceived only as a prelude to the negotiations to be conducted by Ribbentrop in Moscow, presumably leading to a second Ribbentrop–Molotov pact.[23]

Molotov's forty-eight-hour stay in Berlin has been reconstructed by historians in minute detail, and there is little need to recapitulate it here. The prevailing view, however, presents it as a conspiracy to dismantle the British Empire leading to a division of the entire world rather than a reflection of the fierce rivalry over the Balkans which has been unfolded here.[24]

Molotov's negotiations in Berlin stood in sharp contrast to the pomp and circumstance which surrounded his departure from the Belorussia Station in Moscow on 11 November, accompanied by a large Soviet delegation. The dark overcast sky and irritating drizzle which met Molotov the next morning, when his special train pulled into the Anhalter Station in Berlin, was a premonition of things to come. The welcome, however, was cordial and encouraging. Molotov was greeted by Ribbentrop and Field Marshal Keitel. The station was decorated with Soviet and Nazi flags above a large basket of flowers draped in pink. Outside a band struck up 'Deutschland Deutschland über Alles', and the 'Internationale' was played for the first time since 1933. Molotov was then whisked by a black Mercedes limousine to the ostentatious Bellevue Hotel. Little time was wasted and shortly after breakfast the delegation set off for the preliminary talks at the Reichskanzlerei.[25]

Starting with the preliminary meeting with Ribbentrop, Molotov made it clear that the Russians would not be satisfied with Hitler's idea of defining spheres of influence 'along very broad lines'. Considering the terms set out in Molotov's directive, it is hardly surprising that he was not at all tempted by the proposition that Russia seek an outlet in the Persian Gulf. There followed a long discussion on Turkey and the Straits (which is most significantly missing from the German protocols) in which the Russians were offered a revision of the Montreux Convention but without any further securities.[26] The initial impression, as Molotov hastily cabled Stalin, was that the German 'responses during the talk were not always clear and require further clarifications'. Ribbentrop deliberately avoided precise definition of the spheres of influence, preferring the conclusion of an agreement in principle which could serve immediate German interests vis-à-vis England.[27]

Hitler met Molotov with a Nazi salute, 'bending his palm unnaturally'. He invited him to the lounge section of the hall, where Ribbentrop joined them. Hitler was 'surprisingly gracious and friendly . . . eager to win Molotov personally and wanted him to share his views'. Considering Molotov's expectations of rancour, it comes as no surprise that the Soviet Foreign Minister was observed to be 'relieved at Hitler's amiability' when he returned to his hotel.[28] And yet Molotov's unbending stand confirmed Hitler's anxieties about the course of Russia's foreign policy and cast doubt on the possibility of reaching a peaceful arrangement with her. Between their two major meetings a cable from Stalin instructed Molotov not to deviate from the directive, reminding him that 'a peaceful solution will not be tenable without Soviet guarantees to Bulgaria and the admission of Soviet troops into Bulgaria, as means of pressure on Turkey'.[29]

At their following meeting, Hitler was, as Molotov cabled back to Stalin, 'markedly agitated' when Molotov reiterated the demand for the Germans to revoke the guarantees to Rumania, which were 'aimed against the interests of Soviet Russia, if one might express oneself so bluntly'. He went on to convey Stalin's demands, virtually verbatim, for a guarantee to Bulgaria 'under exactly the same conditions as Germany and Italy had given one to Rumania'. Promising non-interference in her domestic affairs, he actually proposed to compensate Bulgaria with access to the Aegean. Such a solution would have impeded Hitler's plans for the occupation of Saloniki.

Molotov further infuriated Hitler when he dug in his heels, alluding to the revision of the Montreux Convention as a paper guarantee while Russia sought 'a tangible one'. He had been instructed by a second cable from Stalin, who was vigilantly monitoring the negotiations from Moscow, to explain to Hitler that Russia was not interested in access to the Mediterranean but rather was vulnerable to a possible attack by the British if they were in a position to navigate unhindered into the Black Sea. Once again the frame of reference was historical. Hitler was to be reminded that 'all the events from the Crimean War in the last century to the landing of foreign troops during the intervention in the Crimea and in Odessa in 1918 and 1919 mean that the security of the Soviet territories on the Black Sea cannot be achieved without a solution of the Straits issue'. Stalin appeared to be still hopeful that a draft agreement on such lines could be prepared in Berlin and the final touches would be put to it later in Moscow.[30]

Hitler, who had been informed about the abortive Soviet approach to King Boris, glossed over the subject, though not without making the sarcastic comment that whereas Rumania had asked for guarantees from Germany and Italy he was not familiar with a similar request made to the Russians by the Bulgarians. He was not reassured by Molotov's serious reservations about the proposals that Russia associate herself with the

Tripartite Pact. Molotov's precondition was that the pact be completely remodelled, as he 'did not object to participating in various activities of the four powers but not in the Tripartite Pact, where the USSR was no more than an object'.

It was left for Ribbentrop to try to pick up the threads in the surrealistic surroundings of the air-raid shelter in Berlin; the heavy British bombing brought the reality of war home and questioned German invincibility. His efforts were directed towards reconciling the Tripartite Pact with the German–Soviet pact through a definition of spheres of influence of which, he admitted, he had only a 'rough idea'. He then drew a folded paper out of his pocket and read aloud the proposed agreement. It was a general document which established the wish of the four powers to define the respective spheres of interests and called for constant mutual consultations. Several secret protocols defined the territorial aspirations of each of the parties. As expected, the Russians were diverted to the Indian Ocean and the only reference to their original aims was a promise to seek a revision of the Straits regime under German auspices. Molotov stipulated that 'paper agreements would not suffice . . . [Russia] would have to insist on effective guarantees of her security.' The guarantees to Bulgaria figured prominently in Molotov's report but only briefly in the German one, most probably in order not to enrage Hitler further.[31]

Hitler's drift towards launching an attack on the Soviet Union was a clear outcome of the intransigence displayed by the Russians in defining what they deemed to be their essential security demands in the Balkans. But he still gave Stalin (as the Russian records though not the German ones reveal) a chance to reverse his policies. Stalin's handling of the Bulgarian issue in the wake of the conference, as we shall see, finally sealed the fate of Russia. Indeed, Ribbentrop and Göring gave reliable testimony to this effect in their interrogations at Nuremberg.[32] Hitler seems to have lost all interest in the talks at that point, indicating that 'he was not . . . absolutely sure' whether the joint plans for the dismemberment of the British Empire 'could be carried out'.[33]

Hitler Opts for War

Despite the early impression gained by the Bulgarians and other keen observers that the negotiations had been successful,[34] Molotov's last cable to Stalin stated unequivocally that the negotiations 'did not produce the desired results'. He then explained that Hitler had 'avoided giving an answer' on Bulgaria by referring the issue to Italy. Equally unsatisfactory was the discussion of the Turkish problem, while Ribbentrop's projected trip to Moscow was no longer mentioned. Molotov wrapped up the report: 'These are the main results. Nothing to boast about, but in any case it does clarify the present mood of Hitler, which one should take into account.'[35] It had become clear, as Molotov explained upon returning to Moscow, that the Germans had hoped 'to lay their hands on Turkey under the pretext of guaranteeing her security similarly to Rumania, while sweetening our lips with a promise of revision of the Montreux Convention in our favour, proposing to us to help them on this matter'. Henceforward the Soviet intention would be to improve the Straits regime in direct negotiations with Turkey and 'not behind her back'. In the corridors of the Kremlin the probability of 'a German expedition against Egypt, through the Straits and Turkey', was actually discussed.[36] As for the German proposals that Russia should encroach on British interests in the Near East, Molotov was most incisive: 'The Germans and the Japanese, it is evident, would very much like to push us towards the Persian Gulf and India. We refused to discuss the matter as we believe that such German recommendations are ill advised.'[37] And yet, rather than causing a sense of irrevocable crisis, the new proposals submitted by Ribbentrop at the last moment[38] led to a short-lived complacency. Negotiations, so it seemed, could proceed at a leisurely pace through 'diplomatic channels'. Molotov was indeed observed to be 'swollen-headed and puffed up' at a welcome party thrown by Rosso for representatives of the 'friendly countries'.[39]

The proponents of the Continental bloc in Ribbentrop's entourage, as well as Schulenburg, still expected that Stalin would eventually yield, given the weakness of the Red Army. 'In my opinion,' commented Weizsäcker, 'we can continue to negotiate with them for a long time. War against Russia is impossible as long as we are busy with England, and afterwards it will be unnecessary.' Even Halder had not abandoned hope of a political solution.[40]

Hitler, however, emerged from the Berlin conference more than ever convinced that British resilience was the result of Soviet intransigence. He was equally disillusioned about the Continental bloc. A prerequisite for conducting a subsidiary strategy, besides agreement with Russia, was Spain's adherence to the Tripartite Pact. On 18 November Hitler had been informed by Ciano that Italy regarded the entry of Spain into the war and the seizure of Gibraltar as vital for inflicting the final blow on the British naval presence in the Mediterranean. Meeting the Spanish Foreign Minister the following day, Hitler lied brazenly, boasting of the successful completion of the preparations for Operation 'Sea-Lion'. Preparations for the operation had in fact petered out during the summer, to a large extent as a result of the Luftwaffe's failure to achieve air supremacy during the Battle of Britain. Though the postponement was conveniently attributed to exceptionally poor weather conditions, the invasion had been postponed 'indefinitely' on 17 September. Germany, Hitler claimed, 'would begin the attack even in winter, if there were a prospect of 3–4 weeks of good weather'. Serrano Suñer, the Spanish Foreign Minister, however, was not to be swayed, announcing Franco's final decision to remain out of the war.[41]

Shortly after meeting Suñer, Hitler drafted a telegram to Mussolini, who had been pressing for assistance after the bungled invasion of Greece on 28 October. Hitler now reluctantly agreed, promising help later in the winter but making the revealing reservation: 'In the spring, by the beginning of May at the latest, I should like, however, to get back my German forces . . .'[42] But he still held his cards close to his chest.

He now spoke for the first time of Russia, which 'hung like a threatening cloud on the horizon and . . . either assumed an imperialist, Russian nationalist appearance or appeared in Communist international guise, depending on the countries involved'. And yet he had not abandoned his idea of creating the 'great worldwide coalition that stretched from Yokohama to Spain'; but he was resolved to hang on to the Balkans, as 'Russia would march in, just as happened in the Baltic. Any vacuum that might develop would be filled immediately by Russia.' He was no longer relying on the agreement with the Russians but 'more on instruments of actual power'. By the spring Germany would have an effective deterrent in the shape of 186 first-class infantry divisions, including twenty armoured divisions. The furthest he intended to go was to revise the Montreux Convention, making the Black Sea 'a kind of gigantic harbour for the adjacent countries, in which these states would have free and unimpeded entry and egress'.[43]

The lesson that Hitler had derived from the conference was that Bulgaria had become the key for the control of the Balkans. To dissuade the Russians from pursuing their hard line, they were informed shortly after the conclusion of the conference that Hungary, Rumania and Slovakia would shortly join the Tripartite Pact.[44] Virtually as Molotov was boarding the train in Berlin Ribbentrop received assurances from Draganov that no prior agreement on mutual assistance had been reached with Moscow. However, he found out from him that although the Bulgarians feared Bolshevization they could not ignore the 'traditional Russian policy on the Balkans – the drive to the Straits. The borders of San Stefano[45] showed that the Russians regarded Adrianople and the whole of Eastern Thrace as a hinterland in defence of the Straits which they hoped would one day be in their own hands.' Ribbentrop's reply that Germany wanted 'peace in the Balkans and with [her] powerful military might [was] in a position to impose it' was prophetic.[46]

Hitler allowed little time for the Russians to digest the repercussions of the Berlin conference. A mere three days after Molotov's departure, King Boris and Popov, his Foreign Minister, were rushed in clandestine fashion to Berchtesgaden to pre-empt a Soviet reaction. Hitler exploited the poor performance of the Italians in the war with Greece to justify his projected intervention in Greece. He had to prevent the airfields in Thrace and Saloniki from falling into British hands and posing a severe threat to the Rumanian oilfields. To Hitler's manifest dismay King Boris, not hiding his fear of a Russian response, 'appeared less inclined than ever' to join the pact. He would not commit himself beyond words to the effect that 'down here you have a small true friend, whom you do not have to disown'. The meeting nonetheless was of significance in that it proved Bulgaria's increasing drift towards Berlin.[47]

It is only too easy to imagine the shock that seized the Kremlin when news of the visit came in. Molotov and Dekanozov, deputy Foreign Minister in charge of the Near East, immediately summoned Stamenov, the Bulgarian ambassador, for an acrimonious meeting in which they left him in no doubt of Soviet determination to conclude a quick agreement before the Bulgarians committed themselves to the Axis. They had no intention of allowing a repeat of the Rumanian syndrome whereby Bulgaria would become a 'legionnaire state'. Molotov, 'friendlily but forcefully', stated that the fate of Bulgaria was 'of interest to the Soviet Union and that faithful to its historical obligation the Soviet Union wished to see a strong Bulgaria'. He first produced the bait, promising to satisfy all Bulgaria's claims against Turkey, Yugoslavia and Greece and moreover to supply material help. He then warned against those forces in the Bulgarian parliament which were trying to make King Boris 'a puppet', regardless of the fact that he was 'clever, fair and genuinely concerned for the interests of the Bulgarian people'. Molotov did not fail to remind Stamenov that 'throughout history Russia had always stood for the independence and sovereignty of Bulgaria'. In that respect 'Russia, in the form of the Soviet Union, maintains that policy, fully supporting Bulgaria's territorial claims against its neighbours'. In reporting home Stamenov saw fit to warn Popov against leaving Russia 'outside to be confronted by a *fait accompli*'.[48] King Boris, however, knew he had succeeded in escaping from Berchtesgaden by the skin of his teeth; on the very night of his return to Sofia he rejected the Soviet proposals, though not before transmitting their gist to Berlin.[49]

Hitler, however, still preferred to believe that Stalin was 'too clever to make Russia England's cannon fodder'. To deter the Russians from the course they had embarked on in Berlin, he hastened to formalize the German presence in the Balkans. General Antonescu now made his own pilgrimage to Germany and was virtually compelled to join the Axis. Ominously, however, the talks with Antonescu revealed to Hitler that the Russians were still refusing to fix their borders with Rumania while demanding free passage for warships in the Danube as far as Braila, behind the Rumanian defence line for Moldavia. This merely confirmed that they were in fact seeking territorial continuity with Bulgaria. Moreover, in conversations with General Keitel it emerged that an imminent

English threat to the Balkans might lead Turkey and Russia to establish their own security arrangements, probably in Bulgaria.[50]

The Germans, therefore, continued to exert pressure. On his way back from Berlin to Ankara Papen stopped over in the Bulgarian capital. He carried with him a warning from Ribbentrop on 'the dangers which Bulgaria may incur' as the result of a guarantee forced on her by Russia, if Bulgaria did not immediately make it plain to the Russians that she had chosen to join the Tripartite Pact. As if oblivious to the German and Russian motives, King Boris still expressed the belief that the dangers could be avoided if he were allowed 'to play the game in such a way that Bulgaria would not become the apple of discord between Germany and Russia'. To prove his commitment to Germany he disclosed Molotov's offer to restore Bulgaria to the borders of San Stefano, while adding that he had no claim to such a crown, which was 'too big for one head'. He planned a polite rejection of the Soviet proposal, reminding them that Bulgaria had no enemies. The Turkish threat was now raised as a further pretext for delaying entry to the Axis, though Papen was reassured that the negative reply to the Russians should leave 'no room for doubt as to Bulgaria's ultimate alignment'.[51]

Though they subserviently passed on to Berlin all their communications with Moscow, the Bulgarians continued to cling to the Russian danger as the main reason for refusing to join the pact.[52] In Berlin Hitler was becoming impatient. The strategic significance of Bulgaria became evident when the Italians were routed by the Greeks in Albania on 24 November. Hitler still hoped to dissuade Stalin from giving guarantees to Bulgaria if the Straits issue could be solved. But, as he told Draganov in Berlin, 'he preferred to create accomplished facts, especially with respect to Russia, and it was his firm conviction that Russia would then try to do business elsewhere'. When Draganov reverted to the Turkish threat, explaining that the Bulgarians did not 'desire to be compelled to beat a glorious retreat in English style before the Greeks or the Turks', Hitler resorted to the brutal language he reserved for such occasions. Constantinople, he told him, was poorly defended and it would 'be wiped out in an instant, just as Coventry and Birmingham had been'. His own plan was simplicity itself. As Stalin professed to have no interest in Bulgaria except for the transfer of troops, the issue could be solved by bringing about a revision of the Montreux Convention. For the time being, it would suffice for Hitler to intimidate the Bulgarians with the threat of a Soviet occupation, which would 'permeate the country with propaganda and terror'.[53]

Rather than waiting passively, the Russians resorted to the German method of establishing a *fait accompli*. Through their covert sources they had found out that King Boris had resisted the German pressure. He was said to believe, in reference to Poland's experience, that a link with one

of the major powers might end in a 'catastrophe for small states' and that
he might still be able to collect the spoils by joining the 'new order' once
it was established, even if he remained neutral.[54] To overcome the King's
refusal to conduct open negotiations, Molotov sent his deputy, Arkady
Sobolev, uninvited to Sofia.[55] To some degree the mission was prompted
by Kollontai, the Soviet ambassador in Stockholm, who had been a fierce
opponent of the Ribbentrop–Molotov Pact and maintained close relations
with Antonov, the Russophile former Bulgarian ambassador in Moscow.
As she told him on the telephone when the news about Sobolev's presence was announced, it was she who had insisted on this urgent step in
order to 'outstrip and avoid the settlement desired by the [Bulgarian]
Government in favour of the Germans'.[56]

The Bulgarians were informed of Sobolev's arrival in Sofia, on a transit
flight to Bucharest, only a couple of hours in advance.[57] 'It is obvious',
Stamenov cabled home, 'that they wanted to surprise Sofia and they were
afraid to be outstripped by Hitler, which is why [Molotov] misled me that
Sobolev was going to Bucharest by plane. My impression is that they are
prepared to do anything if only they could sign a pact with us.'[58] Sobolev
was received by Filov, the Bulgarian Prime Minister, on the morning of
25 November and a meeting with King Boris was fixed for the afternoon.
Sobolev, aware that the Bulgarians were passing on their communications
with the Russians and eager not to provoke Hitler, did not present the
proposals to Filov in a written form but read them out to him.[59] His twelve
points detailed close collaboration, promising to satisfy Bulgarian territorial claims and to assist in the event of war with Turkey. The most
significant clause, however, spoke of the Russians' 'vital interest in the
Straits related to the security needs of their southern borders'. King Boris
should be in no doubt that Moscow could not allow a repetition of 'the
danger that [had] always been present to Russia through the south'.
Sobolev then raised again the offer of a pact of mutual assistance, made
to Bulgaria in September 1939, which would help 'to realize her national
aspirations not only in Western but in Eastern Thrace as well'. Bulgaria
was asked to co-operate with Russia if a real threat emerged 'for the USSR
in the Black Sea or in the Straits'. While the King was later to use this
clause as a justification of his rejection of the agreement, arguing that
Bulgaria was not in a position to render military assistance, it was quite
clear that what the Russians had in mind was permission to transfer their
troops via Bulgaria. This was accompanied by a pledge not to interfere in
the domestic affairs and sovereignty of Bulgaria. So as not to provoke the
Germans, Sobolev was prepared to drop the objections to Bulgaria's
joining the Tripartite Pact. The real enticement, however, was the
announcement that the conclusion of a pact with the Soviet Union might
'very probably, almost certainly', lead to Russia's own entry into the
Axis.[60]

Stunned, the Bulgarian Prime Minister wished to ascertain whether he had correctly understood that Russia did not object to Bulgaria's joining the Axis. However, he was more concerned by the renewed Soviet proposals for a pact of mutual assistance, pretending that he did not even remember the proposals made in September 1939. After being reminded, he stated that the proposal was 'so important that time was needed for it to be studied in depth'. But the general disposition was clear to Sobolev. Filov constantly referred to 'Bulgaria's complicated situation', hinting at Turkey's hostility while refusing to mention either Germany or Italy by name throughout the conversation. He chose this moment to reject the still outstanding Soviet proposals of guarantees.[61] The Bulgarian government, Sobolev cabled home, 'is already committed to Germany to the hilt and that is why it did not want any elucidation from me in connection with the Soviet proposals'. He further warned that King Boris was cunning, maintaining a tight hold over his ministers and direct control of Bulgarian politics.[62]

In making the offer to the Bulgarians, Stalin was increasingly thinking in traditional historical terms. He was careful to make the point that, unlike the case of the Baltic, Russia had no interest in either overrunning the country or Bolshevizing her. To Dimitrov, the head of Comintern, himself a Bulgarian, he explained that the approach was prompted by the threats posed to Russia in the Black Sea. 'Historically the danger has always come from there', Stalin revealed, 'the Crimean War – the capture of Sebastopol – the intervention of Wrangel in 1919 etc.' His main efforts were therefore directed towards Turkey, where he was determined to secure naval bases so that the Straits would 'not be used against Russia'. He believed that at the end of the day the Germans, much as they would have preferred to see the Italians settled there, would have no choice but to recognize the predominance of Soviet interests in the region. Like Hitler, he had no scruples about Turkey's fate were she to interfere. What was Turkey? he asked; 'there are two million Georgians there, one and a half million Armenians, one million Kurds etc. The Turks make up no more than 6–7 million.' If necessary, they could be expelled from Europe. But it was clear to Stalin that Bulgaria stood between him and his objectives. The conclusion of the pact was bound to act as a deterrent for Turkey, altering the whole situation in the Balkans. The subordination of the Comintern to the diplomatic needs of the Soviet Union was once again demonstrated when Dimitrov was instructed by Stalin to run the most energetic campaign in the Bulgarian parliament and in political circles, demanding the 'immediate and unconditional acceptance' of the Soviet offer.

Dimitrov made a serious mistake. Stalin's intention was to mount a seemingly spontaneous popular campaign. Dimitrov's instructions to the Central Committee of the Bulgarian Communist Party, however, disclosed, almost verbatim, Sobolev's proposals, which were printed and the leaflets distributed widely. Most Bulgarian ministers in fact became aware of the proposals from the leaflets. Much more significantly, they found their way to Berlin, where they contributed to Hitler's already soaring indignation about Russia.[63] Molotov was infuriated by the move. 'Our people in Sofia', he reproached Dimitrov over the phone, 'spread hints on the Soviet proposal for Bulgaria. Idiots.'[64]

While Sobolev was presenting his coup in Sofia Schulenburg, determined to remove the obstacles raised at the Berlin meeting, brought Schnurre, head of the Wilhelmstrasse's Economic Division, to Moscow in the hope that an economic agreement might produce favourable conditions for continuing the political talks. But his plans were frustrated when Molotov impatiently reverted to politics, producing a written set of conditions for Russia's adherence to the draft agreement of the Four Powers Pact. Combined with the overtures made by Sobolev in Sofia at that very moment, they indicated that Stalin was not prepared to fulfil the role assigned to him in Hitler's plans for a Continental bloc. Russia continued to demand 'immediate withdrawal' of the German troops from Finland and a change in the regime of the Straits 'within the next few months' through a conclusion of a mutual assistance pact with Bulgaria and the allocation of naval and land bases 'within the range of the Bosphorus and the Dardanelles'. As for the spheres of influence, these were to stretch well into the Balkans, the Black Sea and south of Batum and Baku, rather than in the vague direction of the Indian Ocean as had been envisaged by Hitler. Moreover Russia, Germany and Italy were expected to ensure by military or diplomatic means that Turkey accepted the arrangement. Five secret protocols set down the precise mechanism for the security arrangements and the establishment of the spheres of influence. The Russians thus produced their final and explicit definition of their interests in South-eastern Europe in complete defiance of the German ones. Hitler, victorious and backed by the unscathed Wehrmacht and the industrial potential of Europe, was unlikely to yield. A Soviet concession in Bulgaria and the Straits, however, was bound to render her western front vulnerable and exclude her from European affairs for the first time since the reign of Peter the Great.[65]

The extent of Bulgaria's leanings towards Germany was obvious when Richthofen, the German ambassador in Sofia, was provided with Sobolev's proposals, on the very evening of his visit, and told that they would, 'of course', be rejected.[66] But Sobolev's visit had placed the Bulgarian government in a difficult situation. Popov's complaints of a severe gallbladder attack and Filov's sudden 'illness' could postpone a decision only by a couple of days. When he finally recovered, Filov did not go back on Boris's undertaking to Hitler, but suggested a postponement because in the new circumstances it could be 'viewed as provocation in Moscow'. The episode on the whole seemed to confirm Hitler's doubts about the Russian preparedness to accept his terms.[67]

The written answer to the Russians was submitted by Popov to the Soviet ambassador, leaving no room for doubt about where Bulgaria's priorities lay. Having established guidelines in his talks with Hitler prior to the receipt of the Soviet proposals, he argued, 'the engagement of Bulgaria in negotiations for another pact may cast a shadow on the loyalty of Bulgarian foreign policy and will not only estrange a country friendly to us and the Soviet Union but will even introduce justifiable suspicion'. The apprehensions in Moscow were surely not diminished by assurances that the existence of 'a strong and independent Bulgaria' was an 'effective enough guarantee for Russia' or the flimsy claims that joining the Tripartite Pact with Russia's ally would prevent the war from spreading. Finally, taking the bait in Sobolev's offer but without making the expected response, the Bulgarian government noted 'with satisfaction that the government of the Soviet Union is also posing the question of eventually joining the Tripartite Pact which, it seems to us, shows above all that in this case as well Bulgaria's behaviour could not be interpreted as contrary to the interests of the Soviet Union.' Needless to say, Richthofen was promptly supplied with the written reply to the Russians as well as an almost verbatim account of Popov's conversations with the Soviet ambassador.[68]

Draganov, who had been in Sofia during Sobolev's visit, was now rushed back to Berlin. He hoped to reinstate Bulgaria's allegiance through the disclosure of the Soviet proposals. Hitler, however, 'reacted strongly'; he was being driven towards his fateful decision. He had no interest in the Dardanelles, he assured Draganov, as he could not sail into the Black Sea. However, 'if some day there were a war with Russia he would not attack the Russians across the Black Sea but wherever it suited him along the 2,000 kilometres of their common border'. Germany's intervention was no longer presented as a move against England but rather against Russia, as Hitler could not allow the Balkan Peninsula to be Bolshevized. 'He wanted to trade with the Balkans and for this he preferred a Rumania, a Bulgaria, etc., to a Bolshevized desert such as the Baltic States were now.' Even now he still entertained the hope that, if Bulgaria signed the Tripartite Pact, the Russians would realize they could not accomplish anything, and would 'withdraw, though angry and protesting'.[69]

The very next morning Hitler convened his Chiefs of Staff for the first time since the well-known meeting of 31 July to discuss in detail the plans for an attack on Russia. It was at this meeting that he altered the operational codename from 'Fritz' to 'Barbarossa'. While in the autumn the 'peripheral strategy' had been devised as part of a grand Mediterranean offensive against British dominance, the new plans were confined to the relief of pressure in a series of uncoordinated operations. The change was remarkable: the diversionary action became defensive in nature, while the destruction of Russia became the focal point of a new aggressive strategy.

The invasion of Greece, Halder noted, had been 'taken out of its context and brought into close relationship with the plans for Russia. Its task now was to secure Germany's southern flank and eliminate the imminent danger before the start of the offensive against Russia.' On the same day Hitler informed Mussolini that the entente with Russia could be resumed only after the crisis over Bulgaria had been resolved.[70] The operational aims remained markedly vague, to a large extent reflecting the staff planning of a total war of destruction and Hitler's intention of 'solving the issue of European hegemony'. In the context discussed up to now, the concept of 'European hegemony' related directly to the Russians' steadfast hold on Bulgaria and the Danube and to a lesser degree their claims in the Baltic region. From such a geographical perspective, the southern and northern wings appeared to be the centres of gravity.[71] The divergence between the planners' professional outlook and Hitler's political vision led to his failure to come to terms with their overall objectives, and to oscillate between the Volga–Archangel'sk line and Moscow. This discrepancy cannot be dismissed out of hand, as it accounts for the serious confusion surrounding the implementation of the plans in the very early stages of the campaign in August 1941.[72]

Needless to say, the intransigence of the Russians stiffened Hitler's resolve to resort to force, and racist biases gradually crept in to sustain the decision. But at present, when a clear-cut decision had not yet been taken, the comments were confined to the 'inferiority' of the Soviet soldier and the communist system. Rather than comprising an ideological incentive, they seemed to be an inducement for the army to pursue the planning. Indeed, Halder's awareness a week later that Russia was exploiting every opportunity to weaken Germany was still accompanied by a hope of bridging the gap.[73]

The prospects of reconciliation were receding fast. The Russians not only rejected one by one the arguments presented by the Bulgarians against a pact, but further warned them, though in cryptic form, against joining the Axis. Such a step would be taken as a proof that Bulgaria had 'abandoned its position of neutrality and indicated its active involvement in the orbit of war against the other group of countries', which obviously posed 'a military threat to Bulgaria'. Though he promised to consider the Soviet reservations, Popov gave the clear impression that the die had already been cast. In Bulgaria, he told the ambassador, '[we] are close to the fire of war, and can more clearly feel from where the danger of war may appear for us as well as for the USSR'. Molotov was further discouraged against falling back on the idea of guarantees.[74]

By the same token, the Soviet threats were strong enough to force King Boris to think again. He warned Draganov in Berlin that the Russians did not 'regard the issue as closed' and were still adhering to their former demands.[75] King Boris now desperately clung to neutrality, hoping to

pacify both Russia and Germany. Hitler, however, was infuriated by
the Bulgarians' wavering, which surely emanated from the pressure
exerted on them by the Russians. He was dazed by the incompatibility of
Draganov's account of the negotiations with what had been gathered
through Richthofen. The impression in Sofia was that the Bulgarians were
actually determined to reject the Soviet proposal and join the Axis, though
at an unspecified time in the future. In Berlin Draganov, while not re-
evaluating the commitment to the Axis, wondered whether after all accession to the Tripartite Pact was 'not congruent with conclusion of a pact
with the Soviet Union'. He further recapitulated the reasons against
prompt Bulgarian accession to the Tripartite Pact.[76]

Two factors now decided the course of military strategy. The first was
the failure of the Italians in the Balkans, which brought closer the danger
that the British would succeed in establishing bases in the Saloniki region.
The operations against the British in the Mediterranean, forced on Hitler
by the Italian failure in Greece, were now tied to the campaign against
Russia. In issuing Directive 'Marita' for the war against Greece, Hitler was
conscious of the political implications of the military preparations. The
preparations therefore required 'meticulous direction', which had to be
brought to his personal attention.

However, the most significant factor remained the Russians' refusal
to accept German predominance in Rumania, as manifested in the consolidation of their position on the Danube delta. In the midst of the haggling over Bulgaria the Danubian Conference resumed its sittings.[77]
The Russians persevered and in the early hours of the morning of 17
December Berlin was informed of the deadlock. The Russians had
presented a written statement which bluntly rejected the joint
German–Italian mediation, further declaring their intentions of establishing exclusive control jointly with the Rumanians over the mouth of the
Danube, effectively controlling the exit to the Black Sea. In Berlin this was
received with 'astonishment'. The positions were 'irreconcilable' and
negotiations were 'for the present exhausted'. Hitler brought about the
immediate adjournment of the conference.[78] Keen observers accurately
judged the collapse of the negotiations to be 'the first clash of vital interests between U.S.S.R. and Germany and therefore of first importance'.[79]
A similar trend was traced in Finland, where Soviet interference in the
Finnish elections indicated that they were determined to keep the country
under direct control.[80]

It was no coincidence, therefore, that the decision on the implementation of Directive No. 21, Operation 'Barbarossa', was taken on the
morning after the collapse of the negotiations. The directive instructed the
Wehrmacht 'to be prepared to crush Soviet Russia in a quick campaign,
even before the conclusion of the war against England'. The specific
political, diplomatic and military context in which the decision was taken

casts serious doubt on its ideological dimension. Though the economic advantages were taken into consideration, the operation clearly did not aim at creating *Lebensraum*, as the hinterland had already been established in the Balkans and in the rest of occupied Europe. The purpose was 'to establish a cover against Asiatic Russia from the general line Volga–Archangel', thereby eliminating the potential Russian threat but more specifically allowing the completion of the campaign against Europe, in other words securing the exclusive German domination of Europe.[81]

The deployment of 'Marita' and subsequently 'Barbarossa' started immediately. The skeleton force in Rumania was promptly strengthened while a large task force earmarked for southern Rumania, under the command of Field Marshal List, was assembled. Its task was 'to push through friendly Bulgaria, if necessary, without touching Yugoslav or Turkish territory, toward the Aegean coast . . . thereby eliminating the English in this area'. By the end of January 1941 some seven or eight divisions were earmarked to be stationed in the area and bridgeheads established over the Danube. To allay the Russians' suspicions, they would eventually be informed that Germany could 'not permit the English to gain a foothold in the Balkans'.[82]

Postscript: Preventive War?

The suggestion is occasionally made that the Soviet mobilization in March 1941 prompted the implementation of Operation 'Barbarossa'. We have seen the complex circumstances in which the decisions were taken. It should be borne in mind that the planning of 'Barbarossa' was from its beginning an offensive initiated by the Wehrmacht that completely overlooked the magnitude of the undertaking and arrogantly underestimated the capabilities of the opponent. In comparison with previous campaigns, Hitler assured Keitel, the war with Russia would be 'like child's play in a sand-box'.[83] Consequently, Hitler and the German military *a priori* ruled out the possibility of a Russian pre-emptive strike. General-Major Erich Marcks, who was entrusted with the drafting of the earlier version of the plan, even complained that the Red Army would not do the Germans 'the courtesy of attacking'.[84] The presentation of the war as a preventive measure was first adopted by Hitler in his statement to Stalin on the launching of the war as well as in his address to the army on that same day. He repeated it in October 1941, when he inaugurated an appeal for winter clothing for the soldiers on the Russian front, explaining apologetically that in May 'the situation was so threatening that there could no longer be any doubt that Russia intended to fall upon us at the first opportunity'.[85] The argument certainly had a considerable effect on those in his immediate political entourage, who had not been acquainted with the military plans. Thus, for instance, Rudolf Hess wrote to his mother from captivity in the autumn of 1941: 'A few chosen ones are called upon to decide the aspect of centuries by perhaps one single deed. I have in mind the Führer, who decided to forestall the attack of the Bolshevists: the full significance of his decision will only be completely recognised in later ages.'[86] In a desperate attempt to cover up the difficulties encountered in the execution of the *Blitzkrieg* in Russia, Hitler repeated in May 1942 that if he 'had listened to his badly informed generals and waited, and the Russians, in accordance with these plans of theirs, had stolen a march on us, there would have been hardly a chance of stopping their tanks on the well-constructed road system of Central Europe'.[87]

The presentation of the war as a preventive one was naturally rehabilitated by some of the German generals at the Nuremberg trials. In the appropriate atmosphere of the budding Cold War, they sought to justify their own enthusiastic preparations for Operation 'Barbarossa' by claiming that they had supported Hitler's decision to launch a pre-emptive war intended to contain Soviet expansion.[88] However, German intelligence never pointed in this direction. General von Paulus, who would have been only too happy to produce such evidence at Nuremberg, reluctantly admitted that 'no preparations whatever for an attack by the Soviet Union had come to our attention'. Guderian's memoirs pass a similar verdict. Likewise, Field Marshal von Manstein attested that the Soviet military dispositions did not reveal an intention to strike.[89] As early as September 1940, while the plans for the offensive were being drawn up, Lieutenant-General Köstring informed General Halder that the Red Army was in ruins after the purges and that it would require at least three years to reach its pre-war level.[90] Nor was German intelligence misled by the clandestine mobilization which it was scrutinizing. It expected the Russians to establish 'defensive concentration points', from which they could be expected at best to launch isolated and limited counter-attacks.[91] This assessment was deliberately misconstrued by the propaganda arm of the Wehrmacht to 'convey the impression . . . that the Russians were concentrated and "ready to pounce" and that the German attack was a military imperative'.[92]

The idea of a preventive war as a positive element in military doctrine was deeply embedded in the German rather than the Soviet military tradition. Frederick the Great broached the subject in his *L'Antimachiavel*.[93] Moltke had elaborated the idea of a preventive war in 1886, when he advocated a swift campaign to forestall the Russians in Poland. Count von Schlieffen was in fact relying on his predecessors to provide legitimacy and condone a preventive war when he argued that 'We find ourselves in the same situation as Frederick the Great during the Seven Years' War. Troops have been eliminated from all of Western Russia. Russia has lost its capacity for action for years to come. We could now settle accounts with our most evil and dangerous foe, France, and we enjoy full freedom of action to do so.' Once it dawned on the German General Staff that war on two fronts was inevitable, they recognized that only by resorting to such means could they achieve the swift destruction of one of their opponents and the elimination of a potential threat on that front. This legacy played an important part in the planning of 'Barbarossa'. A 'preventive war' was entirely foreign to Soviet military doctrine. The 'pre-emptive strike', which is a completely different proposition, was one of the manoeuvres incorporated in the 'deep operations' theory, but it was devoid of any expansionist intentions *per se*.[94]

The need to thwart a Russian offensive was entirely a pretext and was marginal in the last six months preceding the war. Hitler's programmatic 'Lebensraum im Osten' concept once more dominated the scene and provided a decisive justification for a war against Russia.[95] Once the decision on 'Barbarossa' had been taken and as the war drew nearer, the ideological creed closely fitted the strategic aim and was always close to the surface. As the Japanese Foreign Minister Matsuoka learnt in Berlin in the spring of 1941, any collaboration by Germany with Russia was excluded 'since the ideological bases of the army, as well as of the rest of the nation, were completely incompatible . . . A union here was as impossible as one between fire and water.'[96] In March 1941 Hitler explained that the war could not be seen strictly from the military aspect but that it was the final blow against 'Jewish Bolshevism'.[97] Addressing Mussolini a day before the invasion, Hitler could heave a sigh of relief:

> In conclusion, let me say one more thing, Duce. Since I struggled through to this decision, I again feel spiritually free. The partnership with the Soviet Union, *in spite of the complete sincerity of the efforts to bring about a final conciliation* [author's italics] was nevertheless often very irksome to me, for in some way or other it seemed to me to be a break with my whole origin, my concepts, and my former obligations. I am happy now to be relieved from these mental agonies.[98]

5

The Curtain Falls on the Balkans

The British Perspective: Co-operation or Embroilment?

The British attempts to revive the trade negotiations after Cripps's arrival in Moscow, though obviously aimed at crippling the German war economy, were also tied in with the developments in the Balkans. Cripps lost no time in alerting Molotov to the danger lying ahead in the Balkans. 'The entire Peninsula', he told him in the summer, would 'be set ablaze' once Yugoslavia and Turkey were drawn into the war. Such warnings were taken from the outset in Moscow as deliberate provocations. Molotov therefore established a pattern, which would remain in force until the Great Patriotic War began, of lightly dismissing the German threat as being 'merely a bluff'. Molotov hastened to warn Maisky not to fall into the trap set by the British, assuring him that if the situation altered drastically the actions of the Soviet Union would be swift.[1]

However, Stalin's readiness to keep the line open to London arose out of the gradual recognition of Hitler's failure to achieve his aims in England by either peaceful or forceful means. Like all foreign observers who lived through the Blitz, Maisky, though a cautious observer, was captivated by the resilience of Londoners and often conveyed to the Kremlin the Churchillian spirit of the Battle of Britain. He described in detail the Luftwaffe's abortive attempts to destroy the transport and industrial infrastructures as a preliminary to an invasion:

All the London bridges are intact. The entire railway system is also functioning though with occasional halts . . . Every night the Germans try to bomb the most important London railway stations but so far without any success. The buses, trams, taxis and Underground are generally speaking running normally. Some damage was inflicted on industry, especially the military, though not of any significance.[2]

Such an impression also emerged from an unusual meeting which Maisky held with Halifax in his cold and damp room, in mid-October, hours after a powerful bomb had exploded in St James's Park and all the windows in the Foreign Office and Buckingham Palace had been shattered. And yet the discussion, conducted in overcoats beside the fire, convinced Maisky that Halifax was still primarily interested in diverting Hitler to the Balkans, where Russia was expected to carry the burden of the fighting – a situation not unfamiliar to the one the Russians had faced in the 1939 negotiations.[3]

England's survival meant that she would still play a role in the peace conference. Subsequent Soviet attempts, therefore, were directed towards the establishment of a common agenda regarding Soviet territorial gains in the Baltic.[4] Keeping an open line to Britain was also aimed at preempting the repeated efforts by Hitler to sue for a separate peace. Indeed, Maisky had gathered from Lord Beaverbrook, the newspaper magnate and Minister of Aircraft Production, that on at least one occasion he had been approached by a messenger from Hitler with a peace proposal. Beaverbrook was confident enough that the offers would be rejected so long as Germany claimed full hegemony in Europe.[5] No less important was the Soviet wish to keep the Germans at bay, as their chargé d'affaires in Moscow found to his dismay when a meeting with Molotov was unexpectedly postponed for one hour 'due to pressure of work'; however, when driving through the gates of the Kremlin, the German diplomat encountered the British ambassador, who was conspicuously leaving after a meeting with Molotov.[6]

It was not, of course, coincidental that the Soviet approach to England followed the worsening conflict in the Balkans, in the wake of the arbitration agreement. Cripps was therefore right in reporting home that 'the resistance of Great Britain is beginning to have its effect on the Soviet Government's attitude' and was responsible for Vyshinsky's 'friendly and forthcoming' disposition. Once again sheer political opportunism, lacking in sentimentalism, continued to be the guideline of Soviet policy. 'We are now living "in the jungle",' remained Maisky's favourite quip; ' "drawing room" language was of no value.' In a more mundane tenor, Vyshinsky explained that 'international relations were essentially fluid and capable of development'.[7]

However, the British and the Russian governments continued to work at cross-purposes in their traditionally hostile mental environment. While the Russians wished to retain their neutrality and cater for their position in the post-war world, the short-term British aim remained to embroil Russia in war. Such, for instance, were the attempts of Rendel, the British ambassador in Sofia, to goad into action his Soviet counterpart Lavrishchev, whom he described with an air of superiority as a 'rather loutish creature, obviously terrified of committing himself, but I think with a good deal of native intelligence'. The 'amicable' conversation 'took place in an atmosphere of Caucasian brandy from Mount Ararat (rather good) and of Soviet cigarettes in cardboard holders (very bad)'. But it is doubtful whether Rendel's success in making Lavrishchev 'as uncomfortable as possible' and in encouraging him 'to watch German activities with an increasingly suspicious eye' served British interests. In all likelihood this was taken as yet further proof of British attempts to spark a conflict between Russia and Germany.[8]

When Schulenburg returned from Germany with what later turned out to be the proposals for the Berlin meeting, the frustrated Cripps sent 'ferocious' telegrams to Halifax. It was clear to him that the only chance of achieving a dialogue with the Russians rested on the post-war arrangements and a recognition that the war was indeed a watershed in international relations. He warned that it was:

> not possible to wipe out the history of the past twenty years, which has taught the Soviet Government to look upon a Government led by those now in the Cabinet as fundamentally hostile to the Soviet Union. They therefore examine the present situation broadly against this background of continued hostility . . . they have, I believe, taken the view – and for this there is plenty of justification in the past – that HMG were not prepared to acknowledge the importance or influence of the Soviet Union in the measure that it deserved. Their exclusion from Munich, their subsequent exclusion from all consultation or exchange of view in the Far East are only two examples of this.

Since the war had done little to convince the Russians that the British attitude had substantially changed, Cripps saw little possibility of bringing about a change unless the British government was prepared to recognize the Soviet absorption of the Baltic States.[9] Negotiations, however, were doomed to failure, as Halifax was at best prepared to raise the Baltic issue as 'a good way of drawing Molotov'. Moreover, with Lend–Lease, the massive American supply programme to Britain, now in full swing and likely to be boosted after the re-election of President Roosevelt, the Kremlin realized that 'the foreign policy of London was increasingly dependent on Washington', and Britain was no longer capable of making any decision on the Baltic States.[10]

Meanwhile, British policy continued to consist of fervent attempts to cause a rift between Germany and Russia. Such attempts were made in the 'acrimonious meeting' of the Danube Commission on the eve of Molotov's departure to Berlin.[11] Instructions were sent to the British missions in the Balkans to seek 'action calculated to inflame differences between Soviet and German Governments over new Danubian regime'. Cripps likewise openly encouraged the Russians to seize unilateral control of the mouth of the Danube. He hoped that the Cabinet would even prevail on Turkey to allow the passage of the Royal Navy through the Straits to assist the Russians. However, the announcement of Molotov's visit to Berlin brought the various efforts to an abrupt end.[12]

Molotov's visit had taken Cripps and most foreign observers in Moscow 'by surprise'. The immediate reaction in Whitehall was to sanction the bombing of the Baku oilfields. Cripps, far less passionate though personally disappointed, attributed Molotov's search for a delimitation of spheres of interest in the Balkans and the control of the Straits to 'a temporary attitude of expediency' and hoped that in the long run, possibly the following year, the 'fundamental hostility' would reassert itself. Halifax persuaded the Cabinet to pursue the moderate line, especially since intelligence sources had revealed that 'not very much had been settled at the discussions between Hitler and Molotov in Berlin'. It was nonetheless proposed to scrap the offer of a trade agreement made to Russia, on the assumption that it had been used by the Russians as a trump card in the Berlin negotiations.[13]

The reshuffle of Churchill's Cabinet on Christmas Eve and Anthony Eden's return to the Foreign Office raised new expectations, especially against the background of the deterioration in German–Soviet relations in the wake of the Berlin conference. Shortly after the holidays Maisky paid a visit to the Foreign Office, to find Eden beaming with excitement. The gloom which had pervaded Halifax's office had been replaced by a bright and orderly atmosphere. Eden projected the image of a triumphant return. He wished to convince Maisky that no major conflict of interest in foreign policy existed between the two countries. The ambassador did not beat about the bush, explaining to Eden that a British recognition of the Soviet absorption of the Baltic States was a prerequisite for a significant improvement in relations. It soon became obvious that the change in the scenery did not entail a change of policy. Like those of his predecessor, Eden's interests remained tactical, aimed at detaching Russia from Germany. However, Maisky, who was eager to exploit the change, deviated from the canon, admitting to Eden that Russia certainly did not wish to see Germany emerging as the victorious power in Europe. Soviet foreign policy, he explained succinctly, rested on three principles:

First, they were concerned with promoting their own national interests. Secondly, his Government wished to remain out of the war. Thirdly, they wished to avoid the extension of the war to any countries neighbouring Russia. In general Soviet policy was not expansionist: the Soviet had already enough territories. Their actions were purely precautionary, to ensure a hold upon essential strategic defensive positions.

Maisky, however, mirrored the Kremlin's conviction that Hitler, 'who was generally cautious', would not encroach on Russian interests in the Balkans. As for the Soviet need to retain good relations with the Balkan States and Turkey, he gained the impression that Eden, who constantly nodded in assent, seemed to wish to intervene and say: 'Well, I also think so.' Maisky certainly did his utmost to convince his masters at home that the change was significant.[14]

The officials at the Northern Department of the Foreign Office were less enthusiastic about reconciliation with Russia, clinging to Cripps's proposal to withdraw the offer of a trade agreement. To Eden, however, it seemed that, if such a communication were made immediately after his arrival at the Foreign Office, the Russians might well conclude that it represented a new policy towards the Soviet Union which he had personally introduced on becoming Foreign Secretary. He therefore urged Cripps to reconsider the decision.[15] It was characteristic of Eden to believe naively that the mere announcement of his appointment would lead to an improvement in relations. He overlooked Cripps's warnings that the absence of 'concrete suggestions' would be interpreted as a sign of weakness by the Russians, whose policy was 'based on the realities of their own situation and not on sentiment'.[16]

As might have been expected, the new and extended German–Soviet trade agreement in January and the appointment of Dekanozov as ambassador to Berlin[17] further sustained the view of the Foreign Office that Molotov's visit had yielded greater achievements than initially perceived. Cripps continued to dispute the assumption that 'the fundamental hostility to Germany or desire to prepare to meet German menace has been diminished'. He therefore advocated a 'flexible' policy, even if Russian policy was bound to be subjected to Germany 'for a long time to come'. His sober evaluation, however, was entirely misconstrued by Sargent, the deputy Under-Secretary, who tried to persuade Eden to bring his initial attempts at rapprochement to an end. The anticipation that Stalin would 'buy off and "appease" the German ogre' reinforced the fatalistic assumption that a German–Soviet agreement was on the verge of conclusion. Britain could effect a change only once 'the British Fleet were able to patrol the Black Sea and British bombers were able to fly over the Caucasus'. He could hardly hide his satisfaction that, until such conditions prevailed, Cripps was bound to 'labour in vain in Moscow'.[18] Eden was further warned against Maisky's 'calculated indiscretions' and his 'notorious . . . journalistic and Parliamentary friends'.[19] All in all, Eden's appointment led to a change in nuance and style but the political concept underlying relations with Russia remained unaltered. Cadogan noted with relief in his diary: 'Glad to find A. [Eden] not "ideological" and quite alive to uselessness of expecting anything from these cynical, blood-stained murderers.' Whether benign or not to the Russians, in the next few months Eden was entirely absorbed in the futile attempt to erect a Balkan bulwark against Germany, displaying hardly any interest in Soviet affairs.[20]

As we have seen Stalin, though ostentatiously adhering to neutrality, expected the war to redress what he regarded as historical grievances inflicted on Russia. For him the yardstick for rapprochement with England was her stand on the Baltic States and Turkey. When, therefore, after months of seclusion, Cripps finally gained access to Molotov but arrived empty-handed, he was rebuffed. As the accumulated experi-ence from 1939 onwards had proved, Molotov stated bitterly, England had failed 'to take into account Soviet interests'. Under such circum-stances he 'showed himself frankly bored and impatient, finally announ-cing that he had no more to say', and that he 'would not personally interest himself in Anglo-Soviet relations' until the outstanding obstacles were removed.

Oblivious to the clear message from Moscow, the Foreign Office refused to reconsider the question even of *de facto* recognition of Soviet control in the Baltic, despite the fact that Hugh Dalton, the Minister of Economic Warfare, had reached the conclusion that such a step would 'not preju-dice our right ultimately to dispute the Soviet position in the Baltic States'. With little straw to construct his bricks Cripps, as it was observed in Moscow, had even stopped 'seeking any contact with the gentlemen in the Kremlin; "now it is up to them to call me if they want something"'. Not quite aware as yet of the extent of the tension between Moscow and Berlin concerning the Balkans, Cripps indeed continued to advocate a 'policy of reserve' until 'developments in various theatres of war or eco-nomic pressure that we can apply in association with America, compel them to seek some closer relation with us'.[21]

In the meantime, in early February 1941, on the eve of Eden's depar-ture for the Middle East, Cripps was finally instructed to withdraw the trade offer 'without delay'.[22] It was followed by the severance of relations with Rumania and the recognition of the Cabinet's Defence Committee that Turkey would not become a belligerent and that her value as an asset therefore lay in her neutrality. But, more significantly, Churchill and Eden now advocated the establishment of a common strategic platform in the Balkans for the defence of Greece. This entailed a halt of operations at Benghazi and the transfer of large forces from Egypt to Greece to meet the expected German attack from Bulgaria.[23] Having lost the initiative and the ability to react to the German encroachment in the Balkans, the Russians became attentive to similar British attempts. Various reports reinforced Stalin's fears that Churchill was fervently seeking to draw the

Russians into action, which in turn would 'bring about a clash of interests between Germany and the Soviet Union'.[24] The obsessive fear of being dragged into the war in the Balkans became a constant feature in Soviet evaluations, diverting the Russians from the genuine threat which they now faced from Germany.

Bulgaria Turns to the Axis

Schulenburg had been shaken by the repercussions of the futile Berlin meeting on the events in the Balkans. Aware of the general direction in which the wind was blowing, he made great efforts to ensure a successful conclusion to the trade negotiations. He returned from Berlin with Schnurre, hoping to placate Hitler by placing 'the big Russian treaty for 1941/2 under the Christmas tree in Berlin'. A personal appeal to Ribbentrop 'and the key military figures' acclaimed the considerable concessions proposed by the Russians, outlining 'the tremendous advantages which Germany would reap from such a treaty with 2.5 million tons of grain as its core'.[25]

The collapse of Sobolev's mission[26] cast a heavy cloud over the Kremlin as well. Stalin remained determined 'to hinder a German penetration into the Balkans which could threaten the Straits'. Molotov seized every opportunity to impress on Schulenburg that the annexation of Bessarabia had 'rendered the Soviet Union a Danubian country and consequently her sovereign right and state interests had to be taken into account'. He came to one of their meetings in early January 1941, armed with a detailed map of the three branches of the Danube, and 'stubbornly and intransigently' demanded that Germany and Italy should prevail on Rumania to accept exclusive Soviet control of navigation at the mouth of the river.[27] Just as persistent were the demands for concessions in the Finnish nickel deposits at Petsamo.[28]

But, to Stalin's dismay, rather than achieving the anticipated negotiations, he was fast losing the battle in Bulgaria without firing a shot. Consequently Dekanozov was rushed to Berlin to replace Shkvartsev, not only as a prominent ambassador but in a special capacity, retaining his position as deputy Foreign Minister. Dekanozov, who was an Armenian, always posed as a Georgian to endear himself to Stalin and Beria.[29] As a confidant of Stalin, he had participated in Molotov's meetings with Hitler while Shkvartsev had been ostentatiously left out. Shkvartsev's dismissal was rumoured to be the result of his failure to keep the Kremlin abreast of the Vienna Arbitration.[30] However, although the Germans had been informed about Dekanozov's assignment he received no preferential treatment and was kept waiting not only for his credentials but even for a short interview with Ribbentrop.[31]

After only a week in Berlin he worriedly urged Moscow to convey to the Germans that he had been assigned a special post and to seek an appointment for him.[32] His anxieties were well founded. When he was finally admitted to Ribbentrop's presence on 12 December, his gift of a signed photograph of Stalin promised during the visit to Moscow was especially ironic, since the final touches were at that moment being put to Directive 'Barbarossa'. Although Ribbentrop professed to admire the portrait, which he promised to place on his desk to commemorate his significant visit in the hope that it would lead 'to success also in the future', he conspicuously avoided contentious issues. In view of Stalin's recourse to diplomatic means to prevent the outbreak of war, attention should be drawn to Ribbentrop's assurances that Germany hoped to bring the war to an end 'within the next year ... with the fewest possible victims'. Ribbentrop further expounded Hitler's intentions of focusing on domestic reconstruction. But, despite the commitment to future negotiations, Dekanozov felt that Ribbentrop was anxious to bring the talk to an early end.[33]

The day after signing Directive 'Barbarossa', Hitler finally allowed Dekanozov to present his credentials at the Reichskanzlerei. After disposing of the formalities Hitler drew the ambassador over to the sofa and offhandedly attributed the delay to the 'incredibly tense international situation'. Efforts by Dekanozov to rekindle the political discussion were simply ignored by Hitler, who 'listened silently and occasionally nodded his head', finally proposing that they should be best discussed 'through official channels'. Dekanozov's insistence that his presence during the Berlin meeting and his familiarity with Molotov's views might hasten the pace of the negotiations evoked little response. Hitler was apparently interested only in Dekanozov's common ethnic origin with Stalin and his exceptionally young age; at forty-one, Hitler remarked, Dekanozov was the youngest ambassador in Berlin, where one had to be sixty-five to assume such a position. It was left for Ribbentrop to suggest, as Dekanozov was taking his leave, that negotiations would continue with him.[34]

As a last resort Molotov now attempted to link the conclusion of the trade agreement with progress made in the political sphere.[35] Hitler's absence from Berlin during the Christmas holidays deferred any immediate decision. Schnurre was instructed to remain in Moscow and iron out the final obstacles, though he was discouraged from entering into any political dialogue. The proponents of the Continental bloc in the German Foreign Ministry had not yet despaired of a concurrent conclusion of the two agreements.[36] They expected the lucrative trade agreement to lubricate the negotiations' wheels. Weizsäcker thus prevented a renewed convention of the Danubian conference to avoid the 'spectacle of a serious dispute between the Germans and Russians before an international audience'.[37] The delay, however, rendered Stalin even more susceptible to the German demands and the trade agreement was finally signed on 10 January.[38]

In an indirect way the agreement contributed to the disinformation campaign that the Germans had just launched. It elaborated in minute detail the deliveries that would be made up to August 1942, giving a false sense of a breathing space in the Kremlin. Moreover, to pacify the Soviet wish to embark on political negotiations, the agreement was accompanied by a secret protocol settling the Soviet claims on the German borders from the River Igorka to the Baltic Sea, including the dispute over the Lithuanian strip.[39]

Once back home Schnurre fulfilled his promise to Schulenburg and presented to Hitler the case for future co-operation with the Russians. Hitler listened to him attentively but it transpired that the Balkans were no longer negotiable, though he preferred to project the impression that much was 'still in suspense'. While he was prepared to receive Schulenburg in Berlin for consultations, the date was deliberately left open and postponed continuously. By early March Schulenburg was lamenting that Ribbentrop had once again shelved his request for leave.[40] It gradually dawned on him that the absence of instructions on future negotiations indicated that Hitler had set his mind on war.[41]

Meanwhile the clash over the Balkans was taking an unpropitious turn. The Bulgarian government found the hug of the two major powers unbearable. Rejecting the Soviet proposals, in mid-December they had pleaded with the Kremlin to understand 'not only logically but also emotionally' how an agreement of mutual assistance was bound to upset the delicate balance of power established in the Balkans.[42] Emotions were unlikely to move Stalin. On a number of occasions Lunin, the GRU resident in Bucharest, cautioned his Bulgarian counterpart that Russia could not ignore the presence of thirteen German divisions on the southern Rumanian border, 'whose objectives stretched beyond the border in the direction of Bulgaria and the Balkans and perhaps even against Russia'. He did not even bother to conceal, as was the habit with Soviet diplomats, that 'relations between Russia and Germany were far from normal', but for obvious reasons wished to give the impression that they were 'developing in a most unfortunate way for Germany'. Russia, he insisted, could no longer remain indifferent to the German penetration into the Balkans. It posed a threat to the Black Sea, which was 'a Russian Sea and which had only one natural exit, the Bosphorus and the Dardanelles, which must remain under Russian control'. King Boris, going attentively through the report, underlined Lunin's bottom line that Bulgaria was 'the country in which [Russia] has the greatest interests. We do not wish to control her, as our enemies claim, thinking of the Baltic countries. There the situation was different as those territories had belonged to the Russian state and today they serve as our living space providing the exit to the Baltic Sea.' Russian interests were confined therefore to Bulgaria's Black Sea coast, along the Varna–Burgaz–Marmara line. Lunin's own transfer from Bucharest to Varna was an ominous reminder to the King of the stakes that Moscow had in the Black Sea littoral and naval ports.[43]

It comes as no surprise, therefore, that the continued fear of Russia led Filov, the Bulgarian Prime Minister, to dig in his heels when he finally recovered from yet another diplomatic illness and made his pilgrimage to Berchtesgaden in early January 1941. While reiterating Bulgaria's agreement in principle to join the Axis, he wished to postpone the decision so as not to provoke the Russians. He tried in vain to impress on Hitler that there was no rush as the Bulgarian government had already undertaken precautionary steps to prevent a Soviet annexation of the Bulgarian Black Sea coast. As usual, Hitler tried to alarm Filov by overplaying the ideological threat which communism posed to Bulgaria. 'The Russian bear', interjected Ribbentrop ominously, 'was trying to stick its paws into the outside world, as it were, through the Dardanelles.' It was therefore necessary to forestall the Russians by clearly demarcating the spheres of interest. But Hitler went one step further: were Stalin to pursue his aims, he would use his troops 'to smash them'. Neither did the Turkish threat hold water. If Ankara made a move, said Hitler, raising his voice, he would 'send his Foreign Minister to Moscow or will call Molotov to Berlin and then an end will be put to Turkey'.[44]

The pressure applied to the Bulgarian government, which was desperately trying to cling to non-involvement, led to conflicting statements. Filov was sent to Ruse on the Danube to deliver 'an astoundingly strong speech' denying suggestions that Bulgaria was becoming 'a legionary country' – a direct response to Sobolev's accusations. At the same time Gabrovsky, the Minister of the Interior, made an equally well-publicized speech in which he stated that 'Bulgaria did not desire to share the fate of the Baltic countries'.[45] But the die had virtually been cast after Filov's visit to Hitler. Shortly after returning to Sofia, Filov advised King Boris to succumb. Boris, to judge from Filov's own account, 'was very agitated and irksome and unusually firm. At first he said that he preferred to abdicate or that we should throw ourselves into Russia's embrace even if we were to be Bolshevized.' However, after delivering a long emotional speech, 'the Tsar gradually calmed down and began to accept the correctness of [Filov's] reflections'.[46]

There was a last attempt to postpone the inevitable, when on specific instructions from King Boris Draganov tried in vain to back off, arguing that to all intents and purposes Bulgaria 'was already a member of the Axis and had even behaved like a silent ally as far as German military wishes were concerned'. But in fact the King had already capitulated and was now trying to exact the price for such a move, an outlet to the Aegean Sea in Turkish Adrianople (without having to fight Turkey) and eventually Saloniki and Greek Macedonia.[47]

The final German clampdown on Bulgaria coincided with the conclusion of the trade agreement, explaining the minor reaction that the agreement evoked in Moscow. Two days after its conclusion, with no further cards to play, Stalin resorted to a communiqué which reiterated his resolve to preserve Russian interests in Bulgaria while preventing the war from spreading further into the Balkans. It denied the rumours, inspired by Berlin, that the entry of German troops into Bulgaria was carried out with 'the full knowledge and consent of the USSR'. In fact the communiqué amounted to a call to the people over the heads of the Bulgarian government to 'expose' the policy of their leaders, while 'carefully avoiding the appearance of provocation' or the impression that the Communist Party was acting 'as a subordinate of the Soviet Union but on its own initiative'.[48] The Bulgarian ambassador was even summoned to Vyshinsky at 2 a.m. with a demand for the publication of the communiqué in the Bulgarian papers; if it were not published, he was warned, it would be 'bad' for the Bulgarians. 'I asked what did he mean by "bad". He answered that we would soon find out.'[49] The communiqué was, as Schulenburg reassured Berlin in a desperate attempt to halt the further deterioration of relations, neither directed against Germany nor couched as an ultimatum, as it failed to specify the measures which the Russian government might take if German troops were moved into Bulgaria.[50]

Having called the Russian bluff, Hitler proceeded with the military planning. After ordering the construction of a bridge over the Danube he wished the troops to be prepared to cross the river by the end of January. Two days after the Russian remonstrations, the Bulgarians were promised an outlet to the Aegean Sea while military talks were initiated in Sofia.[51] So blatant was their misrepresentation of the arrangements that Schulenburg conceded to Molotov that it 'might have satisfied the representatives in Brazil and in Mexico, but for the ambassador in Moscow it was not sufficient, and in fact somewhat ill-omened'. He advised Molotov to instruct Dekanozov to exert further pressure on Ribbentrop.[52] Following Schulenburg's advice, Dekanozov indeed warned Weizsäcker that the Soviet government would 'consider the appearance of any foreign armed forces on the territory of Bulgaria and of the Straits as a violation of the security interests of the USSR'.[53] There was, however, no need to alienate the Russians. The move into Bulgaria was, as expected, presented as an inevitable step to thwart the British. A further attempt was made to lull Stalin with a promise to seek a revision of the Straits Convention 'at the proper time' and resume the political discussions 'in the near future'.[54] On 23 January Filov finally gave the official positive reply to Hitler. From their own sources at the Bulgarian court, the Russians ascertained that once German troops crossed into Bulgaria they were unlikely to face any armed opposition.[55]

By the end of the month, the military and diplomatic moves were synchronized and precautionary steps were being taken against a possible Soviet reaction. Hitler ordered the intensive fortification of Constanza, to protect the oil tanks 'against anonymous bombardment from the sea'. Later on he instructed the German troops in Northern Dobrudja that they would be the first to enter Bulgaria in order to protect the Bulgarian coast. The Bulgarians sought similar measures in Varna and Burgas. The complementary diplomatic measures, executed under German guidance, were the Bulgarian–Turkish declaration of non-aggression[56] and the securing of Yugoslav non-involvement.[57] There was only sporadic resistance to these moves. Moltchilov, the Bulgarian ambassador in London, begged Stalin to intervene. He would eventually resign his post in protest against Bulgaria's 'turning from a potential victim of English or German violence into an accomplice'.[58] King Boris no longer ruled his kingdom. Up to the last minute he still hoped to be able to avoid a situation whereby Bulgaria 'would become the bone of contention between Germany and the USSR'. However, as Draganov put it in a dispatch to the King from Berlin, Boris eschewed even the gesture of 'coating with some sugar this bitter pill' by informing the Russians in advance of the precise date of Bulgaria's accession to the Axis.[59] The British were as helpless as the Russians. Churchill could do little apart from utter the threat that 'condonation of German outrage would condemn Bulgaria to share Germany's ultimate chastisement'.[60]

The signs that events in Bulgaria were coming to a head became obvious when Draganov avoided meeting Dekanozov. When they finally met the Russians seemed to be concerned mostly with the Turkish reaction towards the Bulgarian access to the Tripartite Pact. But they could not conceal the danger that they now faced from Germany. When Draganov suggested that Russia had been exploiting Bulgarian popular sympathy to extend her control over the country, Dekanozov made the point that the Soviet Union 'no longer sought imperialistic aims but in the first place considered its security needs':

We in the Soviet Union often resort to history, especially in order to trace from where Russia has been attacked in the past and where the threat to its existence lies. Yet it is occasionally necessary to revert to more recent examples. If attention is paid to the 'new order' in Europe, of which many as well as the ambassador speak, then we notice that it is self-declared by a certain country and that small countries become economically subordinate to that hegemonic power in Europe. Worse still, the 'new order' is reflected in complete political submission of the small countries to that power, mostly in the military sphere, thus becoming a garrison of that power.

Their historical legacy led the Russians to regard British intervention in Greece and in the Balkans with equal suspicion.[61]

Once the timetable for the transfer of German troops into Bulgaria had been set, the Bulgarian Prime Minister and his Foreign Minister were ordered to come to Vienna for a ceremony to mark Bulgaria's entry into the Axis. Popov felt 'crucified and categorically refused to go to Vienna', as Filov noted in his diary, though he presented a list of excuses for staying behind. King Boris never really became reconciled to his own decision. He blamed Draganov for it and wished him to be withdrawn after he had signed the agreement 'without offering him another appointment'.[62] In desperation the Russians spared no efforts to scare the Bulgarians, but to no avail. Vyshinsky's recriminations were 'harsh and argumentative, hardly allowing [the Bulgarian ambassador] to insert a word'. Citing directly from the Bulgarian papers lying on his desk, Vyshinsky found the change in tone 'shocking'. Zhukov even made feeble attempts to galvanize the Bulgarian army into action over the head of the government.[63]

Finally on 26 February Molotov obtained full and concrete information about the German incursion into Bulgaria.[64] Two days later, as might have been expected, Schulenburg was instructed to present the encroachment in Moscow as a temporary measure aimed at heading off the British in Greece. Once again his brief report home of Molotov's 'obvious concern' over the German move did not reflect the acrimonious nature of the exchange. Molotov refused to accept at face value the reasons produced by Schulenburg, who tried in vain to impress on him that thwarting the British in Greece harmonized with Soviet aims. The fact that Russia had not been informed in advance was clearly another ominous sign.[65] Equally disconcerting was the flood of absurd justifications of the agreement by the Bulgarians as 'an instrument of peace' which should not hamper 'the further development of good relations with the Soviet Union'.[66]

To play down the significance of the move the Germans now hastily convened the International Advisory Committee of the Danube, entrusted with the river north of Braila. They went out of their way to entertain the Russians with lavish dinners, excursions and 'a brilliant opera performance' of Wagner's *Tannhäuser*. Any discussion of the contentious issues, however, was deferred to 30 June, by which time, as was well known to the German negotiators, the Russian claims would become obsolete.[67] When on 1 March Schulenburg officially informed the Russians that Bulgaria was joining the Tripartite Pact there was little left in Molotov's arsenal but to repeat the barren warning that Russia could not 'remain indifferent' to the German move, which undermined Soviet 'security interests'.[68]

Once again Hitler's gamble had paid off. Late in the evening of 1 March Stamenov was summoned by Vyshinsky, who accused Bulgaria of having extended the war to the Balkans. The recent ultimatum was now reduced to a diluted warning that the Soviet Union, 'true to its politics of peace, could not show any support to the Bulgarian government in conducting its present policy'. Molotov did not even have any leverage to combat the Bulgarian press campaign, which he held responsible for spreading mis-leading rumours on alleged Soviet aims.[69] In a way the grave and far-reaching consequences of the fall of Bulgaria and Rumania were slow to sink in. After all, as Maisky put it, neither Bulgaria nor Yugoslavia seemed to be 'a matter of life and death' for Russia. They were only instrumental in the preservation of Russia's genuine strategic target, the Turkish Straits. The Straits, Maisky confided to his diary, were 'a completely different story. One cannot give them up! Anyway the Germans know this very well. I believe that they would therefore not risk seizing the Straits. Germany cannot risk a confrontation with the USSR.'[70]

The Urge for the Straits

The setback inflicted on Molotov in Berlin, the fact that Bulgaria was fast falling into the German net, and the increasing involvement of England in Greece naturally shifted attention to Turkey. Like the Bulgarians and the Rumanians, the Turkish government sought ways of preventing the consolidation of any major power in the Balkans while remaining out of the war. Initially they were clearly relieved by the failure of the Berlin meeting, as any agreement reached would have been at their expense. They particularly frowned upon the idea of sharing control of the Straits with the Russians. 'You give the Russians a finger', complained the Turkish ambassador in Moscow, 'and soon enough they will demand the whole hand and seize full control of the Straits.'[71] Within a month of his visit to Berlin, Molotov found that Hitler was indeed resolved on pre-venting Russia from gaining a foothold in Turkey. Papen appeared to have clarified to Saracoglu the significance Hitler attached to the preservation of Turkey's independence as the key for maintaining the balance of power. Hitler expected Russian interests to be subjected to Germany's and secured under her patronage.[72] Aktay's calming message that Papen was working as an intermediary towards Turkish non-involvement was met by Molotov 'with a wry smile'. The Soviet Foreign Minister expected the Turks to clarify to the Germans that they would take no action in the Black Sea region without consulting the Soviet government.[73] He was far more concerned that the demands he had made in Berlin for the Straits might be leaked to the Turks and he therefore preferred to resort to reconciliation. The problem was that a show of weakness might encourage the Turks to join either the German or the British camp.

The Germans, Bulgarians and British, however, made certain that the Soviet agenda in Berlin came to light.[74] Equally ineffective were Molotov's attempts to misrepresent Sobolev's mission, attributing it to fears resulting from the Italian campaign against Greece. The British provided Saracoglu with sufficient proof that Molotov had intended 'to use Bulgaria as a cat's paw against Turkey' and that the Soviet Union was 'very far from having abandoned her ambitions in the direction of the Straits'.[75] Saracoglu was quick to protest about the proposed Russo-Bulgarian agreement on mutual assistance, claiming that it violated the 1929 agreement on prior consultations between Turkey and Bulgaria. The predominant need to stay out of the conflict, however, led him to the cautious policy of issuing a solemn declaration which denied any belligerent intentions while promising to consult the Russians on issues concerning either Bulgaria or the Black Sea. But suspicions were too deeply embedded to allow for trust-building measures. 'Peace', remarked Molotov sarcastically, 'was only a subject of rumours and negotiations while as far as war was concerned, it unfortunately was a reality.'[76]

Just when the German negotiations with the Russians had reached a stalemate, a new initiative concerning the Straits was launched by the Italians. However, Mussolini's unimpressive muscle-flexing, while his campaign was hitting rock bottom in Greece, only demonstrated to the Russians the fragility of their own situation. Mussolini had been watching with growing trepidation the crisis brewing between Russia and Germany, which improved the position of the latter in the Black Sea and the Mediterranean.[77] In Moscow there was indeed surprise when Mussolini expressed his wish not only to restart negotiations but also to move quickly into the political sphere; he was ready to recognize the Russians' new borders, their 'rights over the Black Sea, Asia and [their] interests in the Balkans'. In exchange the Italians sought recognition of their own rights in the Mediterranean. They even urged that talks should start immediately, either in Moscow or in Rome, at foreign ministerial or ambassadorial level.[78]

Molotov promptly gave his blessing, though insisting that the negotiations be carried out in Moscow, far from the scrutinizing eyes of the Germans.[79] Within days Rosso confirmed his government's readiness to adopt the proposals made in June 1940.[80] The Italians were further prepared to allow Bulgaria access to the Aegean, while claiming for Italy and Germany the Rumanian oil and economic assets. Molotov in return put forward the claim for control of the mouth of the Danube. But the major Soviet prize was of course the Turkish Straits. Strangely enough, the dialogue with the Italians, as well as the subsequent approach to the Turks,

was motivated by a fear of renewed British involvement in the region if
Germany were to assist Italy in the war. The Straits, as Molotov asserted
in the familiar vein, were connected 'with the issues of the security of the
Black Sea borders of the Soviet Union. Russia has suffered an invasion
from the Straits not once and not twice. During the Crimean war the
enemy descended on Russia through the Straits. In 1918 the intervention
against Russia was executed through the Straits. In 1919 the French
attacked Russia through the Straits.' He could easily see how the expansion of the war into Bulgaria might force the British, who had been maintaining a low profile, to interfere. 'The situation then', Molotov explained
to Rosso over dinner:

> will sharpen and the question of Soviet security will become more
> serious. Turkey will scarcely keep out of the conflict as it has a Pact with
> England. Besides England already has an air base and submarines in
> Lemnos at the gates to the Straits. The war will be carried out to the
> Black Sea, and this, obviously, will affect Turkey's stand on the Straits.
> Such a development is not unlikely in view of the nature of the rela-
> tions between Turkey and England.

But he left Rosso in no doubt that Russia intended to realize her interests
in the Straits 'by hook or by crook'.[81]
    The fact that Hitler was concealing from Mussolini his decision to
attack Russia only encouraged the latter to make the overture to Moscow.
Hitler had in fact assured him at the end of December that Germany's
relations with the Soviet Union were 'very good' and he did not expect
them to take 'any step to our detriment as long as Stalin lives'. The Duce
chose to ignore Hitler's warning, though, that it was not in Germany's
interest 'to deliver Bulgaria or the Straits themselves to Bolshevism'. But
Rosso, who initially disapproved of the policy pursued by Ciano, made
sure that the precise contents of the proposals were neatly transmitted to
Schulenburg.[82]
    Ribbentrop was amazed to find out how far negotiations had pro-
gressed. In his notoriously crude style he ridiculed the Italian negotiators
for waiving their right to enter the Black Sea while encouraging the
Russians to sail their warships into the Mediterranean. 'The Balkan
policy', he coached Alfieri, the Italian ambassador in Berlin, 'must not be
shackled by too hasty an agreement with the Russians.' Alfieri had in fact
to concede that he 'realized very well that Germany did not want Russia
to get into the Balkans again through the window by the roundabout way
of an agreement with Italy, so to speak, when she had just been ushered
out through the door'. In case the message was not explicit enough,
Ribbentrop chose the occasion to reveal the Soviet attempts to exclude the
Italians from the Danubian Commission.[83]

Hitler finally invited Mussolini to Berchtesgaden at the end of January 1941, when he crushed his fading hopes of independence. The Russians, he warned him, deliberately kept their treaties flexible; 'like Jewish lawyers, they preferred vague formulations and . . . ambiguous definitions' upon which they made new claims. Though continuing to conceal from his ally his plan to attack Russia, he vindicated the German presence in Rumania as a measure to counter a Soviet attack on either the oilfields or the Rumanian ports. Mussolini was further humiliated by written instructions from the German Foreign Ministry that awaited him in Rome, prohibiting him from pursuing 'any final formulation and commitment' of policies with the Russians without prior consultations.[84] Even with his feathers plucked, Mussolini continued his pitiful efforts to regain manoeuvrability by offering Molotov a revision of the Montreux Convention. This offer, however, which Molotov found to be 'unclear', coincided with Cripps's attempts at the end of February to mediate between the Russians and the Turks, and was allowed to lapse.[85] The Italians kept the ball in play but confined their conversations to trade.[86]

The realization that they might be the next victim of the Germans led the Turks to modify their attitude to Moscow throughout January. Their embassies abroad provided Moscow with detailed intelligence on the German build-up in Rumania, which was believed to reflect a German plan to cross the Danube into Bulgaria and jointly with them attack Turkey. The sharp about-turn was, as might be expected, regarded in Moscow with suspicion, particularly as the seizure of the Straits was presented as a component in an overall plan to attack the Soviet Union. The Germans, the Russians were told, 'aimed at preventing the British from rendering assistance to Russia'. Stalin was now torn between the fear of a German move to the south and the entrenched concept[87] that Britain was seeking, behind the scenes, to embroil Russia in war with Germany. The Russian ambassador in Bucharest, well attuned to his masters' voice, therefore passed the detailed information through such filters, suggesting that the occupation of the Straits was more likely to be a prelude to an assault on Egypt and Syria. Similar interpretations accompanied Dekanozov's reports from Berlin that Turkey would be used as a springboard to take Baku.[88]

There is no doubt, however, that the Kremlin seemed to have been seized by panic that the Germans might be tempted to continue their march to the Straits in a mirror image of the Russian objectives. In London Maisky declared that it was certain that 'his government did not wish to see any Great Power established in the Balkans', but it seemed to Eden that he was 'less confident than in the past that this unwelcome event would not occur'.[89] Schulenburg tried in vain to convince Molotov that this was unlikely to happen unless the Turks entered the war. Molotov was far more concerned by the fact that the Soviet counter-proposals for a settlement, submitted after the Berlin conference, had been left unanswered for over two months.[90]

Lacking a viable military option, as had been demonstrated during the war games conducted by the Russian military in January 1941,[91] Stalin now resorted to his favourite diplomatic games. There at least he did not feel he was hindered by incompetent and untrustworthy generals but held all the threads in his own hands. Away from the limelight, Maisky had already been urgently instructed in early January to set the ball rolling in London through Aras, the Turkish ambassador there. The bait was the conclusion of a mutual assistance pact. So compelling was the fear that Maisky had urged Aras to contact Ankara by telephone; but the ambassador appeared evasive, proposing to send a courier instead. Maisky judged correctly that the efforts were 'not serious!', reminiscent of Admiral Drax's abortive military mission by the slow sea route to Moscow in August 1939. The long-awaited negative reply from Saracoglu arrived a month later, expressing fear of making a premature move.[92]

The encroachment into Bulgaria threatened to place the Germans, rather than the Russians, in Adrianople, just around the corner from the Straits. The Turks clung desperately to non-intervention. Their mutual declaration of non-aggression with Bulgaria was conspicuously motivated by the concrete German threat, and was aimed at preventing Bulgaria from becoming a German pawn.[93] It also served as 'a convenient weapon' against British attempts to get Turkey involved in war, thus opening the Straits to the British navy.[94] They preferred, however, to present it as a guarantee against Russia. According to Aktay, Bulgaria wished to avoid any conflict with Turkey but 'more significantly ... had finally realized what the friendship with the Soviet Union entailed'.[95] The Russians, however, were not fooled. They knew perfectly well, as Dekanozov explained to Draganov in Berlin, that the declaration was motivated by a German 'threat to the Straits thereby transgressing Russian interests'. But at the same time they continued, at least outwardly, to 'categorically exclude a conflict between Germany and Soviet Russia'. While admittedly resigned to the fate of Bulgaria, they now 'established a new red line which was Turkey's involvement in the war'. According to the revised 1936 Montreux Convention, once involved in war the Turks could open the Straits at will to whatever naval force they saw fit.[96]

The likelihood of Bulgaria's joining the Axis by the end of January hastened an understanding between England, Russia and Turkey to bar the Germans from advancing to the Straits. Despite the unavoidable ups and downs in mood, reflecting the harsh conditions of diplomatic life in Moscow, Cripps maintained an unyielding conviction that Russia's benevolent neutrality towards Germany was motivated only by a need to boost her military preparedness for a clash which he regarded as inevitable.[97] Though he did not expect the Russians to prevent the Germans from reaching the Dardanelles by force, he thought they could be induced to do so by diplomatic means.[98] He easily swayed the 'Club', Aktay and the Greek and Yugoslav ambassadors, round to his point of view. On Cripps's advice Aktay indeed made such an overture to Molotov, who conceded that the situation was 'grave and complicated', grumbling that 'with the eating comes the appetite – German troops are already on the Bulgarian frontier'. For the first time he now overtly encouraged the Turks to resist the pressure.

Similar feelers were sent to the British, stating that it 'was not in the Soviet interest that German influence should spread in the Balkans' and that no policy was 'perpetual or eternal'.[99] The Foreign Office, however, remained sceptical and suspicious. Like British intelligence,[100] it continued to dismiss any suggestion that mutual hostility and varying interests might result in a head-on clash between Russia and Germany. In terms which betrayed ideological perceptions and wishful thinking, it repeated the well-known doctrine that Russia and Germany were bound together in regarding Britain as their ultimate enemy. In fact it did not put it past Stalin to make 'some bargain with Hitler whereby in return for Stalin abandoning Russian interests in the Balkans + Bulgaria to Germany, Hitler undertook to give Stalin full support if Stalin tries to wrest the Straits from Turkey'.[101]

It is not hard to imagine the anxiety which seized Stalin and Molotov when by the end of February Bulgaria's entry into the Tripartite Pact materialized. As a keen observer of the Kremlin, Cripps thought conditions were now most propitious for a new move to draw the Russians closer to the Allies. The presence of Eden in Turkey, where he was making a last-ditch attempt to reassemble the shattered remnants of the Balkan bloc, could facilitate a clandestine meeting in the Crimea with Molotov. Cripps impressed on Eden the significance of such a visit. Provided they 'were not too frightened to request a visit', the Russians would be 'flattered' and it could 'encourage our friends in South-East Europe'. The Foreign Office, however, persevered in its opinion that Stalin was in fact on the verge of concluding a new agreement with Germany. It not only resented Cripps's initiative but in fact wished to summon him immediately to London for consultations.[102] Churchill would not hear of such a visit, as he was not prepared to trust the Russians with Eden's 'personal safety or liberty'.[103]

Eden, who was later to collude with Cripps in an attempt to challenge Churchill's leadership,[104] was more attentive to Cripps, whose proposals fitted in well with his own plans. Like Stalin, since taking office Eden had been convinced that the 'Drang nach Osten' might after all be executed through the Balkans and across Anatolia, thus threatening Egypt. The control of Rumania appeared therefore to be designed 'not only to defend the oilfields from any possible air attack on our part, but also to provide jumping off points for an attack on the Straits'. For a while suggestions that Eden might visit Ankara to establish a Balkan bloc with the partici- pation of Turkey and Russia were muted in Cabinet. But shortly after assuming office Eden informed Knatchbull-Hugessen, the British ambas- sador in Turkey, that he expected the Turkish attitude to hinge 'on their appreciation of the probable attitude of the Soviet Government'. 'Past history', he concluded, 'has made it plain that they will do their utmost to avoid a conflict with Russia, and the key to the situation probably resides in the degree to which the Russians may acquiesce in, or actively support, the German scheme.'[105]

As was his habit, Cripps started the move on his own initiative, but his informal feelers encountered a negative 'official' reply from the Kremlin, using the pretext that 'time was not yet ripe for the solution of major issues by way of a meeting . . . more so before it was prepared politically'. When inquiring whether 'not yet ripe' meant that 'such a moment might occur in the future', he was given to understand that 'the arrival of such a moment was not excluded, but it was difficult to tell the future'. Cripps, however, went one step further, asking the Russians to arrange for him to fly to Istanbul to meet Eden and bring about a Turco-Soviet under- standing. The Russians appeared keen to facilitate his mission. Clearly they hoped firstly to sustain a new Balkan bloc, perhaps to deter the Bulgarians from putting their final signature on the agreement with Germany, and secondly to prevent closer Anglo-Turkish co-operation from which they would be excluded. For a moment the gesture was perceived in London by the very few supporters of Russia in the Foreign Office as a breakthrough in Anglo-Soviet relations, so much so that Maisky found them to be 'excessively naive'. 'Do they really think', he confided in his diary, 'that we can express overt exceptional interest in the negotiations between Eden and Cripps in Ankara in the present state of Anglo-Soviet relations?' Nonetheless it could hardly be denied that the fervent interest in his journey evinced, more forcefully than ever before, the awareness of the German danger.[106]

Early the next morning,[107] Cripps was ushered into a large twin- engined Douglas, especially assigned for his mission, at Moscow's inter- national airport. This was by no means routine, since air travel was restricted by stringent war regulations and this was in fact the inaugural flight to Istanbul across the Black Sea. It was no coincidence that the first fuelling stop was made at an enormous air force base where some eighty or more fighter planes were out in what seemed a deliberate display. The fear of a British bombing of Baku had not subsided. The rest of the flight, at a good altitude just above the clouds in the direction of Kherson and Burgas, was uneventful. Landing, Cripps could recognize the narrow entrance to the Bosphorus Straits, that very crucial water passage. Flying low over the hills surrounding Istanbul, the plane finally glided over the Sea of Marmara towards Yeshilköy, missing by only ten minutes a fierce gale and thunderstorm. There was a large welcoming party of military, naval and air personnel and civilians. After racing through the narrow streets of the old town and crossing to the eastern side on board the British ambassador's yacht, Cripps just caught the night train to Ankara.

Cripps reached Ankara in the early hours of the morning and immediately conferred with Knatchbull-Hugessen. Eden, who had been entertained at a cabaret until 5 a.m., turned up only later in the morning, obsessed with his favourite plan of forming a Balkan bloc with Yugoslavia. Eden seemed to Cripps to have been influenced by the lavish hospitality bestowed on him to believe an agreement with Turkey was in his pocket. The talks, however, did not get very far, as lunch at the embassy was a crowded occasion. The evening was taken up by a folk-lore show arranged specifically for Eden. Cripps, however, was not so easily discouraged. He embarked on the special night train taking Eden to Istanbul, hoping to be able to raise the Russian issue *en route*.

The journey was camouflaged as a return to Egypt. After 'a magnificent send off with bands troops & a cheering crowd' the train set off on the Adana line to the east. After three quarters of an hour it returned, blinds down, at full speed through Ankara station on the line westwards to Istanbul. The luxurious train was well stocked with food, drinks and smoking facilities, which made it conducive for Cripps to persuade Eden to reconsider the decision concerning the Baltic States. Though polite and attentive, Eden did not commit himself but promised to reach a decision within days of his return to London.

Cripps spent a good deal of his day in Istanbul 'seeing all sorts & kinds of people from refugees & secret service agents to members of our staff & journalists'[108] and even paid a short visit to the Sultan's Palace, which was opened specially for him. He then boarded the night train to Ankara, where he was due to meet Vinogradov, the Russian ambassador. Vinogradov had been little impressed by his brief and perfunctory encounter with Eden during a ball thrown in his honour by the Turks. He thought Eden created a 'tremendous superficial clamour' while talking 'in generalities', completely oblivious to Balkan intricacies. Moreover, he entertained a gullible 'faith in Turkey's loyalty'. He did not appear too keen to discuss Russian affairs, leaving them for Cripps to take care of.[109] Cripps found the young Vinogradov to be 'lively and very pleasant – also I should think intelligent'; their talks culminated in a joint memorandum for Saracoglu's consideration. Vinogradov's co-operation gave the unmistakable impression that the Russians had become anxious to re-establish closer contact with Turkey and in fact were eager to discuss material and military aid to her. Cripps left Ankara in the evening, 'fourth successive night to be spent on the line!!', convinced that 'a useful piece of work' had been done which 'at least reopens the chances of some improvements in the Turco-Russian position'.

The consequences of Cripps's initiative could barely be perceived at the time. Eden's reluctance to take on any tangible commitments, coupled with his manifest impotence, enhanced the growing suspicion in Moscow that together with Churchill he was trying to save England's skin by dragging Russia into the war.[110] At least this was the impression made on Vinogradov by the considerable British efforts to induce the Russians to issue a public declaration of support for Turkey, inevitably directed against Germany, and based on the somewhat dubious hunch that Eden's visit had confirmed the 'loyalty of the Turkish Government to the obligations it had taken on itself'. Cripps and Knatchbull-Hugessen expected that the Turks would immediately deploy their troops in Thrace. The Russians preferred the Turks to produce concrete proposals and even implied that the Soviet government would 'consider sympathetically' a Turkish request for war materials.[111]

The Russian archives reveal that, like Britain and the Balkan countries, the Russians were indeed seriously concerned about the future moves of Germany. The fear of England lingered on, as she had now become directly involved in the Balkans and the abandoning of 'Sea-Lion' revived the prospects of a separate peace. The Turkish hope of thwarting the German threat rested on an Anglo-Soviet collaboration which might bolster Yugoslavia's resolve to resist Germany, checking her further expansion.

Stalin used dubious means in seeking a rapprochement with Turkey through British mediation. On the one hand he wished the Anglo-Turkish co-operation to remain powerful enough to stop Hitler's advance beyond Adrianople. On the other hand England remained a potential enemy in the region and her own occupation of the Straits had to be prevented. The impression that 'Eden had failed to receive from Turkey an undertaking to join England if Germany moved into Greece' was therefore received with considerable relief. And yet attempts by friends of Russia, like R. A. Butler, to impress on Stalin that the entrance of Germany into the Middle East 'posed tremendous dangers not only for England but also for the USSR' was conceived simply as a deliberate attempt at provocation.[112]

The convoluted Turkish manoeuvres conducted indirectly through the embassy in London vaguely hinted at a possible 'Soviet–Turkish "alliance"'. Such moves were actually meant to discourage the Russians from executing unilateral military actions while also serving as a deterrent against Hitler. With the threat now no longer theoretical Maisky did not swallow the bait, insisting that any alliance had to culminate in a military agreement.[113] The likelihood of such an agreement under British sponsorship was in any case small, as Churchill had never been an enthusiastic supporter of the Balkan bloc.[114] He discouraged Eden, who was still hopping from one capital to another in the Middle East, by conveying the pessimistic evaluation of the Defence Committee about the likelihood of averting the 'fate of Greece unless Turkey and/or Yugoslavia come in which seems most improbable'. The British had in fact become resigned to their 'ignominious ejection' from Greece and the Balkans.[115]

Nothing, however, could stop Cripps. Immediately upon his return to Moscow, on 6 March, he was received most cordially by Vyshinsky for an unusual two-hour talk. Vyshinsky was eager to find out whether 'the Turks would resist a possible German attempt to occupy the Straits'; he was no less obsessed with the idea that Turkey too might join the Axis, which Cripps vehemently denied. Vyshinsky not only feared provocation but was concerned by the fact that Cripps had actually returned from his meeting with Eden empty-handed. Nor had the Turks put forward any concrete proposals, while Cripps was virtually trying to revive the old proposal to form a Balkan bloc put to Stalin in July 1940. Impetuous by nature, Cripps harmed his own case by driving home his belief that the Balkan episode was only a prelude to 'the more important plan of attacking the Soviet Union'. The message relating to Turkey must have been read in that context; Cripps warned Vyshinsky that the continued survival of Turkey depended entirely 'on the material and moral support which England and Russia could render'. Whether it was taken to be credible is doubtful, since Cripps admitted he had gathered it from rumours. Cripps now produced his double-edged weapon, raising the alarm in Moscow to new heights, in the form of a warning that an attack on the Soviet Union would 'enable the Germans to reach a peace with England whereby they would abandon Belgium and France for the sake of the Soviet Union'. Not only were Cripps's motives questioned by the Kremlin, but he faced stiff criticism at home. The Foreign Office, perhaps correctly, anticipated that 'part of the price the Soviet Government might expect Turkey to pay for any assistance would be concessions at the Straits'.[116] On the other hand, the Kremlin had ascertained from its own sources in the Balkans that, though the Turks did not intend to fight outside their borders, they would 'not abandon even one inch of their territory without a fight'. The Turkish military attaché was questioned at the Soviet Ministry of Defence about the possible Turkish reaction to a German advance into Thrace and then to the Straits. His answer too was unequivocal: 'Naturally defend ourselves!' But again the question of provocation came up when he warned the Turks that were the Germans to reach the Bosphorus Soviet interests would 'be at stake as well . . . it would clearly be only a first step in an overall plan to attack the Soviet Union and then the British would not be able to help you'.[117]

Stalin was now torn between his wish to prevent the Germans from reaching the Straits and his fear of being provoked by the British into entering the war prematurely. The fallacious forecast that the Germans would proceed with the occupation of the Straits prior to mounting an attack on Russia only enhanced his suspicions of British provocation. The intrinsic interests in the Straits, however, overcame the hesitations. Despite the fear of a rebuff, the Russians finally made the initial move. On 9 March Aktay, the ambassador in Moscow, was handed a declaration which stated that 'should Turkey be subjected to an attack by any foreign power and needed to resort to arms to defend its borders, it could count on her non-aggression pact with the Soviet Union and on the full under-standing and neutrality of the Soviet government'. The assurance reflected Stalin's wish for the best of both worlds. Gone were the not too far distant days when he had hoped to seek a revision of the Straits regime with German co-operation. While tenaciously adhering to neutrality, he sounded a faint warning to Berlin. It was received with obvious relief by Aktay, as 'the silence of the Soviet Union left room for various guesses and apprehensions'.[118]

Cripps was informed of the declaration minutes after it had been deliv-ered to Aktay in an 'unexpectedly cordial and long' meeting with Vyshinsky. To him it was 'indicative of a decision taken during the last few days . . . to increase [Soviet] resistance to German penetration in the Balkans rather than of any compliance by the Soviet government or any decision to reach a fresh arrangement with Germany on the question'. Though not attaching undue significance to the declaration, he believed it was important in a country 'where everything is done indirectly and by hint or suggestion'. As long as the balance of relations was tilted against Russia, however, he did not expect any dramatic changes: 'a fine day in late winter', he cabled home, 'is often heralded as the beginning of spring when in reality spring is far off'. But, as a man of vision, he insisted that 'the situation is so fluid that . . . we must be prepared to take immediate advantage of any change that occurs in the political atmos-phere here'. The British government, as he concluded a long and argu-mentative telegram to Eden, were 'bound, as realists, to accept the *fait accompli* in the Baltic States'. In Eden's absence the Foreign Office regarded the declaration merely as one of benevolent neutrality, an under-taking not to 'seize the opportunity of stabbing [Turkey] in the back'. The genuine aim was 'to draw Turkey into the Balkan war'.[119]

Churchill would not even hear of pressure on Turkey. Before the Cabinet was due to discuss Cripps's proposals he told Cadogan that he 'didn't like it. He thought this Russian declaration shd. be a comfort to the Turks, but he doubted whether the latter shd. be encouraged to push the Soviet further – that might only result in a recoil.'[120]

Hitler swiftly nipped the new alignments in the bud. Saracoglu was informed that the presence of German troops in Bulgaria was a precau-tionary move taken to 'eliminate the British influence on the European

Continent'. He was assured that the measure was in no way 'directed against the territorial or political integrity of Turkey'; Hitler had specifically ordered the troops to be deployed at some distance from the Turkish border and he expected the Turkish troops to act likewise. The exchange of letters excluding the use of force between Hitler and Inönü, the President of the Turkish Republic, paralysed the Russians completely, the more so when Inönü went one step further, undertaking not to cede territory to any foreign power.[121]

The intense suspicions led Stalin to assume, once Hitler's letter had entered the public domain, that the development had actually been devised by the British to ensnare the Soviet Union in war. Besides, the Russians were only too eager to avoid an overt conflict with the Germans. Vinogradov therefore was quick to change the tune, rejecting the widespread rumours that the Germans planned to seize the Straits 'with a view to ultimate conflict with the Soviet Union'. As if oblivious to the reasons which had led to the Soviet initiative a mere two weeks earlier, he was convinced that 'Germany had always given assurances of good intentions towards the Soviet Union', but he did not neglect to mention that the Soviet Union 'was admittedly keeping her eyes open'; though resolved to keep neutral she 'would not remain idle if her interests were threatened'. The possibility of a British conspiracy to involve Russia in war was revitalized, as was the alternative of peace overtures to Germany.[122] And yet, with Hitler's commitment now in their pocket, the Turks somewhat defused the tension by finally acknowledging the Soviet declaration on 17 March, reciprocating with a similar undertaking to refrain from hostile activities if the Soviet Union were to find herself at war.[123]

The new understanding were immediately undermined by Hitler, who seized the occasion to disclose to the Turkish ambassador in Berlin in great detail the demands made by Molotov to him in November for bases on the Dardanelles and the positioning of troops in Bulgaria. Indeed, in Ankara 'the greatest impression was made by the Führer's statements that Russia had demanded the right to intervene at the straits as a condition for accession to the Tripartite Pact'. A victorious Hitler found it only too easy to appear the guardian of Turkish interests by preventing 'the liquidation of the Balkans and Turkey by Russia'.[124]

The situation was further complicated by the awareness that in certain circumstances the agreement for mutual assistance between Turkey and Britain might be diverted against the Soviet Union in the Black Sea region and the Caucasus. It was precisely such an occurrence which the declaration set out to prevent. Indeed, in secret talks with Eden in Nicosia it was agreed that if Turkey were invaded by Germany RAF fighters could at once use the airfields in Thrace and Yeshilköy, the main airport of Istanbul, not to mention those in Antalya.[125] Merkulov, the head of the NKGB, had assembled for the Kremlin a pile of reports on activities of

clearly anti-Soviet character carried out by Turkish intelligence in northern Turkey and the Caucasus. A special bureau had been set up in
Erzerum to co-ordinate the work of the agents involved in the espionage.
The bureau was indeed working on plans to transform the Caucasus into
an autonomous region under Turkish protection. The most concrete information related to instructions by the Turkish General Staff to its intelligence arm to collect material on the dislocation and deployment of the
Red Army in the Caucasus area, as well as on the state of the railways,
roads and bridges leading from the Caucasus to Turkey. They further
sought information on the positioning of Soviet artillery and naval forces
in the region and displayed particular interest in the fire-fighting facilities in the oil-production regions.[126]

    All the Russians could do was resort to verbal protests. The exchange
of undertakings to honour the non-aggression pact between the two countries received wide publication in the Soviet papers on 25 March.[127] In his
endless efforts to salvage the shattered relations between Germany and
Russia Schulenburg went out of his way to dismiss the declaration as 'an
insignificant episode', but Rosso, always more outspoken, could not but
see in it an expression of Russia's dissatisfaction with the German position on the Balkans. It was a warning to Germany, related to the negotiations under way with Yugoslavia,[128] and a 'platonic help to Turkey'.
Hitler clearly did not share Schulenburg's view. To him it was an
'unfriendly act', but his response lay in the divisions deployed on the
border rather than in a paper agreement.[129]

6

The Red Army on Alert

The Soviet Defence Plans

The euphoria and sense of relief which were briefly evident after the signature of the Ribbentrop–Molotov Pact quickly evaporated when the ineptitude of the Red Army became apparent in the conduct of what were essentially minor battles in Poland and Finland. It gradually sank in that the time and space gained by the pact would barely be sufficient. The effects of the purges on the preparedness of the army were suddenly exposed. Stalin could hardly ignore the drain on the officer corps. Between May 1937 and September 1938, some 36,700 men had been purged in the army and 3,000 in the navy: 90 per cent of district chiefs of staff and deputies, 80 per cent of corps and divisional commanders and 90 per cent of staff officers and chiefs of staff. There was also a marked decline in the educational and intellectual standard of the survivors. By the time of the German attack 75 per cent of the officers and 70 per cent of the political officers had been in active service for less than one year.[1] Indeed, the training and experience necessary before command of a division was given required a number of years, but the pressure of circumstances forced undeserved early promotions. However, even in the dire circumstances the reconstruction of the army had to be a gradual process which ruled out adventurous strategies, even if these had been contemplated.

Equally damaging to the war preparedness was the undermining of the unique Soviet military doctrine during the purges. A short digression is called for here. In devising a new approach in the stimulating revolutionary environment of the 1920s and early 1930s, the architects of the Red Army had conceived an entirely original doctrine which addressed both universal requirements and the specific features of Soviet national needs. These radical innovations were developed by the prodigious trio of Generals Tukhachevsky, Triandafilov and Isserson. The salient characteristic of the doctrine was the refinement of the prevalent Clausewitzian categorization of warfare into strategic and tactical levels by the introduction of an intermediate level, labelled the 'operational'.[2]

What distinguished the doctrine was not only the invention of a new 'operational level', comfortably tucked in between 'strategy' and 'tactics'; it was the theoretical assumption of the existence of ingrained tension between the two levels, between the 'goal' and the 'means' used to accomplish it, between pinning down the enemy (*skovyvanie*) and the strike (*udar*). Thus, unlike the European notion, which distinguished rather mechanically between defensive and offensive means of war, the Russian established a cognitive harmonious relation between the two. 'Operational skill' was the ability to recognize the existence of such tensions and reconcile them in a given situation in order to attain the objective. From the early 1920s it was fully recognized that a basic component in the exploitation of the inherent tension was the study and implementation of defence as a prerequisite for a successful offence.

The introduction of the 1929 *Polevoi Ustav* (Field Regulations) assigned the forward detachments, the light screen groupings, with a combination of tasks ranging from reconnaissance to allow for regrouping of the main thrust, to actual engagements aimed at preventing the enemy from seizing key positions and introducing chaos into its offensive deployment. The range of activities of the forward detachments depended on the degree of mechanization, as they would need to maintain close contact with the main covering force for support.[3]

In 1936 Tukhachevsky published his *Problems Concerning the Defence of the USSR*, which analysed these problems. There was nothing sinister, aggressive or ideological in the comprehensive association of defence and offence; the two were in fact intertwined. Even if the strategic goal was defensive in nature, the operational manoeuvres of 'deep operations' employed in achieving it could assume a dynamic orientation.[4] Thus Soviet strategy in the event of an invasion was committed, rather ambitiously, to the prompt transfer of the war to the enemy's territory. The objective of the defence was to seize the initiative from the opponent and establish preconditions for a counter-offensive.[5] These concepts were incorporated in the 1936 Field Regulations, which visualized the 'simultaneous use of tank, mechanized, air and air assault forces to strike and penetrate the entire depth of the enemy's defences, through its tactical defences, into its operational depths'. The prerequisite for the successful implementation of such a goal was the creation of an effective mobile force, which in turn necessitated rapid industrialization and a major reform in the armed forces. This in itself required a major expansion of the armoured corps and the creation of airborne divisions co-operating with the ground forces. It must be remembered that industrialization was not aimed at boosting the military. The technological revolution in weaponry was a spin-off of industrialization and not the main cause of it. By 1933 the change was marked by the development of multiple groupings of mechanized and tank forces which were to be engaged in both operational and tactical combat.[6]

The concept reached its maturity with the introduction of 'deep operations', which exploited the tension inherent in the operational level. It envisaged the deployment of armoured and mechanized formations, echeloned in depth, co-operating jointly with infantry and artillery in an attempt to break through the enemy lines and subsequently to exploit the initial success by developing operational manoeuvre activities in the rear of the enemy's deployment. To break through the impasse, the theory created suitable conditions for the covering forces on the border to initiate a swift counter-offensive with the aim of destroying the main body of the enemy's forces on his own territory. The key to the effective conversion of tactical successes into victories lay in the pursuit of successive operational manoeuvres.[7]

The army was therefore deployed in depth to start with. The covering forces were positioned in a linear fashion along the border, around the strongholds. The mechanized formations and infantry divisions were concentrated as a second echelon in depth, and the third echelon served as the base for the recruitment of further troops while the operations were in progress. The task of the forward detachments was therefore to absorb and mitigate the initial shock while identifying the general trends of the enemy's manoeuvres. Their activities served as the anvil upon which the initial counter-offensive of the first echelon could be mounted to disrupt the deployment and manoeuvres of the enemy. The third stage led to the deployment of the second echelon (mostly mechanized and armoured) in counter-offensives in depth leading to the removal of the threat posed by the opponent.[8]

Recognition of the severe deficiencies of the military led to a swift reorganization of the army's High Command shortly after the Winter War. The meeting of the plenum of the Central Committee of the Party on 28 March 1940 witnessed a sensational event when Defence Commissar Voroshilov 'spoke quite frankly about [the army's] shortcomings'. The entire Chiefs of Staff were seated on the stage and subjected to criticism of their performance. The attempt to blame it on the harsh wintry conditions was seen as a poor excuse. Russia, they were reproached, was a northern country and the greatest victories had been achieved in winter: 'Alexander Nevsky against the Swedes, Peter the First against the Swedes and Finns, Alexander the First and the victory over Napoleon. There were very many good traditions in the old army, which need to be utilized.'

The key to recovery lay in competent military leadership, but the plenum established that the reality was grim: 'The commanders – 60 per cent are good; 40 per cent idiots, characterless, cowards, etc.'[9]

On 8 May, Timoshenko, who had commanded the Karelian troops in the Russo-Finnish war with remarkable success, was promoted to marshal and replaced Voroshilov as Commissar of Defence. Both Hitler and Stalin continued to overestimate British power and watched with alarm the British foothold on Narvik, which was in fact precarious. Above all Hitler's defeat of Denmark had introduced uneasiness and confusion in Moscow. The General Staff had been in the middle of implementing demobilization plans and addressing the shortcomings revealed during the Winter War, and no new operational plans were contemplated.[10] The demobilization plan of 9 May, which had been prepared by Voroshilov, is of the utmost historical significance. It was submitted to Stalin the day before the German attack on France and reveals that the Red Army had been preparing a massive demobilization which had been interrupted by the diversionary wars in Poland and Finland. After the conclusion of the war on 4 April, efforts were renewed to reduce the troops in the Caucasus and the Odessa and Kiev military regions to their previous strengths. As a result of the mobilization carried out during the Polish and Finnish campaigns, the army had increased by 1,736,164 soldiers. However, rather than continuing to swell the ranks, efforts were made to reduce further the size of the army through demobilization 'in order to discharge the extra people called up from the reserves'. As far as the artillery was concerned, specific recommendations were made to place 'the status of all corps on a peacetime level', with the sole exception of four corps which were diverted to the Caucasus. Altogether 153,000 gunners were to remain mobilized in peacetime. Corresponding measures were taken in the cavalry. Both the air force and the tank divisions, the Politburo determined, 'which have been on a war footing, [should] be returned to peacetime status'. The sole exception to this trend was the creation of three tank brigades to be stationed in the Baltic countries and two in the Caucasus region. All in all, 686,329 soldiers out of a total of 3,200,000 were to be immediately discharged.[11] This demonstrates that no master plan for exploiting the attrition of the belligerents for military expansion had existed in the earlier stages of the war.

The war in France abruptly changed Soviet perceptions and produced a major shift in policy. The measures taken by Stalin from mid-May onwards were triggered by the realization of the growing German menace. The urgent reorganization measures taken by the military during the second half of May were clearly prompted by the sensational victory of the Wehrmacht, which to all intents and purposes meant the collapse of the western front. They were embarked upon as soon as the extent of the German success in France was understood and gathered momentum after the fall of Paris. In his memoirs Khrushchev vividly depicts the panic that seized Stalin when the news of the occupation of Paris reached the Kremlin; Stalin, he recalled, 'let fly with some choice Russian curses and said that now Hitler was sure to beat our brains in'.[12]

The extent of the deterioration of Soviet–German relations in the wake of the peace of Compiègne is often overlooked. It is highly debatable whether Stalin's apparent compliance with the German successes indicated that he was 'blinded by ideological preconceptions' and unable to distinguish between major and minor dangers. It is equally questionable whether he viewed the annexation of the Baltic States as a 'reward for loyalty to Hitler'.[13] The more likely explanation, as was astutely observed by the American chargé d'affaires in Moscow, is that Soviet policy was 'largely defensive and based upon the fear of possible aggression by Allied or associated powers . . . and possibly upon uneasiness over the prospects of a victorious Germany'.[14]

Facing the almost unscathed Wehrmacht, the Russians placated the Germans and avoided any provocation.[15] Molotov's congratulations to Schulenburg on the 'splendid success of the German Wehrmacht', given great prominence in Churchill's history of the war, reflects a desperate attempt to mollify the Germans and forestall any move eastwards. Molotov's words were only a preface to the flimsy explanation of the annexation of the Baltic States and the 'extremely urgent' demand for a solution of the Bessarabian question.[16] In any case, the diplomatic acquiescence went hand in hand with the hasty reinforcement of Soviet defences.[17] It is patently obvious that the assumption of control of the Baltic States on 15 and 16 June was connected with events in France. The anti-German aspects of the headlong transfer of troops to the western front, the overnight conversion of public institutions into military establishments and the transfer of the command of the Baltic fleet to the forward naval bases in Tallinn could hardly be concealed and were not lost on the Germans.

The occupation of the Baltic States lengthened the contiguous border with Germany and in theory made it more difficult to defend. However, it redressed the problem of the disappearance of the buffer zone which had previously fulfilled the needs of Soviet defence. It clearly improved Russia's strategic position by preventing the formation of a 'Baltic bridgehead' which could serve as a springboard for an attack against Leningrad or Minsk, as had indeed occurred during the Civil War. Moreover, despite his claim, Stalin made intensive efforts to expand the fortified positions along both the new and the old Soviet borders.[18]

The occupation of the Baltic countries poses serious moral questions. The Sovietization of the three states had little to do with ideology, but it was a rather mendacious and cynical method of gaining control over the occupied territories. The oppressive means so characteristically employed by Stalin aggravated the injustice and had a long-lasting effect on Moscow's relations with these countries. However, while the occupation can and should be condemned on moral grounds, it was dominated by the threat hanging over the Soviet Union.[19]

When the prospect of war was suddenly driven home, the Russian leadership, committed to remaining out of the war, became seriously concerned about its initial phase. The brilliant German execution of *Blitzkrieg* tactics in the West and later in the Balkans raised the possibility of a surprise attack which might undermine the Russian army's ability to seize the initiative. It was no longer improbable that the Germans would complete their deployment before corresponding measures were carried out on the Russian side. Zhukov and others attest to how after the fall of France the General Staff spent sleepless nights devising plans which would accommodate the 'operation in depth' with the defence requirements of the projected battlefield. The new mobilization plans were embarked upon in earnest only on 22 May, when the German army appeared invincible, and therefore they can hardly reflect an aggressive disposition. They reversed the trend which had been in force up till then of discharging a large part of the army. On the same day, plans were hastily laid for speeding up the construction of the T-34s to replace the Russians' vast stocks of obsolete tanks now that the contribution of the German armour to the successful *Blitzkrieg* had been fully comprehended. The plan, obviously an emergency one, was updated in early July.[20]

In none of the reforms can revolutionary jargon or practice be detected. Voroshilov, who had proved his inability to command large formations, was replaced as Defence Commissar in the second week of May by Timoshenko, who was promoted to the rank of Marshal of the Soviet Union. This was followed by the final restoration of the old imperial ranks in the army and the release from prison of some 4,000 officers detained during the purges, who took up command posts. One of those released was Colonel, later Marshal, K. K. Rokosovsky, who was to assume command of a newly formed mechanized corps. Among the 1,000 officers promoted in June were K. A. Meretskov and G. K. Zhukov, who were now promoted to the rank of army generals on the way to their consecutive appointments as Chief of Staff. Newly appointed lieutenant-generals who were to gain reputations later in the war were Koniev, Vatutin, Yeremenko, Sokolovsky, Chuikov and Golikov. The High Command of the navy, which had suffered severe casualties during the purges, was similarly restored with the appointment of Nikolay G. Kuznetsov as Chief of the Naval Forces and L. M. Galler and I. S. Isakov as new admirals. None of them had gained sufficient experience to function adequately in their new posts by the time the Great Patriotic War broke out.

Equally significant was the introduction of a new disciplinary code. A rigidly traditional approach replaced the communist code, which assumed egalitarianism and motivation through ideological commitment. Indeed, Timoshenko's concluding address to the Military Conference of December 1940 focused on the need to instil discipline and raise the morale of the armed forces as a precondition for success in what was now termed 'modern war'.[21] In addition, all 'bourgeois' forms and courtesies, notably the salute, were reinstated. All the changes were incorporated in the 'Disciplinary Regulation' of August 1940. This was followed up by the abolition of the dual command, depriving the political commissar of the power and control he had enjoyed over his military counterpart.[22]

Rather than maintaining the major western theatre of war, which could have served as a springboard if the Russians were to strike against the German concentrations, four new groups were created, while the western one was divided into the Leningrad, Baltic, Special Western, Special Kiev and Odessa military districts. Each of these was to be transformed into a forward headquarters entrusted with the defence of that zone.

The only defence plan that preceded the outbreak of the Second World War was composed by Marshal V. M. Shaposhnikov, the Chief of Staff, in 1938 and assumed a threat on two fronts: the predominant one of Germany, Italy, Finland and the Baltic countries in the western sector, and the subsidiary Japanese one in the east. The threat on the western front could be translated into two variants, either a German strike north of the Pripet Marshes along the Minsk–Smolensk axis heading to Moscow, or a move to the south if economic considerations were in fact preponderant.[23] The state was indeed gradually moving on to a war footing but in a markedly defensive manner. In July the newly formed Chief War Council finally brought the 1938 plans in line with the situation as it was evolving after the fall of France.[24] They were reviewed by General A. M. Vassilevsky on Shaposhnikov's instructions on 19 August, still anticipating rather elusive potential dangers to Russia in the west and east. The new directive, however, took into account the fact that the consequences of the secret protocol of the Ribbentrop–Molotov Pact now drove Italy, Hungary, Rumania and Finland into the German camp, forcing Russia to face a coalition which extended the geographic arena. The political and strategic turmoil in the Balkans was thus gradually shifting the focus from the centre to the flanks. But Shaposhnikov's directive still anticipated the main blow to fall on the central sector, north of the River San, along the Vilnius–Minsk and Brest–Baranovichi axes. A German advance towards Kiev and Lublin seemed less likely. The task of the Soviet military was therefore defined in very general terms as 'bringing about the defeat of German power, concentrated in Western Prussia and in the Warsaw region'.[25]

The intensifying conflict in the Balkans in the next month led to a modification of the plan by Timoshenko and the newly appointed Chief of Staff K. A. Meretskov. It was presented to Stalin on 19 September. As we have seen,[26] collation of information by the GRU towards the end of August indicated that the German build-up indeed posed a genuine threat to Russia. However, with the redeployment of German troops in the East now in full swing, General Jödl reinforced Stalin's mistaken evaluation through a disinformation campaign which depicted 'the main point of deployment as the southern sector while forces in the north remained relatively small'.[27] The tendency was now to explain the concentration as a move to reinforce Germany's eastern borders with the USSR, which had been neglected during the campaign in France. However, the patterns of the build-up drove home the alarming fact that Hitler was encroaching on vital Russian interests in the Balkans. This seems to have contributed in autumn 1940 to the diversion of the Soviet effort to the southern borders.[28]

In mid-August the first extensive report on the redeployment of the German troops in the East since the conclusion of the campaign in France was prepared by the border NKVD. Despite earlier warnings, the report was passed over in favour of an assessment which related to the events in the Balkans. 'It is noted among the German wire operators (radio-telegraph) and the civilian population', the report concluded, 'that some of the troops transferred from France will be directed to the Balkan peninsula, against the British, with the aim of seizing the naval ports of Rumania.'[29] The agents of the GRU in the Balkans corroborated the political appreciation, pointing out that the Balkans remained 'the decisive centre of political events, particularly since a direct clash of intrinsic German and Soviet interests arose there'. They quoted the German ambassador in Belgrade, who had told a small circle of confidants: 'For the Germans the Balkans are the most significant asset and they ought to be included in the new order of Europe; but as the USSR would never agree to that a war with her was inevitable.' Dozens of rumours in this vein were circulating freely in the diplomatic community.[30]

In shifting attention to the southern arena, the planners now to some extent revived the ideas developed in the early 1930s by Svechin, the prominent military theoretician. Svechin had assumed an Anglo-French coalition to be the major threat to the USSR. Drawing on the experience of the Crimean and the Civil Wars, he expected the main thrust to come from the Black Sea while the strike in the Ukraine was considered to be a complementary one. Auxiliary strikes were anticipated across the Pripet Marshes and in the Baltic. The theory had been discarded by Tukhachevsky when the Nazi menace became dominant. However, it continued to prevail even after Germany replaced Britain as the main threat in the region towards the end of 1940, clearly reinforced by the German incursion into the Balkan peninsula.[31]

Like its predecessor in August, the directive assumed an acute German threat. It was governed not only by the stormy relations in the Balkans but also by the early concentration of nearly 100 German divisions on Rumania's northern border. The two major variants of the German offensive remained a major strike from Prussia north of the River San and a drive in the south towards Kiev, with supporting action in the north. But the shift of the centre of gravity to South-eastern Europe had significant ramifications. The pattern of their concentration put Hitler in a convenient position to pursue the two variants. He could collaborate with the Italians by deploying them in the Balkans, thus presenting the Russians 'with a considerable threat'. Such a coalition would be augmented by the incorporation of the armed forces of Hungary and Rumania in the war effort and the full exploitation of the economic resources of the Balkan States. Moreover Hitler could use the deployment as a bridgehead for an invasion of the rich agricultural and industrial territory of the Ukraine. It was, as the directive indicated, in the south-western sector that 'one ought to expect the main strike of the united forces of the opponent'. The shift to the south had a lasting impact; in fact the deployment directives issued by the army's chief planner, General Vatutin, on 13 June 1941[32] still failed to recognize the most lethal threat and organized the main reserve force of the second echelon in a south-western direction. When the Germans launched their offensive north of the Pripet Marshes, the Red Army had to execute complicated manoeuvres in an attempt to transfer the troops from Kiev to the main western front.

The relative scarcity of the troops, now facing a threat extending from the south to the north along the entire border, produced severe tension in the defensive system. With the political events in the Balkans firmly entrenched in their minds, the planners wavered, producing two alternatives. Events in the Balkans, nonetheless, gave precedence to the southern variant, which in a way was geared to remove the tension on both sectors, by deploying the 'main force of the Red Army . . . south of Brest-Litovsk so that a powerful strike in the direction of Lublin, Cracow and further to Breslau in the first stage of the war would cut off Germany from the Balkan States, tear her away from her important economic base, and produce a decisive influence on the Balkan States on the issue of their participation in the war'. Tearing Germany from the Balkan States acquired 'exclusively a political significance'. The second variant followed the previous directive and proposed to deploy the army north of Brest-Litovsk, with the task of 'inflicting a defeat on the main forces of the German army within the limits of Eastern Prussia and seizing the latter'. The planner however showed his own preference by pointing to the unpreparedness of the arena and the difficulties involved in carrying out the blow which were bound to encourage the Balkan States to join the war against Russia, opening a front in the south.

While the emphasis thus swung to the south, the fluidity of the situation was recognized as well as the fact that the deployment would 'depend on the political conditions existing in the opening stages of the war'. The directive reflected the contentions in the Balkans but preceded the German unilateral arbitration on 30 August[33] which paved the way for their complete domination of the peninsula. Following the arbitration Timoshenko and Zhukov, commander of the Kiev Military District, introduced to Stalin in early October alterations to the plan, which set the priorities by establishing the south-western front as the major arena. Measures were now taken to hasten the fortification of the new 'Molotov line', so that 'in the future, on account of the hopefully established new defence zones in occupied Poland, more troops could be released to strengthen the basic concentration in the south-east'. Likewise special measures were taken to improve the railway and road communications leading to the south-west.[34] By December, when news of Hitler's decision on 'Barbarossa' started trickling in, it was already taken for granted that 'the main strike of the unified power of the opponents' would come from the Balkans.[35]

The predominance of the south-western deployment, therefore, was not, as is occasionally suggested, a simple premeditated attempt to overrun and occupy the Rumanian oilfields. Rather, it was a concentration of troops at the spot where the major threat, a German occupation of the Rumanian oilfields and a swift drive into the Ukraine and Baku, was anticipated. From autumn 1940 to spring 1941 the build-up of the troops on that flank was indeed logical. After all, it was only on 17 March 1941 that Hitler abandoned his idea of a double encirclement–pincer manoeuvre in the Ukraine and opted for a major concentrated thrust in the central sector.[36] Consequently the plans underwent only minor alterations in February 1941 following the war games of January, and served as the basis for the mobilization plan.[37]

The Bankruptcy of the Military

The initial complacency in the Kremlin following the Berlin conference was soon overridden by the looming threat as the struggle for the Balkans intensified. On the morning of 5 December 1940 Dekanozov, the newly appointed ambassador to Berlin, went through the mail as was his daily practice. He was suddenly struck by an anonymous letter containing significant military information about Hitler's intentions of attacking the Soviet Union in the spring of 1941.[38] A week later Stalin was made familiar with the contents of a speech delivered by General Keitel in Berlin to corps and division commanders. Though admitting that a neutral Russia 'did not pose a danger for Germany in the East', he reconfirmed

Hitler's irritation at Stalin's 'refusal to pursue negotiations on the "new European order" and in general on the division of the world into "spheres of influence"'. The information further disclosed Hitler's resolve to seize Saloniki and transfer troops through Bulgaria 'regardless of whether Russia agreed or not'.[39] Stalin's attention was apparently also drawn to Hitler's speech to his High Command on 18 December, which was rich in anti-Soviet innuendoes and mentioned the war in the East as the aspiration of the Third Reich.[40]

The most dramatic piece of intelligence, however, reached Stalin in the middle of a conference of the High Command which he summoned in mid-December to discuss a long list of shortcomings unveiled by a special committee of the Central Committee. A mere eleven days after the issue of Directive 21 on Operation 'Barbarossa', General Tupikov, the military attaché in Berlin, alerted Moscow to its existence:

TO THE CHIEF OF THE INTELLIGENCE SERVICE OF
THE GENERAL STAFF OF THE RED ARMY
BERLIN, 29 December 1940

[name deleted] informed that [name deleted] has learnt from most well-informed high military circles that Hitler has given the order to prepare for war with the USSR. War will be declared in March 1941.

Instructions have been issued to verify the information.

Confirmation swiftly followed: Tupikov stood by his sources, which were 'based not on rumours, but on a special written directive by Hitler' that was 'exceedingly secret and known only to a few people'. Molotov's visit to Berlin reminded the informants of the 1939 trip by Colonel Beck, the Polish Foreign Minister, summoned to Berlin to negotiate with Hitler after the plans for the occupation of Poland had already been finalized. Both the letter and the evaluation were dispatched to Stalin personally.[41] He was also aware of instructions to the Luftwaffe to initiate an extensive programme of reconnaissance flights over Soviet territory in the border regions.[42]

A summary survey by the Ukrainian and Belorussian chiefs of the NKGB depicted the establishment of an Army Quarters Command post in Warsaw, massive transfers of troops and conversion of civilian institutions into barracks, fortification of major rail junctions and installation of anti-aircraft defences. Of similar significance was the dramatic rise in border incidents with the Germans: while there were twenty-two minor incidents, which were quickly solved by the local commanders, between the signing of the agreements with Germany up to June 1940, this number had risen to 187 in the second part of 1940.[43] An intercepted telegram from the Japanese embassy in Bucharest disclosed information from the German ambassador: 'The situation has reached the decisive phase. Germany has completed its full deployment from Finland to the Black Sea and is convinced of an easy victory. Rumania, too, as far as possible, is carrying out preparations so that she will be in a position to take part immediately.'[44]

Alarmingly, the threats were accompanied by reports on the unpreparedness of the Red Army for war. In early December Timoshenko even complained to the Central Committee that no operative plan for war had been deposited with the Ministry of Defence. Moreover, the Chief of Staff had not been briefed about the situation on the borders. In a subsequent report Merkulov warned about the dismal state of the troops on the eastern borders.[45] Stalin reacted by convening an extraordinary conference of the High Command of the Red Army at the end of December in Moscow.[46] The intensive sessions touched on all aspects of the reorganization of the armed forces: the training programme, 'operational art', the armoured and mechanized units, the air force and so on. Though the various lectures showed remnants of the sophistication reached by the Soviet military in the 1930s, an oppressive atmosphere and Stalin's instructions on the need to devise 'new war ideologies' led at the end of the day to a general confusion.

Despite the taboo against Tukhachevsky, Zhukov, as well as Timoshenko, clung to his theories like a life belt. They expected the Red Army to be able to contain the enemy in the initial phase of the war and later to exploit the success while inflicting the 'main strike' (*udar*). However, confidence in the doctrine had been somewhat undermined by fear of Stalin and even more so by fascination with the *Blitzkrieg* tactics employed in the West. Worse still, since most of the architects of the novel theory had been purged, the ability to grasp the doctrine fully and translate it into action was limited. It was not until the Battle of Kursk in summer 1943 that it was finally restored to its full scope, paving the way for impressive Russian victories.[47] The temptation to transfer elements of the 'miraculous' German prescription into what Stalin and some of his generals termed the 'modern contemporary war' was almost irresistible. Generals Romanenko, Stern, Pavlov and Zhukov now almost fanatically advocated the augmentation of the armoured formations, complaining about the slow pace of production.[48]

Zhukov, and to some degree Timoshenko in his concluding words, came closest to advocating full rehabilitation of Tukhachevsky's theories. Zhukov could see no substitute for the creation of a proper operational defensive zone, in which it would be possible to reorganize the rear effectively and recruit forces for operational manoeuvres. The manoeuvres were to be conducted at a depth ranging from 8–10 kilometres for an infantry division to 80–100 kilometres for an army. Defence was therefore to be pursued in stages: first the containment of the enemy, then the disruption of the offensive logic and the counter-offensive leading to the annihilation of the opponent, and finally synchronized strikes to extend the breakthrough in various directions.[49]

In closing the conference, Timoshenko did nothing to play down the direct danger posed to the Russians by the 'most powerful' army in the world. Nonetheless, it was probably fear of Stalin that led him to put on a display of confidence, conveying to those present the feeling that 'although the war with Germany might be difficult and long, the country had all it needed for a struggle to full victory'. This conclusion to a certain extent diverted attention from the rather severe shortcomings which had been revealed during the conference, especially by Zhukov's outspoken criticism of the Defence Ministry.[50]

Hardly had the conference ended when the commanders were summoned unexpectedly to the Kremlin. Stalin wore a grim look; Zhukov could not fail to notice that 'it was not the same Stalin' that he had met after his victory over the Japanese at the Battle of Khalkin-Gol in autumn 1939. Members of the Politburo were present as well. Stalin opened rather ominously by describing how he had spent a sleepless night following Timoshenko's concluding talk. He cut short Timoshenko's comment that the lecture had been submitted to him in advance: 'You don't really think I have time to read every paper which is tossed at me.' Molotov then proposed that Timoshenko prepare a new directive for the Red Army. This new directive, inspired by the war games that followed shortly, led to the spring mobilization and the deployment of the army on the western front on the eve of the war.[51]

Of the two war games conducted during the first two weeks of January 1941, the second, which has come to light only recently, was the most significant. In this game, as will be discussed in some detail below, Zhukov led the 'Reds' counter-attacking on the south-western front. This had been the scenario most dreaded by Stalin. The eventual build-up and deployment of the troops was derived from the games. When the three operational directives issued on 22–23 June 1941 are carefully scrutinized, it is apparent that they were lifted directly from the war game documents. Indeed, Anfilov, the renowned Russian military historian, concedes that when General Pavlov, commander of the western front, was faced with the German thrust, he took out the 1941 war game papers and tried to make sense of them while preparing his response.[52]

The significance of the war games can hardly be overestimated.[53] They tested the plans which had been diligently worked out beforehand, examining the major theoretical questions of offence and defence in the context of potential external threats. They further comprise an accurate representation of the state of Soviet strategic thinking on the eve of the war. Neither of the two major games presumed a Soviet aggressive or preemptive strike. On the contrary, 'the set-up created for the games', as attested by General Zakharov, 'was marked by dramatic episodes for the eastern side; it very much resembled the events which occurred on our borders in June 1941 following the treacherous attack of the German–Fascist forces on the Soviet Union'.[54]

Both games, therefore, postulated a German offensive on various fronts and explored defensive responses.[55] The first, on 2–6 January, anticipated that the Germans would strike in the central and northern sectors. The main thrust of the 'Blues' (the Germans) was carried out by about 160 divisions under Zhukov's command south of Brest and towards Vladimir-Volynsky and Tarnopol'. A diversionary attack was executed in the north by sixty divisions, aimed at distracting the Reds from the main drive. The force was launched from East Prussia towards Riga and Dvinsk and from the Suwaki and Brest region towards Baranovichi. The Soviet defence was under Pavlov's command. Though the Germans penetrated deep into the Soviet defences, they failed to develop the offensive manoeuvres and the attack petered out. But the alarm was raised when Pavlov was unable to repel the enemy and the game ended inconclusively with the Germans well established inside the Soviet defences.

The second game was wider in scope and was conducted on 8–11 January. Pavlov and Zhukov now changed roles. While the first game focused on a narrow sector comprising the Baltic countries, the second was based on the revised operational plan, assuming that the south-western front and the Balkans would be the main theatre of war. They handled larger battle orders which assumed that the main strike would be delivered in the south, posing a serious threat in the rear. Unlike Pavlov, Zhukov conducted the defence according to the 'deep operations' doctrine; containing the main attack in the south, he inflicted his main strike on the Blue troops, virtually in the rear of the opponent, creating a split between the main German thrust and the rear and causing a major disruption. However, he failed in his subsequent attempts to use the reserve troops to roll up the German offence through manoeuvring, mostly because of the huge space which had to be covered.[56]

The games shook the confidence displayed at the conference and exposed the vulnerability and deficiencies of the defence. The umpires of the games drew unflattering conclusions about the performance of the army:

> The results of the first game demonstrated that the operative–strategic outlook of most of the commanders of the highest level was far from perfect and demanded further painstaking and persistent effort in sharpening the sense of direction and management of large formations, thorough mastering of the character of current operations, their organization and planning, and then executing them in practice.

In view of this harsh judgment Stalin could have had few hopes of conducting a military adventure. The most that might be achieved was that the basic deficiencies of the defence as exposed in the games could be rectified before the Germans moved on to the offensive.[57]

To varying degrees, both games brought about a 'dramatic moment' for the Red forces, resembling the situation which they eventually encountered on 22 June 1941. The senior officers who had participated in the games were about to return to their units when they were summoned to the Kremlin on 13 January. Once again members of the Politburo were present as well. Obviously shaken by the results of the games, Meretskov gave a confused, illogical and inadequate report. Stalin interrupted him halfway through, remarking that in war it was necessary not just 'to do arithmetical calculations but also to take into account the operational art of the commanders'. An attempt by Pavlov to defuse the tension, declaring in a jocular way that the setback to the Reds had happened 'only in war games', made Stalin lose all interest in the rest of his presentation. Meretskov was then subjected to a merciless rebuke by Stalin. 'The trouble', he concluded, 'is that we do not have a proper Chief of Staff,' and he there and then dismissed the stunned Meretskov. The next afternoon, Zhukov was rushed to the Kremlin directly from the war games and informed of the Politburo's decision to appoint him as the Chief of Staff. He assumed his position, after collecting his gear from Kiev, on 31 January, though not before a wide purge of the High Command and the transfer of various senior commanders from command posts.[58] Though Zhukov had been criticized during the conference for his uncritical adherence to the offensive theories, his relative success in the war games and particularly in the crucial south-western wing, together with the prestige he had gained at Khalkin-Gol, seems to have won Stalin's approval. Zhukov was also the only officer present at the meeting who attempted to draw concrete lessons from the games, reviving the modernized operational theory and advocating the establishment of the strongholds (*ukraplenie raiony*, or URs) at some distance from the front, increasing the manoeuvrability of the operational level and preventing a static defensive war.[59] Neither the games nor the military conference succeeded in solving the essential strategic problems that arose once it was recognized that the Soviet Union was already facing the 'most threatening war period'. Specifically, it continued to be assumed that 'defence will essentially play an auxiliary supportive role in the achievement of the designated goals'. Little attention, therefore, was paid to the possibility of fighting a battle to escape an encirclement.[60]

The unpreparedness of the armed forces as revealed by the conference and the war games, coupled with the NKVD reports on the state of the fronts, helps explain Stalin's desperate attempts to postpone the war, and his cautious handling of the deployment in the months preceding the war.[61] Likewise, the resort to diplomacy as the best means of out-manoeuvring Hitler became even more pronounced after the loss of the Balkans. An equally significant factor was the realization that industry could not cope with the new demands at such short notice. An investigation carried out by the NKVD during the war games disclosed that the master plan for the construction of railways had fallen far behind. Nor had the emergency plans ordered by the Red Army's Chief of Staff been fulfilled: no co-ordinated plan existed for the administration of the railways during the first months of the war. The handling of the mobilization plans in this context had not even been discussed, and the railways leading to the front line could not handle more than 30 per cent of the traffic anticipated. In the central sector of Minsk, for instance, no more than 16.7 per cent of the budget allocated for the improvement of the railways had been used. On average less than 12 per cent of the plans for the expansion of the railways had been accomplished. Heavy tanks had to be transferred to the front on 60-ton platforms; only 387 such platforms were available, and not a single one had been constructed in 1940. Only about 50 per cent of supplies indispensable for the construction of an adequate transport system to the front, such as rails, telegraph posts and railway sleepers, were available. Finally, the alarm was sounded that work on the Baltic mobilization system had 'not even started'.[62] Intensive measures were indeed taken by the SNK to give a boost to the 'production of defensive materials' throughout 1941, placing great emphasis on the construction of new industrial complexes which could cater for the new demands.[63]

The Gathering Clouds

Contrary to the prevailing view, the Soviet intelligence community preceded its Western counterparts in providing precise and accurate information on German intentions at the end of 1940.[64] The rapid pace of events in the closing months of 1940 gave way to a temporary lull in early 1941. This was partly a result of the suspension of the diplomatic dialogue with Germany. On the military side it reflected the fact that winter conditions prevented major troop movements, giving rise to speculation.

But the lull did not lead to complacency. The recognition of the imminent danger and the need to combat it effectively by improved intelligence and counter-intelligence led to a major reform of the security services in early February. The Ministry of the Interior was divided: the NKVD was entrusted with interior affairs while the NKGB focused on external issues.[65] Merkulov, the newly appointed director of the NKGB, was quick to draw Stalin's attention to the fact that the German High Command was 'pursuing systematic preparations for a war against the

Soviet Union'. A briefing of senior German officers, with the aid of operational maps, revealed that the intention was to detach the European part of the USSR from Leningrad to the Black Sea and to establish there a state with a government friendly to Germany. The war aimed at ensuring complete control of the industrial centres of Russia.[66] The general report was backed up by numerous items of strategic intelligence. A typical case was the report of a visit paid by an Obergruppenführer, wearing the Iron Cross, to a doctor in Bucharest. Once loosened up he confided that the plans for an attack on England had been abandoned. The German army, he explained, consisted of 10 million drafted men who were 'bored' and longing for battle. The war machine could not remain 'unemployed'. He then unfolded the plans:

> We shall march through the Ukraine and the Baltic regions. The entire continent of Europe will fall under our influence. The Bolsheviks will have no space but beyond the Urals; the Führer has decided to strike and free Europe from the enemies of today and tomorrow. Our campaign against Russia will be a military walkover. Governors of Odessa, Kiev and other major cities have already been appointed.[67]

From Berlin 'Starshina' warned that air surveillance of the Soviet Union 'was proceeding at a full pace'. The planes, taking off from Bucharest, Königsberg and Kirkenes, were covering the entire length of the border. The photographs were collated in the Intelligence Department of the air force. The possibility of Russian resistance was dismissed out of hand, and the common belief was that the Red Army would collapse within eight days. Stalin's continued focus on his south-western borders was fully justified, as most of the information indicated Hitler's intention of depriving Russia of her economic and industrial basis in the Ukraine. Once the Ukraine collapsed, the Wehrmacht was expected to move into the Caucasus and northwards towards the Ural Mountains, completing the operation within twenty-five days.[68] The appreciation vindicated 'Corsicanets', who had concluded that Halder was confident of a 'lightning seizure' of the Ukraine and considered the capture of the Baku oil industries intact to be a 'light task'. Moreover, a four-year planning committee had been instructed to prepare a list of the economic resources which Germany might gain from an occupation of European Russia.[69]

The still vague strategic intelligence was more than compensated for by concrete operational information. The GRU adhered to the view that the German High Command was 'continuing with great intensity the work on the engineering preparations of the war theatre against the USSR and on the replacement of old units with increasingly fresh ones'. It was now estimated that the reorganization of the Wehrmacht would substantially augment the German war machine to 250–60 infantry divisions, twenty tank divisions and fifteen motorized ones.[70] In mid-February, Kobulov, the Berlin resident of the NKGB, dispatched a special intelligence report which was circulated to the Politburo and the Central Committee. It revealed the strenuous efforts of the Wehrmacht to increase the army to eight million men by recruiting and mobilizing the resources of the occupied territories: over a short period twenty-five new infantry divisions, five tank divisions and five motorized divisions had been created. Similar trends were discerned in all the countries bordering Germany. The report warned that with the approach of spring Russia would encounter strong measures of mobilization on all fronts, leading to the expansion of the armies along the border.[71]

In mid-March, Golikov sent Stalin a most alarming report, this time focusing on Germany's industrial potential, which raised the possibility that she might be able to conduct war on two fronts simultaneously. Golikov was now daily receiving disturbing reports in this vein from his attachés in various capitals. The emphasis placed on the economic side of the campaign in these reports, did not, however, detract from their political significance. The military attaché in Bucharest, for instance, reported that a German major had told a friend: 'We have completely altered our plans. We aim at the East, at the USSR. We shall seize the Soviet grain, coal and oil. We shall then be invincible and will be able to continue the war against England and the United States.' The Wehrmacht appeared to be synchronizing the attack on the Soviet Union with the Rumanian army, scheduling its commencement for within three months.[72]

The reports by Golikov continued to depict in sombre colours the reorganization and expansion of the German armed forces during the winter months. Since September 1940, he warned, the number of infantry divisions had increased from 228 to 263. Five new tank divisions had been added to the fifteen in existence while five motorized divisions had been added to the previous ten. He then provided exact figures on their allocation within the various units, adding illuminating tables to drive home the message. He found the increase to be noteworthy, bearing in mind that during the Battle of France the Germans had had only two or three tank divisions. Golikov further warned of the large strides taken by the Luftwaffe in the development and production of new types of aircraft. Here too a minutely detailed table exhibited the improvements and innovations introduced to aircraft such as the Heinkel N-113, the Focke-Wulf FB-187 and 198 and the Messerschmitt 'Jaguar'. Golikov overestimated the German production capabilities, expecting them to release some 25,000–30,000 planes within a year. He also expected the German air force to produce bombers with a range of 1,700–2,000 kilometres, able to fly at an altitude of 6,000–7,000 metres and at a speed of 750 k.m.h. Further ominous information indicated that the Germans had accelerated the production of the advanced Mark VII tanks and had improved the heavy ones seized by the Germans in France. Equally horrifying was the minute description of the development of chemical warfare, to the extent that 'the military chemical industry can envisage the mass usage of gas at any moment'.[73]

Shortly afterwards the NKVD informed the government (usually a euphemism for Stalin and Molotov and occasionally the Politburo) and the Central Committee that information obtained from within the German headquarters revealed that Halder did not expect any difficulties in overpowering the Russians. The report attributed the anticipated campaign to the need for raw materials, which Germany hoped to derive from the Ukraine. Such reports are particularly striking when compared with the general and circumstantial nature of the information available to British intelligence at the time, dwarfing the significance of Churchill's warning:[74]

The Chief of Staff of the Ground Forces, Lt.-Gen. Halder, predicts certain success and the swift occupation by German forces of the Soviet Union, and above all of the Ukraine, where according to Halder's estimate successful operations will be facilitated by the better condition of the railways and roads. Halder also sees as an easy task the occupation of Baku and its oil industry, which the German will apparently be able to restore quickly following war damage. Halder feels that the Red Army will not be in a position to put up any serious resistance to a lightning attack by German forces and will not even be successful in destroying their stores.

The estimates of Col. Bekker, on the other hand, underline the enormous economic effect that will be achieved as a result of military operations against the USSR.[75]

Concurrently counter-intelligence reported a significant rise in the rumours indicating that a German offensive against Russia might indeed precede the subjugation of Britain. Cripps was quoted as having received such assurances from General John Dill, the Chief of the Imperial General Staff, and Eden during his visit to Ankara.[76] When the focus of attention shifted to South-eastern Europe, military attachés in the Balkans confirmed that the Germans had decided to postpone the attack on the British Isles and together with Hungary, Rumania and Bulgaria to seize the Ukraine and push towards Baku in April–May.[77] A German informant disclosed in Bucharest that Hitler, backed by a vast military machine craving action, was determined 'to strike and liberate Europe from today's foes. Our advance into Russia will be a military stroll.' He dismissed out of hand the suggestion that Hitler was determined to avoid a war on two fronts and mocked the idea that he was committed to friendship between the two countries: 'That is how it was before, but now we do not have two fronts. Now the situation has changed. We will smash the English little by little with air power and submarines. England is no longer a front.'[78] So far as the nature of the blow was concerned, information originating from the Luftwaffe staff suggested that the Germans might launch an air strike at the end of April or beginning of May.[79]

The trickle of operational intelligence turned into a flood in mid-March, reflecting the German encroachment into the Balkans in preparation for Operation 'Marita'. The intelligence reinforced the Soviet obsession with the threat they faced in the south-western theatre. Stalin seems to have been entirely overwhelmed by the events unfolding in the south, which he undoubtedly hoped would pin Hitler down. A largely accurate assessment of the German build-up in the Balkans reached Moscow in mid-March. It depicted the intensity of the process, which had caused severe traffic congestion.

It would be wrong to assume, however, that the corresponding build-up on Russia's western borders was overlooked. The reports continued to depict, though laconically, the concentration there of some 100 divisions.[80] From Berlin Stalin was informed that the Luftwaffe had speeded up its consolidation in the eastern arena. Sources close to the General Staff disclosed that 'the decision has been taken by the Germans to take military action against the Soviet Union in the spring of this year. The Germans are counting on the fact that the Red Army will be routed and will not be in a position to destroy the grain.'[81] Reports from Paris revealed that the infantry had been transferred to the East and replaced by inexperienced troops.[82] The move was corroborated by reports from Vichy of the transfer of infantry and tank divisions, which had been earmarked to participate in the invasion of Britain, from northern France to Rumania and Bulgaria.[83] Just as alarming was a report from Vienna that General Antonescu had discussed with Göring the possible participation of Rumania in a German offensive against the USSR.[84]

An easy judgment would therefore be to present Stalin, as Churchill does in his memoirs, as a 'simpleton'. However, although much of the data conveyed a fairly coherent picture of the German menace, a supplementary body of evidence, while not dismissing the danger, questioned the inevitability of war and raised various scenarios relating to the conditions in which such a war would erupt. The all too familiar human flaw of intelligence now came into play; the information was either tailored to confirm the views held at the top, or was presented in an ambiguous way so as to accommodate political expectations through selective reading. The yardstick for both was the overbearing fear of a premature and unnecessary embroilment in the Balkans.

The 'war season' opened in spring 1941 with Hitler's engagements in the Balkans, which *a priori* confirmed the assumption that war against the Soviet Union was 'unthinkable prior to the defeat of England'.[85] Such an appraisal did not follow strategic logic but rather fell prey to Hitler's intensive disinformation campaign diverting attention from the regrouping of the troops, paralleled by the resumption of air raids on London.[86] As was most aptly put by the Soviet military attaché in Budapest, the rumours of war were 'fabricated' by British propaganda. For Germany the war with England was 'ample', and she was only 'interested in peaceful economic relations with the Soviet Union'.[87]

In presenting his fortnightly report on 20 March Golikov promptly set the tone for the Kremlin's evaluation: 'The majority of the intelligence reports which indicate the likelihood of war with the Soviet Union in spring 1941 emerge from Anglo-American sources, the immediate purpose of which is undoubtedly to seek the worsening of relations between the USSR and Germany.' He now presented, without further commentary, sixteen reports which he thought deserved 'special attention'. These, however, were heavily edited to conform with what he believed to be Stalin's preconceptions. The almost axiomatic assumption of the summarized reports was the belief that Germany would not launch an attack on Russia before England was defeated. Some focused on a struggle presumed to be taking place within the German leadership on the issue of war.[88] The long report played down information concerning the actual German plans for the campaign, as it was assumed that war could still be averted or at least postponed by diplomatic means. On the whole it corresponded to the evaluation which had directed the war games in January. The only marked divergence was fresh information gleaned from Swedish sources in Berlin, which later proved to be totally accurate. Its reliability, however, appeared suspect, coming as it did from Cripps.[89] It actually depicted with great precision the three thrusts along the entire front, with the focus now moving to the centre, even naming the commanders in charge and pinpointing the date of the attack to 20 May (Hitler was later forced to revise the date because of the Balkan diversion and delays in the deployment). But Golikov gave more prominence to 'other sources' which assumed that Germany would attack the Soviet Union only 'after the victory over England', striking from two directions, in the north, probably from Finland, and from the Balkans. Golikov did take some precautions, mentioning the dissonant views from Rumania that Hitler had actually changed his plans and intended to attack the Soviet Union before completing the campaign against England, as the front in the West had virtually ceased to exist. However, one should not place too much weight on this digression, which paled in comparison with the fact that the entire document was summed up with the definite conclusion that 'the opening of hostilities against the Soviet

Union will occur in the wake of the victory over England or after the conclusion with her of a peace advantageous to Germany'. Even more insidious was the firm assessment that 'rumours and documents suggesting the inevitability of war against the Soviet Union this spring should be evaluated as disinformation, emanating from the British and also possibly from German intelligence'.[90] These, then, were the prevalent views in Moscow as the curtain fell on Yugoslavia in early April, demonstrating even more starkly the threat of war.

7

At the Crossroads:
The Yugoslav Coup d'Etat

Following his usual custom, Hitler diverted his attention to Yugoslavia as soon as Bulgaria fell in his net. In the spring of 1941 control of Yugoslavia became crucial for his operational plans: the country was destined to provide a shield against Russia on the left wing in the forthcoming campaign in Greece and the right wing in Operation 'Barbarossa'. This was dictated by the exigencies of Operation 'Marita', the occupation of Greece. The build-up had fallen behind schedule and the transfer of troops via Yugoslavia was critical if Operation 'Barbarossa' was to be embarked upon in early summer. Control of Yugoslavia was expected to shorten the length of the campaign by allowing a rapid occupation of Saloniki, thus keeping Operation 'Barbarossa' more or less on schedule.[1]

Milan Gavrilović, the leftist leader of the Serbian Agrarian Party, arrived in Moscow in June 1940, shortly after the fall of France, eager to enlist Soviet support in detaching the Regent Prince Paul from Germany. During his first visit to the Russian Foreign Ministry he went as far as to advocate the creation of a Balkan Union governed by Slavophile ideas, in which the Russian language would replace the diverse Slavic dialects. In his memoirs General Sudoplatov, the deputy director of Foreign Intelligence, claims that together with Fedotov, the director of Counter-Intelligence, he 'formally recruited' Gavrilović as an agent.[2] Whether or not this is true, Gavrilović certainly co-operated closely with the Kremlin, though he was suspected from the outset of conniving with Cripps to embroil Russia in war with Germany.

Because of their fear of provocation the Russians at first ostentatiously confined their conversations with Gavrilović to 'ethnography, geography, literature, art, linguistics and a historical debate on the origins of the Serbian people'.[3] Virtually in exile and estranged from his own Foreign

Ministry, Gavrilović gradually inspired the Russians to seek the support of the Yugoslav military, which disapproved of the government's veering towards Germany. Clandestine talks were indeed initiated in Paris at the end of September 1940;[4] the Yugoslav Chief of Staff wasted little time in submitting his shopping list. In an unprecedented move the newly appointed Yugoslav military attaché was received by Marshal Timoshenko, the Defence Minister, and the Chief of Staff General Meretskov.[5] After the fiasco of Molotov's visit to Berlin, the offer of armaments assumed a more concrete form. Lieutenant-Colonel Bozhina Simić, who had fought with the Red Army during the Civil War, was selected to lead a military mission to Moscow. Reports from the Soviet mission in Belgrade testified that 'in parades and in the barracks, the officers are openly singing our military songs in praise of Stalin'.[6] Feelers were also made through the Yugoslav embassy in Ankara. The German guarantees to Rumania had certainly brought the two countries together by barring Soviet movement into the Balkans, now placed under total German domination.[7]

Hitler, however, took swift measures to nip Soviet influence in Yugoslavia in the bud. Shortly after Molotov's visit to Berlin Cincar-Marković, the Yugoslav Foreign Minister, followed the well-worn path trodden by the other Balkan leaders to Berchtesgaden, where he was warned by Hitler of Russia's Pan-Slavic ambitions, 'borrowed from the testaments of Peter the Great and the Empress Catherine'.[8] By then, however, Yugoslavia's subservience to Germany had been determined, as the German minister in Belgrade informed Berlin, by the 'unqualified recognition of Germany's military supremacy on the Continent, and growing realization of the senselessness of Russophile tendencies'.[9] For the time being Hitler's wish to harness Yugoslavia to the Tripartite Pact was frustrated by the fear of her armed forces that Yugoslavia would be used as a springboard for the invasion of Greece.[10] The split between the military and the politicians was to play a major role in Yugoslavia's relations with Russia following the dramatic coup in March 1941.

The continued drift of the Yugoslav government towards Germany in early 1941 led the Russians to stall the armaments transaction. To avoid provocation which might lead to a collision with Germany, Molotov cautioned Soviet diplomats in Belgrade against British and German attempts to 'draw them into conversations which might later give them a basis for speculation making use of the Soviet Union in their own interests'.[11] The harsh measures taken in Belgrade against 'communist subversion' and the expulsion of the Tass correspondent there did little to ease the atmosphere.[12]

With time running short for Hitler after Bulgaria's entry into the Axis, the Yugoslav Prime Minister Cvetković was ordered to Berchtesgaden together with Cincar-Marković. Cvetković, in the now predictable pattern, tried in vain to defer a decision on joining the Axis by pointing out the Soviet concern and exploiting the increasing Soviet–German tension. Ribbentrop not only dismissed such suggestions but assured his guests that Stalin was 'a sensible, clear-thinking man' who knew perfectly well that a conflict with Germany would 'lead to the destruction of his regime and his country'. Hitler cunningly discouraged Cvetković from playing the Russian card by disclosing to him that in Berlin Molotov had offered Bulgaria territorial changes at Yugoslavia's expense. By the end of the visit the scene was set for a meeting of Hitler with Prince Paul, who was also subjected to Hitler's regular mixture of threats and cajoling.[13]

The diplomatic game, at which Stalin had so far excelled, was faltering in early 1941. With Rumania and Bulgaria already orbiting Germany, Yugoslavia alone stood between Russia and Germany in the Balkans. Stalin had been carefully monitoring the strategic debate in London concerning British assistance to Greece. It did not escape him that on their own the British could not possibly reactivate the Balkans against the 'unemployed German army'. Eden, for instance, had been inciting Maisky, warning that Yugoslavia's drift to Germany and 'the loss of Salonika would be a threat to the Straits, in the future of which Russia had a historic interest'. Stalin therefore had become increasingly obsessed with what he conceived to be a British scheme to lead Russia into a pre-mature confrontation with the Germans in the Balkans. Moreover, by focusing his attention on the British and the Yugoslavs he underrated the real danger lurking around the corner.[14]

Stalin had been informed about the guarantees which Hitler was offering Yugoslavia in return for joining the Axis. As he expected the Yugoslav politicians and court to yield to the pressure, he attributed the forthcoming visit to Moscow of the military delegation headed by Simić to a British plot.[15] Moreover, the popular sympathy for Russia in Yugoslavia seemed to be effectively checked by Prince Paul's pro-British sentiments and Cincar-Marković's pro-German leanings. Gavrilović's proposals for co-operation were dismissed therefore as feelers 'of an exploratory nature'; after all, his standing with the Yugoslav government was poor while his skills in diplomacy were said to be 'confined at best to playing chess'.[16] Within the Cabinet Tupanjanin, deputy leader of the Agrarian Party, himself on the NKVD's payroll, questioned the sincerity of the Yugoslav initiative, as the two countries had 'only just got on to nodding terms'.[17]

In the meantime Stalin was briefed by 'Sophocles', the military attaché in Belgrade, about Prince Paul's agreement to join the Axis during his meeting with Hitler in early March. Reliable sources in the palace revealed that, in an attempt to discourage the Yugoslavs from playing the Russian card, Hitler had disclosed to the Prince his intentions of abandoning the plans for war against England in favour of seizing the Ukraine and Baku in April–May. But equally significant was the disclosure by 'Sophocles' that 'the real power in Yugoslavia now lies in the hands of the General Staff, without whom the Council of Ministers will undertake nothing'.[18] The apparent defiance of the government by the armed forces raised new hopes. These were reinforced by Simiç's attitude in his secret talks at the Ministry of Defence, where he favourably considered co-operation to counter the German threat. Moreover, suspicion of England was somewhat alleviated by the Yugoslav refusal to allow Eden and General Dill to visit Belgrade, which indicated their intention of 'holding the scales even'.[19] The German ambassador himself forewarned the Wilhelmstrasse that the Yugoslav government was sitting in continuous session, 'and not for drinking coffee'.[20]

As in the Bulgarian case, Soviet efforts were directed towards the mobilization of popular support in Belgrade; this was done both through diplomatic channels and through the Comintern. Lebedev, the Soviet ambassador in Yugoslavia, was charged with exposing the insincerity of the Yugoslav government's overtures to Russia, which concealed the German–Yugoslav activities 'behind the scene'.[21] Tito, the leader of the Yugoslav Communist Party, was instructed 'to mobilize the Party against the capitulation to the Germans. Support the movement for a mass opposition to the incursion of the German military into Yugoslavia. Demand friendship with the Soviet Union.'[22] Public opinion was moulded in Belgrade to press the government to make concrete propositions. Concurrently, Tupanjanin, following instructions from Moscow, leaked information on the forthcoming negotiations with the military. Gavriloviç exerted direct pressure on Cincar-Markoviç, pointing to the severe domestic repercussions which the failure of the negotiations might have. He tried to lure the Prime Minister, suggesting that if proposals made by the government were eventually rejected in Moscow the people would then blame the Russians and not the government at home. He further suggested that the government would be exonerated if the Russians were to agree in principle but impose harsh conditions and drag out the negotiations. But it seems that his main objective in setting the negotiations in motion was to put the Russians to the test: to find out to what extent the manifest discontent of the Soviet military with the Germans was endorsed by the Kremlin.[23]

The British Foreign Office was not far off the mark in suspecting Stalin of 'playing with Yugoslavia . . . in order to impress Hitler with a view to extracting better conditions from him'.[24] The military negotiations in Moscow were marked by the Soviet resolve to establish a military alliance which would restore the equilibrium with Germany and force Hitler to the negotiating table.[25] There is a certain similarity to the motives which had led Chamberlain to guarantee Poland after the German occupation of Prague in March 1939. Both sides, however, acted prudently. Stalin, perhaps in a mirror image, continued to suspect the Yugoslavs of using the negotiations with the Russians as a card in their negotiations with the Germans, and the British of trying to ensnare Russia in war. He was fully aware of Eden's efforts during his prolonged tour of the Middle East to form a defensive bloc of Turkey, Greece and Yugoslavia.[26]

This was only aggravated by Cripps's unceasing attempts to alert the Russians to the German danger. Unaware that the die had been cast by Prince Paul, Cripps pursued his attempts to enlist Russia's help. Already during his consultations with Vinogradov in Ankara he had suggested that the Germans might carry out their advance against Greece through Yugoslavia. He did not exclude the possibility that the Yugoslav army, which was 'not bad', might even give assistance to Britain. He was of course hoping to give Eden's idea of a Balkan bloc a new lease of life. Cripps suggested that England take part in the clandestine military talks under way in Moscow, the existence of which Vinogradov of course would not admit.[27] Shortly after his return from Turkey, Cripps indeed found out from Gavrilović that Simiç's talks had revealed that the military authorities in Moscow were 'most anxious' to reach a military agreement with Yugoslavia.[28]

Cripps sprang into action as soon as news of the Regent's decision to join the Tripartite Pact reached the embassy in the afternoon of 22 March 1941. He depicted the German objectives to Vyshinsky in sombre colours, as had become his habit. Vyshinsky, who received the news 'very seriously', promised to communicate with his government. Cripps did not stop there, sending Gavrilović to Vyshinsky with a proposal to issue a communiqué which would repudiate the common belief that the Soviet Union was 'abandoning the Balkans and Yugoslavia to Germany's sphere of interests'.[29] Cripps's zeal did little but invigorate Stalin's suspicion of a British plot. On Cripps's return to the Kremlin in the evening, expecting to continue the 'friendly discussion', he was snubbed by Vyshinsky when he started elaborating the obstacles to German designs in the Balkans if Yugoslavia were to be encouraged by the Russians to preserve her independence. Vyshinsky also chose this moment to produce a catalogue of supposedly hostile British acts against Moscow.[30] Gavrilović himself was recalled to the Foreign Ministry at midnight, where he found Vyshinsky to be 'obviously anxious and sympathetic but also afraid'. Vyshinsky seemed to fear that the efforts to induce Russia to intervene after the irreversible decision had been taken by Yugoslavia were a trap.[31]

German disinformation convinced Stalin of the wisdom of his policies. In Ankara, Papen, the German ambassador, strongly denied the rumours of German intentions to use Yugoslavia as a springboard to occupy the Straits. He went further to mollify the Russians, suggesting that the association with Yugoslavia was exclusively aimed at checking the British in the Balkans and the Black Sea, and that Germany could 'win the war only if it went hand in hand with the Russians'.[32]

The cards, however, were reshuffled on 27 March; General Sushan Simović, the commander of the Yugoslav air force, executed a bloodless coup in Belgrade with the support of the armed forces. Prince Paul was deposed and exiled while the young King Peter was installed on the throne. To close observers it was patently clear that the coup came as a surprise in Moscow. There could hardly be a 'covert or overt' Soviet involvement in a coup orchestrated by the British Special Operations Executive. Although General Solomon Milstein, deputy director of the GRU, accompanied by a few 'illegals' had been especially sent to Belgrade, his task in the affair, if any, was confined to monitoring 'British plots'.[33]

Despite his excellent sources, Stalin had not been privy to Hitler's harsh and irrevocable decision to 'smash Yugoslavia militarily and as a state', even if Operation 'Barbarossa' had to be postponed by four weeks. Hitler, however, faced a surprise as well, since he assumed that Russia would not react.[34] Stalin found it increasingly difficult not to be swayed by the popular support enjoyed by the insurgents. The Yugoslav government were at a loss in their attempts to curb the widespread demonstrations against the pact. The Soviet ambassador could hardly hide his excitement in reporting home that 'the entire population of Belgrade swarmed the streets, waving the national flags' and was allowed to 'openly express its feelings'. Moreover, the masses seemed to be pinning their hopes on the Soviet Union. The association with Moscow, Lebedev commented, was related to expectations of an 'abrogation of the shameful pact with the Axis and in particular with hated Germany . . . From the early hours of the morning thousands of people had been gathering in front of the Soviet embassy raising banners calling for an "Alliance with the Soviet Union!"' Later on the demonstrators moved to the neighbouring German embassy, shouting hostile slogans and breaking the windows of the German tourist bureau. The numbers of demonstrators 'increased so markedly that by the evening the crowds could no longer reach the embassy but they continued to call for an "Alliance with the Soviet Union!"'[35]

Further reports reflected the bitter criticism of the government's pro-German policies. The army was being mobilized when the Yugoslav delegation returned from Vienna in disguise, avoiding Belgrade's main railway station. Carried away by the defiant spirit of Belgrade, Lebedev rather prematurely supposed that the coup had brought an end to the extensive German political presence in Yugoslavia; he already cherished the hope that it would lead to a dramatic reversal of the political trend not only in the Balkan States but over the entire European Continent.[36]

The impression was corroborated by General Golikov, the director of Military Intelligence. He too emphasized the pro-Soviet nature of the demonstrations, which were dominated by slogans such as 'For a union with the Soviet Union' and 'To the health of Stalin and Molotov'. He now expected the army to reject the secret clauses of the agreement, which granted German troops free passage in the south of the country, and did not exclude the possibility that Yugoslavia might withdraw from the Axis. His appreciation that the forty-eight divisions just mobilized were determined and competent to thwart a German invasion certainly enjoyed the support of the Chief of Staff.[37]

Though undoubtedly relieved, Stalin was not quick to display the brazen military defiance of Germany that is commonly portrayed in the literature. He remained cautious, as it was an open secret that the coup had not brought about a full reversal of Yugoslav policies. After assuming power Simoviç informed the King of his intention of adhering to the Axis. He was quick to reassure the German ambassador that Yugoslavia stood for 'continued co-operation with the Axis Powers, particularly with Germany', and a 'return as far as possible to a policy of neutrality'.[38] Stalin's limited objective remained therefore to manipulate the surge of popular support as a means of deterring Hitler from spreading the war, and the British from exploiting the volatile situation. In the absence of a direct dialogue with the Belgrade government prior to the coup, Russian attempts to inhibit Yugoslavia from joining the Axis were conducted through the Communist Party. In the new circumstances urgent steps were taken to dampen popular enthusiasm. Dimitrov, the President of the Comintern, was promptly instructed by Molotov to call off street demonstrations which, he feared, might be 'exploited by the British as well as by the domestic reactionaries'.[39] Tito was instructed to watch over 'the unruly British warmongers and Great Serbian chauvinists, who are pushing the country into military slaughter by their provocations'. Stalin clearly hoped to redress the shifting balance of power by preserving Yugoslavia's sovereignty, preventing her from becoming 'ammunition in the hands of the British imperialists as well as . . . the slaves of the German and Italian aggressors'.[40]

In the meantime Gavriloviç's standing in Moscow was enhanced by his appointment to a ministerial post in the newly formed Cabinet. By sheer chance his departure home, in protest against the signature of the pact, had been prevented by bad weather.[41] As soon as the new regime had established itself Simoviç sent the Russians an oral offer of a mutual assistance pact which was tantamount to a 'real alliance'. A stronger appeal was made the same evening by the new Defence Minister in a clandestine meeting with the Soviet ambassador which took place at his own lodgings. Iliç reiterated his intention of establishing 'full political and military co-operation with the Soviet Union'; he pledged the army's resolve to 'resist to the end' a German invasion. The breach between the government and the armed forces seemed to be growing.[42]

On 31 March a landslide of intelligence reports, including a major one by Merkulov corroborating an alarming report by Golikov about the possibility of war, arrived on Stalin's desk.[43] The pressure from the Ministry of Defence to pursue the Yugoslav negotiations increased. In the early hours of the following day, Lebedev arrived at Simoviç's apartment accompanied by Sukhonin, the military attaché, and a translator. He informed the Prime Minister that Molotov had just accepted the offer of a pact and wished a delegation to proceed swiftly to Moscow to conclude the agreement. Simoviç wasted no time in telephoning Ninciç, his Foreign Minister, instructing him to appoint Gavriloviç as the head of the delegation so that negotiations could start even before the arrival of its other members.[44]

When Lebedev met Ninciç the next morning, he gained the impression that the Cabinet was split. He suspected that in a last-ditch attempt to avert the conflict the Yugoslav government wished to use the Soviet leverage in Berlin. Somewhat naively, they anticipated that Hitler would leave Yugoslavia alone if Stalin were to notify him that 'the Soviet Union had immense sympathy towards the Yugoslav people'. On the other hand, the fact that the Cabinet was determined to resist the British pressure to open a new front in the Balkans certainly put Stalin's mind at rest.[45] In Moscow feelings were mixed about the possibilities raised by the coup. Timoshenko seemed to entertain high hopes of the Yugoslavs' ability to resist a German invasion, while Stalin perceived a limited agreement as a card in his complex diplomatic game. Maintaining Russia's neutrality and achieving recognition of her spheres of interests remained his prime aim. The limited objectives were reflected even in Zhdanov's guidance to the Comintern. 'The Balkan events', he stated, 'do not alter the general situation . . . We do not endorse the German expansion into the Balkans. This does not mean that we withdraw from the pact with Germany and stand by England.'[46] The coup offered a heaven-sent opportunity of deferring confrontation with Germany: a prudent agreement with the Yugoslavs might deter Hitler and lead him to the negotiating table. If, however, hostilities were to break out, Russia could still adhere to neutrality while ensuring that the Yugoslavs tied down the Wehrmacht for two months or more, thus postponing the war with Russia for at least a year. This explains the Soviet offer of munitions and supplies to Yugoslavia before the magnitude of the defeat had become apparent.[47] Thus the parameters for the negotiations were established prior to the arrival of the Yugoslav delegation in Moscow. They were subordinated to the common wish of both governments to avert war rather than mount effective resistance to Hitler. Far from annulling the agreement with Germany, efforts were made to modify it to 'conform with Yugoslav interests'.[48]

In the meantime hasty arrangements were made for the Yugoslav delegation to reach Moscow via Istanbul. However, visa formalities absorbed an entire morning and the two officers were able to start their journey aboard a special plane only around midday on 2 April. Torn between their wish to react and fear of provocation, the Russians asked for the identifying marks to be removed from the plane to prevent its recognition. After a flight from Belgrade over Saloniki to Istanbul, the delegates were diverted by an incomprehensible mistake to Ankara. A short delay occurred before they could proceed to Odessa, finally landing in Moscow in the early afternoon of 4 April.[49]

Stalin had hoped that a mere demonstration of solidarity with Yugoslavia would suffice to inhibit Hitler from attacking her. While the delegation was on its way the situation had altered dramatically. An increasing flow of ominous intelligence unveiling the offensive German deployment on their borders led the Yugoslavs to raise the stakes by seeking a full military–political alliance with Russia. Naturally the proposal had to be brought before Stalin, but Vyshinsky had little doubt that 'it was scarcely expedient to sign such agreements'. It was better for the Yugoslavs to watch out for provocations, whether British or German, while displaying a show of force, as 'the independence of a country was best protected by a strong army'. Gavriloviç insisted, however, that his government 'firmly wished and expected an alliance with the Soviet Union'.[50] Indeed, Lebedev was summoned by the Prime Minister and confronted with a *fait accompli*: the Yugoslav government regarded the agreement as 'already in existence even if in practice it may have not yet been signed'. Simoviç counted on Stalin to present 'a strong Soviet démarche in Berlin to stop a German intervention, or in any case provide Yugoslavia with time to complete the mobilization'. As the outbreak of hostilities could no longer be ruled out, the Russians were invited to place troops and munitions in Yugoslavia. To goad Stalin into action Simoviç even parted with fresh information obtained from Prince Paul, who had been told by Hitler during their recent meeting about his intention of attacking Russia.[51]

The dilemma facing Stalin became acute during 2–4 April in view of a flow of startling intelligence. From inside Göring's headquarters the agent 'Corsicanets' revealed that events in Yugoslavia were taken 'most seriously' by the military. The Luftwaffe staff was 'conducting active preparations for actions against Yugoslavia', which he expected to occur imminently. The extensive campaign had even led them 'provisionally' to abandon the preparations against Russia. He further raised expectations in Moscow by suggesting that the Luftwaffe staff feared that the campaign might last three or four weeks, 'delay the attack on the Soviet Union and even threaten to miss the opportune moment for action against the Soviet Union'.[52] From Belgrade 'Sophocles' suggested that the

Germans were applying psychological pressure on the Yugoslavs to discourage them from further association with Russia. The Yugoslavs were informed of Hitler's intention to 'start a war with the Soviet Union in May and within 7 days reach Moscow'. Their military attaché in Berlin gleaned the information that the offensive would be conducted by three army groups, under Field Marshals Rundstedt, List and Beck, which eventually turned out to be the precise German plan. However, Stalin's tactics could still be defended, as the report assumed that an offensive would be preceded by an ultimatum to the Soviet Union to join the Axis and to offer economic concessions. It was now vital not to make any false move.[53]

Negotiations with the Yugoslav mission were opened under the shadow of these reports in the early afternoon of 4 April. It was now apparent that the Russians were utterly opposed to the idea of a military alliance which the Germans were bound to perceive as a blatant provocation. They clung to the feeble technical excuse that such an agreement required 'a serious mutual examination of the forces available for such an arrangement'. Instead they opted for a treaty of friendship and non-aggression. To test the water Molotov informed Schulenburg, as the clauses of the Ribbentrop–Molotov Pact required, of the decision to sign such a pact. Schulenburg's report home deliberately glossed over the dramatic tenor of the conversation. The turn of events in Yugoslavia now threatened to jeopardize his efforts to enthrone Hitler as the modern Bismarck. In his earlier reports Schulenburg had dismissed the rumours of Soviet military intervention as an 'evil Yugoslav intrigue'.[54] Hoping to dissuade the Russians from proceeding with the negotiations, he warned that the proximity of the agreement to the events in Belgrade might 'create an undesirable impression in Berlin'. Molotov sought to emphasize the limits of the agreement, which 'was not even as far-reaching as the German–Yugoslav Treaty', and implied the continued adherence of the Yugoslavs to the Axis.

The Russian records, however, reveal the intense and sour tone which characterized the meeting. Schulenburg apparently warned Molotov that the violent demonstrations in Belgrade against Germany were bound to be viewed in Berlin as a 'hostile act'. He dropped strong hints about German intentions, expressing his doubts about the validity of the Yugoslav–German Pact, whose signatories had already been imprisoned in Belgrade. Molotov's vehement attempts to defend the Russians' own agreement, which had been arrived at 'after prolonged deliberations' and aimed at maintaining good relations with Germany, fell on deaf ears. Schulenburg could only 'hope that Molotov and not he was right'. To his colleagues he expressed the fear that this time the Soviet protest went 'too far'. The news of his imminent departure to Berlin for consultations could of course be taken either as a sign that the new policy of containment was producing results or, more likely, as a warning that relations were steadily deteriorating.[55]

As a precautionary measure Vyshinsky prompted Gavrilović to put Schulenburg's mind at rest. But their meeting further revealed the inaccuracy of the Kremlin's evaluation. Assuming that Hitler had not been 'receiving sufficient and reliable information from his closest associates about the situation',[56] Gavrilović used his new ministerial position to insist that the message reach the German leader personally. Gavrilović spared no effort to admonish the Germans for the force employed in coercing the Yugoslavs to adhere to the Axis. It was 'too much', he protested, 'to ask from the people, that you regard as being a lower race, and who have a serious debt to the Allies, not only to abandon their neutrality, which we wish to keep, but to help you to fight precisely those Allies and love you'. But the personal message to Hitler dovetailed with the Soviet position. While reaffirming the commitment to the Axis, he nonetheless demanded that the pact should not 'harm Yugoslavia's vital interests and honour'. He ended with a warning 'against committing larger mistakes than the first one. We shall fight with the courage of desperation for every inch of our territory and to the last soldier. We do not claim that we shall be able to defeat Germany but soon enough we shall put Germany and Italy in a very difficult situation.' Gavrilović made a similar approach to Rosso, expecting Mussolini 'to use his influence on Berlin to avoid a clash that will be very serious for both countries'.[57]

The negotiations had become so delicate that telegrams between Moscow and Belgrade were now shown only to Stalin and Molotov personally, while Vyshinsky, in charge of the negotiations, was acquainted only with their general content. As we have seen, Stalin's display of force over Yugoslavia was aimed at bringing Hitler back to the negotiating table. The meeting with Schulenburg, corroborated by the latest intelligence reports, sounded the alarm. He therefore now seriously wavered between the fear of provocation and the wish to see Yugoslavia fight. Russia could not possibly acquiesce to Constanza, Burgas and now the Yugoslav tributaries of the Danube being in German hands. As the last independent stronghold in the Balkans, Yugoslavia's collapse would open the way for the Germans to proceed straight to the Turkish Straits, while shielding their right wing if they should proceed against Russia. However, the fear of provocation, intensified by Schulenburg's warning, and the suspicion that Gavrilović was acting 'under the influence of Cripps' remained overwhelming.[58]

The little hope still entertained by Gavrilović was thus dashed when he was summoned again to Vyshinsky in the late afternoon. He was amazed to discover that without prior warning the Russians had modified the main clause of the agreement, virtually reducing it to a statement of neutrality rather than a non-aggression and friendship pact. He was not impressed by Vyshinsky's assurance that the 'mere public announcement constituted an important step towards the reinforcement of peace in the Balkans', and the meeting ended inconclusively. In a follow-up meeting the 'highly strung' Gavrilović condemned the new Russian proposal as a substantially watered-down version of the original proposal of a political–military alliance. He therefore postponed the signing of the agreement set for the next day, pending further consultations with Belgrade. For the Russians a hasty conclusion of the agreement before Germany made any military move was essential to clear the air in their dealings with her; Gavrilović was warned before taking his leave that time was running out and that 'what was possible today, could be impossible tomorrow'.[59] At Stalin's dacha members of the Politburo gathered that night and endorsed the agreement, expecting the Yugoslav government to follow suit.[60]

The next morning found Stalin confident that he had shrewdly beaten the Germans and the British at their own game. He had succeeded in establishing Soviet interests vis-à-vis Hitler without firing a single shot, avoiding the pitfall of being dragged into a premature war. Indeed, it was noticed in the Russian Foreign Ministry that in comparison with the last few days Molotov appeared 'excited and quite optimistic'. He made it clear that General Simović's 'dreams about a pact of mutual assistance' were incongruous with Soviet aims.[61] The optimism, however, was short-lived, as the earlier disagreements between the Yugoslavs now resurfaced. When negotiations resumed the Yugoslav mission persisted in its demands for the original friendship agreement to be reinstated. Now that Russia was not to be involved directly in hostilities, Vyshinsky was prepared to concede that a supplementary agreement between Yugoslavia and Britain would be 'expedient'; it could eliminate the likelihood of a separate peace and defer the danger of a German attack on Russia.[62]

With the probability of war increasing by the hour, the Yugoslav government was little encouraged by Lebedev's noncommittal statements that 'the Soviet Union was already pursuing a struggle to secure peace for Yugoslavia, and was endeavouring to lay the necessary political foundations to consolidate such a peace in the future'. Negotiations had in fact been put on hold, as Lebedev learnt in the evening. Rather than lifting the despondent spirits of the people, the agreement was likely to 'worsen Yugoslavia's position'.[63] A treaty of neutrality could not possibly serve Yugoslav interests, as it in fact gave Hitler a free hand in a war against Yugoslavia. The offer was therefore rejected and Gavrilović was instructed to insist on the conclusion of a friendship and non-aggression pact. The Yugoslavs had in fact made a last-ditch attempt to reconcile the Germans, who were informed that the negotiations in Moscow had been sparked by the momentary 'excitement' of the uprising but had been opposed by the entire Cabinet, which 'did not want an understanding with Moscow, but one with Berlin'.[64]

The signing of the agreement had originally been scheduled for 10 p.m. on 5 April. By midnight Dekanozov informed Stalin from Berlin that a German invasion of Yugoslavia was imminent.[65] Inquiries at the Ministry of Communication revealed that no telegram had reached the Yugoslav delegation that night. Feverish activities followed. At one o'clock in the morning Gavrilović, who was taking refuge at a late-night reception organized by the American ambassador, was located.[66] He was, however, evasive and disinclined to co-operate, informing Vyshinsky on the phone that he did not expect the government to respond until later in the morning. Vyshinsky would not take no for an answer. Special arrangements were made for Gavrilović to speak directly to Simović by phone from his own embassy.[67]

Gavrilović had become so suspicious that he could not discount the possibility that the Russians were in fact setting a trap for him. The conversation therefore assumed a rather surreal character:

'This is General Simović.'
'From where are you speaking, General?'
'From where? Why do you ask?'
'Where are you, General? At home or in the office?'
'But why are you asking that?'
'I have to know, General.'
'I am at home.'
'In which street? What is the number of the house?'
'But you know very well where I live! We are neighbours!'
'It does not matter. Just give me your address.'
'2 Gladstone Street.'

'Good,' replied Gavrilović, only now convinced at last that he was indeed speaking to the Prime Minister. Very quickly a profound disagreement emerged. The Prime Minister, who had had no response from the Germans and was constantly primed with intelligence on the forthcoming assault, was now desperate to conclude the agreement:

'Sign whatever the Russians are proposing to you.'
'I cannot, General. I know what is my duty and what is my job.'
'You have to sign.'
'I cannot, General, trust me.'
'Sign, Gavrilović!'
'I know what I am doing, General. I cannot sign this document.'
'All right. If you want an order, then I am ordering you to sign.'

'I know what I am doing, trust me.'
Gavrilović then slammed down the receiver.[68]

Within a minute the phone rang again. Novikov, the head of the Near Eastern Department of the Soviet Foreign Ministry, was at the other end. Gavrilović insisted that the line was poor and he could not ascertain whether he had actually spoken to General Simović. He 'thought' that he had been instructed to sign the agreement, but he 'nonetheless wished that the mention of neutrality be removed'. When Vyshinsky appealed to him Gavrilović persevered, now attributing to his government the wish 'to exclude the mention of neutrality from the agreement'. Gavrilović, however, knew perfectly well that the 'telephone conversation had undoubtedly been recorded and reported to Stalin'. This was probably why Vyshinsky persisted in his demand that the entire delegation assemble at the Kremlin at 2.30 a.m. Gavrilović resorted to delaying tactics, regretting that the members of the delegation could not be located. This hardly proved a serious challenge to the 'Protocol Department' of the Foreign Ministry, which worked closely with the NKVD in shadowing foreign diplomats, and the Yugoslavs were promptly traced to the Moscow Restaurant, the American embassy and so on. To avoid any further hitches Novikov himself was ordered to drive them to the Kremlin. On the way he learnt from Gavrilović that 'the mission did not expect to receive the instructions from the government, and did not contemplate signing the pact', a message which he duly passed on to his superiors.

Fearing the worst, Gavrilović was ushered into Molotov's office where he was pleasantly surprised to find an easy-going and cheerful Stalin. Turning to Stalin, Molotov unexpectedly announced that he proposed to 'make an amendment by removing the word "neutrality" throughout'; he pinned the blame for the bungle on Vyshinsky. They appeared so anxious to conclude the agreement that there was no time for the revised version to be translated into Serbo-Croat, and the retyped Russian one was signed around 3 a.m. on 6 April. As the main addressee was Germany, the signing was announced on the radio within an hour. Stalin insisted, however, that the date of the signing should be 5 April, so as not to suggest that it had been signed with preknowledge of or concurrently with the German invasion of Yugoslavia.[69]

The participants then retired to watch a newsreel while Molotov improvised a banquet which lasted until 7 a.m. Stalin's nonchalant reaction to the German threat to Yugoslavia and Russia, 'Let them come. We have strong nerves!' is widely quoted but not in the right context. As we have seen, it was fear of the invasion which had led Stalin to seek the agreement. The Russian objective was to deter Germany; now that the invasion of Yugoslavia seemed inevitable the aim was to prolong the breathing space and defer the attack on Russia by stiffening Yugoslav resistance. Stalin went out of his way to display exaggerated confidence; he described in great detail the innovations introduced into the Red Army and its ability to assist the Yugoslavs. His personal intervention was certainly effective, as it brought about a dramatic change in Gavriloviç's view of him: 'He has a superb will, he controls everything, he grasps everything, his soul is full of force and energy. The incomparable Stalin, oh *velikij* (great) Stalin.'[70]

In negotiating with the Yugoslavs Stalin had reluctantly accepted the views of the military and Molotov that an agreement might still deter Hitler from a long war of attrition. As the Yugoslavs were parting from Stalin in jubilant spirits, Hitler unleashed the attack on Yugoslavia in a ferocious bombardment of Belgrade which turned the city into ruins. Despite the intelligence he had received, Stalin appeared to be surprised when news of the German attack came in.[71] Two hours after leaving the Kremlin he called Molotov from his dacha. An argumentative conversation followed in which Stalin urged Molotov to cancel the banquet scheduled for the evening. Stalin argued that the attack had put the agreement in a new perspective and that the banquet was bound to have a 'brazenly provocative character'.[72] The fact that neither *Pravda* nor *Izvestiia* appeared that morning until nearly midday reflected the disagreements and apprehensions. When the papers came out Molotov's line still prevailed and attempts were made to extract the utmost from the agreement without provoking Germany. Observers perceived it as a 'significant moral and political support for Yugoslavia's policies of resistance', reflected by the 'unusual measure of publishing a 5 column photograph of the ceremony . . . such a picture has not appeared since the signing of the Ribbentrop–Molotov Pact'.[73] But the commentary was most carefully tailored for transmission to both Yugoslavia and Germany, going out of its way to explain that the friendship clause was aimed at 'strengthening the peace and preventing the spread of war'. The frenzied activities which had led to the conclusion of the agreement were concealed, while attempts were made to present it as a natural outcome of the breakthrough in relations achieved a year earlier. But at the same time it was a statement of the Soviet stakes in Yugoslavia, where 'the main tributaries of the Danube constitute the main roads leading from Italy, Germany and Hungary through Belgrade to Saloniki and Istanbul'. But perhaps most significant was the concealed warning of a prolonged war if hostilities were not brought to a speedy end.[74]

At the same time Stalin's ever-present fear that the British were trying to entangle him in war resurfaced. The ink on the signature had hardly dried when Simiç was asked to 'promptly replace' the Yugoslav military attaché because of his alleged pro-British leanings. A month later Timoshenko bluntly accused the Yugoslav military mission of 'serving as

British provocateurs' by misleading the Russians into believing that the signature of the agreement would 'contribute to peace and strengthen the Yugoslavs' will to resist and increase the German reservations against an attack' while in fact leaning towards Britain.[75]

In the meantime attempts to bolster the Yugoslav resistance without implicating the Soviet Union directly continued. The Ministry of Defence immediately offered a rather impressive list of fighter planes, both short and long range, anti-tank and anti-aircraft guns, a number of mountain batteries, and mortars. The explicit preference for equipment which could be used effectively in mountain warfare reflected the Soviet hopes of a prolonged war of attrition.[76] The Yugoslavs were further led to understand that the reversion to the 'friendship' formula was made so as not to give the Yugoslavs the impression that if war broke out the Soviet Union would 'simply wash its hands and be indifferent to the fate of the country'.[77] The initial boldness of the Russians can be partly attributed to the mild German reaction. With Operation 'Marita' rolling, the Germans made great efforts to keep Stalin at bay. Schulenburg was instructed to inform Molotov of the operation 'without any special emphasis, in an objective and dispassionate manner'. Significantly, there was no allusion to the fresh Soviet–Yugoslav agreement, while the invasion was presented as a measure of forestalling Anglo-Yugoslav co-operation. Moreover, to disguise the plans for 'Barbarossa' the Germans announced their intention of withdrawing from Yugoslavia as soon as their aims in the Balkans were achieved.[78]

But the shocking realization that the German campaign in South-east Europe was progressing even more effectively than the previous one in France drove home the severity of Russia's plight. Within three days of the savage bombardment of Belgrade the German forces had cut through the Yugoslav resistance in Skopje and captured Saloniki. Owing to the success gained on this front and General Kleist's armoured advance on Belgrade, the main thrust of the 2nd Army commenced ahead of plan. On the evening of 10 April, two days early, German troops completed the occupation of Zagreb and by 13 April they were in full control of Belgrade. The war in Greece was conducted in similar fashion and on 23 April, after the Greek Prime Minister had committed suicide, the army surrendered. The British fared no better. They started their retreat on 16 April; by 25 April the swastika was hoisted over the Acropolis and four days later the double campaign against Yugoslavia and Greece was completed with the arrival of German forces at the southern tip of the Peloponnese. The aftermath was the descent of German paratroopers on Crete on 20 May. Cania fell on 27 May and by 1 June the last British soldier was evacuated from Souda Bay.[79]

While the campaign was drawing to a quick conclusion, Stalin was informed by the NKVD sources within the German embassy about

Schulenburg's concern that the agreement was 'a significant change in the course of Soviet foreign policy'. Schulenburg had been pondering what on earth had possessed Stalin to conclude an agreement with a power which was on the verge of being annihilated.[80] Stalin watched with great trepidation the fate of Belgrade, the swift advance of the Germans and the occupation of Skopje a mere two days after the outbreak of hostilities.[81] Two days later he was informed that the Greeks too were 'extremely pessimistic' about their ability to resist. The 100,000-strong British army in Greece had not been engaged and the prevailing view in Athens was that all the British plans for Europe had collapsed.[82] At midnight on 11 April Gavriloviç confirmed reports from various Yugoslav embassies abroad about the gravity of the situation; most of them, including that in Moscow, had been cut off from Belgrade.[83] The next morning Stalin flexed his muscles for the last time, warning Hungary in the pages of *Izvestiia* against exploiting the situation and joining the plunder.[84]

The Yugoslav episode had serious repercussions. Stalin's varied manoeuvres to renew the negotiations with Hitler from a position of strength collapsed once Yugoslavia and Greece had been devastated. The miscalculation was obvious; he now confronted the almost untouched Wehrmacht deployed earlier than he had expected along his entire border before the dialogue he sought with Hitler had been opened. His subsequent desperate attempt to remedy matters and appease Hitler while avoiding provocation was perhaps the most significant direct cause of the calamity which befell the Russians on 22 June. It further worsened the already hazardous relations between Stalin and the military. Before his expulsion from Russia, at the end of May, the Yugoslav military attaché was summoned to the Ministry of Defence. Timoshenko did not conceal from him that he expected a war to break out. He was further explicitly told that his expulsion reflected a need to pacify the Germans. He emerged from the meeting convinced that Timoshenko's position had been shaken by his staunch support of the agreement with Yugoslavia and his belief that the Yugoslav army would be able to withstand a German onslaught for at least a month to be followed by protracted guerrilla warfare. Consequently his name had almost disappeared from the papers, even from the army's *Red Star*.[85]

At the height of Glasnost, the Soviet Ministry of Foreign Affairs released some documents related to the negotiations.[86] It misled the reader into assuming that the title 'Pact of Friendship and Non-Aggression' was extraordinary in itself. As we have seen, Stalin had gone out of his way to reject the military alliance proposed by the Yugoslav armed forces and even attempted to downgrade the friendship agreement to a neutrality pact. Throughout the conflict, the leaders of the Yugoslav coup were split on the nature of their association with Russia. They ended up by playing the German, British and Soviet cards simultaneously and seeing their political achievement crumble within a week. History, however, has applauded both sides, presenting a rather romanticized myth of a last-minute resolve to hold back the onslaught of Nazi Germany.

8

Churchill's Warning to Stalin

British Intelligence and 'Barbarossa'

The belief in Moscow that Churchill had set out to draw Russia into the war was strengthened by the crushing defeats inflicted on Britain on the battlefield. It was against this background that Churchill sent Stalin his famous warning about German intentions. Churchill's powerful account of his abortive message overshadows the abundance of the other, far more important evidence about 'Barbarossa' which did reach Stalin.[1] His interpretation of the dramatic events surrounding the warning has been uncritically repeated ever since. The warning is the event which first comes to mind when the drama leading to the war is unfolded. Prior to the opening of the vast material on the Second World War in the British archives in the mid-1970s, Churchill's voluminous history of the Second World War, with its persuasive but excessively self-centred and therefore occasionally misleading interpretation of events, was regarded as authoritative and was even frequently quoted by Soviet historians. The relations with Russia on the eve of the Great Patriotic War, in which Cripps played a prominent part, are a typical example. They were portrayed in the light of the Cold War, Cripps's major political challenge to Churchill in 1942 and their continued political rivalry after the war. The warning provides Churchill with a starting point for a highly tendentious account of the events leading up to the German invasion of Russia which has since captured the imagination and minds of readers. He passes judgment on Stalin and his commissars as the 'most completely out-witted bunglers of the Second World War' while glossing over the British failure to consider the significance of Russia as a potential ally in the war.[2]

Cripps's rancorous squabbles with Churchill should be viewed within the framework of the protracted debate in England on the course of Anglo-Soviet relations, described earlier.[3] In Ankara Cripps had urged Eden to dispel the Soviet suspicion that Britain was conducting a 'hopelessly hostile policy towards Russia through conclusion of a political settlement of the Baltic issue'. He also took the unusual step of appealing directly to the Cabinet, warning that it would be 'disastrous to lose an opportunity here through the lack of instructions'.[4] The Cabinet had not even touched on relations with Russia for months until Attlee brought up Cripps's telegram on 31 March. By then Churchill, to judge from his own account of the warning to Stalin, had come to realize the significance that Russia was to assume in the next phase of the war. However, his alleged foresight is not perceptible in the records of the discussion in Cabinet, and the issue remained within the jurisdiction of the Foreign Office.[5] Eden, still in Athens, casually endorsed the Foreign Office's advice to reject Cripps's 'imprudent and useless initiative'.[6]

The evaluation of intelligence on German intentions was held back by the political concept entrenched in the Foreign Office.[7] The analysis of the ample intelligence on the German deployment and intentions, some of which emanated from decrypts of the German code, was hindered by these preconceived ideas. Since the beginning of the war Military Intelligence had remained in close touch with the Foreign Office and had adopted a corresponding appreciation of Soviet–German relations. Cadogan, the permanent Under-Secretary who in the absence of Eden represented the Foreign Office in Cabinet, was in almost daily direct contact with the Chiefs of Staff. Victor Cavendish-Bentinck was not only the Foreign Office's representative on the Joint Intelligence Committee but also chaired it. Moreover, the Foreign Office's weekly summaries were circulated among the different intelligence branches, forming a political guideline for the collators.[8]

The evaluation of the forthcoming conflict was also hampered by the extremely poor information available on the Red Army, summarized by a highly prejudiced Chief of Staff. Military Intelligence was influenced not only by the prevailing political concept but also by an enduring image of the Russian army; this had been reiterated in dozens of assessments, some going back to the Crimean War but most dating to the First World War. The assessments had not been modified in light of the vast theoretical, technological, structural and strategic reforms which the Red Army had undergone since the revolution. A disparaging attitude was thus inherent and did not stem only, as is commonly argued, from the purges of 1937–8. The rather timeworn final verdict, based on similar papers written in the 1920s and in 1935, stated that 'though the forces are large, much of their equipment is obsolescent. They suffer from certain inherent failings which would serve them ill against the Germans, and their value for war is low.

They are, however, at their best in defence, and, on land, have vast territories on which to fall back.'[9]

Thus early reports from varied sources on Hitler's bellicose designs in the East were dismissed out of hand. These were held to be based on 'misleading rumours' serving the interests of 'wishful thinkers'. The explanation arrived at, in harmony with the political concept, was that the Russians' collaboration with Germany was in fact so close that they were 'ready to yield to the mere threat of force'.[10] An alternative explanation attributed the unusual deployment of German troops in the Balkans to a defensive move against Russia. Information from Moscow that the January war games of the Soviet General Staff were based on the assumption of a German attack on Russia was discounted.[11]

More pronounced rumours of an impending German invasion of Russia came in March from several capitals and suggested that a German turn eastwards was 'within the bounds of possibility'. Cavendish-Bentinck did not rule out a German invasion: 'Hitler may occasionally for opportunist motives depart from the principles laid down in Mein Kampf, but sooner or later they are proved to be the basis of his policy.' But such rare heresies were disregarded. The 'doubtful just anonymous talk', explained Cadogan, was disseminated by the Germans to 'intimidate' the Russians and therefore could not serve as a 'very sure guide' for re-evaluation.[12] A detailed account from Stockholm of the German intentions, concluding that 'all military circles in Berlin are convinced of conflict with Russia this spring and consider success certain', was passed over by the Foreign Office, dismissed as 'the usual contradictory rumours'.[13]

When the growing traffic of intelligence could no longer be ignored it was conveniently attributed to a 'war of nerves' waged by the Germans; its aim was 'to produce an atmosphere of nervousness in Moscow which would militate against any possible Russian interference in the Balkan project, or to prepare the ground for an attempt to squeeze further accommodation from the Soviet Government'. Doubt was expressed whether 'Red Riding Hood will now pluck up courage to face these dangers'; Russia was rather expected 'to appease the big bad wolf by a policy of further accommodation'.[14]

Cripps's different political outlook enabled him to perceive the German menace to Russia. In early March 1941 he returned from his short visit to Ankara[15] firmly convinced, as he told fellow ambassadors, that Russia and Germany would be at war 'before summer'. Cripps expected Hitler to overcome the opposition to a war on two fronts and attack Russia before England became too strong for Germany to form another front. In an off-the-record press conference Cripps predicted that Hitler would attack Russia 'not later than the end of June'. Cripps's first explicit report to the Foreign Office about the German intentions was transmitted on 24 March, at a time of growing tension over Yugoslavia. This information was both prophetic and accurate, considering the early date of its origins, and was obtained from a source in Berlin through Vilhelm Assarasson, the well-informed Swedish minister in Moscow.[16] The evaluation of the information and the ideas for its exploitation illustrate the British assessment of the brewing conflict and the repercussions on Soviet foreign policy, and are worth examining at some length. The gist of the report confirmed Cripps's impression that the Germans were determined to 'attack Russia by a blitz and to get hold of all Russia up to the Urals':[17]

> 6. German plan is as follows: the attack on England will be continued with U-boats and from the air, but there will be no invasion. At the same time a drive against Russia will take place.
> 7. This drive will be by three large armies: the first based at Warsaw under von Bock, the second based at Königsberg, the third based at Cracow under List.[18]
> 8. Everything is being arranged with the greatest care so that the attack can be launched at a moment's notice. It would not be surprising if the attack took place in May.[19]

Cripps hoped that if employed cautiously and wisely the information could draw the Soviet Union closer to England. It was just about possible that the Russians might comprehend their difficult situation and consider changing their attitude. Cripps, however, maintained that the information should be disclosed indirectly to Maisky through a third party, such as the Chinese or the Turkish ambassador. An 'indirect and secret' approach, he advised, 'would be more impressive than a direct communication, the motive of which they would suspect'. His proposal was immediately brushed aside by senior officials, who regarded the information as 'part of the "war of nerves" against Russia, designed to force her into a closer partnership with Germany'. The chairman of the Joint Intelligence Committee, Cavendish-Bentinck, rejected the report. From the German point of view, the occupation of Russia was 'rather a large mouthful. The War Office have no confirmation of any increase in the German forces facing Russia, nor has there been the slightest movement of German aircraft in that direction. It would therefore appear that these German threats against Russia are intended to intimidate the Soviet Government into making an alliance with Germany . . . and mislead us.' Although the information continued to turn up from various quarters, Military Intelligence, faithful to its concept, dismissed it as a plant by the Germans.[20] A more even-handed appreciation of German intentions did circulate in the different branches of Military Intelligence, but in the existing climate it was written off as 'not convincing'.[21]

The 'Cryptic' Warning

According to Churchill, it was with 'relief and excitement' that he came across a report from one of Britain's 'most trusted sources' that 'illuminated the whole Eastern scene like a lightning flash'. The reference is to information obtained by the British through Ultra, the machine they had devised to decipher intercepts of German signal traffic. The intercepts indicated that three armoured divisions and other key forces had been ordered to move from the Balkans to the Cracow area the day after Yugoslavia joined the Axis[22] and had been recalled when the Germans learnt of the ensuing coup in Belgrade. The sudden transportation of massive armoured formations to Poland and then swiftly back to the Balkans, argued Churchill, could 'only mean Hitler's intention to invade Russia in May . . . The fact that the Belgrade revolution had required their return to Roumania involved perhaps a delay from May to June.'[23] But was Churchill's perception really a stroke of genius? Was this particular report indeed the sole reason for his change of mind about the German intentions and for the decision to send a personal warning to Stalin? Had Churchill become aware, unlike the rest of the intelligence community and the Foreign Office, of the danger lurking for Russia around the corner? How did Churchill come to predict June as the likely date for the invasion? The answers to these questions reveal the devastating impact which Churchill's warning had on Stalin's own evaluation of the danger lying ahead.

Like Stalin, Churchill had established a procedure whereby raw intelligence reports were collated for him. These were further sifted by Major Desmond Morton and presented to Churchill daily in a special red box. The intelligence included intercepted telegrams from hostile as well as friendly embassies, but above all intercepts of the German signals traffic obtained through Enigma. While the naval code had been broken and information was flowing regularly and smoothly to Bletchley Park, where the vast deciphering operation was taking place, the Wehrmacht's communications traffic was still difficult to decrypt. Up to Operation 'Barbarossa' only fragmentary reports on the German build-up were submitted to Churchill.

In view of the dramatic events in Yugoslavia, Churchill was preoccupied by the desperate attempts being made by Eden and General Dill to raise an effective barrier against Germany's penetration into the Middle East and South-eastern Europe, and particularly to divert her from Turkey.[24] Like Stalin, Churchill examined Germany's intentions towards Russia in relation to the developments in that region. Late in the evening of 28 March he relayed to Eden, then in Athens, detailed instructions on Britain's overall strategy. Only the final item made a passing and highly hypothetical reference to the possibility of a German–Soviet confrontation. 'Is it not possible', he suggested, 'that if a front were formed in the Balkan peninsula Germany might think it better business to take it out of Russia?'[25] In other words, the Balkans and the Middle East were perceived by Churchill to be Hitler's main objectives, while effective resistance in the Balkans might divert Hitler to Russia.

The next morning, however, Churchill reverted to his previous appreciation when he was presented by Major-General Sir Stewart Menzies, the Chief ('C') of MI6, the Secret Intelligence Service, with an intercept from Enigma. The intercept included the transit orders from Rumania to the Cracow area for three of the five armoured divisions located in the southeast and for two motorized divisions, including the SS division. The movement was to commence on 3 April and to end by the 29th. As we can deduce from the now-available intelligence reports to Churchill, it was 'C' who, in his usual succinct language, enlightened Churchill to the fact that the directive was issued prior to the Yugoslav *coup d'état* and that 'it would therefore be of interest to see if it is still carried out'.[26] Churchill, however, did not immediately see the implications for the German plans vis-à-vis the Soviet Union. He most certainly, despite his retrospective claim, did not send the 'momentous news at once' to Stalin. Instead he hastened to transmit the gist of the information to Eden, assuming that Eden could do with a trump card to convince the reluctant Greeks, Turks and Yugoslavs to form a solid front against Hitler. His reading, therefore, stressed the southward direction of the German movement, which he believed would divert the Wehrmacht, at least temporarily, from Russia:

> The bad man concentrated very large armoured forces etc to over-awe Yugo and Greece and hoped to get former or both without fighting. The moment he was sure Yugo was in the Axis he moved three of the five Panthers towards the Bear believing that what was left would be enough to finish Greek affair. However Belgrade revolution upset this picture and caused orders for northward move to be arrested in transit. This can only mean in my opinion intention to attack Yugo at earliest or alternatively act against the Turk. It looks as if heavy forces will be used in Balkan Peninsula and that Bear will be kept waiting a bit.[27]

It needed time, but even more significantly outside influence, to really drive home the full implications of the intelligence before Churchill acted on it. It should be noted that Churchill replaced Eden at the Foreign Office during his prolonged absence in the Middle East and was therefore shown all important communications. It was when he drafted the telegram on strategy to Eden that his attention was drawn by Cadogan to information corroborating the Enigma reports.[28] Cripps's most detailed telegram on the subject was shown to him as well; both the projected date of the invasion and the decision to alert the Russians correspond to Cripps's telegram rather than to the Enigma decrypt. A definite shift of policy occurred no earlier than 30 March, when the possibility of a German invasion of Russia figured more prominently in a second telegram from Churchill to Eden. However, this was only after both Air Intelligence and the government code and cipher school had analysed the Enigma report and reached a similar conclusion. Even then Churchill refrained from active participation in the long-delayed discussion on Anglo-Soviet relations of 31 March described above.[29]

The decision to adopt Cripps's proposal and present the Russians with the accumulated evidence took even longer to materialize. Churchill was most likely influenced by further reports received from Belgrade on 30 March and from Sumner Welles, the American Under-Secretary of State, on 2 April. They confirmed news from Athens, where Prince Paul had sought refuge after the coup, that Hitler had revealed to him during their meeting at Berchtesgaden on 4 March his intention to take military action against Russia. It also emerged that Göring had disclosed to Matsuoka, the Japanese Foreign Minister, during the latter's visit to Berlin that Germany intended to attack Russia in the spring regardless of the outcome of the campaign against England.[30] Cripps, convinced that the German threat was real and as usual itching to act, suggested on 31 March that, if confirmed, the revelations could 'be used here to good effect'.

A careful distinction should be made at this juncture between Cripps's reservations about passing on the information and those of the Foreign Office. Cripps was mostly concerned that the Russians might interpret it as an attempt to drag them into the war. The Foreign Office did not expect a German attack and was therefore reluctant to initiate a step which might play into German hands in the phantom negotiations. The new information threatened to undermine the entrenched concept that a Soviet–German alliance was in the making. If the Russians were to accept the warning, an Anglo-Soviet rapprochement would become the order of the day. No wonder, therefore, that on the very day that Churchill was contemplating his warning to Stalin, Cadogan, fully supported by Laurence Collier, the head of the Northern Department at the Foreign Office, objected to the proposals made by Cripps and Halifax to alert the Russians to the danger. There was no point, he noted in the final minute, of repeating warnings to the Russians unless this was likely to have 'a good effect, from our point of view, if they interpret it as meaning that they will be attacked *in any case*, and regardless of any concession which they may make to Hitler'. In short, the transmission of intelligence would be useless until the Russians were 'strong enough to react in the right way to it'.[31] By now the political concept had infiltrated the intelligence agencies and come to dominate their thinking. On 1 April

Military Intelligence concluded that 'the object of the movement of German armoured and motorized forces was undoubtedly to exert military pressure on Russia to prevent Russian interference in German Balkan plans'.[32]

When considering Churchill's warning to Stalin, it should be borne in mind that the Prime Minister had hitherto displayed an almost complete lack of interest in Russian affairs.[33] Moreover, his zeal in warning the Russians stood in sharp contrast to the position he had previously maintained. In February, when British prospects seemed brighter, he had opposed the half-measure of alerting the Russians, 'while odds seem heavily against Britain in Greece'.[34] His intervention now was motivated by the thought that Germany might have altered her overall strategy. Churchill's sudden entry into the arena, however, was somewhat capricious and did not take account of the delicate political framework into which his message was to fit. His move set Moscow on a course which would soon take a serious toll in the response to the German threat. The message which was intended to draw Stalin's attention to the change was finally drafted only on 3 April and ran as follows:

> I have sure information from a trusted agent that when the Germans thought they had got Yugoslavia in the net, that is to say, after March 20, they began to move three out of the five Panzer divisions from Roumania to Southern Poland. The moment they heard of the Serbian revolution this movement was countermanded. Your Excellency will readily appreciate the significance of these facts.

It was, as aptly described by Churchill, 'short and cryptic'; its 'brevity and exceptional character' were intended, as he recalled later on, to 'give it special significance and arrest Stalin's attention'.[35] Cripps was asked to submit the warning if it could be delivered to Stalin 'personally'.[36]

The Foreign Office, which acted as the communication channel between Churchill and his ambassador in Moscow, was entrenched in its concept and reluctant to accept the new turn of events. Sargent and Cadogan, obviously anxious that Cripps might commit himself further than desired if allowed unhindered access to Stalin, hastened to provide him with a 'line on which to speak'. As Cripps did not know the source of the evidence, the Foreign Office's briefing only weakened the very effect which Churchill had intended for the message. The instructions embodied two schools of thought: Churchill's own and the sceptical position of the Foreign Office. Cadogan started by recapturing the essence of Churchill's warning:

> The change in German military dispositions surely implies that Hitler through the action of Yugoslavia has now postponed his previous

plans for threatening Soviet Government. If so it should be possible for Soviet Government to use this opportunity to strengthen their own position. This delay shows that the enemy forces are not unlimited, and illustrates the advantages that will follow anything like a united front.

The ambivalence, however, was striking. In the second paragraph Cadogan argued that by applying substantial pressure Hitler hoped to extract further concessions without really intending to attack Russia. The first draft was so unsatisfactory that Churchill himself replaced the paragraph, stressing the military significance of the information. Even then the instructions did not reflect Churchill's sense of urgency or his interpretation of the fresh intelligence. Moreover, while Churchill's warning conformed with Cripps's advice not to imply an appeal to relieve Britain from her distress in South-east Europe, the instructions clearly did so:

2. Obvious way of Soviet Government strengthening its own position would be to furnish material help to Turkey and Greece and through latter to Yugoslavia. This help might increase German difficulties in Balkans and still further delay the German attack on Soviet Union of which there are so many signs. If, however, opportunity is not now taken to put every possible spoke in the German wheel danger might revive in a few months' time.

3. You would not of course imply that we ourselves required any assistance from Soviet Government or that they would be acting in any interests but their own. What we want them to realise, however, is that Hitler intends to attack them sooner or later, if he can . . .[37]

Churchill misleads the reader into believing that he did not hear from Cripps until 12 April.[38] Just as puzzling is his deliberate omission of the dramatic signature of the Soviet–Yugoslav treaty on the very day that his warning reached the British embassy in Moscow, rendering it obsolete. The agreement clearly indicated that Stalin was conscious of the looming German menace, terrified of any attempt to provoke the Germans and equally suspicious of British attempts to embroil Russia in war.[39]

As early as 5 April Cripps informed Churchill that it was 'quite out of the question in the present circumstances to try to deliver personally any message to Stalin'. He reminded Churchill that he had been prevented from seeing Stalin since their first and only meeting in July 1940. Convinced by the force of the argument, Churchill agreed that the message should be handed to Molotov instead.[40] His telegram, however, crossed another one sent by Cripps. Developments in Yugoslavia had raised serious reservations about the wisdom of handing over the warning. Cripps informed Churchill of the steps taken by the Russians to publicize the Yugoslav agreement and the significance attached to it. In view of the obvious Russian awareness of the German danger, Cripps pressed Churchill to reconsider the dispatch of the warning. He and the Greek, Turkish and Yugoslav ambassadors had been feeding Stalin with similar information. 'In existing circumstances,' he stated emphatically, 'I think it wiser not to interfere further at the moment as all is going as well as possible in our direction.' The Foreign Office, which for entirely different reasons was reluctant to alert the Russians, was quick to acquiesce in Cripps's forceful arguments in favour of withdrawal of the message.[41]

The matter was allowed to lapse. The Foreign Office's reluctance to alter its outlook as a result of the events in the Balkans was all too evident. Churchill's intervention raised the suggestion of providing Cripps with a compilation of fresh reports which might be invaluable if the Russians were to respond favourably. But the unchallenged assumption of an impending Soviet–German agreement continued to impede a balanced judgment. In view of the importance attributed by Churchill to alerting the Russians, it is worth quoting at some length the evaluation of the reports by the Joint Intelligence Committee, the essence of which was as follows:

Following considerations must however be borne in mind:
(1) These reports may be put out by Germans as part of the war of nerves.
(2) A German invasion would probably result in such chaos throughout Soviet Union that the Germans would have to reorganise everything in the occupied territory and would meanwhile lose supplies which they are now drawing from the Soviet Union at any rate for a long time to come . . .
(3) Germany's resources, though immense, would not permit her to continue her campaign in the Balkans, to maintain the present scale of air attack against this country, to continue her offensive against Egypt and at the same time to invade, occupy and reorganise a large part of the Soviet Union.
(4) As yet no information has been received of movements of German aircraft towards the Soviet frontier, an indispensable preliminary to a campaign against the Soviet Union . . .
(5) There have been indications that German General Staff are opposed to war on two fronts and in favour of disposing of Great Britain before attacking Soviet Union.
(6) Soviet–German agreement for supply of oil during 1941 has just been concluded.

Cavendish-Bentinck finally rejected the idea of passing the material to Russia, as the reports were no more than a 'hotch-potch of pretty unconfirmed and probably untrue information'. The scanty evidence was confined to 'preparations as distinct from intentions'. The political concept, which rejected the evidence of an impending German–Soviet clash, clung tenaciously to unconfirmed fragments of evidence pointing to a forthcoming German–Soviet alliance.[42]

While this evaluation was taking place in London, Cripps had exploited the favourable climate to convey to Stalin, through Gavriloviç, the information obtained from Prince Paul about his meeting with Hitler. The Yugoslav ambassador attested that it was taken seriously by the Russians. Indeed, the NKVD's intercepts of the telegrams of Aktay, the Turkish ambassador, confirmed the information obtained through the Swedes and Hitler's revelations to Paul. In fact most of the sources which served the British, apart from Enigma which in any case could not be disclosed, were at the Russians' disposal.[43] Seeking a special interview with Molotov, Cripps protested, would mislead him into assuming that 'I was trying to make trouble with Germany. It might very well diminish seriously the strong effect of Prince Paul's conversation.' Unexpectedly Churchill overruled Cripps's reservations, insisting that it was his 'duty' to make Stalin reflect, even if he had the information from other sources, that 'the engagement of German armoured divisions in Balkans has deferred that threat and given Russia breathing space. The more support that can be given to Balkan States, the longer will Hitler's forces be tied up there.' Once again the warning was clearly connected to the support which Stalin was expected to render to the British in the Balkans.[44]

On 8 April, in response to a suggestion that he should approach Molotov, Cripps reiterated his previous argument, supported by evidence that the Russians had been briefed about the content of Prince Paul's interview with Hitler, 'which they obviously believed and of which they took great notice'. Further evidence indeed came in from the military attachés in Moscow and Ankara that a partial mobilization had been carried out in the Red Army. If he were to seek a special interview with Stalin, Cripps argued, the Soviet leader would be bound to relate it to events in Yugoslavia and assume that Britain was 'trying to make trouble with Germany'.[45]

As Cripps had been left without definite instructions in reply to his first communication, Cadogan was now inclined to countermand the delivery of the warning altogether. In the meantime Eden had returned to England from his extended Middle Eastern tour. A decision on the recognition of Soviet annexations in the Baltic was now long overdue. It was 'a difficult hand to play', Eden conceded, but he swiftly succumbed to the view held in the Office that under heavy pressure from Germany Stalin would 'prefer to yield to Hitler's threats and blandishments rather than risk an open breach which such a policy would involve'. Concessions in the Baltic were therefore destined to be 'the seal for a rapprochement and in no sense an attempt to buy such a rapprochement'. For this reason he tended to agree with Cripps that the warnings would be counter-productive.[46]

Unexpectedly, however, Churchill again intervened; ignoring Cripps's arguments, he stated once again that it was his 'duty' to convey the facts to Stalin. It was irrelevant to the importance of the facts if they or their message were 'unwelcomed'. Instructions on these lines were accordingly sent to Cripps, stressing the military significance of the breathing space which Russia had gained while Hitler was tied up in the Balkans. Although Churchill's instructions were mandatory, Eden, on his first day in the Foreign Office after the Middle East mission, went through the file and in a last-minute alteration directed Cripps to forward the message but still left the final decision to his discretion. Curiously enough, the blatant haggling is entirely absent from Churchill's account.[47]

Although Churchill presents the warning as of paramount significance, it should be borne in mind that the prolonged wrangle over its delivery was only incidental to the intensive activity on the international scene, which was suppressed in the memoirs. Cripps had in vain been pressing the government to define their policy towards Russia in the event of a change in the international constellation. After the signature of the Yugoslav–Soviet pact, coinciding with Churchill's message to Stalin, Cripps resumed his canvassing in favour of a *de facto* recognition of Russian control of the Baltic. In his memoirs Eden competes with Churchill for the distinction of having been the first to lay the foundations of the Grand Alliance. The evidence of German intentions and Russia's varied attempts to stem German aggression proved that 'the time had come for a smoothing out of relations' with Russia which, Eden assures us, ranked high on his list of priorities.[48] This, however, was not the case. Cadogan easily convinced Eden to reject Cripps's proposals. The events referred to in Eden's memoirs were not considered to be 'definite evidence' showing that the Russians had abandoned the policy of co-operation with Germany. On the contrary, Eden still presumed that Stalin was likely to yield to Hitler's threats rather than risk an open breach, and was reluctant to 'indulge in useless gestures'. Cripps's role was reduced to close observation of events in order to discern the turning point, when it might be possible to effect a change in relations.

Sensing that an opportunity had slipped away, Cripps now complained bitterly that he had been provided with 'few cards to play here, but most of the possible ones had been taken away by His Majesty's Government'. Left to his own devices, he was set, as he wrote home, to do 'my best on my own initiative if I can get these people to listen to me'.[49] It was easier said than done; with Yugoslavia tottering towards collapse, the Russians became even more sensitive to any attempt to drag them into the war. None of the pretexts used by Cripps led to a meeting with Vyshinsky. Finally, after a 'rather stiff letter' to Vyshinsky, he was summoned to the Foreign Ministry in the middle of a lunch given by the Swedish ambassador on 9 April. Cripps, however, was not permitted even to start a political conversation; Vyshinsky seemed to have withdrawn into his shell. On his return to the embassy Cripps wrote a personal letter to Vyshinsky.[50] The letter, more than ten pages long, deplored the Soviet habit of seeking security zones for their own frontiers rather than securing the neutrality of the Balkans as a bloc. Though the letter preceded the major setbacks to the British forces in Greece, when seen against the background of the calamity there it was bound to enhance Stalin's suspicion of attempts to bring him into the war in order to relieve the pressure on Britain. The most striking sentence in Cripps's letter, therefore, was his recommendation that:

> the current moment is the most crucial from the point of view of the Soviet Government, because inevitably the question arises of whether it would be better to wait and meet the undivided might of the German armies alone, when they can choose the time to take the initiative, or whether it would be better to take immediate measures to unite Soviet forces with the still undefeated armies of Greece, Yugoslavia and Turkey, with feeble British assistance in manpower and resources. These armies would number over 3 million men and would trap a very great number of German forces in difficult terrain.

Cripps was in fact driving home the essence of Churchill's message, that it was 'perhaps the last opportunity for the Soviet Government to take action to prevent a direct attack upon its frontiers by the German armies'.[51]

It was only after delivering his own warning that Cripps received Eden's instructions to go ahead with the delivery of Churchill's warning. Cripps now dropped one of his customary bombshells, disclosing the private warning he had just given to Vyshinsky. He feared that in the new circumstances the Russians would not understand 'why so short and fragmentary a commentary, on facts of which they are certainly well aware, without any definite request for explanation of Soviet Government's attitude or suggestion for action by them, should be conveyed in so formal a manner'. Delivery of the message, he stated emphatically, 'would be not merely ineffectual but a serious tactical mistake'. While great amazement was expressed in the Foreign Office at Cripps's inexplicable action in producing his own full-dress political letter to Vyshinsky, it was agreed that there was no point in pursuing the matter any further. On 15 April Eden presented Churchill with Cripps's reply, together with a short note concurring that 'there may be some force in Sir S. Cripps's arguments against the delivery of your message'. Churchill, however, overruled all these reservations. He informed Eden that he 'set special importance on the delivery of this personal message from me to Stalin. I cannot understand why it should be resisted. The Ambassador is not alive to the military significance of the facts. Pray, oblige me.' There was another short delay while Eden was out of London until Cripps was finally instructed on 18 April to deliver the warning despite his reservations. He was to use any channel and include such of the supplementary comments of the Foreign Office as were 'still applicable'.[52] The warning finally found its way to Stalin in the Kremlin only on 21 April.

Churchill's and Eden's retrospective claim that the warning was intrinsically connected with the laying of the foundations for the Grand Alliance is arguable. The ruling political concept at the Foreign Office had not been shaken by the dramatic events, the accumulating intelligence reports or Churchill's intervention. A marked 'strict reserve' attitude and a refusal to initiate fresh negotiations remained the declared policy of the government. Goaded by Cripps, Eden did inform Cabinet on 21 April of his intentions to embark on fresh negotiations, but added that he 'was not very sanguine of good results'. He did not intend 'to put the Soviets in good humour' with Britain in the hope that 'something might emerge'.[53] Churchill, as if oblivious of the motives which had prompted him to insist on the delivery of his warning to Stalin, was not in favour of proceeding with 'frantic efforts' to demonstrate 'love' but rather advocated 'sombre restraint'.[54] Eden hastened therefore to concur with the Prime Minister that there was 'nothing to be gained from further attempts with Russia now'.[55]

The doggedness with which Churchill clung to his warning is easy to understand if examined in the context of the disastrous military setbacks inflicted on Britain. The need to enlist Russia was dictated by the reverberations of these events on the domestic front as well as on British stature in the Balkans and the Middle East. It was no coincidence that Churchill's interest in the Enigma intercept increased on 1 April, just as he received General Wavell's cable depicting the success of Rommel's offensive in Cyrenaica, 'rather sooner and in more strength' than he had expected, forcing him to retreat. Churchill was immediately struck by the consequences of the defeat, hastening to warn Wavell that 'far more important than the loss of ground is the idea that we cannot face the Germans and that their appearance is enough to drive us back many scores of miles. This may react most evilly throughout Balkans and Turkey . . . By all means make the best plan of manoeuvre, but anyhow fight.'[56] The early haggling over the delivery of the warning coincided with the decision to bring the faltering offensive in the Western Desert to a temporary halt while diverting troops to Greece. The decision was geared in many ways to rally a despondent public opinion rather than follow tactical or strategic considerations. Obviously, the only chance of checking the Germans in Greece, especially after the opening of the Yugoslav front on 6 April, was through the introduction of a Russian threat in the rear.[57]

Wavell proved unable to stabilize the line, conceding the acute danger facing Tobruk on 7 April. Churchill reacted swiftly, accusing Wavell of a failure to 'strike the right note for our public'; London was the place 'where opinion has to be held'. The atmosphere at home had become so oppressive that Wavell was instructed by Churchill to hold Tobruk 'to the death without thought of retirement'.[58] The brevity and cryptic drafting of the message to Stalin had been explained by Churchill as a means of attracting Stalin's attention and establishing confidential contact with him. After 10 April, when the battle in Greece took a turn for the worse, he no longer seems to have attached much significance to this argument. On that day Eden returned empty-handed from the Middle East and a gloomy Cabinet learnt that 2,000 men, among them three generals, had been taken captive in Libya. The prevailing feeling of despair was reinforced by the renewed bombing of London. The prospect of a sudden dramatic event on the eastern front provided the only ray of hope. Bearing this in mind, and completely unconcerned about the effect on the Russians of a public declaration of supposedly secret information, Churchill expressed his belief on the radio on 9 April and again in Parliament on the 27th that Hitler might suddenly divert his campaign in the Balkans to seize 'the granary of the Ukraine and the oilfields of the Caucasus'.[59] This corollary to the supposedly secret message entirely cancelled its effect.

On 15 April Churchill admitted that the Germans appeared to be so successful in their offensive that they now posed a serious threat to Egypt. He could not both maintain the defence of Egypt and pursue the resistance in Greece.[60] By the time of the delivery of the warning the situation had become so severe that Churchill was gravely concerned about 'the fate of the war in the Middle East, the loss of the Suez Canal, the frustration or confusion of the enormous forces we have built up in Egypt, the closing of all prospects of American co-operation through the Red Sea'. Finally on 22 April Wavell regretfully informed Churchill that the 'time has come to prepare public in official communiqué for impending Greek collapse'.[61] For Churchill the possible loss of Egypt and the Middle East amounted to 'a disaster of the first magnitude to Great Britain, second only to successful invasion and final conquest'. The situation had become so acute that Wavell was instructed that in the ensuing battle 'no surrenders by officers and men will be considered tolerable unless at least 50 per cent casualties are sustained by the Unit or force in question . . . Generals and Staff Officers surprised by the enemy are to use their pistols in self-defence.'[62]

Rumours of War and a Separate Peace

Mistrust of British intentions increased in direct proportion to the worsening military situation. During the winter, when military operations had
come to a halt, the Russians anticipated that Hitler would consolidate
Germany's economic position by executing selective military operations
in the Middle East. Once the 'war season' opened he was expected to
concentrate the decisive effort against Britain. By April, however, it had
become obvious that a stalemate had occurred on the Anglo-German
front. On the other hand, after the defeat inflicted on England in Greece,
it did not seem conceivable that the British would ever be in a position
to force a decision on the battlefield. A compromise peace seemed
plausible.[63]

The crucial task of Soviet diplomacy and intelligence, therefore, was the
early detection of any signs pointing to a separate peace. Maisky was one
of the few Mensheviks holding high office to survive the purges; his
popularity in London at the height of the policy of collective security
probably saved his life, and he was fully conscious of this. His former
association with the Mensheviks had taught him prudence and he went
out of his way to demonstrate his loyalty to Stalin. He was rewarded for
this when in February 1941 he was elected a full member of the Central
Committee of the Party. His appointment, Molotov stressed, reflected the
appreciation that Maisky 'performs well as the ambassador plenipoten-
tiary in difficult conditions and it is necessary to show that the Party
values diplomats who implement the will of the Party'.[64] The significance
of Maisky's reports has been underrated. Few diplomats were so well
regarded in London. His intimate knowledge of the political scene in
England was crucial for the Kremlin's assessment of British policies on
the eve of the war.

Once the Balkans were set ablaze Maisky's reaction was that of extreme
caution and reserve. 'Let us live and see' became his favourite catch-
phrase; it was 'difficult to be a prophet these days' and he had no intentions of making 'a guess through a coffee cup'. And yet a careful
examination of his contacts, diary entries and telegrams to Moscow gives
a clear insight into the views held by the Kremlin. The most important
task of Soviet diplomacy was to neutralize the bad blood which threatened to impair German–Soviet relations.[65] Most of Maisky's visitors,
among them Vansittart, the former permanent Under-Secretary at the
Foreign Office, went out of their way to impress on him that the Soviet
Union might well be the next victim. Maisky, well attuned to the Kremlin,
tended to see in such approaches the British obsession with seeing
Germans everywhere, 'even under the bed'. He faithfully informed
Moscow of his firm handling of such blunt efforts to involve Russia in
war.[66]

Maisky was undoubtedly sceptical about the likelihood that Churchill might sue for peace. He nonetheless purported to have detected a well-orchestrated campaign of the British government and press to 'frighten the Soviet Union with Germany'. He was particularly disturbed by Churchill's public announcements on 9 and 27 April, mentioned above, in which he warned of a future German move against Russia. 'Since when', Maisky wryly asked Churchill's intimate adviser Brendan Bracken, 'does Churchill tend to take the interests of the Soviet Union so closely to his heart?' In the complicated situation, warned Maisky, Churchill's statements were 'a source of embarrassment and even tactless. They were having an opposite effect in Moscow to what he intends.' Maisky's suspicions were only reinforced when he found out that Churchill did not really possess any concrete evidence about the German intentions. It was clear, concluded Maisky, 'that the campaign of the British Government and the English press on the approaching German attack on the Soviet Union was unsubstantiated and evidence that: "Der Wunsch ist der Vater des Gedankens." '[67] Lloyd George told Maisky that he found the Prime Minister 'depressed and restless'. Neither the defeats in Libya nor the tremendous German successes in the Balkans had been anticipated by him. Churchill, he thought, was living 'in the certainty of a German assault on the Ukraine and is only waiting for the USSR to fall into the English basket like a "ripe fruit" '.[68]

When in early May Churchill was asked by a sceptical Prytz, the Swedish ambassador to London, how England intended to win the war, Churchill responded with a charming fable:

There were two frogs, an optimist and a pessimist. One evening they were hopping around the meadow and happened to notice a wonderful smell of milk from a nearby dairy. The frogs were tempted and jumped through an open window. They thought they were in luck and jumped right into a large jar of milk. What could they do? The pessimistic frog swam round in circles, saw that the sides of the jar were high and slippery and could not be climbed, and so became panic-stricken. It turned over on to its back, folded its legs, and sank to the bottom. The optimistic frog did not want to perish in such an inglorious way. It also saw the high, smooth sides of the container, but resolved to put up a fight. Throughout the night the frog swam and thrashed its legs in the milk until it was thoroughly churned up. And what happened then? As you might have guessed, by morning the optimistic frog had churned a large piece of butter from the milk and so was saved.

In Maisky's memoirs, with obvious hindsight, he uses the tale to depict Churchill as the leader who stood firm against all odds. But at the time,

as is obvious from his diaries, he formed a different impression. While
the memoirs end with that heroic story, the diaries reveal that Prytz was
little impressed by Churchill's sense of drama. He told Maisky explicitly
that Churchill lacked any grand strategy and relied on improvisation. He
seemed to have little idea of how to win the war. In the absence of any
concrete gains for Churchill to point to, Priutz formed the impression that
the imminent clash between Germany and Russia had indeed become the
British Prime Minister's fixation. In the case of a German–Soviet war
Churchill was 'prepared to enter into an alliance with anyone who might
be advantageous, be that the devil, Satan himself'. Maisky had therefore
become convinced that the lack of alternatives was increasingly prompt-
ing Churchill to ensnare Russia in the war through the spreading of
rumours.[69]

In view of the growing German concern over the rumours,[70] urgent
measures were taken to dispel them. At a reception held at the Soviet
embassy in Washington, the ambassador, Umansky, drew Halifax aside
and several times complained bitterly that 'hostility to Soviet Russia
survived in British Government circles, as also the spirit of Munich'.
Umansky launched a virulent attack on Churchill, commenting that in his
last broadcast he had made what could be, 'with respect, only described
as a gaffe. He had spoken as though Germany not only would but could
swallow the Ukraine with the greatest of ease. This was both absurd
and offensive.' With members of the German embassy within earshot,
Umansky boasted of the achievements of the Red Army at Khalkin-Gol,
emphasizing that Russia was not Daladier's France.[71]

The sense among the Russians that one false move, a military provocation or a diplomatic blunder, might begin a war now led to prudence
bordering on paranoia. Incidentally or not, Maisky's actions were clearly
curtailed after the fall of Yugoslavia and Churchill's warning, with the
rising fears of provocation and a separate peace. Like the rest of the Soviet
diplomatic staff, he was closely monitored by a large contingent of NKGB
at the embassy. He could hardly conduct an interview without an eaves-
dropper and often had to take his guests for a stroll to the end of the back
garden of the embassy if he wished to speak freely.[72] After his meeting
with Eden on 16 April, he was always accompanied, undoubtedly under
instructions from Moscow, by his new counsellor, K. V. Novikov, who
seemed to Eden to be 'a Kremlin watch-dog'. Maisky noted Novikov's
presence at all his meetings, even in his shorter reports. Whether Novikov
was employed by the security forces or by Narkomindel to watch over
Maisky, this unprecedented procedure clearly hindered his contacts with
Eden, as he himself suggested in jocular fashion in his diary:

> Eden telephoned, invited me and asked me to come alone, because
> E[den] would be alone. I answered him that I did not see any reason

not to bring N[ovikov] with me. When we were in the reception area, the secretary emerged and stated that it would be better for N. to wait in the reception area. However, I went in to see E. with N. Seeing us together, E. blushed deeply with irritation, which I had never seen in him so far, and shouted: 'I don't want to be rude, but it should be said, that today's invitation is for the ambassador alone, not for the ambassador and the counsellor.' I replied that there were no secrets between me and N., and I did not understand why he could not accompany me in the discussions. E. heatedly said that he had no personal animosity towards N., but that he could not set an undesirable precedent; if the Soviet ambassador could arrive with his counsellor, then other ambassadors could also do the same. If it was possible to bring a counsellor, then why not bring 2–3 secretaries? Then the ambassador would not come alone, but bring an entire delegation. That would be unworkable. E. had never received an ambassador other than on his own, and he had no intention of changing his practice. I shrugged my shoulders. N. remained, but E. sat red-faced and sullen throughout our conversation. The situation ended up by being impossible. If such a scene is repeated, I will have to take my leave and return to the embassy.[73]

There was little question as to whom Maisky feared more, Stalin or Eden.

The Bogy of a Separate Peace

The belated attempts to secure Soviet involvement in the Balkans, epitomized by Churchill's warning, undoubtedly revived in Moscow the memories of the events of the late summer of 1939 and enhanced the suspicion of an attempt to shift the war to the eastern borders. This coincided with the revival of fears of a separate peace. On 17 April, before receiving Churchill's final instructions to deliver his warning, Cripps complained to Eden that a perilous situation had arisen, due to a large extent to the government's failure to make up its mind whether it was prepared to make 'any or what bid for close relations' with Russia. Consequently, as a result of the débâcle in South-eastern Europe, Russia became more susceptible to pressure from the Axis. Without waiting for instructions from London, Cripps now addressed Molotov with a fourteen-page memorandum of inducements and threats as a last resort to bring the Russians into the Allied orbit. This impulsive approach, it should be stressed, was dictated by a wish to thwart the activities of Schulenburg, who had left unexpectedly for urgent consultations in Berlin.[74] Cripps feared, as he forewarned Eden, that Schulenburg might return from Berlin 'very soon with a new offer to Soviet Union on a large scale in exchange for her whole-hearted economic co-operation with

Germany, and with an alternative veiled threat as to what will happen if the Soviet Union refused'.[75]

In delivering the message Cripps, in his characteristic sermonizing style, lectured Vyshinsky on the policy that he believed Russia should follow. All the ingredients savoured of provocation. Cripps did not confine himself to alerting the Russians to the danger, which he believed was no longer a hypothesis but rather concrete German plans for the spring. He resorted to what he recognized as the 'delicate' device of drawing the Russians towards Britain by playing on their fears of a separate peace. As events soon proved, the Foreign Office was right in objecting to the use of this 'double-edged weapon which may encourage Stalin to cling more tenaciously to his policy of appeasement'.[76]

His insinuations of a possible separate peace if Russia did not alter her policy had lasting if not fatal consequences:

> It was not outside the bounds of possibility, if the war were protracted for a long period, that there might be a temptation for Great Britain (and especially for certain circles in Great Britain) to come to some arrangement to end the war on the sort of basis which has again recently been suggested in certain German quarters, that is, that Western Europe should be returned to its former status, while Germany should be unhampered in the expansion of her 'living space' to the east. Such a suggestion might also receive a response in the United States of America. In this connection it must be remembered that the maintenance of the integrity of the Soviet Union is not a direct interest of the British government as is the maintenance of the integrity of France and some other Western European countries.

He was, however, careful to add, though this would be entirely lost on Stalin, that 'at the moment there was no question whatever of the possibility of such a negotiated peace so far as His Majesty's Government are concerned'. Vyshinsky did not feel the need to consult his government before turning down Cripps's memorandum, which embodied the lethal combination of both a 'separate peace' and an attempt to drag Russia into the war. He rejected it explicitly on the ground that the 'necessary prerequisites for discussing wide political problems did not exist'. Vyshinsky had also prepared for Cripps a reply to his detailed personal letter of 11 April which comprised only four lines in much the same vein.[77]

So deep-seated now were the Russian apprehensions and preconceived views that in reporting personally to Stalin Vyshinsky claimed to have noticed that Cripps acted with 'nervousness which could hardly be concealed'. The ambassador complained of his treatment and regretted having disclosed the information about the German threat. Hardly concealing his own hostility, Vyshinsky had advised Cripps that it was 'up to him' to decide what information to disclose, but he would hardly encourage him to make extraordinary approaches before the conditions were ripe for a political discussion. The Bulgarian ambassador was told bluntly by Vyshinsky on the same day that Stalin 'would not allow the Soviet Union to become involved in the war'. Stalin had also gleaned from inside the British embassy that the rumours of war were being spread 'with the aim of intimidating the neutral states, and the Soviet Union in particular'.[78]

These threats only reinforced a report from the NKGB informant within the embassy about Cripps's off-the-record press conference on 6 March, after his return from Ankara, in which he expressed his belief that Hitler might attack Russia, risking a war on two fronts. But it was equally likely that he might:

> attempt to conclude a peace with England on the following terms: the restoration of France, Belgium and Holland and the seizure of the USSR. Such terms of peace stand good chances of being accepted in England, because, as in America, there are influential circles who would like to see the USSR destroyed, and if the situation in England worsened, they will compel the Government to accept Hitler's peace terms.[79]

Cripps had indeed confided in his American counterpart, Steinhardt, as well that he could easily envisage his government's connivance in a German invasion of Russia in return for peace.[80] That he genuinely believed in the possibility of a separate peace was to a large extent a result of his isolation in Russia and his absence from London during the Blitz, when Churchill had established unshakeable authority as a national leader. As a witness of Churchill's 'finest hour', Maisky was inclined to play down the possibility of a separate peace in defiance of the views held at the Kremlin.[81] This led him to waver perpetually between his own convictions and the views which he thought Stalin expected to receive. Consequently, as will become clear, his vacillation too contributed to the Kremlin's false appreciation of the approaching dangers.

The day after raising with Molotov the possibility of a separate peace, Cripps was finally forced to transmit Churchill's message. In view of his letter to Vyshinsky of 11 April and the interview with him on 18 April, he did not find it advisable to pass on the additional information, which could only be seen as repetitive.[82] Uneasy after the ill-fated accord with Yugoslavia, the Russians had become obsessed with the thought that Churchill was attempting to drive a wedge between them and Germany. To rule out any clandestine collusion with Britain they were quick to leak the essence of Cripps's memorandum to the Germans.[83] The official reaction was expressed by blunt accusations in *Pravda* against the United States and Britain in the same spirit.[84] The fear that Britain might obstruct a political solution with Germany also stemmed from the sense of hope-lessness in London which, as Maisky noted in his conversations with British leaders, was overwhelming.[85] The prediction of the Northern Department of the Foreign Office that after the dispatch of the warning 'further approaches to the Soviet Government will be worse than useless, since they will be taken as proof that our position was desperate and thus reinforce the tendencies of Molotov to compromise with the Germans' was indeed borne out.[86] Widespread rumours, some of them planted on Soviet intelligence, only intensified the feeling in the Kremlin that the British might not even assist Russia in the event of a German attack: they would 'either rapidly conclude peace with Germany or halt military action against her'.[87] By the time Churchill's warning reached Stalin it clearly had an adverse effect, only deepening Soviet suspicions. 'Look at that,' Stalin told Zhukov, 'we are being threatened with the Germans, and the Germans with the Soviet Union, and they are playing us off against one another. It is a subtle political game.'[88]

Maisky was assigned the task of verifying with Eden the contents of Cripps's memorandum, which had clearly paralysed Moscow. In an unprecedented move it had been transmitted to Maisky *in toto*. The warn-ings and memorandums were perceived in Moscow to be a deliberate attempt to embroil Russia in war on the side of Britain by creating a sem-blance of negotiations. The second memorandum was particularly dis-concerting in that Maisky had warned Eden only a week earlier that such documents were couched 'in the wrong sort of terms to make any appeal at all'; the new one sounded 'like a bad joke'. Diverting the discussion from the Balkans to the Baltic issue was expected to put British intentions to the test. A British statement on this issue would have been a snub to the Germans and proof that a separate peace was not on the agenda. In the same vein Maisky steered the discussion to the Middle East in an effort to find out whether the army had deliberately slackened its efforts. Butler displayed a clearly defeatist outlook, confessing that after the fall of Yugoslavia the situation of the Anglo-Greek forces 'is becoming cata-strophic'. His rather vague optimism that 'hard months lie ahead for England but that in the final account she will nevertheless emerge victori-ous' was hardly a solace.[89]

Aftermath

It is doubtful whether Churchill's message to Stalin constituted a warning. The military significance which Churchill attached to his message is also disputable. He insisted all along that, rather than being a warning of German intentions, the note to Stalin was an exposition of the deficiencies and weaknesses of the German army. Had the Russians acted upon it, they might still have faced similar consequences, as was clearly demonstrated by the brilliant double campaign of the Wehrmacht in Yugoslavia and Greece. When Operation 'Marita' was contemplated the Wehrmacht had an ample pool of troops to draw on. Naturally preparations for 'Barbarossa' were disrupted, but only fifteen divisions out of the enormous force of 152 earmarked for Russia were actually diverted for the operations in Yugoslavia and Greece. Because of the leisurely pace of the build-up for 'Barbarossa'[90] most of the divisions assigned for Russia had not yet departed. In practice only four divisions were detached and sent to the south ahead of their scheduled deployment in the East. Only the 14th Division out of the five divisions earmarked for the south, whose movement had alerted Churchill, had started rolling east before being ordered to change course. As the military historian M. van Creveld has most convincingly proved in his debunking of the established myth,[91] the Greek diversion, far from overstretching the Wehrmacht, only produced a negligible delay of the build-up for 'Barbarossa'.[92]

The circumstances of Churchill's somewhat distorted presentation of his warning are closely linked to two critical developments which coincided in October 1941: Cripps's unprecedented challenge to his leadership and Stalin's mounting dismay at the absence of a major concrete British contribution to the war effort against the background of the renewed German assault on Moscow. The combination was particularly threatening in view of the massive popular support of Russia in Britain and dissatisfaction within the War Cabinet among Churchill's closest colleagues, notably Beaverbrook and Eden. There is virtually no reference to the challenge in Churchill's memoirs. Cripps complained of the 'petulant and irrelevant telegrams' which were not 'worthy' of Churchill. He continued to oppose Churchill's strategy, which he described as the execution of 'two relatively unrelated wars to the great benefit of Hitler instead of a single war upon the basis of a combined plan'. To Churchill it had become evident, as he told Beaverbrook, that Cripps was 'preparing his case against us'.[93] Cripps's ceaseless pressure for diversionary action reached its peak in mid-October when the Defence Committee, hitherto Churchill's stronghold, considered favourably the redeployment deep in the Caucasus of two divisions originally earmarked for North Africa.[94]

The origins of Churchill's published version of his warning to Stalin date from this turbulent period. It was sparked by Beaverbrook's recollection of Stalin's complaints at the Moscow conference at the beginning of the month of not having been warned about 'Barbarossa'. In a note to Beaverbrook Churchill now exploded in a denunciation of Cripps's 'effrontery' in withholding the message in April. Reflecting on the whole episode, Churchill assigned 'great responsibility' to Cripps for his 'obstinate, obstructive handling of this matter'.[95] The fury had of course little to do with the warning but reflected the recent bickerings and bitter exchanges. Churchill also used the occasion to exonerate himself from blame for the low ebb to which his relations with Stalin had sunk. Had Cripps followed his instructions, he argued, 'some kind of relationship would have been constructed between him and Stalin'. This interpretation, a mere six months after the events, already ignored the political atmosphere in mid-April. Churchill's accusations seemed so far from the mark that they were contested even by Eden, despite his well-known timidity in communications with Churchill. At the time, he put it delicately to Churchill, 'the Russians were most reluctant to receive messages of any kind . . . The same attitude was adopted towards the later messages which I gave to Maisky.'[96] Notwithstanding those reservations, the exchanges with Beaverbrook were incorporated almost verbatim, except for Eden's defence of Cripps, in Churchill's war memoirs.

It is interesting to compare Cripps's dilemma with that of Laurence Steinhardt, the American ambassador in Moscow, who was placed in a similar situation in early March. The still neutral Americans had better intelligence sources in Berlin and throughout South-east Europe. By the beginning of March they had sufficient indications of an offensive German deployment to warrant an approach to the Soviet government. Weighing the pros and cons, Steinhardt dissuaded Cordell Hull, the American Secretary of State, from taking this course, arguing that the move would be regarded by the Russians as 'neither sincere nor independent'.[97]

9

Japan: The Avenue to Germany

Russia's abortive stand on Yugoslavia and Hitler's punitive campaign in the Balkans shattered Stalin's dream of establishing Soviet predominance in the region. Worse still, the reality of the danger now facing Russia was being driven home. Intelligence reports from varying sources had been accumulating on Stalin's desk. At the end of March the Director of Foreign Intelligence of the NKGB warned Marshal Timoshenko of the seriousness of the German intentions. He cited twenty-one clear indications of movement and concentration on the border of German troops since the end of February and especially during March.[1] On the same day he informed Stalin unequivocally that NKGB's undercover agents and corroborating evidence revealed 'the acceleration of the transfer of the German troops to the Soviet border'. The railway system, as well as requisitioned transport, was employed to full capacity to achieve the transfer not only of troops but also of artillery and ammunition from inside Germany to the border. Hasty measures were being taken to improve the roads leading to the border regions.[2]

By mid-April the NKGB had compiled such a long and impressive file on German troop concentrations that it felt confident enough, regardless of Stalin's known views, to enlighten Military Intelligence. This was followed a week later by the incredible report of forty-three fresh violations of air space by German flights. The sheer number of flights in less than a fortnight, and the fact that in many cases they penetrated more than 220 kilometres into Soviet territory, ruled out the possibility that they were the results of navigation errors.[3] Despite his tendency to agree with Stalin, Golikov conceded that in the first two weeks of April alone a massive movement of troops from Germany towards the Russian borders had been detected; they were now encamped in the Warsaw and Lublin districts. The intelligence led to an unequivocal conclusion: 'The transfer of forces and the stockpiling of ammunition and fuel are continuing on the borders with the USSR.'[4] The trend could no longer be ignored; the figures presented to Stalin showed that since February the Germans had increased their presence on the border by thirty-seven infantry divisions, three or four tank divisions and two motorized divisions.

However, German disinformation, confusion over troop movements during the subsidiary campaign in Greece and Yugoslavia and the leisurely pace of the deployment still made it possible for Stalin to doubt Hitler's ultimate personal objective, of which he barely had any information. The effectiveness of intelligence is determined by the access of the policy-makers to the collators and the ability of the latter to sustain a high degree of autonomy. Generally speaking, and in Stalin's case even more markedly, the collation of intelligence tends to be governed by a conceptual framework projected by the politicians downwards. The providers of the intelligence sift through the sea of information at their disposal, seeking to present the leadership with adequate responses to the issues that engross them. The selection process thus inevitably deflects the providers, and in turn the politicians, from the more vital data. The results are often counter-productive and indeed disastrous.

What obsessed Stalin after the fall of Yugoslavia was less the likelihood of war and more the prospect of averting a military clash through the creation of a climate conducive to a political settlement. The archival material supports Sudoplatov's recollections that almost half of the information available to the GRU and the Russian security services suggested that war could be avoided, and that rumours of war were being spread in an attempt to embroil Russia. 'The thickness of this file', he attests, 'grew day by day, as we received further reports of British activity to stimulate fear among the German leadership that the Soviet Union was coming into the war.'[5] It is necessary therefore to precede any discussion of Stalin's attempts at appeasement with a review of those files.[6]

From mid-April onwards, the nature of the reports presented to Stalin resembled an *à-la-carte* menu, from which he could choose the most appealing intelligence. Merkulov, the chief of the NKGB, chose to present Stalin with every piece of intelligence, to a large extent the reports of 'Starshina', which suggested the existence of a split between the political and military leadership in Germany. Comparison of the warnings in their raw state with the final ones submitted to Stalin indicates that by and large they were geared to the sustaining of the appeasement process. Information from within the German establishment was misconstrued to create an atmosphere conducive to further negotiations with Hitler.

Since the outbreak of war the Soviet legation in Berlin had been suggesting the existence of a breach within the leadership. Sustained by the 'powerful industrialists', Hitler seemed to be bent on continued co-operation with the Soviet Union. Only a negligible hard core of Nazi ideologists were believed to be motivated by anti-Soviet designs in their desire to expand the Third Reich.[7] In early March 1941 the various intelligence agencies naturally focused their attention on the growing evidence and rumours of a German plan to invade Russia. The prevalent tendency was to admit that though some circles in Berlin might be advocating war, and perhaps even making war plans, it was inconceivable that the German leadership, aware of the might of the Red Army, would condone such an outcome.

This imaginary rift within the German leadership had two supplementary consequences: it appeared to open a window of opportunity for a political settlement, while rendering the Russians excessively suspicious of British attempts to provoke them into a premature war.[8] Faced with the conflicting intelligence, Stalin increasingly favoured the reports which depicted a breach. It was no coincidence that the wave of rumours of war was compared by the Russians to what they believed had been a similar campaign pursued deliberately by the Western democracies after Munich to divert Germany to the East.[9] At the same time, the vociferous rumours within the diplomatic community in Moscow of an imminent war 'aimed at the southern districts of the USSR, rich in grain, coal and oil', were to a large extent dismissed as a deliberate provocation, attributed to Eden's fervent attempts to form a Balkan bloc.[10]

Stalin's attention was drawn to a report from 'Corsicanets' that Ribbentrop, and presumably Hitler, supported the unanimous recommendations of the four-year planning committee that Germany 'stood to gain much more' by pursuing trade with Russia than through the occupation of her territories. The real threat seemed to be from the armed forces, which were examining the issue from a strict military–strategic point of view and appeared to be trigger-happy. Though the preparations for war were obviously continuing and the deployment of the German army on the Soviet border closely resembled its deployment on the Dutch border before the invasion of the Low Countries, the danger did not seem imminent, as Turkey was marked as the next victim before Germany turned against Russia.[11]

The Soviet spy Richard Sorge, because of the romantic aura surrounding his activities, is often quoted as the most reliable source of the warnings. As a confidant of Ott, the German ambassador in Tokyo, and his military attaché, Sorge had access to precious information. With few exceptions his reports to Moscow have been quoted selectively by historians, highlighting those fragments which eventually turned out to be accurate. However, what in retrospect may be recognized as perfectly reliable data were mixed with misleading trends, reflecting the German embassy's partial and often false recognition of the reality. As always, rumours and evaluations were interwoven. The contradictory nature of the information therefore would allow Stalin to follow his policy of appeasement, vindicating his hope to avoid the outbreak of hostilities.

Sorge's first significant report, on 10 March 1941, focused on the pressure exerted on Japan to 'invigorate her role in the Tripartite Pact' against the Soviet Union rather than making a move southward. The information, obtained from a special courier who had just arrived from Berlin, added that such an approach was 'particularly prevalent in military circles', corroborating the erring assessment in the Kremlin of the situation in Berlin. The warning was further watered down by the axiomatic assumption that the German military would launch a war only 'once the present one was over'. From Stalin's point of view, therefore, such information, though indeed exposing the danger, suggested that the breathing space until England's defeat could be exploited if the split within Germany were encouraged.[12] In May Sorge briefed Moscow that Hitler was resolved 'to crush the Soviet Union and keep the European part of the Soviet Union in his hands as the raw material and grain resources necessary for the German control of Europe'. The statement, however, was modified to leave room for diplomatic manoeuvres, suggesting that war would become 'inevitable' only if the Russians were to cause further problems. The disparaging attitude of the German generals towards the Red Army and its defensive capabilities could also be addressed through a careful show of force and confidence, such as that evinced in Stalin's speech to the graduates of the war academies on 5 May.[13] Later in the month Sorge told his superiors that a group of German officials, fresh from Berlin, were convinced that war would start at the end of May; they were instructed to return to Berlin, on the Trans-Siberian express, before that date. But the same dignitaries also expressed their opinion that the danger of war in 1941 had receded.[14]

Finally, in one of his most famous reports, Sorge hastened to warn Moscow in early June that the German ambassador in Tokyo had been informed by Berlin that 'the attack against the Soviet Union will begin in the second part of June'. He was '95 per cent certain' of the outbreak of war. The ambassador had been convinced of such a development by instructions to him to minimize the transmission of important data via Russia and to reduce the transportation of rubber through the Soviet Union to the minimum. A follow-up telegram, of which the original has not come to light so far, somewhat reduced the significance of the information. Sorge traced its origin to Lieutenant-Colonel Scholl, the German military attaché, who had left Berlin almost a month earlier, on 6 May. From Stalin's point of view, this date was prior to the 'breakthrough' in the 'negotiations' with the Germans. When pressed by Sorge, the German ambassador in Tokyo admitted that he possessed no corroborating information from Berlin. Scholl, however, had revealed to him that the planned attack was prompted by 'a major tactical mistake' by the Red Army; the Soviet army was deployed in a linear form rather than in depth.[15]

The illusion of a breach within the German camp was deeply rooted not only in Moscow. In mid-March, Stalin was shown a report from an agent within the British embassy of a confidential press conference held by Cripps. Cripps told the journalist that relations between the Soviet Union and Germany had 'deteriorated markedly' and war had become 'inevitable'. But, more significantly, he too now elaborated the 'split' between the German military and Hitler, who was opposed to a war on two fronts. Cripps expected Hitler to seek, and perhaps achieve, a separate peace with England, thus paving the way for a campaign in the East. Paradoxically such information, coupled with similar innuendoes made directly by Cripps, only encouraged Stalin to seek a rapprochement with Hitler to forestall such an agreement.[16]

Rumours of Soviet–German negotiations emanating from the well-informed Swedish legation in Berlin were widespread among diplomats in Moscow. Virtually all of them described in their reports the two tendencies discernible in Germany: 'one favouring rapprochement with the USSR by combining diplomatic and military threats, and the other advocating a direct military seizure of the economic resources of the USSR'. The almost unanimous view was that while the German army and people 'favoured action against Russia', it seemed that Hitler preferred to achieve his aims with his customary techniques of intimidation and cajoling. The month of May was therefore expected to witness either war or full co-operation.[17] This assumption had become so popular that in May Halifax transmitted to London information originating in Berlin, according to which:

> Russia, feeling her weakness vis-à-vis Germany, was gradually giving way and was preparing to give Germany economic privileges in the Ukraine and Baku area. Ribbentrop was believed to be in favour of such an arrangement but the German military were said to oppose it since they felt it would give Russia a breathing spell in which to strengthen her military position. These quarters thought it would be more to Germany's advantage to attack Russia now while she was still unprepared. Hitler was said to be still undecided between these two theories.[18]

In his extensive report to Stalin on 20 March,[19] Golikov elaborated at length the hypothesis of the split. He argued that two tendencies were prevalent among the Germans:

> The first – the USSR at present is weak both in military and domestic affairs and therefore it is wise to seize the convenient moment and

together with Japan get rid of the USSR and Soviet propaganda, and the sword of Damocles which is constantly hanging over Germany; the second – the USSR is not weak, the Russian soldiers are strong in defence as history has demonstrated. One should never take risks. It is better to maintain good relations with the Soviet Union.

Roughly speaking the German armed forces, led by Göring, were believed to be pressing for war against Russia and advocating a separate peace with Britain. Some reports had indeed suggested the existence of clandestine conversations and feelers on both sides; tracking such efforts would obviously become uppermost in the order of priorities of the intelligence agencies. Hitler and Ribbentrop were believed to be more cautious, and Hitler's decision therefore was not conceived as a foregone conclusion. Some reports, well represented in the pot-pourri, suggested that Hitler had been weighing three alternatives as to where he should employ his idle 228 divisions in 1941: he could invade England, attack in North Africa or indeed turn against the Soviet Union. Ample room was given to those reports that suggested that the war aims would be limited, such as giving assistance to Rumania and Finland in regaining the territories they had lost to the Soviet Union.[20]

The prominent position of 'Starshina' in the German Air Ministry, an obvious asset, was also a drawback. While he was well placed to provide a steady flow of both strategic and operational information, 'Starshina' in fact portrayed a one-sided picture seen from the Ministry's perspective. His relative ignorance of developments in other arms of the military led him to inflate the role of the air force as the spearhead in the campaign against Russia. He promptly postulated a scenario whereby Göring appeared as the most vocal advocate of the anti-Soviet camp, often pressing for war against Hitler's will. In his reports to Moscow he depicted in lively colours the clash between Göring and Ribbentrop, a clash that had 'gone so far as to sour their personal relations'. This view naturally led him to unfounded speculation, such as his theory that, while Brauchitsch seemed to propagate the idea of war, 'the majority of the German officer' corps was opposed to Hitler and among them the idea of an attack against Russia was not popular'.[21]

A week later Merkulov submitted to Stalin and Timoshenko a digested review of the latest intelligence, formulated in such a way as to silence the 'warmongers' and facilitate reconciliation with Germany. While the first part of the report did not dismiss the danger of war, it suggested that the German victories in North Africa were reviving their hopes of 'winning the war against England by way of striking their communication lifelines and oil resources in the Middle East'. In the second and most important part, the report from 'Starshina' of the rift between the armed forces and the politicians was given prominence. However, the presumed weariness of the troops led him to the conclusion that the strike power of the Wehrmacht had declined in comparison to 1939. The third section chose to bring to the fore a report which described the despondency within the Luftwaffe in face of the qualitative superiority of the Russian bombers and fighter planes.[22]

Stalin's reading of the foreign intelligence also enhanced his interpretation. Via Anthony Blunt, one of the 'Cambridge Five', he was able to lay his hands on at least some of the Foreign Office's weekly intelligence reports. The report he received for the week of 16–23 April indicated that 'the German preparations for war against Russia continue, though so far there is no absolute evidence that the Germans intend to attack the Soviet Union in summer 1941'.[23] Indeed, a synopsis of reports gathered by the residency in London on the British intelligence evaluation of German intentions corroborated the split theory. The intelligence paper on 'German Plans and Perspectives', covering the period of 4–11 May, disclosed from sources close to Himmler that a lightning campaign was aimed at occupying Moscow and setting up a government which would collaborate with Germany. If these were the aims of the war, Stalin could still hope to convince Hitler that he was his best partner if negotiations were resumed. More significant from Stalin's point of view was the additional information, contradicting the earlier evaluation, which supported the prevailing view in London that Germany was seeking to come to terms with Russia. The report disclosed that, while the German army was pressing for war, the politicians advocated negotiations. 'Led by Ribbentrop,' it concluded, 'they claim that in negotiations with Russia it is possible to obtain all that Germany needed, i.e. participation in the economic and administrative control of the Ukraine and the Caucasus. Germany will gain more from a peaceful solution than from control of occupied territory, deprived of the Soviet administrative apparatus.'[24]

Deliberate disinformation also contributed to the faulty evaluation, spreading rumours of the Wehrmacht's continued preparation and concentration of forces for an invasion of Britain.[25] But the disinformation that bolstered the self-deception proved the most effective. 'Litseist' continued to send his usual blend of accurate and false information. After giving fairly accurate though general information about the size of the forces facing Russia, he resorted to a soothing message. War between the Soviet Union and Germany, he assured the residency, was 'unlikely', despite the popular support it enjoyed in Germany. Hitler could not risk a war 'which might break the unity of the Party'. Working effectively on Soviet susceptibilities, he explained that Hitler was opposed to a war which might cost him at least six weeks, even if he were to be the victor, since during this time England might become stronger with the help of the United States. The concentration of troops was therefore merely a demonstration of the 'resolve to act'. Hitler assumed that Stalin was 'compliant' and would do everything to bring to an end the intrigues against Germany, and in the first place 'increase the dispatch of goods and in particular oil'. Germany stood to gain little from the war, as it was bound to introduce havoc in Russia. True, the Germans were confident of their ability to beat the Russian army, which had proved itself 'entirely unfit' both in Finland and in Poland; if forced to fight the Germans would find themselves in the Soviet capital and in control of the entire European part of the Soviet Union within six weeks. However, 'Litseist' dismissed the idea as a contingency plan.[26]

Very swiftly the 'split theory' was elaborated and incorporated into an 'ultimatum theory'. As early as 2 April 'Starshina' transmitted information emanating from 'Litseist' that Hitler was determined to 'use the grain and oil resources of the Soviet government'. As a sophisticated double agent, 'Litseist' was of course forwarding a mixed bag. It was clear that in the mood prevailing in the Kremlin the word 'use' might imply negotiations, while the build-up could be explained as a means of pressure. 'Starshina' himself attributed the war preparations to a 'demonstration' of German resolve. The focus of Stalin's attention was obviously directed to his appreciation that 'the actual initiation of military activities will be preceded by an ultimatum to the Soviet government with a proposition to join the Tripartite Pact'. Hitler was expected to launch the war only if Stalin 'refused to fulfil the German demands'. The need to act prudently was dictated by the suggestion that the ultimatum would be presented as soon as the battle of Yugoslavia and Greece was decided. The telegrams were withheld from Stalin until 14 April, when his miscalculations in Yugoslavia were exposed with the victorious entry of the Wehrmacht into Belgrade. Beria and Merkulov overruled the decision of the three-member analytical committee of Foreign Intelligence not to disseminate the information on war which did not tally with the view held at the top. Within days, indeed, a second telegram again referred to an ultimatum. The 'ultimatum theory' was thereafter adopted by the NKGB and fitted in only too well with Stalin's own views.[27] Very shortly a similar interpretation spilled over into the diplomatic community, inflaming it even further.[28]

A month later, on the eve of the negotiations with the Germans, described below, the Berlin residency conveyed a soothing message, originating from within the Ministry of Economy, that 'the Soviet Union will be asked to join the war against Britain on the side of the Axis. As a guarantee she will be asked to cede the Ukraine, and perhaps the Baltic countries.' Such a report naturally devalued contradictory information, such as that Hitler had told high-ranking officers: 'In the near future extraordinary events will take place which will appear to some to be completely incomprehensible. But the measures which we contemplate are a necessity, as the red mob raises its head over Europe.'[29]

The primary task which Stalin would henceforth set for his intelligence agencies would be to glean the nature of the demands Germany was likely to present. By and large, these focused on the German need to ensure a more intensive flow of Soviet deliveries. 'Litseist' continued to provide sophisticated disinformation, treading the thin line between credibility and deception. As the deployment could no longer be concealed, he admitted that the army was already fully prepared for the war and only waiting for marching orders. But the related data could be interpreted in varied ways. The German connivance in the pact with Japan was explained as a manoeuvre to gain time. Hitler seemed to be concerned that Japan, following the Italian precedent, might despite her weakness launch an adventurous war against Russia and drag Germany into a premature conflict. The wish to avoid war rendered Stalin susceptible to any information which suggested that Hitler was prepared to convert the military solution into a political one. According to 'Litseist', Hitler was motivated by the scarcity of commodities, mostly oil and wheat, for which he had to rely on the Soviet resources. For him the Ukraine was 'the granary of the entire European Continent'. Moreover, a breathing space was assured by Hitler's decision to postpone the war 'pending the developments in the Balkans and the success of the campaign against Egypt'.[30]

Shortly after the invasion of Yugoslavia, the residency passed on to Moscow information extracted from a major, designated 'X', that Hitler had made up his mind to attack the Soviet Union now that the war with Britain was being protracted, so as not to face a stronger Russia in the future. The possibility that war with Russia would precede the war with Britain now gained prominence but was cushioned by the ultimatum theory. Corroborating information was abundant. For instance, a certain Franz Kosh, a worker in one of the electricity factories in Berlin and a provider of reliable information, insisted that Hitler was aiming at a comprehensive trade agreement for ninety years, in return for which Germany would agree to Turkey and Finland becoming Soviet republics.[31] 'Mazut', a former Latvian and a director of one of the leading Rumanian oil companies, reported that the German disappointment with the trade relations with Russia was leading them to seek in Europe 'conditions which would force the USSR to make considerable concessions to Germany'.[32]

Stalin was acquainted with such reports while impatiently waiting the outcome of Schulenburg's consultations with Hitler in Berlin.[33] Indeed corroborating information from a reliable source suggested that the special planning committee in Berlin had reached the conclusion that the shortage of economic resources would force Germany 'to exploit the bread and oil reservoir of the Soviet state'. Some even suggested he might seek the creation of a free Ukrainian state, subservient to Germany.[34]

By early May many intelligence reports were going all out to accommodate the Kremlin. While the overwhelming evidence pointed to war in mid-May, 'Starshina' continued to adhere to the damaging evaluation that 'initially Germany will present the Soviet Union with an ultimatum with demands for wider exports to Germany and the cessation of communist propaganda. In order to fulfil these demands German commissars will be sent to the industrial and agricultural centres in the Ukraine and several Ukrainian regions will be occupied by the German army.' The suggestions of what the terms might be provide an insight into the extent of the submission that Stalin was considering when embarking on the false negotiations with Schulenburg. The 'war of nerves', as a further telegram from Kobulov explained, was carried out through misleading rumours. 'Starshina' still assumed the majority of the Germans officers, and some circles within the Nazi Party, to 'really be opposed to a war with the Soviet Union'. Such a war made no sense and could 'lead to Hitler's downfall'.[35]

On instructions from Moscow the embassy in Bucharest dismissed information about German consultations with the Rumanian Chiefs of Staff as a stage in the 'so-called German preparation of an attack against our state'. Moreover, the 'tendentious and unreliable' rumours were traced to English sources. It was even suggested that 'the British had deliberately allowed the Germans to occupy the Greek islands situated near the Straits, thereby posing a threat to the Soviet Union and dragging her into the war'. The British thus hoped to achieve two aims: 'on the one hand the destruction of the USSR, and on the other, the weakening of Germany. Both suited them.'[36] Indeed, this seemed to be confirmed in a series of intercepted telegrams from Cripps which were transmitted to Stalin. Cripps impressed on Eden that Hitler's next steps depended to a large extent on whether he could obtain complete obedience from Russia, which he believed would 'become obvious in the near future', a clear reference to Schulenburg's return from Berlin. He believed that so long as Russia did not provoke the Germans Hitler was likely to defer war. For that same reason he suggested a number of measures to drive a wedge between Germany and Russia, measures which would alarm Stalin and certainly divert him from the genuine danger.[37]

The diversion of the war to the Balkans and the Anglo-German entanglement in Greece encouraged speculation that Turkey might be the next victim, perhaps paving the way for the seizure of Egypt, the Suez Canal, Syria and Iran and possibly also Spain and Gibraltar.[38] Even reliable agents, like 'Dora' in Zurich who later gained fame for his accurate warnings, submitted misleading information. His sources in Berlin suggested that war would break out only once the entry of the British navy to the Black Sea was blocked and the Germans were settled in Asia Minor. It seemed therefore that Gibraltar and the Suez Canal were

Hitler's next objective in an attempt to expel the Royal Navy from the Mediterranean.[39] Partially at least the concentration on Russia's south-western border was explained as pressure to allow the transfer of German troops through southern Russia to Iran and Iraq. Such an axis, threatening British imperial assets, might also divert the British from an objective appreciation of the German threat.[40]

Upon Schulenburg's return to Moscow 'Starshina' anxiously informed the Soviet government that he had found out from the office liaising between the Air and Foreign Ministries that a decision had 'finally been taken for an attack on the Soviet Union' which was expected 'any day'. Even more disconcerting was the suggestion that Ribbentrop, 'who so far has not been a supporter of an attack on the USSR, recognizing Hitler's strong resolve on this question, has now assumed a position in support of an attack against Russia'. Moreover staff talks were in progress with the Finnish air force while the Bulgarians, Hungarians and Rumanians had been asking for defensive measures.[41] It is most likely, however, that Stalin was not even shown the telegram. On the other hand, he was briefed on that very day that Funk, the Minister of the Economy in Berlin, had completed a survey of German economic resources. His conclusions certainly delighted Stalin; they stated that, unless peace with England were concluded within the year and economic co-operation restored, Germany would have to 'widen the economic ties with Japan and the Soviet Union, particularly with the latter, by force if peaceful means fail'. The future co-operation depended on the Soviet ability to increase deliveries of raw material.[42]

Facing the obvious dangers, Stalin had to strike a delicate balance between submission to Germany and a display of self-confidence in order to discourage the Germans from reacting to his weakness. His intricate political game, which in hindsight, against the background of the invasion, seems absurd, was grounded in the logic of the unfolding events. Stalin was rarely challenged by his entourage, since his 'divide and rule' method of government and his projection of his own reasoning on to that of his rivals, coupled with extreme suspicion even of potential allies, led to self-deception of colossal proportions. The increasingly reduced alternatives led him to adhere more tenaciously to his own convictions, stifling divergent opinions and coercing the entire political and military system to conform to his views.[43] Moreover the evaluation was sustained by ample evidence which confirmed his political outlook. Only a marginal part of it was the result of deliberate deception by Hitler.[44] Far more significant were misleading directions presented to him by opponents of Hitler's policy, Schulenburg in the first place and to some extent even Ribbentrop. Ultimately Stalin remained convinced that sophisticated political manoeuvres could avert or at least postpone the war. This he hoped to achieve through the revival of Ribbentrop's invitation for Russia to join the Axis, submitted to Molotov in Berlin prior to his departure in November 1940.

The decision to avoid a conflict with Germany at all costs seems to have been reached a mere two days after the conclusion of the pact with Yugoslavia. Molotov ordered Dekanozov to renew negotiations cautiously with Weizsäcker for bilateral relations. Weizsäcker for his part noted that Dekanozov 'did not utter one word of criticism of our intervention in Yugoslavia'; on the contrary, he seemed to be interested in the visit of the Japanese Foreign Minister, Matsuoka, to Berlin, which he was assured was a continuation of efforts to expand the Tripartite Pact which had as 'its purpose to prevent the war from spreading'.[45] The ambassador in Vichy was used to convey to the Germans the Soviet intentions of adhering to the letter of the Ribbentrop–Molotov Pact. Russia pledged not to make 'any obligation either military or political with respect to Yugoslavia', and strongly wished to avoid the experience of 1914 when defence of Serbia dragged her into war.[46]

The most significant reaction to the fall of Yugoslavia was the hasty conclusion of a neutrality pact with Japan on 13 April, during Matsuoka's return trip from Berlin via the Russian capital. The conclusion of the Ribbentrop–Molotov Pact had had immediate and direct repercussions on Soviet policy in the Far East. The close collaboration with China petered out. Chiang Kai-shek, the leader of the Kuomintang and head of state of nationalist China, failed even to tempt the Russians with a proposal for a military alliance and the right for Russia to place garrison forces on Chinese territory.[47] His special military envoy, who arrived in Moscow in late April 1940 with a more concrete proposal to form a common platform 'to crush Japanese aggression', was denied access to Stalin and returned to China empty-handed.[48] These approaches were perceived by Stalin as British attempts to ensnare Russia in war.[49]

The gradual drift away from China coincided with reconciliatory approaches to Japan.[50] Molotov was cautious in responding to the Japanese initiatives, fearing, as he frankly revealed to Togo, the Japanese ambassador in Moscow, that it might be used by the Japanese as leverage in their talks with the Americans.[51] He changed his tune, however, when the fall of France appeared imminent. Rather than the bilateral relations which had hitherto been on the agenda, he now wished to move to the 'major issues, linked with the various changes which occur in the international situation and those which may happen in the future'.[52] This led to a quick demarcation of the Manchurian border, to the dismay of the Chinese, which Molotov anticipated would hasten the dissolution of the old 'Anti-Comintern Pact'.[53] These early moves cleared the air and encouraged further co-operation when Prince Fumimaro Konoe became the Prime Minister in July 1940 and brought about an improvement in relations with both Germany and Russia. The new tripartite understanding, he hoped, would provide Japan with a 'golden opportunity' to exploit the upheaval in the international arena to expand southward. Matsuoka, who as representative of Japan in the League of Nations had proved to be an enthusiastic proponent of better relations with Russia, was appointed the new Foreign Minister.[54] Matsuoka's grand designs in foreign policy matched those of Stalin and Ribbentrop. He hoped that the conclusion of a Tripartite Axis would pave the way for the creation of a 'four-power entente' with the Soviet Union. He shared Ribbentrop's vision of the new world order in which Europe, Asia and Africa would be divided into spheres of influence of the four powers. He expected the Germans to act as the brokers in bringing about the new order. The move southward against the British imperial assets was strongly encouraged by Berlin. The German ambassador promised the new Foreign Minister that Germany would 'do everything within her power to promote a friendly understanding and will at any time offer her good offices to this end'.[55]

But it was really the increasing tension in the Balkans and the creation of the Axis in autumn 1940 which led to a more active Russian policy. In a rare move Molotov invited Togo for breakfast during which both finally agreed that in order for Russia to be associated one way or another with the Tripartite Pact the differences between the two countries should be resolved.[56] Stalin had been informed by Beria of Hitler's intentions of effecting a pact between the Soviet Union and Japan 'to demonstrate to the world the full ties and unity of purpose between the four powers' and thus discourage the United States from assisting Britain.[57] Stalin, however, did not wish to commit himself to the neutrality pact proposed to him by the outgoing ambassador in Moscow before he gained a clearer impression of Hitler's plans during Molotov's forthcoming trip to Berlin.[58]

Matsuoka wasted little time. Lieutenant-General Tatekawa, professing to be 'a strong man seeking to reason with the Russians without a diplomatic turn of phrase', was sent to Moscow to effect a change. To the Swedish ambassador he seemed like 'one of those Buddha statues that can be bought in the market for a couple of rubles – but his stomach is majestic and is the only vital thing in the otherwise immobile little person'. Tatekawa's appearance was misleading, because it concealed a dynamic personality. He saw an advantage in his military position, as he believed that in time of war 'countries could only communicate with each other holding a sword in the hand'.[59] Already at his first meeting with Molotov on 1 November he proposed a non-aggression pact analogous to the Ribbentrop–Molotov one. Aware of Konoe's need to remove the threat of a second front in the north, Stalin was not in a hurry. Himself preoccupied with the post-war arrangements which he hoped would soon be settled in Berlin, he wished to receive an appropriate price:

Japanese recognition of Russia's sovereignty over northern Sakhalin and of her fishing rights, thus reversing the humiliating Portsmouth Agreement in 1905 following the destruction of the Russian navy. Such terms, Molotov impressed on the ambassador, were only 'fair compensation' for allowing Japan 'to have her hands free to move south', while Russia was risking alienation of the United States and China.[60]

After the failure of Molotov's negotiations in Berlin Stalin remained cautious, reluctant to bring down on himself the wrath of both the British and the Americans. Moreover, the Japanese, eager to conclude the agreement, had reverted to their proposal of a neutrality pact while deferring the contentious issues to a later date. Stalin therefore adopted delaying tactics, drawing the Japanese into exhaustive and tedious negotiations on the fishing rights.[61] Once the fishing convention was concluded at the end of January Stalin moved on to equally arduous negotiations on a trade agreement.[62]

On the whole the negotiations with the Japanese mirrored the developments on the western front, which since mid-February had presented an imminent threat. The stalemate in the negotiations and the circulating rumours of a war which might draw Japan into hostilities with Russia led Matsuoka to take the reins in his hands. Ostensibly, the European tour he now made was aimed at co-ordinating Japan's moves with those of her Axis allies. But over 'a cup of tea' at his own residence Matsuoka confided to the Russian ambassador that he regarded the meeting with the Soviet leadership during a stopover in Moscow as 'the most important aim of his trip'. He ascribed the secrecy of the meetings in Moscow to the opposition at home, though in reality it was directed at the Germans, who he feared might exert pressure on Japan to move against Russia. A keen traveller, he asked the Russians to provide him with a railway carriage with a kitchen and a sleeper to facilitate the long trans-Siberian journey.[63] During his trip he drank vodka and evinced confidence in his diplomatic ability by telling his entourage how he would 'make puppets of Hitler and Stalin'. As the train ploughed through the barren snow-covered plains, Matsuoka 'composed short poems, full of subtle twists of thought, or meditated silently while sipping weak powdered tea'.[64]

For Stalin, who was set on exploiting his diplomatic skills to avert the danger of war, the proposed visit was a godsend in his efforts to restart the dialogue with Hitler, stalled since Molotov's visit to Berlin. He certainly was encouraged by Matsuoka's announcement in parliament that he intended to make a 'serious effort to bring about a fundamentally improved relationship' with Russia, in harmony with the ideas of the Tripartite Pact.[65] Tatekawa was thus informed in Moscow that the time had come to 'move from the small issues to the regulation of cardinal questions'. Tatekawa indeed hoped this could be accomplished during Matsuoka's stopover in Moscow.[66] There was certainly a sense of collusion when Schulenburg and Rosso were excluded from a series of dinners to which the Japanese ambassador invited Molotov on his own.[67]

Matsuoka's concern about the Germans was relieved to some extent by Ribbentrop himself. Still cultivating his dream of establishing the Continental bloc through the raising of the 'Great Wall' from the Atlantic to the Pacific Oceans, he continued to press the Japanese to capture Singapore and divert the war effort to the Pacific. To do so he had to conceal from the Japanese the plans to attack Russia, which might pose a threat to Japan as Germany's ally and involve her in an unwanted war. Ribbentrop even confessed to Oshima, the Japanese ambassador in Berlin, his hopes of reviving the negotiations with Russia and achieving her inclusion in the Axis.[68] Consequently the level of negotiations was raised just before Matsuoka's departure; arrangements were made for unprecedented meetings between the Japanese Foreign Minister and Stalin, both on the former's way to Berlin and on his way back.[69] On his arrival in Moscow on 24 March, Matsuoka cautiously raised with Molotov the idea of a non-aggression pact. However, the Foreign Ministry had drawn Molotov's attention to the fact that the 1937 non-aggression pact with China prohibited the Russians from concluding a similar one with Japan. He therefore proposed a neutrality agreement instead.[70]

At his meeting with Stalin Matsuoka recalled his efforts to bring about a non-aggression pact with Russia in 1932, which had been foiled by hostile public opinion at home. He and Konoe were now 'determined to bring about the improvement of relations between the two countries'. Matsuoka appeared extremely eager to win Stalin over, developing an elaborate theory which depicted the Japanese system of government, though ruled by an emperor in a capitalist environment, as 'moral communism'. The present government sought through its association with the Tripartite Pact to bring about 'the destruction of the Anglo-Saxons' and with it 'capitalism and individualism'. If Stalin shared such views, he suggested, Japan would be 'prepared to walk together hand in hand' with him. Stalin was certainly amused by the exposition but was aware of the more practical openings. He clearly wished to use Matsuoka as a go-between, asking him to convey to Ribbentrop the message that the Anglo-Saxons had never been Russia's 'friends, and nowadays he most likely would not wish to befriend them'.

Stalin further stressed that differing ideological outlooks should not be an obstacle to rapprochement between the two countries. It was evident, however, that Matsuoka preferred to defer the actual negotiations until after he had sounded out Hitler.[71] The prospects seemed bright. At a reception given for the Japanese Foreign Minister that same evening he openly spoke of the need to cement the Axis and find an appropriate way for Russia to join it. He strongly hinted at his intentions of paving the way for such an arrangement during his trip to Berlin.[72] Moreover, Stalin's suspicion, fed by wild rumours that Matsuoka might visit London in search of an agreement with the British which would free his hands to fight Russia together with Germany, was countered by denials from Maisky in London.[73]

Matsuoka's meetings in Berlin between 27 and 29 March coincided with the coup in Yugoslavia. It placed the German leadership in an uneasy position. While wishing to discourage Japan from signing the agreement in Moscow, the Germans were equally eager for her to launch an attack on Singapore. The Japanese clearly deemed it necessary to conclude an agreement with Russia before embarking on war. Hitler therefore concealed from Matsuoka the plans to attack Russia, which might tempt the Japanese to postpone the expedition south and claim booty in Russia. But Matsuoka soon realized that the larger scheme of recruiting Russia to the crusade against the Anglo-Saxon world would not be realized. The Soviet position on the Balkans, Ribbentrop complained to him, was unacceptable, as 'Germany needed the Balkan Peninsula above all for her own economy and had not been inclined to let it come under Russian domination.' If Stalin, whom at one point he described as 'sly', did not work in harmony with what the Führer considered 'to be right, he would crush Russia'. Matsuoka did make unsuccessful attempts, in his typical roundabout way, to reverse the trend, disclosing to Hitler that during his conversations with Stalin he had been told that 'Soviet Russia had never got along well with Great Britain and never would'. But he was advised rather firmly not to bring up the issue of Russia's accession to the Axis in the talks in Moscow, 'since this probably would not altogether fit into the framework of the present situation'. In the last meeting, Ribbentrop, probably under the impact of the events in Yugoslavia and under direct instructions from Hitler, cautioned Matsuoka more specifically not to conclude a non-aggression pact with Russia, as Germany could engage Russia if there were a Russian attack on Japan while the latter pursued her goals in the south. His final words upon their departure contained a clear hint at 'Barbarossa', though maintaining the ambivalence. He could not assure the Japanese Emperor 'that a conflict between Germany and Russia was inconceivable. On the contrary, as matters stood, such a conflict, though not probable, still would have to be designated as possible.'[74]

Matsuoka certainly received the message. Though Hitler hardly touched on the issue during their meeting on 1 April, Matsuoka went out of his way to apologize for the miniature conference which had taken place in Moscow. He failed to mention that the initiative had come from him but zealously calculated that if the translations were taken into account, then he had 'conversed with Molotov for perhaps ten minutes and with Stalin for twenty-five minutes'. While giving a fairly accurate account of the talks, he significantly neglected to mention that he had offered Stalin a non-aggression pact.[75] Matsuoka drew some encouragement from his talks in Rome with Ciano, who never tired of gnawing at the German drive to supremacy. Matsuoka was in fact praised for his efforts to explore the possibilities for extending the Tripartite Pact and encouraged to further 'clarify and improve the relations between Japan and the USSR'.[76]

Matsuoka returned to Moscow on 6 April and met Molotov the following morning. The dramatic events in Yugoslavia between the two visits had brought about a marked change in Stalin's outlook.[77] By the time of Matsuoka's departure on 13 April, the day the Wehrmacht entered Belgrade, Stalin had come to grips with the German menace and his desperate need to resume negotiations with Berlin. The Japanese avenue, therefore, had become a vital one. No wonder therefore that Matsuoka found Molotov at their first meeting to be 'considerably softer'.[78] Matsuoka no longer beat about the bush; he had no interest in negotiations on trade and fishing rights, which he was leaving for his ambassador to handle. His visit was motivated 'not by coincidental current mutual interests but by the wish to improve relations for the next 50–100 years'. In short his 'uppermost desire was to conclude a non-aggression pact, overlooking other outstanding issues'. He was certainly not reluctant to exploit the tension in German–Soviet relations, suggesting that 'to conclude the pact now would produce a good master's strike – that which in a baseball game is called a "master-hit", when the ball is hit, with maximum strength, and directed with a strike in the right direction'.

The obvious appeal for the Kremlin was that the move would considerably improve its bargaining position vis-à-vis Germany. Matsuoka further lulled the Russians by suggesting that the possibility of a joint attack on the Soviet Union had not been discussed in Berlin. Molotov however continued to make the conclusion of a neutrality pact conditional on the return of southern Sakhalin, which Russia had lost in the 1905 war with Japan: in other words the revision of the Portsmouth Agreement, giving Russia full control of the Sakhalin Islands. Those conditions, which had prevented the conclusion of the agreement for more than a year, clearly demonstrate the prominence attached by Stalin to a comprehensive agreement which would be part and parcel of the final post-war order. The meeting therefore ended inconclusively, though not before Matsuoka revealed his intention to postpone his departure by one week to the 13th, the next weekly departure of the trans-Siberian express.[79]

After preliminary consultations, Matsuoka appeared ready to settle for the neutrality pact but Molotov, well aware of Japan's desperate need to conclude such an agreement, made it conditional on the liquidation of the Japanese concessions in northern Sakhalin. Unwilling to compromise, Matsuoka revived the German offer for Russian access to the warm waters of the Persian Gulf and the Indian Ocean, which he believed would reduce the concession in northern Sakhalin to a 'small issue'. Negotiations had clearly reached a stalemate. That night, after dinner with Molotov, Matsuoka boarded the 'Krasnaya strela' train to Leningrad. He certainly hoped that his absence from the capital would exert pressure on the Kremlin to reconsider its decision.[80]

On his return to Moscow on 11 April Matsuoka conveyed to Molotov the Emperor's readiness to conclude the neutrality agreement, but refused even to consider the liquidation of the Japanese concessions in Sakhalin. Molotov gambled on the urgent Japanese need to neutralize the Russian threat by bringing the talks to an end, regretting that it would be 'necessary to wait for more conducive circumstances to conclude a political agreement'. Matsuoka played his cards with iron nerves. He presented Molotov with a draft letter he had composed on the train from Leningrad which he suggested Molotov should submit on the day the neutrality agreement was signed, expressing a hope that a similar one relating to the concession issue would be signed before long. He displayed no anxiety when Molotov dug in his heels. The rest of his time in Moscow until the departure of the trans-Siberian express was spent on touring the city, visiting technological institutes of the Academy of Science and the motor industry and even paying a visit to a reticent Zhukov, the arch-enemy and hero of Khalkin-Gol, on whom he made a 'bad impression'. The evening of 12 April was spent at the theatre enjoying a production of Chekhov's *The Three Sisters*.[81]

While Matsuoka savoured the treasures of the Hermitage and the Kremlin and reviewed the technological innovations in Moscow, Stalin witnessed with growing concern the disastrous consequences of his miscalculations over the Yugoslav issue. He had just received reports that the Greeks had become 'extremely pessimistic' about their ability to resist, while the 100,000-strong British army in Greece had not yet engaged the Wehrmacht. The view in Athens was that the entire British plan for Europe had 'collapsed and great concern was expressed over the future course of the war'.[82] Moreover, a stream of intelligence reports indicated the intention of the Wehrmacht to pursue the 'Drang nach Osten' as soon as the Balkan campaign was concluded. According to the residency in Berlin, Matsuoka was believed to have come there to confirm the fulfilment of the alleged promise of a war against Russia made to Japan when she joined the Tripartite Pact.[83] The futile show of force in Yugoslavia, about which he had had serious reservations to start with, now gave way to an urgent need to appease the Axis.

Emerging from the theatre, Matsuoka was whisked off to the Kremlin, where Stalin was waiting for him. Matsuoka repeated his desire to conclude the neutrality agreement, which he believed to be 'useful and expedient not only for Japan, but also for the USSR', but 'without any attached conditions and produced as a diplomatic *Blitzkrieg'*. Stalin feared that the Tripartite Pact was the main stumbling-block for the conclusion of the agreement. Matsuoka, however, put his mind at rest, leading him to believe that Ribbentrop had impressed on him that the agreement was bound to improve German–Soviet relations. On the whole, as in his previous meeting with Molotov, Matsuoka was keen to present the neutrality pact as a component in the overall scheme of integrating Russia in the tripartite arrangements. In an attempt to divert the Russians from the Sakhalin issue, he elaborated once again the arrangements proposed to Molotov in Berlin to divide Asia into spheres of interests between the two countries. This interested Stalin far more than Matsuoka's descriptions of Japan's 'moral communism'. The significance he attached to the agreement was not the expansion of the creed but rather the fact that 'cooperation between Japan, Germany and Italy on the major issues was possible'. For the moment he attributed Hitler's reluctance to turn the Tripartite Pact into a four-power pact to a conviction that he could win the war on his own. The moment chosen for the conclusion of the neutrality pact with Japan, therefore, not only reflected Stalin's fear of a war on two fronts; he truly saw in it 'a first step, and a serious one, to future co-operation on major issues'. Stalin confessed that he had had his suspicions about Japanese aims, but he was now convinced that there were no 'diplomatic games', and that Japan was 'genuinely and seriously interested in improving relations with the Soviet Union'. Stalin then praised Matsuoka for his 'sincere and direct speech'. It was 'very rare to find a diplomat who speaks openly what is on his mind. What Talleyrand told Napoleon was well known, that "the tongue was given to a diplomat so that he could conceal his thoughts". We, Russians and Bolsheviks, think differently and believe that also in the diplomatic arena it is possible to be open and sincere.'[84] Extraordinary efforts were made to secure a swift confirmation by the Emperor of the agreement, which was signed in a jubilant mood in the afternoon of 13 April; unusual photographs of Stalin and Matsuoka, arm in arm, were to adorn the papers the next morning.

The rather surreal farewell scene at the Yaroslavsky railway station deserves to be described in detail, as it conveys vividly the growing self-deception which now marked Stalin's hope of avoiding calamity.[85] Stalin was convinced that he had succeeded by a masterly stroke in outwitting his opponents. In his eagerness to see Russia embroiled in war with Germany, Cripps interpreted the agreement and Stalin's boosting of Matsuoka's vanity at the station as a proof of the 'lengths to which Russia would go to try and secure her Eastern frontier in the light of the danger in the West'.[86] This interpretation was common at the time and has been repeated since, to a large extent by Russian historians, who prefer to see in the gesture, as in the case of the agreement with Yugoslavia, a stand against Hitler rather than excessive appeasement of Germany.[87]

The weekly trans-Siberian train had been kept waiting for an hour and a half while the celebrations continued at the Kremlin. When Matsuoka and Tatekawa finally arrived at the station, around 6 p.m., they were woozy from the refreshments consumed at the Kremlin during an impromptu banquet following the conclusion of the agreement. They had hardly entered the station when, to the amazement of the large corps of diplomats and journalists, Stalin, who was rarely seen in public and had certainly never seen off any of his guests, appeared at the station. He was dressed in his military coat, leather boots and overshoes and his brown-visored cap. Staggering a couple of steps behind him was Molotov, who 'kept saluting all the time, shouting: I am a pioneer, I am ready!' If we are to accept the judgment of the Bulgarian ambassador, he was 'the least drunk' of the participants.

An alert journalist left an accurate and lively description of what followed:

> Stalin began embracing the Japs, patting them on the shoulders and exchanging expressions of intimate friendship. As few of the Japs or Russians could speak each other's language, the most frequently heard remark was 'ah . . . ah'. Stalin went up to the aged and diminu-tive Japanese Ambassador-General, punched him on the shoulder rather hard, with a grin and an 'ah . . . ah', so that the General, who has a bald and freckled pate, and is not more than four feet ten in height, staggered back three or four steps, which caused Matsuoka to laugh in glee.

But the most significant gesture occurred when Stalin, noticing Colonel Krebs of the German embassy, suddenly detached himself from the Japanese group. Tapping Krebs on the chest and looking up at his face searchingly for a few seconds, he asked him: 'German?' The six-foot German officer, towering over the diminutive Stalin, stood at attention and mumbled an embarrassed affirmative in poor Russian. Slapping him on the back and shaking his hand, Stalin declared with deep conviction, 'We have been friends with you and we shall remain friends with you', to which Krebs answered, 'I am sure of that', though the Swedish military attaché noticed that he 'did not seem so convinced of it'.[88] It immediately dawned on the Bulgarian ambassador, who was fluent in Russian and a keen observer of the Kremlin, that Stalin was sending signals about his decision to associate himself with the Axis. He wondered whether Matsuoka 'did not play the part of a mediator between Russia and Germany'.[89] Indeed, when Stalin took leave of Matsuoka for the third time, he shook his hand firmly and embraced him, declaring in a some-what cracked voice: 'We shall organize Europe and Asia.' Stalin then personally accompanied Matsuoka into his carriage and stayed on the

platform until the train left the station. The members of the Japanese delegation were so touched by the special honour bestowed on them that
they accompanied Stalin to his car; as the Rumanian ambassador noticed,
'the little Ambassador, Tatekawa, standing on a bench, waved his hand-
kerchief and cried in a strident voice: "Spassibo! Spassibo! (Thank you!
Thank you!)" '[90]

Before leaving Soviet territory Matsuoka sent a warm personal letter to
Stalin from the Manchurian border station which well conveys the historical significance of the episode. He described the great impression he
had formed of Russia, her people and her achievements. 'The unofficial
yet heartfelt scene on the occasion of the conclusion of the Pact remains,
undoubtedly, one of the happiest moments of my entire life. The kind-
ness of your Highness, expressed in your personal appearance at the
station to see me off, will always be valued as a sign of genuine goodwill
not only towards me but towards my people.' Another letter followed the
ratification of the agreement, congratulating Stalin on his courage in the
execution of the 'diplomatic *Blitzkrieg*'.[91]

The agreement was an avenue for the revival of the talks with the
Germans. 'The Balkan victories', the Turkish envoy Aktay reported
home, 'have penetrated with lightning effect the dark skulls of the
Soviets . . . the flattering of the Japanese by Stalin in the Soviet–Japanese
agreement has been done purely and simply to win the heart of Germany.'
Stalin, he concluded, was 'about to become a blind tool of Germany'.[92]
Matsuoka was indeed genuinely interested, like Ciano, in warding off a
German attack on Russia once Japan was set on the drive southward. The
Japanese spared no effort in impressing on Ott, the German ambassador
in Tokyo, that Matsuoka had 'found Stalin to be absolutely desirous of
peace. Stalin . . . had assured him that there could be no question of Russia
making a deal with the Anglo-Saxon powers.'[93] A further telegram from
the German embassy in Tokyo emphasized that the Russians now
appeared to be impressed by the German successes and 'had become
ready to conclude a pact. Therefore Russia decided on going hand in hand
with the Powers of the Tripartite Pact. The Tripartite Pact has only now
become the sterling instrument of the policy of the Axis Powers and Japan
through the long sought for Russo-Japanese Agreement.'[94]

It was hardly a coincidence that Stalin chose this crucial moment, following Matsuoka's visit and during Schulenburg's visit to Berlin,[95] to free
himself from the ideological constraints which limited his political
manoeuvrability. The German invasion of Yugoslavia had brought about
a split within the Yugoslav Communist Party on the issue of whether the
war should be defined as a defensive one. Earlier it had proved impossible to harness the Party to Moscow and restrain it from acting against
the Germans in the wake of the coup. The ideological haggling seemed
too hazardous; the benefits reaped from communist supporters in general

were marginal and in the case of Yugoslavia and Bulgaria even counter-productive.[96] The unequivocal message now was that state interests rather than Messianism dominated the Kremlin. It was high time, urged the Russian ambassador to Vichy France, 'to stop seeing the hand and eye of Moscow everywhere'. The Soviet Union, he succinctly explained, was pursuing a realistic rather than a sentimental policy. Sentiments, he said, 'we save for small children and little animals, but in practice we do not conduct a sentimental policy in relation to any country, be it Slav or not, be it small or big'.[97]

At midnight on 20 April, after an exuberant performance by Tadjikii dancers at the Bolshoi,[98] the members of the Politburo returned to the Kremlin for a routine nocturnal meeting to which Dimitrov, the President of the Comintern, was summoned as well. Stalin chose the occasion to propound his latest views on the prospects for world communism, which shook the foundations of the Comintern by advocating 'national communism':

> the Communist parties should become completely independent rather than sections of the C[ommunist] I[nternational]. They should be trans-formed into national Communist parties, under different names – Workers' Party, Marxist Party, etc. The name is not important. It is important that they should focus on their own people and concentrate on their own basic and specific tasks. All of them should have a Com-munist programme, they should be based on Marxist analysis but not dependent on Moscow, for us to solve all the current problems which vary in the individual countries. The International was created under Marx in the expectation of an approaching international revolution. The Comintern was created by Lenin in such a period too. Today, *national* tasks for each country have top priority. Do not hold on to what was *yesterday*. Take into account exactly the new conditions which have been created.[99]

Little time was lost in implementing the decision. The next morning Dimitrov and members of the Praesidium of the Comintern started drafting the new conditions for admission to the Comintern which were to replace the militant Twenty-one Conditions introduced by Lenin in 1921. They now emphasized: 'the *full independence* of the various Com-munist Parties, their transformation into *national* parties of Communists in the given countries, guided by a Communist programme, not deciding on the concrete tasks by their own convictions but in accordance with the conditions of their countries, and taking responsibility for their own decisions and actions'.[100] Stalin next saw to it that the usual com-munist slogans on display in the May Day celebrations were replaced by ones which emphasized values of nationalism and national liberation.[101]

Dimitrov was warned by Zhdanov that Stalin regarded 'uncritical cosmopolitanism' as a 'fertile ground for spies and for agents of the enemy'; he expected the changes to be 'implemented genuinely, so that they do not seem as if only the clothes are changed but the rest stays the same. It should not look as if the Executive Committee of the Comintern is dismissed but in fact there continues to exist an international directing centre'.[102] Stalin's position on the very morning of 22 June demonstrates how far was his mind from a revolutionary war. He was indubitably relieved to instruct Dimitrov that though the Comintern might still remain open 'for a while ... the parties in the regions may create a movement for the defence of the USSR. Do not bring up the question of the socialist revolution. The Soviet people will carry out a patriotic war against Fascist Germany. The issue at hand is the defeat of Fascism.'[103]

10

'Appeasement':
A New German–Soviet Pact?

The overwhelming need to pacify Germany was symbolized by Stalin's unprecedented appearance at the station to see Matsuoka off. The act was of particular significance as it was known that Schulenburg, 'uneasy and disturbed by dark forebodings', was leaving that same evening for Berlin, hoping to 'defer any hurried and ill-considered decision'.[1] It was Schulenburg who had initiated the consultations in Berlin, although both Ribbentrop and Weizsäcker later claimed to have fathered the idea.[2] The urgency was dictated by the realization that Stalin's stand on Yugoslavia had finally provided Hitler with the pretext for pushing ahead his plans to solve the conflict with Russia by force. The opposition to this course briefly created an uneasy alliance within the Foreign Ministry. Hitler, like Stalin, exercised power by driving wedges between the military, the politicians and the civil service.[3] It was hard not to be aware in Berlin of the growing rumours of an impending military campaign which plainly reflected Hitler's intense suspicion of Russia.[4] However, neither Ribbentrop nor his Foreign Ministry was aware of the extent of the military preparations under way, let alone the directives on 'Barbarossa'. All they knew was that Hitler had lost interest in the diplomatic process, and he was manifestly keeping his distance from the Foreign Ministry. Consequently, the advocates of the Continental bloc lost much ground but still sought ways of reversing the decision.

The increasingly isolated Ribbentrop reluctantly joined hands in spring 1941 with his professional diplomats in a last, though pitiful, attempt to dissuade Hitler from attacking Russia. Various sporadic and uncoordinated attempts were made to deflect Hitler from the course he had taken. Both Weizsäcker and Ribbentrop seem to have entertained hopes that Germany's allies in the Axis could be recruited to deter Hitler. However,

Hitler concealed his plans from his allies to forestall an open debate on his strategy. The opposition's moves could obviously be pursued only in a covert fashion through insinuations. Weizsäcker, for instance, had repeatedly approached Dino Alfieri, the Italian ambassador in Berlin (and an influential member of the Fascist Council in Rome), with hints of a possible war. In a meeting with Ribbentrop on 15 May Mussolini commented that 'it seemed to him advantageous that a policy of co-operation with Russia should be pursued',[5] though he also clearly relished the idea that the Germans might 'lose a good many feathers in Russia'.[6] Perhaps more significant were the attempts made by Weizsäcker to enlighten Matsuoka, who was also deliberately kept in the dark about German intentions during his visit to Berlin. Both Ott, the German ambassador in Tokyo, and Admiral Raeder, Commander-in-Chief of the German Naval Forces, conspired in this move.[7]

Schulenburg could not bring himself to believe that Hitler had opted for war and was even doubtful whether he was 'aware of the rumours of war'. He despised Ribbentrop, whom he blamed for 'trying systematically to isolate Hitler from him and make him depend on his own information and advice'. Since the appointment of Ribbentrop Schulenburg had exchanged only a couple of words with Hitler when they bumped into one another by sheer chance during Molotov's visit to Berlin.[8] Before setting out for his mission, Schulenburg produced a forceful memorandum jointly with the senior members of his staff: Hilger, counsellor at the embassy; Tippelskirch, his deputy; and General Köstring, the military attaché, advancing arguments against an invasion of Russia. Schulenburg held on to his belief that what united Russia and Germany was the wish to prevent the Anglo-Saxon bloc from assuming dominance in Europe. He tended therefore to dismiss the rumours of war as 'pure fantasy', a product of British propaganda. He strongly believed that 'anything the Germans stood to gain from a war with the Soviet Union could be obtained in an easier and safer way through peaceful negotiations'. Though Schulenburg shared the common belief that the Wehrmacht could crush the Red Army, he warned that an occupation would introduce uncontrollable chaos into Russia. Personally he did not believe that Hitler would launch an attack 'before England was defeated'. While sharing these appreciations, Rosso, more cynical and less idealistic, gave a forlorn warning, which Schulenburg tended to dismiss, that 'we have seen sufficient examples that the fools who now rule the world are capable of committing any folly'.[9]

Schulenburg further distorted, as had become his habit, a report to the Wilhelmstrasse on the Japanese pact. It was worded in such a way as to enhance his own credentials during the forthcoming visit to Berlin by faithfully reporting Stalin's own views. He underlined the conciliatory nature of Stalin's moves, relaying his pledge to Matsuoka that 'he was a convinced adherent of the Axis and an opponent of England and America'. Schulenburg then described in most dramatic fashion Stalin's meeting with Krebs. But, more significantly, he pointed out that Stalin had also specifically looked out for him and manifestly threw his arms around his shoulders and said: 'We must remain friends and *you must now do everything to that end!*'[10]

Schulenburg's colleagues at the embassy continued to bolster his efforts after his departure through a series of telegrams which stressed the co-operative Russian attitude. On 15 April they informed the Foreign Ministry that the Russians were now pressing for a solution of the boundary dispute in the Baltic area in conformity with the proposals previously made by the embassy. It was, they pointed out, an 'unconditional acceptance of the German demand'; they added that the Soviet attitude seemed 'very remarkable'.[11] A similar approach was made on the same day to solve the border disputes with Rumania.[12] A day later Tippelskirch telegraphed once again, for no apparent reason other than to convey the view held by members of the Japanese embassy in Moscow that the pact was 'advantageous not only to Japan but also to the Axis, that the Soviet Union's relations with the Axis will be favourably affected by it, and that the Soviet Union is prepared to co-operate with the Axis'. He again referred to the extraordinary scene at the railway station on the day of Matsuoka's departure, which to him indicated that Stalin had exploited the opportunity 'to show his attitude towards Germany in the presence of the foreign diplomats and press'.[13] A week later he informed Berlin that relations between Finland and the Soviet Union had 'recently become more serene' and that the Russians were no longer pressing for concessions in the nickel mines of Petsamo.[14]

When Krebs complained to the liaison officer of the Red Army that Yugoslav officers were continuing to appear in Moscow in uniform, Gavriloviç was promptly asked to evacuate them from Russia. Krebs was reassured that their presence in Moscow 'had no political relevance as the Yugoslav army and government had now ceased to exist'.[15] An important incentive for a breakthrough in Berlin was a Tass communiqué, published on 19 April, which clearly bore the trademark of Stalin. It went a long way to expose the Soviet desire for a new agreement with Germany. The agreement with Japan was attributed not to the German threat but rather to the proposals made to Molotov in Berlin the previous November 'that the Soviet Union should join the Three-Power Pact'. 'The Soviet government', it continued, 'did not *at that time* [author's italics] think it was possible to accept the proposals', clearly implying that circumstances had changed.[16]

Prompted by Schulenburg's arrival in Berlin, the German Foreign Ministry seized upon Stalin's new conciliatory attitude to broach the

topic directly with Hitler and the Wehrmacht. Karl Schnurre, the architect of the trade agreements with Russia, participated in these moves.
On 21 April he approached the High Command of the Wehrmacht and
conveyed the 'complaints' of Alexei Krutikov, the Deputy People's
Commissar for Foreign Trade, who happened to be visiting Berlin, that
'Germany did not provide enough rolling stock for transporting the goods
delivered by the Soviet Union from the German–Soviet border'. He even
mentioned the possibility of increasing Soviet deliveries.[17]

Hitler repeatedly deferred seeing Schulenburg.[18] On 21 April
Weizsäcker, who had 'almost entirely got out of the habit of trying to
achieve [his] aims through Ribbentrop', swallowed his pride; behaving,
as he put it, 'like a sneaking crawling creature without claws', he sought
an urgent interview with Ribbentrop. Despite Ribbentrop's reluctance to
meet him, Weizsäcker arrived in Vienna for a ten-hour stay and conferred
with him at the Imperial Hotel that very evening. Weizsäcker fully
endorsed Schulenburg's memorandum, which had been transmitted to
Hitler, and warned Ribbentrop that a war against Russia 'would end in
disaster'. Though Ribbentrop remained noncommittal, Weizsäcker gathered from his entourage that he by no means shared Hitler's views.[19]

The efforts finally bore fruit when Ribbentrop intervened personally
with Hitler and secured an interview for Schulenburg.[20] By the time the
meeting took place, Ribbentrop seemed to have been firmly converted to
the cause. He was, however, playing his cards cautiously, preferring to
gain an impression of Hitler's state of mind before committing himself
any further. On the eve of the meeting he sent instructions to Schulenburg from his special train to take notes of his conversation with Hitler
and to dispatch them promptly to him.[21] In the meantime he urgently
contacted Weizsäcker by telephone from Salzburg and requested the
Ministry's views on Schulenburg's memorandum, as he himself was contemplating a paper for Hitler on the subject. Weizsäcker had approached
Ribbentrop with elaborate arguments against a war at least twice during
the winter of 1941. On 6 March he had prepared a long memorandum in
which he set out his arguments against the war in Russia and had even
advocated a military alliance. The memorandum, however, had never
been transmitted to Ribbentrop. He now dictated the gist of it on the telephone, maintaining that 'Germany could not expect to beat England in
Russia.' His main reasoning ran as follows: 'A German attack on Russia
would only give the English a new moral lift. It would be interpreted
there as German uncertainty as to the success of our fight against
England. We would thereby not only be admitting that the war was going
to last a long time yet, but we might actually prolong it in this way, instead
of shortening it.'[22]

Little is known, however, about the nature of Schulenburg's meetings
during his fortnight's stay in Berlin. Although Hitler's military directives

were not laid before him, one may surmise that Schulenburg was exposed to the myriad rumours circulating in Berlin and was able to gather information through his circle of friends in high places, both in the army and in the Foreign Ministry. On the eve of his meeting with Hitler he had dinner at Schnurre's home. Schnurre, who had made an abortive approach to Hitler earlier, appeared most sceptical of Schulenburg's ability to move Hitler.[23]

On the afternoon of 28 April Schulenburg was finally received by Hitler on his own at the Reich Chancellery. His memorandum lay sealed in an envelope on the desk. Throughout the meeting Hitler ignored it, instead making general observations on the international situation.[24] Mistrustful of Schulenburg, and careful not to divulge his genuine plans, Hitler was scornful of the Russians, wondering 'what kind of devil had possessed them' in concluding a friendship pact with Yugoslavia. Hitler restrained his overzealous ambassador by levelling various accusations against Stalin which would later be employed as pretexts for the attack on Russia. Stalin's meddling in the Balkans was one such subject, but the main invective focused on the alleged Russian mobilization. Hitler, as Weizsäcker recalled later, 'had the effrontery on this occasion to pretend to Schulenburg, in the same way as he had to Matsuoka, that the German military preparations in the East were defensive'.[25] When Schulenburg insisted that those moves were guided by Russia's 'urge for 300 per cent security', this was immediately repudiated. Schulenburg attempted unsuccessfully to draw Hitler out by suggesting that 'Russia was very apprehensive at the rumours predicting a German attack on Russia'. Nor was he able to impress on Hitler that Stalin was anxious to conclude an agreement and was prepared to make further concessions. Barely half an hour after its beginning the Führer brought the meeting to an end, though not before dropping the casual remark: 'Oh, one more thing: I do not intend a war against Russia!'[26]

Schulenburg left for Moscow, on Ribbentrop's personal plane, in time for the May Day celebrations at the Kremlin. Hilger, the counsellor at the German embassy, writing his memoirs long after the events described here, when his memory had been refreshed by a historian, recalled how Schulenburg drew him aside as soon as he landed in Moscow and told him that 'the die was cast' and that Hitler had deliberately lied to him.[27] This statement has diverted historians for decades from the final and crucial chapter in Schulenburg's efforts to avert Hitler's move. Though sceptical about Hitler's sincerity, Schulenburg was still hopeful that he could produce a coup in Moscow. In the end he achieved the exact opposite, reinforcing Stalin's mistaken but convenient belief that it was still possible to prevent the war. As the dramatic events of the following days would testify, Schulenburg undoubtedly entertained hopes of persuading

Stalin to launch a personal initiative which might dispel Hitler's manifest suspicion and restore mutual trust.

Schulenburg returned from Berlin armed with what would prove to be a lethal conviction, reinforcing Stalin's erroneous assessment, that 'certain people in Hitler's entourage prevailed on him once and for all to have a showdown with the Soviet Union, but others, among them Ribbentrop, resolutely advised him against such a move, in any case not before England was brought to her knees. Hitler seemed to be leaning towards the latter view but was of course resolved to keep his options open.' Walther, counsellor at the embassy, who had accompanied Schulenburg to Berlin, further revealed upon his return that an armed conflict with Germany 'was improbable this year'. If the Russians were to proceed with provocations similar to that in Yugoslavia, then 'he would not know what the Führer would be forced to do'. In the present circumstances he expected Germany to come to an understanding with the Russians, though they would hardly be in a position 'to say anything in these matters'. However, as Schulenburg did not bring any concrete proposals he at first did not initiate any approach and waited to be summoned to the Kremlin.[28]

Stalin continued to work tenaciously to ward off the German danger. Fear of Germany had become so acute that Zhdanov even implored Stalin to postpone the May Day parade in Red Square so as not to provide the Germans with 'the pretext to attack'. But the more urgent problem facing Stalin was to quash the wild rumours about the inevitability of war, especially those which belittled the might of the Red Army, suggesting that the Wehrmacht could 'cut through Russia like a knife through butter'. The rumours might easily tip the scales in favour of an adventurous crusade against Russia.[29] Negotiations towards a pact with Germany had to be pursued from a position of strength. In mid-April Stalin had ordered the security services to accompany the German military attaché on an extensive tour of the Soviet military–industrial plants in Siberia and to spread information in Berlin about Soviet technical and military might.[30] Since the fall of Yugoslavia, when the threat of war had become imminent, Soviet ambassadors had been instructed to deny resolutely the rumours of war and at the same time to remind their interlocutors that they surely were 'oblivious to the might of the Red Army, to its fighting capacity'.[31] Kollontai, renowned for her anti-Nazi stand, was sent to the Swedish Foreign Ministry to dismiss the rumours of a possible war as 'completely groundless'. Even more remarkable was her rebuttal of suggestions that Russia contemplated 'any counter-measures to the German actions in the Balkans . . . even if Germany attacked Turkey'. This was a particularly embarrassing submission, considering that the entire squabble with Germany in the past year had revolved around control of the Straits. Her admission was no coincidence, as Vinogradov too 'resolutely' assured the Turks that were

Germany to interfere in Turkey the Soviet Union would remain 'totally passive'.[32] When, for instance, a most reliable source enlightened the Soviet ambassador in Bucharest about the massive German concentration on the Moldavian border, the 'rumours' were nonchalantly dismissed as 'exaggerated, hardly reflecting the intentions of German military circles, as the latter can overlook neither the military might of the Soviet Union nor the danger which faced them' were they to attack Russia.[33] In Washington Umansky too made efforts when in the company of German officials to show confidence in the ability of the Red Army to face the Wehrmacht.[34] In Moscow Vyshinsky dismissed a warning by Steinhardt, insisting that relations with Germany were governed by agreements which were fully observed. The Russians were not 'faint-hearted people' and were 'powerful enough to defend themselves'.[35]

It is within this framework that Stalin delivered his now famous speech to the graduates of the Military Academy on 5 May. The speech and the following toasts have been the focus of bizarre interpretations suggesting that Stalin was preparing the Red Army for an aggressive war against Germany.[36] The speech, however, was delivered at the height of the appeasement campaign and neatly dovetailed with it. Its aim was to act as a deliberate deterrent, discouraging the Germans from launching the war through a brazen show of confidence, while at the same time invigorating the army in case a war did break out. Because of its demonstrative nature the gist of the speech was deliberately leaked and was reported by the foreign legations.[37] It reflected the need to confront the increasing rumours of the dismal state of the Red Army. Numerous reports warned that the Wehrmacht was 'drunk with success'; the predominance of the German mechanized forces meant that the occupation of the country up to Moscow and the Urals should not 'pose serious difficulties'. The belief in the weakness of the Red Army, therefore, was encouraging the Wehrmacht to advocate a war with Russia before the completion of the campaign in England.[38]

The speech thus mirrored the instructions mentioned earlier for the Soviet diplomats to inflate the strength of the Red Army. It further sought to bolster morale in the army. Earlier in the year Zhdanov had been warned by the military that the peace-oriented propaganda and the 'pacifist mood' were diminishing the 'war spirit . . . and the nation's awareness of the capitalist encirclement'. It was therefore recommended that the 'essential international tasks' of the army should be geared towards 'the defence of the Soviet Union – the motherland of the world proletariat'. The press and the schools were entrusted with a campaign to prepare the population for war. However, rather than using revolutionary themes, traditional ones glorifying Russia's heritage were revived. The showing of plays like *Suvorov* or *Field Marshal Kutuzov* and the study of the war of 1812 and the defence of Sebastopol were encouraged.[39]

Stalin, Minister of Defence Voroshilov and politburo members at
Stalin's dacha.

Foreign Minister Molotov at his desk.

Churchill and Maisky at a lunch party in the Winter Garden of the
Soviet Embassy, London.

Ambassador Maisky with his aides at the Embassy.

Count von Schulenburg with Molotov at the signature of the
Ribbentrop–Molotov Pact.

Milan Gavriloviç, the Yugoslav ambassador in Moscow with his daughter,
returning to Moscow after the *coup* in Belgrade to take charge of the
negotiations on a neutrality pact.

Defence Minister, Marshal Timoshenko, examining artillery units, watched by Chief of Staff, General Meretskov (*right*), and his successor, General Zhukov, in the summer of 1940.

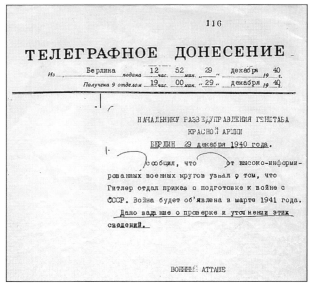

116

ТЕЛЕГРАФНОЕ ДОНЕСЕНИЕ

Из ____ Берлина _подана_ 12 _час._ 52 _мин._ „29" декабря 19 40 _г._
Получена 9 отделом 19 _час._ 00 _мин._ „29„ декабря 19 40

НАЧАЛЬНИКУ РАЗВЕДУПРАВЛЕНИЯ ГЕНШТАБА
КРАСНОЙ АРМИИ

БЕРЛИН 29 декабря 1940 года.

....сообщил, что ....от высоко-информи-
рованных военных кругов узнал о том, что
Гитлер отдал приказ о подготовке к войне с
СССР. Война будет об'явлена в марте 1941 года.

Дано задание о проверке и уточнении этих
сведений.

ВОЕННЫЙ АТТАШЕ

The warning to Stalin about Hitler's decision on 'Barbarossa', from the soviet military attaché in Berlin, 29 December 1940.

Molotov reviewing the guard of honour in Berlin railway station, November 1940.

Molotov entertained by Hitler in Berlin, November 1940.

The Luftwaffe's bombing of Belgrade, 6 April 1941.

King Boris of Bulgaria visiting Hitler at Berchtesgaden.

The Japanese Foreign Minister, Matsuoka, boarding the trans-Siberian train at Vladivostock heading for Moscow.

Matsuoka watches over Molotov signing the pact of neutrality with Japan in April 1941.

General Zhukov at the front, May 1941.

The former British ambassador to Belgrade Sir Ronald Campbell (*left*) and Sir Stafford Cripps, recalled for consultations by the Foreign Office, 12 June 1941.

The threat of an imminent war clearly required drastic indoctrination of the armed forces, who had been brainwashed by slogans of 'non-involvement' and 'peace'. Following the lead taken by Stalin in his speech to the cadets, Shcherbakov, the newly appointed Politruk (political commander) of the Red Army, set the trend. In a major directive he revived Lenin's justifications of a war which would extricate the Soviet Union from capitalist encirclement and 'hasten the final victory of socialism'. Regardless of the clearly geopolitical and pragmatic considerations which had led to the division of Poland, the absorption of Bessarabia and the Baltic States, these were now presented to the ranks as the ultimate victory and achievement of Leninist ideas. But Lenin's ideas of 1915, when he had actually deplored the idea of a 'defensive war' and advocated non-intervention in the imperialist war, were now twisted to justify the 'offensive' spirit.

Defence through strategic retreat and exploitation of depth had been inherent in the Soviet military doctrine as a preliminary to a counter-offensive. Defence and offence were therefore tied together in insepa-rable continuous operational manoeuvres. However, since the purges of the military the academies had been prohibited by Stalin from pursuing theoretical studies. Simplistic slogans had virtually replaced doctrine in an attempt to conceal the bankruptcy of the military. 'Shedding little blood and on foreign territory', Molotov wryly reflected on this period, 'was already a propaganda slogan. Agitation governed our ordinary policy, and it was necessary, nothing was done without it.'[40] The revival of Lenin's corrupted slogans therefore should be examined in the context of the imminent German threat, rather than as the fulfilment of a mes-sianic dream. Indeed, the slogans emphasized the need to indoctrinate the troops in 'the spirit of fiery patriotism, revolutionary resoluteness, and steadfast preparedness to launch a shattering attack on the enemy'. This could be best achieved through 'revitalizing the feeling of patriotism among the people, the infinite love of the Socialist motherland, in the spirit of fearless readiness to make sacrifices'. The directive stressed the need to idolize courage and eradicate fear of the enemy.[41]

In the speech Stalin expounded at great length and in minute detail the tremendous strides made by the Red Army from the technological and operational points of view. He then cast doubt on the invincibility of the Germans. According to him, Germany's weakness was due to her failure to recruit allies, alluding, as he had done during the negotiations with Matsuoka, to Russia's possible role. The short toasts proposed by Stalin are what have attracted undue attention. They were aimed mostly at boosting morale and indeed raising the alarm in view of the threat facing Russia. When in early June Timoshenko tried to exploit the speech to activate the operational plan, he was told explicitly by Stalin: 'This I said for the people, it is necessary to raise their vigilance, and you must understand that Germany will never fight on her own against Russia.'[42] The first two toasts were in the nature of slogans, calling for the intensification of theoretical studies and exalting the artillery, which was 'the god of modern warfare'. The third one, however, much in line with the main speech, stated confidently that with the completion of the modernization and reconstruction of the army, it could 'move from defence to attack'. However, the text, quite apart from the context of the speech, remained defensive in nature, concluding that 'the defence of our country must be carried out in an attacking fashion . . . The Red Army is a modern army, and a modern army is an army of attack.'[43] This of course was little more than a rather crude revival of the operational theories discussed earlier, which had been suppressed during the purges, a boost of morale and more significantly a clear message to Germany.

Confidence had been manifested in a similar way in the open. In his traditional speech on May Day Timoshenko too intertwined in a sophisticated manner a show of force with a call for the 'liquidation of war and the restoration of peace . . . the faster the better'. The Germans were expected to recognize in the Red Army a force which had to be reckoned with, especially now that it had been put on 'war readiness' footing.[44] The resort to deterrence may have been a result of a report by 'Starshina', submitted to Stalin, on the impressions gained by a delegation of the Luftwaffe to Moscow. The Germans had been struck by the advanced production line of the new Iliushin-18 with its 1,200 h.p. engine, of which they did not have an equivalent. Apparently their report had come as a 'nasty surprise' to Göring, who followed the 'clear course in support of a war against the USSR', as it pointed to the 'risks and the futility of such an adventure'.[45]

The attempts at deterrence, however, paled in comparison with the efforts to appease the Germans, for instance the ardent flirtation with Vichy France. In the middle of the crisis over Yugoslavia a new ambassador arrived in Moscow from Vichy. Bergery, who had started on the left with Léon Blum, had made a considerable move to the right. 'An advocate of a 100 per cent co-operation with Germany', he provided an excellent channel for Stalin to sound out the Germans, the more so as it was an open secret in Moscow that he intended to use his ambassadorship as a springboard to the position of Foreign Minister.[46] In Vichy the new but experienced Soviet ambassador Bogomolov wasted little time in stating that France, being 'lonely and isolated', would appreciate 'the friendship of a major power like Soviet Russia'. The Russians, he stated, cultivated good relations with the Germans and desired similar relations with France.[47]

What particularly appealed to the Russians was Bergery's search, with German connivance, for manoeuvrability. He expected the Germans to realize that a European bloc could not be achieved under the hegemony of a single nation but only with the 'co-operation of various nations'. 'The new Europe', according to him, would necessitate 'the co-operation of France and Russia . . . it was impossible to reconstruct Europe without the intellect and resources of Russia.'[48] The investment seemed to pay off during the meeting of Admiral Darlan, the deputy of Pétain, with Hitler in Vichy in mid-May, which was closely scrutinized by Bogomolov. When Bogomolov returned to Moscow to report to Stalin in person, Bergery used the occasion to impress on him, with his 'rhetorical elegance and logical sharpness', that Russia should participate actively in the schemes for a revised Europe. He even produced from his briefcase the six-point proposals on co-operation submitted to Hitler, the essence of which was the maintenance of France's economic independence and co-operation with respect to a peacetime rather than wartime economy.[49]

But appeasement was primarily directed towards Germany. In the expectation that Schulenburg would bring concrete proposals from Berlin, Stalin assumed the premiership of the Soviet Union on 5 May. The lessons of the bungle over Yugoslavia clearly contributed to his decision. It was the necessity of removing the constraints which his position as General Secretary of the Communist Party imposed on the conduct of the delicate negotiations with the Germans, rather than Stalin's wish to take control of the military, which motivated his assumption of the role of Prime Minister. Only he could project with full credibility the loyalty to Germany which would deprive her of any excuse to reproach Moscow. Already during the negotiations with the Japanese Stalin seems to have assumed the position of head of state, which he was so careful not to do earlier on, preserving the separation between the state and the Party. The communiqué of 17 April on the agreement with the Japanese stated that 'Comrade Stalin had on 12 April a conversation on Soviet–Japanese relations with the Japanese Foreign Minister, Molotov *was present* [author's italics]'. As a complementary step a couple of days later the Red Army reinstated the old tsarist forms and withdrew the revolutionary jargon and symbols, while the Soviet 'polpreds' abroad regained their traditional ambassadorial status.[50]

Indeed, when endorsing the decision on 4 May, the Plenum of the Central Committee, after disposing of the customary clichés on the need to achieve 'full co-ordination of the workings of the Soviet and Party organizations', spoke of the need to enhance the 'authority of the Soviet organs in the present strained international situation' in fortifying the 'defence of the country'.[51]

These events fitted in only too well with Schulenburg's own ploy. On 3 May he informed Berlin that the front page of the latest *Pravda* displayed a photograph of the government's tribune at the May Day parade, where Dekanozov was given the honour of standing next to Stalin. He impressed on his superiors that it certainly indicated 'the special recognition accorded to the ambassador in Berlin'.[52] Stalin's assumption of the premiership came as a godsend, confirming that his 'realistic policy' towards Germany would continue and be fostered.[53]

On 7 May Schulenburg took the unusual step of inviting Dekanozov and Pavlov, the director of the Western Department of Narkomindel, for breakfast at his own residence, away from potential informers in the embassy. Various historians have claimed that during their clandestine meeting Schulenburg divulged to Dekanozov Hitler's intention of attacking Russia. A. Mikoyan, the Politburo member and Commissar of Foreign Trade, whose memoirs have given rise to a number of false interpretations of Stalin's policies at the time, suggested that Schulenburg gave Dekanozov a clear-cut warning. Over breakfast, Schulenburg is supposed to have approached Dekanozov and to have rather bluntly told him: 'Mr Ambassador, perhaps this has not ever occurred in the history of diplomacy, as I am about to disclose to you the state secret number one: convey it to Mr Molotov, and he, I hope, will inform Mr Stalin that Hitler has decided to launch an attack against the Soviet Union on 22 June. You will ask me why am I doing it? I was brought up in the spirit of Bismarck, and he always objected to a war with Russia . . .' When informed of the meeting, Stalin is alleged to have told the Politburo in the evening that 'We must consider that disinformation has reached the level of ambassadors.'[54]

Much as this revelation captures the imagination, it is not borne out at all by the actual records of the meeting. It also contradicts Hilger's evidence that Schulenburg was reluctant to embark on the initiative, fearing that he would be 'tried for treason if it leaked out that we were about to warn the Russians'. It seems that both eventually made an approach with the intention not of actually warning the Russians but of indicating, as Hilger attests, 'the seriousness of the situation' and attempting to push Stalin into a diplomatic initiative which would 'involve Hitler in negotiations which would rob him, for the time being, of all pretexts for military action'.[55] This conforms with Molotov's seemingly accurate recollection that Schulenburg 'did not warn, he hinted. A tremendous number of people hinted that a conflict was imminent. But to believe Schulenburg . . . so many rumours were being spread!'[56]

The initiative was, of course, not a dramatic warning, though this was what he wished the reader to believe; Hilger was writing too close for comfort to the Nuremberg trials. Rather it was a result of Schulenburg's extended attempt to prevent the war. There were in fact three meetings, on 5, 9 and 12 May, which he telescoped into a single one, introducing further confusion.[57] The dynamics between the three meetings are crucial for the understanding of the policies pursued by the Kremlin in the month preceding the conflict.

Over breakfast Schulenburg produced the bait by referring to Hitler's most recent speech, which summed up the campaign in the Balkans.[58]

Hitler, he impressed on Dekanozov, had reiterated the statement made to Molotov in Berlin that Germany entertained neither territorial nor direct political ambitions in the region, and was only reacting to the events taking place there. It is indeed striking that Schulenburg deliberately concealed from Dekanozov the extent of Hitler's fury over the Neutrality Pact with Yugoslavia. In doing so he was eager to re-establish a common platform for renewed negotiations. He disclosed only that during his visit to Berlin, Hitler had been puzzled by the agreement, which he found 'difficult to comprehend and strange'. Dekanozov did not deny that the pact with Yugoslavia had been aimed at advancing Soviet interests in the Balkans, which the Russians hoped to achieve through a dialogue with the Germans. He reminded Schulenburg that before concluding the agreement with Yugoslavia the Soviet Union had received assurances that the Yugoslav government 'was set on preserving its good relations with Germany and wished to live in peace with all its neighbours but in the first place with Germany, and that the Yugoslav government had not therefore renounced its adherence to the Tripartite Pact'.

Schulenburg hinted at the severity of the situation, conceding that although he had tried hard to convince Hitler that Soviet policy was aimed at preserving normal relations with her neighbours he had not succeeded in doing so '100 per cent, and he was left with a somewhat unpleasant resentment about the recent activities of the Soviet government'. But this comment, rather than comprising a warning, served as a prelude to the scheme he now devised to shore up the crumbling relationship. Slightly twisting the line of Hitler's argument, Schulenburg impressed on Dekanozov that Hitler had justified the German concentration of troops as a counter-measure to the recent rumours of the Russian mobilization and deployment of the Red Army and the inevitability of an armed conflict. The memory of the Russian mobilization of 1914 which had hastened the outbreak of war was undoubtedly still uppermost in his mind. Schulenburg clearly hoped that by resorting to personal diplomacy he might be able to prod the Russians into initiating measures which could help to undo the obvious damage in Berlin caused by Russia's recent moves in the Balkans. Stalin's overtures of appeasement convinced him that it was still possible to solve the intensifying conflict in the realm of diplomacy. The move, however, had to be initiated by Stalin personally.

Having been provided with little straw to build his bricks, Schulenburg chose to focus on the rumours. The use of the 'rumours' as the springboard for a more general agreement was sensible. Schulenburg's long absence in Berlin had given rise to speculation in Moscow and London. This seemed to have deflected both Stalin and the British from a correct evaluation of the prospects ahead. The German disinformation effort after Schulenburg's return to Moscow was particularly directed at the ambassador himself and the Russians. Berlin seemed most anxious to quell the wave of rumours of an impending war, and such rumours were firmly denied in correspondence with Schulenburg. He was thus misled into believing that the German concentration was 'a rear cover for the Balkan operations'. During his visit to Berlin he gained the impression that the rumours were being spread by forces interested in the outbreak of hostilities and were intensifying Hitler's mistrust of Russia. Going through the papers which had accumulated on his desk during his long absence in Berlin, Schulenburg's attention had been drawn to an urgent directive of the Chief of Staff which warned him that the 'rumour-mongering' was 'very detrimental to the further peaceful development of German–Russian relations'. The embassy was instructed to quell and deny the rumours.[59]

On the very eve of the meeting Schulenburg was urged by the head of the Political Department of the Foreign Ministry to quash the rumours, which were being deliberately spread by the British 'to poison the wells'. He was even led to believe that eight divisions would be transported from east to west in the first half of May.[60] His practical advice to Dekanozov, therefore, was to defuse official pronouncements, such as the Tass communiqués, which seemed 'to pop up like mushrooms after rain' in the wake of any development in the Balkans. Rather than displaying a conviction that Hitler was set on war, Schulenburg referred a couple of times to Hitler's restraint and explained that the 'precautionary measures' on Russia's western front were a reaction to her own mobilization. This partly explains Stalin's reluctance to deploy Russian forces in an overt and effective way which might be conceived as provocation in Berlin.

Schulenburg therefore wasted little time after breakfast in conveying to Dekanozov his impression of the disastrous effects which the rumours were having. He warned him strongly that 'rumours of an imminent war between the Soviet Union and Germany were of an "explosive nature" and should be suppressed and "broken to the bones"'. He did not fail to mention, though, that the initiative was his own and was not sanctioned by the government. It was left to the Russians to advance concrete proposals. Thus from Schulenburg's point of view the unprecedented approach set the scene for improving relations rather than betraying state secrets. Dekanozov, who found it difficult to believe that such an important communication had been made on Schulenburg's own initiative, certainly saw the importance of the event. He too took advantage of the general tone of the conversation to revive negotiations, reminding Schulenburg that Moscow was still expecting a reply to the November proposals. Most significantly, it was decided to reconvene this informal forum.

The call to counter the rumours fell on fertile ground. Two conflicting sets of rumours concerning the German concentration of troops were circulating. The first assumed that the concentration was a lever in the forth-coming negotiations which might possibly end in a military alliance. The other assumed that a war was imminent, but in Moscow these rumours were attributed to incessant attempts by Britain to embroil Russia in war. While the campaigns in the Balkans could be explained in rational terms, the war against Russia would be conducted for entirely different motives. The lack of definition of the military objectives of the campaign meant that means and ends were interwoven. This peculiar characteristic of the planning made it extremely difficult for the Kremlin to perceive the exact nature of the German threat, even when intelligence was abundant. The evaluation of the German deployment, as well as of the various diplo-matic overtures, was further undertaken by Stalin with the fear of war in mind and coincided with growing public criticism, in Britain, of Churchill. In Southern Europe the remnants of the British expeditionary force had been withdrawn to Crete, where a disastrous battle was about to commence. The earlier British victories over the Italian forces in North Africa had turned into a rout once General Erwin Rommel had bypassed the besieged fortress of Tobruk and started his advance towards Cairo and the Suez Canal. The Germans had mastery of the skies in the Mediterranean, imposing an effective siege on the strategic British naval base at Malta. Meanwhile heavy losses were being inflicted on the mer-chant navy in the Atlantic, threatening England's lifeline.

Considering Stalin's frame of mind at the time, it is most likely that he suspected Hitler was using Schulenburg, as part of the war of nerves, to secure better terms in the forthcoming negotiations. And yet, as in 1939, when informal feelers had been made in Berlin by the Russians, Stalin was afraid that an overt statement might be used against him in possible German–British negotiations and that he would become a laughing-stock. However, far from dismissing the information obtained from Schulenburg, Stalin now acted on it. Within a day *Pravda* published a denial of the allegations that the strong concentrations of military forces on the western border of the Soviet Union signalled a change in relations with Germany. The campaign to crush the rumours was executed system-atically. The Japanese ambassador, for instance, was told by Molotov 'that the rumours of an impending German attack on the U.S.S.R. were simply British and American propaganda and entirely without foundation. On the contrary, relations between the two countries were excellent.'[61]

Schulenburg related Stalin's assumption of the premiership to his own initiative but could not inform Berlin of his unauthorized move. After his traumatic meeting with Hitler in Berlin, he realized that the only hope of averting war now rested on a direct dialogue between Stalin and Hitler. He remembered the only positive observation by Hitler during their meeting – that Stalin was 'the soul of Russian consensus politics and of mutual understanding with Germany'.[62] He now contemplated a campaign on two fronts. In Moscow he would encourage Stalin to approach Hitler directly, while in his reporting to Berlin he would assume the point of view of a detached observer and emphasize the conciliatory Russian attitude, thus preparing the ground for Stalin's approach. His telegrams to Berlin should therefore be read in this vein. As Hitler seemed to be implacable about the events in Yugoslavia, it was essential for Schulenburg to erase the memory of recent developments and present them as a deviation. Molotov was chosen as the scapegoat. Schulenburg presented the changes in the Russian government as 'a considerable abridgment of his former authority'. He attributed it to 'the recent mistakes in foreign policy which had led to a cooling of the cordiality of German–Soviet relations [a clear hint at the Soviet pact with Yugoslavia], for the creation and preservation of which Stalin had consciously striven, while Molotov's own initiative often expended itself in an obstinate defence of individual positions'. After reiterating the significance of Stalin's new appointment, Schulenburg prepared Berlin for his next coup by predicting that 'Stalin will use his new position in order to take part personally in the maintenance and development of good relations between the Soviets and Germany'. He also chose the occasion to convey Bergery's ideas on the need to incorporate the Soviet Union in a reconstructed Europe.[63]

Still waiting for a response from Berlin, Schulenburg was invited by Dekanozov for breakfast at the magnificent guesthouse of the Foreign Ministry at Spiridonovka on 9 May. While Schulenburg appeared impatient and eager to exploit Stalin's new position to advance his plans, Dekanozov, on instructions from Stalin, acted cautiously, trying to strike a delicate balance between a display of confidence in the forthcoming negotiations and a readiness to yield. Aware of Hitler's complaints, Dekanozov launched into a speech on Soviet grievances but was cut short by Schulenburg. 'After all,' he reminded him, 'we have not met with the view of conducting a legal debate. At present, as diplomats and politicians, we ought to deal with the situation that is arising and contemplate which counter-measures can be taken.'

This was the signal for Dekanozov to move ahead with a well-thought-out plan which was clearly sanctioned if not devised by Stalin. A feeler, in response to Schulenburg's suggestion of the previous meeting, had been published in the press that same morning, dismissing the rumours of alleged concentrations of Soviet troops on the western border as 'a sick fantasy'. Stalin, it stated, had 'set himself a foreign policy goal of overwhelming importance for the Soviet Union, which he hopes to attain by his personal efforts'.[64] Dekanozov now advocated the publication of a joint German–Soviet communiqué which would establish that the recent rumours of the deterioration in German–Soviet relations and even the possibility of a military conflict were groundless and spread by elements hostile to Russia. Indeed, the quashing of rumours as a prerequisite for any later agreement stood behind the infamous communiqué of 13 June.[65]

Schulenburg, however, was anxious to raise the stakes and create the maximum impact in Berlin for Stalin's new position. His suggestion was that Stalin should address Matsuoka, Mussolini and Hitler with identical personal letters which would explicitly state that he had assumed the premiership to ensure that the USSR would 'conduct in the future a friendly policy towards them'. It was suggested that in the second part of the letter to Hitler Stalin should propose a joint denial of the rumours of the impending attack, in the spirit of Dekanozov's proposal; 'The Führer will then send a reply, and in the opinion of S[chulenburg] the issue will be resolved.' While luring the Russians to act Schulenburg no longer conveyed, as has been suggested, that his approach was a personal initiative. On the contrary, he appeared confident that were Stalin to realize his intention of addressing Hitler personally with a letter, Hitler would dispatch a courier in a special plane and the matter would 'proceed very fast'. Dekanozov could hardly be expected to exceed his authority and obviously had to consult Stalin. Arrangements were therefore made for a prompt third and decisive meeting.[66]

Stalin acted forcefully to back up his conciliatory diplomacy. He hastened to send a Soviet representative to Baghdad to the rebellious government of Rashid Ali. The latter, sustained by the Germans, had seized power in Baghdad on 3 April. On 8 May, the Norwegian and Belgian ministers at Moscow received arrogant notes that their credentials were no longer valid. They were promptly expelled from Moscow and recognition of their governments-in-exile withdrawn. The new governments were recognized by Stalin instantly. While the clandestine talks were taking place Gavrilović was unexpectedly summoned by Vyshinsky and informed of the decision to withdraw recognition of his government. Gavrilović was indeed in a 'bad mood and aggravated'. He nonetheless confessed that he 'well understood what Soviet diplomacy was attempting to achieve'.[67]

Unknown to Schulenburg, events had been following a completely different course in Berlin. As Schulenburg was heading from Moscow airport to his residence, Ribbentrop's special train pulled into Friedrichstrasse station. On the evening of 29 April a courier had flown to Ribbentrop in Vienna with the report prepared by Schulenburg of his conversations with the Führer.[68] Though the tone was ominous, Ribbentrop still hoped he could sway Hitler, as he had done after Molotov's visit, from the course contemplated. To his great concern he found Hitler determined to nip the negotiations in the bud and not to allow them to undermine the preparations for 'Barbarossa'. Hitler demanded that Ribbentrop 'support his attitude unambiguously'; he warned him 'against further *démarche*, and forbade me to talk to anyone about it; no diplomacy, he said, would make him change his mind about Russia's attitude, which was quite clear to him, and it might well deprive him of the weapon of tactical surprise for an attack'.[69]

Faced with Hitler's intransigence, Ribbentrop adopted a typically yielding posture. Ribbentrop transferred his frustration to Weizsäcker, blaming him for adopting a 'negative attitude' at the crucial turns of history. Weizsäcker, however, continued to believe, even after Hitler's rejection of the memorandum, that Ribbentrop remained 'in principle opposed to war with Russia'.[70] Indeed, on the very eve of 'Barbarossa' Ciano found Ribbentrop resigned to the idea of a war, though he was 'less ebullient than usual, and had the nerve to recall his enthusiastic praise of the Moscow agreement and of the Communist leaders, whom he compared with those of the old Nazi party'.[71]

Weizsäcker was left in no doubt of Hitler's determination and Ribbentrop's subservience. On 1 May he was told by an informant in Hitler's entourage (probably General Geyer) that the Führer had decided that 'Russia can be defeated as it were incidentally and without affecting the war against England. England will be defeated this year, with or without the Russian war. The British Empire will then have to be sustained, but Russia will have to be rendered innocuous.'[72]

Schulenburg, who had left Berlin in great haste, was not briefed about the aftermath of his interview with Hitler.[73] With his initiative gaining momentum, he had sent feelers to Weizsäcker in a personal telegram on 7 May. Wishing to render his clandestine overtures semi-official, he hinted at the possibility of conveying to Stalin the German government's congratulations. Moreover, playing on Hitler's anxiety about relations with Vichy France,[74] he exerted pressure by conveying the essence of his conversations with Bergery, who was openly advocating a Continental bloc 'in which the great Soviet Union and its abundance of raw materials must be included'. Rather cunningly, Schulenburg also used the whip. In Berlin he had been exposed to the evaluation that a lightning campaign in Russia might lead to a swift occupation of Moscow and the toppling of the communist regime. However, as he had gathered in Berlin from Werizsäcker, the army was of the opinion that, while it would be relatively easy to take Moscow, any campaign towards the Urals would encounter severe difficulties.[75] He therefore added a postscript, disclosing in a detached manner that the absence of air-raid drills in Moscow confirmed information that 'the Soviet government has for some time already prepared a wartime capital "somewhere", equipped with all the frills (means of inter-communication, etc.) which it can reach in a very short time. It will in any event not remain in Moscow.' This was a clear allusion to Napoleon's disastrous experience when he encountered the scorched-earth tactics of Alexander II in 1812. Finally, sounding out Berlin about the possibility that preparations for war were continuing unhindered, Schulenburg referred to the need to make the necessary arrangements to safeguard the safety of the employees of the embassy if hostilities did break out.[76]

On 12 May, Dekanozov returned to Schulenburg's apartment for their third breakfast meeting inside a week. This time he seized the initiative at the outset, solemnly announcing Stalin's and Molotov's agreement to send the personal letter to Hitler. Stalin's impatience is attested by his request that, in view of Dekanozov's departure for Berlin on the same day, Schulenburg and Molotov should waste little time and jointly draft the text of the letter.[77] However, an hour or so before Dekanozov's arrival Schulenburg had received two unexpected communications by courier from Berlin,[78] which seemed to undo his efforts. The brief one from Weizsäcker indicated only too clearly which way the wind was blowing. The only suggestion of Schulenburg's communication which had been acted upon was his suggestion that arrangements be made for the safe evacuation of his staff in case of the outbreak of hostilities; 'at a given time', he was now told, this suggestion 'will be brought to light'. Schulenburg was then informed laconically but very bluntly that the rest of his proposals had not been presented to Ribbentrop 'because this would not have been a rewarding thing'. The second letter, from Ernst Wörmann, director of the Political Department of the Foreign Ministry, demonstrated that following his confrontation with Hitler Schulenburg's moves were now being closely watched. He was reprimanded for his disclosure in Moscow of the nature of his talks in Berlin, and for the manifest pessimism reflected in rumours that Schulenburg was 'packing [his] private belongings in cases'.[79]

Reconstructing the conversation, Dekanozov reported that from the outset of the meeting Schulenburg 'did not take the initiative and did not strike up a conversation on the subject of our previous talks. He only mentioned that he had a pile of dispatches that morning including a letter from Weizsäcker and Wörmann which, however, did not hold anything new or interesting'. Schulenburg listened, 'quite emotionless', to Dekanozov's proposals, which he obviously assumed to be a major breakthrough, and answered that he had conducted the negotiations in the last couple of days 'on his own initiative and without authority'. He was not empowered to conduct negotiations with Molotov and was 'also doubtful whether he was likely to receive such instructions'. He appeared rather concerned that reports of Stalin's latest moves to reconcile Germany were conspicuously missing from the German press.

The tenor of the conversation was a strange blend of hints about the likelihood of war with equally persuasive attempts by Schulenburg to maintain the momentum and disinformation. All this was to add to the already confused state of mind at the Kremlin. As they sat down for breakfast Schulenburg and Hilger made cynical and jocular comments which Dekanozov perceived as hints about 'the retirement of Schulenburg from the political scene'. And yet Schulenburg was eager to salvage his initiative by raising a number of alternatives:

> It would be good if Stalin himself were on his own initiative and spontaneously to approach Hitler with a letter. He, Schulenburg, would be visiting Molotov in the near future (on topics concerning arrangements in the Baltic Sea), but he has no authority and has not got the right to discuss those issues in his meeting. It would be good if Molotov himself could open his meeting with him [Schulenburg], raising this issue or perhaps I [Dekanozov] would receive consent here in Moscow to make a similar proposal in Berlin to Weizsäcker or to Ribbentrop.

This restraint, contrasting with the offers made a couple of days earlier, undoubtedly baffled Stalin. On the one hand Schulenburg, just back from his conference with Hitler, might indeed have been reflecting the German attitude but simply trying to exert pressure in an attempt to achieve better terms. It was equally possible to assume that the issue was not yet settled in Germany and that a cautious policy might yield an agreement. On the other hand it might just as well prove to be a trap set for Russia, and a premature approach might be used as a trump card in future negotiations with Britain. Indeed, during the meeting Schulenburg made the entirely speculative assessment that 'in his own opinion the day was not far off' when England and Germany were 'bound to reach an agreement and bring the calamity and destruction and bombing of their cities to an end'.[80] This statement was no doubt repeatedly re-examined in the Kremlin that very evening, when news came on Radio Berlin of Rudolf Hess's flight to Scotland on a self-appointed peace mission.[81]

Schulenburg had been most hesitant in pursuing his activities in the first place,[82] and the reprimand from Berlin produced an immediate effect. Shortly after Dekanozov's departure he composed two letters. The reply to Wörmann was highly defensive, denying the various accusations. He assured him that his 'very costly rugs' were still 'lying in their old place, the pictures of my parents and other relatives are hanging on the walls as before and in my residence nothing at all has changed, as every visitor can see for himself'. He then made a gesture which had never been his practice, ending the letter with a 'Heil Hitler' greeting. Weizsäcker in Berlin acted similarly, complaining that Schulenburg's moves were naturally held against him, and admitting that perhaps he should have followed the recipe of the opposition in the army by 'avoiding raising doubts'. He then went on to express his confidence in the triumph of the Wehrmacht.[83] In a letter to his friends the Herwarths, Schulenburg confided that same day that 'the matter of great interest to us is still as threatening as ever. We expect the crisis to come to a head around the end of June.' There was therefore 'no longer much work to be done . . . The awesome silence appears to us frightening: is it the lull before the storm?' As he had hinted to Dekanozov earlier that day, he was already resigned to returning to Germany and furnishing the Falkenberg castle which he had just acquired.[84]

In his second telegram to the Foreign Ministry Schulenburg still persevered in his efforts to defuse the crisis. It prepared the ground for the possibility that Stalin might initiate a move through Dekanozov. Berlin's attention was therefore once again drawn to the 'extraordinary' appointment of Stalin as Prime Minister and to the 'prominence given to Dekanozov' during the May Day parade, which should be regarded 'as a special mark of confidence on the part of Stalin'. There followed a forceful presentation of the conciliatory Soviet moves, completely overlooking Schulenburg's own role in them, leading to the inescapable conclusion that:

> It may be assumed with certainty that Stalin has set himself a foreign policy goal of overwhelming importance for the Soviet Union, which he hopes to attain by his personal efforts. I firmly believe that, in an international situation which he considers serious, Stalin has set himself the goal of preserving the Soviet Union from a conflict with Germany.[85]

The same message appeared in the report of his meeting with Molotov on 22 May. He did not cease to impress on Berlin that the moment Stalin became Prime Minister he and Molotov, 'the two strongest men in the Soviet Union', held positions which were 'decisive for the foreign policy of the Soviet Union' and their policy was, 'above all, directed at the avoidance of a conflict with Germany'.[86] Later on he provided Berlin with a one-sided report of Stalin's speech to graduates of military academies, concluding that he appeared 'anxious to prepare his followers for a "new compromise" with Germany'.[87]

In the final analysis Schulenburg's activities in early 1941, and particularly in the crucial month of May 1941, kept alive Stalin's hope of a possible diplomatic solution to the conflict and diverted him from the lethal danger lurking around the corner. Moreover, Stalin had become even more convinced that in desperation Churchill was now trying to drag Russia into the conflict by spreading the rumours of an 'inevitable war'.[88] Rather than providing a warning, as is often believed, the clandestine negotiations reinforced Stalin's belief in the likelihood of appeasing Hitler. Suspicious as ever, Stalin even mounted a bold operation to intercept the German couriers carrying the diplomatic bags at the Hotel Metropole. While one was locked in a bathroom, the other was jammed in a lift as the contents of the bag were photographed. Schulenburg's reports stressed, as we have seen, his confidence in Stalin's wish to pursue negotiations.[89]

It is therefore quite understandable that in Moscow Tatekawa expected Hitler and Stalin 'to meet somewhere on the border'.[90] According to Zhukov, when he came to see Stalin in early June, he saw on his desk the letter addressed to Hitler.[91] When Dekanozov failed to reach Ribbentrop after his return to Berlin on 14 May, he sought the good offices of Meissner, who had forged close relations with Kobulov, the NKGB resident in Berlin. Fluent in Russian which he had acquired during a long stay in Russia, Meissner was a man of the 'old school' who had served under President Hindenburg and was considered to be close to Hitler.[92] He had participated, though as a minor and marginal figure, in the talks with Molotov in Berlin.[93] The semblance of negotiations, which petered out by the first week of June, briefly continued to beguile Stalin as to the possibility of reaching a new agreement with the Germans. According to Berezhkov, the young first secretary at the Soviet embassy in Berlin, he actually 'hinted that the Reichskanzlerei was working out some new proposals for strengthening Soviet–German relations, which the Führer intended shortly to present to Moscow'.[94]

However, the sense that a single false move, whether a military provocation or a diplomatic blunder, might trigger a war now led Stalin to prudence bordering on paranoia. It further hampered the work of the intelligence agencies as war drew closer. Schulenburg's suggestion in his talks with Dekanozov that the rumours might be a trigger for war introduced a further complication, inhibiting the embassies from seeking information on German intentions and robbing the Russians of crucial information. The outstanding case was the desperate and futile attempt made by the British to pass to Maisky information obtained from 'Ultra' on the very eve of the war.[95] But this happened in every Soviet embassy: the ambassadors simply adhered fanatically to their instructions and information was sieved and crudely interpreted to fit in with the views held at the top. For instance, when the Finnish ambassador in Istanbul provided his Russian colleague with precise information on the presence of 125 divisions on the Russian border, he was cut short by a cynical reaction from Vinogradov: 'Perhaps Mr Ambassador could tell us whether he personally counted the divisions?' Rather than pursuing the conversation, he proudly and obediently reported to Moscow that he 'had no intention of continuing the talk on that subject and diverted it to a different topic'.[96]

The bulk of the intelligence submitted to Stalin on German intentions, as distinct from the actual preparations for war on the ground, increasingly assumed ambiguous meanings when read against the preconceived ideas. A case in point was a meeting between the Turkish President Inönü and Papen, in which the former displayed concern about a possible meeting of Hitler and Stalin. The German ambassador put his mind at rest, suggesting that even if 'mutual relations between Germany and Russia were improved' Germany would 'continue to check Russia and was strong enough to conduct a war also on the eastern front'. Rather than identifying the threat, obvious to us in view of the eventual German invasion, Stalin tended to see in the report proof that such a meeting and the improvement of relations were indeed on the agenda.[97]

Even intelligence which in retrospect seems to us decisive could in the present state of mind in the Kremlin be regarded as ambivalent. The reliable and skilled military attaché in Bucharest gleaned from an informer who had been a guest of the German General Staff that the rigorous preparations for the campaign had been completed and the outbreak of war was expected in June. He believed that if war did not come in 1941 it could be considered a 'miracle'. But he then raised the possibility, which would prove more attractive to Stalin, that Hitler 'was playing an extremely subtle game'. This was accentuated by the fact that Hitler seemed to be avoiding making any clear statements on his intentions vis-à-vis Moscow or holding negotiations with countries bordering on Russia. Neither did he discuss the war with the Japanese. The information that 'not even a single person has the slightest doubt of a quick victory over the USSR' could be perceived as part of the war of nerves. Such an interpretation was further corroborated by the admission that it was recognized in Berlin that an occupation of the Soviet Union might lead to a disastrous disruption of the economy. It was therefore left to Stalin to agree or disagree with the informer's 'belief' that war had become 'inevitable' and that the German army would be in Moscow 'earlier than assumed'.[98]

It is not surprising therefore that when four German deserters from the infantry, artillery and navy crossed the lines and gave an accurate and detailed description of the German pattern of deployment, Merkulov preferred to give a rather tendentious description of the mood and political attitude of the soldiers. He stressed the weariness of the troops and their craving for home. At least twenty of their comrades had been court-martialled for desertion. Many of the soldiers 'evinced sympathy towards the Soviet Union' and were afraid of facing 'the strong Red Army, with its abundant fleet of planes and tanks, over a huge territory'. In the naval unit fascist propaganda was most effective but coupled with it was 'a growing anti-war feeling'. Some soldiers expressed their view that Hitler was 'dragging Germany into a war, from which the working class would gain nothing'. It was coupled with subdued information about some units which 'still preserve the war spirit and are prepared to fulfil all the directives of their commanders . . . among them they mention "the imminent war" with the Soviet Union'.[99]

What Dekanozov chose to bring out in his reports home was the general belief that German industrialists were opposed to the war and that the

Soviet Union intended to concede territory to Germany. The Russian wife of the Chinese counsellor, who was sitting next to Dekanozov at a dinner in Berlin, told him that 'she would hate to see the Ukraine given to Germany . . . she had heard of it from the Germans themselves'. Likewise the daughter of the Turkish counsellor felt 'very sorry for the Caucasus', which would be given to Germany. Dekanozov chose to quote at length the views of Gerde, the Turkish ambassador, who believed that the German government was in a 'hopeless situation', short of oil and grain and possessing a huge unemployed army. The deployment of the troops in the Balkans and in Rumania was directed to the north, but he assumed that it was aimed 'at exerting pressure on the Soviet Union'. He further misled Dekanozov by suggesting that General Brauchitsch had been inspecting the trains directed to the West, leading him to the conclusion that the 'move of troops to the Soviet border was done with the aim of diverting attention from the activity contemplated in the West'. Anticipating fresh negotiations, Dekanozov was eager to trace the origins of the rumours and the extent to which they mirrored the views held by the government.[100] In a subsequent report he notified the Kremlin that:

> Parallel to the rumours circulating about the imminent war between Germany and the Soviet Union, rumours were spread in Germany of a rapprochement between Germany and the Soviet Union, either on the basis of far-reaching 'concessions' on the part of the Soviet Union, or on the basis of 'division of spheres of influence' and undertakings on the part of the Soviet Union not to interfere in European affairs. This is related to Stalin's assumption of the premiership.

He clung to commentaries in this vein on the neutrality agreement with Japan and Stalin's most recent recognition of the governments in the occupied territories.

That the Kremlin was indeed geared towards the resumption of negotiations is clear from Dekanozov's long citations from those newspapers which pointed out that, as he put it, 'the present policy of the USSR fully supports the "new order" in Europe'. He was just as zealous in forwarding information which suggested a growing rift within Germany. According to him the 'smarter and more solid people (in the first place the German industrialists) appeared worried by the worsening relations with the Soviet Union, stressing their satisfaction with the present economic ties with the USSR. On the other hand, the military circles . . . took a more aggressive stance towards relations with the Soviet Union.' As far as the terms of the agreement were concerned, Dekanozov suggested that the most frequent rumours, coming from various directions, spoke about 'the leasing of the Ukraine for 5, 35 and 99 years'. Perhaps the most significant observation was his stated belief that the rumours emanated from and were spread by the German government. However, the sheer volume of the rumours introduced enough doubt in his mind to suggest that it might after all be 'a continuation of the ideological (and concrete) preparation for a war against the Soviet Union'.[101]

At the end of May Timoshenko and Zhukov were summoned to the Kremlin, and they assumed that Stalin was at last prepared to allow them to put the army on 'war readiness' status in view of the alarming intelligence reports. They were dumbfounded when Stalin passed on to them Schulenburg's appeal to allow groups of Germans to search for graves of German soldiers who had perished in the First World War. It was plain to Zhukov, as he angrily pointed out to Zhdanov, that the purpose was a survey of the regions which the Germans intended to attack. Timoshenko seized the opportunity to raise the increasing infringements of Soviet air space and asked for permission to shoot down the German planes. Yet Stalin clung to the belief that the German army was acting on its own initiative. 'I am not sure', he said as he brought the discussion to an end, 'that Hitler knows about those flights.' Overriding Zhukov's reservations, he seemed satisfied by Hitler's recent explanation that inexperienced young pilots were encountering navigation problems. Moreover, he informed Zhukov of a secret personal meeting which Dekanozov had had with Hitler, who had assured him that the transfer of the troops to the border was aimed at regrouping them for the offensive against the West and misleading London. The 'ultimatum theory' was further recruited to suggest that the Germans might be trying 'to scare us'. Even when the number of flights increased dramatically in early June, Stalin suggested that Molotov should acquaint Hitler through Schulenburg with the state of affairs.[102]

The need to conform with the Kremlin had now become overriding. In his concluding report for May Golikov, as if unaware of the hard facts accumulating on his desk, revised his earlier appreciation of the German priorities in the wake of the Balkan campaign. The German High Command was now carrying out, in the following order: first, the restoration of the western groupings for the struggle with England; second, an augmentation of the force against the USSR; third, consolidation of the reserves placed at the disposal of the High Command. He grossly exaggerated the number of divisions earmarked for the invasion of Britain, fixing them at 122 to 126, as compared with the 120 to 122 divisions which were deployed against the Soviet Union, while forty-four to forty-eight were kept in reserve. The deployment of the troops on the Russian border still gave prominence to the south-western front. The twenty-nine divisions in the Middle East, he argued, were adequate to continue operations there while simultaneously regrouping in the West, in anticipation of a main operation against the British Isles. Finally, by establishing that 'the regrouping of the German army, in the wake of the campaign in the

Balkans, has essentially been completed', he turned a blind eye to the significant transfer of troops to the borders in the three weeks preceding the attack.[103]

The security services were now faltering as well. During a banquet given by the Japanese ambassador the increasing probability of a German attack was rumoured, with 15 or 20 June tipped as likely dates. Various scenarios for the attack were discussed. However, the chillingly accurate information was then fitted into the conceptual framework of the Kremlin, assuming that the war would follow an Anglo-German agreement, possibly on the basis of the proposals submitted by Hess in London. Moreover, it was almost taken for granted that war would be preceded by severe demands for the Soviet Union to join the Axis and render Germany 'more effective economic support'. In the final analysis, it seemed that the 'threat of war' was employed 'to exert pressure' on the Soviet Union.[104]

11

'The Special Threatening Military Period'

On the Alert

There were no means by which the full extent of the German build-up could be grasped on the ground before the second half of April. The initial phase of the German deployment was confined to mobilization and the creation of infrastructures for deployment. It was executed at a slow pace from mid-December to March. The second phase proceeded at moderate speed from mid-March to mid-April, while the massive third and fourth phases, including the transfer of the motorized units, commenced at the end of April. The movement of the reserves was to start only after hostilities had actually begun.[1] The gradual but systematic Russian mobilization and deployment were a direct response to the German menace, now clearly reflected by abundant military intelligence.[2]

Zhukov, barely installed in his new post as Chief of Staff, was increasingly disturbed by the intelligence pouring in. He was particularly frustrated by the limitations imposed on him. The minute attention paid by Stalin to the diplomatic 'great game', through which he hoped to spare Russia from war, contrasted sharply with the scant interest he displayed in military affairs and in the activities of his new Chief of Staff. Stalin's totalitarian regime was based on separation of the various governmental bodies. The Red Army was not, therefore, acquainted with the political process and was rarely aware of its implications. Stalin's dacha, his office in the Kremlin and to a lesser degree the Politburo were perhaps the only places where the military and political spheres converged, but both Zhukov and Timoshenko were only occasionally present there. In fact, as the war drew nearer, significant items of intelligence seem to have been withheld from the army, presumably to deter it from pressing for action.[3]

At the end of February Timoshenko arranged for Zhukov to meet Stalin. 'Take into consideration', he warned Zhukov, as they set out for Stalin's dacha, 'that he will not listen to a long lecture. All that you have told me in three hours has to be said in ten minutes.' Stalin was entertaining Molotov and other members of the Politburo. The Chief of Staff's work was not made any easier by the fact that Stalin was now leaning heavily on his old comrades, Generals Mekhlis and Kulik, devoted and servile but lacking any substantial military record. Zhdanov and Voroshilov were also kept on hand to bolster Stalin's own outlook on military affairs.[4] Intimidated by his surroundings, Zhukov confined himself to the short comment that 'considering the complicated military–political situation it was necessary to take urgent measures in time to remedy shortcomings on the western front'. 'Are you eager to fight the Germans?' interjected Molotov, but Stalin hushed him, allowing Zhukov to complete his presentation before dinner was served. The atmosphere at the dacha did not mirror Zhukov's trepidation. Dinner, as was the case with Stalin when entertaining at home, was simple: thick Ukrainian borsch, buckwheat porridge ('kasha') and plenty of stewed meat, followed by stewed and fresh fruit. Stalin was in a jovial mood, cracking jokes and sipping the light Georgian wine, Khvanchkara, which he offered around, though the majority preferred brandy. On taking leave of Zhukov Stalin encouraged him to proceed with the planning, though warning him against 'wild unrealistic plans for which Russia lacked the means'.[5]

The initial deployment plan, therefore, was diffuse and restrained. The revised timetable called for completion of the mobilization by 15 July.[6] To a large extent the planners were working, not unlike their counterparts in Germany, in a political void. However, unlike the Germans, they did not enjoy the leadership's support, and were therefore deterred from using their imagination and initiative in seeking ways to counter the threat. The plan, as submitted to Stalin by longhand in a single copy on 11 March, was a natural outcome of the mobilization order and lacked ingenuity. Only when the threat became concrete from April onwards did Zhukov persistently though unsuccessfully attempt to alter it. Up to the outbreak of war the plan underwent only minor modifications to accommodate the speed, volume and position of the German troops, in line with the detailed fortnightly reports provided by Golikov. Those, as we have seen, were increasingly tailored to conform with the views held at the top.

The framework of the March plan was remarkably defensive. It established at the outset that 'the highly complex political situation in Europe compels us to turn our undivided attention to the defence of our western borders'. In evaluating the threats facing Russia, Zhukov stressed the continued threat of a war on two fronts: 'Under such circumstances, the Soviet Union needs to be ready for a war on two fronts: in the West –

against Germany, supported by Italy, Hungary, Rumania and Finland, and in the East – against Japan, as an overt enemy or as an enemy assuming the position of "armed neutrality", which can always be turned into open conflict.' The German threat was still conceived as a potential one, as Zhukov admittedly lacked any documentary evidence of the German operational plans, but it was certainly the overwhelming one. If Germany were to abandon the plans to attack Britain she could muster some 200 divisions, including 165 infantry, twenty tank and fifteen motorized divisions, for deployment on the Soviet border. Zhukov seems to have overestimated the vast force that might face Russia, assuming that together with her allies Germany could deploy some 233 infantry divisions, more than twenty tank divisions comprising 10,810 tanks, and fifteen motorized divisions, supported by 11,600 planes and 20,050 guns. The estimate of the Panzer *Gruppe* would have been right in the May 1940 terms, assuming that each division comprised some 500 tanks. Unknown to the Russians the Germans had doubled the number of their tank divisions in 1941 by cutting the number of tanks in each division by half.

The assumption, still based on the plans of October 1940,[7] was that the Germans would launch an offensive in the south-western sector with the final objective of seizing the Ukraine. Such a strike might be assisted by supportive strikes in the centre and north from East Prussia in the direction of Riga and Dvinsk or in the central sector in the direction of Brest. But, in contrast to the commonly held opinion, it should be stressed that Zhukov did not exclude the possibility that the major blow might originate from Warsaw and fall on the central sector on the Riga–Dvinsk axis. The decision taken was to deploy most of the army in the west and south-western sectors, leaving only a strong skeleton force in the east to deter the Japanese and paralyse their offensive if they were to launch a war. Forty infantry divisions, of which six were mechanized and seven armoured, were assigned to the East, while Zhukov was left with 171 infantry, twenty-seven motorized, fifty-three tank and seven cavalry divisions to cover the entire western front.[8] Stalin's initial reaction was to reject even the amorphous plan presented to him, fearing that it might provoke the Germans. However, he gave the plan his blessing when faced with the accumulating intelligence by the end of March, the time of the German move against Yugoslavia and Greece.[9]

To understand Zhukov's shift towards a more vigorous deployment from the end of April onwards, attention should be paid to the evolving nature of the intelligence landing on his desk. The warnings of agents like Sorge and 'Starshina' have gained them a romantic aura. However, the most vital military intelligence came from the hundreds of observers dispersed along the entire German side of the western border at the pivotal rail and road junctions. They painstakingly delivered to Moscow an updated and precise picture of the German deployment. Likewise, the military attachés and Military Intelligence submitted a steady stream of fairly accurate information. Although, as we have seen,[10] the strategic intelligence directly affected Stalin in his attempts to avert war through diplomatic means, the hard facts provided by the observers were scrutinized by Zhukov and his staff and determined the nature of the army's response. The army enjoyed some latitude in devising the means to encounter the threat, of which Stalin was of course fully informed, as long as it did not impinge on his political manoeuvrability.

In mid-March the NKGB, which handled the monitoring activities, instructed the agent 'Sidrov' to collate the evidence accumulated in the field. His vivid and detailed report drew attention to the numerous trains allotted for the transfer of troops to destinations in the East along the entire Soviet border. He witnessed the tremendous congestion which the additional military traffic was inflicting on the main lines running east from Germany, Vienna and Budapest. Much of the traffic originated not in Germany but in the occupied Western countries.[11] The traffic from Berlin to former Poland was now almost exclusively reserved for the military, and civilians needed special permission to travel. The movement was conducted mostly at night to conceal its magnitude. Since 3 March some three or four train echelons had made the daily journey from west to east carrying troops and equipment, while boats were unloading military material in the Polish ports.[12]

The pressure on the key railway stations in former Poland increased during April and the construction of new hangars and airstrips in the border regions, as well as great efforts in widening and improving the roads and railway networks, were observed.[13] The close watch kept on the traffic disclosed in mid-April the return of troops who had been engaged in Yugoslavia through Budapest to Vienna. After a short recuperation they were redeployed in Poland and on the Russian border. The Hungarian army had been put on alert, while the soldiers spoke freely of a campaign to seize the Ukrainian Carpathians.[14]

In the last week of March 'Corsicanets' revealed that the Germans were continuing to make an extensive photographic survey of the border areas, especially in the vicinity of Kiev. He expected the war to erupt at the end of April or beginning of May. The choice of the date was governed by the wish to attack while the wheat was still green to prevent the retreating Red Army from setting fire to it. However, the reader should remember the ambivalent nature of the reports from Berlin.[15] While Timoshenko and Zhukov would regard the reports as deadly serious, Stalin and Beria tended to focus on the final verdict of 'Starshina' that 'the likelihood of war is only 50 per cent, and can still be attributed to a "bluff" policy'.[16]

Another significant disclosure, made by 'Starshina' early in April, was that the planning division of the German air force had completed its plans for the attack on the Soviet Union. The war would start with a

heavy bombardment of railway junctions, crossroads and communication centres and concentrations of troops, rather than industrial targets,
which the Germans hoped to seize intact and exploit after the short
campaign. The bombardment was aimed at disrupting communication
lines and the transfer of the reserves to the front. 'Starshina' stood by
the authenticity of the information, which he drew from documents
passing through his own hands. However, in view of Stalin's conviction
that a split existed within the German leadership, it should be noted
that 'Starshina' did not definitely establish whether war would break out,
noting that 'the final decision, to which he was not made privy, rested
with Hitler'. Though 'Starshina' described the attack as 'imminent',
he did not exclude the possibility that the anticipated campaign in
Yugoslavia might bring about a delay. As far as the planning was
concerned, he continued to misinform Moscow that the main effort would
be towards the Ukraine with supportive action from Prussia.[17] The gist
of the information was accurately transmitted to the Red Army, though
it was given to understand that it did not yet 'provide a sufficient base
to assume that the offensive had been finally decided by the supreme
leadership'.[18]

The military attachés, especially those posted in the Balkan countries,
constantly supplied exceptional information. A great part of it never
reached Stalin but found its way to the armed forces. Towards the end of
March, for instance, a childhood friend of Antonescu's nephew disclosed
that Hitler had revealed to the Rumanian leader during their meeting in
January his decision to attack Russia, and the information was confirmed
by Göring during their recent meeting in Vienna. May was tipped as the
critical month.[19]

In his fortnightly report in early April Golikov made no effort to conceal
the grave threat posed by the build-up of the German war machine along
the entire border. Moreover, he recognized a clear shift towards the central
western front, where eighty-four divisions had already been identified.
New headquarters had already been established in Allenstein in Prussia
and in Zakopane, some eighty-five kilometres from Cracow.[20]

The increasing number of reconnaissance flights deep into Soviet territory was most disconcerting. At the end of the month the Russians captured from a pilot who made a forced landing near Rovno exposed films
and a torn map of the Soviet border districts which clearly indicated the
object of his flight. Anxiously waiting for Schulenburg to bring new proposals, Stalin forced Timoshenko to make 'an exception . . . and give the
border troops orders not to fire on German planes flying over Soviet territory so long as such flights do not occur frequently'.[21]

On 15 April, following the fiasco in Yugoslavia, Golikov submitted a
second portentous report. Though lacking any analytical assessment, the
laconic document was detailed enough to depict the significant change in

the pattern of the German deployment. Golikov's opening sentence, as was his practice, set the tone for the entire report:

A major transfer of troops has taken place by railway, roads, motor columns and organized marches between 1 and 15 April, from the heart of Germany, from the western districts of East Prussia and from the General Gubernia [Poland] towards the Soviet borders. The concentrations are mainly in East Prussia, in the vicinity of Warsaw and in the districts south of Lublin. Within 15 days the German army in the eastern borders has increased by three infantry divisions, two motorized ones and seventeen thousand armed Ukrainian nationalists and one formation of paratroopers. The total number of German divisions of all sorts in E. Prussia and Poland alone amounts to 78 divisions.

Golikov then identified the various formations and their locations, ending with the ominous conclusion that 'the transfer of troops is continuing, as well as the accumulation of ammunition and oil on the borders of the USSR'.[22] A couple of days later the military attaché in Budapest found out from a trusted source that the Germans now possessed 265 divisions: 180 infantry, ten motorized, eighteen tank, five paratroop, six mountaineer and two to three cavalry divisions, and some forty unspecified divisions. Of these he believed only seventy-five remained on Russia's western front, and forty-five were concentrated in the Balkans. The bulk of the army confronted the Russian central and northern sectors.[23]

Zhukov could hardly afford to remain idle when confronted by this ominous intelligence. However, in the Kremlin Stalin continued to be obsessed with efforts to reconcile the Germans and was engulfed by deep suspicion of the British efforts to embroil Russia in war. Zhukov therefore set out to accomplish the impossible task of boosting the defensive plan of the previous month without aggravating the Kremlin. The conciliatory introduction of his new directive to General Pavlov, the commander of the western front, was aimed at Stalin and assumed that the non-aggression pact with Germany 'safeguards peace in our western borders. The Soviet Union does not intend to attack Germany and Italy. Nor does it appear that those States intend to attack the Soviet Union in the near future.' Zhukov went to great lengths to reconcile Stalin's obsessive fear of provocation with the genuine threat posed by Germany. Tongue in cheek, he pointed out the danger posed to Russia 'not only by such opponents as Finland, Rumania and England, but also possible opponents such as Germany, Italy and Japan'. But he dwelt on the recent events in the Balkans, the German incursions into Bulgaria, Rumania and Finland, the continued concentration of the German troops on the Russian border, and the growing power of the Axis which under different circumstances could be diverted against the Soviet Union. Consequently, the directive drove home the military's main concern: that the defence of the western borders of the Soviet Union had assumed 'exceptional significance'.

Zhukov presumed that the Germans would be able to muster for the campaign in the East some 200 divisions, comprising 165 infantry, twenty tank and fifteen motorized divisions. Misled by their incursion into the Balkans and Southern Europe, and assuming Hitler to be driven by economic interests, Zhukov expected him to 'try to seize the Ukraine' by delivering a major blow in the area enclosed between Berdichev and Kiev. The offensive could be sustained through subsidiary assaults from West Prussia to Dvinsk and Riga, or from Brest to Volkovysk and Baranovichi. However, Zhukov did not exclude the possibility that the main assault might be carried out from Prussia, via Warsaw, in the direction of Riga or Kovno and Dvinsk, with supportive action towards Minsk.

The main challenge for Zhukov, which he was unable to meet until the outbreak of war, was the need to cope with the double threat in the central and southern regions, in view of the tremendous extent of the battlefield. It should be borne in mind however that one reason for the failure of the Russians to perceive the German intentions sprang from the unresolved dispute within the German High Command on the final aims of the campaign. While Guderian sought to deliver a mortal blow on Moscow, Hitler strove to occupy the Ukraine and Leningrad. The compromise plan provided for a war in two stages. The success of the plan depended on the ability of the Wehrmacht to destroy the bulk of the Soviet army and prevent it from retreating in an orderly way across the Dniepr and then regrouping. To gloss over the conflicting views, it was decided to re-examine the objectives once the German army had regrouped on the Leningrad–Orsha–Dniepr line. The forces were therefore initially distributed more or less evenly between the three military districts. Army Group North under Field Marshal von Leeb, comprising an armoured striking force, a Panzer *Gruppe* and the 16th and 18th Armies, was entrusted with the destruction of the Soviet troops in the Baltic countries and the capture of Leningrad. The powerful Army Group Centre, under Field Marshal von Bock, consisted of thirty-five infantry, nine armoured and six motorized divisions. Their orders were to break through the Brest–Grodno–Vilna–Smolensk line and capture Smolensk. Army Group South under the command of Field Marshal Gerd von Rundstedt, with thirty-two infantry, five armoured and three motorized divisions, was expected to strike at Kiev. Pondering with his advisers on the pattern of the German deployment, Stalin could obviously reach a variety of conclusions, none of which necessarily involved a shift to the centre or north. He received little assistance from Soviet intelligence which, as we have seen, continued to produce conflicting evidence.[24]

The specific directive to General Pavlov elaborated the vague guide-lines of the March deployment plans. One should not lose sight of the fact that the directive was drafted in the midst of Stalin's appeasement efforts and, as we have seen, Zhukov was forced in the opening phase of the document to water down the threat considerably to conform with the Kremlin's views. Since he was robbed of the initiative, such as a pre-emptive strike, Zhukov had to devise a response to a German attack. Even under such circumstances he adhered strictly to the 'deep operations' principles introduced by Tukhachevsky[25] in devising his master stroke. In the initial stage of the war, assuming a German attack, the covering forces based in the strongholds (ukraplenie raiony) were expected to contain the enemy, absorb the extensive blow and conduct 'a stubborn defence'. To counter the two German efforts, he planned to move on to the offensive by striking at the concentration of the enemy in the Lublin–Radom region, moving on to occupy the crossing points on the River Visla. To sustain the main effort an auxiliary blow would be delivered in the direction of Warsaw leading to its occupation and establishing the defence on the River Narev. The success of such operations was bound to lead to the encirclement and annihilation of the main German concentration east of the Visla. By the tenth day of the operation the Red Army was expected to be settled on the Visla.

Considering the exigencies under which Zhukov was acting, only a single copy of the directive, handwritten by General Vassilevsky, deputy Chief of Staff and head of the Planning Division, went out and Pavlov was instructed to keep it under lock and key. The plan was to be put into action once a ciphered telegram with the words 'start implementing' reached his headquarters. Only then would the war machine start rolling, putting into effect the following stages: first, the plan for the covering of the borders and defence during the entire period of the concentration; second, the plan of concentration and deployment; third, the plan for the implementation of the first operation by the 13th and 4th Armies and the plan for the defence of the 3rd and 10th Armies.[26] For the moment, anticipating the negotiations with Schulenburg,[27] Stalin confined himself to administrative measures. On the evening of 23 April at his offices in the Kremlin, he discussed with Zhukov and Meretskov, and the ubiquitous General Kulik, the formation of three army groups to cope with the potential German threat.[28] For the moment Zhukov took only the emergency, though marginal, step of reinforcing the central sector through the deployment of the 231st and 224th rifle divisions in full battle readiness.[29]

The euphoric expectations of a breakthrough on the diplomatic front at the beginning of May turned by the end of the month into despondency. The ominous silence in Berlin was broken only by the deafening sound of the colossal German war machine settling along the entire length of the

Russian border. It was becoming well nigh impossible for Golikov to manoeuvre between Zhukov, alarmed by the signals of an imminent war, and Stalin, seeking a window of opportunity to start the negotiations with the Germans. At the end of April Golikov sought from the military attaché in Berlin, General Tupikov, an overall appraisal of German intentions. Pondering over the 150 telegrams and the two dozen reports which he had sent to the GRU in the previous three months, Tupikov marked the continuous and steady transfer of troops to the eastern front as the single most important and persistent feature of German policy. His report was backed up by an accurate table of the deployment of the German troops, giving preference to the northern and central sectors of the Russian border over the south-western, Balkan or Middle Eastern theatres. Just as indicative and alarming for him was Hitler's brazen disregard of Russian interests, mostly in the Balkans. But even his report was not void of ambivalence which could encourage an alternative appraisal. Tupikov recognized in the Ribbentrop–Molotov Pact an effective stabilizing force in relations with Germany, though he believed it to be a temporary respite. Tupikov too tended to attribute the incomprehensible German undertaking to a desperate need to control the economic resources of Russia, quoting Göring's aides that 'when rats are hungry they will gnaw through steel armour to reach their bread'. The situation had become so acute that German scientists were purported to be 'working on trans-forming sewage into edible food'. Tupikov, who was set on warning Stalin about the military danger, failed to realize that such an appraisal still left the door in the Kremlin wide open for an agreement on further conces-sions through political means and undermined Zhukov's position. But the bottom line clearly established that 'in the immediate German plans for the war, the USSR is next in the queue'.[30]

Another ominous sign was evidence of systematic German attempts at recruiting Russia's neighbours. An internal memorandum at the Foreign Ministry described Antonescu's overt hostility towards Russia; he was being encouraged by the Germans to revive the revisionist claim to Bessarabia. The reports from the region pointed to the 'German rein-forcement of the Rumanian border and the Black Sea shores and the con-centration of troops in Moldava while measures were undertaken to defend the oil regions from air attacks'. There was little doubt about 'how far the plans of immediate war and the preparedness of Germany for war against the Soviet Union have gone'.[31] German officers in Rumania even disclosed that the war against Russia would take place in mid-June. Under German supervision new airbases were being quickly built, while co-ordination was established with the Rumanian officers in preparation for the occupation of Bessarabia.[32] Precisely accurate information sup-plied by the NKGB depicted the various measures taken by the Germans 'to hasten the preparation of the theatre of war' on the Soviet–Hungarian border. High-ranking German officers were surveying the region and photographing the Soviet posts and bridges on the River Bug. This information went hand in hand with the well-documented systematic transfer of troops to the border since 27 March. Factories had been converted to produce scarce war materials and were now working 'around the clock'. Metal domes to shield guns had been stripped from the Maginot Line in France and transferred to the Russian border. Reconnaissance flights were on the increase. Agents had been instructed to obtain information on the location of staff headquarters, radio stations and airfields. Finally, when meeting local peasants on 10 April, the German commander of a border post was alleged to have said: 'Greece has surrendered, soon we shall seize Yugoslavia . . . One month of rest and we start a war against Russia.'[33]

For the moment, Golikov persisted in alerting the Kremlin to the 'intensifying concentrations against the Soviet Union along the entire length of the western and south-western borders, including Rumania and also Finland'. The schizophrenic situation was reflected in his periodical report of 5 May. On the one hand he dwelt on the stupendous German efforts: the fact that they had increased their forces in two months by thirty-seven divisions, while doubling their armoured divisions from six to twelve. And yet he also diverted attention to the extension of operations against England in the Near East (Turkey and Iraq) and North Africa, not excluding the possibility that Spain would be the next victim.[34]

The residency in Warsaw described how preparations for war were being conducted openly in the city and its vicinity. Between 10 and 20 April, troop formations were seen marching eastwards through the city's main streets, day and night, while artillery, planes and heavy machines were transferred to the front on shuttle trains. Warsaw was preparing for air raids: car lamps were blackened, windows blocked and civil defence organized. Vehicles had been confiscated, while schools had closed early for the summer vacation and other civilian institutions were being converted into military hospitals. The German officers in former Poland were studying the Russian language and exploring topographic maps of Russia. Todt, the famous engineer of the Siegfried Line, had been put in charge of the construction of fortifications on the border which employed no fewer than 35,000 Jews on forced labour.[35] The unceasing flow of accurate field intelligence increased from mid-May onwards. It dovetailed the final stages of the German deployment. A typical report consisted of dozens of short snippets of accurate information such as: 'on 25.4.41 8 infantry divisions were spotted and identified making their way to Sokalsky'. In addition, the Ukrainian NKGB provided precise information on road construction, the fortification of railway stations and junctions, and related preparations for war.[36]

Emergency Deployment

The formidable German concentration placed Zhukov and Timoshenko in a serious dilemma: the pace, volume and extent of the German deployment appeared to be outstripping the corresponding Russian efforts. They desperately sought means of closing the gap. On the night of 12 May, after discussing with Dekanozov the disappointing consequences of his last clandestine meeting with Schulenburg, and perhaps even as a reaction to the hints dropped by Schulenburg on Hitler's intentions, Stalin ordered the two generals to the Kremlin. In a meeting which lasted for almost two hours and which was attended by Molotov as well, Stalin reluctantly consented to restricted measures to bolster the defence mostly of the Kiev and Western Military Districts. The next morning the 16th, 19th, 21st and 22nd Armies, a total of about 800,000 troops, supported by the 21st Motorized Division, were ordered to move from the rear to the front. Well aware of Stalin's sensitivity, Zhukov conducted the transfer in an exceedingly discreet fashion to avoid provocation.[37]

The deployment seems particularly restrained compared to the plans issued by Zhukov a month earlier,[38] when his identification of the weaker links in the German deployment had led him to propose a counter-offensive once war broke out. The present directives seemed primarily to address the need to react to the German deployment by covering the entire border space in anticipation of an onslaught. The plans defined the most susceptible regions and sought means of thwarting the German threat. The deployment orders divided each military region into five or six covering districts. The framework set for the instructions, delivered to the various front commanders, assumed a German offensive and instructed the troops, somewhat optimistically, to:

> prohibit enemy land and air intrusion, cover and protect the mobilization and deployment of the main force by conducting a stubborn defence along the borders, detect enemy mobilization and deployment, gain air superiority and disrupt enemy force concentration, protect Soviet mobilization and concentration of forces against enemy air attack, and block any actions by enemy air assault or reconnaissance-diversionary groups.

The troops were allocated their specific covering regions and placed in the appropriate strongholds. They were instructed to bring the strongholds to war readiness while creating the necessary conditions for the deployment of the covering forces in the buffer zone leading to the border, to confront and engage the Germans once hostilities erupted. The recognition of the vulnerability of the Siavena–Yassy–Beltsy–Bapniarka axis, overshadowing the danger posed to Kishynev, Galatz, Volgrad and

Tiraspol, exemplified the shift from the Balkans to the Ukraine as the perceived ultimate objective of the German plans.

The deployment orders for the Odessa military region called for the
formation of a defensive line from Korzhenits to the mouth of the Danube
at Kilia and along the Black Sea shores up to the Straits. The naval
forces in the Black Sea were ordered to intercept a naval assault in the
direction of Odessa, the Crimea and the Caucasus, reflecting Stalin's continued fear of British connivance in a German attack. The constraints
under which Zhukov was operating are clearly discernible. In executing
the deployment he warned the front commanders that 'the first crossing
of the state borders' would be undertaken only by a 'specific instruction
of the Chief of Staff', coming into effect on receipt of a cipher telegram
with the words 'start carrying out the covering plan for 1941'. The directives themselves were issued in only two copies in longhand, one remaining with Zhukov and the other deposited in the safes of the commanders
of the various fronts.[39] On the field level the new deployment orders were
amalgamated with Zhukov's April directive. Indeed, on 14 May General
Pavlov issued more specific instructions to the army commanders. The
commander of the Grodno area was specifically ordered to contain the
Germans while generating favourable conditions for a counter-strike
by the mechanized corps. Even then, the strike at the rear of the enemy
was aimed specifically at disrupting the German ability to pursue their
attack.[40]

There is little doubt that, given sufficient time to deploy the army effectively on the border, Zhukov would have organized the defence in the
only fashion which Soviet doctrine recognized: a combination of defensive and offensive measures. Indeed, a mere three days after implementing the additional deployment measures and against the background of
the Yugoslav fiasco, Zhukov attempted to persuade Stalin to seize the initiative. Since he was not privy to the intricate diplomatic game, Zhukov
was becoming increasingly restless about the cautious mobilization plan
imposed on him. On 15 May, he and Timoshenko prepared yet another
directive, a direct sequel to that of April. Whereas in April he had still left
very vague the crucial issue of the 'early period of the war', the timing
of the counter-blow, this time Zhukov wished to seize the initiative in executing a pre-emptive strike. His point of departure was in no way ideologically motivated or expansionist. The plan had the clearly defined and
limited aim of pre-empting the German blow which he now believed to
be inevitable. Rather than seeking the destruction of the German state or
even armed forces, the plan sought the disruption of the German offensive. Zhukov may have raised the idea with Stalin at their meeting in the
Kremlin at midnight on 14 May, but it was more likely to have been
discussed in a two-hour meeting together with the deputy head of the
Planning Division, General Vatutin, on 19 May.[41] The idea clearly origi-

nated with the military and was rejected by Stalin outright, as it jeopardized his attempts to bring about a political solution.

Stalin's failure to prepare for the German onslaught primarily reflected the unappealing political choices which the Soviet Union faced both before the Second World War, in 1939, and on the eve of the Great Patriotic War, in 1941. Only with hindsight is it perhaps possible to point to alternatives which might have been pursued. Even then the blow could at best have been softened, but not averted. The extent of the German military successes both in France and in the Balkans were unforeseen by all the players in what Stalin referred to as the 'great game'. Even before the war Stalin believed, according to Molotov, 'that only by 1943 could we meet the Germans on an equal footing'.[42] Stalin's prudence in the conduct of the military preparations was dictated to a great extent by the belief that astute politics and adequate preparations might delay if not avert hostilities. Once the reality of war sank in, rather than resorting boldly to the newly devised doctrine or allowing the military to do so, Stalin in his typical style of leadership issued muddled instructions which responded to changing circumstances. He thus failed to create the proper environment for military planning which would have reconciled the doctrine with the strategic goals.

Zhukov's pre-emptive plan is in fact an unsigned draft, with corrections inserted in the margins by Zhukov himself. Its limited aims can be inferred from the framework set for the operation in the opening paragraph:

> Considering that at present Germany is keeping its army fully mobilized, with the rear deployed, it is in a position to circumvent us by mounting a surprise attack. To prevent this, I think it is essential not to allow the German High Command to seize the initiative on any account, to forestall the deployment of the enemy, and to attack the German army at the moment when it is in the middle of deployment and before it has successfully completed the organization of the front and the co-ordination of the movement of the various forces.

Zhukov probably hoped to repeat the relative success he had scored during the second war game in January, when his south-western front was in a position to drive westwards to the River Vistula. The plan contained elements of the 'deep operations' theory which he had implemented successfully in the Battle of Khalkin-Gol.

Zhukov envisaged that the Red Army would be able to confront the estimated 100 German divisions, assembled in depth in the central western sector from the borders to Warsaw, with 152 of its own. The execution of vast encirclement battles through tactical manoeuvrings was expected to cause havoc among the German concentrations in the central western sector and isolate them from their left wing. While executing the manoeuvres the Red Army was expected to gain control of the German part of Poland and East Prussia. The initial success would pave the way for successful battles of encirclement against both the northern and southern flanks of the German army.[43]

In an unusual move Stalin summoned to the Kremlin on 24 May the High Command, among them Timoshenko, Zhukov, Admiral Kuznetsov, Vatutin and the commanders of the major fronts, General Kirponos (including the senior members of his staff), commander of the Kiev Military Region, and Pavlov. In a meeting which lasted for almost three hours they most probably discussed the problems related to the German threat and the measures to counter it. Stalin, however, refused to go beyond the emergency measures already undertaken.[44]

It has been suggested that if Stalin had accepted the recommendations Russia would have fared better in the initial stage of the war. But Stalin's caution appeared reasonable, not only because of the political considerations described here but also in military terms. Zhukov's estimate was based on the concentration of the German forces in mid-May. He could not complete his own deployment before the end of June, by which time his forces would have been greatly outnumbered by the Germans. Perhaps even more sobering were the lessons drawn from the war games, which had exposed the unprepared state of the Russian army. In retrospect Zhukov admitted that his proposal had been a terrible mistake: if the Red Army had been allowed to strike at that time it would have been destroyed instantly.[45] Zhukov later challenged Marshal Vassilevsky, who in an interview which was suppressed for almost twenty years had argued that Stalin made a mistake by not deploying the entire covering forces and the second echelon on the border. Zhukov marked in the margins of the interview, which is deposited with the Politburo archives, that 'Vassilevsky's opinion does not fully correspond with reality. I believe that the Soviet Union would have been beaten, early on, if we had deployed all our forces on the borders on the eve of the war, and the German troops would have been able to accomplish their plan, encircle and destroy them at the border . . . Then Hitler's troops could have stepped up the campaign and Moscow and Leningrad would have fallen in 1941.'[46]

The deployment, as an emergency measure, was conducted in great haste and in a most disorderly fashion. It was executed prematurely, while the armies and their auxiliary forces had not yet been built up to their war strength, and were poorly equipped. This was well understood in Moscow and enhanced Stalin's resolve to postpone the war as long as possible. As early as 29 April Kirponos warned Zhukov that the February mobilization plan 'was not being fully completed'. Four days after the mobilization had been ordered Lieutenant-General Purkaev informed Zhukov from Kiev that the plans for supplying the armies with ammunition and provisions were proceeding 'extremely slowly'. It looked as if the supply programme for the entire year would not be attained. On 6 June, the commander of the 5th Tank Division complained that although mobilization orders had been issued his manpower was far from the required strength and he did not possess any operational instructions. He concluded therefore that the 'delay in the increase of staff does not render it possible to complete the implementation of the mobilization orders in accordance with the mobilization plan for 1941'. On the same day the Deputy Chief of the Baltic Military District informed Zhukov that the logistical difficulties, failure to establish the proper material infrastructure and lack of communications 'do not allow for the fulfilment of the mobilization plan'.[47]

The reluctance to embark on a bold defensive policy is hardly surprising. On 17 May Zhukov and Timoshenko, in co-operation with Zhdanov, issued a report on 'the results of battle training inspection for the winter period of 1941 and orders for the summer period'. The report exposed the shortcomings uncovered in the inspection of the army in the winter of 1941. These failings cast further doubt on the ability of the Red Army to execute a pre-emptive strike at this stage. The inspection revealed that the army on the whole did not display particular vigilance, battle-readiness, steadfastness in defence or preparations to repel an armoured invasion. The report reflects a desperate attempt to put the house in order. A reappraisal of the defensive goals brought home the gloomy realization that only a few of them had been attained throughout the winter. The surveys carried out by the Defence Commissariat and the military districts established that most units had failed to implement the directives on mobilization. Consequently, a new set of orders which were expected to form the basis for training during the summer of 1941 clearly displays a defensive disposition and the ineptitude of the armed forces. The orders of the commanders of the motorized infantry and the tank corps show even more bluntly that very basic techniques, including communications and co-ordination, accuracy of fire and night combat, had not been mastered.[48]

An effective defence relied on a system of strongholds which were hastily raised along the new 'Molotov Line', some 300 kilometres west of the former border. The vital task of these URs, constructed at some distance from the border, was to serve as the outposts for the covering forces of the first echelon, and provide them with logistic and fire support in the initial stage of the war. The covering forces were expected to seize the area leading to the border, contain the enemy, absorb the first blow and create favourable conditions for the second echelon to deliver counter-blows. The plan had been worked out in the autumn of 1940 but failed to 'address the new political and military problems' arising out of the Ribbentrop–Molotov Pact. It was further hampered by the major

242 *Grand Delusion*

strategic mistake of assuming Hitler's main strike to be directed against Kiev rather than the Belorussian front.[49]

During 1938 thirteen strongholds, manned by twenty-five machine-gun battalions totalling 18,000 men, had been established. Eight more were added before the German invasion of Poland. The introduction of the new strategic plans in 1940–1 was accompanied by the construction of twenty densely fortified regions along the new border. The decision to dismantle the old line and remove the guns to the new ones was taken personally by Stalin. The project, however, encountered endless technical problems in the transfer of the equipment from the old fortifications to the new ones.[50]

The Military Council of the Red Army met twice in February and March 1941 to discuss means of accelerating the construction of new fortifications. In early March the Politburo exerted further pressure in an attempt to remove the obstacles which seemed to be hindering the completion of the defence posts. Responsibility for their construction was duly stripped from the Engineers' Corps and entrusted directly to the former Chief of Staff, Shaposhnikov.[51] In mid-April the political authorities of the Red Army reviewed the dire situation of the URs and reached the grave conclusion that 'overwhelmingly they are not militarily ready'. The Defence Ministry was blamed for the failure to furnish the strongholds with the adequate weaponry systems and equipment. The General Staff duly issued a directive on the need to accelerate construction, in which some 140,000 labourers were engaged daily. The directive opened by conceding that 'despite the series of orders placed by the General Staff of the Red Army, the installation of the fortified defences in the long-term military constructions and the bringing of those fortifications to military readiness are proceeding at an unacceptably slow pace'.[52]

The government allocated 10 million rubles, a tremendous sum in those days, to hasten construction of the fortifications on the new line. As late as 4 June, the Politburo intervened, pressing for the hasty completion of the URs by October 1941. The first ones, to be staffed by 45,000 men, were expected to be ready on 1 July and the remainder, accommodating 75,000 men, in October. The effort was well under way when it was disrupted by the German invasion.[53] Alarming gaps of 50–60 kilometres continued to exist between the strongholds, leaving the covering forces without protection. The failure was not only a result of the shifting borders but was due to the absence of construction materials such as concrete, timber and barbed wire, aggravated by the lack of time.[54]

Until May Stalin sided with Voznesensky, the head of State Planning and deputy Prime Minister, who had long found the demands of the General Staff excessive. In view of the pressure mounted by the Chief of Staff in the spring, Stalin agreed to increase production considerably to provide for the newly mobilized armies.[55] Only in early May did Stalin agree to introduce major changes in the armoured formation through the creation of twenty new mechanized corps. Putting the economy on a war footing, the stupendous effort to increase the production of armaments and ammunition during the second half of 1941, and the hasty conversion of industries followed. The lion's share of the production of the new KV3 and improved T-34 tanks was to be accomplished towards the end of the year, clearly reflecting Stalin's recognition that he had no adequate response to the Germans in the summer of 1941 and the belief that he could postpone the war to the following year. Even so, the Russians could at best produce 2,800 T-34s by the end of the year.[56]

There was little to commend in the state of the air force. In April the government conceded in a report to the Politburo that 'the accidents and disasters in the Red Army's air force have not only not been reduced, but in fact increased because of the slackness of the pilots and the commanding officers which has brought about the breakdown of the basic flying regulations'. The 'lack of discipline' led to the death of two or three pilots in accidents per day. Timoshenko was further reprimanded for having assisted Rychagov, the air force commander, in deliberately concealing from the Politburo the poor state of the air force.[57] As for the production of the LAGG-3 fighter plane, 593 of which should have been constructed, the Chief of the Air Force conceded to Stalin that progress was not being made according to the plan. Out of the mere 158 manufactured, many were found to be defective.[58]

At the end of May, a couple of days after the miniature military conference at the Kremlin, Zhukov and Timoshenko were summoned to a Politburo meeting at which they expected at long last to be briefed about the looming danger. Stalin informed them that:

> The German ambassador von Schulenburg has approached us with a request from the German government to allow them to conduct a search for the graves of soldiers and officers who perished in the First World War in combat with the old Russian army. For the search for these graves the Germans have formed several groups, which will assemble at agreed points marked on this border map. You are to arrange control to ensure that the Germans do not extend their search deeper or wider than the designated areas. Order the districts to maintain tight contact with our border guards, who have already been briefed.[59]

At that meeting Zhukov and Timoshenko did eventually air their concern about the German build-up and repeated their wish at least to intercept the increasing number of German aircraft flying reconnaissance flights over Russia. Stalin objected, advancing Schulenburg's explanation that these were errors of navigation by inexperienced and newly recruited German pilots.

Zhukov nonetheless passed a rather lenient verdict on Stalin's behaviour. Though pinning the blame on him, he was quick to explain that 'There is nothing simpler than providing a new interpretation of events when the past and its consequences are already known. And there is nothing more complex than investigating the intricate issues, weighing the varying opposing forces, the multitude of conflicting opinions, information, and facts which were available at a given historical moment.'[60] Zhukov eventually reached the conclusion that in Stalin's mind 'loomed the threat of war with fascist Germany, and his entire thoughts and actions were based on a single desire – to avoid war or to delay its outbreak, which he was certain he could achieve . . . In these difficult circumstances J. V. Stalin's desire to prevent war was transformed into a belief that he could successfully wipe out the danger of war by peaceful means. Counting on his "wisdom", he proved to be too clever by half and did not comprehend the devious tactics and plans of Hitler's government.'[61]

Until the end of May 1941, the various channels of intelligence tended to submit balanced and fairly accurate reports on the German deployment. However, Stalin's refusal to come to terms with the magnitude of the danger and the priority he gave to the efforts to avoid provocation were making their mark on the intelligence agencies. Golikov's fortnightly report of 15 May was a turning point. While not oblivious to the imminent danger, he now chose to dwell on the reinforcement of the German forces earmarked for action against England in the Middle East and Africa.[62] At the end of the month, Golikov presented Stalin with a detailed chart of the German deployment that was bound to lead to an ambiguous reading of the situation. It can plausibly be surmised that by that time he had become aware, against the background of the deepening rift between Stalin and the Chief of Staff, that Stalin was on edge whenever a suggestion was made that the Germans might be on the brink of war. Consequently it became increasingly difficult to distinguish between what Stalin dismissed as 'rumours' and 'hard facts', even if they conveyed the same message. This ambivalence was reflected in the incongruous attempts to see parity between the German deployment in the West and in the East.

According to Golikov's numerical estimates (he did not attempt to evaluate the quality), the Germans possessed 122 to 126 divisions earmarked for the war against England in the West and a similar number, 120 to 122 divisions, on the eastern front. The picture was not entirely balanced, as forty-four to forty-eight divisions were kept by Hitler in reserve close to the front and could be thrown into the battle at short notice. The divisions in Norway could also be lined up against Russia. All in all, three spearheads now threatened Russia: in western Russia twenty-three to twenty-four divisions (eighteen or nineteen infantry, two armoured and three motorized divisions); in the central sector twenty-nine divisions (twenty-four infantry, four armoured and one motorized); in the Lublin–Krakovsky region thirty-six to thirty-eight divisions (twenty-four or twenty-five infantry, six armoured and five motorized); in Slovakia five mountaineer divisions; while four divisions were deployed on the Ukrainian Carpathian border. The remaining forces were allied troops.

Golikov now went out of his way to attune himself to Stalin's preconceived ideas, concluding rather bluntly that the Germans had exhausted their efforts in the Middle East and were regrouping their forces in France for 'launching a major operation against the British Isles'. Considering, however, that the armies were equally divided between two fronts, the final analysis left the alternatives wide open. It simply noted that 'the regrouping of German forces after the Balkan campaign has essentially been completed'. Obviously such reporting proved fertile ground for the cultivation of the erring concepts in the Kremlin.[63]

The conflicting appreciations were mirrored by the diplomatic community in Moscow. Gafencu had learnt from Bucharest that the 'inevitable and imminent' attack would start on 15 June. The Turkish ambassador, Aktay, held a similar view. Even the new Vichy ambassador, Bergery, claimed to have authentic information that Hitler had decided to embark on a holy crusade against Bolshevism. Cripps, who found it 'too good to be true', also relied on similar information originating in Stockholm that war would erupt on 15 June. On the other hand, Schulenburg and his staff were showing 'happy and satisfied faces' as if denying the existence of the threat. Rosso received a telegram from Berlin stating, according to a well-known source, that 'negotiations were going on between Russian and German negotiators in Königsberg, touching among other topics on the right of transfer of German troops through the Ukraine'. The Swedish ambassador, a veteran and keen Kremlin-watcher, wondered whether the fact that the rumours had surfaced both in Bucharest and in Stockholm did not indicate that they emanated from German sources, and were 'aimed at keeping Moscow in a state of tension which might reduce Stalin's resilience in the event of German pressure . . . This is why the German embassy on the face of it denies knowledge of the initiation of any Soviet–German negotiations. Such contacts may well be taking place not through official channels.'[64]

12

The Flight of Rudolf Hess to England

The Conspiracy

The flight of Rudolf Hess, Hitler's deputy, on a peace mission to England on 10 May 1941 is one of the most bizarre episodes of the Second World War. A significant aspect of the affair, largely overlooked by historians, is the impact it had on the Soviet evaluation of British and German intentions on the eve of 22 June 1941. In Moscow the mission was examined against the background of Churchill's warning, Cripps's incessant threats of a separate peace and Schulenburg's fresh overture. The persisting belief in some sort of Anglo-German collusion, and the failure to eradicate the mutual suspicion between the new allies after the German invasion of the Soviet Union accounts for Stalin's obsessive demand that Hess should be kept imprisoned in Spandau until his death, long after the other war criminals had been released. The extent of Stalin's suspicion of Hess first emerged in the autumn of 1942. At the peak of the debate on the opening of the second front, he accused Churchill of keeping Hess 'in reserve'.[1] Cripps, then a member of the War Cabinet, was instructed to prepare a most comprehensive and accurate account of the event, which did not put Stalin's mind at rest, perhaps because the censor insisted on the omission of references to the interviews conducted by Lord Simon and Lord Beaverbrook with Hess in 1941. The fact that such interviews had taken place was well known to Stalin.[2]

Stalin's interpretation of the Hess affair, perpetuating the Soviet obsession about British schemes to compel Germany to fight Russia, came to the fore during Churchill's visit to Moscow in October 1944. After the two leaders had carved up Eastern Europe in precise percentages, wined and dined, Stalin reverted to Hess. Churchill gave a light-hearted, though accurate, account of the ensuing conversation, in which he said:

Hess thought he could be the man to save England for Germany. So Hess, who had been forbidden to use any aircraft at any time because he was crazy, managed to get hold of a machine and flew over. Hoped to use the Duke of Hamilton, who was Lord Steward!! to be taken directly to the King. Stalin then rather unexpectedly proposed a toast to the health of the British Intelligence Service which had inveigled Hess into coming to England. He could not have landed without being given signals. The Intelligence Service must have been behind it.

Stalin would not budge from this position, despite Churchill's indignation. He simply argued that British intelligence might not have shared the information with Churchill. After all, the Russian Intelligence Service, he insisted, 'often did not inform the Soviet Government of its intentions and only did so after their work was accomplished . . .'[3]

This notion coincided with numerous conspiracy theories which have gained respectability in the West. The theories have run wild, ranging from a suggestion that it was actually not Hess but a 'duplicate' who made the mission to England to an accusation by highly acclaimed historians that Hess did not die a natural death in jail but was poisoned by his captors. Outstanding in this genre is *Ten Days to Destiny: The Secret Story of the Hess Peace Initiative and British Efforts to Strike a Deal with Hitler* by John Costello, which was published in 1991 and immediately translated into Russian. The book epitomized and perpetuated the various conspiracy theories which have since been discredited with the opening of the closed British files on Hess in the summer of 1992.[4]

The 18,000 pages of documents on the Hess affair made available by the British Public Record Office, when read in conjunction with archival material of the Russian security services, reveal a deliberate disinformation campaign carried out by British intelligence which misfired and led to misinterpretations both at that time and subsequently. And yet the huge collection basically confirms the two crucial assertions made in Churchill's account of the episode in his memoirs. Hess, Churchill wrote, 'came to us of his own free will, and, though without authority, had something of the quality of an envoy'. His second verdict, which is most relevant for our story, is that 'considering how closely Hess was knit to Hitler, it is surprising that he did not know of, or that if he knew he did not disclose, the impending attack on Russia . . .'[5] The archival material, however, does make a remarkable revelation, which had previously been hinted at only by fragments of evidence,[6] that the affair was manipulated by the British Foreign Office and British intelligence in an attempt to disrupt the negotiations that they believed were about to start between Hitler and Stalin. The impact of the resulting statements on Moscow at the time was undoubtedly much more significant than the issues which became the pivots of the conspiracy theories.

The Mission

Hess took off in a Messerschmitt Bf110, an aircraft which the British called the ME 110, from Augsburg at 5.45 p.m. on 10 May. The daring flight and the navigation involved considerable skill. Hess parachuted out over Eaglesham in Scotland, dressed in the uniform of a captain of the German air force, after dark had fallen. He landed 12 miles from the Duke of Hamilton's estate. Despite later attempts to claim that he carried a formal peace proposal with him, no documents were found on him other than a photograph of himself and his son and the visiting card of the celebrated expert on geopolitics, Professor Karl Haushofer, whose son Albrecht was most probably the driving force behind the mission.[7]

The archival material establishes beyond doubt that the Royal Air Force was not expecting Hess and therefore did not set up a secure corridor for him. Moreover, the defences in that region were by no means as dense as is often suggested. The plane was in fact detected at 15,000 feet just after 10 p.m. and was pursued by two patrolling Spitfires, which lost touch with him as their speed was slower than his. By the time Hess had reached the west coast of Scotland he was also chased by a 'Defiant' night fighter, which was just about to catch up with the Messerschmitt when Hess baled out.[8]

If indeed, as is claimed by Costello and others, Hess's landing was anticipated in Scotland by SIS (also known as MI6), this would have been reflected in the treatment he received in the early hours after his arrival. It should be remembered that Hess landed very close to the Duke of Hamilton's estate, and that if he was expected he could not possibly have been 'lost' for hours. His reception, however, was totally bungled, which demonstrates more than anything else the bewilderment which his arrival caused. The information regarding Hess's parachuting reached the Home Guard through the Giffnock police station, which had in turn been informed by passing observers that a plane had crashed near Eaglesham House at 23.12. Hess's capture was a completely uncoordinated affair. An officer who resided at the scene took two gunners from the nearby camp and set off for the scene of the crash. By then Hess had been detained in the cottage of the ploughman on to whose land he had parachuted. The parachutist, identifying himself as Alfred Horn, was taken by car to the Home Guard headquarters.

Shortly after midnight the Home Guard approached the Argyll and Sutherland Highlanders with a request for an escort to transfer the pilot into the army's custody. Surely no one was expecting Hess, for the duty officer instructed the Home Guard to place him in the Giffnock police cell for the night, despite their remonstrations that Horn seemed to be 'of some importance and that he should be taken in care by a Military Unit'. An inquiry by Military Intelligence into the affair later discovered major flaws in the handling of Hess which would not have occurred had his arrival in England been orchestrated by the Secret Intelligence Service. Little was done to establish that the prisoner was an officer and therefore had to be interrogated in an appropriate fashion. Air Intelligence completely ignored the information submitted to them at 1 a.m. on 11 May that the prisoner claimed to be an important figure and was anxious to make a statement to them.[9] Finally, after further urging backed up by the information that the pilot was carrying a message for the Duke of Hamilton and was willing to talk to the right party, the army agreed to receive him. The police detective inspector who had come to collect him withdrew only after he had conducted his own private investigation and examined Hess's belongings.

This interrogation was carried out with the assistance of a certain Group-Captain Donald, who happened to be on the scene when Hess was brought in. Donald drafted Roman Battaglia, a member of the Polish consulate in Glasgow, to act as an interpreter. 'It seems incredible', reproached 'C', the head of SIS, 'that this should have been permitted.' Battaglia noticed that the pilot was the spitting image of Hess but this was denied by him. Hess was on the whole calm but slightly distressed, probably as a result of being interrogated by Battaglia, who spoke English 'somewhat stiltedly', in the presence of some fifteen or twenty Home Guards. As the early stages of a prisoner's interrogation are obviously vital, it is perhaps worth describing the ambience of the scene as recorded in Battaglia's debriefing by Military Intelligence. He was puzzled:

> that no attempt was made, so far as he knew, to check up on [Hess's] own identity or integrity; that of the fifteen or twenty persons present there seemed to be no official interrogator, and that he [Battaglia] was asked to put questions from all corners of the room, some of which he considered offensive and which he refused to ask. No accurate report was made of the interrogation, and people wandered round the room inspecting the prisoner and his belongings at their leisure.

It gradually dawned on those present that the prisoner was not an ordinary pilot, as his uniform was of particularly good quality and had not seen service. Accordingly, 'a certain measure of extra courtesy' was now afforded to Hess, who was conducted to Maryhill Barracks at about 2 a.m.[10]

Once Hess's identity had been established, Military Intelligence was taken to task by 'C' over the mishandling of the affair. He was particularly indignant about the interrogations after midnight despite Hess's insistence that he was carrying an important message. Intelligence was quick to shift the blame on to the Duke of Hamilton, stating that 'it can only be assumed that the decision to do nothing until [later in] the morning was taken by Wing Commander the Duke of Hamilton'. This suggestion has persisted and has given rise to extravagant claims that Hamilton was involved in the machinations of SIS; it may have derived from a letter which Albrecht Haushofer, the renowned German expert on geopolitics, had sent to Hamilton in the autumn of 1940 and which had been intercepted and examined by Military Intelligence. By sheer coincidence the letter, which was a peace feeler, had reached its destination a couple of days before Hess's arrival. A coincidence does not necessarily amount to conspiracy.

There may have been a number of reasons for the fact that Hamilton did not immediately interrogate the prisoner at 3 a.m. To start with, it is entirely possible that Hamilton was not informed on the phone that the pilot identifying himself as Alfred Horn was carrying a political message. Hess was not the only German who was shot down that night in one of the heaviest German night raids. It was by no means normal practice for a station commander to carry out an interrogation in the small hours. Moreover, Hamilton retired to bed only after going through a list of Luftwaffe officers he had met during the Olympic Games in 1936, but he could not find a Horn there. The delay, therefore, was negligence at worst.[11]

There is another facet to the episode which should be discussed in this connection. Even if Hamilton did guess that the pilot was Hess, which is most unlikely, his reaction would not be surprising. As a respected wing commander who was trying to shake off his past association with the appeasers, he was suddenly faced with the embarrassing reality of being the object of Nazi peace overtures. The Hess affair threatened to release the genie from the bottle.[12] His embarrassment was to be aggravated when a German public announcement linked him with Hess's mission, creating an unfounded impression of complicity. Random letters examined by the censor reflected this feeling. The following is just one example: 'I wonder if there is any truth in the tale that this wretched man was intimate with the Duke of Hamilton. There seem to be far too many of our nobility mixed up with the Nazis.'[13] Hamilton's sensitivity was so acute that he put the government in an awkward position by suing the veteran communist leader Harry Pollitt for his statement that he, Hamilton, was 'a friend of Hess'. In view of their suspicion the communists, probably on instructions from Moscow, saw here an unusual opportunity for Hess to be subpoenaed and cross-examined in public.[14] Indeed, the need to 'help to clear the Duke of Hamilton from the unfortunate and ignorant suspicions that have surrounded him' was fully recognized.[15] When Cripps prepared a report on the affair for the Cabinet in November 1942 he made a point of exonerating Hamilton, mentioning that 'the Duke's conduct in relation to Rudolf Hess had been in every respect honourable and proper'.

Hamilton finally met the imprisoned pilot at 10 a.m. the next day, when Hess revealed his true identity. Hamilton, however, was unable or unwilling to remember meeting Hess during his visit to Berlin. He certainly had not had any contact with him since. During their private conversation Hess divulged the gist of the information he had come to impart, stating that he was 'on a mission of humanity and that the Führer did not want to defeat England and wished to stop fighting'. Though he emphasized that his views were close to those of Hitler, Hess insisted that the mission was his own initiative.[16] This statement, which would be constantly repeated,[17] leads us to the critical issue of Hitler's alleged connivance in the mission. Maisky preferred to leave the question open in his memoirs: 'Who is Hess? A camouflaged emissary from Hitler or a solitary psychopath? or is he the representative of some grouping within the Nazi top leadership, disturbed at the prospect that the war may drag out too long?'[18] The British archival material now released contradicts the frenzied speculations which had proliferated over the years and to a considerable degree harmed Anglo-Soviet relations. Some desperate attempts are still being made to salvage segments of such theories, but to no avail. In his recent work on Hess,[19] Peter Padfield incorporated many of the ideas raised by Costello. But by the time the book was ready for publication the archives had been opened and he was obliged to add an extensive epilogue which disavowed the bulk of his earlier arguments. He did, however, attempt to salvage the theory that Hess had come with Hitler's connivance by enlisting evidence obtained by a French war correspondent, a certain André Guerber, shortly after the war. Guerber claimed in a newspaper article to have found documents 'in the ruins of the Berlin Chancellery at the end of the war which definitely established that it was Hitler himself who decided to send Hess to Britain'. He alleged that Hess had actually been provided with a draft peace treaty, printed on Chancellery paper, which was confiscated from him shortly after his arrival. Guerber's version, comprising a four-point draft agreement, has never been produced. On his own admission, only the fourth point differed substantially from the oral proposals actually made by Hess: it purportedly proposed that Britain should maintain an attitude of benevolent neutrality towards Germany during the German–Russian war.[20]

Once the British archival material had been released and proved to be entirely innocuous, only unfettered speculation could sustain the old conspiracy theories. Padfield quotes the testimony of a certain John Howell who told him of a man of German origin, whose name cannot be divulged, who was invited with a couple of other German-speakers by Ivone Kirkpatrick, a German expert at the Foreign Office, to analyse the terms of the precise peace proposal which Hess brought with him from Germany. They were written in German on Chancellery paper together with an English translation. The committee, he further claims, met in extremely clandestine circumstances at the BBC headquarters in Portland Place. According to the informant, the 'first two pages of the proposals detailed Hitler's aims in Russia, outlining his precise plans for conquest in the east and the destruction of Bolshevism'.[21] The informant may well have confused the paper with the one prepared by Hess for his meeting with Lord Simon, which is the occasion on which he put his ideas down in writing.[22]

It is argued that the existence of formal proposals from Hess proved such an embarrassment to Churchill or to British intelligence that they simply ordered their removal from the inventory of Hess's belongings upon arrival. The report of the Home Guard on the detention of Hess specified: 'Captain Barrie took with him the articles which had been taken from the prisoner and which were inventoried. Copy of the inventory is attached to this report.'[23] The consecutive numbering of the pages in the original Military Intelligence file shows that it has not been tampered with. The file itself, as compared to those of the Foreign Office, was tattered to start with. It is most likely that the inventory list had not been attached to it in the first place.

Those who claim that Hess came as part of an elaborate scheme devised in Berlin are eager to show continuity. One such claim is that Hess had been sent to Madrid by Hitler on 20 April in an attempt to establish contact with the British government. It most probably relies on the fact that the British ambassador in Madrid, Sir Samuel Hoare, was a notorious appeaser and would have welcomed such an approach.[24] A close examination of the archives repudiates such a claim. The Foreign Office approached the embassy in Madrid with a request for information regarding the 'reports from Vichy that Hess has flown to Madrid with a personal letter from Hitler to Franco'. The rumours referred to an arrangement concerning the right of passage of German troops to Gibraltar. The second telegram of 25 April rejected such rumours. Frank Roberts, a future ambassador to Moscow then at the European Department of the Foreign Office, stated that 'the scare of last weekend has turned out to be at least premature'. This referred, however, not to Hess's visit but to the threat to Gibraltar, which obsessed the British at the time. The information was actually contradictory in nature. A visit by Hess to Spain would have been associated with possible clandestine contacts with British intelligence sources or even with the British ambassador, Sir Samuel Hoare, but the right of transfer of troops naturally implied belligerent action against Britain. In response to a query put by Military Intelligence, Frank Roberts, rather than giving credence to the rumours, clearly stated that he could not 'confirm report that Hess has met German Ambassador in Barcelona. If Hess has come here his arrival has been kept remarkably secret and his presence in town is not even rumoured yet.' He further commented that Hoare would have reported 'automatically' if such rumours had a basis.[25] The view in Moscow was that the rumours concerning Hess's peace negotiations in Spain were mischievously spread by the British to divert attention from the grievous situation and ensnare Russia in war.[26]

The archival material tends to prove that Hess did not come with Hitler's authorization, nor was he lured by British intelligence. Moreover, he did not carry with him any formal proposals. On the first anniversary of Hess's arrival in England, after he had been interrogated and put under twenty-four-hour surveillance and monitoring, Cadogan passed a clear-cut verdict: 'By now, it is pretty clear that Hess's escapade was a mad venture on his own, and that the German authorities knew nothing about it beforehand.'[27] Cadogan must have known; he had been placed in charge of co-ordinating the handling of Hess by all departments including the security services. Hess himself confessed in a letter to Haushofer that 'There is no denying that I have failed. But there is no denying that *I was my own pilot* [author's italics]. I have nothing to reproach myself with in this respect. At any rate I was at the helm.'[28]

One source which seemed to sustain the idea that Hess had left Germany with Hitler's full knowledge was a newspaper interview with his wife at the end of the war. But her evidence was based on her recollection of Hess's last meeting with Hitler in Berlin on 4 May, when 'their voices were raised but . . . they did not actually quarrel'.[29] The fragmentary nature of the evidence stands in contrast to Hess's voluminous correspondence with his family during the war and does not lend force to such claims. In a long letter to his mother Hess described the meticulous preparations for the flight, stressing that 'the many evenings which I spent *secretly* [author's italics] with maps, tables, slide-ruler and drawing board were worth while'. In another letter he gave his reason for not taking off from Berlin; Hitler had apparently prohibited him from flying from there without prior permission. 'I might just as well', he explained to her, 'have had myself taken into custody right away. But it was fortunate that nothing came of the flying near Berlin. I could not have hidden my activities and the Führer would have heard about them sooner or later. My plan would have been stopped and I should have blamed myself for carelessness.'[30] Even if by some remote chance it does turn out that Hess's mission had official German backing, it is patently clear that the British government had no knowledge of this, nor did they assume Hess to be Hitler's official emissary.

The real inspiration behind Hess's mission was almost certainly Haushofer. The extent of Haushofer's direct and immediate involvement is still somewhat obscure, but the letter he was forced to write in Berchtesgaden on the day of the flight demonstrates his influence on Hess and the contacts which Hess was to make in England.[31] The recent book by

Lord James Douglas-Hamilton shows very clearly the line leading from Haushofer to Hess. At his very first meeting with the Duke of Hamilton Hess credited the Haushofers with the mission.[32] Hess later repeated this information in casual conversations which he held with his medical officer.[33] In the first letter to his wife from prison, Hess asked her to 'write to the General [Haushofer] – of whose dreams I often think'.[34] The inspiration he received from Haushofer comes through in a letter Hess addressed to him: 'you said you did not think I was mad but "sometimes daring". You can believe me when I say I have not regretted for one moment my madness and daring. Some day, the last part of your dream which was so dangerous for my plan will be fulfilled and I shall appear before you.'[35] Equally revealing was his disclosure that the decision matured in December 1940 and that he had already made a number of abortive attempts to fly to England. It is indeed possible that he made up his mind once Hitler reached the decision to attack Russia (if he was aware of it) and after the collapse of the Berlin talks in which he took part. Alternatively he may have been appalled by Ribbentrop's idea of the Continental bloc, which envisaged the participation of the Soviet Union in the carving up of the British Empire.

Fictitious Negotiations

After Hamilton's debriefing of Hess, attention shifted to London. Cadogan, who would be personally entrusted with the handling of the affair and to whom 'C' and other branches of intelligence were made subordinate, learnt of the affair later on 11 May, though the identity of Hess was still kept secret: 'a German pilot landed near Glasgow, asked for the Duke of Hamilton. Latter so impressed he is flying to London & wants to see me at No 10 tonight . . . Half an hour later heard P.M. was sending to meet His Grace at airfield and wd bring him to Chequers.'[36]

Hamilton's initial idea was to see the King. He flew his own plane to London on the evening of 11 May but upon arrival was persuaded by Cadogan to see Churchill first.[37] He was driven late at night to see the Prime Minister at Ditchley, where Churchill was watching an American film with close friends. Before even taking off his flying jacket, Hamilton insisted on drawing Churchill aside and revealing to him the pilot's identity. All the evidence points to the fact that Churchill was taken completely by surprise. He treated Hamilton as 'though he were suffering from war strain and hallucinations'. In characteristic fashion, Churchill then welcomed him in and said, 'Well, Hess or no Hess I am going to see the Marx Brothers.' However, once the film had ended at midnight, he spent over three hours questioning Hamilton and pondering on the repercussions of Hess's presence in Britain.[38]

It should be emphasized that at no time did Churchill even envisage negotiations with Hess. At this challenging crossroads it was essential to extract the utmost propaganda value from the mission and avoid making a false move. From the outset he insisted that Hess 'like other Nazi leaders is potentially a war-criminal and he and his confederates may well be declared outlaws at the close of the war'. He was further determined to prevent a pilgrimage of politicians who might be entertaining a hope of an early peace. He therefore instructed that Hess 'be strictly isolated in a convenient house not too far from London, fitted by "C" with the necessary appliances, and every endeavour should be made to study his mentality and get anything worthwhile out of him'.[39] A few days after his arrival Churchill ordered the transfer of 'my prisoner', as he now called Hess, to London. Incidentally, those who still adhere to the conspiracy theory should note that as soon as Hess was declared a prisoner of war he passed into the custody of the army rather than the security services.[40] Churchill demanded that he should be 'informed before any visitors are allowed', a move clearly designed to prevent visits by appeasers. He instructed that Hess be kept 'in the strictest seclusion, and those in charge of him should refrain from conversation'. 'The public', he warned, would 'not stand any pampering except for intelligence purposes with this notorious war criminal'.[41] Churchill later pledged in communications with Roosevelt that he would not consider Hess's proposals, which he defined as 'the old invitation to us to desert all our friends in order to save temporarily the greater part of our skin'.[42]

On the morning of 12 May Eden took Hamilton across from 10 Downing Street to Whitehall and together with Ivone Kirkpatrick of the Foreign Office, who had met Hess in Berlin, they examined the array of photographs brought along by Hamilton and established that they appeared to be of Hess. As a precautionary measure Kirkpatrick flew back with Hamilton to Scotland to identify Hess personally. For the time being the press was not briefed on the unfolding drama. Kirkpatrick not only recognized Hess but also won his confidence; Hess probably gained the fleeting impression that his offer was being taken seriously. Still unaware that he had made the wrong bid, Hess expounded the reasons which had led him to fly to England. Skilfully guided by Kirkpatrick to the subjects which interested the government, Hess insisted that he 'had come here without the knowledge of Hitler in order to convince responsible persons that since England could not win the war, the wisest course was to make peace now. But he emphasized his long acquaintance with Hitler and that the views reflected his.' Hess further elaborated the plan whereby England would give Germany 'a free hand in Europe, and Germany would give England a completely free hand in the Empire . . .'

Kirkpatrick was less successful in drawing Hess out on Russia. He set a trap by contending that Hitler would not be at liberty to deal with

Russia if she belonged to the Asian continent. Hess avoided the issue by making the cryptic and misleading comment, reflecting his ignorance of the plans, that 'Germany had certain demands to make of Russia which would have to be satisfied, either by negotiation or as the result of a war.' He saw fit to add, however, that 'there was no foundation for the rumours now being spread that Hitler was contemplating an early attack on Russia'. Hitler's policy was to make the utmost use of Russia while she could be of service to him; and he would select the moment for presenting his demands. The reader should bear in mind, in view of the various conspiracy theories which have emerged, that this was the most extensive comment Hess ever made on Russia, and as such it concealed more than it revealed of Hitler's genuine plans. More significantly, it confirmed the evaluation of Military Intelligence that negotiations would precede war.[43] It should be mentioned that Hess was indeed astonished when news of the attack was broken to him, muttering: 'so they have attacked after all'.[44]

All the evidence from Hitler's headquarters depicts very vividly the surprise and rage with which the news of Hess's disappearance was received. Schmidt, his interpreter, reported that it was 'as though a bomb had hit the Berghof' (the Führer's villa at Berchtesgaden). Similar testimony was provided by Generals Keitel and Halder and by Albert Speer. The harsh treatment given to Hess's adjutants, Pintsch and Leitgen, by the Gestapo is yet another indicator. Arrests were also made among the staff of the Augsburg airfield. Later on, when Hess's association with astrologers and anthroposophists had been established, numerous arrests were made and the organizations suppressed. Albrecht Haushofer, who had inspired Hess in the first place, was rushed to Hitler and forced to write down a detailed account of his contacts with Hess.

The initial British hope of exploiting the confusion in Germany by maintaining silence did not materialize. To steal a march on the British, the Germans released the news on the radio at 8 p.m. on 12 May. They announced that Hess, 'apparently in a fit of madness', had taken off in a plane and was missing. The announcement was deliberately vague, as the Germans possessed no information whatsoever on his fate. Hitler had in fact been assured by the Luftwaffe that his chances of reaching England were slim.[45] As soon as the news came on the German radio, Churchill, 'immensely excited', called Eden, eager 'to issue something at once', and indeed a statement was made around midnight.[46] The Germans hit back with a detailed communiqué the next morning. They further released the contents of the letter Hess had left for Hitler, expressing his devotion to the Führer. The disclosure of genuine information was the Germans' best hope for disrupting possible British propaganda, which might imply that the flight indicated a growing rift within the German leadership.[47]

Churchill had hoped to derive the utmost benefit from Hess in his favourite way, by making a dramatic announcement in Parliament, diverting criticism and buoying up optimism. The people, he explained, could be 'both entertained and cheered by this remarkable episode, and it is certain that the action taken by the Deputy Führer in quitting Germany and his chief at this juncture will be the cause of deep-seated bewilderment and consternation throughout the ranks of the German armed forces and throughout the Nazi party and the German people'.[48] As soon as the Germans had made their revelations, Churchill dictated and then meticulously edited a six-page statement. If he had delivered the speech, many of the unfortunate and long-lasting consequences of the affair might have been averted. But the statement remained on paper. It does, however, reflect the extent to which Churchill was prepared to divulge the truth about Hess and the precise nature of his proposals, including his offer of a division into spheres of influence and the uncomfortable claim that he had come to England because of the prevailing feeling 'that there was a strong peace or defeatist movement in Great Britain with which he might negotiate'. Churchill further intended to dispel the disastrous rumours, which endured until the opening of the archives in 1992, by disclosing that Hess 'represented himself as undertaking a self imposed mission to save the British nation from destruction'. Moreover, the statement would have displayed the government's resolve to reject negotiations with Hess, whom Churchill intended to describe as 'the confederate and accomplice of Herr Hitler in all the murders, treacheries and cruelties by which the Nazi regime imposed itself on Germany as it now seeks to impose itself on Europe'. The status of Hess as a 'war-criminal whose ultimate fate must, together with that of other leaders of the Nazi movement, be reserved for the decision of the Allied nations when victory has been won' would have been established. The point should be made here that Churchill's main consideration was the impact of the revelations on Germany and the United States, while that on Russia was completely overlooked. Typically for Churchill, the only important detail that he did not disclose was Hess's condition that Churchill's government be toppled before negotiations were opened.[49]

The statement which was finally released from 10 Downing Street, together with a brief radio announcement, was hardly reassuring. The public was left gasping for information by the pledge that 'as soon as [Hess] is recovered from his injury his statement will be carefully examined'. Churchill further fuelled the public imagination with his admission that so far it was impossible to 'account for Hess's escapade'. He expected Parliament to understand that even if an explanation was forthcoming it might 'not be in the public interest that I should at once disclose its nature'. In supporting Churchill's wish to come out with a detailed statement, Major Desmond Morton, his closest adviser on intelligence, foresaw the consequences of maintaining silence: 'In my opinion great value could accrue were an official statement and propaganda to be issued at once. The longer we wait the rottener the apple.'[50] But Cadogan had already succeeded in convincing Eden that it was best to keep Germany guessing and draw out more from Hess 'by pretending to negotiate and avoiding making a hero out of him'.[51]

The brevity and restraint which characterized the statement only raised questions and fuelled the conspiracy theories. The public, deprived of the gist of Hess's proposals, was left in the dark about the nature of the mission and the government's reaction to it. Indeed, the Minister of Information Duff Cooper had earlier advised Churchill that 'the interest in the Rudolph Hess story has assumed such proportions that he considers it most important to issue information about it in instalments whenever possible'.

The thirst for news was phenomenal. Roosevelt implored Churchill to provide him with information, as 'from this distance I can assure you that the Hess flight has captured the American imagination and the story should be kept alive for just as many days or even weeks as possible'. Similar suggestions were made by Halifax from Washington.[52] Roosevelt's comments accurately reflected the tension in Moscow. On 14 May Churchill reiterated his intention of addressing Parliament. The Foreign Office, however, stood fast. An uneasy feeling prevailed in the Office in view of the resemblance between Hess's revelations to Kirkpatrick and the 'comparatively accurate German account of the ostensible reasons' for Hess's flight to Britain. It was argued that the proposed statement would 'confirm the German wireless'. The German people were likely to 'heave a sigh of relief and say "So that really is the reason why our dear Rudolf left us. Foolish of him: but he's not a traitor and we must not fear he is betraying our secrets."' Churchill's statement also conflicted with the Office's intention of launching a disinformation campaign, focusing on a fancied rift within the higher Nazi echelons. Churchill, however, prevailed in his wish to make the statement. Late at night he called Eden again and dictated to him the statement he intended to make. Eden left a vivid picture of what then happened:

> I struggled out of bed & redrafted it & telephoned it. A few minutes later Winston telephoned he did not like it & Duff [Cooper] was most upset. On the other hand Max [Beaverbrook] agreed with me. Which was it to be – his original statement or no statement? I replied 'no statement'. 'Alright no statement' (crossly!) & telephone was crashed down.[53]

The line adopted, therefore, was to 'give out very little and so leave the Germans guessing as to what Hess may be doing – and saying'.[54] To

Eden's amazement, Churchill made one more attempt to issue a structured statement in Cabinet on 19 May, but with Beaverbrook's help he succeeded in 'strangling the baby' a third time.[55]

Eden returned to bed, convinced that he had dissuaded the Prime Minister from the idea. The Ministry of Information, however, could not resist exploiting the opportunity to the best of their ability. They continued to exert pressure on Churchill to reap the utmost advantage from Hess through a personal statement.[56] The following day Beaverbrook briefed the press over lunch and confidentially disclosed that Churchill had refrained from making a public statement because 'what was wanted at the moment was as much speculation, rumour, and discussion about Hess as possible'. Although the draft telegram prepared for Churchill to Roosevelt recommended that 'it is desirable that the press should not romanticise him and his adventure', Churchill added in longhand: 'we think it best to let the Press have a good run for a bit & keep the Germans guessing'.[57] The leading papers naturally embellished the news, especially when Hess was transferred from Scotland to the Tower of London. To some it signalled an imminent interview with the Prime Minister. This new wave of rumours fitted in all too well with the rumours and speculations which had been paramount since mid-April. As often happened with Churchill, he lost much of his interest in Hess once he was not allowed to have his own way. Besides, he had become totally engrossed in the war in Crete and the great naval battles which would culminate in the sinking of HMS *Hood* and the *Bismarck*. His only involvement was an attempt to satisfy Roosevelt's curiosity by providing him with an accurate digest of the interviews conducted with Hess so far.[58] On the whole the diplomatic corps in London tended to reject the idea of a separate peace, but many remained convinced that Hess had co-ordinated his mission with Hitler. To a great extent this was the result of a lamentable speech by Ernest Bevin, a Labour leader and member of the War Cabinet, which they tended to regard as representing the official view in the absence of an official statement.[59]

Shortly after Hess's arrival Kirkpatrick had suggested that 'in view of the reservation that Germany could not negotiate with the present Government, it might be possible to let Hess think that there was a chance of turning out the present administration and if he could be put in touch with perhaps a member of the Conservative Party who would give him the impression that he was tempted by the idea of getting rid of the present administration, it might be that Hess would open up freely'.[60] The idea was taken up when it was observed that Hess had sunk into a depression once he realized that his plan had misfired. He constantly professed anxiety that he had 'fallen into the hands of a clique of the Secret Service' and was being treated as an ordinary prisoner of war. Cadogan's correspondence with Churchill proves beyond doubt that Hess had not brought any plans from Hitler's Chancellery. One of the major tasks, therefore, was to 'obtain light on the question whether Hess was sent here by Hitler as part of any plan for a peace offensive'.[61]

On 26 May Eden asked Lord Simon, the Lord Chancellor, to interview Hess. Simon was told to admit to Hess that the government was aware of the interview, but he was to imply that his relations with Churchill and Eden were strained. The ploy did not comprise genuine negotiations. The framework for the interview was clearly set up by Simon, who insisted on its being a 'piece of "intelligence" work' with the clear and limited aim of giving Hess 'a favourable opportunity of talking freely about his "mission" and of seeing whether in the course of unburdening himself he is led to give any useful information as to the enemy strategy and intentions'. Like Hamilton, Simon was extremely susceptible to insinuations about his past association with the appeasers and therefore sought assurances that 'in no circumstances would the interview be known outside'.[62]

Churchill hoped that Simon would be able to find out the reasons for Hess's obvious concern about the international scene and why he 'so earnestly desire[d] a patched-up peace now'.[63] Although Cadogan and 'C' entertained only scant hopes, the Foreign Office intended to draw Hess out, particularly on Hitler's intentions towards Russia.[64] Coaching Simon before his interview, Kirkpatrick worded the questions he was to put to Hess. They were markedly influenced by the prevailing Foreign Office concept. Simon was advised to provoke Hess by asking him what was the use of concluding peace with Britain if Germany was 'going to sign up with Russia and bring Russian bolshevism into Europe. If Germany was solely interested in Europe she should abandon her designs against Russia since Russia was an Asiatic Power outside Germany's sphere of influence.' By posing the question in such a manner, it was hoped that Hess would reveal whether Germany was indeed seeking an agreement with Russia or preparing for war.[65]

Lord Simon indeed stood the best chance of drawing out information from Hess, and their interview therefore deserves close scrutiny. Before Simon's identity was disclosed Hess appeared most suspicious. He demanded that two German witnesses be present as well as the Duke of Hamilton, whom he assumed to be 'outside the political clique or Secret Service ring which is preventing him from meeting the proper Peace people and the King'.[66] In due course Hess was informed that the negotiator would be Lord Simon. He was led to believe that, as Lord Chancellor, Simon enjoyed a measure of constitutional independence. Hess was also reminded that the two had met in Berlin when Simon, then Foreign Secretary, had visited Hitler. Hess was delighted and 'appeared to be a changed man . . . he had an agreeable recollection of the chief negotiator'.[67]

After a poor morning, refusing to eat his lunch and complaining that his breakfast milk had disagreed with him, Hess was fortified by a glass of port and a little glucose. Simon was driven to the Tower by 'C' in the early afternoon. He entered with Kirkpatrick, under the respective pseudonyms of Drs Guthrie and McKenzie, and conversed for three hours with Hess, who assumed the cover name of 'Jonathan'. Why the pseudonyms were necessary is a mystery, since Hess knew their real identities. David Irving says that they were used to fool the guards, but in that case it is unclear why Hess himself needed a pseudonym. Nevertheless, Simon had studied all the material supplied by Hess and was well versed in it. He was told that Hess had arrived with no formal proposals. Once Hess had learnt of the forthcoming 'negotiations', he had jotted down copious notes. These he would later submit to Simon as his official proposals.[68]

The opening round of their conversation convinced Simon that the statement which Hess had prepared so assiduously for a couple of days in anticipation of their meeting contained little that was new. The scribbled outline he submitted to Simon does not at all tally with suggestions that Hess had brought with him written proposals which included clear references to Operation 'Barbarossa' and the future of Russia.[69] Simon's categorical judgment was, as he reported to Churchill, that 'Hess has come on his own initiative. He has not flown over on the orders, or with the permission or previous knowledge, of Hitler. It is a venture of his own. If he achieved his purpose and got us to negotiate with a vision to the sort of peace Hitler wants, he would have justified himself and served the Führer well.' He further gained the correct impression that Hess had been outside the circle of politicians conducting the war, and knew little of strategic plans, as his sphere was really party management. Hess's plan was at best a 'genuine effort to reproduce Hitler's own mind, as expressed to him in many conversations'. Analysing the interview, MI6 experts formed the opinion that Hess was in fact incapable of countering any arguments, especially of a political nature.[70] This dovetailed with the impressions gained by Sumner Welles, the American Under-Secretary of State, from his meeting with Hess on 3 March. Welles had been shocked by Hess, whom he had expected to possess 'a powerful and determining influence in German affairs'. It had turned out that Hess 'was merely repeating what he had been told to say to me . . . and that he had neither explored the issues at stake nor thought anything for himself'.[71] Thus the failure to extract information from Hess finally put the seal on the 'semi-official conversations'. In Cadogan's blunt words, Hess had become a 'gramophone record'.[72]

Any suggestion, therefore, that the silence and disinformation were a sinister cover-up of Hess's debriefing is not borne out by the evidence now available. As the German troops were crossing the Soviet border, SIS conducted a thorough examination of the scanty material obtained from Hess and reached the conclusion that it had been 'sucked quite dry, and no more flesh can be got off these bones'.[73] The mishandling of the affair resulted from disagreements about its potential for publicity and propaganda. The thought of a cover-up was not raised at any stage, simply because there was little to conceal. Major Desmond Morton, reflecting Churchill's own thoughts, advocated an official statement which would incorporate the accumulated evidence. If it were up to him, he told Eden, then 'whoever is put in charge of the publicity on the subject should have access to *all* the documents in the case and . . . it will not be a matter of one stilted Government communiqué'.[74] Going through the extensive 'Guthrie–Jonathan' transcripts, Churchill reached the conclusion that Hess's statements were 'like conversation with a mentally defective child who has been guilty of murder or arson'. He did not even share the common view that Hess was 'in fact reflecting Hitler's inner mind' but was amused by the fact that 'he gives us some of the atmosphere of Berchtesgaden, which is at once artificial and fetid'. By now Churchill had lost interest in making a public statement.[75]

It should be assumed that the consistency of Hess's statements in scores of interrogations, and the constant recording by SIS of even his least audible mumbles, verifies his version of events. The chief psychologist of the British army, who was called in to observe Hess, gained 'a strong impression that the story was in general true'. He further noted that Hess's lack of fluency in English made it difficult for him to tell a convincing story that was completely untrue. He also suspected that his mental condition was far from stable: 'he is of a somewhat paranoid type. He has an abnormal lack of insight or self criticism. He is also of an introspective and somewhat hypochondriacal type. This man gives me the impression of being lacking in balance, a psychopathic personality . . .'[76]

'Running the Bolshevik Hare'

Britain's failure to extract useful information for propaganda meant that all efforts were directed towards the exploitation of Hess in the Russian context. Even before a decision was taken to exploit Hess vis-à-vis the Russians, the silence maintained by the British over the affair had given rise to rumours which were to affect the Kremlin long after it had ended. In October 1942 Sir Archibald Clark Kerr, Cripps's successor as British ambassador in Moscow, related the suspicions to the fact that the Russians had been left in the dark. He asked Churchill how he would feel if Ribbentrop were to fly to Russia while England was left guessing about the nature of his mission.[77] Hess, as Clark Kerr explained, was like 'a skeleton in the cupboard' whose occasional rattlings continued to disturb the public mind. It seemed as if Hess was deliberately being kept by Churchill as a trump card for negotiations on a separate peace if the war reached a critical stage.[78]

The diversion of the Hess affair to the Russian sphere should be related to the final decision taken on the night of 14–15 May 1941 by Eden and Beaverbrook, in which Churchill grudgingly acquiesced, to play up the propaganda value of the Hess mission. The stage was set for the complex game of using Hess in an attempt to alter Soviet policies. As soon as Hess landed in Britain, Cripps informed the Foreign Office of the interest which the Hess mission had evoked in Moscow. Fully aware of the explosive nature of the Hess affair, he proposed to use the 'golden opportunity' either to play on Soviet fears or to allay them:

1. Hess incident has no doubt intrigued the Soviet government quite as much as anybody else and may well have aroused their old fears of a peaceable deal at their expense.

2. I am, of course, unaware to what extent, if at all, Hess is prepared to talk. But on the assumption that he is, I very much hope you will consider urgently the possibility of using his revelations to stiffen the Soviet resistance to German pressure either (a) by increasing their fears of being left alone to face the music or (b) by encouraging them to think that the music, if faced now and in company, will not be so formidable after all; or preferably by both, for the two things are not really incompatible.

Halifax too favoured the idea of exploiting any information which pointed to a split within the German leadership to exert pressure on the Russians. At that point Sargent, the architect of the Foreign Office concept governing Anglo-Soviet relations, appeared to be resolutely opposed to the idea of alluding to a separate Anglo-German peace which might drive the panic-stricken Stalin into German arms. Cripps was therefore to sit tight and wait to see when and whether any information from Hess would be available.[79]

However, when within a few days it was realized that the prospects of exploiting Hess for propaganda purposes in Germany were limited, Sargent reverted to Cripps's own idea. As Hess was withholding whatever information he had on German intentions in Russia, this could be done only through the deliberate spreading of disinformation. The proposed disinformation would indicate the existence of a split within the Nazi leadership regarding the German plans in Russia. It would state that Hess, unlike Göring and Ribbentrop, whom he seemed to abhor, remained 'one of the most fanatical of the Nazis'. He was determined to prevent any agreement between Russia and Germany in his capacity as the custodian of the pure doctrine of Nazism.[80]

The eagerness to embark on such a course, regardless of the obvious risks involved, is closely tied to the intelligence evaluation of the German build-up on the Russian frontier. One should remember that the exploitation of the Hess affair against Russia was motivated to a large extent by the mistaken evaluation of British intelligence, which like Stalin did not fully grasp the likelihood of a German–Soviet war until the end of May 1941. It still held fast to the view that the German deployment in the East was a prelude to negotiations with the Soviet Union. The Joint Intelligence Committee pointed to some indications which suggested 'that a new agreement between the two countries may be nearly complete'. The most up-to-date information suggested that 'Hitler and Stalin may have decided to conclude a far-reaching agreement, the basis of which is not yet clear, for political, economic, and even military collaboration'. The possibility of war was therefore confined to 'a Soviet failure either to agree to German demands or to implement any agreement reached'. The resentment and frustration prevailing at the Foreign Office was a recognition that diplomacy was 'completely hamstrung'. In the case of Russia, grudgingly confided Cadogan, one could do nothing 'unless you can (a) threaten (b) bribe it. Russia has (a) no fear of us *whatever* and (b) we have *nothing* to offer her. Then you can juggle with words and jiggle with drafts as much as you like and you'll get nowhere.'[81] This conclusion finally led both the Foreign Office and the security services to the idea of exploiting Hess 'mendaciously',[82] to discourage the Russians from concluding an agreement with Hitler. The effectiveness of such a policy, needless to say, depended on the actual existence of such negotiations. As Stalin himself had just been misled by Schulenburg into believing that reconciliation was indeed the order of the day, the Hess affair reassured him of the correctness of his own evaluation while raising the constant fear that England and Germany might indeed close ranks. Considering that the debriefing of Hess virtually lasted until the German attack on Russia, the affair clearly had disastrous repercussions on Stalin's state of mind in the crucial month leading up to the German–Soviet war.

On 16 May Sargent returned with a new paper which formulated his views more succinctly and effectively. The disinformation he wished to employ against the Russians rested on the following premises:

> Hess considers himself the custodian of the true and original Nazi doctrine, the fundamental tenet of which is that Nazism is intended to save Germany and Europe from Bolshevism; Hitler has now been persuaded by the later adherents of the Party, who are mere opportunists, and by the Army to try and reach a settlement with the Soviet Union to the extent of bringing her in as a full Axis partner; this was more than Hess could stand and hence his flight to this country.

If this was effectively transmitted to Stalin, he could be led to believe that Hitler was luring him into the German orbit simply in order to obtain a foothold in Russia. Once Hitler had improved his position he would attempt to topple Stalin and thus appease the more extreme elements in the Party. A Foreign Office decision on this course was delayed, however, not because of the possible implications for the Russians, but because of the fear that the disinformation might reach the Germans, whom the Office still wished to keep guessing. Moreover, Eden rightly foresaw that disinformation might actually encourage the Russians to seek an agreement with the Germans more vigorously once they found out that Hitler was set on negotiations.[83]

And yet it soon emerged that Hess's debriefing was not yielding any material and Hess was 'saying nothing of note!' The only alternative therefore was to use him against the Russians by the release of snippets of disinformation. It now occurred to Sargent, itching to act, that the best method of deceiving the Russians would be to use 'some underground channel'. Cadogan enthusiastically endorsed the idea provided it would not 'simply scare the Russians too much!' Following in Eden's footsteps, he was clearly alluding to the much dreaded German–Soviet military alliance.[84]

The directive to MI6 'for the exploitation of the Hess incident through underground channels abroad' was finally endorsed by the Foreign Office on 23 May. It was welcomed as 'a clear warning to the Soviet Government to beware of Hitler's present offers of collaboration and friendship'. In many ways the hint, as seen from the Kremlin, resembled Churchill's warning and the threats made by Cripps in Moscow. It warned them that if they succumbed to German demands Hitler would reap benefits from the agreement, but the Russians would eventually be left to fight on their own. Cavendish-Bentinck, the chairman of the Joint Intelligence Committee, took effective steps 'to ensure that the above whisper reaches Soviet ears forthwith' through SOE and other channels. The appropriate directives for the 'whisper campaign' were sent to the British embassies in Stockholm, New York and Istanbul on 23 May; it was 'designed for Russia only and to be spread only through channels leading direct to Soviet'. The campaign was backed by 'as many "whispers" as possible', spread independently in co-ordination with the guidelines set in the directive.[85]

The Political Intelligence Department at the Foreign Office also felt that no real dividends were being received from the Hess affair. They exerted pressure to extract the utmost from Hess's anti-Bolshevik feelings. The question facing the Foreign Office was whether to persist with the 'whisper campaign' which had just been launched, or whether to alert the Russians officially to Hess's genuine information. The views of Eden and Cadogan prevailed, despite attempts by Duff Cooper to present the issue for discussion at ministerial level, and the 'whisper campaign' continued unhindered until it was finally annulled by the German invasion of Russia.[86]

The new line very soon started circulating freely. Eden briefed the leading representatives of the British press at the Foreign Office and impressed on them that 'Hess was very earnest about his mission, and that the mission indicated a split within the German leadership.' The representative of *The Times* came out of the meeting convinced that Hess was trying to 'get a peace plan over' and that he had been officially authorized by Hitler to do so. Such views now circulated more widely in London.[87] By 10 June, just as Simon was interviewing Hess, the disinformation was no longer confined to 'whispers'. Eden misled Maisky into believing that 'Hess fled from Germany because of a quarrel he had, not with Hitler himself, but with several senior personages in his entourage, such as Ribbentrop and Himmler'.[88] Paradoxically, this line suited only too well Stalin's self-deception concerning his ability to defer the war.

The 'whisper campaign' had only just been initiated when Cripps, who had not been informed of the trivial nature of Hess's debriefing, made his own bid to exploit the affair. As usual, his acute observation and analysis of the situation did not match his restless mode of operation. 'I am left fairly hopeful that the Soviet Government would not concede anything that would vitally affect their war preparedness or preparations,' he cabled to Eden, 'since I believe them to have no illusions about Germany's ultimate intentions where they are concerned and to be determined to resist at points where in their own estimation they must either do so or go under.' He was convinced that 'in view of the Soviet Government's evident reluctance to face a war with Germany at the present stage, the temptation to "run things too fine" in border-line cases must be very great'. Cripps therefore estimated that the Russians' action in such cases depended on their evaluation of relative British and German strength. He hoped to use the information gleaned from Hess to 'influence Soviet Government's decision on such border-line cases and particularly to discourage them from speculating on extraneous factor mentioned above – in other words to convince them that they have something to dig their toes into now, but may have nothing that will hold them later on'.[89]

Although Cripps was discouraged from initiating independent moves, he was duly briefed about the disinformation, which on the face of it seemed to follow his advice:

> We are putting it about through covert channels that Hess's flight indicates growing split over Hitler's policy of collaboration with the Soviet Union and that if pursued he will insist on short term benefits knowing that he will be forced to abandon it and to break any promises which he may have made to the Soviet Union, so that in the end their last state

will be worse than their first. They will have lost potential friends and made concessions and will be left to face Germany single handed in a weakened state.[90]

The friction between Duff Cooper and Eden continued throughout May. Eden was under constant pressure from Maisky to curtail the rumours and was determined to stop the semi-official leaks from the Foreign Ministry. On 5 June Eden reimposed the official guideline of observing silence over the affair, while the Foreign Office retained the right to use secret propaganda and 'invent and run Bolshevik and other hares'. Little attention was paid to Cadogan's wry comment that 'whispers can be much more irresponsible and even, without disadvantage, conflicting and confusing'.[91] Eden's attempts to rein in Military Intelligence and the Ministry of Information were ineffective; up to the German invasion both worked hard to alter the decision. To Military Intelligence it seemed that if the main object was 'to keep the Germans guessing' then 'silence is no good and *something* must go out'. Likewise Duff Cooper continued to deluge Churchill with requests to make a public statement.[92]

Hess as Perceived by the Kremlin

Khrushchev reminisced that, when news reached the Kremlin of Hess's flight, Stalin agreed with him that he was 'on a secret mission from Hitler to negotiate with the British means of cutting short the war in the West to free Hitler's hands for the push East'.[93] Such a thought certainly crossed Stalin's mind, but the Hess mission posed a much more serious challenge to him. If Hess was Hitler's emissary, then the nightmare of England and Germany closing ranks in a crusade against Bolshevik Russia would materialize and the vast German deployment on the Soviet border would assume a new and menacing posture. However, Stalin's self-deception inevitably led to a differing conclusion: paradoxically, the mission reinforced the assessment of a split within the German leadership which might hasten the opening of the 'negotiations' with Germany.[94] The silence and secrecy surrounding the mission fitted in only too well with what were conceived in Moscow to be the ceaseless British attempts to bring Russia into the war. However, the possibility of a separate peace could not be taken too lightly. The tendency in the Kremlin was therefore on the one hand to play down any suggestion that Hess was on an official mission, and on the other to belittle his potential as a British tool in the search for a separate peace.

The first information which came under scrutiny in Moscow was the official British statement. The heavily pencilled markings of the NKGB's

senior officer on a copy of the statement seemed to discount the possibility that Hess was acting on Hitler's orders. Duff Cooper's assertion
that the flight in the first place manifested 'the differences of opinion
within the National-Socialist movement' was underlined. Similar attention was drawn to reports from the Swedish press explaining the mission
against the background of an ongoing debate within the German leadership and economic and industrial circles there. A powerful group, associated with Göring, was supposed to be 'striving all along to reach peace
with England'. Significantly, the NKGB then emphasized that the reports
of Hess's arrival in England coincided with current rumours of a possible meeting between Stalin and Hitler. Hess was presented as 'the opponent of Hitler's policy of friendship with the USSR' who sought a
dialogue with the British 'before the meeting of the dictators took place'.
The final marking endorsed the assumption that Hess was 'making a personal attempt to conclude peace' in order to forestall the German–Soviet
agreement.[95]

Hess had already been identified as an obstacle to rapprochement
with Germany during his brief meeting with Molotov in Berlin.[96] The
NKVD had then inquired into his standing within the leadership and
came up with a most denigrating report. They could not find anyone who
would attest to his 'propaganda or administrative talents'; he was simply
described as a 'trustful person' who enjoyed Hitler's sympathy. 'Perhaps
he has some extraordinary capabilities,' the NKVD officer in charge of the
investigation ironically summed up, 'but as it happens no one has yet
detected them.' He merely saw fit to note, perhaps for purposes of future
extortion, Hess's 'scandalous' past. Hess, he explained, 'used to belong to
a group of "hots" (homosexuals) who nicknamed him "Black Bertha", by
which he is known not only in Munich but also in Berlin. Marriage has
not helped Hess much, as Berliners refer to his wife as "he" and to him
as "she".' In short, Hess was 'an insignificant person in a most conspicuous position', whose influence was declining.[97]

A day after Hess's landing in London 'Litseist', the Gestapo double
agent working for the Berlin residency, contributed his small but cus-
tomarily effective input. The intricate intelligence of 'Litseist' had been
working on two themes: the existence of a split within the German leadership and the idea that any military action would be preceded by negotiations. He now presented Hess as a lunatic who had spent four to seven
months in the past two years in sanatoriums, and confirmed that he had
been devoid of actual power for some time. As a 'bitter opponent of the
Soviet Union' and 'an enthusiastic supporter of England', he had developed the *idée fixe* that he could become 'the new Christ and save the
world'.[98]

Kobulov, the head of station in Berlin, who had been informed by
Dekanozov, just back from Moscow, about the 'negotiations' currently

under way, made full use of the fragments in the reports of 'Starshina' which drove home the 'existence of discord at the top'. The widely circulating rumours in Berlin suggested that Hess was 'connected with Göring'. His information, attuned to Stalin's perceptions, suggested that the participation of Göring at Hitler's press conference on Hess's flight was merely a demonstration aimed at refuting such rumours and presenting a united front at the top.[99]

In a subsequent report Kobulov covered himself by raising the possibility that Hess had flown to England 'in an excellent state and . . . with the definite knowledge and at the suggestion of the German Government'. He had been informed by the agent 'Frankfurter' that he had learnt over dinner with an unnamed general that the flight 'was not an escape but was done with Hitler's connivance; a mission with peace offers to England'. However, the lion's share of his reports pointed out that as 'an uncompromising enemy of communism and an opponent of rapprochement with the USSR', Hess had flown 'on his own initiative' to convince the British to bring the war to an end and allow the transfer of troops to the East.[100]

While the information from Germany, despite some ambiguity, tended to confirm Stalin's belief that the mission indeed exposed the split within the German leadership, the reports from London were far less decisive. Maisky was of course aware that the salient and lasting feature of Stalin's foreign policy in the inter-war period, originating in the Allied intervention during the Civil War, was a pathological suspicion of an Anglo-German crusade against Russia. Since the fall of France, Stalin had been particularly exasperated by the continued inclusion in Churchill's Cabinet of the 'Men of Munich', who might tip the scale towards a peace with Germany. Cripps had been harping on these fears for some time. After the fall of France he had in desperation persuaded Halifax that Maisky should be led to believe that the British response to peace overtures by Hitler would depend on the progress made in the negotiations between Russia and Britain.[101]

Soviet intelligence had been keeping a close watch on all possible harbingers of a separate peace. For instance, it had suggested in July 1940: 'The former English King Edward together with his wife Simpson is currently in Madrid, from where he maintains ties with Hitler. Edward is discussing with Hitler the possibility of the formation of a new English government and the conclusion of peace with Germany, on the condition of the creation of a military alliance against the USSR.'[102] The new insinuations of a separate peace during the last week of April 1941 caused unprecedented anxiety in Moscow which Maisky could hardly ignore. After the débâcle in Greece and Crete, which provoked mounting criticism and dissatisfaction in England, Maisky was instructed to keep vigilant watch on the appeasers in the government.[103] He fervently sought to dispel the rumours of peace feelers in a series of meetings with Beatrice Webb, R. A. Butler, the Parliamentary Under-Secretary, and Sir Walter Monckton.[104]

Maisky's difficulty in assessing the situation and reconciling his observations with the concepts prevailing in Moscow became more acute as the rumours of an impending war gained momentum. The events of the month preceding Hess's arrival were complicated by Churchill's warning and Cripps's ultimatums. With a host of circulating theories to choose from, Stalin read the reports of his ambassadors selectively. In turn the ambassadors, and Maisky in particular, had become experts at accommodating the Kremlin by providing the desired commodity veiled in ambiguity. As we have seen, throughout the second part of 1940 Maisky maintained that Churchill enjoyed massive support for continuing the war 'at least for now', while the appeasers were 'still' not playing an important part. He did not, however, believe for a moment that Churchill's staunch resistance was a matter of principle; Churchill was simply reluctant to conclude an agreement which might perpetuate Britain's lack of success on the battlefield. But Maisky no longer ruled out the possibility that a shocking defeat which undermined the British Empire (he was undoubtedly alluding to the fall of Egypt) might lead to the 'betrayal of the ruling class, somewhat similar to that of Pétain and his group'.[105] In the new circumstances, in the spring of 1941, he confided in his diary that the situation was too fluid to allow the Russians to feel comfortable since 'at present, when the English bourgeoisie wants to carry on with the war, Churchill appears to them to be a godsend. But later on he could become a great obstacle if and when they desire to conclude peace.'[106]

It comes as no surprise, therefore, that Maisky's normally assiduous entries in his diary, which was constantly under observation, were suspended for a while. His dispatches in the wake of Hess's arrival in England make an outstandingly slim volume. Maisky's sparse reports contrast with the extremely busy schedule he maintained in an attempt to make sense of the affair. Stunned by the news on the wireless of Hess's arrival in England, Maisky encountered only speculation; no one could say 'anything plainly'.[107] At the Foreign Office Butler was puzzled and reticent, informing the ambassador that conversations with Hess had 'not yet begun', and expecting them to start within two or three days.[108] In the absence of any tangible information, Maisky made only a brief commentary on the Hess affair in his dispatch to Moscow of 15 May. The impressionistic evaluation was aimed at echoing the expectations in Moscow that 'a very strong anti-Soviet' attitude characterized the debriefings; Hess appeared to be very critical of the Ribbentrop–Molotov Pact. It was however difficult to draw any working conclusion from his dispatch, except for the second part, which relayed

Hess's admission that he had come on his own initiative and that he had not divulged any secrets to the British. Like the rest of the world, Moscow impatiently awaited information concerning Hitler's intentions towards Russia.[109]

Overwhelmed by the ominous silence, Maisky returned to Butler on the pretext of the urgent need to discuss the repatriation of Soviet sailors and boats held in British ports. Although he himself had not yet been given authoritative information, Butler now expressed his personal opinion that Hess had come to England on his own initiative and not as Hitler's emissary. He then developed a hypothesis which was later adopted as deliberate disinformation: he could not exclude the possibility that in launching his mission Hess might have been backed by a powerful group within the higher echelons of the Party. The mission seemed to indicate, therefore, that support for Hitler was not unanimous. Butler further reiterated his belief in the government's strong resolve to carry on the war. If Hess had 'the strange idea that he would find a mass of "Quislings" here waiting only for Germany to stretch out its hand, then he is already or soon will be convinced of his mistake'. He further ruled out a meeting with Churchill. A few days later, Butler elaborated his theory even further by suggesting, of his own volition, 'that there was a quarrel between Hess and Hitler, as a result of which Hess decided to make his flight to England in the hope that here he would succeed in finding influential circles prepared to make peace with Germany'. Maisky now felt confident enough to dismiss Hess's hopes as a 'fantasy'.[110]

The NKGB's reports from London dovetailed with those of Maisky. Anatole Gorske, who ran Burgess, Maclean and Philby (of the 'Cambridge Five'), transmitted a report from Philby ('Sonnchen') that Hess had 'arrived in England declaring he intended first of all to appeal to Hamilton . . . a member of the so-called Cliveden set'. He appeared to be well informed on Kirkpatrick's initial interview with Hess but failed to provide details of any peace proposals that Hess might have been bearing. His report led to instructions to the various NKGB stations to verify what was the nature of the offer and whether it had received Hitler's blessing or perhaps that of the military who were opposed to Hitler.[111] After further probing, the London residency regretfully admitted that they were 'not in possession of precise information concerning Hess's stay in England'. Philby, however, had succeeded in extracting some information from Tom Dupree, the deputy chief of the Press Department of the Foreign Office, though he could not verify it. According to his source, up to the evening of 14 May Hess had not given his interrogators any valuable information concerning his flight. In conversations with officers of British Military Intelligence, Hess declared that he had arrived in Britain to 'conclude a compromise peace which would halt the attrition of both belligerents and prevent the final destruction of the British Empire, preserving it as a stabilizing force'. The disconcerting element from Stalin's point of view was Hess's declared loyalty to Hitler and the false information about a secret visit paid by Beaverbrook and Eden to Hess. Dupree assumed that Hess was actually 'aiming at the creation of an Anglo-German alliance against the Soviet Union'. Seizing on Churchill's announcement in Parliament that 'Hess is my prisoner', Philby believed 'that the time for peace negotiations had not yet arrived, but that later in the course of the war Hess could become the centre of intrigues for a compromise peace and would therefore be useful for the peace party in England and for Hitler'. Significantly, this part of the telegram was strongly marked for attention at the Lubianka, the headquarters of the NKVD in Moscow.[112]

The effect of the 'whisper campaign' could be clearly discerned in early June, when the NKVD established for the first time that there was 'good reason to believe' that Hess had been involved with the British 'Intelligence Service'. It appeared that 'the ruling circle (Hitler, Ribbentrop, Himmler and Keitel) are pursuing the so-called "policy of Bismarck" in relation to the USSR and their hand has been strengthened after the flight of Hess. The group (Göring, Brauchitsch, Rosenberg) of the pro-British tendency continue to impress on Hitler the disastrous policy of co-operation with the Soviet Union.'[113]

As seen from the Kremlin, Hess's mission was dramatic in the sense that it might augur the long-sought-for negotiations with the Germans, if indeed Hess had not come on Hitler's authority and represented those segments of the Nazi elite who were opposed to the conciliatory Rapallo line pursued by Hitler. Alternatively, he might indeed be a genuine envoy paving the way for a coalition war against Russia. As was his habit on such occasions, Maisky clearly preferred to sit on the fence, as he found it difficult to 'sift the most probable from the mass of tales, reports, guesses, suppositions, rumours, etc., surrounding this strange, almost romantic story'.[114] To follow the wishful thinking of Moscow was dangerous in view of Cripps's extemporaneous warning of mid-April, which suddenly seemed to be substantiated. During an intimate dinner with the Webbs on 23 May, Maisky reverted to Cripps's long memorandum which, he claimed, had irritated his government. He then made the obvious connection by attempting to elicit the Webbs' reaction to the possibility of a separate peace:

> Would England hold out – would there not be a powerful section of the ruling class in favour of a negotiated peace with Hitler? He gave us what he believed to be the truth about the Hess affair. Hess had been quite frank about his mission; though he refused to say that it was with the assent of Hitler. He wanted to persuade the British government to give way: the British and the Allies would be beaten in the war for the domination of Europe, though it would exhaust Germany in doing it.

Germany must remain the dominating force in Europe; Great Britain
must keep her Empire, except a few minor concessions in Africa. Then
Germany and Great Britain could stop the spread of Bolshevism which
was a Devil.[115]

He emerged even more concerned from a dinner which he had *à deux*
with Lord Beaverbrook, the powerful associate of Churchill in the War
Cabinet. When probed about the mission, 'Beaverbrook unhesitatingly
answered: "Oh, of course, Hess is an emissary of Hitler."' Beaverbrook
then paraphrased Hess's 'peace with honour' proposals but distorted
their context by inflating their anti-Soviet bias, claiming that the proposals were presented as a defence of civilization against Bolshevik bar-
barism. Beaverbrook also remained noncommittal when the prospects of
a separate peace were discussed. True, he dismissed out of hand the
present overture: 'Hess apparently thought that he would only have to
unfold his plan to make all those dukes run to the king, dump Churchill,
and create a "reasonable government". Idiot!' However, he suggested
that Churchill believed that Hitler genuinely wished for peace. Playing
the German card like Cripps before him, Beaverbrook concluded
ominously that the future would show whether peace would materialize.
He merely conveyed his belief that the British government 'would consider peace with Germany on "acceptable terms"', though he was sceptical whether such terms were 'likely to be offered at this stage'. What
Maisky deduced from the talk was that a vigorous prosecution of the war
depended not on Churchill's inflexible will but rather on the nature of the
German proposals.[116]

Though the thought of a split within the German leadership conformed
with Stalin's own evaluation, the confusing and contradictory information kept him most apprehensive about Hess. By mid-June the intelligence
reports on the German build-up had spilled over into the press, which
frenziedly produced diametrically opposed assessments. These coincided
with the disinformation planted on Soviet intelligence about the coun-
terfeit negotiations with Simon. As a result of various comments by Eden
at the beginning of the month, the Kremlin became apprehensive that the
British might be tempted to sign a separate peace if they assumed that
negotiations between Russia and Germany had begun. On 5 June Maisky
informed Eden that 'no negotiations were under way' between Germany
and the Soviet Union but failed to convince him. Eden insisted that he
possessed information indicating 'serious negotiations on questions of
tremendous significance' between Russia and Germany.[117]

On the very day that Hess was interviewed by Lord Simon, Maisky
bumped into Lloyd George in the corridors of the House of Commons.
Lloyd George appeared disheartened about the course of the war. 'The
time has come', he confessed to Maisky,

to think about a compromise peace. On what terms? Lloyd George proposed that the conclusion of peace might become possible if Hitler were to agree that Danzig, Silesia, Austria and Alsace-Lorraine would be included in [Germany's] territory, plus a protectorate over some portions of Europe and Poland and in addition some sort of 'adjustments' in Belgium and Holland. The proposals produced by Hess were absolutely unacceptable – categorically answered the old man – if Hitler were to insist on them, the continuation of the war was inevitable.[118]

A few hours later in Whitehall, Maisky learnt from Eden that no negotiations were contemplated. Eden stated solemnly: 'Hess is destined to spend some time in an English jail – until the end of the war.' But within a few days Maisky would learn to his horror from Beatrice Webb that Lord Simon, the apostle of 'appeasement', had been entrusted with Hess's debriefing.[119]

The evaluation which most accurately reflected Maisky's genuine views about Hess in the wake of the German invasion was his belief that Hitler had wished to enlist British support in the war against Russia by presenting himself as the saviour of Western civilization in the crusade against communism. The objective of Hess's flight therefore seemed to be to prepare the ground for an Anglo-German alliance on the eve of that war or during its initial stages. The final verdict in Moscow was that Hess had come on Hitler's orders with peace proposals which were related to Operation 'Barbarossa' but that he had miscalculated the British response.[120] This misapprehension was in fact shared by the Russians up until the conflict but was dispelled by Churchill's famous speech on 22 June, promising British aid, to the Russians' great relief. Tragically, it had distracted Stalin's vigilance on the eve of war and diverted him from the real danger lurking around the corner.

13

On the Eve of War

'Mobilization Is War!'

The recently released uncensored version of Zhukov's memoirs, and the fragmentary reminiscences of Timoshenko, give a vivid picture of the Kremlin on the eve of the war. Reading them together with the directives of the General Staff in the fortnight preceding the attack, one is left in no doubt that the two were fully alert to the danger lurking around the corner. They sought in vain to disrupt the offensive German deployment by fully implementing their mobilization and deployment plans. However, after the mobilization of mid-May, Stalin consistently restrained his Chief of Staff, fearing that the situation might quickly get out of hand.

The urge to act in the Defence Ministry reflected the alarming nature of the intelligence. On 2 June Beria transmitted to the government disconcerting evidence of the 'war measures' undertaken by the Germans along the entire Soviet border. The report, a collation of material from NKGB sources from Belorussia, the Ukraine and Moldavia, showed the exact location of the various German armies, their headquarters and their patterns of deployment. Beria further disclosed that in early May Hitler, accompanied by Göring and General Halder, had attended naval manoeuvres in the Baltic Sea, and later in the month had spoken to a gathering of 600 high-ranking officers in Warsaw. But the sombre assessment was unlikely to shake the Kremlin, as its corollary assumption was: 'With the capture of Crete the next stage of the Anglo-German war will come to an end. If Germany really starts a war against the Soviet Union, then it will probably be the result of an Anglo-German agreement which will lead to an immediate cessation of hostilities between Germany and

England. It is possible that this may indeed be the proposal of peace between Germany and England which Hess has brought to England.' This was more likely to intensify Stalin's desire to steal a march on the British and reach an understanding with the Germans.[1] The firm evidence from the Ukraine of the massive build-up continued to be represented as a prelude to an ultimatum.[2]

From early June it had become increasingly difficult to turn a blind eye to the massive deployment in the border area. Golikov, whose factual reports were disparaged by the political leadership, felt particularly vulnerable. He therefore sought the assistance of the NKGB in validating his ominous discoveries. Above all he wished to deduce 'the plans for military operations against the Soviet Union (in a variety of forms such as documents, rumours etc.)'.[3] Impressive as it was, the intelligence was largely tactical, while strategic information was rare and inconsistent. Formidable detailed reports arrived within days from the Ukrainian and Baltic NKGB. On 5 June alone, 100 heavy tanks were spotted moving east from Warsaw. Infantry divisions were individually identified, precisely enough to draw up a detailed map of the German deployment facing the Kiev Military District. Equally precise was the information originating in the Baltic region, where train spotters traced the congested traffic of both troops and armaments from the Warsaw region to the border. The remarkably illustrative catalogue ran as follows: 'On 25 April the 35th infantry division reached West Prussia from Bulgaria. The staff of the 34th regiment of that division is established in Gelenburg, the staff of the 3rd battalion in Kolmafeld, the staff of the 10th companies of the 34th regiment in Rostenburg . . .' and so on. There was also evidence of logistical preparations: the refurbishing of airfields and hangars in the border areas and the creation of depots of petrol and ammunition. The intentions could be construed indirectly: the German commanders spoke openly of the imminence of war against the USSR. At a ball given by one of the German divisions stationed in Rumania, to which Rumanian officers were also invited, the commanding general said: 'Gentlemen officers, the time has come to unite our forces to return Bessarabia and Northern Bukovina and seize the Ukraine. This is our aim – a battle against communism.'[4] A colossal transfer by rail of two motorized divisions and reservists from the north to the Soviet border was detected, followed by precise information on the recruitment of reservists on a massive scale in Finland.[5]

A special agent of the NKGB travelling by train from Berlin to Moscow through Poland brought home his candid impressions. He found the border area to be saturated with strong German formations, many hidden in the forests. Along the entire Soviet border, to a depth of some 200 kilometres, extensive works were in progress to replace the rail tracks with the German gauges, while strategic roads were repaired and paved. All bridges were fortified and guarded by light artillery. Dozens of echelons of soldiers were marching to the front, in full gear and armed. They gave him the impression of being young and fit, twenty to thirty years old, 'properly dressed and well nourished'. They appeared to be 'strike units which had already tasted battle'. Numerous long convoys, each consisting of 20–100 vehicles, were on their way to the borders. Between the stations of Kolo and Kanin he observed a column, some twenty kilometres long, of large trucks at a fixed distance from one another of ten to fifteen metres.[6]

The various reports were rounded up and presented to Stalin in a more concise form on 12 June. In a nutshell they depicted the intensified German efforts to achieve dense deployment of the troops in the regions bordering the Soviet Union. Oil and supplies were organized in special depots near the border. He was also informed that a further batch of twenty-three high-ranking officers had visited the border area, carefully observing and photographing its Soviet side.[7] The NKGB further prepared a compelling memorandum which reviewed the flagrant violation of Russian air space by German planes since October 1940. Of 185 reconnaissance flights, ninety-one had occurred between May and mid-June. Similar complaints reached Zhukov from the Northern Fleet. The flights, penetrating to a depth of 100 kilometres, happened to be over large concentrations of the Red Army. On the ground almost 10 per cent of the 2,080 people who had crossed the border illegally turned out to be agents of German intelligence.[8] Intercepted telegrams wrapped up the picture. The Japanese consul in Königsberg provided useful observations from one of the major junctions through which the Germans were transferring the main forces from Berlin to the eastern front. Thus on a single day, on 9 June, he witnessed seventeen special military trains in transit (twelve carrying mechanized units, three tanks, one field artillery and one medical equipment).[9]

The steady and massive transfer of troops to Poland coincided with information on mobilization in the Balkans; the civilian population was warned of possible prolonged air raids.[10] Perhaps most significant was Golikov's sudden recognition of the need to pay 'SPECIAL ATTENTION . . . to the continued increase of the German troops on Polish territory'. Hence, a mere fortnight before the invasion, Soviet intelligence finally considered the possibility that the blow might fall in the central sector, on the Minsk–Moscow line, rather than in the Ukraine.[11] Kobulov in Berlin was of a similar opinion. He identified the presence of the main headquarters of the army groups in Königsberg, Allenstein, Warsaw, Lublin and in the region of Zamost–Krasnostav–Yanov south of Cracow. Moreover, the crack German units were earmarked for Chenstokov, Katowitz, Cracow, Lodz, Poznan, Breslau, Danzig, Stettin and Bromberg, in the central–western sector. Nevertheless the Achilles heel of his report was the failure to obtain the actual plans; only 'Starshina' could lay his hands on these, but at the risk of compromising the entire Berlin intelligence net.[12]

The steady stream of intelligence was not ignored by Zhukov and Timoshenko or by the commanders in the field. Zhukov was forced to cancel an order which, the NKGB complained to Stalin, had been issued by Kirponos to the commanders of the covering forces, to deploy their troops in the buffer zone between the strongholds and the border. Such an order, Zhukov warned in tune with Stalin, might 'drive the Germans to an armed confrontation'.[13] Kirponos, however, was still restless and asked for permission to carry out special measures to strengthen the 'war readiness' of the Kiev Military District. By 1 July he intended to move a number of rifle divisions to a forward position and bring into full operation the new airfields constructed on the border. He believed that with great effort he could secure an effective defence of his front by October–November. For the moment, however, he even lacked the half million rubles he desperately needed for building the infrastructure for the reinforcement.[14]

While restraining the local commanders from initiating unilateral moves, Zhukov encouraged them to pursue their preparations as long as these did not provoke Stalin's rage. To shorten the time needed to bring the covering forces to combat readiness once the war alert was sounded, the local commanders were instructed to organize and prepare the munitions and equipment for war. The feedings of the machine-gun belts, which had been piled in boxes in storage, had become damp and needed drying. In the emergency situation they were to be dried and changed every two months. Half of the shells and hand grenades in the reserve stores were to be unpacked and distributed to the artillery units of the covering forces, which were to be kept at full readiness. Food was to be prepared and packed in personal kits, and field kitchens and other logistics set up. Half of the tank units were ordered to be fuelled and ready for combat action. The time of war alert was reduced to two hours for the rifle divisions and three for the motorized and artillery divisions.[15]

A re-examination of the state of mobilization by Vatutin, in charge of the Planning Division of the Red Army, revealed that 303 divisions had been mobilized so far. Of these, 186 divisions were deployed along the western front, out of which 120 were rifle, forty tank, twenty mechanized and six cavalry divisions. They were more or less evenly divided between the southern, central and northern fronts. The second strategic echelon, a reserve placed at the disposal of the Supreme Command in the Moscow vicinity, was still in an embryonic state. As for the air force, out of the 159 wings in the West, eighteen were positioned in the north, thirteen in the north-west and twenty-one on the central western front (fifty-two altogether), as compared with eighty-five placed on the south-western front and twenty-nine left at the disposal of the Supreme Command. Mobilization was therefore still incomplete in the sense that a second echelon had not yet been formed, while the need to secure a long border led to a thin cover of troops and dangerous gaps.[16]

On the night of 11–12 June, Zhukov and Timoshenko requested to put into motion the deployment plan which they had devised during April and May. It would have allowed the covering forces to move into the most forward position and create favourable conditions for conducting the defensive war. Stalin rejected their proposals outright, suggesting they should consult the press the following day. One can only imagine how flabbergasted they were by the Tass communiqué of the next morning denying the likelihood of war.[17] The responsibility for readying the army for battle, however, rested on their shoulders. When they persisted in their demands to put the troops on war alert, they were told by Stalin that 'we have a non-aggression pact with Germany; Germany is busy up to her ears with the war in the West and I am certain that Hitler will not risk creating a second front by attacking the Soviet Union. Hitler is not such an idiot and understands that the Soviet Union is not Poland, not France and not even England.' Stalin flew into a rage: 'Are you proposing to carry out mobilization in the country, alert the troops now and move them to the western borders? That means war!' Timoshenko and Zhukov left the Kremlin with heavy hearts.[18]

On 13 June Zhukov and Timoshenko brought up to date the defence plan for the covering forces in the Baltic and Western Districts. The plan assumed that the Germans had completed their build-up, and recognized that the main threat emanated from the central sector. The tasks set for the district commanders clearly reflect the nature of the threat and the defensive disposition of the troops:

II. Tasks of the Covering Forces

a) Holding off an incursion, whether by land or by airborne forces, of the enemy into the territory of the Baltic Military Defence District.

b) Tenacious defence along the state frontiers and borders of the fortified areas to halt the attack of the enemy and to permit the mobilization, build-up, and deployment of the forces of that district.

c) Establishing the defence of the coastline and the islands of Dago and Ezel in collaboration with the Kiev Military District front to prevent the landing of enemy naval commandos . . .

The other instructions followed the same pattern. The rest of the document dealt with the actual deployment of various covering forces and their co-ordination with the URs. The shortcoming of the plan was the heavy concentration of large forces close to the border, detached from the strongholds and yet too far from the regions which they were to defend.

The option of earmarking the first echelon for operations in depth in counter-offensive fashion, which had been the key to Zhukov's operational system, was not adequately exploited.[19]

Stalin's refusal to allow the covering forces to assume combat positions was compensated for by the reinforcement of the first echelon of the various fronts. The reinforcement was carried out under the strict constraints imposed by Stalin. As a result of a late-night meeting with Stalin on 11 June, Zhukov was permitted to transfer to the western front the 51st Rifle Corps incorporating the 98th, 112th and 153rd Divisions, and the 63rd Corps incorporating the 53rd and 148th Divisions, together with the 22nd Engineers Regiment. The transfer was to be completed by 2 July. The conditions set for the reinforcement were stringent measures to conceal the move so that it would not be conceived by the Germans as a provocation. Only members of the Military Council of the Western District were to be acquainted with the transfer, and no mention of the units' arrival over the telephone or telegraph was permitted. The logistical support with which they were provided at the front was assigned to them not by the numbers of the units but by special codes.[20]

Within a day Zhukov undertook similar hasty measures to bolster the defence of the Kiev Military District through the deployment of the 16th Army there. The movement, scheduled to commence immediately, was expected to be completed by 10 July. Strict measures were undertaken to enforce the secrecy of the move. Specially selected officers were put in charge of the disembarkation of the troops. Draconian disciplinary measures were imposed on the station and the immediate neighbourhood. The echelons were to scatter immediately upon arrival at their various destinations. All marching was to be carried out in small formations rather than waiting for entire divisions to concentrate. Zhukov requested daily reports on the progress of the deployment and the fulfilment of the instructions.[21] The following day, having restrained Kirponos from implementing the defence plan, Zhukov nonetheless issued instruction for putting the district on 'war preparedness' by 1 July.[22] Less attention was directed to the north, though the Baltic regions were reinforced by three light armoured trains.[23]

Finally, on 19 June, Zhukov issued emergency directives to ensure the camouflaging of military installations. Now that an armed clash seemed imminent, it appeared that the fighter planes had not been properly camouflaged. The artillery and mechanized units too were defenceless, positioned in large groups in set linear patterns that made them an easy prey for the enemy. The tanks and armoured cars had been painted in bright shiny colours and could therefore be detected not only from the air but also from the ground. Warehouses and other military structures were not properly camouflaged. An immense scheme was drawn up to correct all those shortcomings: grass was to be planted at all airfields by 1 July to make them harmonize with the natural surroundings, airstrips were to be coloured and the whole airbase made to match the surroundings. All buildings were to be painted, while the oil tanks were to be dug underground. The planes were to be dispersed within the airfields and camouflaged. Mock airfields were to be constructed at distances of 500 kilometres along the borders, with forty to fifty dummy planes on each of them. The operation was to be completed by 15 July.[24]

A Middle East Diversion: The Flaw in British Intelligence

Basking in their own misconception of an imminent German–Soviet alliance, the British never seriously considered a war in the East as a source of salvation; they had rather pursued their futile efforts to contain Hitler in the Balkans, hopefully with the help of Turkey. No major shift in British strategy, and certainly not in the European arena, was considered when the probability of an imminent war sank in, a mere fortnight before the German attack. The Middle East and North Africa continued to be regarded as the arena where Germany could ultimately be defeated. The developing conflict on the Soviet borders was consequently examined in the framework of the peripheral strategy, aimed at maintaining the predominance in the Middle East.[25]

What the British and the Russians shared on the eve of the German–Soviet war was a conviction that a German ultimatum and possibly an agreement would precede hostilities. Even when Cripps conveyed accurate information on the German plans to Eden early in March,[26] he undermined the effectiveness of his warning by suggesting that it might be 'a part of the war of nerves . . . the Germans are arranging this campaign whereby through promises and intimidation they would force [Russia] finally into an alliance. Attack will be made only if pressure fails in its effect.' The 'war of nerves' theory conformed so well with the dominant British concept that it inhibited the Foreign Office from passing on warnings to Moscow, fearing they might be 'playing the German game'.[27]

Just as was happening in Moscow, the evaluations of the Joint Intelligence Committee infiltrated into the various embassies, where they gave rise to reports in much the same spirit. The thick files at the Foreign Office that hold the warnings are full of such reports. On 1 May, to take just one example, the British ambassador in Japan informed Eden that he had learnt 'from a reliable source' that 'German attack on Soviet Russia is not imminent but that recent rumours have been put about by German Government: a) To increase Soviet fear of invasion, b) To force Soviet to join Tripartite Pact, and c) To stimulate deliveries of raw material.' The overbearing concept distorted even the most straightforward information by denying the inevitable. ' "Max's" outfit thinks', the ambassador related to his sources, that 'invasion is certain but believes there is at least an even chance that Stalin will not resist', thus assuming *a priori* the existence of the ultimatum syndrome. Even when German sources 'scouted the idea that this was all part of war of nerves', the ambassador insisted that 'this nevertheless would seem to be the more likely explanation'.[28]

A few eyebrows were raised at the complacency, in view of the vast preparations undertaken by the Germans. Professor Postan, the renowned medievalist from Cambridge and head of the Russian Department of the Ministry of Economic Warfare, dared to suggest that Hitler was set on war 'almost entirely for military reasons, i.e. because it was desired to settle with the Soviets, and from a military standpoint the present campaigning season was held to be a far more favourable occasion than in subsequent years'. To reconcile the increasing stream of hard information with the preconceived concept, the intelligence agencies preferred to sit on the fence, assuming that no decision had yet been taken 'as to whether Russia should be attacked or merely persuaded by threats to comply with German wishes'.[29] Though he did not press home his arguments, Cavendish-Bentinck, the chairman of the Joint Intelligence Committee, wondered why the German High Command was putting such a heavy strain on the economy by augmenting the size of the army to 250 divisions. 'The Russians', he commented:

> are at the best of times maddening people to deal with and Hitler, who is both revengeful and spiteful, must have a number of scores to pay off as a result of the chicanery and double-crossing which the Russians have doubtless perpetrated since August 1939 whilst they felt that they had the Germans at a disadvantage. Moreover Hitler has a tendency sooner or later to revert to the tenets enunciated in 'Mein Kampf': on revient toujours a ses premiers amours![30]

Churchill likewise pondered whether the massive concentration did not indicate Hitler's resolve to seize the Ukraine and Caucasus, 'thus making sure of corn and oil'. But he too wavered, suggesting that 'either war or a show-down' was near.[31]

Any evidence which challenged the concept was cast aside. When, for instance, a Swedish businessman reported that Göring had revealed that Germany would attack Russia on about 15 June, Eden nonchalantly commented: 'June 15th has been tipped so often that it is becoming suspicious.' Similar information from Kollontai, the Soviet ambassador in Stockholm, was rejected on the ground that 'Mme. Kollontai's denial of knowledge of political conversations does not count for much.'[32] Even when the likelihood of an invasion was finally driven home, it was given a different meaning in the Foreign Office: 'Our latest intelligence of military movements etc. points definitely to final German preparations for an attack upon Soviet territory; in other words, it points to a German intention to put such far-reaching demands to Stalin that he will either have to fight or to agree to a "Munich".'[33] In the month preceding the German attack British efforts were therefore primarily directed to forestalling the phantom negotiations. Ironically their blatant efforts only strengthened Stalin's illusions of the viability of such an agreement. Consequently, by way of feedback both the British and Soviet intelligence systems were nourishing the other's erring appreciations.

Eden and Cripps were tireless in their efforts to obstruct the 'agreement' which they expected Schulenburg to conclude after his return from Berlin in early May. Hitler was believed to be preparing some sort of a showdown with Stalin, sustained by a considerable troop concentration on the border. He would then summon Stalin to the border and present an ultimatum for immediate acceptance. Cripps, at least, expected Stalin to go a long way to appease Hitler out of fear of an Anglo-German reconciliation.[34] Rumours in Moscow of Schulenburg's despondency after his return from Berlin did little to undermine the concept. The fact that he was already packing his belongings could mean that he was being 'replaced by a more hard-boiled Nazi who will be better at threats and pressure'.[35]

To reduce to the minimum the damage such an agreement would inflict it was necessary to anticipate its terms. Misled by the dynamics of the war, whereby Hitler seemed to be systematically building a springboard for extending the war into the Middle East, many observers expected Turkey to be the next victim. Such an eventuality could lead to disastrous consequences for British strategy by allowing the Germans to sweep into the Middle East through the back door.[36] Though professing to possess only a 'vague' idea about German intentions, Saracoglu, the Turkish Foreign Minister, was insisting that the Germans and Russians were 'already in *pour parler* or . . . are on the point of opening conversations which might even lead to alliance to war'. He expected Russia to reach an agreement which would be 'made on the back of a certain number of countries amongst which Turkey must be counted'.[37] As rumours and reliable information had by now become totally intermingled, it was no time before Cripps too suggested that 'conversations of some sort' were being conducted in Berlin, and their likely outcome would be an arrangement for the Germans to transfer troops via southern Russia to the Middle East and Iran.[38]

On 23 May the Joint Intelligence Committee noted rather worriedly that 'whereas a few weeks ago rumours were current throughout Europe of an impending German attack on the U.S.S.R., the contrary is now the case. There are some indications which suggest that a new agreement between the two countries may be nearly complete.' The 'far reaching agreement' seemed to encompass 'economic, political and military issues'. The political co-operation, they established, was 'directed towards the seizure of the Middle East'.[39] Three days later, Military Intelligence felt confident enough to suggest that the essence of the agreement was 'the delimitation of spheres of influence in the Middle East, and . . . German troops assembling at Lvov are to move through the Soviet Union to Iran with Russian consent'.[40] The first measures taken were therefore to warn the Turks of the 'German trap' and advise them to do 'nothing likely to arouse Soviet suspicion or resentment or to drive Stalin nearer to Germany'.[41]

The crushing defeat in Greece and Crete, however, reduced Britain's leverage on Turkey. For Hitler, on the other hand, a non-aggression pact with Turkey had become vital for executing Operation 'Barbarossa'. Such an agreement, undermining Turkey's association with Britain, would eliminate a potential threat to his right wing. The bait was an offer of Greek Thrace in return for the right to transfer troops and war materials via Turkey. Like the Bulgarians, the Turks persisted in their opposition to any terms which might compromise their relations with the Russians. They feared that such an agreement might either prompt an Anglo-Soviet collaboration or lead to an uprising, similar to that which had occurred in Yugoslavia.[42]

Eden was caught off-guard. He had failed to grasp the extent of the Turkish suspicion of Russia since Molotov's visit to Berlin; moreover, he was bent on the idea that a Soviet–German agreement at Turkey's expense was in the making. His desperate attempt to bring Turkey and Russia together ran aground. The Turks, as was noted in the Foreign Office, had made 'the most of their case for distrusting the Russians'. On 16 June Cadogan had to admit a failure in the belated attempt to resuscitate the remnants of the Balkan entente. He had realized that the Turks were 'on the point of signing an agreement with the Germans without, apparently, saying anything to Moscow'.[43]

Hitler postponed the pact with Turkey until the very eve of Operation 'Barbarossa'. A demand was then made to the Turks to sign the agreement 'at once'. As a means of inhibiting a Soviet reaction, as well as softening up the Turks, the claims Molotov had made earlier to bases on the Bosphorus were leaked to the press. The haste with which the agreement was signed allowed the Turks to confine themselves to a strict non-aggression pact, maintaining their neutral position and avoiding the notorious secret treaties to which their Balkan neighbours had been subjected.[44] The Turks were manifestly relieved by the announcement of war. Saracoglu, as Papen informed Berlin, 'had to disconnect his telephone in order to escape from congratulations'. Until the very last moment they had obviously feared a Soviet–German agreement on the lines proposed by Molotov during his visit to Berlin, which would divert the war to the Mediterranean and compromise Turkey's sovereignty.[45] This was undoubtedly a remarkable achievement for Turkish diplomacy, though in the final account, as in the nineteenth century, Turkey's vital geopolitical position rendered her a playground for the great powers. Her ability to retain her neutrality throughout the war was a result not only of ingenious diplomacy but also of the unexpected breakdown of the German war machine on the Russian front.

The British government were resolved to prevent a German–Soviet agreement which would undermine their Middle Eastern strategy. Stalin had attempted to placate Germany by his recognition of Rashid Ali's German-oriented government after the *coup d'état* in Iraq in early May, and this lent force to the idea that a new Soviet–German community of interests was in the making. Maisky was warned by Butler that such moves made an 'extremely unfavourable impression'.[46] However, efforts by Eden to extract information on Stalin's intentions from Maisky in their meeting on 27 May were fruitless. Maisky, clearly in a straitjacket, accompanied by his 'shadow' Novikov, resorted to the customary complaints about the press campaign which encouraged rumours ranging from suggestions that negotiations on a German–Soviet military alliance were under way to a warning of an imminent German attack on the Ukraine and the Caucasus. While Eden was hardly comforted by such an approach, Maisky was not reassured by Eden's announcement of the forthcoming evacuation of Crete, which obviously put England in a vulnerable position as far as a possible peace with Germany was concerned.[47]

By June the British examination of the brewing conflict on the eastern front was undertaken almost exclusively from the Middle Eastern perspective. Cripps feared that after the crushing defeats inflicted on Britain Stalin no longer felt inhibited from pursuing dynamic policies in the Middle East. Rather than making 'really dangerous economic concessions', he was likely to be tempted to allow the Germans to transfer troops through southern Russia to Persia and the Near East. Only a 'vigorous policy in the Middle East' could stave off such a development.[48] He told Eden that Stalin was not 'affected by any pro-German or pro-anything feeling except pro-Soviet and pro-Stalin. He is no more friendly or antagonistic to us than to Germany and he will always use any country that he can to attain his objective which is to keep out of the war as long as he can without jeopardising his regime or Soviet power in so doing.' Both however agreed that the clue to future events lay in developments in the Near East.[49] The Cabinet was alerted to the possibility that Stalin might yield to German demands and undermine British interests by allowing the Wehrmacht a 'free passage for troops North of the Black Sea and through the Caucasus into Iraq or Iran. Such a move would turn the flank of our position in the Middle East, and if carried out in the near future might develop before we could take effective steps to counter it.'[50]

Eden's pressing concern was to avert a German–Soviet agreement without arousing suspicion in Moscow that he was trying to embroil Russia in war. His anxiety was acute, as he believed that the German pressure on the Russians had reached such dimensions that they would 'give way unless their skin [was] asked of them'.[51] In his conversations with Maisky he tried to project the feeling that England had the 'power and determination to preserve [her] position and interests in the Middle East'. Obviously the sudden diversion to the Middle East was entirely lost on the Russians, who in fact were not engaged in negotiations with the Germans. The British Commander-in-Chief in the Middle East was instructed to prepare for the occupation of Iraq, which would enable the Royal Air Force to make 'the biggest blaze ever' in the Baku oilfields. The idea of threatening Russia with the bombing of Baku, which might have had disastrous consequences for the Grand Alliance, was dropped once again only because of considerations related to the violation of Turkish and Iranian air space.[52]

Mutual suspicion was now leading both sides to fatal misunderstandings, further deflecting them from a proper evaluation of the danger looming ahead. The need to maintain supremacy in the Near East was demonstrated by the occupation of Syria in early June and by Churchill's constant badgering of General Wavell to launch Operation 'Battleaxe', his counter-offensive against Rommel, in the middle of the month.[53] Referring to the Soviet recognition of the rebellious regime of Rashid Ali in Iraq, Eden reiterated to Maisky at their meeting on 2 June the British government's resolve to maintain supremacy throughout the Middle East, including Iran and Afghanistan. He hoped that Germany would not succeed in introducing a conflict between Russia and Britain in that region. Maisky was far more interested in finding out whether England intended to submit to Germany in the Middle East as she had done in Greece and Crete. Familiar with Stalin's frame of mind, he hastened to inform him of seemingly conflicting interpretations in Cabinet of the German intentions towards Russia. Churchill apparently was now suggesting that concrete evidence, rather than rumours, showed clearly that the German army was offensively deployed on the Soviet borders. This could only confirm the suspicion in Moscow that *in extremis* Churchill was trying to draw Russia into war, at the very crucial and delicate moment when Hitler's proposals were eagerly anticipated in the Kremlin. Maisky therefore underlined the other view, expressed by Eden, that the deployment looked like 'the prelude to an attack on the Soviet Union' though he was inclined 'to think that the given concentration is one of Hitler's chess moves in the "war of nerves" with the Soviet Union and Turkey'. Under these circumstances, rather than focusing on the substance of the warning and in line with strict instructions from Molotov, all Maisky could do was to insist that 'Comrade Stalin is not a coward' and that therefore there was no point in scaring Russia with Germany. The Red Army, he reminded Eden, was well equipped 'and would not have to fight with sticks as it did last time'. To Eden it seemed that 'while Mr. Maisky delivered this statement with emphasis, I had a feeling that he might be trying to convince himself as he went along'.[54]

The Tass Communiqué

In view of the threat posed to British interests in the Middle East by the hypothetical German–Soviet accord, Cripps was unexpectedly rushed home for consultations. His recall was aimed not at laying the foundations for an Anglo-Soviet alliance in view of the anticipated war (as has been subsequently suggested), but rather at finding ways to discourage the Russians from making concessions to Germany in the Middle East.[55] The manner in which the decision was executed is indeed puzzling. When Eden had returned from the Middle East in mid-April, an almost open rebellion erupted in the Northern Department against Cripps's 'occasional unwillingness to carry out his instructions, combined with his tendency to take independent and unannounced action'. The demand was then made for Cripps to return home without delay, not only for consultations but mostly for 'instruction'. Eden however ruled out such a course, probably impressed by the suggestion that once in London Cripps might be 'bitten by politics here and not wish to return'. Cadogan also expressed mild concern about the interpretation which the Russians might give to Cripps's recall. It was thus admitted that Cripps 'should not give up his post under a cloud and therefore a hurried evacuation of his piggery seems fairly difficult to arrange'.[56]

Considerations of Cripps's personal safety on his flight to England were behind the decision to withhold the announcement of his recall. However, once the news was leaked to the press, Soviet sensibilities were not taken into account. The announcement was carried by all the news agencies on 6 June and 'caused considerable sensation among journalists of all nationalities in London and speculation as to the reason for the journey became wild'. The speculation generally assumed a 'sudden worsening of Anglo-Russian relations'. After all, it was widely believed that the Russians were in the midst of intensive negotiations with the Germans, and it never crossed the minds of officials in Whitehall that the Russians themselves might suspect that similar negotiations were taking place in London.[57]

Maisky promptly sought reassurance from Whitehall; his suspicion, however, was further aroused when Eden nonchalantly explained that it was the 'habit to seek to maintain contact with the more distant Embassies' and that 'it would be most useful for all concerned if [Cripps] could come home and get a view of the picture here'. The statement conflicted with information Maisky had received from the Foreign Ministry in Moscow. In a last-ditch attempt to prevent the Russians from submitting to the purported German demands, Cripps had made what turned out to be yet another unauthorized threat to Vyshinsky during a fifteen-minute meeting. Convinced that the Russians were on the brink of concluding an agreement with Germany, he revealed that he was leaving for consultations but might never resume his post in Moscow. Stalin and Molotov were given another chance to consult him if they so wished before his departure. Cripps took his leave by thanking Vyshinsky 'for the barren year'.[58] His departure coincided with the evacuation of employees and families of the embassy staff amid growing rumours of an imminent German–Soviet clash. Lady Cripps herself accompanied her husband, while his daughter was evacuated to Teheran. Cripps's recall was accompanied by a vociferous British press campaign which was leading the Russian government to 'a different conclusion', that the British were indeed set on ensnaring Russia in war. Maisky urged Eden again to control the press as a precondition for any rapprochement.[59]

Maisky was so concerned that he hastened to ascertain the reasons for Cripps's return. The prominence given to the Hess affair during his conversations leaves one in little doubt as to the repercussions it had on the interpretation of the recall. Maisky further displayed a marked interest in the British reaction to German involvement in Syria and Iraq, which had become a test case for British determination to remain on the battlefield. He wished to know why the British army was not 'already acting vigorously in Syria. A timid policy would not only be likely to fail, but would have unfavourable effects in various countries including Russia.'[60]

The interpretation given to Cripps's recall coincided with circumstantial evidence implying that the Americans were pressing Churchill to consider the German peace feelers and sacrifice Russia. On almost the same day that Cripps left Moscow, John Winant, the recently appointed American ambassador to London, departed to Washington for consultations. This revived speculations, triggered by the Hess affair, that a separate peace was being discussed.[61] Such rumours emanated from credible sources like ex-President Herbert Hoover. What further alarmed the Russians was that Winant's arrival precipitated a marked deterioration in American–Soviet relations: on 10 June two Soviet assistant military attachés were ordered to leave the United States.[62]

There was also a revival of interest in Hess, who was then being interviewed by Lord Simon. Given the extreme suspicion prevailing in Moscow, the recall of Cripps, combined with the disinformation on the nature of his journey spread by the Foreign Office, seemed to lend force to the hypothesis that some kind of arrangement might after all be worked out behind the scenes, allowing Hitler a free hand in the East.

There was always an outside possibility that, even if the peace proposals were left unanswered, Britain might signal to the Germans her wish to remain uninvolved if war with the Soviet Union broke out. Moreover, the Germans might be provoked into a diversion to the East if they suspected that Cripps's recall indicated consultations about a possible Anglo-Soviet rapprochement. The memory of the punishment inflicted on Yugoslavia for her approach to Russia was still vivid.[63] This reinforced the feeling in Moscow that Germany was being encouraged to resolve her conflict with Russia by force.

The risks run by Stalin had now reached a new peak. He could hardly contain the military from initiating active defensive measures while the intelligence agencies, under tremendous pressure, were bringing home terrifying news. He could no longer turn a blind eye to the German deployment. Pushed into a corner, he now tended even more vigorously than before to displace the danger by regarding the British as the genuine villains, set on depriving him of political gains by triggering a premature war. The only munition left in his dwindling arsenal was the initiative he had contemplated with Schulenburg a month earlier. If it were successful the issue of a Tass *démenti* might trigger a German reaction. The two-fold aim of the communiqué were therefore to draw a denial from the Germans and to demonstrate to them that Russia was not colluding with the British but was conforming with Hitler's wish to quash such rumours. Molotov gave an accurate, though succinct and incomplete, explanation of the reasons which led Stalin to issue the communiqué: 'The affair of the Tass communiqué was a last resort. If we had succeeded in delaying the war beyond the summer it would have been very difficult to start it in the autumn. So far diplomacy had proved successful in delaying war, but no one could predict when it would fail. However, keeping silent would certainly provoke an attack'.[64]

In his memoirs Maisky exaggerates his own warnings to Stalin. He deliberately deludes the reader into believing that on 10 June he transmitted to Moscow an 'urgent' ciphered telegram of specific intelligence he had obtained from Cadogan, the British permanent Under-Secretary at the Foreign Office. He claims therefore that it was with 'extreme amazement' that he received Stalin's response in the form of the communiqué published on 14 June. The communiqué, however, was a logical culmination of Maisky's own views, which attributed the rumours to Churchill and the British government. The meeting with Cadogan, which raised doubts about the validity of his appreciation, took place only on 16 June.[65] Maisky repeats a couple of times in his memoirs that 'the shaft in the direction of Britain with which the Tass communiqué began left no room for doubt that it was the reply to the warning given by Cadogan'.[66] His obsession with the communiqué stands in sharp contrast to the skimpy coverage of the events leading to the war. The emphasis conceals the fact

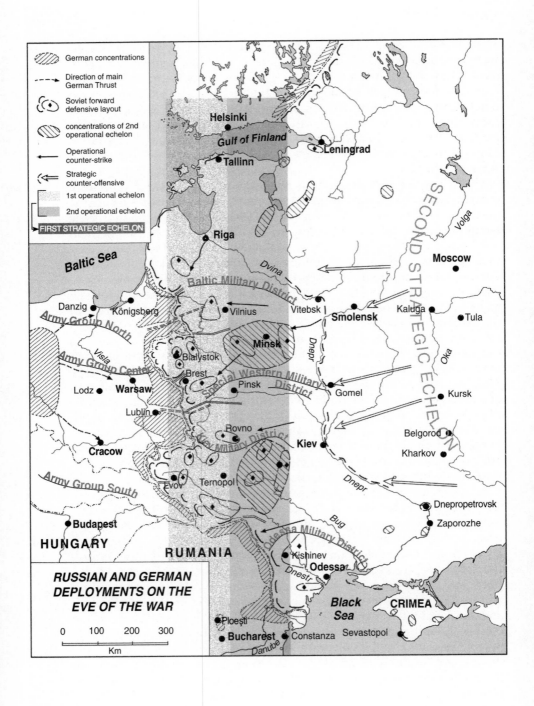

Legend:
- German concentrations
- Direction of main German Thrust
- Soviet forward defensive layout
- concentrations of 2nd operational echelon
- Operational counter-strike
- Strategic counter-offensive
- 1st operational echelon
- 2nd operational echelon
- FIRST STRATEGIC ECHELON

SECOND STRATEGIC ECHELON

Helsinki

Gulf of Finland

Leningrad

Tallinn

Moscow

Riga

Baltic Sea

Dvina

Baltic Military District

Danzig

Königsberg

Vilnius

Vitebsk

Smolensk

Kaluga

Tula

Army Group North

Visla

Army Group Center

Bialystok

Minsk

Dnepr

Brest

Special Western Military District

Pinsk

Gomel

Kursk

Lodz

Warsaw

Lublin

Rovno

Kiev

Belgorod

Kharkov

Kiev Military District

Army Group South

Lvov

Ternopol

Dnepr

Cracow

Bug

Dnepropetrovsk

Zaporozhe

Budapest

HUNGARY

RUMANIA

Odessa Military District

Kishinev

Odessa

Dnestr

Black Sea

CRIMEA

RUSSIAN AND GERMAN DEPLOYMENTS ON THE EVE OF THE WAR

0   100   200   300

Km

Ploesti

Bucharest   Constanza

Sevastopol

Danube

Volga

Oka

that the significant meeting with Cadogan, in which he received the detailed evidence on German concentrations, took place not on 10 June, as he claims, but rather on 16 June, after the publication of the communiqué. Maisky's blatant falsehood is aimed at covering his own contribution to the self-deception which affected the Kremlin on the eve of the war.

The clue to his distortion is to be found in the communiqué's frame of reference and its extremely careful wording. The 'shaft' which supposedly puzzled Maisky read: 'Since before Cripps's arrival in London and *especially after he had arrived there* [author's italics] there have been more and more rumours of an "early war" between the Soviet Union and Germany . . . All this is nothing but clumsy propaganda by forces interested in an extension of the war.' Indeed Vyshinsky insisted in retrospect that 'following Cripps's arrival in London the British press started disseminating rumours on the forthcoming attack of Germany on the Soviet Union'. The communiqué referred therefore to rumours from London 'before and after the arrival of Cripps to London'.[67]

Cripps had reached London only on the night of 11 June, and the communiqué referred to headlines in the British press on 12 June which implied that 'a certain sharpening of German–Soviet relations was discernible'.[68] Under the headline 'Sir S. Cripps Returns; Possible Talks with Russia; Hope of Better Relations', the *Sunday Times*, for instance, commented that Russia was striving to improve relations with Britain to thwart German aggression.[69] In practice it would have been Maisky himself who compiled and evaluated the British press's commentary for Moscow's benefit. Indeed, in a conversation with I. McDonald, the political correspondent of *The Times*, on the evening of 12 June, Maisky bitterly deplored what he believed to be the 'Foreign Office stunt in all the newspapers of yesterday morning. Such an official campaign . . . would be bound to have the worst possible effect in Moscow'. McDonald's efforts to establish his independent standing fell on deaf ears. 'The Ambassador', concluded McDonald, 'seemed a little hurt that I should try to pitch such a cock-and-bull story at him; he clearly disbelieved it.'[70]

Fully tuned to the Kremlin, Maisky attributed to Churchill the swelling wave of rumours prompted by Cripps's sudden arrival in London. In a letter to Eden he confirmed that the communiqué was prompted by the rumours concerning an impending war which had been circulating since Cripps's return 'and particularly in connection with the press report that in his talk with the Prime Minister, Sir Stafford expressed the opinion that war between the U.S.S.R. and Germany was unavoidable in the near future'.[71] He was driven to that conclusion by Churchill's briefing to the chief editors of the national dailies on 7 June. Hard pressed on the progress of the war, Churchill proposed 'that it was best to follow the natural course of events. A clash between Germany and the Soviet Union is inevitable. The concentration of German forces on the Soviet border is proceeding at an accelerated rate. We need to bide our time . . .' Maisky believed that Churchill there and then instructed Duff Cooper, the Minister of Information, to launch a campaign about the imminent conflict.[72] The News Department of the Foreign Office gained the clear impression from their contacts with the Tass representative in London that the Soviet embassy suspected the government of spreading the reports of an imminent clash in an attempt to push Russia into the war. The belief in the Kremlin that in desperation Churchill was trying to drag Russia into war had become so overwhelming that an internal Foreign Ministry memorandum scrutinizing Maisky's telegrams of the entire year detected clear hostility as the guideline of British policy.[73]

Maisky thus echoed his master's voice from the Kremlin in continuing to believe that Churchill was the obstacle to Soviet accommodation with Germany. In conversation with a British diplomat, he further provided a reasonably accurate picture of the terms of the agreement Stalin anticipated:

> if it was a mere matter of supplying three million or four million more tons of fodder – here he waved his hand contemptuously towards the mountains of imaginary fodder which he saw littering Kensington Palace Gardens [where the Soviet embassy in London was located] – Moscow might be ready to give it. 'We are always ready to drive away the fires of war when they approach our threshold,' he said, 'and we choose the means that best suit our interests. But we certainly would not allow inspectors on our railroads or technicians in our factories. That is a foolish suggestion and Stalin would certainly not agree to it.'[74]

On the following day, still before the issue of the *démenti*, Maisky expressed to Eden his concern over the 'type of reports' which were unlikely to be taken by his government to represent independent opinions.[75] There was obviously a grain of truth in this assumption. Unknown to Cripps and possibly to Eden, the press had been briefed on the subject by the Foreign Office itself.[76] The motive for the release can only be guessed at but Cadogan at least cherished the hidden hope, intimated in his diary, that the Russians would not 'give way and sign on the dotted line . . . as I should love to see Germany expanding her strength there'.[77] The rumours might indeed prompt suspicion that Britain aimed at encouraging the Germans to push east; they especially seemed to reflect the intelligence appreciation that the *Blitzkrieg* in Russia would be 'a campaign of little difficulty', estimating that the capture of Moscow and rounding up of Soviet forces would be completed in between '3 and 6 weeks'.[78]

As is now obvious, the object of the subtle Tass communiqué issued on 14 June was to ward off provocation and conciliate Berlin. The Foreign Office could not but notice the 'grovelling attitude' of Stalin, which was more suited to 'a small Balkan country than a great Power'. Kollontai was perceived to have 'changed her tone; she was no longer harping on Soviet Union's strength to resist all attacks, but rather upon the fact that Soviet Union's relations with Germany were perfectly friendly'.[79] The accusing finger was clearly pointed at Britain, though she was not named; the rumours were ascribed to forces 'hostile to the Soviet Union and Germany, interested in the further extension and spreading of the war'. The bait was put out for Germany to place her demands in the forthcoming negotiations. In the meantime, to avoid any provocation, the German concentration of troops was ascribed to the redeployment of troops after the Balkan campaign, whose objectives were 'not related to Soviet–German relations'. An advocate of peace, the Soviet Union remained loyal to the neutrality pact with Germany and the rumours of war were 'false and provocative'. The Soviet counter-measures were then attributed to the summer manoeuvres of the Red Army.[80]

The unequivocal message that no Soviet–British entente was in the making was at the least expected to produce in London a confirmation and further quashing of the rumours. In Berlin it was expected to evoke a German denial of belligerent intentions, if not to draw Hitler to the negotiating table. However, it was not even reproduced by the German papers. The only reaction to the communiqué came from Wehrmacht circles, where it was 'seen as highly ironical'.[81] On the night of 14 June Vyshinsky was sent to chat with Schulenburg but the conversation, which dealt with minor bilateral matters, failed to elicit from Schulenburg 'even a single word' in response to the communiqué.[82] In England the communiqué resulted in a harsh official remonstration against the accusations levelled against Cripps, as the rumours seemed to have originated 'from the Soviet side of the frontier'.[83]

14

Calamity

Self-Deception

The tension mounted in Moscow with the continued flow of intelligence pointing to an imminent outbreak of hostilities. It had become extremely difficult for the collators of intelligence in Berlin to ignore the evidence of Hitler's intentions. The confusion surrounding the events leading to the war and Stalin's misplaced confidence in his ability to avert the war are seen only too well in Dekanozov's reporting from Berlin shortly after his return from Moscow. While in the past he had been punctilious in alerting Stalin to the danger ahead, he now, like Golikov, appeared extremely cautious. He carefully cited the two sets of rumours circulating in Berlin. The first pointed to the inevitability of a war between Germany and Russia. The other predicted a revival of the old tradition of rapprochement between the two, based on a renewed division into spheres of influence and the Soviet Union's undertaking not to interfere in European affairs. Stalin's assumption of the premiership and recognition of the governments of the countries occupied by Germany were hailed as a prelude to the resumption of talks. On the other hand, Dekanozov was informed of Hitler's and Keitel's recent trip to Danzig and the transfer of the army's headquarters to the East. But in his final assessment Dekanozov played down the information, which was 'partially disseminated through the rumours of war with the Soviet Union'. Though attempting to cater to Stalin's known prejudices, Dekanozov could hardly conceal his own evaluation that the German government was 'clearly preparing the country for a war with the Soviet Union, drawing the attention of the population to the resources of the Ukraine and spreading rumours of the weakness of the Soviet Union, while simultaneously examining the reaction of the

German people'. Indeed, a week later he was on track again, with a bleak survey of the 170 to 180 divisions, the bulk of the German army, confronting the Red Army along the entire border. While until the end of May the transfers to the front had mostly consisted of motorized vehicles, since then they had been replaced by heavy artillery, tanks and planes. His agents had witnessed with horror a massive transport of troops and equipment on the night of 12–13 June.[1]

The Germans now boosted their disinformation efforts, which proved a lethal weapon in the atmosphere of increasing suspicion and uncertainty. The conflicting sets of rumours in Moscow and in London played into Goebbels's hands. In his diary he commented with great satisfaction that as far as Russia was concerned, 'we have been successful in producing a tremendous torrent of false reports. The newspapers' speculations have confused issues and they can no longer confirm what is true and what is false. This is the atmosphere we need.'[2] I. F. Filitov, the Tass correspondent in Germany, and according to German intelligence sources the deputy head of the NKGB residency in Berlin, was instructed on 12 June 'to clarify whether or not Germany is actively pursuing negotiations on peace with England and whether or not to expect an attempt in the longer term to secure a compromise with the United States'. He was to give the impression that 'we are all convinced that it is indeed possible to maintain our peace policy. There is still time . . .'[3] Unlike Dekanozov, who watered down his reports but still warned of the danger, Filitov produced an appreciation of the rumours which fitted in well with Stalin's expectations. He qualified the danger by stating his firm belief that Hitler had produced 'a gigantic bluff'. He did not expect war to 'suddenly erupt tomorrow' but rather the Germans to exert pressure 'in the hope of deriving some benefits which Hitler needs for continuing the war . . .'[4]

The rumours turned out to be a godsend for Hitler. With the Führer's blessing Goebbels wrote a long article entitled 'Crete as an Example', elaborating on the presumed German preparations for a war in the Mediterranean. It attracted much attention and was widely quoted before the edition was abruptly withdrawn from the newspaper kiosks, creating the impression that the article disclosed state secrets. It was in fact so clever, Goebbels boasted, that 'it was possible to extract from it anything that an enemy might wish to believe at a given moment'. The Germans further exploited to the utmost the press campaign in England by the publication of scores of articles which implied that adequate foundations had been laid for continued negotiations with Moscow. While the communiqué from Moscow was ignored, Goebbels encouraged the 'uninterrupted spreading of rumours: peace with Moscow, Stalin is expected in Berlin, an attack against England itself will be mounted in the near future'.[5]

On 9 June Kobulov informed Stalin that 'Starshina' believed that the rumours on negotiations were being deliberately spread by the

Wehrmacht and the Ministry of Propaganda to conceal the preparations for war. But the accurate information was still overshadowed by the 'ultimatum theory'. Lieutenant-Colonel Heimann, head of the Russian section of the Air Staff, was quoted as saying that Hitler would 'present the Soviet Union with demands for German economic control over the Ukraine, delivery of bread and oil and the use of the Soviet fleet against Britain'.[6] It was followed two days later by a revelation that the final decision to invade Russia had been taken, but whether it would be preceded by demands on the Soviet Union was 'unknown'. Göring's staff was ordered to transfer his headquarters from Berlin to Rumania. The second line of the air force was transferred from France to the Poznan region. The German and the Finnish General Staffs were believed to be in the midst of 'intensive negotiations'. Documents which had passed through the hands of 'Starshina' revealed that the Germans would invade Russia in the north from West Prussia and in the south from Rumania, creating large pincer movements which would lead to the encirclement and annihilation of the Red Army. To understand the pressure under which Kobulov ('Zakhar') was working, attention should be drawn to his desperate attempts to convince Stalin in concluding his reports that the recommendation of 'Starshina' to pre-empt the Germans was not a 'provocation', but rather words 'straight from the heart'.[7]

The following day Kobulov reinforced the warning with fresh evidence from 'Starshina' concerning the 'conclusiveness of the decision on a surprise attack'. He quoted directly from 'Starshina': 'the leading circles of the German Ministry of Aviation and in the Staff of the Air Force are convinced that the issue of the attack by Germany on the Soviet Union is definitely decided. Regardless of whether any demands are put to the Soviet Union in advance – we should take into account the possibility of a surprise attack.'[8]

When Merkulov presented Stalin on 16 June with further evidence from 'Starshina' which indicated that the final measures for the attack had been taken, Stalin exploded, suggesting that 'the "source" in the Staff of the German Air Force should be sent to his f****** mother! This is no source but a *disinformer*.' He further dismissed out of hand the revelation that Rosenberg, the notorious author of Hitler's anti-Soviet chapter in *Mein Kampf*, had already selected the various administrators who would run the Soviet economy after the occupation. According to 'Starshina', Rosenberg had promised that 'the name of Russia would be wiped off the geographical maps'.[9] When on 9 June Timoshenko and Zhukov discussed with Stalin a wide array of intelligence, Stalin was scarcely moved; 'And I have different documents', he interrupted and tossed back their compilation of intelligence reports. He further dismissed the information provided by Sorge, joking that in Japan Sorge had 'set himself up with some small factories and brothels and even deigned to report the date of the German attack as 22 June. Are you suggesting I should believe him, too?'[10]

And yet the harsh reactions only proved that Stalin's confidence had been shaken. When compelling reports on the imminent war finally reached Stalin on 17 June, coinciding with the information obtained from London, Stalin hastily summoned Merkulov and Fitin, the head of Foreign Intelligence, to the Kremlin. Stalin wished the reports to be redrafted, as they seemed 'contradictory'. They were 'ordered to prepare a more convincing and conclusive summary of all intelligence information'.[11] The document 'Calendar of information obtained through "Corsicanets" and "Starshina" from 6 September 1940 to 16 June 1941' was consequently prepared on 20 June. It reached Merkulov's hands hours after the Germans attacked. Subsequently it was returned by Fitin to the head of the German department of Foreign Intelligence and buried in the archives for posterity.

Stalin simply refused to come to grips with the reports, challenging as they did the wisdom of his politics in the preceding two years. Obviously a large number of the reports were now tailored to his whims, while the agents had to find a way to retain their integrity and perform their duties by conveying the warnings as well. The final result, however, was counter-productive. While pointing to the likelihood of war, they kindled the hope in the Kremlin that it would still be possible to delay the war. Stalin now clung to scanty and contradictory intelligence which depicted shortcomings in the combat readiness of the Wehrmacht. He further argued that the Germans were unlikely to start hostilities while their armour, air force and artillery units were still stationed far from the border.[12]

He also clung to the fact that varied dates for the invasion were being proposed. The contradictory data seemed to justify Stalin's cautiousness in implementing the deployment plans.[13] The surveillance of Schulenburg also led to equivocal conclusions. On 9 June, for instance, Stalin gleaned from an intercepted telegram that although Schulenburg had received no instructions to start negotiations, he had not been informed about possible hostilities. Moreover, the German ambassador kept reiterating that Russia was 'painstakingly fulfilling its obligations which would make it difficult for Germany to pick a pretext for an attack on the Soviet Union'.[14]

Though seriously fettered, the intelligence agencies continued to drive home the danger in a fairly unequivocal way in the last few days leading to the war. On 18 June the NKGB reported the hasty evacuation since 10 June of thirty-four members of the German embassy, together with their wives and children and personal belongings. The exodus was continuing, and visas had been sought for more members. Secret Service papers had been sent to Berlin in advance, while others were being burned in the embassy's courtyard. The evacuation, Stalin was told, reflected the 'intense nervousness and concern in Moscow in connection with the prevailing opinion that the relations between Germany and the USSR have worsened, and that a war will break out in the next few days'. On 12 June, the employees of the embassy had been assembled and given instructions for their departure from Moscow. The communiqué had brought a temporary relief, but the absence of a reaction hastened the evacuation.[15] Intourist was flooded with requests from the various German missions for seats on outgoing flights.[16] Schulenburg was reported to be 'in a very pessimistic mood', fearing that as a result of his rebuff by Hitler during their meeting in Berlin he might shortly find himself in a concentration camp. He could not even exclude the possibility that within a week he would 'not be among the living'.[17] His personal messenger returned to Moscow empty-handed. Consequently members of the German embassy accelerated their packing while making arrangements for evacuating their families. In a telegram intercepted by Soviet intelligence, Rosso informed Rome that 'an armed conflict was inevitable and that it might occur within two to three days, perhaps on Sunday [22 June]'.[18]

Sorge's output increased as well. The courier from Berlin had informed the German military attaché in Tokyo that 'he was convinced that the war against the Soviet Union would be postponed to the end of June at the latest'.[19] On the very eve of the war Sorge hastened to inform Golikov that Ott, the German ambassador to Tokyo, had disclosed to him that war with Russia had become 'inevitable'. The Japanese General Staff was already discussing what would be Japan's position once war broke out.[20] On the day before the invasion, the NKGB produced its now customary crop of fresh information on the 'unceasing transfer of troops, armoured divisions and mechanized forces from deep in Germany through Warsaw to the Soviet borders'. The number of trains was specified with their exact location, and the German troop units were identified by their numbers and affiliations. As the NKGB had discovered, the last-minute task assigned to German agents was to inform on the state of the railway system and roads in Russia, the pattern of deployment of the Red Army, the armaments used by the units deployed on the border and so on. German officers were conducting intensive indoctrination of their troops, focusing on the betrayal by the Soviet Union and the approach of war.[21]

As we have seen, Zhukov and Timoshenko had been pressing Stalin since 10 June to put the army on full alert. On 18 June the two pursued the argument further in a meeting which lasted for more than three hours in Stalin's offices, in the presence of members of the Politburo. Timoshenko's retrospective recollections of the meeting leave a vivid impression of Stalin's process of decision-making and his ruthless, impatient and insulting handling of the military. Timoshenko and Zhukov arrived in the Kremlin equipped with maps which depicted in minute detail the German concentrations. The poised Zhukov spoke first, describing the anxiety among the Soviet troops and pleading with Stalin to put them 'in full military readiness'. The more he spoke, the more irritable Stalin became, knocking out his pipe nervously on the table. He finally sprang up, walked towards Zhukov and shouted at him: 'And what, have you come to scare us with war, or do you want a war, as you are not sufficiently decorated or your rank is not high enough?' Zhukov immediately lost his composure and sat down. Timoshenko, however, persisted in warning that to leave the troops in the present state of deployment would produce havoc if the Wehrmacht struck. This provoked Stalin into a tirade which reveals his brutality but provides a glimpse into his inner thoughts:

> Stalin returned to the table and spoke harshly: 'It's all Timoshenko's work, he's preparing everyone for war, he ought to have been shot, but I've known him as a good soldier since the civil war . . .' I told [Stalin] what he had told everyone at the meeting with the Academy graduates, that war is inevitable. 'So you see,' – Stalin said addressing the Politburo – 'Timoshenko is a fine man, with a big head, but apparently a small brain' – at this he showed his thumb. 'I said it for the people, we have to raise their alertness, while you have to realize that Germany on her own will never fight Russia. You must understand this.' And he left.
>
> Then he opened the door and stuck his pock-marked face round it and uttered in a loud voice: 'If you're going to provoke the Germans on the frontier by moving troops there without our permission, then heads will roll, mark my words,' and he slammed the door.[22]

Preventing provocation had obviously become vital for Stalin in his attempts to avoid the war. His restless mind and ruthless style of government sought means to avoid the pitfall. Since April the local NKGB had reported that Ukrainian nationalists were 'spreading provocative rumours'. These suggested either that the Soviet Union 'was preparing an attack on Germany', linking it with the conclusion of the neutrality pact with Yugoslavia, or alternatively that Germany was 'preparing an attack on the Soviet Union'.[23] Ukrainian schools, Stalin was further informed, were being encouraged to teach the history and geography of 'Independent Ukraine', maps of which were hung on the walls of many educational institutions in Cracow. Rumours had it that 200 active Ukrainian nationalists had been sent to special courses in Berlin to prepare them to administer the 'Independent Ukraine'.[24]

Early on, the head of the Ukrainian NKGB had expressed his fear that in time of war those nationalists might act as a fifth column. Under the leadership of Stephan Bendera, a 1,000-strong force had been armed by various criminal elements and was already engaged in hostile activities against the Soviet regime by terrorizing the local population. Hiding in the forests during the day, the organization terrorized the kolkhoz population at night, targeting especially the unprotected homes of those who had been sentenced during the purges.[25] An intercepted telegram from the Japanese consul in Königsberg seemed to confirm these suspicions. Apparently various courses in Russian had been organized by the Germans at local universities. Some 2,000 members of the 'Ukrainian Union', who had been working at the Siemens factory in Berlin, were returned to Poland. Indeed six of these, who were finally sent to the Lvov area, were arrested by a Red Army border patrol.[26] Later in May, 120 members of various kolkhozes at a distance of sixteen kilometres from the border were reported as not leaving for work in the fields in view of 'the provocative rumours on the imminent outbreak of war with Germany'. In Moldavia, the report noted, 'hostile elements spread provocative rumours on market day that the Red Army, retreating under the threat of a German invasion, was stealing the peasants' livestock on the way. The peasants fled the market place in panic back to their villages to lock in their livestock.'[27]

The negotiations with Schulenburg in mid-May had alerted Stalin to the danger that rumours and provocations might in fact trigger a war not desired by Hitler.[28] The activities of the nationalists seemed particularly hazardous, as they could be exploited by the German army which, Stalin believed, was eager to drag Hitler into war. Clutching at his concept, and assuming that the activities of the 'counter-revolutionary elements' were being used by 'foreign intelligence for spying purposes', Stalin instructed the NKGB to arrest 'provocateurs' and imprison them in special camps for periods ranging between five and twenty years. Five categories of people were specified, among them members of nationalist organizations, former counter-revolutionaries, policemen and former governmental officials. Nor were their families spared. Merkulov ordered the immediate construction of special camps to which the suspects would be 'quickly dispatched'. This operation, wide in scope, took priority even over the gathering of intelligence at this very crucial stage of the Wehrmacht's deployment. Merkulov took charge personally, assisted by 208 officers who were released from their training at the higher school of the NKGB in these provinces. The whole operation was to be wound up within three days.[29] On 22 May Beria issued instructions to the border NKGB to launch a sweeping operation aimed at 'bandits, spies and anti-Soviet revolutionaries'. Some 12,000 suspects and their families were rounded up that very night and sent to camps in the East. In the next two weeks the NKGB harnessed all its resources to curtail the activities of these organizations in the hope of eliminating the threat of provocation.[30]

The lack of adequate military or diplomatic means to deal with the ominous situation sidetracked Stalin into attempts to eliminate the danger of provocation. A working paper of Foreign Intelligence suggested that the subversive activities of the Ukrainians and particularly the Poles were led by former Polish officers whose hope was to exploit an armed conflict with Germany to achieve their aims. The activities of those organizations was alleged to be co-ordinated by German intelligence. Strangely enough, all Jewish and Zionist organizations were marked as subversive anti-Soviet elements rather than potential victims of Nazism. This was based, in addition to deep-rooted anti-Semitism, on an assumption that the 'Revisionist' wing of the Zionist movement was a 'Fascist Jewish Organization' with pro-British leanings. Their party was alleged to be modelled on Italian fascism. Moreover, they were bourgeois in their outlook, and if Russia became involved in war with Britain they could be expected to join hands with her in sabotaging the Red Army in the rear.[31]

On 16 June Sudoplatov, deputy director of Foreign Intelligence, was ordered by his superior, Fitin, just back from consultations at the Kremlin, to create a special task force to counter any German attempts at provocations on the border of the sort which had triggered the war in Poland. The next day Merkulov proudly announced the successful purge of the 'anti-Soviet social elements' in the newly absorbed Baltic territories. In the course of the campaign, 14,467 people were arrested in the Baltic republics alone, while 25,711 were exiled to Siberia. Until the very last minute, the NKGB continued to invest great efforts in identifying the alleged sources of subversion and sabotage inspired by Germany.[32]

London: 'This Avalanche Breathing Fire and Death'

On 9 June British intelligence came across fresh evidence which led it to the conclusion that 'German concentrations against Russia are being pressed with the utmost speed and vigour'. Eden decided to release the information in order to 'encourage Russian resistance', obviously to a German ultimatum.[33] From his ambassador in Stockholm he learnt that 'while Soviet–German relations have been strained during the last three weeks a solution is likely to be found soon and a delegation of Soviet Military representatives is expected in Berlin to sign a Soviet–German Military pact. The message is unofficial and presumably sent in order to ascertain whether Soviet authorities will deny it, affirm it or remain silent.'[34] Hitler's 'apparent decision not to drive home the advantages gained by his conquest of Greece and Crete, but to stage a major threat to Russia' was indeed difficult for the Foreign Office to digest. It seemed, as Eden admitted, 'the most astonishing development on the grand scale since the war began'. Indeed Cadogan, who had assumed that there was 'always method in [Hitler's] madness', confessed that he too was puzzled by the intelligence. Eden remained sceptical: 'But *if* Russia fights, a big *if*,' he commented.[35]

To discourage the British from assuming that German–Soviet negotiations were in progress and therefore hastening their own negotiations with the Germans, Maisky informed Eden on 10 June that 'no military alliance was in existence between Germany and Russia, nor was one contemplated. More than that, the Soviet Government were not at present in negotiation with the German Government about any new agreement, either economic or political.' The volunteering of this information posed, however, a serious dilemma. If the concentration meant war the British might be tempted to initiate their own peace effort or encourage Germany to turn east.[36] The Russians obviously hoped that their assurances would encourage the press to drop the topic. Instead they were faced with a plethora of speculation revolving around Cripps's recall.

Maisky's hunch that Britain was desperately trying to entangle Russia in war seemed to be confirmed by his interview with Eden after Cripps's return on 13 June, just before the release of the Tass communiqué. Maisky was under the strong impression that there was a 'campaign in the press related to the arrival of Cripps . . . and he expressed regret that the measures undertaken by Eden to put to a stop the "speculations" in the papers on this subject, about which he had informed me on 5 June, had not been successful'. It obviously confirmed his feeling that Churchill was drumming up the rumours. Maisky warned Eden, even before the publication of the communiqué, that 'the type of reports which had appeared yesterday would not be understood in Moscow and would be resented there'. Eden, however, had summoned Maisky this time to inform him of the increasing flow of intelligence in the previous forty-eight hours. The concentrations, he stressed, 'might be for the purpose of a war of nerves, or they might be for the purpose of an attack on Russia'. He appeared desperate to impress on Maisky his conviction that the nature of the intelligence now showed that the Germans did plan to attack. However, against the background of the press campaign, Maisky was quick to reject Eden's proposal of assistance, which could have been yet another attempt to embroil Russia in war. The offer, he remarked, presupposed 'intimate collaboration' between the two countries, which he believed was 'premature'. Eden, however, persevered, explaining that, whereas previously he had shared Maisky's interpretation, the newly available information had made him change his views. Burdened with the heavy responsibility of correctly assessing the nature of the information, Maisky pressed Eden for further evidence on the German intentions 'at an early date, either today or during the week-end'. The urgency of Maisky's request was lost on Eden, who had promised to consult Churchill and the General Staff before transmitting the intelligence.[37]

The decision to part with momentous evidence obtained through Enigma was finally sanctioned by Churchill late on Sunday 15 June, a week before the German attack. The Joint Intelligence Committee handed Cadogan the latest and most up-to-date paper on the likelihood of war, which was based on the collation of all available intelligence, including the Enigma reports. This was an extremely generous gesture, as the report could, if studied carefully, compromise the source of the intelligence. They further provided him with a map showing a conservative estimate of the forces facing each other on the border, with the sarcastic comment that 'a comparison of this map and M. Maisky's remarks to the Secretary of State during their last interview is very funny'. As Maisky was away for the weekend, the transfer of the information was delayed until the next morning.[38]

Maisky was therefore astounded when he was summoned to the Foreign Office on Monday morning to face Cadogan's detached and monotonous recital of 'precise and concrete' evidence. What disturbed Maisky was not so much the realization, subsequently so graphically depicted in his memoirs, that 'this avalanche, breathing fire and death, was at any moment to descend' upon Russia, but rather the soothing content of his previous communications. He therefore hastened to cable Moscow, reversing his earlier appreciations.[39] Even then Maisky, as attested in his memoirs, was inhibited from making a precise report by the perceptions prevailing in Moscow:

Of course, I did not accept Cadogan's communication as 100 per cent true. Information from military intelligence is not always accurate; the British were interested in war being let loose in the east, and might deliberately heighten the colours in order to have a bigger effect on the Soviet government. For these reasons I made a considerable discount in my mind from what Cadogan had told me. Nevertheless, the Under-Secretary's information was so serious, and the reports he had communicated were so precise and concrete, that (it seemed to me) they should give Stalin serious food for thought, and lead him urgently to check them and, in any case, give strict instructions to our Western frontier to be on guard!

Despite the censorship, Maisky's cable gave rather accurate information on the various stages of the German build-up on the Soviet borders in May and June. The British Chiefs of Staff, however, seriously underestimated the magnitude of the deployment in comparison with the information available to the Russians, and assumed that the Germans possessed eighty divisions in Poland, thirty in Rumania and five in Finland and northern Norway, 115 divisions in all, excluding the mobilized Rumanian army.[40]

The Russians were skating on thin ice by winning over the Germans but undermining their position in England. That could be particularly dangerous if negotiations on a separate Anglo-German peace were in full swing. They were now clearly wavering in their appreciation. The attitude of the British government to the developing crisis had been central to the Kremlin's own evaluation. Despite the atmosphere of despair prevailing in the Kremlin, Stalin's belief in British provocation on the one hand and in a German ultimatum which would precede an attack on the other remained unshaken. This was discouraging his entourage, intelligence sources as well as Maisky, from formulating a clear-cut evaluation. Maisky's appraisals between 10 and 15 June therefore played on Stalin's obsession with provocation, as echoed in the famous communiqué, and lulled him into ignoring the real danger in the military sphere.

Pondering with his advisers on the absence of reaction to the communiqué, Stalin was faced on 16 June with Maisky's revised appreciation after his talks with Cadogan. The repercussions were swift. On the evening of 16 June the British chargé d'affaires made a courtesy call at the Kremlin, his first since Cripps's departure. In an attempt to minimize the effect of the communiqué, Vyshinsky assured him that the reference to Cripps was not personal vindictiveness; it 'merely registered a fact and did so in careful words'. It was possible that Cripps's arrival in London 'had stimulated [newspaper editors'] imagination', as it was remarkable that after his arrival on 11 June the British press 'gave more prominence to these reports than before'.[41] When Cripps warned Maisky on 18 June that his return to Moscow would be 'largely influenced' by Soviet explanations of the references to him in the communiqué, he was assured of the Russians' 'greatest personal regard' for him.[42] Within hours Maisky addressed Eden with an apologetic and conciliatory message almost identical in wording to that given in Moscow.[43]

The stopover in Stockholm had cast some doubt on Cripps's belief in an imminent agreement. During dinner at the home of the British ambassador in Stockholm, the general director of the Swedish Foreign Ministry was startled by Cripps's theories of a possible Soviet–German agreement. To enlighten the British government he told Cripps of intercepts of the Wehrmacht's orders to the troops in Norway. He argued 'with great emphasis' that the Germans were set on attacking Russia during the week between 20 and 25 June.[44]

Cripps was invited to present his views to the War Cabinet, which discussed Russia for the last time before the outbreak of hostilities on 16 June. Eden and the Chiefs of Staff treated Cripps to lunch at the Savoy beforehand. The outlook still remained most uncertain. The army expected Hitler to destroy the Russian military immediately. Cripps thought Britain would be better off 'if Soviet is not involved this year & remains a potential threat', but Eden did not believe Hitler would permit it. Faithful to the collective wisdom of his Office, he anticipated that Russia would 'accept harsh terms of "collaboration", or be attacked'.[45] It was 'not outside the bounds of possibility', Sargent continued to believe, 'that in a few days' time Stalin and Hitler will reach an agreement according to which, in return for the concessions which the Soviet Government will have to make to Germany, Stalin will be allowed to recoup himself by annexing Turkish territory beyond the Caucasus or by asserting a privileged position in the Dardanelles'.[46] Churchill continued to waver, hardly expecting hope to emerge from the East. 'According to all the information I have been able to gather,' he wrote to the South African Prime Minister, 'Hitler is going to take what he wants from Russia, and the only question is whether Stalin will attempt a vain resistance. I have increasingly good hopes of the United States.'[47]

The absence of any concrete information led the Cabinet to adopt the view that 'Germany intended to deliver an ultimatum to Russia when her military concentrations were complete.' Maisky was accurately informed of the Cabinet's views by Brendan Bracken, Churchill's unruly adviser. Two schools of thought seemed to have emerged. Cripps, as the Soviet ambassador had learnt from him before, feared that although the Wehrmacht was at its peak the Red Army needed another year to rehabilitate itself. He showed sympathy for Stalin in recommending that the Russians stay out of the war for a while. Churchill, on the other hand, believed that the Red Army could pose some challenge to Germany, which might be 'a great help for Britain'. This confirmed Maisky's fears that Churchill's appreciations were still coloured by 'wishful thinking', a desire to see Russia involved in war. Until the very eve of the war Maisky therefore continued to warn Stalin, with some justification, that the Cabinet as a whole was 'eager for the USSR to take part in the war'.[48] He was, however, becoming increasingly nervous about the nature of his reports, especially since his meeting with Cadogan.

Two days after the Cabinet meeting, Maisky lunched with Cripps and his wife Isobel. Maisky put it to them bluntly that Britain wished to get Russia involved in the war against Germany. Cripps not only denied this but told Maisky that all he desired was for Russia to display towards Britain 75 per cent of the neutrality that she did towards Germany. As Maisky hastily informed Molotov, Cripps had now become convinced, despite his performance in Cabinet, 'of the inevitability of a military conflict between Germany and the Soviet Union, which will occur no later than mid-July'. Maisky still tried to put on a brave face while curiously clinging to the concept held by the Foreign Office: the build-up was simply 'one of Hitler's moves in the "war of nerves" . . . But a war? An assault? An attack? I find it difficult to believe. It would be crazy!' Maisky's feeble denials 'did not make a great impression' on Cripps, who produced powerful arguments which certainly unsettled Maisky who ended by saying that he:

> possessed absolutely reliable information concerning Hitler's plans. And if he were successful in defeating the Soviet Union, then afterwards he would turn with his entire might on England. The members of the British government with whom Cripps discussed this fact feel that before an attack on the Soviet Union, Hitler will present us with a definite ultimatum. Cripps doesn't agree with this. Hitler will simply attack us without prior warning, because he is interested not in this or that quantity of goods, resources, etc. which he wants to obtain from the Soviet Union, but in the destruction of our country itself and the annihilation of the Red Army.[49]

Cripps formed the distinct impression that, compared to their meeting a few days earlier, Maisky 'seemed much less confident that there would not be a war'. He nonchalantly concluded that their conversation had brought about 'a complete deflation of the Soviet Ambassador who now seemed very depressed'.[50] The same impression was gained by Geoffrey Dawson, the editor of *The Times*, who found Maisky suddenly convinced of a German invasion.[51]

22 June 1941: The Long Weekend

Assarasson, the Swedish ambassador to Moscow, doyen of the diplomatic community in Moscow and a keen Kremlin-watcher, provided the best description of the atmosphere in the Kremlin on the last days of peace:

> No one either knows or is prepared to say a thing about what is happening, if anything is indeed happening on the diplomatic front. One suggests that negotiations are under way, a second that they have not started yet, and a third that there won't be any negotiations but an ultimatum. Some say that the demands, whether they have been made or not, concern the Ukraine and the Baku oil wells, while others suggest they are concerned with different issues. Some suggest that the demobilization and disarming of the Ukraine are part of the demands. Most believe that war is inevitable and imminent; some believe that a war is intended and desired by the German side. A few think that there won't be a war, at least not presently, and that Stalin will make extensive concessions in order to avoid the war. The only certain thing is that we face either a battle of global significance between the Third Reich and the Soviet Empire or the most gigantic case of blackmail in world history.[52]

Stalin seemed to be suppressing all thoughts of war. His behaviour, however, displayed to people like Khrushchev that he was restless and seriously worried. He now took to heavy bouts of drinking, to which he also subjected his entourage. Moreover, unlike his usual habit he sought constant company, which seemed to banish from his mind the night-marish thoughts of an imminent war. Prolonged dinners and gatherings at his dacha replaced the working sessions in the Kremlin which had pre-viously characterized his routine.[53] Up to the very last minute Stalin con-tinued to believe that the German army was trying to provoke the conflict. As Kollontai admitted on the day of the invasion, Stalin 'certainly hoped and believed that a war would not break out without prior negotiations during which a solution to avoid war would be found'.[54] He had, however, lost the initiative and was practically paralysed.

The 'total silence' from the Kremlin and the reticence of the national press reflected the wish to prevent even the semblance of provocation.[55] Since the issue of the communiqué, Gafencu wrote home, Moscow had been living 'under the silence of Hitler. The war of nerves is at full blast, worsened by the news from Finland and Rumania about more and more significant military preparations.'[56] Schulenburg was living under the same shadow, convinced that a war would not serve German interests. But the common view in the German embassy, with which Stalin certainly concurred, was that 'when the gun is loaded it may go off even if not intended'; they entertained the illusion that it was Hitler's tactics 'to keep the King in constant check without forcing a checkmate'. Schulenburg had even sent his counsellor, Walther, as a last resort to Berlin to find out whether a meeting could be arranged between Hitler and Stalin.[57]

In the lull Stalin continued to contemplate the arrangements which he might be able to extract in the peace agreements. Bogomolov, his trusted ambassador in Vichy, who had just returned from consultations at home, explained that 'the new partition of the territories in Europe and the estab-lishment of new States in place of those which existed before the war will not become definite until the new frontiers are confirmed by the peace treaties involving the countries directly interested'. Stalin had been visu-alizing two scenarios. If Germany were to emerge as the victor of the war, Poland 'would be wiped off the map'; if Germany were defeated it was obvious that 'Poland would be reconstituted as an independent State and its borders fixed by treaty with the Soviet Union'.[58] Over tea at the Quai d'Orsay General Sousloparov, Bogomolov's military attaché, expressed the 'profound conviction that the Germans will not attack the Soviet Union and further refuted the existence of tension between Berlin and Moscow'. He admitted that it had originally appeared that the British were spreading the rumours, but it was now 'incontestable that the rumours have been propagated if not directly through the German infor-mation services then certainly with their consent'. He reflected accurately the views held by Stalin that the reason for the rumours seemed to be the 'pressure which the German Government is expected to exert on Moscow to increase considerably the delivery of grain, oil products and other raw materials, indispensable for continuing the war'.[59]

Maisky was spending the unusually hot weekend at Bovington, the house of his friend the former Republican ambassador of Spain. He was not beguiled by the serenity of the British countryside. The burden of responsibility which had fallen on him in the previous two months was difficult to bear. The most recent disclosures of Cadogan and Cripps questioned the essence of his consistent reports to Moscow. Many other Soviet ambassadors may well have shared that feeling. Pondering on the rumours, statements, cajolery and threats of the last month, Maisky, like Stalin, continued to vacillate:

> But perhaps this is artificially inflated by British speculations? Maybe this is British 'wishful thinking'? Yet another attempt to disrupt our relations with Germany and drag us into war on their side? Frankly speaking, I don't really believe that Hitler will attack us. To make war on Russia has always been very difficult. An invasion always ends tragically for the initiators. One only has to recall the Poles (during the Time of Troubles), Charles XII, Napoleon, the Kaiser in 1918. Russian geography has not changed all that much. And in addition, and this is especially important, we have a powerful army, and we have tanks, aircraft, artillery . . . We have the same instruments of war which Germany has and which, for example, France did not possess. We are strongly united at home in a way that France was not. We will be able to stand up for ourselves. Is it at all possible that in such circumstances Hitler will risk an attack on us? You know that would be tantamount to suicide.

Shortly after lunch Maisky was recalled to London, where Cripps gave him further evidence of the forthcoming attack, which was duly dispatched to Moscow. Cripps disclosed that information obtained from a reliable intelligence source (the source was Enigma) 'bears witness to the rapid approach of the moment of "action" on the part of Germany. That all German ships berthed in Abo and other Finnish ports had received orders to set sail.' He expected Hitler to attack the next morning or the following Sunday. Hitler, Cripps explained to Maisky, would derive a slight advantage from attacking on a Sunday when the enemy was in a lower state of alert. Cripps promised Maisky, though it would be taken in Moscow with a grain of salt, that Britain 'would not slacken its war effort'. In a manifestly schizophrenic fashion Maisky continued to dismiss the likelihood of war, much as he had done during his conversations with Eden on 13 June, suggesting that 'the entire scene, as illuminated by you, looks no more than highly hypothetical'.[60]

The winter had been unusually long in Moscow and snow had still fallen in the second week of June. On this particular Saturday the warm sun suddenly broke through and crowds thronged the parks on this long white night. The air of uncertainty weighed heavily on the Kremlin during this weekend. 'The situation is unclear,' the distressed Molotov confessed to Dimitrov, 'a great game is being played. Not everything depends on us.'[61] Although he admitted in conversation with the Turkish ambassador that the situation had become 'confused and uncertain', he too was under orders from Stalin to display robust confidence that the 'Soviet Union had no reason for anxiety'.[62] Stalin arrived at the Kremlin in the early hours of the afternoon well aware that he was no longer the master of events.

The precautionary and surreptitious military moves were accompanied by desperate diplomatic efforts to impress on the Germans what the communiqué had failed to do. Saturday 21 June was an exceptionally warm and pleasant day in Berlin too. Most members of the Russian embassy were resting and swimming in the serene surroundings of the Potsdam and Wannsee parks. The few left at the embassy were suddenly alerted and set to frenzied activity. A protest at the increase of German reconnaissance flights over Soviet territory was to be lodged personally with Ribbentrop, significantly accompanied by expressions of Soviet readiness to embark on negotiations. The hectic efforts to open a dialogue in Berlin were aimed at gaining direct access to Hitler, to acquaint him with the gravity of the situation. Dekanozov had failed to do so in a meeting he forced on Weizsäcker on the evening of 18 June. All efforts, however, to establish contact with the Wilhelmstrasse were futile now. Ribbentrop had deliberately left Berlin early in the morning, giving specific instructions that Dekanozov be kept at arm's length.[63] The Russian ambassador was to be told that as soon as he returned from the country Ribbentrop would contact him. The constant telephone calls from Moscow urging the staff of the embassy to expedite communication brought no response.

Consequently Schulenburg was rushed to the Kremlin at 6 p.m. Molotov had clearly lost much of his composure, complaining about the massive German violations of Soviet air space. He wished to find out why members of the German embassy and their wives had left Russia, giving rise to rumours of imminent war. Why did the German government not react to the 'peace-loving' Tass communiqué? What had caused German discontent with the Soviet Union, 'if it actually exists'? Molotov was unable to get any response to his pleas. Schulenburg, however, dropped his final hint about the German intentions, which obviously he did not report home. He admitted that 'posing those issues was justified', but unfortunately he was in no position to answer, as Berlin 'kept him entirely in the dark'. Rather pathetically, Molotov whined that 'there was no reason for the German government to be dissatisfied with Russia'.

Schulenburg ominously repeated that he was in no position to answer the questions. His own ray of hope was the news he had heard on the British radio that Dekanozov had met Ribbentrop a couple of times during the day. But Molotov, who had also been tuned in to the BBC, regretfully denied such developments, parting from Schulenburg even more baffled.[64] Dekanozov finally forced a meeting with Weizsäcker at 9.30 p.m. and handed him a note, similar to the one Schulenburg had received in Moscow, specifying some 180 cases of German reconnaissance flights over Soviet territory since the latest Soviet complaint in April. The flights, the note stated, 'had assumed a systematic and intentional character'. The expression of confidence that 'the German government will take steps to put an end to these border violations' clearly reflected the conviction in Moscow that Hitler could curb the army. Weizsäcker gained time by proposing that Dekanozov await the official response.[65]

Zhukov was spending the day with Timoshenko at the Ministry of Defence. As Molotov was conferring with the German ambassador, Zhukov received an urgent call from the Chief of Staff of the Kiev District, informing him of a German sergeant-major who had just crossed the border and revealed the attack plans for the next morning. Stalin, anxiously waiting to hear from Molotov, suggested that he should come to the Kremlin together with the Defence Minister in forty-five minutes. When they reached the Kremlin at around 7 p.m. Stalin met them on his own. He now seemed worried but was still toying with the idea that the German generals had sent the defector deliberately 'to provoke a conflict'. Some members of the Politburo had assembled in the meantime and in response to a query by Stalin Timoshenko proposed to activate the directive setting the covering forces in motion. Stalin found it to be too blunt: 'It is premature to issue the directive, as it is perhaps still possible to solve the problem by peaceful means.' He preferred to issue a shorter, more general warning which Zhukov hastened to prepare. The last-minute instructions to the commanders of the 3rd, 4th and 10th Armies, sent at 2.30 a.m., though still drafted prudently to satisfy Stalin's obsession with avoiding provocation, nonetheless stirred the covering forces:

1. A surprise attack by the Germans is possible during 22–23 June 1941 on the LVO (Leningrad Military District [M. D.]), PRIBOVO (Baltic M. D.), ZAPOVO (Special Western M. D.), KOVO (Kiev M. D.), ODVO (Odessa M. D.) fronts. The attack may be preceded by a provocative action.

2. The task of our forces is to refrain from any kind of provocative action which might result in serious complications.

3. I order that:

a) During the night of 22 June 1941 the firing positions of the fortified regions on the state border are to be occupied secretly.

b) Before dawn of 22 June 1941 all aircraft stationed in the field aerodrome are to be dispersed and carefully camouflaged.

c) All units are to be put in a state of military preparedness without calling up supplementary troops. Undertake measures to ensure black-out of cities and targets. No further measures are to be carried out without specific instructions.[66]

Some steps, however, were taken. Zhukov was assigned overall command of the south-western and southern fronts, where the main German onslaught was still expected to fall. His predecessor as Chief of Staff, Meretskov, was appointed commander of the northern front.[67]

Stalin had been subjected to endless warnings since the beginning of the month, and had been pressed during the entire week to issue directives alerting the troops. That Sunday, disconcerting as it might have been, did not seem different to him. After conversing for another fifteen minutes with Molotov and Beria, he felt confident enough to return early to his dacha at 11 p.m.[68] Zhukov and Timoshenko felt differently. They returned from the Kremlin to the Ministry of Defence and communicated with the various fronts, keeping them all alert. Around midnight their attention was drawn by Kirponos to a second deserter who had swum across the river and informed the NKGB border police that the attack would start at 4 a.m. Stalin, who was promptly informed at his dacha, was little moved and retired to bed.

At 3.30 a.m. the coded telephones started ringing at the Ministry of Defence, bringing news of heavy German shelling along the entire frontier. Stalin was speechless when Zhukov contacted him on the phone; only his heavy breathing could be heard. Despite Zhukov's insistence he refused to sanction any counter-measures. By 4.30 a.m., when Zhukov and Timoshenko were on their way to the Kremlin, the German artillery had been pounding Soviet cities, the Soviet air force had been annihilated on the ground and the war machine had started rolling into Russia. At the Kremlin the two Soviet commanders encountered a 'very pale' Stalin, 'sitting at the table clutching a loaded unlit pipe in both hands'. Present were also the ubiquitous Mekhlis and Voroshilov, Molotov and Beria. Stalin was clearly 'bewildered' but desperately hanging on to his misconception, suggesting it might still be 'a provocation of the German officers'. He was little moved by Timoshenko's attempts to bring him down to earth, and ignored the Marshal's insistence that rather than being a local incident this was an all-out offensive along the entire front. Stalin simply dug in his heels, suggesting that 'if it were necessary to organize a provocation, then the German generals would bomb their own cities'. After some reflection he added, 'Hitler surely does not know about it.' As a last resort he wished Molotov to speak to Schulenburg.

In the meantime Schulenburg himself was seeking an urgent meeting with Molotov. Between 3 and 4 a.m. a phone call had arrived at Molotov's secretariat from Schulenburg's office. Stalin's all-powerful secretary Poskrebyshev received the information and alerted Stalin and Molotov. Molotov left Stalin's office and went upstairs to his office.[69] Schulenburg had received a top-secret telegram instructing him to destroy the embassy's radio set and all the cipher material. He was to meet Molotov at 4 a.m. as the first salvo landed on the Soviet troops, and make to him a detailed statement underlining alleged Soviet hostile acts against Germany since the signature of the Ribbentrop–Molotov Pact. Hitler deliberately did not couch the statement as a declaration of war, wishing to present the attack as a defensive reaction to alleged Soviet aggression.[70]

While Molotov was meeting Schulenburg Stalin continue to ward off Zhukov's pleas to activate the deployment plans. At exactly the same time Dekanozov was rushed to see Ribbentrop in an official car put at his disposal by the Germans. He was informed that 'under the impression of the serious threat of a political and military nature which was emanating from Soviet Russia, Germany had since this morning taken the appropriate counter-measures in the military spheres'. The war which Stalin had been so anxious to avert had now descended on Russia. As he was taking his leave, Dekanozov was pursued by Ribbentrop, who was in a manifestly distressed and maudlin state. The Foreign Minister begged the ambassador to impress on Moscow that he had tried to no avail to prevent Hitler from embarking on war. Throughout the war, Hilger later attested, Ribbentrop would seize opportunities of recapturing 'something of his moments of glory . . . he never ceased dreaming about another chance to talk with Stalin'.[71]

Schulenburg drove to the Kremlin at around 5 a.m. He found Molotov 'wearing a tired and worn-out expression'. Even at this trying moment, Schulenburg retained his integrity. He skipped the catalogue of accusations, informing Molotov that it was 'with the deepest regret' that he had to inform him of what he himself had not known when he had met him a couple of hours earlier, that the German government felt obliged to take 'military measures' to counter the Soviet concentration of troops on the border. He added that he could 'hardly conceal his despondency, caused by the inexcusable and unexpected action of his own government'. He reminded Molotov of the utmost efforts he had made to preserve peace and friendship with the USSR. Still hoping that the situation was a prelude to negotiations, Molotov wished to know what was the status of the oral note, as it obviously was not an official declaration of war. Schulenburg, however, robbed him of any hope, bluntly telling him 'that he believed it meant the beginning of war'. Molotov tried in vain to explain that the concentrations were only part of the summer manoeuvres. He further revealed the Kremlin's state of mind by complaining that 'until the very last minute the German government had not presented any demand to the Soviet government'. Showing little interest in the arrangements for the evacuation of the two embassies from Moscow and Berlin, all Molotov wished to know was 'why did Germany conclude a pact of non-aggression, if she so easily breached it?' Schulenburg then took leave of Molotov 'in silence, but with the customary handshake'.[72]

Even when Molotov returned with the bleak news Stalin inhibited the military from implementing the defensive plans, endorsing a special directive which still specifically forbade the troops 'with the sole exception of the air force' to cross the German lines. He was clearly under the illusion that the war could be delayed. But, given the surprise attack and the absence of preliminary preparations, it was impossible to implement the deployment directives effectively.[73]

By seven o'clock members of the Politburo had gathered at their Kremlin offices. Stalin was discussing the situation in an adjoining room with Molotov, Voroshilov, Kaganovich and Malenkov. Though Stalin appeared calm and self-confident, he entrusted Molotov with the official announcement on the radio. It was only then that the various diplomatic efforts to redress the situation were abandoned and the various theatres received the green light to implement the deployment directives. They called for the execution of 'deep operations' in which the air force, which had just been struck a terrible blow by the Luftwaffe, was expected to take the lead in disrupting the deployment of the German forces and air force in the rear at a depth of 100–150 kilometres.[74] These orders were never carried out.

* * *

Well into the morning of 22 June Stalin did not exclude the possibility that Russia was being intimidated into political submission. As Molotov confessed to Cripps a week after the eruption of war, the Kremlin had not anticipated that war 'would come without any discussion or ultimatum'.[75] It is interesting to note Stalin's reaction of surprise to the ominous news from the front on the morning of 22 June. The Germans, he grumbled, 'just descended on us, without using any pretexts, not carrying out any negotiations; simply attacked basely like thieves'. He also seemed to justify his policy on the eve of the war by producing Schulenburg's explanation for the attack, which claimed that the Germans 'consider themselves threatened by the concentration of Soviet forces on their eastern borders and have implemented counter-measures'.[76]

Stalin was equally puzzled by the fact that Britain had not joined in a crusade against Russia. As long as he believed he could avert war, the probability of an alliance with Britain seemed remote. Mesmerized by the recent German successes in the Balkans, he was even more reluctant to make the slightest move which might be interpreted by the Germans as provocation. His suspicion of Britain had been intensified by the Hess affair and the various warnings by Cripps and Churchill. When the British chargé d'affaires paid a visit to the Kremlin early on Sunday 22 June, he found the Russians not only, as might have been expected, 'exceedingly nervous', but also 'excessively cautious'.[77] This explains the silence and confusion which engulfed Maisky in the early days of the war. Maisky heard of the invasion on the BBC morning news and even had to post-pone a meeting with Eden until he became acquainted with Soviet policy through Molotov's radio address.[78]

Over the weekend preceding the attack, Churchill had for the first time displayed some interest in the Russian war. Operation 'Battleaxe' against Rommel had just foundered and a war in the East, as Eden suggested, could prove useful: 'We need a breathing space & could use it.'[79] Churchill was preoccupied with how to renew the attempt 'to regain the initiative in Libya and disengage Tobruk'. He hoped he would be able to send the crucial 100 cruiser tanks with a special convoy 'if and when the enemy is engaged against Russia'.[80]

When the Soviet–German war broke out Maisky posed Eden a series of questions which betrayed the same concern: 'Could he assure his Gov-ernment that our position and our policy were unchanged? He felt sure that Germany would seek to combine offensive action on Russia with a peace move towards the Western Powers. Could the Soviet Government be assured that our war effort would not slacken?' Churchill gladly responded to Maisky's modest request. He had never considered the peace proposals, and would be less likely to do so now that Germany was tied up on the eastern front. His rhetoric in the famous broadcast speech on the day of the invasion concealed the absence of any major shift in strategy by referring to the more pressing Soviet anxiety, the Russians' astonishing belief in British connivance in the German attack: 'We will never parley, we will never negotiate, with Hitler or any of his gang. We shall fight him by land, we shall fight him by sea, we shall fight him by air . . .'[81] Maisky's reaction to the speech in his diary clearly reflects his relief: 'A powerful presentation! A wonderful presentation . . . The essence of his speech – a warlike, decisive speech, no compromises or agreements! War to the end! This is exactly what is needed today.'[82]

The Politburo of the British Communist Party issued a statement on the same day, before it had been briefed by Moscow and before hearing Churchill's pledge of assistance, claiming that Hitler's attack was 'the sequel of the secret moves which have been taking place behind the curtain of the Hess mission'.[83] Soviet suspicion of British connivance in the German attack was expressed by prominent members of the Soviet embassy in London on several occasions, even after Churchill's speech. If Churchill and Eden were forced to retire, they insisted, those who would take over 'would make a separate peace with Germany at the expense of

Russia'.[84] Nor was Cripps surprised to find Stalin, at their first meeting after the invasion, apprehensive about a possible separate peace. After all, he disclosed in his diary, 'we have tried to make them [apprehensive] in the past so as to prevent them going too far with the Germans'.[85] 'All believed', recalled Litvinov in Washington a few months later, 'that the British fleet was steaming up the North Sea for a joint attack, with Hitler, on Leningrad and Kronstadt.'[86]

Conclusion

Stalin was little affected by sentiment or ideology in the pursuit of foreign policy. His statesmanship was rooted in Russia's tsarist legacy, and responded to imperatives deep within its history. 'I am reading at break-fast now a life of Tsar Alexander and his entanglement with Napoleon at the time of Tilsit & after,' wrote Stafford Cripps in his diary a mere month before the German invasion, 'and it is really very remarkable how similar the strategy of Hitler is vis-à-vis Russia to that of Napoleon vis-à-vis Alexander! It looks very much sometimes as if history would repeat itself.'[1]

True, Stalin's system of government was characterized by an idiosyn-cratic and despotic choice of methods. Who would dispute the disastrous impact of Stalin's purges of the military in the 1930s and his meddling in the workings of the High Command? Yet it would be a mistake to attribute Soviet foreign policy in the wake of the Ribbentrop–Molotov Pact either to the whims of a tyrant or to relentless ideological expansionism.

Stalin's policy appears to have been rational and level-headed – an unscrupulous *Realpolitik* serving well-defined geopolitical interests. Marx's battle cry for the international proletariat in 1848, that they had 'little to lose in this revolution but their own chains', evoked far less resonance in Stalin than Palmerston's famous dictum of the same year that 'we have no eternal allies and we have no perpetual enemies. Our interests are eternal and perpetual, and these interests it is our duty to follow.' As Henry Kissinger put it in his characteristically succinct way, 'Richelieu or Bismarck would have had no difficulty understanding [Stalin's] strategy.' And yet the traditional 'unrestrained balance-of-power policy' was blended with a Metternich-like belief that relations between states 'had to be determined by consensus among like-minded rulers'.[2] It is not surprising that in the execution of his foreign policy Machiavelli rather than Lenin was Stalin's idol; here was a man who had *The Prince* specially translated for him.

Strict neutrality rather than commitment to Germany was regarded by Stalin as the crowning success of the Ribbentrop–Molotov Pact. Having signed the pact under duress, Stalin was evidently determined to extract the utmost from it. He sought to redress the imbalances which he felt had been inflicted on Russia not only at the Versailles peace conference and in the inter-war period, but also throughout the nineteenth-century struggle for the mastery of Europe. Stalin did not expect that Germany and England would exhaust themselves in the war, but he certainly hoped that they would lose a few feathers. While establishing his own agenda for the peace conference, he believed he had secured a sufficient breathing space to improve the military preparedness of the Red Army, a vital bargaining counter in the anticipated negotiations. The policy was exclusively geared towards the attainment of what he regarded as Russia's national interests. The gist of this policy was the idea of 'spheres of influence', which *ipso facto* undermined sovereignty. The creation of a buffer zone along the entire Western border was a legacy of the Russian tsars, who perceived free access to the Black Sea in the south, the Baltic Sea in the north and the Pacific Ocean in the east as fundamental to Russia's status as a major European power and the defence of her vulnerable borders. The smaller states, tucked uncomfortably between Russia and Germany along the entire buffer zone from Finland in the north to Turkey in the south, had adapted their policies to the realities dictated by geopolitical factors. Failure to do so led to disastrous consequences and usually ensued from a mistaken evaluation of their ability to resist or of the extent of the support they were likely to receive from a third party. Ultimately the victims of the 'power game' could at best enlist international indignation.

During the Phoney War Stalin appeared confident of the arrangements he had secured along his Western and Northern European borders. Moreover the breathing space he had gained seemed to allow him sufficient time to bolster his military machine. His gaze, however, was directed at the Balkans, the Turkish Straits, the Okhotsk Sea and the Kuril Islands in the Far East.

In view of the eventual formation of the Grand Alliance, it is rarely recognized by historians that the Russians regarded the Germans and the British with equal suspicion. Churchill's assumption of the premiership in May 1940 was not reassuring to the Russians. He did little to challenge the Foreign Office's fatalistic concept which excluded the possibility of collaboration with Russia for the duration of the war. In London it was taken for granted that the neutrality pact would eventually mutate into a military alliance between Russia and Germany. The effect of hostilities between Britain and Russia on the grand strategy of the war received only perfunctory consideration. Indeed, the Soviet Union was twice brought to the threshold of war with Britain: during the Soviet–Finnish war and again when the Allies decided to bomb the Soviet oilfields in Baku. Such plans, in which Churchill was personally involved, were forestalled only by the German occupation of Norway, Denmark and France.

The appointment of Sir Stafford Cripps as ambassador to Moscow was a last-ditch attempt to prevent the crystallization of a Soviet–German bloc after the disastrous collapse of France. But it was also, as Stalin accurately perceived, an attempt to drive a wedge between Russia and Germany in the Balkans. Cripps, whose ideas on post-war Europe coincided with the views held in Moscow, was however an outspoken opponent of his own government. His bitter haggling with Churchill and the civil servants at the Foreign Office, observed by Stalin, culminated in the execution of conflicting policies, further obfuscating the picture in the paranoiac atmosphere in the Kremlin.

Well into 1940 it was British naval predominance in the Mediterranean, rather than the German threat, which seemed to oppress Stalin. Drawing on the historical experiences of the Crimean War and the Allied intervention in the Civil War, he feared that Turkey might serve as a springboard for an Allied attack against the Soviet Union. From his vantage point only full control of the Black Sea littoral and the mouth of the Danube could complete the security arrangements he had achieved through the Ribbentrop–Molotov Pact.

The dazzling victory of the Wehrmacht in France shattered Stalin's confidence. He now faced the bleak prospect of being either left out of the peace arrangements or crushed by German supremacy unless he took the initiative to safeguard Russia's interests. The threat that Hitler might establish hegemony over Europe by sheer military predominance drew Stalin closer to Mussolini. By presenting a united front they hoped to consolidate their common interests in the Balkans, the Mediterranean and the Black Sea, with Germany's blessing. The new community of interests further arose out of the vacuum created by the fading Anglo-French presence in the Mediterranean and the Balkans. Yet once the Germans diverted their attention to the Balkans, and in particular the economic resources of Rumania, their overwhelming power was brought to bear on Italy, finishing off the collaboration with Russia.

It was the growing Soviet–Italian understanding which paved the way for the Russian occupation of Bessarabia. The expansion to the mouth of the Danube, rather than being an irredentist move, gave the Russians control of the river and served as a springboard for a further advance towards the Straits. For Stalin, securing the land-bridge was pivotal for the implementation of any revised arrangement concerning the Straits.

Most alarming for the Russians was their deliberate exclusion from the arbitration arrangements forced on Rumania, Hungary and Bulgaria in Vienna on 30 August, arrangements which determined the borders of Rumania and set the mechanism for the control of the River Danube. Those arrangements undermined the status of the Soviet Union as a major European power, exposed a vital gap in her security arrangements and terminated her aspirations in the Black Sea.

There is therefore little to support the claim that, during his visit to Berlin in November 1940, Molotov conspired with Hitler to divide the entire world. The directive for the talks, dictated to Molotov in Stalin's dacha and taken in longhand, was confined to intrinsic Soviet interests in the Balkans and the Turkish Straits and dominated by considerations of security. It is indisputable, though, that security was to be achieved partly through the annexation of territories with little respect for their sovereignty. Stalin specifically opposed the dismemberment of the British Empire, which he anticipated at the peace conference.

From the Berlin meeting onwards Stalin was torn between a desire to prevent the Germans from reaching the Straits and a fear that any association with the British in the Balkans might provoke the Germans and be deliberately used by the British to embroil Russia in a war. Stalin's resort to elaborate diplomatic moves reflected his awareness of the weakness of the Red Army, seriously crippled by the purges of 1937–8. Steady preparations were therefore under way to improve Russia's military preparedness and, far more significantly, her bargaining power in the impending peace conference, which he hoped would topple the Versailles order and restore Russia's position as a major power. By the time the peace conference convened, Stalin expected Russia to be powerful enough to redress her past and present grievances.

The acute sense of a German threat to Russia led Stalin to walk a tightrope, desperately seeking both a political arrangement and a remedy for the Red Army. The key directives of the General Staff for 1941, examined here for the first time, reveal that Stalin, who was fully informed of the extent of German deployment, made frantic attempts to reform the army in the spring of 1941. Those measures were debated in great detail at a special meeting of the High Command in the Kremlin in December and put to the test in two complex war games in early 1941. Both assumed a German invasion of Russia and their conclusions were implemented in the mobilization and deployment plans which were prepared by General Zhukov, the newly appointed Chief of Staff, in the spring of 1941. The sophisticated new military doctrine, devised in the mid-1930s under the leadership of the ill-fated General Tukhachevsky, was now revived. Great efforts were made to hasten the fortification of the borders acquired in 1939–40, but this had been only partially achieved when the Germans attacked.

In mid-April 1941 the head of Military Intelligence, General Golikov, submitted to Stalin an alarming report on the massive movement of German troops towards the Russian borders. Stalin conceded that, despite vast strides, the Red Army was far from ready for battle. The turnover in the High Command had disrupted the reconstruction of the army: three Chiefs of Staff served in the single year preceding the war. A stream of reports from division commanders revealed severe shortcomings. The only solution therefore was a temporary accommodation with the Germans. The conclusion of the Friendship Agreement with Yugoslavia in early April 1941 was not a rebuff to Hitler, as other writers have maintained hitherto. Riding the wave of popular support in Belgrade after a *coup d'état* had brought a non-compliant government to power, Stalin hoped to deter Hitler from carrying the war further east and lead him back to the peace conference. The dramatic negotiations between the Yugoslavs and the Russians were in fact subordinated to their common wish to avert war rather than mount effective resistance to Hitler. If, however, hostilities were to break out, Stalin could still revert to neutrality while encouraging the Yugoslavs to tie down the Wehrmacht for at least two months, after which weather conditions would force the Germans to postpone the campaign until the next spring. The high expectations of the Ministry of Defence, backed by Molotov, proved unfounded when Yugoslavia was occupied a mere ten days after the German invasion. Stalin was confronted by an almost untouched Wehrmacht, deployed earlier than expected along the entire border before the dialogue with Hitler had begun.

Attention should be drawn to two aspects of Stalin's appeasement. One was the dramatic decision to dissolve the Comintern, which was regarded as a major stumbling-block to future collaboration with Germany. The other was the Neutrality Pact with Japan, signed in April 1941. The significance of the pact was not, as has hitherto been suggested, in relieving the threat of war on two fronts. Rather it was a positive move, sustained by similar attempts to reconcile Italy and revive Ribbentrop's idea that Russia should join the Axis. A surprising discovery from the Russian archives is the fact that these forlorn hopes were cultivated by the German ambassador in Moscow, Count Werner von Schulenburg, later a leading member of the attempted coup against Hitler in 1944. After failing to convince Hitler of the folly of a war against Russia, Schulenburg made unauthorized overtures in Moscow to prevent the war. Over a number of clandestine breakfast meetings with the Soviet leadership, he encouraged Stalin to take measures which he believed might lead to a renewal of the negotiations started by Molotov in Berlin in the previous autumn. Schulenburg, like Cripps and Maisky, deflected Stalin from the real danger by constantly stressing the need to placate Germany through the quashing of rumours of war originating in London. He reinforced Stalin's well-founded suspicion that, after the fiascos in Greece and North Africa, Churchill was keen to see Russia dragged into the war to alleviate the German pressure on Britain.

Stalin's refusal to reckon with the potential consequences of a miscalculation, while adamantly pursuing his appeasement and avoiding provocation at all costs, was perhaps the single most significant factor in the calamity which befell the Russians on 22 June 1941. It had severe repercussions in that it increased the mistrust he harboured towards the military in the crucial month preceding the German attack on Russia. More than ever he now clung to diplomacy in an attempt to appease Hitler and delay if not avoid a war. The Yugoslav episode marked a watershed. Like Chamberlain before him, Stalin was mesmerized by the German might and opted for the diplomatic solution. But, drawing on the experience of British 'appeasement', he did not neglect the military and was in the process of restoring the army when war erupted.

The wish to seek an agreement with Germany at all costs was also strongly motivated by the fear that British provocation might entangle Russia in war. Contrary to Churchill's account, the massive German concentration in the East was consistently interpreted in London, as late as the first week of June 1941, as pressure mounted by the Germans to secure positive results in the negotiations that Britain imagined must be under way with Russia. The evidence presented here shows that Churchill's warning to Stalin of the German deployment in April, rather than being a landmark in the formation of the Grand Alliance, in fact achieved the opposite. Stalin was diverted from the main danger, suspecting that Churchill was bent on drawing Russia into the hostilities. His false evaluation was reinforced by Cripps's unauthorized diplomatic initiatives. Cripps believed that the only effective method of bringing the Russians closer to Britain was to play on Soviet fears of a separate peace. The warnings, backed by rumours which derived from the Foreign Office, were extremely ill-advised, as they played on Stalin's underlying fears.

Despite the purges which had crippled the Soviet intelligence services, they remained very effective. However, they were not immune to the universal limitations of intelligence: the way in which it is analysed, sifted and forwarded to the leadership, and misperceptions which lead to tendentious reading of the material. There was sufficient ambiguity in the vast intelligence offered to Stalin for him to be convinced that the attack might be deferred, or at best unleashed at a time of his own choosing, if he played his diplomatic cards well. The intelligence indicated a possible split between Hitler and the Wehrmacht: while Hitler hoped to achieve his aims through negotiations, the Wehrmacht sought war. This only strengthened Stalin's belief that to declare a general mobilization and deployment on the border would be tantamount to an act of war. Stalin was not really misled by German intelligence or by his own services. He was clearly suffering from self-delusion, constantly inventing rational justifications for his misconceptions.

In the light of these events, the flight of Rudolf Hess to Scotland on 12 May 1941 on a peace mission emerges as a key to the understanding of the Soviet attitude to the approaching conflict. The most recent documents released by the British government reveal an incredible attempt by MI6, encouraged by the Foreign Office, to use Hess 'mendaciously' through covert intelligence sources to prevent the Russians from concluding an agreement with Germany. This disinformation seemed to corroborate Stalin's evaluation that a split indeed existed within the German leadership, and that Hess was seeking peace with Britain in order to convince Hitler to withdraw his reservations about a campaign against Russia. British intelligence hoped that the information would inspire Stalin to join forces with Britain before it was too late, rather than seeking an agreement with Germany. The message had the opposite effect in the Kremlin, enhancing the belief that the rumours of war were indeed fabricated in London in an attempt to involve Russia in an unnecessary conflict.

This, then, is the context in which Zhukov's directive of 15 May for a pre-emptive strike against Germany should be examined. The directive is of course a centrepiece in the case produced by the 'revisionists'. They assume that the plan had originated with Stalin himself and was 'appropriately signed', thus proving Soviet strategy to be 'offensive', that is aggressive. And yet the directive was never even initialled, while the following day Zhukov issued a signed second directive for a defensive deployment of the Red Army in anticipation of a German attack. It is this directive which, with minor alterations, remained in force until 22 June. Moreover, a thorough analysis of Zhukov's proposal divests it of its sinister character. Adopting the highly sophisticated doctrine of 'operational art' devised in the mid-1930s by the prodigiously talented Generals Tukhachevsky and Triandafilov, the directive called for an *udar*, a well-defined and restricted strike, deep into the rear of the German concentration. It was conceived not as a springboard towards the seizure of the heart of Europe, but as a limited operation aimed at disrupting the German build-up and therefore of a defensive nature.

The events on the very eve of the war assumed a dramatic and menacing character. The effective German disinformation campaign and the misunderstandings coincided with Cripps's sudden recall to London for consultations in suspicious circumstances in early June. This lent force to the hypothesis that some kind of arrangement was being worked out behind the scenes, allowing Hitler a free hand in the East. Just as alarming was circumstantial evidence implying that American pressure was being exerted on Churchill and Eden to sacrifice Russia in exchange for peace proposals. Finally there was always an outside possibility that, even if the peace proposals were left unanswered, Britain might signal to the Germans her wish to remain uninvolved if war with the Soviet Union broke out. But to Stalin, who now realized he could not face a military encounter, the more likely hypothesis was the split theory. While the army and the ardent Nazis were pressing for war, Hitler and Ribbentrop still adhered to the spirit of the pact with the Soviet Union and believed they could obtain from Stalin both commodities and perhaps even tacit support against the British by peaceful means. Stalin remained unshaken in his belief that the British were attempting a provocation and that no German attack would take place without a previous ultimatum. His known views paralysed his immediate entourage, the various branches of the intelligence services and his ambassador in Berlin from pressing home the extent of the danger. The devastating nature of the intelligence, the obsessive fear of provocation and the realization that the Red Army could do little to hold off the Wehrmacht contributed to the calamity which befell the Russians at dawn on 22 June 1941.

When Zhukov telephoned Stalin at his dacha to inform him of the German attack, Stalin still appeared to believe that the Wehrmacht was provoking a war without Hitler's authorization. His first directive therefore prohibited the army from fully implementing the deployment orders. Once the reality of war sank in, he was convinced that the British had connived in the attack. It was only two weeks later, after a severe nervous breakdown and a recognition of his miscalculations, that Stalin was able to regain the reins of power and embark upon the arduous road of restoring his leadership and harnessing national support in the defence of the 'Motherland'.

Stalin's failure to prepare for the German onslaught primarily reflected the unappealing political choices which the Soviet Union faced before the outbreak of the Second World War, and even more so on the eve of the Great Patriotic War. It was however aggravated by Stalin's self-deception and miscalculation, a reflection of his authoritarian rule. And yet, even with hindsight, it is hard to devise alternatives which Stalin could have safely pursued. If he had made a pre-emptive strike, the blow would at best have been softened but definitely not averted. The extent of the German military successes both in France and in the Balkans was unforeseen by all the players in what Stalin referred to as the 'great game'.[3] Even before the war, Molotov attested, Stalin 'had felt that only by 1943 could we meet the Germans on an equal footing'.[4] It is even more likely that his initial hope was for Russia to avoid the war altogether and reap the fruits of the peace conference which he anticipated would be convened some time in late 1941.

Notes

Preface

1. P. M. H. Bell, *John Bull and the Bear: British Public Opinion, Foreign Policy and the Soviet Union, 1941–1945* (London, 1990); see also striking examples in A. Hillgruber, *Hitlers Strategie* (Frankfurt, 1965), p. 105, and L. Maury, 'Stalin the Appeaser: Before 22 June, 1941', *Survey*, 76 (1970), p. 76. Those episodes gain prominence in the voluminous work of A. Read and D. Fisher, *The Deadly Embrace: Hitler, Stalin and the Nazi–Soviet Pact, 1939–1941* (London, 1988). It reinforces the previous misleading interpretation, anecdotal in nature, by perpetuating as a guideline statements by Molotov such as that 'The friendship of the peoples of Germany and the Soviet Union, sealed in blood, has every reason to be lasting and firm' (see p. 426). In fact merely 150 pages of the voluminous book deal with the period from the signing of the pact to the invasion of Russia, none of which is based on Soviet sources. A similar disposition is in in A. M. Nekrich, *Pariahs, Partners, Predators: German–Soviet Relations, 1922–1941* (New York, 1997).

2. V. Suvorov, *Icebreaker: Who Started the Second World War* (London, 1990), pp. 344–5 and 327. The staunchest support of his views in Russia is in V. A. Nevezhin, *Gotovil li Stalin nastupatel'nuiu voinu protiv Gitlera?* (Moscow, 1995), and by the same author, *Sindrom nastupatel'noi voiny* (Moscow, 1997). A representative differing view is E. I. Ziuzin, 'Gotovil li SSSR preventivnyi udar?', *Voenno-istoricheskii zhurnal* (hereafter *VIZh*), 1 (1992), and Iu. A. Gor'kov, 'Gotovil li Stalin uprezhdaiushchii udar protiv Gitlera v 1941 g.', *Novaia i noveishaia istoriia*, 3 (1993).

3. See, for instance, G. Gorodetsky, 'Was Stalin Planning to Attack Hitler in June 1941?', *Journal of the Royal United Services Institute*, 131/3 (1986), pp. 19–30.

4. *Mif 'Ledokola': nakanune voiny* (Moscow, 1995).

5. For a fascinating, most powerful presentation of this problem, see N. Tumarkin, *The Living and the Dead: The Rise and Fall of the Cult of World War II in Russia* (New York, 1994). I have taken the liberty of reproducing some of her ideas in this section.

6. Gunter Gillessen, 'Der Krieg der Diktatoren: ein erstes Resümee der Debatte über Hitlers Angriff im Osten', *Frankfurter Allgemeine Zeitung*, 25 Feb. 1987. Similar interpretations had earlier passed almost unnoticed. See, for instance, H. Seraphim, *Die deutsch-russischen Beziehungen, 1939–1941* (Hamburg, 1949), p. 38; P. Fabry, *Der Hitler–Stalin Pakt, 1939–1941* (Darmstadt, 1962), pp. 427–30, and see a thoughtful critique in H. Koch, 'Hitler's Programme and the Genesis of Operation "Barbarossa" ', *Historical Journal*, 26/4 (1983).

7. Nolte, 'Vergangenheit, die nicht vergehen will'. The major contributions to the debate were compiled in *'Historikerstreit': Die Dokumentation der Kontroverse um die Einzigartigkeit der nationalsozialistischen Judenvernichtung* (Munich, 1987); W. Maser, *Der Wortbruch, Hitler, Stalin und der Zweite Weltkrieg* (Munich, 1994); W. Post, *Unternehmen Barbarossa: Deutsche und sowjetische Angriffspläne 1940–1* (Berlin, 1996). Nolte has been indirectly assisted by recent works of distinguished Sovietologists who have been attempting to equate Stalin's extermination of the Kulaks with Hitler's Final Solution; an illustrious example is R. Conquest, *The Harvest of Sorrow* (New York, 1986). The obvious political and ideological penchant of the debate explains why the *Frankfurter Allgemeine Zeitung* and *Der Spiegel* had been digesting it *ad nauseam*. Hoffman's work, within the framework of the official history of the German armed forces is 'Die Rote Armee bis Kriegsbeginn 1941', in *Das Deutsche Reich und der Zweite Weltkrieg, herausgegeben vom Militärgeschichtlichen Forschungsamt. Bd. 4: Der Angriff auf die Sowjetunion* (Stuttgart, 1983). Hoffman's predispositions and bias could be distinctly detected in his earlier book *Die Geschichte der Wlassow-Armee* (Freiburg, 1984); see in particular pp. 307–8. A rather critical view of the Centre's handling of 'Barbarossa' is in Berghahn, 'Das MilitärgeschichtlicheForschungsamt in Freiburg', *Geschichte und Gesellschaft*, 14 (1988). An extensive cover story in *Spiegel*, 6 (1996), was devoted to the exposition of those views.

8. E. Topitsch, *Stalin's War: A Radical New Theory of the Origins of the Second World War* (New York, 1987). See a discussion of the problem in my ' "Unternehmen Barbarossa": Eine Auseinandersetzung mit der Legende vom deutschen Präventivschlag', *Vierteljahrshefte für Zeitgeschichte*, 4 (1989), pp. 645–73. R. C. Raack, *Stalin's Drive to the West, 1938–1945: The Origins of the Cold War* (Stanford, 1995), and 'Stalin Plans for World-War-II', *Journal of Contemporary History*, 26/2 (1991).

9. A critical survey of the current drifts is in B. Pietrow, 'Deutschland im Juni 1941 – ein Opfer sowjetischer Aggression?', *Geschichte und Gesellschaft*, 14 (1988). Pietrow rightly observes (p. 119) that Hoffman's evidence emanates mostly from unrepresentative samples of debriefings of prisoners of war, a suspicious source to start with.

10. Especially the works of H. Arendt and K. Friedrich. A most recent example, though a refined one, is the otherwise insightful book by Alan Bullock, *Hitler and Stalin: Parallel Lives* (London, 1991).

11. W. Churchill, *The Second World War*, vols I–IV (London, 1948–50), III, p. 316.

12. The best compilation of their views is in S. Bialer, *Stalin and his Generals: Soviet Military Memoirs of World War II* (New York, 1969).

13. See for instance a discussion of this in the still authoritative and eye-opening study of J. Erickson, *The Road to Stalingrad* (London, 1975), p. 77. A reflection of the spectrum of the prevalent opinions

can be seen in the journal *Soviet Union*, 18/1–3 (1991), devoted to the issue with articles by leading historians of Soviet foreign policy such as A. Dallin, J. Haslam and G. Weinberg.

14. See Bibliography for details of the archives and collections.

15. A pioneering and inspiring work, which set a new standard for diplomatic history by extending the scope of the geographic and thematic themes is D. C. Watt, *How War Came: The Immediate Origins of the Second World War, 1938–1939* (London, 1989), especially chs 16 and 17.

16. See L. Bezymensky, 'The Secret Protocols of 1939 as a Problem of Soviet Historiography', in G. Gorodetsky (ed.), *Soviet Foreign Policy, 1917–1991: A Retrospective* (London, 1994).

17. A first breakthrough was in G. Roberts, *The Soviet Union and the Origins of the Second World War: Russo-German Relations and the Road to War, 1933–1941* (London, 1995), and a much less satisfactory treatment in Nekrich, *Pariahs, Partners, Predators*.

18. Archives of the Russian Foreign Ministry (hereafter AVP RF), f.017a, Maisky's diary, op.1 p.2. d.8.

Introduction: The Premises of Stalin's Foreign Policy

1. Public Record Office, Foreign Office (hereafter FO) 371 11779 N319 and N560/53/38, minutes, 27 Jan. and 11 Feb. 1926.

2. I. Deutscher, *The Prophet Armed: Trotsky, 1879–1921* (Oxford, 1970), p. 327.

3. *Piatyi vsemirnyi kongress Kommunisticheskogo Internatsionala, stenograficheskii otchet*, II (Moscow, 1925), pp. 33–4 and 66.

4. By far the best overall survey of Soviet foreign policy in the 1920s is Teddy J. Uldricks, 'Russia and Europe: Diplomacy, Revolution, and Economic Development in the 1920s', *International History Review*, 1 (1979), on which this summary draws. The standard and balanced work on collective security is still I. Haslam, *The Soviet Union and the Struggle for Collective Security, 1933–39* (London, 1984). For an analytical approach to the debate see B. R. Posen, 'Competing Images of the Soviet Union', *World Politics*, July 1987.

5. R. A. Savushkin, *Razvitie Sovetskikh vooruzhennykh sil i voennogo iskusstva v mezhvoenny period (1921–1941)* (Moscow, 1989), pp. 9–10.

6. Suvorov, *Icebreaker*. A typical similar view in the West is in Robert C. Tucker, *Stalin in Power: The Revolution from Above, 1928–1941* (New York, 1990), chs 10–21. I have made extensive use of the brilliant and (overall) balanced view of the period by T. Uldricks in 'Soviet Security Policy in the 1930s', in Gorodetsky (ed.), *Soviet Foreign Policy*. As significant and level-headed is the contribution by G. Roberts, *The Unholy Alliance: Stalin's Pact with Hitler* (London, 1989).

7. See the authoritative work of Anita Prazmowska, *Britain, Poland and the Eastern Front, 1939* (Cambridge, 1987), and her essay 'The Eastern Front and the British Guarantee to Poland of March 1939', *European History Quarterly*, 14 (1984).

8. Two recent works which bring forth a revised and updated account of appeasement are J. Charmley, *Chamberlain and the Lost Peace* (London, 1989), and A. Parker, *Chamberlain and Appeasement: British Policy and the Coming of the Second World War* (London, 1993).

9. Suvorov, *Icebreaker*, p. 27. See a more subtle way of presenting the same message in W. Leonhard, *Betrayal: The Hitler–Stalin Pact of 1939* (New York, 1989).

10. E. L. Woodward (ed.), *Documents on British Foreign Policy, 1919–1939,* 3rd Ser., V (London, 1952), p. 104.

11. FO 800/279 Su/39/221, Henderson to Sargent.

12. C. A. Macdonald, *The United States, Britain and Appeasement, 1936–1939* (Oxford, 1981); W. J. Mommawn and L. Kettenacker, *The Fascist Challenge and the Policy of Appeasement* (London, 1983); T. Taylor, *Munich: The Price of Peace* (London, 1979).

13. A. Ulam, *Expansion and Coexistence* (New York, 1975), pp. 250–64. On the Soviet fear of continued appeasement see for example S. G. Desiatskov, 'Uitkholl i Miunkhenskaiia politika', *Novaia i noveishaia istoriia,* 3 (1979), and E. M. Zhukov, 'Proiskhozhdenie vtoroi mirovoi voiny', *Novaia i noveishaia istoriia,* 1 (1980).

14. Russian proposals submitted to Halifax on 18 April in Woodward, *Documents on British Foreign Policy, 1919–1939,* V, pp. 228–9.

15. *Ibid.,* pp. 205–6.

16. Russian Military Archives, papers of the Military Intelligence (hereafter GRU GSh RF), op.9157 d.2 ll.418–31. Stalin was further provided with intercepts of Schulenburg's telegrams of that time which confirmed the information. See for example *ibid.,* ll.447, 453 and 454.

17. D. Volkogonov, *Stalin: Triumph and Tragedy* (London, 1992), p. 351. See also 'Alternativy 1939-go', *Izvestiia,* 21 Aug. 1989. Another illuminating and fresh interpretation is in 'Ribbentrop–Molotov', *Voprosy istorii KPSS,* 8 (1988).

18. See the excellent discussion in I. Fleischhauer, *Diplomatischer Widerstand gegen 'Unternehmen Barbarossa'* (Berlin, 1991), pp. 14–28.

19. On Stalin's realism in pursuing foreign policy see Conclusion, pp. 13–14.

20. This is argued forcefully by J. Haslam, *The Soviet Union and the Struggle for Collective Security in Europe, 1933–39* (London, 1984).

See also S. Pons, *Stalin e la guerra inevitabile, 1936–1941* (Turin, 1995).

21. On the danger see below, pp. 89–94.

22. AVP RF, f.077 op.20 p.109 d.3 l.15–17, record of meeting between Sharonov, Soviet ambassador in Budapest, with Rashichev, Yugoslav representative in Budapest, 11 Jan. 1940. See also *Komintern i vtoraia mirovaia voina* (Moscow, 1994), pp. 122–4, the Executive Committee of the Communist International on the war in the Balkans, 28 Sept. 1939, J. Attfield and S. Williams (eds), *1939: The Communist Party of Great Britain and the War* (London, 1984), and David Childs, 'The British Communist Party and the War, 1939–41: Old Slogans Revived', *Journal of Contemporary History,* 12/12 (1977).

23. Dimitrov's diary, 7 Sept. 1939. See also F. I. Firsov, 'Arkhivy Kominterna i vneshniaia politika SSSR 1939–1941 gg.', *Novaia i noveishaia istoriia,* 6 (1992), p. 25.

24. *Komintern i vtoraia mirovaia voina,* I, pp. 88–9, 99–101 and 113–14. See also a description of the meeting in Dimitrov's diary, 25 Oct. 1940.

25. Dimitrov's diary, 21 Jan. 1940.

26. See for example 'Alternativy 1939-go', and 'Ribbentrop–Molotov'. Bezymensky, 'Secret Protocols', pp. 75–86.

27. T. Uldricks, 'Evolving Soviet Views of the Nazi–Soviet Pact', in R. Frucht (ed.), *Labyrinth of Nationalism: Complexities of Diplomacy* (Columbus, Ohio, 1992), pp. 331–60.

1. *'Potential Enemies': London and Moscow at Loggerheads*

1. FO 371 24855 N1523/1523/38, 11 Mar. 1940.

2. Public Record Office, Cabinet Papers (hereafter CAB) 66/2 and 3, WP(39) 90 and 134, 13 and 20 Nov.

1939. See also the whole file FO 371 24851 N*/181/38.

3. FO 837/1098, 25 Apr. 1940.

4. CAB 84/8 JP(39)49, and CAB 65/1 43(39)6, 6 and 10 Oct. 1939.

5. FO 800/279 Su/39/221.

6. For a survey of Franco-Soviet relations see FO 371 24853 N3413/ 341/38, Halifax to Campbell, 18 Mar. 1940, and CAB 21/1051, Halifax to Campbell, 11 Dec. 1939. On the expulsion see CAB 21/1051, Butler to Halifax, 22 Dec.; CAB 65/2 105 and 108, and 112(39), 6 and 8, 12 Dec. 1939. On the Baku episode see below, pp. 18–19.

7. See Bell, *John Bull and the Bear*.

8. *Documents on German Foreign Policy* (hereafter *DGFP*), VIII, p. 79.

9. CAB 21/962, 30 Mar. 1940. Kipling's poem is quoted as it appeared in Ismay's document.

10. FO 371 23678 N4571 and 5240/ 57/38, FO minutes 18 Sept. and 17 Oct. 1939.

11. CAB 65/6 66(40)1, 12 Mar.; Chamberlain papers, NC 18/1/1144, letter to Ida, 23 Feb. 1940.

12. Presidential Archives, Moscow, f.45 op.1 d.298 l.11–18, Stalin's conversation at the Kremlin, 29 Jan. 1940.

13. The Archives of the Swedish Foreign Ministry (hereafter UD:s Arkiv 1920 ARS), HP/517/LXXI, Assarasson to FM, Oct. 1939.

14. MID, *Dokumenty vneshnei politiki, 1939 god* (hereafter *DVP, 1939*), XXII, 2, p. 12, Molotov to Terentiev, 3 Sept. 1939.

15. L. H. Curtright, 'Great Britain, the Balkans, and Turkey in the Autumn of 1939', *International History Review*, 3 (1988), p. 436. The most informative and comprehensive analysis of Turkey's foreign policy is in B. R. Kuniholm, *The Origins of the Cold War in the Near East: Great Power Conflict and Diplomacy in Iran, Turkey, and Greece* (Princeton, 1994).

16. *DVP, 1939*, XXII, 2, pp. 146–53, record of Saracoglu's meeting with Stalin and Molotov, 1 Oct., and p.

717, Potemkin on meeting Aktay, 25 Oct. 1939. Two useful works on the 1939 tripartite negotiations are F. Marzari, 'Western–Soviet Rivalry in Turkey, 1939', *Middle Eastern Studies*, 7 (1971), pp. 63–80, 201–20, and Curtright, 'Great Britain, the Balkans, and Turkey'; see also A. L. Macfie, *Turco-Soviet Talks*, pp. 431–4, who quotes the report leaked by the Turks to the Germans concealing that their own approach was actually directed against Germany. On the Soviet perception of the British threat see V. Ia. Sipols, 'Tainye dokumenty "strannoi voiny"', *Novaia i noveishaia istoriia*, 2 (1993).

17. Selim Deringil, 'The Preservation of Turkey's Neutrality during the Second World War: 1940', *Middle Eastern Studies*, 18/1 (1982), p. 30.

18. *DVP, 1939*, XXII, 2, pp. 35–7, 7 Sept. 1939.

19. Curtright, 'Great Britain, the Balkans, and Turkey', pp. 443–55, and Deringil, 'Preservation of Turkey's Neutrality', p. 30. A. L. Macfie, 'The Turkish Straits in the Second World War, 1939–45', *Middle Eastern Studies*, 25/2 (1989), p. 238.

20. *DVP, 1939*, XXII, 2, pp. 263–70 and 373–80, Terentiev to Stalin, Molotov and Voroshilov, 6 Nov. and 7 Dec. 1939.

21. *Ibid.*, pp. 92–3, Prasolov, chargé d'affaires in Sofia, to FM, 16 Sept. 1939.

22. *Ibid.*, pp. 273–4, report by Maisky, 8 Nov. 1939.

23. D. Dilks (ed.), *The Diaries of Alexander Cadogan, 1938–1945* (London, 1971), pp. 247–8.

24. CAB 84/2, 19 Feb. 1941.

25. M. Kitchen, *British Policy towards the Soviet Union during the Second World War* (New York, 1986), p. 19. Kitchen's typically lively and entertaining style does not conceal a most penetrating and critical view of British policy.

26. AVP RF, f.069 op.24 p.68 d.7 l.9–19, Maisky to Molotov on meeting

Butler, 26 and 30 Jan., and FO 371 24843 N1390/30/38, Butler on meeting Maisky, 30 Jan. See also AVP RF, f.06 op.2 p.1 d.8 l.18–21, Molotov on meeting Aktay, 11 Jan. 1940.

27. Dalton, the British Minister of Economic Warfare, in Dalton papers, Box II 5/2, memorandum by Boothby, on meeting Maisky, 17 Sept.; FO 371 23678 N5297/57/38, 5 Oct. 1939. On Maisky's extraordinary position in London see S. Aster, 'Ivan Maisky and Parliamentary Anti-Appeasement, 1938–39', in A. J. P. Taylor (ed.), *Lloyd George* (London, 1971).

28. AVP RF, f.059 op.1 p.326 d.2238 l.44–53, Molotov to Maisky, 21 Feb. 1940.

29. AVP RF, f.06 op.2 p.11 d.109 l.3–8, record of Cripps meeting with Molotov, 16 Feb. 1940.

30. See for example instructions to the Austrian and Czech CP, 31 Jan. 1940, in *Komintern i vtoraia mirovaia voina*, I, pp. 252–7 and 277–80.

31. CAB 70(40) in FO 371 24887 R3518/5/67, 16 Mar.; Public Record Office, War Office (hereafter WO) 208/1754, report by Major Kirkman, 6 Mar. 1940.

32. FO 371 25014 R1777 and 2781/242/44, Admiral Philip to Halifax, 7 Feb. 1940.

33. AVP RF, f.077 op.20 p.109 d.3 l.26–8, Sharonov (Hungary) to FM on meeting Csàky, 13 Feb., and f.084 op.20 p.131 d.5 l.29–32, record of Sergeev's (the Soviet chargé d'affaires in Athens) meeting with Papadakis, the head of the Information Section of the Greek FM, 21 Feb. 1940.

34. AVP RF, f.06 op.2 p.1 d.9 l.1–4, record of Molotov's meeting with Aktay, 2 Mar. 1940.

35. FO 371 25014 R3636/242/44, Knatchbull-Hugessen to FO, 21 Mar. 1940.

36. FO 371 24887 R3285/5/67, Knatchbull-Hugessen to FO, 13 Mar. 1940; FO 371 24887 R3681 and

R3769/5/67, Le Rougetel to FO, 23 Mar. 1940.

37. AVP RF, f.082 op.23 p.95 d.4 l.148–54, record of Tikhomirov's (first counsellor in Berlin) meeting with M. F. Kleis, 4 Mar. 1940.

38. *Istoriia Velikoi Otechestvennoi Voiny Sovetskogo Soiuza, 1941–1945* (Moscow, 1961), I, pp. 74 and 741.

39. AVP RF, f.06 op.2 p.14 d.155 l.3–8, Molotov's record of meeting Schulenburg, 7 Jan.; see also Filimov, Soviet ambassador in Iran, to FM, on meeting Ettel, the German ambassador in Iran, 4 Mar. 1940, in AVP RF, f.059 op.1 p.333 d.2284 l.97–100.

40. Charles Richardson, 'French Plans for Allied Attacks on the Caucasus Oil Fields January–April 1940', *French Historical Studies*, 8/1 (1973).

41. FO 371 24846 N3698/40/38, 25 Mar. 1940.

42. The plans are in FO 371 24846 N3698/40/38, 23 Mar., and see minutes by Sargent and Cadogan on 26 Mar. 1940 in 24887 R3836/5/67.

43. FO 371 24887 R3940/5/67; see also Deringil, 'Preservation of Turkey's Neutrality', p. 31, and Macfie, 'The Turkish Straits in the Second World War', p. 240.

44. FO 371 24887 R3963, R4010 and R4130/5/67, FO minutes, 31 Mar. 1940.

45. AVP RF, f.059 op.1 p.325 d.2233 l.306–7, Maisky to FM, 5 Apr. 1940.

46. FO 371 24888 R4466/5/67, memorandum on Allied military policy in the Balkans, 6 Apr. 1940.

47. FO 371 24888 R4666/5/67, Chiefs of Staff (hereafter COS) memorandum to the Head of Missions Meeting in London, 9 Apr. 1940.

48. FO 371 24888 R4467/5/67, record of the Meeting of British Head of Missions from South East Europe, 8 Apr. and CAB 99/3 SWC(39/40), 22 Apr. 1940.

49. CAB 99/3 SWC(39/40), 22 Apr. The extent to which the Russians were aware of the plans is clear from

AVP RF, f.059 op.1 p.325 d.2234 l.50–1, Maisky to FM, 20 Apr. 1940.

50. See Chapter 2.

51. FO 371 24847 N5689/40/38, 29475 N/941/29/38 and 24849 N5788/ 93/38, FO minutes, 2, 4, 10 June 1940. See also Churchill, *Second World War*, I, p. 118.

52. J. Wedgwood papers, note by Wedgwood's daughter Helen on a letter from Cripps, 27 Feb. 1942. Churchill, *Second World War*, II, p. 118.

53. AVP RF, f.017a, Maisky's diary, 2 Mar. 1941; see Sargent's minute in FO 371 24844 N5853/30/38, 28 June 1940.

54. Letters by Cripps in Monckton papers, Box 3, pp. 75–7, 115–18, 2 and 25 Sept. 1940, Box 4, p. 68, 13 Feb. 1941, and in Cripps papers, letters to Monckton, 5 and 20 Jan. 1941. On Cripps's mission see H. Hanak, 'Sir Stafford Cripps as British Ambassador in Moscow, June 1941–January 1942', *English Historical Review*, 370 (1979) and 383 (1982).

55. FO 800/322, Cripps to Halifax, 10 Oct. 1940.

56. Monckton papers, Box 3, pp. 75–7, 115–18, 2 and 25 Sept. 1940, Box 4, p. 68, 13 Feb. 1941; Cripps papers, letters to Monckton, 5 and 20 Jan. 1941.

57. Churchill, *Second World War*, IV, p. 56.

58. Monckton papers, Box 3, p. 118, 25 Sept. 1940.

59. FO 371 24841 N5812/5/38, Butler on meeting Maisky and FO minutes on appointment of Cripps, 16 May, and CAB 65/7 127(40)1, 18 May 1940.

60. UD:s Arkiv 1920 ARS, HP/516/ LXVIII, Assarasson to FM, 15 May 1940; on Cripps's abortive efforts see my *Stafford Cripps' Mission to Moscow* (Cambridge, 1984). G. Weinberg in his undeniably impressive and enlightening *A World at Arms: A Global History of World War II* (Cambridge, 1994), pp. 162–4,

suggests that Cripps, who rather naively expected Stalin to align with England, became disillusioned in Moscow. The leading thread of Weinberg's approach is based on his earlier book *Germany and the Soviet Union, 1939–1941* (Leiden, 1954).

61. FO 371 24582 N6029/243/38, memorandum by Sargent, 17 July, minute by Halifax, 18 July. Other typical examples are FO 371 24844, 24846, N2779/40/38 and N5937/ 30/38, FO minutes 8, 11 and 13 Mar., 3 July; 24853 N7279/283/38, memorandum, 24 Nov. 1940; 29135 W53/53/50, 'Weekly Intelligence Summary', 15 Jan.; 29479 N1316 and 1324/78/38, minutes, 3 Apr.; 29481 N2171 and 2466/78/38, minutes 13 and 27 May; WO 208/1761 Joint Intelligence Committee (hereafter JIC) (41)218, 23 May 1941.

2. The Scramble for the Balkans

1. See for instance the position of Turkey, Afghanistan and the Scandinavian countries in AVP RF, f.06 op.2 p.1 d.10 l.46–8 and 54–5, record of Molotov's meetings with Assarasson and with O. Maseng, Norwegian ambassador in Moscow, 25 Mar., f.059 op.1 p.314 d.2160 l.221–3, telegram from Terent'ev to FM, 19 Mar., and f.071 op.22 p.192 d.6 l.59–61, record of Mikhailov's (Soviet ambassador in Afghanistan) meeting with Hans Pilger, the German ambassador there, 21 Mar. 1940. M. Hauner sheds light on the perceptions of the threat in his 'The Soviet Threat to Afghanistan and India, 1938–1940', *Modern Asian Studies*, 15/2 (1981), pp. 287–309.

2. AVP RF, f.06 op.2 p.14 d.155 l.35–43, record of the meeting, 5 Mar. 1940.

3. AVP RF, f.082 op.23 p.95 d.4 l.190–1, a note by Shkvartsev on meeting Weizsäcker, 15 Mar. 1940.

4. Presidential Archives, f.3 op.64 d.668 l.49–56, Tevosian on meeting Göring, 29 Mar. 1940.

5. AVP RF, f.059 op.1 p.315 d.2174 l.156–60, Shkvartsev to Molotov, 6 Mar., and f.06 op.2 p.14 d.155 l.54–9, record of Molotov's meeting with Schulenburg, 11 Mar. 1940.

6. Presidential Archives, f.3 op.64 d.668 l.72–8, record of Mikoyan's meeting with Hilger, 21 Apr. 1940. See the works of G. M. Ivanitsky, 'Sovetsko-germanskie torgovo-ekonomicheskie otnosheniia v 1939–1941 gg.', *Novaia i noveishaia istoriia*, 5 (1989), pp. 28–39, and especially V. Ia. Sipols, 'Torgovo-ekonomicheskie otnosheniia mezhdu SSSR i Germaniei v 1939–1941 gg. v svete novykh arkhivnykh dokumentov', *Novaia i noveishaia istoriia*, 1 (1997), pp. 29–41.

7. Presidential Archives, f.3 op.64 d.668 l.58–64, Mikoyan on meeting Schulenburg, 5 Apr. 1940.

8. Presidential Archives, f.56 op.1 p.298 l.29–32, record of Stalin's meeting with Ritter, 8 Feb., and AVP RF, f.059 op.1 p.315 d.2174 l.153–4, Shkvartsev to FM, 5 Mar. 1940.

9. Presidential Archives, f.03 op.64 d.668 l.68–70, and *DGFP*, IX, pp. 157–8, records of Tevosian's meetings with Ritter, 12 Apr. 1940.

10. *DGFP*, IX, pp. 82–3 and 110–12, Schulenburg to FM and response by Ritter, 6 Apr. 1940.

11. FO 837/1127, Dalton on meeting Maisky, 25 May 1940; see also V. Assarasson, *I skuggan av Stalin* (Stockholm, 1963), pp. 28–9.

12. AVP RF, f.082 op.23 p.95 d.5 l.16–17, Shkvartsev on a breakfast meeting with Schulenburg and Hilger at the German embassy in Moscow, 5 Apr. 1940.

13. AVP RF, f.082 op.23 p.95 d.5 l.6, report by Pavlov, Soviet chargé d'affaires in Berlin, 26 Mar., and UD:s Arkiv 1920 ARS, HP/516/ LXVII, Assarasson to FM, 8 Mar. 1940.

14. AVP RF, f.082 op.23 p.95 d.5 l.41–2, Skavrets to FM on meeting Skirpa, Lithuanian ambassador in Berlin, 19 Apr. 1940.

15. AVP RF, f.059 op.1 p.315 d.2174 l.264–6, Shkvartsev to FM on meeting Ribbentrop, 20 Apr. 1940.

16. See for instance, Archives of the Bulgarian Foreign Ministry (hereafter AMVnR), d.40 p.34 op.1t pop.272 l.82.

17. A discussion of the seizure of the Baltics and the military repercussions is on pp. 119–20.

18. AVP RF, f.06 op.2 p.14 d.155 l.206–8; *DGFP*, IX, p. 154, record of Molotov's meeting with Schulenburg, 17 June 1940.

19. AVP RF, f.082 op.23 p.95 d.5 l.120–1, Tikhomiro to FM, 7 June 1940.

20. AVP RF, f.059 op.1 p.329 d.2266 l.149–50, Gelfand to FM, 25 Feb., and FO 371 24968 R462/9/37, Hoare to FO, 8 Jan. 1940. See also earlier revelations by F. Marzari, 'Prospects for an Italian-led Balkan Bloc of Neutrals', *Historical Journal*, 4 (1970).

21. *DVP, 1939*, XXII, 2, p. 328, Kukolev, Soviet chargé d'affaires in Bucharest, to FM, 22 Nov. 1939, and AVP RF, f.059 op.1 p.329 d.2266 l.5–6 and 53–4, Gelfand to FM, 3 and 18 Jan., and p.330 d.2269 l.1 and 7, Potemkin to Gelfand, 5 and 16 Jan. 1940.

22. See pp. 15–16.

23. See pp. 39–40, 68–71.

24. AVP RF, f.059 op.1 p.329 d.2266 l.196, Gelfand to FM, 11 Mar., p.315 d.2174 l.175–9, Shkvartsev to FM on meeting Ribbentrop, 14 Mar.; op.2 p.14 d.155 l.115–18, and *DGFP*, IX, p. 317, records of Molotov's meeting with Schulenburg, 5 May 1940.

25. AVP RF, f.059 op.1 p.330 d.2267 l.49–54, Gelfand to FM on meeting Ciano, 29 Apr. 1940. See the Bessarabian affair on p. 29f.

26. *DGFP*, IX, pp. 471–3, Ribbentrop to FM, 30 May 1940.

27. AVP RF, f.059 op.1 p.330 d.2269

l.57–8, Molotov to Gelfand, 1 May, and f.06 op.2 p.14 d.155 l.189–94, and *DGFP*, IX, p. 359, records of Molotov's meeting with Schulenburg, 31 May 1940.

28. UD:s Arkiv 1920 ARS, HP/1547/ XXX, Assarasson to FM, 27 May 1940.

29. AVP RF, f.06 op.2 p.14 d.155 l.197–8. See also *DGFP*, IX, p. 512, record of Molotov's meeting with Schulenburg, 3 June 1940.

30. AVP RF, f.077 op.20 p.109 d.3 l.60–2, record of Sharonov's meeting with Csàky, 11 June 1940.

31. AVP RF, f.06 op.2 p.20 d.228 l.1–2, record of Molotov's meeting with Rosso, Italian ambassador in Moscow, 13 June 1940.

32. UD:s Arkiv 1920 ARS, HP/516/ LXVII, Assarasson to FM on conversations with Rosso, 10 June 1940.

33. AVP RF, f.06 op.2 p.20 d.226 l.3–4, Gorelkin, Soviet ambassador in Rome, to FM on meeting Ciano, 22 June 1940.

34. AVP RF, f.059 op.1 p.330 d.2267 l.190–1, Gorelkin to FM on meeting Anfuzo, 18 June 1940.

35. AVP RF, f.059 op.1 p.316 d.2175 l.301–2, Shkvartsev to FM, on meeting Kleist, head of Ribbentrop's bureau, 12 July, and f.0125 op.24 p.118 d.5 l.67, Lavrentev to FM on meeting Gidzhi, Italian ambassador in Bucharest, 22 July 1940.

36. AVP RF, f.06 op.02 p.20 d.226 l.24–6, Gorelkin to FM on meeting Mussolini, 24 July, and d.14 l.140–1, record of Molotov's meeting with Lorenzo, 24 July 1940. G. Petracchi, 'Pinocchio, the Cat, and the Fox: Italy between Germany and the Soviet Union, 1939–1941', in B. Wegner (ed.), *From Peace to War: Germany, Soviet Russia and the World, 1939–1941* (Oxford, 1997), pp. 499–523, gives a lucid view of the negotiations but unjustifiably plays down the significance of the June–December 1940 overtures.

M. Knox, *Mussolini Unleashed, 1939–1941: Politics and Strategy in Fascist Italy's Last War* (Cambridge, 1982), tends to overlook the episode which was a cornerstone in the diplomacy of both countries, even if proved barren in retrospect.

37. See below, p. 29. On the association between the invasion and the rapprochement see M. Toscano, *Designs in Diplomacy* (London, 1970), pp. 164–5.

38. AVP RF, f.3a d.6, Yugoslavia, exchange of notes between the Soviet Union and Yugoslavia on the establishment of diplomatic relations, 24 June 1940. See also N. V. Novikov, *Vospominaniia diplomata: zapiski 1938–1947* (Moscow, 1989), p. 39.

39. *DGFP*, X, pp. 215–16, Herren to FM, 23 July 1940.

40. AVP RF, f.06 op.2 p.20 d.229 l.1–6, record of Molotov's meeting with Rosso, 20 June, and f.059 op.1 p.330 d.2269 l.84–5, Molotov to Gorelkin, 27 June. See also AMVnR, d.40 p.34 o.1t p.272 l.141–2, Tilev, Bulgarian ambassador in London, to FM, 27 June 1940. The Italian text is given in full by Toscano, *Designs in Diplomacy*, pp. 150–8.

41. *DGFP*, X, pp. 416–19, 486–7, 495–6 and 501–2, exchange of telegrams between Mackensen and Ribbentrop, Aug. 1940.

42. AVP RF, f.06 op.2 p.20 d.229 l.9–12, record of Molotov's meeting with Rosso, 25 June 1940.

43. AVP RF, f.059 op.1 p.316 d.2175 l.71–3, Shkvartsev to FM on meeting Weizsäcker and Ribbentrop, 10 May 1940.

44. AVP RF, f.06 op.2 p.14 d.155 l.122–4 and l.170–5, records of Molotov's meetings with Schulenburg, 10 and 17 May 1940.

45. AVP RF, f.082 op.23 p.95 d.5 l.64–8, Shkvartsev to FM on meeting Ribbentrop, 4 May 1940; based also on an unpublished paper on the Russian security services by General Sergei A. Kondrashev.

46. AVP RF, f.0129 op.2 p.23 d.293 l.10–12, record of Umansky's meeting with Welles, 13 May; see also f.059 op.1 p.320 d.2199 l.12–15, Umansky to FM (shown to Stalin), 1 June 1940.

47. *DVP, 1939*, XXII, 2, pp. 132–3, Kukolev, 27 Sept. 1939.

48. AVP RF, f.06 op.2 p.14 d.155 l.10–15, record of Molotov's meeting with Schulenburg, 25 Jan. 1940.

49. *DVP, 1939*, XXII, 2, pp. 224–6, Terentiev to FM, 26 Oct. 1939.

50. *Ibid.*, pp. 235–8, Terentiev to FM, 27 Oct. 1939.

51. *Ibid.*, pp. 347–9, Maisky to FM, 29 Nov. 1939.

52. FO 371 24968 R9/9/37, Halifax to Hoare (Bucharest) on Cadogan's meeting with Tilea, Rumanian ambassador in London, 9 Jan. 1940.

53. *DVP, 1939*, XXII, 2, pp. 396–8, Kukolev to Molotov, 11 Dec. 1939.

54. FO 371 24890 R6246/5/67, Halifax to Hoare on conversations with Tilea, 22 May 1940; and further proposals in AVP RF, f.06 op.2 p.1 d.10 l.82–3, Molotov on meeting Davidescu, Rumanian ambassador in Moscow, 2 Apr. 1940.

55. FO 371 24887 R3236 and R3531/5/67, Hoare to FO, 8 Mar. 1940.

56. FO 371 24968 R6751/9/37, Halifax to Cripps, 26 June, and R5673/9/37, Hoare to FM, 24 Apr. 1940.

57. Novikov, *Vospominaniia diplomata*, p. 43.

58. AMVnR, d.40 p.34 op.1t pop.272 l.147, Tilev to FM, 4 July 1940; see also *DGFP*, X, p. 26, Schulenburg to FM, 26 June 1940.

59. AVP RF, f.0125 op.24 p.118 d.3 l.24–7, record of Molotov's meeting with Davidescu, 9 Apr.; and FO 371 24968 R4887/9/37, Ankara chancellery to Southern Department of FO, 13 Apr. 1940.

60. AVP RF, f.082 op.23 p.95 d.5 l.106–7, Shkvartsev to FM, 28 May 1940. On Italy see p. 29.

61. AVP RF, f.059 op.1 p.318 d.2191 l.104–7, Kukolev to Dekanozov,

24 May, and Novikov, *Vospominaniia diplomata*, p. 45. See also similar impressions gained by Schulenburg and Köstring in *DGFP*, IX, pp. 396–7, 21 May, and of Campbell in Belgrade, in FO 371 24889 R5894/5/7, 8 May. See also UD:s Arkiv 1920 ARS, HP/1548/XXXIII, Assarasson to FM, 14 June 1940.

62. GRU GSh RF, op.918 d.4 l.119–20, report by the 5th Dept of the RKKA, 23 June 1940.

63. AVP RF, f.06 op.2 p.14 d.155 l.181–4 and f.059 op.1 p.319 d.2194 l.86, telegram from Molotov to Lavrentev, 23 June 1940. See also *DGFP*, IX, pp. 412–14, record of Molotov's meeting with Schulenburg, 25 May 1940.

64. Presidential Archives, f.3 op.64 d.674 l.128, record of Osetrov's (Ministry of Defence) meeting with the German military attaché, General Ernst Köstring, 21 June 1940.

65. AVP RF, f.06 op.2 p.14 d.155 l.209–15, and *DGFP*, X, pp. 3–4, record of Molotov's meeting with Schulenburg, 23 June 1940.

66. UD:s Arkiv 1920 ARS, HP/516/LXVII, report by Assarasson to the FM on a meeting with Schulenburg, 28 June 1940.

67. *DGFP*, X, pp. 7–9 and 12–13, instructions to Moscow and Bucharest by Weizsäcker, 24 June 1940.

68. An excellent description is in Novikov, *Vospominaniia diplomata*, p. 41.

69. *DGFP*, X, pp. 19–20, Fabricius to FM, 26 June 1940.

70. AVP RF, f.059 op.1 p.319 d.2194 l.89–90, Molotov to Lavrentev on meeting Davidescu, 27 June 1940.

71. *DGFP*, X, p. 32, Schulenburg to FM, 27 June 1940.

72. *Ibid.*, pp. 34–5, Ribbentrop to Fabricius, 27 June 1940.

73. AVP RF, f.059 op.1 p.318 d.2191 l.159, Lavrentev to FM, 28 June 1940.

74. FO 371 24968 R6648/9/37, various

telegrams and minutes related to
the annexation of Bessarabia, 1 July
1940.

75. AVP RF, f.059 op.1 p.319 d.2194
l.91–2, Molotov to Levrentev on
meeting Davidescu, 28 June 1940.

76. *DGFP*, X, pp. 33–4, German minister in Bucharest to FM, 27 June
1940.

77. See for instance V. K. Volkov,
'Sovetsko-iugoslavskie otnosheniia
v nachal'nyi period vtoroi mirovoi
voiny v kontekste mirovykh sobytii
(1939–1941 gg.)', *Sovetskoe slavianovedenie*, 6 (1990).

78. Churchill, *Second World War*, I, p.
403, radio speech, 1 Oct 1941.

79. *DVP, 1939*, XXII, 2, pp. 167–9,
Maisky to FM, 7 Oct. 1939.

80. Webb papers, diary, pp. 6880–8, 20
May 1940.

81. AVP RF, f.069 op.24 p.70 d.43 l.6–10
and 19–23, and FO 371 24840
N4625/5/38 WP(40)106, records
of Halifax's meeting with Maisky,
15 and 29 Apr.; and AVP RF, f.059
op.1 p.326 d.2238 l.101–3, Molotov
to Maisky, 21 May 1940.

82. AVP RF, f.059 op.1 p.325 d.2235
l.28–33 and 55–8, Maisky to FM, 22
and 28 June 1940.

83. *Komintern i vtoraia mirovaia voina*,
I, p. 343, Dimitrov to Stalin and
Molotov, 22 May 1940.

84. FSB, *Organy Gosudarstvennoi
Bezopasnosti SSSR v Velikoi Otechestvennoi Voine. Stornik dokumentov*,
2 vols (Moscow, 1995), I(1), pp.
187–9, a memorandum by Osokin,
head of the Border NKVD, and
Savchenko, head of the 5th Dept of
the NKVD, 16 May 1940.

85. AVP RF, f.082 op.23 p.95 d.5 l.64–8,
Shkvartsev on meeting Gerde, 4
May 1940.

86. FO 371 24841 N5812/5/38, and
24849 N5729/93/38, reports by
Butler on meeting Maisky, and FO
minutes, 16 and 29 May 1940; and
FO 837/1127, Dalton on meeting
Maisky, 25 May 1940.

87. FO 371 24877 R6099/7/4, Rendell
to FO, 7 May 1940.

88. FO 371 24890 R6597/5/67, Campbell to FO, 18 June 1940.

89. UD:s Arkiv 1920 ARS, HP/1548/
XXXIII, Assarasson to FM, 14 June
1940.

90. FO 371 24841 N5840/5/38, Cripps
on meeting Molotov, 14 June 1940.

91. AVP RF, f.06 op.2 p.26 d.339 l.7–11,
14 June, and p.20 d.229 l.1–6,
records of Molotov's meetings with
Labonne and Rosso, 14 and 20 June
1940 respectively.

92. Public Record Office, Prime Minister's Papers (hereafter PREM) 3,
395/1, pp. 16–17, Churchill to
Cripps, 22 June 1940.

93. AVP RF, f.06 op.2 p.10 d.100
l.4–7, record of Molotov's meeting
with Cripps, 26 June 1940; see pp.
23–9.

94. FO 800/322 pp. 353–60, Cripps to
Halifax, 10 Oct. 1940.

95. CAB 79/6 COS(40)256(3) and CAB
80/16 COS (40)649, 9 and 28 Aug.;
FO 371 24852 N6458/283/38,
Cripps to Halifax and minutes by
Sargent, 31 Aug. 1940.

96. Significantly this proposal is
missing in the Russian record of
the conversation, as well as in the
leakage to the Germans; see FO
371 24844 N5937/30/38; Russian
version in *Diplomaticheskii vestnik*,
21–3 (1993), record of Cripps's
meeting with Stalin, 1 July 1940.

97. AMVnR, d.40 p.34 op.1t pop.272
l.151, Stamenov, Bulgarian ambassador in Moscow, to FM, 14 July
1940.

98. For a discussion on Soviet intelligence, see below, pp. 52–6. Presidential Archives, f.45 op.1 d.435
l.39–51, Proskurov to Stalin, 4 June,
and AVP RF, f.082 op.23 p.95 d.5
l.112–14, record by Shkvartsev on
meeting Ritter, 1 June 1940.

99. On the decision see pp. 48–52.

100. Archives of the Russian Security
Services – counter-intelligence
(hereafter TsA SVR RF), d.21616 t.1
l.14–15, memo by Fitin, deputy
director of the NKVD, 5th Dept,
and GRU GSh RF, op.22424 d.4

l.261, 'Meteor', Berlin, to the NKVD, 9 July; see also TsA SVR RF d.21616 t.1 l.21–2, deputy director of the Border NKVD to the Centre, 13 July 1941.

101. GRU GSh RF, op.918 d.3 l.159–63, special report by the 5th Dept of the RKKA, 13 June 1940. On the tendency to suppress the threat see FSB, *Organy Gosudarstvennoi Bezopasnosti SSSR*, I(1), pp. 236–7, Savchenko, deputy director Border NKVD to the Centre, 26 June 1940.

102. G. Gorodetsky, 'Filip Ivanovich Golikov', in H. Shukman (ed.), *Stalin's Generals* (London, 1993), pp. 77–90.

103. Central Archives of the Security Services (hereafter TsA FSB RF), f.3 op.7 pop.23 l.223–5, Golikov to Timoshenko, 20 July 1940.

104. Central Archives of the Security Services' Foreign Intelligence (hereafter TsA SVR RF), d. 21616 t.1 l.23–5 and 89–90, Beria to Stalin and Molotov, 17 Aug. See also the Directorate of Ukrainian Frontier Guard, NKVD, 5 Aug. 1940, reproduced in *Izvestiia TsK KPSS*, 4 (1990), pp. 199–201.

105. AVP RF, f.06 op.2 p.2 d.12 l.173–4, record of Molotov's meeting with Le Rougetel, 31 May 1940.

106. *DGFP*, IX, pp. 470–1, Schulenburg to FM, 29 May 1940.

107. *DGFP*, X, pp. 79–85, record of a meeting between Hitler, Alfieri and Keitel, 1 July 1940. On Hitler's decision to attack Russia see pp. 48–52.

108. M. van Creveld, *The Balkan Clue: Hitler's Strategy, 1940–1941* (Cambridge, 1973), p. 70.

109. UD:s Arkiv 1920 ARS, HP/516/ LXVII and LXVIII, Assarasson to FM, 20 June and 10 July 1940.

110. AVP RF, f.06 op.2 p.2 d.14 l.95–106, Molotov on meeting Togo, 2 July; see also *DGFP*, X, pp. 136–7, record of a meeting between Ribbentrop and Sato, 9 July 1940. On relations with Russia see chap. 9.

111. *DGFP*, X, pp. 195–6, Schulenburg to FM, 11 July, AVP RF, f.059 op.1 p.317 d.2180 l.140–1, Molotov to Shkvartsev on meeting Schulenburg, 13 July, and f.082 op.23 p.95 d.5 l.139–41, Kobulov to FM, 6 July 1940. On the alternative of the Continental bloc see G. T. Waddington, 'Ribbentrop and the Soviet Union 1937–1941', in J. Erickson and D. Dilks (eds), *Barbarossa: The Axis and the Allies* (Edinburgh, 1994).

112. *DGFP*, X, pp. 207–8, Schulenburg to FM, 13 July; see also HP/516/ LXVIII, Assarasson to Schulenburg, 5 Aug. 1940.

113. B. A. Leach, *German Strategy against Russia, 1939–1941* (Oxford, 1973), pp. 60–1 and 70–1.

114. AVP RF, f.059 op.1 p.339 d.2267 l.211a–216, Gorelkin to Molotov on meeting Ciano, 26 June. *DGFP*, X, pp. 18–19, Mackensen to FM, 26 June 1940.

115. *DGFP*, X, pp. 217–21 and 226 f., Hitler's directive and letter to King Carol, 15 and 16 July 1940.

116. AMVnR, d.40 p.34 op.1t pop.272 l.127, Christov to FM, 5 June, and AVP RF, f.059 op.1 p.314 d.2161 l.290–4, Terentiev to FM on meeting Kirov, Bulgarian ambassador in Ankara, 20 June; see also a detailed analysis in Swedish Military Archives (hereafter Krigsarkivet), Fo..rsvarsstaben, Ser. E/II/15/1, report no. 54 by the military attaché on conversations with the Bulgarian military attaché, 1 Nov. 1940.

117. AVP RF, f.059 op.1 p.316 d.2175 l.275–7, Shkvartsev to FM, 8 July 1940.

118. AMVnR, d.40 p.34 op.1t pop.272, and op.1sh pop.272 l.181–3, Stamenov to FM, 7 and 9 Sept. 1940.

119. TsA SVR RF, d.21616 t.1 l.14–15, Savchenko, the deputy director of the Border NKVD, to the GRU, 12 July; GRU GSh RF, op.817 d.4 l.119–20, report of the 5th Dept of the RKKA, 9 Aug. 1940.

120. FSB, *Organy Gosudarstvennoi*

Bezopasnosti SSSR, I(1), pp. 245–6, head of the Foreign Intelligence of the border NKVD to the Centre, 24 Aug. 1940.

121. Bulgarian Central National Archives (hereafter TsDA MVR), f.176 op.8 a.e.906 l.143–5, Antonov (Stockholm) to FM, 14 Sept. 1940.

122. AMVnR, d.40 p.34 op.1t pop.272 l.152, Stamenov to FM, 16 July 1940; *DGFP*, X, p. 77, Ribbentrop to Fabricius, 1 July 1940.

123. See the most authoritative book by M. L. Miller, *Bulgaria during the Second World War* (Stanford, 1975), pp. 13–15 and 24–6, and see also D. Sirkov, *V'nshnata politika na B'lgariia, 1938–1941* (Sofia, 1979). It is attested in *DVP, 1939*, XXII, 2, pp. 263–70, Terentiev to Molotov, 6 Nov. 1939.

124. AMVnR, d.40 pop.142 l.50–3, Antonov, Bulgarian ambassador in Moscow, to FM, 20 Sept. 1939.

125. *DVP, 1939*, XXII, 2, pp. 412–13, Dekanozov on meeting Antonov, 15 Dec. A highly informative account of the events is in UD:s Arkiv 1920 ARS, HP/516/LXVII, Assarasson to FM, 2 Mar. 1940.

126. AVP RF, f.074 op.25 p.109 d.22 l.1–4, Lavrentev to Dekanozov, 3 Jan. 1940.

127. AMVnR, d.40 p.34 op.1t pop.272 l.48 and d.40 p.34 op.1t pop.272 l.56–64, Christov to FM, 21 Feb. 1940. Miller, *Bulgaria during the Second World War*, pp. 21–3.

128. *DGFP*, X, pp. 54–5, Richthofen to FM, 29 June 1940. On the Italian episode see above, p. 23.

129. AMVnR, d.40 p.34 op.1t pop.272 l.122–3, Christov to FM, 7 June 1940.

130. *DGFP*, X, pp. 37–8 and 47, memorandum by Wortman on meetings with Draganov on 26 and 27 June 1940. On the Soviet expectations see UD:s Arkiv 1920 ARS, HP/516/LXVIII, Assarasson to FM, 26 June 1940.

131. *DGFP*, X, pp. 332–41, record of a meeting between Filov and Hitler and Ribbentrop, 27 July 1940.

132. *Izvestiia*, 2 Aug. See evaluations by Stamenov in AMVnR, d.40 p.34 op.1t pop.272 l.156–7, 2 and 3 Aug., and FO 371 24845 N6243/30/38, Cripps to Halifax, 2 Aug. 1940.

133. AVP RF, f.06 op.2 p.2 d.14 l.154–6, and *DGFP*, X, pp. 349 and 367, records of Molotov's meetings with Schulenburg, 29 and 31 July 1940.

134. *Vedomosti Verkhovnogo Soveta SSSR* (Moscow, 1940), No. 31, and AVP RF, f.059 op.1 p.336 d.2271 l.262, Lavrishchev to FM, 2 Aug. 1940.

135. AVP RF, f.074 op.25 p.108 d.6 l.22–3, record of Lavrishchev's meeting with Popov, 15 Aug. 1940.

136. FO 371 24877 R788/259/7, 26 Aug. 1940.

137. *DGFP*, XI, pp. 8–10, Ribbentrop to Schulenburg, 3 Sept. 1940.

138. AVP RF, f.059 op.1 p.316 d.2176 l.185–7, Shkvartsev to Molotov, 2 Sept., and *DGFP*, XI, pp. 8–10 and 44–6, exchange between Schulenburg and Ribbentrop, 2 and 3 Sept. 1940.

139. *DGFP*, XI, pp. 22–5 and 28, 29–30, exchanges between Ribbentrop and Fabricius, 5 and 6 Sept. 1940; see also Miller, *Bulgaria during the Second World War*, pp. 29–30.

140. AMVnR, d.40 p.34 op.1sh pop.272 l.177–9, Stamenov to FM on meeting Dekanozov, 13 Sept. 1940.

141. See a tremendous insight in G. Gafencu, *Prelude to the Russian Campaign* (London, 1945), pp. 66–8, and his *Misiune la Moscova, 1940–41: Culegere de dokumente* (Bucharest, 1995), pp. 67–8, Gafencu to the FM, tel. 2305, 16 Sept., and AVP RF, f.0144 op.20 p.105 d.3 l.11–12, record of Vyshinsky's meeting with Gavrilović, 5 Nov. 1940.

142. Gafencu, *Prelude to the Russian Campaign*, pp. 67–8. *DGFP*, XI, pp. 73–4, Schulenburg to FM, 14 Sept. 1940.

143. FO 371 25229 W8797/183/96 and W6469/183/96, Campbell to FO, 8 and 16 June 1940.

144. AVP RF, f.0125 op.24 p.118 d.5 l.41–5, record of Lavrentev's meeting with Tanriover, Turkish

ambassador, 12 July, and FSB, *Organy Gosudarstvennoi Bezopasnosti SSSR*, I(1), pp. 223–4, memorandum by Savchenko, deputy director, Border NKVD, 12 July 1940.

145. *DGFP*, XI, pp. 30–2, Ribbentrop to Schulenburg, 6 Sept., and Gafencu, *Misiune la Moscova*, pp. 64–7, tel. 2302, Gafencu to FM, 16 Sept. 1940.

146. AVP RF, f.082 op.23 p.95 d.6 l.65–7, and f.059 op.1 p.316 d.2176 l.232–3, p.317 d.2181 l.92–3 and 124, AVP RF f.059 op.1 p.317 d.2181 l.92–3 and 124, exchanges between Molotov and Shkvartsev, 6, 9, 12 and 16 Sept.; see also *DGFP*, XI, pp. 64–5, Schulenburg to FM, 12 Sept. 1940.

147. AVP RF, f.0125 op.24 p.118 d.5 l.76–9, record of Lavrentev's meeting with Hankey, 29 July 1940.

148. *Izvestiia*, 13 Sept.; see also Cripps's evaluation in FO 371 25230 W10404/215/96. On the relevance of the shooting incidents see Gafencu's views in UD:s Arkiv 1920 ARS, HP/516/LXVIII, Assarasson to FM, 13 Sept., and AMVnR, d.40 p.34 op.1sh pop.272 l.185, Stamenov to FM, 14 Sept. 1940.

149. See AVP RF, f.059 op.1 p.331 d.2275 l.47–8, Vyshinsky to Lavrishchev, 18 Sept., and Gafencu, *Misiune la Moscova*, tel. 2309, pp. 68–9, Gafencu to the FM, 17 Sept. 1940.

150. *DGFP*, XI, pp. 287–8, memorandum by the director of the Economic Policy Department, 11 Oct., and FO 371 25231 W10814 and W10543/215/96, Cripps and Campbell to FO, 19 and 27 Sept. 1940 respectively.

151. *DGFP*, XI, pp. 287–8, memorandum by the director of the Economic Policy Department, 11 Oct., and FO 371 25229 W10967/183/96, Campbell to FO, 8 Oct. 1940.

152. AVP RF, f.06 op.2 p.15 d.157 l.47–51, record of Molotov's meeting with Schulenburg, 17 Oct. 1940.

153. Novikov, *Vospominaniia diplomata*, pp. 52–67, and AVP RF, f.059 op.1 p.319 d.2193l.22, telegram from

Lavrentev to FM, 1 Nov. See also Gafencu, *Misiune la Moscova*, p. 100, tel. 2791, 1 Nov., and FO 371 25231 W11435/215/96, Cripps to FO, 2 Nov. 1940.

154. Gafencu, *Misiune la Moscova*, tel. 3042, pp. 102–3, Gafencu to FM, 13 Nov. 1940, and UD:s Arkiv 1920 ARS, HP/517/LXIX, Assarasson to FM on conversations with Gafencu, 13 Jan. 1941.

155. *DGFP*, XI, pp. 424–5, 458–9 and 461, Fabricius to FM on meetings with Sobolev, 29 Oct. and 3 Nov. 1940. See similar impressions gained by the Soviet ambassador in Bucharest, AVP RF, f.059 op.1 p.319 d.2193l.22, Lavrentev to FM, 1 Nov. 1940.

3. On a Collision Course

1. Quoted in T. Higgins, *Hitler and Russia: The Third Reich in a Two-Front War, 1937–1943* (New York, 1966), Introduction.

2. R. Cecil, *Hitler's Decision to Invade Russia, 1941* (London, 1975), p. 167.

3. J. Förster, 'Barbarossa Revisited: Strategy and Ideology in the East', *Jewish Social Studies*, 50/1–2 (1992), and W. Murray, 'Barbarossa', *Quarterly Journal of Military History*, 4/3 (1992), pp. 8–17.

4. G. R. Ueberschaer, 'Hitlers Entschluss zum "Lebensraum"-Krieg im Osten. Programmatisches Ziel oder militärisches Kalkül?', *UB*, pp. 94–5, and B. R. Kroener, 'Der "erfrorene Blitzkrieg". Strategische Planungen der deutschen Führung gegen die Sowjetunion und die Ursachen ihres Scheiterns', in B. Wegner (ed.), *Zwei Wege nach Moskau vom Hitler-Stalin-Pakt bis zum 'Unternehmen Barbarossa'* (Munich, 1991), pp. 137–8.

5. F. Halder, *Kriegstagebuch* (Stuttgart, 1963), II, pp. 46–50; see also Ueberschaer, 'Hitlers Entschluss', p. 102, and E. Klink, 'Die militärische Konzeption des Krieges gegen die Sowjetunion', *DRuZW*, p. 216.

6. *DGFP*, X, pp. 79–85, record of a meeting between Hitler, Alfieri and Keitel, 1 July 1940.
7. See p. 37.
8. *DGFP*, X, pp. 147–5, record of a meeting between Hitler, Ribbentrop and Ciano, 8 July 1940.
9. Kroener, 'Der "erfrorene Blitzkrieg"', p. 138.
10. *DGFP*, X, p. 263, Wörmann to the embassies in Ankara and Moscow, 22 July 1940.
11. General Armand de Caulaincourt, *With Napoleon in Russia* (New York, 1935), p. 23.
12. J. Tauber, 'Die Planung des "Unternehmen Barbarossa". Bemerkungen zum Forschungsstand', in H. H. Nolte (ed.), *'Der Mensch gegen den Menschen': Überlegungen und Forschungen zum deutschen Überfall auf die Sowjetunion 1941* (Hanover, 1992), pp. 160–91. Halder, *Kriegstagebuch*, II, pp. 49–50.
13. On this point see J. Förster, 'Das Unternehmen "Barbarossa" als Eroberungs und Vernichtungskrieg', *DRuZW*, p. 415.
14. R. D. Müller, 'Das "Unternehmen Barbarossa" als wirtschaftlicher Raubkrieg', *UB*, p. 177, and *Der Prozess gegen die Hauptkriegsverbrecher vor dem Internationalen Militärgerichtshoe* (Nuremberg, 1947), VII, pp. 278–80, and X, p. 589; see also Klink, 'Die militärische Konzeption', p. 214.
15. J. Förster, 'Hitlers Entscheidung für den Krieg gegen die Sowjetunion', *DRuZW*, pp. 14–16. Förster in most of his work on the subject and W. Deist, 'Die militärische Planung des "Unternehmens Barbarossa"', *UB*, pp. 110–11, present the decision as a symbiosis of power-oriented policies and ideology. In the final judgment they may well be right but while the pragmatic considerations are easily detected the ideological ones remain very much a matter of assumption.
16. J. Förster, 'Hitler Turns East – German War Policy in 1940 and 1941', in Wegner (ed.), *From Peace to War*, pp. 117–21.
17. Ueberschaer, 'Hitlers Entschluss', p. 98.
18. On the Continental bloc see pp. 48–9.
19. Deist, 'Die militärische Planung', p. 113.
20. Ueberschaer, 'Hitlers Entschluss', p. 102: Paulus's account is in *Der Prozess gegen die Hauptkriegsverbrecher*, VII, pp. 284–6.
21. *DGFP*, X, pp. 549–50, excerpts from the War Diary of the Wehrmacht Operations Staff, 26 Aug. 1940.
22. *DGFP*, XI, pp. 144–6, High Command of the Wehrmacht to FM, 20 Sept. 1940.
23. *Der Prozess gegen die Hauptkriegsverbrecher*, VII, pp. 284–6 and 324–5; see also Cecil, *Hitler's Decision to Invade Russia*, p. 111.
24. W. Hubatsch (ed.), *Hitlers Weisungen für die Kriegsführung, 1939–1945* (Munich, 1965), pp. 77–85. See also the comments of Professor Hans-Adolf Jacobsen, the editor of Halder's diary in *Kriegstagebuch*, p. 165.
25. Hitler's Directive No. 18, 12 Nov. 1940 in *DGFP*, XI, pp. 527–8.
26. Halder, *Kriegstagebuch*, pp. 129–30 and 147–8, 8 and 23 Oct. 1940.
27. M. Milstein, 'According to Intelligence Reports . . .', *New Times*, 26 (1990).
28. On this see C. Andrew and O. Gordievsky, *KGB: The Inside Story* (London, 1991), pp. 253–4, and V. Berezhkov, *History in the Making* (Moscow, 1983), pp. 100–3.
29. Both are mentioned by their code names throughout the book.
30. FSB, *Organy Gosudarstvennoi Bezopasnosti SSSR*, I(2), pp. ii and 73, and FSB, *Sekrety Gitlera, ha stole u Stalina: razvedka i kontrrazvedka o podgotovke germanskoi agressii protiv SSSR, mart-iiun' 1941 g.* (Moscow, 1995), p. 218. See also unpublished article by L. Bezymensky on 'The Soviet Security Forces and the German Attack on Russia'.

31. F. I. Chuev, *Sto sorok besed s Molotovym: iz dnevnika F. Chueva* (Moscow, 1991), pp. 31–2.
32. F. I. Golikov, *Krasnye orly (Iz dnevnikov 1918–1920 gg.)* (Moscow, 1959).
33. 'Marshal Sovetskogo Soiuza F. I. Golikov (K 80-letiiu so dnia rozhdeniia)', *VIZh*, 7 (1980), pp. 86–8. I am grateful for an informative interview with the late General Milstein, who was Golikov's deputy in the GRU.
34. Dimitrov's diary, 20 Feb. 1941.
35. *Ibid.*, 21 Jan. 1941.
36. Attested by V. A. Novobranets, who was the head of the Information Department of the RKKA, in *Znamia*, 6 (1990), and Zhukov, 'Iz neopublikovannykh vospominanii', *Kommunist*, 14 (1988), p. 98.
37. Volkogonov papers, Archival material from the GRU prepared for the TsK. The unprecedented Russian release of material prepared by Khrushchev but never released before is in O. Gorchakov, 'Nakanune, ili tragediia Kassandry: povest' v dokumentakh', *Nedelia*, 42–4 (1988).
38. See for instance GRU to Foreign Intelligence, 29 Mar. 1941, reproduced in *Izvestiia TsK KPSS*, 4 (1990), p. 208.
39. AVP RF, f.059 op.1 p.328 d.2253 l.100–1, 144, 153, 163, 173 and 267–9, Ivanov to FM, 14 and 26 Sept., 7, 10 and 11 Oct. and 9 Nov. 1940.
40. P. Sudoplatov, *Special Tasks: The Memoirs of an Unwanted Witness – a Soviet Spymaster* (London, 1994), pp. 116–17.
41. GRU GSh RF, f.37967 op.6 d.2551 l.156; special intelligence review by the director of the Western Front Intelligence to Golikov, 19 Sept. 1940.
42. TSa SVR RF, d.21616 t.1 l.174–5, deputy director of the Ukrainian NKGB to Golikov, 26 Sept. 1940.
43. FSB, *Organy Gosudarstvennoi Bezopasnosti SSSR*, I(1), pp. 278–9; also AVP RF, op.23 n.104 d.57 l.202–3, Tikhomirov to FM, and TsA SVR RF, d.21616 t.1 l.353–6, NKVD Memorandum on German War Preparations, 5 Nov. 1940.
44. *Izvestiia TsK KPSS*, 4 (1990), pp. 203–5, report by the 5th Dept of the NKVD on German intentions, 6 Nov. 1940.
45. AVP RF, f.082 op.23 p.104 d.57 l.202–3, Tikhomirov, first secretary of the Berlin embassy, on 'The situation in Germany after a year of war', 4 Nov. 1940.
46. GRU GSh RF, op.918 d.6 l.20–2, special report by Golikov, No. 252610, 9 Nov. 1940.
47. GRU GSh RF, op.22424 d.4 l.402–4, 29 Sept. 1940.
48. TsA SVR RF, d.21606 t.1 l.301–3, Beria to Stalin, 24 Oct. 1940.
49. Gafencu, *Misiune la Moscova*, raport 2384, pp. 69–78, Gafencu to Sturdza, 21 Sept. 1940. The only work focusing on the significance of the Turkish straits is T. V. Lavrova, *Chernomorskie prolivy* (Rostov, 1997).
50. COS(40)853 in FO 371 24892 R8227/5/67, 21 Oct. 1940.
51. Attested by Chuev, *Sto sorole besed s Molotovym*.
52. See a revealing talk between Vyshinsky and Cripps in FO 371 24848 N7173/40/38, Cripps on meeting Vyshinsky, 11 Nov. 1940, and Chuev, *Sto sorok besed s Molotovym*, pp. 101–3.
53. See pp. 63–6.
54. AVP RF, f.059 op.1 p.326 d.2239 l.50–2, Molotov to Maisky, 6 Oct., and AMVnR, d.40 p.34 op.1sh pop.272 l.213–14, Stamenov to FM, 7 Oct. 1940.
55. AVP RF, f.06 op.2 p.15 d.157 l.67–8, Maisky to FM, 3 Nov.; see also a discussion of the appreciation of England's resilience, pp. 59, 89–90.
56. Presidential Archive, copy of the handwritten notes by Molotov, 9 Nov.; AVP RF, f.059 op.1 p.338 d.2314 l.2, Stalin to Molotov, 11 Nov. 1940.

57. AVP RF, f.084 op.22 p.132 d.5 l.18–25, Dekanozov to FM, on meeting the Greek ambassador in Germany, 14 Jan. 1941.
58. CAB 65/10 288(40)3, 13 Nov.; AVP RF, f.059 op.1 p.325 d.2237 l.117–19, Maisky to FM, 15 Nov. 1940.
59. Quai d'Orsay Archives, 834/Z/312/1, pp. 29–31, a memorandum by Nemanov on meeting Bogomolov, 4 Dec. 1940.
60. Gorodetsky, *Cripps' Mission to Moscow*, pp. 24–31. FO 371 24841 N5808/30/38 and N5840/5/38, telegrams from Cripps, 14 and 17 June; Cripps papers, letter to daughter Diane, 18 Sept. 1940.
61. Cripps papers, letter to Knatchbull-Hugessen, British ambassador in Ankara, 23 Oct. 1940.
62. AVP RF, f.059 op.1 p.328 d.2253 l.153, Ivanov (Paris) to FM, 7 Oct., and op.1 p.319 d.2192 l.240–1, Lavrentev to FM on meeting Tanrioera, Turkish minister in Bucharest, 10 Oct. 1940. See also a round table reproduced in 'Mezhdunarodnye otnosheniia i strany tsentral'noi i Iugo-Vostochnoi evropy v nachale vtoroi mirovoi voiny: sentiabr' 1939-avgust 1940 gg.', *Sovetskoe slavianovedenie*, 1 (1991), pp. 3–27.
63. AVP RF, f.059 op.1 p.314 d.2162 l.47–50, Terentiev to FM, 6 July; see also diplomatic efforts in this vein in f.0125 op.24 p.118 d.5 l.63–6, record of Lavrentev's meeting with Tanrier, 19 July 1940.
64. Assarasson, *I skuggan av Stalin*, pp. 37–8.
65. AVP RF, f.06 op.2 p.2 d.15 l.34–7, and f.059 op.1 p.315 d.2165 l.13–18, records of Molotov's meetings with Aktay, 9 and 13 Aug. 1940.
66. AVP RF, f.059 op.1 p.314 d.2162 l.169–71, telegram from Vinogradov to Molotov on meeting Saracoglu, 4 Sept. 1940.
67. AVP RF, f.0125 op.24 p.118 d.5 l.131–8, record of Lavrentev's meeting with Fabricius, 13 Sept. 1940.
68. S. Wegner-Korfes, 'Ambassador Count Schulenburg and the Preparations for "Barbarossa"', in Wegner (ed.), *From Peace to War*, p. 118.
69. AMVnR, d.40 p.34 op.1sh pop.272 l.207–8, Stamenov to FM, 20 Oct., and TsDA MVR, f.316 op.1 ae.273 l.77, Popov to Draganov, 17 and 21 Oct. UD:s Arkiv 1920 ARS, HP/517/LXIX, and HP/516/LXVIII, Assarasson to FM, 10 July and 21 Oct. 1940.
70. FO 371 25015 R7626 and 8117/242/37, Cripps to FO, 30 Oct. 1940.
71. AVP RF, f.059 op.1 p.314 d.2163 l.126–8, Vinogradov to FM, 21 Nov. 1940.
72. AVP RF, f.059 op.1 p.315 d.2165 l.70–2, Vyshinsky to Vinogradov on meeting Aktay, 4 Nov. 1940.
73. AVP RF, f.059 op.1 p.315 d.2165 l.73–4, 75–6, Vyshinsky to Vinogradov, 4 Nov. 1940.
74. *DGFP*, XI, pp. 482–3, Papen on meeting Gerde in Berlin, 6 Nov. 1940.
75. AVP RF, f.0132 op.23 p.232 d.6 l.74–7, record of Vinogradov's meeting with Aktay, 25 Sept., and f.059 op.1 p.314 d.2163 l.51–4 and p.315 d.2165 l.62–3, exchange of telegrams between Molotov and Vinogradov, 12 and 15 Oct.; see also UD:s Arkiv 1920 ARS, HP/516/LXVIII, Assarasson to FM, 17 Oct. 1940.
76. FSB, *Organy Gosudarstvennoi Bezopasnosti SSSR*, I(1), pp. 270–8, memorandum by Beria on the situation in Turkey, 5 Nov. 1940.
77. AVP RF, f.059 op.1 p.318 d.2189 l.200–2, Sharonov to Molotov on meeting Csàky, 28 Oct. 1940.
78. AMVnR, d.40 p.34 op.1t pop.272 l.157, Stamenov to FM, 3 Aug. 1940.
79. *DGFP*, X, pp. 410–11, Richthofen to FM, 4 Aug. 1940.
80. TsDA MVR, f.316 op. 1 ae.273 l.149–50, Draganov to FM on meeting Ribbentrop, 9 Sept. 1940.
81. AVP RF, f.074 op.1 p.331 d.2272 l.17–18, Lavrishchev to Molotov on meeting Popov, 26 Aug. 1940.
82. *DGFP*, XI, pp. 29–30, Ribbentrop to Bucharest legation, 5 Sept. 1940.

83. AVP RF, f.o6 op.2 p.3 d.16 l.34, and AMVnR, d.40 p.34 op.1sh pop.272 l.174, Stamenov to FM on meeting Molotov, 10 Sept. 1940.

84. AMVnR, d.40 p.34 op.1sh pop.272 l.213–14 and 207–12, Stamenov to FM, 7 and 20 Oct., and TsDA MVR, f.316 op.1 ae.273 l.77, Popov to Draganov, 17 Oct. 1940.

85. *DGFP*, XI, pp. 364–6, King Boris to Hitler, 22 Oct.; TsDA MVR, f.316 op. 1 ae.273 l.71, Popov to Draganov, 20 Oct. 1940.

86. On this see pp. 83–6.

87. TsDA MVR, f.316 op.1 ae.273 l.47–8, Draganov to Popov, 20 Oct. 1940.

88. *Ibid.*, l.65, Popov to Draganov, 30 Oct. 1940.

89. *Ibid.*, l.38, Draganov to FM, 31 Oct., and AMVnR, d.40 p.34 op.1sh pop.272 l.217, Stamenov to FM, 30 Oct. 1940.

90. AMVnR, d.40 p.34 op.1sh pop.272 l.217 and 222, Stamenov to FM, 30 Oct. and 5 Nov. 1940.

91. *DGFP*, XI, pp. 479–80, Ritter to Bucharest legation, 6 Nov. 1940.

92. On this see for example *DGFP*, XI, p. 408, Bismarck, chargé d'affaires in Rome, to FM, 27 Oct., and TsDA MVR, f.316 op.1 ae.273 l.37, Draganov to FM, 4 Nov. 1940.

93. AVP RF, f.059 op.1 p.315 d.2165 l.70–2, Vyshinsky to Vinogradov on meeting Aktay, 4 Nov. 1940.

94. See p. 81.

95. AVP RF, f.0100 op.24 p.196 d.8 l.427–9, well expounded in Paniushkin's meeting with Bai Chzhunsi, Chinese Deputy Chief of Staff, 31 Oct.; and f.059 op.1 p.315 d.2165 l.73–4, 75–6, Vyshinsky to Vinogradov, 4 Nov. 1940.

96. TsDA MVR, f.316k op.1 ae.273 l.19, Popov to Draganov, 9 Nov. 1940.

4. The Road to 'Barbarossa'

1. A typical approach is Cecil, *Hitler's Decision to Invade Russia*, p. 110.

2. UD:s Arkiv 1920 ARS, HP/ 516/LXVIII, Assarasson to FM, 10 Sept. 1940; Klink, 'Die militärische Konzeption', p. 195–6; J. von Herwarth, *Against Two Evils: Memoirs of a Diplomat–Soldier during the Third Reich* (London, 1981), pp. 182–4.

3. AVP RF, f.o6 op.2 p.15 d.157 l.1–5; *DGFP*, XI, p. 47, record of Molotov's meeting with Schulenburg, 9 Sept. On Schulenburg's concern see also Gafencu, *Misiune la Moscova*, tel. 2287, pp. 63–4, Gafencu to FM, 13 Sept. 1940.

4. AVP RF, f.o6 op.2 p.15 d.157 l.16–27, and *DGFP*, XI, pp. 137–43, records of Molotov's meeting with Schulenburg, 21 Sept. The Russian press presented Russia as 'a new Danubian State', Gafencu, *Misiune la Moscova*, tel. 2273–4, pp. 59–3, Gafencu to FM, 13 Sept. 1940.

5. L. E. Hill (ed.), *Die Weizsäcker-Papiere, 1933–1950* (Frankfurt, 1974), p. 216.

6. *DGFP*, XI, pp. 221–3, memorandum by Schnurre, 28 Sept. 1940.

7. *Ibid.*, pp. 102–5, Hitler to Mussolini, 17 Sept. 1940.

8. Wegner-Korfes, 'Ambassador Count Schulenburg', pp. 118–19.

9. AMVnR, d.40 p.34 op.1sh pop.272 l.237, Stamenov to FM, 12 Nov. 1940.

10. Wegner-Korfes, 'Ambassador Count Schulenburg', p. 195.

11. *Weizsäcker-Papiere*, p. 226.

12. *DGFP*, XI, pp. 521–3, memorandum by Weizsäcker, 11 Nov. 1940.

13. *Ibid.*, pp. 113–23, memorandum on Ribbentrop's meeting with Mussolini, 20 Sept. 1940.

14. AVP RF, f.059 op.1 p.316 d.2177 l.6–8. See also *DGFP*, XI, pp. 276–7 and 279, reports of Shkvartsev's meeting with Ribbentrop, and a circular to German missions in the Balkans, 9 Oct.; *DGFP*, XI, pp. 245–59, 297–301 and 411–22, records of Hitler's meetings with Mussolini, 4, 15 and 28 Oct. Halder, *Kriegstagebuch*, II, pp. 135–9, 15 Oct. 1940.

15. TsDA MVR, f.176 op.8 ae.17 l.67–70, Draganov to FM on meeting Papen, 6 Nov., and a reconfirmation in F. von Papen, *Memoirs* (London, 1952), pp. 465–7, and see also AMVnR, p.42 op.1sh pop.315 l.29–31, Draganov to FM, 11 Nov. 1940.

16. *DGFP*, XI, pp. 150–2 and 164, record of Ribbentrop meeting with Mussolini, 22 Sept. Indeed clause V stipulated that the agreement in no way 'affects the political status which exists at present as between each of the three contracting parties and Soviet Russia'. See also *ibid.*, pp. 187–8, Ribbentrop to Molotov, 26 Sept., and AVP RF, f.059 op.1 p.316 d.2176 l.311–12, Shkvartsev to FM, 28 Sept. 1940.

17. *Weizsäcker-Papiere*, p. 219; AVP RF, f.059 op.1 p.316 d.2176 l.311–12, Shkvartsev to FM, 28 Sept. 1940.

18. *DGFP*, XI, pp. 187–8, Ribbentrop to Molotov, 26 Sept. 1940.

19. *Ibid.*, pp. 236–8, Ribbentrop to the Moscow embassy, 2 Oct. 1940.

20. AVP RF, f.059 op.1 p.316 d.2177 l.6–8, report by Shkvartsev of meeting Ribbentrop; see also *DGFP*, XI, pp. 276–7 and 279, a circular letter by Ribbentrop, 9 Oct. 1940.

21. AVP RF, f.06 op.2 p.15 d.157 l.47–51; *DGFP*, XI, pp. 291–7 and 317, Ribbentrop to Stalin, 13 Oct., and reports of Molotov's meeting with Schulenburg, 17 Oct. 1941. On Schulenburg's continued optimism see Gafencu, *Misiune la Moscova*, raport 2714, pp. 91–9, report by Gafencu to Sturdza, 21 Oct. 1940.

22. AVP RF, f.06 op.2 p.15 d.157 l.55–8 and 61–2, and *DGFP*, XI, pp. 327–8 and 334–7, records of Molotov meetings with Schulenburg, 19 and 21 Oct. 1940.

23. Presidential Archives, f.3 op.64 d.675 l.1; *DGFP*, XI, pp. 353–4, Stalin's letter to Ribbentrop, 21 Oct. 1940.

24. In his monumental *A World at Arms*, which set the standards for research

on the war, Weinberg naturally assumes that the Russians 'were always happy to assist the Germans in stirring up trouble for the British in Asia', and that Molotov's visit reflected the 'continued fruitful cooperation between them against Great Britain'; but, as the Russian documents demonstrate, this was not their main objective. He further maintains that Molotov pressed for 'real and immediate Soviet advances toward the Straits and thus to the Mediterranean'; while, as we have seen, the move to the Straits was confined to the Bosphorus, reflecting a concern for control of the Black Sea rather than interest in the Dardanelles, which would have implied a southward ambition in the Mediterranean.

25. Berezhkov, *History in the Making*, pp. 7–50.

26. Presidential Archives, f.03 op.64 d.675 l.21–30, and *DGFP*, XI, pp. 533–41, record of Molotov's meeting with Ribbentrop, 12 Nov. 1940.

27. AVP RF, f.059 op.1 p.338 d.2314 l.11–18, Molotov to Stalin, 13 Nov. 1940.

28. G. Hilger and A. G. Meyer, *The Incompatible Allies: A Memoir-History of German–Soviet Relations, 1918–1941* (New York, 1971), p. 323.

29. AVP RF, f.059 op.1 p.339 d.2315 l.35–6, Stalin to Molotov, 13 Nov. 1940.

30. AVP RF, f.3 op. 64 d.675 l.49–67, report of meeting between Molotov and Hitler, 13 Nov., and f.059 op.1 p.339 d.2315 l.29–30, Stalin to Molotov, 13 Nov. 1940.

31. Presidential Archives, f.3 op.64 d.675 l.68–83, and *DGFP*, XI, pp. 562–70, records of Molotov's meeting with Ribbentrop, 13 Nov. 1940.

32. For this see *Der Prozess gegen die Hauptkriegsverbrecher*, IX, pp. 328–30 and 383–5.

33. Presidential Archives, f.3 op.64 d.675 l.31–41 and 49–67, and *DGFP*, XI, pp. 541–9 and 550–62, records of Molotov's meetings with Hitler on

12 and 13 Nov. 1940. See also Hilger and Meyer, *Incompatible Allies*, p. 323.

34. See for instance AMVnR, d.40 p.34 op.1sh pop.272 l.233–4, Stamenov to FM, 13 Nov. 1940.

35. AVP RF, f.059 op.1 p.338 d.2314 l.36–8, Molotov to Stalin, 13 Nov. 1940.

36. See the evidence of General Sousloparov, Soviet military attaché in Vichy, Quai d'Orsay Archives, 834/Z/312/1 pp. 73–5.

37. AVP RF, f.059 op.1 p.326 d.2239 l.112–14, Molotov to Maisky, 17 Nov. 1940.

38. See p. 75.

39. On this see AMVnR, p.42 op.1sh pop.315 l.34, Stamenov to FM, 16 Nov. 1940.

40. *Weizsäcker-Papiere*, pp. 220 and 227, and Halder, *Kriegstagebuch*, II, pp. 182–3, 16 Nov. 1940.

41. *DGFP*, XI, pp. 598–609, memorandum on conversation between Hitler and Ciano on 18 Nov. and with the Spanish Foreign Minister, Serrano Suñer, 19 Nov. 1940.

42. *Ibid.*, pp. 637–43 and 654–70, Hitler to Mussolini, and record of meeting with Antonescu, 20 Nov. 1940.

43. *Ibid.*, XI, pp. 632–6, memorandum on Hitler's meeting with the Hungarian Minister President, Count Teleki, and Count Csàky in Vienna, 20 Nov. 1940.

44. *Ibid.*, p. 432, 17 Nov. 1940.

45. The Treaty of San Stefano, 3 March 1878, established an independent Bulgaria the borders of which comprised the territory lying between the Danube, the Black Sea and the Aegean, including Rumelia and Macedonia but excluding Saloniki.

46. AMVnR, p.42 op.1sh pop.315 l.20–8, Draganov to FM, 14 Nov. See also p.34 op.1sh pop.272 l.237, Stamenov to FM, 17 Nov. 1940.

47. *DGFP*, XI, pp. 606–10 and 652, n. 2, 19 Nov. 1940. B. Filov, *Dnevnik* (Sofia, 1986), p. 199.

48. AMVnR, d.40 p.34 op.1sh pop.

272 l.238, and AVP RF, f.059 op.1 p.331 d.2275 l.105–13, records of Molotov's meeting with Stamenov, 18 Nov. 1940. On the Soviet policy see also P. P. Sevost'ianov, 'Nakanune velikoi bitvy', *Novaia i noveishaia istoriia*, 4 (1981), pp. 99–128, and O. N. Reshetnikova, *Mezhdunarodnye otnosheniia i strany Tsentral'noi i Iugo-Vostochnoi Evropy v period fashistskoi agressii na Balkanakh i podgotovki napadeniia na SSSR* (Moscow, 1992).

49. Filov, *Dnevnik*, p. 199, and *DGFP*, XI, pp. 652, n. 2, and 653–4, 18 Nov. 1940.

50. *DGFP*, XI, pp. 654–70 and 680–4, record of Antonescu's talks with Hitler, Keitel and Ribbentrop in Berlin, 23 and 25 Nov.; the Russians were well briefed about the talk, see AVP RF, f.059 op.1 p.3196 d.2193 l.131–5, Lavrentev to FM, 21 Nov. 1940. See an earlier identification of the Balkans as the key to understanding the German–Soviet clash in E. Presseisen, 'Prelude to "Barbarossa": Germany and the Balkans, 1940–1941', *Journal of Modern History*, 4 (1960).

51. *DGFP*, XI, pp. 651–3, Richthofen to FM, 22 Nov. 1940.

52. *Ibid.*, pp. 691–70, Richthofen to FM, 24 Nov. 1940.

53. *Ibid.*, pp. 672–8, report of Hitler's meeting with Draganov, 23 Nov. 1940.

54. AVP RF, f.059 op.1 p.331 d.2272 l.155–6, Lavrishchev to FM on meeting Popov, 20 Nov. 1940. On the King's Hobson's choice see Rendell, British ambassador in Sofia, in his G. Rendell, *The Sword and the Olive: Recollections of Diplomacy and the Foreign Service* (London, 1957), p. 183.

55. AMVnR, d.40 p.34 op.1sh pop.272 l.248, Stamenov to FM, 26 Nov. 1940.

56. TsDA MVR, f.176 op.8 a.e.17 l.104, and AMVnR, p.42 op.1sh pop.315 l.5, Antonov to FM, 24 and 29 Nov. 1940 respectively.

57. AMVnR, PREII/1/3 pap.1 op.2sh pop.1 l.1, Stamenov to FM, 23 Nov. 1940.
58. AMVnR, d.40 p.34 op.1sh pop.272 l.246, Stamenov to FM, 26 Nov. See also Molotov's record of his meeting with Aktay on 10 Dec. 1940, in AVP RF, f.06 op.2 p.3 d.19 l.10–14.
59. A less likely explanation for the oral delivery is that a written one would have constituted an abrogation of the 1925 agreement with Turkey on mutual consultations – at least this is the excuse used by Molotov when reproached by the Turks, see *Foreign Relations of the United States* (hereafter *FRUS*), I (1941), pp. 287–9, MacMurray, US ambassador in Ankara, to Secretary of State, 22 Feb. 1941.
60. AMVnR, PREII/1/3 pap.1 op.2sh pop.1 l.7, report by D. Shishmanov, general secretary of the Bulgarian FM, 25 Nov. 1940.
61. AVP RF, f.059 op.1 p.331 d.2272 l.167–8, telegram from Sobolev to Molotov, 25 Nov. 1940.
62. Dimitrov's diary, 11 Jan. 1941.
63. Dimitrov's diary, and *Komintern i vtoraia mirovaia voina*, p. 454, telegram from Dimitrov to the CC of the Bulgarian CP, 25 Nov. 1940; AMVnR, PREII/1/3 pap.1 op.2sh pop.1 l.19, anonymous pamphlet distributed in Sofia, 27 Nov. On the diplomatic setback in Sofia see AMVnR, PREII/1/3 pap.1 op.2sh pop.1 l.11, Popov to Stamenov, 1 Dec. 1940.
64. Dimitrov's diary, and *Komintern i vtoraia mirovaia voina*, pp. 461–2, 28 Nov. 1940.
65. AVP RF, f.3 op.64 p. d.675 l.108–16, record of a meeting between Schnurre, Schulenburg and Molotov, 25 Nov. 1940, and *DGFP*, XI, pp. 714–15 and 716–17, notes by Molotov to Schulenburg and by Schulenburg to FM.
66. Filov, *Dnevnik*, pp. 199–200, and *DGFP*, XI, pp. 712–14, Richthofen to FM, 26 Nov. 1940.

67. *DGFP*, XI, pp. 726–7, Richthofen to FM, 28 Nov. 1940.
68. AMVnR, PREII/1/3 pap.1 op.2sh pop.1 l.8–9 and 10, exchange of telegrams between Popov and Stamenov, 30 Nov. and 1 Dec.; AVP RF, f.059 op.1 p.331 d.2272 l.192–9, Lavrishchev to Molotov, 30 Nov. 1940. Richthofen's reports are in *DGFP*, XI, pp. 756–7.
69. TsDA MVR, f.316 op.1 a.e.273 l.25, and *DGFP*, XI, pp. 767–73, records of Hitler's meeting with Draganov, 3 Dec. 1940.
70. *DGFP*, XI, pp. 789–91, Hitler to Mussolini, 5 Dec. 1940.
71. See pp. 121–3.
72. Some historians suggest that it was customary for Hitler to gloss over this contentious issue with the military; but there are no signs of a prior dispute between Hitler and the army: see Klink, 'Die militärische Konzeption', pp. 236–7.
73. Halder, *Kriegstagebuch*, II, pp. 213–14 and 227–8, 13 Dec. 1940.
74. AMVnR, PREII/1/3 pap.1 op.2sh pop.1 l.12, Shishmanov, minute on meeting Lavrishchev, 6 Dec.; TsDA MVR, f.176 op.8 ae.17 l.42, Popov to Stamenov, 9 Dec. 1940.
75. TsDA MVR, f.176 op.8 a.e.17 l.41, Popov to Draganov, 8 Dec. 1940.
76. *Ibid.*, l.106, and *DGFP*, XI, pp. 806–7 and 833–5, Richthofen to FM, 7 and 10 Dec., and Draganov to FM and record by Wörmann, director of the Political Department of the German FM, 10 Dec. 1940.
77. See above, pp. 44–7.
78. *DGFP*, XI, pp. 838–9, 879–81 and 883–4, Fabricius to FM, 11 and 16 Dec. 1940. See also Novikov, *Vospominaniia diplomata*, pp. 67–8.
79. FO 371 25231 W12425 and W12738/215/96, Campbell to FO, 6 Dec. 1940.
80. *DGFP*, XI, pp. 841–2, Blucher (Helsinki) to FM, 11 Dec. 1940.
81. *Ibid.*, XI, pp. 899–902, 18 Dec. 1940.
82. *Ibid.*, XI, pp. 937–41, Ritter to

FM (submitted personally to Ribbentrop and Hitler) and a memorandum by General Jödl on 'German Military Preparations in the Balkans', 23 Dec. 1940.

83. A. Speer, *Inside the Third Reich* (New York, 1970), p. 173. A review of the process of decision-making is in E. M. Robertson, 'Hitler Turns from the West to Russia, May–December 1940', in R. Boys and E. M. Robertson (eds), *Paths to War: New Essays on the Origins of the Second World War* (New York, 1989).

84. 'Der operationsentwurf Ost' des Generalmajors Marcks vom 5. August 1940', in F. Klein and I. Lachnit (eds), *Wehrforschung*, 4 (1972), p. 116.

85. Quoted in Cecil, *Hitler's Decision to Invade Russia*, p. 169.

86. FO 1093/2 fol. 14.

87. Cecil, *Hitler's Decision to Invade Russia*, p. 105.

88. See for instance the study of Hitler's Chief of Staff F. Halder, *Hitler as Warlord* (London, 1950).

89. Cecil, *Hitler's Decision to Invade Russia*, p. 171.

90. *Ibid.*, p. 121.

91. See Erickson, *Road to Stalingrad*, p. 85.

92. Quoted in Förster, 'Hitler Turns East', p. 20.

93. The following is based on a most informative article by I. Tsukertort, 'Germanskii militarism i legenda o "preventivnoi voine" gitlerovskoi Germanii protiv SSSR', *VIZh*, 5 (1991), pp. 16–24.

94. For more on this see pp. 115–17. See S. Naveh, *In Pursuit of Military Excellence: The Evolution of Operational Theory* (London, 1997).

95. Ueberschör, 'Hitlers Entschluss', pp. 83–9.

96. *DGFP*, XII, pp. 386–94, 405–9 and 413–20, Matsuoka's conversations with Hitler and Ribbentrop in Berlin, 31 Mar. 1941.

97. Quoted in Förster, 'Hitler Turns East', p. 22.

98. *DGFP*, XII, p. 1069.

5. The Curtain Falls on the Balkans

1. AVP RF, f.06 op.2 p.2 d.715 l.107–19, record of Molotov's meeting with Cripps, 24 Aug., and f.059 op.1 p.326 d.2239 l.14–15, Molotov to Maisky, 25 Aug. 1940.

2. AVP RF, f.059 op.1 p.325 d.2236 l.92–7 and 192–3, and f.069 op.24 p.70 d.43 l.91–3, Maisky to Molotov, 14 Sep., 1 and 7 Oct. 1940.

3. AVP RF, f.069 op.24 p.70 d.43 l.95–9, record of Maisky's meeting with Halifax, 17 Oct. 1940.

4. AVP RF, f.07 op.1 p.2 d.22 l.4–7, and FO 418/86 N6594/2039/59, reports of Cripps's meeting with Vyshinsky, 14 Sept. 1940.

5. AVP RF, f.059 op.1 p.325 d.2236 l.163–7, Maisky to FM on meeting Beaverbrook, 25 Sept. 1940.

6. AVP RF, f.06 op.2 p.15 d.157 l.35–6, and *DGFP*, XI, pp. 244–5, records of Molotov's meeting with Tippelskirch, 4 Oct. 1940.

7. AVP RF, f.07 op.1 p.2 d.22 l.8–10, and FO 371 24841 N6681/5/38, records of Cripps's meeting with Vyshinsky, 20 Sept.; see also FO 371 24848 N7348/40/38, Halifax to Cripps, 27 Nov. 1940.

8. FO 371 24870 R7763/4/7, Rendell to FO, 28 Sept. 1940.

9. Cripps papers, and FO 371 24848 N6838/40/38, official and private letters to Halifax, 10 and 11 Oct., and diary entry for 10 Oct. 1940.

10. CAB 65/9 269(40)8, 10 Oct.; AVP RF, f.059 op.1 p.320 d.2202 l.131–4, Vyshinsky to Umansky, 24 Dec. 1940.

11. See pp. 44–6.

12. FO 371 25231 W12004/215/96, Hoare to FO, 21 Nov., and 25015 R8202/242/37, Cripps to FO and minutes, 3 Nov. 1940. A marvellous and insightful examination of Churchill's strategy and politics in the Balkans is in S. Lawlor, *Churchill and the Politics of War* (Cambridge, 1994).

13. FO 371 24852 N7163/22/38, Cripps to FM, 10 Nov., and minutes by Cadogan and Halifax, 13 and 25 Nov.; on the withdrawal of the offer see 24849 N7387/40/38, Cripps to Halifax, 8 Dec., CAB 65/10 295(40)3 and FO 837/1133, Ministry of Economic Warfare (hereafter MEW) minutes, 26 Dec. See also Maisky's talk with Halifax on the Berlin meeting in the same vein in FO 371 24848 N7348/40/38, Halifax to Cripps, 27 Nov. 1940.

14. FO 371 24849 N7548/40/38, and AVP RF, f.069 op.24 p.70 d.43 l.132–7, record of Maisky's meeting with Eden, 27 Dec., and a comment by Cripps, 29 Dec.; Maisky gained a similar impression of Eden's ineffectiveness from Lloyd George, see AVP RF, f.059 op.1 p.325 d.2237 l.323–7, Maisky to FM, 29 Dec. 1940.

15. FO 371 24849 N7500/40/38, Eden to Cripps. Also Cripps to Eden, 19 Dec. 1940. Eden to Dalton, 3 Jan. 1941, and minute by Cadogan, 27 Dec. 1940.

16. FO 371 29463 N29/3/38, Cripps to FO and minutes by Eden, 31 Dec. 1940.

17. See pp. 95–6.

18. FO 371 29497 N159/88/38, Cripps to the FO, and minutes, 11 Jan. 1941.

19. FO 371 24849 N7484/40/38, FO minutes, 22 Jan., and CAB 65/17 5(41)2, 13 Jan. 1941.

20. Dilks (ed.), *Cadogan Diaries*, pp. 345, 347, 372; See also W. P. Crozier, *Off the Record: Political Interviews, 1939–44* (London, 1973), p. 208. On the myth of Eden's staunch support of the Soviet Union see D. Carlton, *Anthony Eden: A Biography* (London, 1981), pp. 16, 63, 86–8 and 149, and on the Middle East, 170–2.

21. FO 837/1098, Cripps to FM, 12 and 20 Feb., and minutes. UD:s Arkiv 1920 ARS, HP/517/LXIX, Assarasson to FM, 9 Jan. 1940.

22. AVP RF, f.06 op.3 p.8 d.81 l.2–5, and FO 371 29463 N402 and N411/3/38, and 29473 N759/22/38, exchange of telegrams between Cripps and Eden, Cripps to Mikoyan, and FO minutes, 1, 20 and 21 Feb. 1941.

23. CAB 69/2 DO (41)7, 10 Feb. 1941.

24. AVP RF, f.0125 op.27 p.122 d.4 l.105–6, Lavrentev to Molotov, 11 Feb. 1941.

25. AVP RF, f.06 op.2 p.15 d.158 l.18–22, and *DGFP*, XI, pp. 723–4, record of Molotov's meeting with Schulenburg, 28 Nov., and pp. 746–8, Schnurre to Ritter, 29 Nov. 1940.

26. See above, pp. 80–2.

27. AVP RF, f.059 op.1 p.317 d.2128 l.188–90, and *DGFP*, XI, pp. 979–80 and 1013–15, reports of meetings between Molotov and Schulenburg, 29 Dec. 1940 and 3 Jan. 1941. See also Gafencu, *Misiune la Moscova*, tel. 3, pp. 127–8, Gafencu to FM, 2 Jan. 1941, and similar detailed views by General Sousloparov, military attaché in Vichy, Quai d'Orsay Archives, 834/Z/312/1, pp. 66–7, 3 Jan. 1941.

28. *DGFP*, XI, pp. 1137–8, memorandum by Wiehl, director of the Economic Policy Department, 19 Jan. See also AVP RF, f.07 op.2 p.9 d.27 l.6–7 and 9, Vyshinsky on meeting Pasikivii, 21 and 24 Jan. 1941.

29. On this episode see also J. Barros and R. Gregor, *Double Deception: Stalin, Hitler, and the Invasion of Russia* (1995), pp. 48–51. *Double Deception* gives a most persuasive account of Stalin's politics in the spring of 1941. However, it appeared before the opening of the Russian archives and therefore suffers inevitable lacunae and occasional inaccuracies.

30. UD:s Arkiv 1920 ARS, HP/517/LXIX, Assarasson to FM, 25 Nov., Krigsarkivet, Fo..rsvarsstaben, Ser. E/II/15/1, military attaché's report, no. 2, 25 Nov., AMVnR, p.42 op.1sh pop.315 l.5, Antonov to FM, 29 Nov., and FO 371 24853 N7347/

283/38, Cripps to Halifax, 29 Nov. 1940.

31. *DGFP*, XI, p. 854, Ribbentrop to Schulenburg, 12 Dec. 1940.

32. AVP RF, f.059 op.1 p.319 d.2193 l.204, telegram from Dekanozov to FM, 6 Dec. 1940.

33. AVP RF, f.082 op.23 p.95 d.6 l.285–90, and *DGFP*, XI, pp. 854–6 and 864–5, records of Dekanozov's meeting with Ribbentrop, 12 Dec. 1940.

34. AVP RF, f.082 op.23 p.95 d.6 l.268–72, record of Dekanozov's meeting with Hitler, 19 Dec. 1940.

35. AVP RF, f.06 op.2 p.15 d.158 l.48–52, and *DGFP*, XI, pp. 928–9, records of Molotov's meeting with Schulenburg, 21 Dec. 1940.

36. *DGFP*, XI, pp. 943–4, Weizsäcker to Schulenburg, 24 Dec. 1940.

37. *Ibid.*, pp. 1044–5, Weizsäcker to Ribbentrop, 7 Jan. 1941.

38. AVP RF, f.06 op.3 p.1 d.4 l. 1–6; *DGFP*, XI, pp. 1000–1, records of Molotov's meeting with Schulenburg, 2 Jan., and p. 1040, Schulenburg to Ribbentrop, 7 Jan. 1941.

39. *DGFP*, XI, pp. 1066–9, Trade Agreement between USSR and Germany, 10 Jan. 1941.

40. *Ibid.*, XII, pp. 4–5 and 8, telegrams to Schulenburg, 3 Feb., and minute by him, 1 Feb., and AVP RF, f.07 op.2 p.9 d.22 l.19–20, record of Vyshinsky's meeting with Tippelskirch, 4 Feb. 1941.

41. Herwarth, *Against Two Evils*, pp. 188–9.

42. AVP RF, f.059 op.1 p.331 d.2272 l.238–9, Lavrishchev to Molotov, 18 Dec.; AMVnR, PREII/1/3 pap.1 op.2sh pop.1 l.14–16, report by Popov on meeting Lavrishchev, 18 Dec., and Dimitrov's diary, 20 Dec. 1940.

43. TsDA MVR, f.176 op.15 ae.1 l.55–9, and op.8 ae.962 l.6, reports by Petrov, the Bulgarian naval and air attaché in Bucharest, on conversations with Lavrentev and Lunin, 4 and 11 Jan. 1941.

44. *DGFP*, XI, pp. 1018–27 (actual date of document 4 Jan.), memorandum on Hitler's meeting with Filov, 4 Jan., and Filov, *Dnevnik*, pp. 200–8, 4 Jan. 1941. Even at the height of the 'ideologized' period of Bulgarian historiography it was recognized that the drive for revisionism was bound to lead Bulgaria towards the German camp; see I. Dimitrov, 'Bulgaria in European Politics between the Two World Wars: Certain Preliminary Inferences', *Southeastern Europe*, 8/1–2 (1981).

45. *FRUS*, I (1941), p. 278, Earle, US ambassador in Sofia, to Secretary of State, 12 Jan. 1941.

46. Filov, *Dnevnik*, pp. 209–11, 7 Jan. 1941.

47. TsDA MVR, f.176 op.15 ae.1 l.132–9, and *DGFP*, XI, pp. 1081–5, records of Weizsäcker's meeting with Draganov, 13 Jan. 1941.

48. *Izvestiia*, 11 Jan.; Dimitrov's diary, 12 and 13 Jan., and AMVnR, d.51 p.45 op.1sh pop.333 l.10, Stamenov to FM, 13 Jan. An analysis of the Russian position is also in FO 371 29500 N262/122/38, Eden to Cripps on Butler's meeting with Maisky, 15 Jan. 1941.

49. AMVnR, d.51 p.45 op.1sh pop.333 l.11, Stamenov to FM, 14 Jan. 1941.

50. *DGFP*, XI, pp. 1100–1, Schulenburg to FM, 14 Jan. 1941.

51. *Ibid.*, pp. 1104–5 and 1076, Weizsäcker to Ribbentrop, 15 Jan., and head of Foreign Intelligence, OKW, to FM, 11 Jan. 1941.

52. AVP RF, f.06 op.3 p.1 d.4 l.37–41, Molotov's meeting with Schulenburg, 17 Jan. 1941.

53. *DGFP*, XI, pp. 1122–3.

54. *Ibid.*, pp. 1122–3 and 1155–6, Weizsäcker to Ribbentrop on meeting Dekanozov, 17 Jan., and Ribbentrop to Weizsäcker, 21 Jan. 1941.

55. AVP RF, f.074 op.26 p.110 d.6 l.26–7, record of Lavrishchev's meeting with Gurev, King Boris's adviser, 24 Jan. 1941.

56. See p. 106.

57. *DGFP*, XI, pp. 1210–12 and

1216–17, 1236–7, memorandum by
Ambassador Ritter, Berlin; Field
Marshal Jödl to Ritter, 28 Jan.
Directive of the High Command
of the Wehrmacht, 27 Jan. 1941.

58. AVP RF, f. 017a, Maisky's diary,
l.23, 11 Feb., and TsDA MVR, f.176
op.8 ae.1016a l.55, Moltchilov to
FM, 1 Mar. 1941.

59. TsDA MVR, f.176 op.8 ae.962 l.13,
and *DGFP*, XII, pp. 73–4, reports
by Draganov and Ritter on their
meeting, 9 Feb., and TsDA MVR,
f.176 op.8 ae.17 l.46–7, exchange
of telegrams between Popov and
Draganov, 13, 17 and 18 Feb. 1941.

60. FO 371 29724 R1562/36/7, minute
by Churchill on meeting Moltchilov,
20 Feb. 1941.

61. AVP RF, f.082 op.24 p.105 d.6 l.124–
30, record of Dekanozov's meeting
with Draganov, 18 Feb. 1941.

62. Filov, *Dnevnik*, pp. 249–50; on Hitler
and King Boris see Miller, *Bulgaria
during the Second World War*, p. 46.

63. AMVnR, d.51 p.45 op.1sh pop.333
l.36 and 39–41, Stamenov to FM, 24
Feb. 1941.

64. Dimitrov's diary, 26 Feb. 1941.

65. AVP RF, f.06 op.3 p.1 d.4 l.28–32,
and *DGFP*, XII, p. 195, records of
Molotov's meeting with Schulenburg, 28 Feb. 1941.

66. AVP RF, f.074 op.26 p.110 d.6 l.45,
Lavrishchev on meeting Shishmanov, general director of Bulgarian FM, 28 Feb. See also *ibid.*, l.47–8,
Lavrishchev on meeting Altinov,
head of the Political Department of
the Bulgarian FM, 1 Mar., and
TsDA MVR, f.176 op.8 ae.17 l.24,
Popov to Stamenov, 1 Mar. 1941.

67. *DGFP*, XII, pp. 191–4, Maritius to
FM, 28 Feb. 1941.

68. AVP RF, f.06 op.3 p.1 d.4 l.63–6, and
DGFP, XII, pp. 213–16, records of
Molotov's meeting with Schulen-
burg, 1 Mar. 1941.

69. AMVnR, d.51 p.45 op.1sh pop.333
l.47, Stamenov to FM, 4 Mar. He was
forced to resort to yet another ineffective Tass communiqué, *Izvestiia*,
4 Mar. 1941.

70. AVP RF, f. 017a, Maisky's diary,
l.41–6, 1 Mar. 1941.

71. UD:s Arkiv 1920 ARS, HP/
517/LXIX, Assarasson to FM on
conversations with Aktay, 21 Nov.
1940.

72. AVP RF, f.06 op.2 p.3 d.19 l.50–7,
Molotov on meeting Aktay, 14 Dec.;
additional information in UD:s
Arkiv 1920 ARS, HP/517/LXIX,
Assarasson to FM, 14 Dec. 1940.

73. FO 371 24871 R8945/4/7, Cripps
to FO, 14 Dec. 1940. Aktay was
a confidant of Cripps; they met
almost daily in what they termed
the 'Club', together with the
Yugoslav and Greek ambassadors.

74. AVP RF, f.059 op.1 p.314 d.2163
l.182–5, Vinogradov to FM on
meeting Saracoglu, 17 Dec. 1940.

75. FO 371 24871 R8909/4/7, Rendell
to FO, 11 Dec. 1940.

76. AVP RF, f.059 op.1 p.314 d.2163
l.170–4, Vinogradov to FM, 13 Dec.,
and f.06 op.2 p.3 d.19 l.10–14,
Molotov report on meeting Aktay;
see also Steinhardt on meeting
Aktay in *FRUS*, I (1941), pp. 276–7,
10 Dec. 1940.

77. *DGFP*, XI, pp. 54–6, Mackensen
to Ribbentrop, 10 Sept. Initially
Molotov was happy enough to
resume trade negotiations; those
could serve as a deterrent to the
Germans and a vehicle for reopening political discussions between
Russia and the Axis, see AVP RF,
f.059 op.1 p.330 d.2269 l.182,
Molotov to Gorelkin, 14 Dec. 1940.

78. AVP RF, f.0596 op.1 p.330 d.2268
l.160–1, Gorelkin to FM on meeting
Ciano, 26 Dec. 1940. The Italian
documents on the overture are in
Toscano, *Designs in Diplomacy*, pp.
201–9.

79. AVP RF, f.06 op.2 p.16 d.205 l.10–11,
record of Gorelkin's meeting Ciano,
28 Dec. 1940.

80. See p. 27.

81. AVP RF, f.06 op.3 p.17 d.208 l.1–7,
and op.2 p.20 d.229 l.15–21, records
of Molotov's meetings with Rosso,
30 Dec. 1940, and 27 Jan.; UD:s

Arkiv 1920 ARS, HP/517/LXX, Assarasson to FM, 5 Feb. 1941.

82. *DGFP*, XI, pp. 990–4, 996–9 and 1011, Hitler to Mussolini, 31 Dec. 1940, and Mackensen to Ribbentrop, 1 and 3 Jan.; on Rosso see AMVnR, d.51 p.45 op.1sh pop. 333 l.20, Stamenov to FM, 1 Feb. 1941.

83. See p. 46. *DGFP*, XI, pp. 1030–3, record of Ribbentrop's meeting with Alfieri in Berlin, 7 Jan. 1941, and the Italian version of the negotiations in Toscano, *Designs in Diplomacy*, pp. 201–35.

84. *DGFP*, XI, pp. 1127–33, Hitler's meeting with Mussolini at Berchtesgaden, 21 Jan., *DGFP*, XI, pp. 1163–7, and XII, pp. 45–6, unsigned memorandum, probably from Ribbentrop to Ciano, 22 Jan., and note by Weizsäcker, 6 Feb. 1941.

85. AVP RF, f.06 op.3 p.1 d.4 l.55–7, record of Molotov's meeting with Rosso, 24 Feb. 1941. See also Toscano, *Designs in Diplomacy*, pp. 241–4.

86. AVP RF, f.06 op.3 p.4 d.35 l.48–50, Lozovsky on meeting Rosso, 19 Mar. 1941.

87. See pp. 91–2.

88. AVP RF, f.0125 op.27 p.122 d.4 l.68–71, report on Lavrentev's meeting with Kokatürk, Turkish military attaché in Bucharest, 6 Jan.; and AVP RF, f.07 op.2 p.10 d.25 l.2–4, Dekanozov on meeting with Alkend, the Turkish chargé d'affaires in Berlin, 13 Jan. 1941.

89. FO 371 29463 N382/3/38 and 29777 R/700/113/67, Eden to Cripps, 29 Jan. 1941.

90. *DGFP*, XI, pp. 1124–5 and 1172, and AVP RF, f.06 op.3 p.1 d.4 l.37–41 and 42–7, records of Molotov's meetings with Schulenburg, 17 and 23 Jan. 1941.

91. See below, pp. 127–8.

92. AVP RF, f. 017a, Maisky's diary, l.15, 21, 29–30, 27 Jan., 10 and 19 Feb. 1941.

93. See revelations by the Turkish military attaché in Moscow, in

Krigsarkivet, Fo..rsvarsstaben, Ser. E/II/15/1, military attaché's report, no. 4, 5 Feb. 1941.

94. *DGFP*, XII, p. 120, Papen to Ribbentrop, 20 Feb. 1941.

95. UD:s Arkiv 1920 ARS, HP/517/LXX, Assarasson to FM, 30 Jan. 1941.

96. TsDA MVR, f.176 op.8 ae.1016a l.40–3a, Draganov to FM on meeting Dekanozov, 21 and 22 Feb. See also AVP RF, f.07 op.2 p.9 d.24 l.1–2, record of Vyshinsky's meeting with Aktay, 20 Feb., and UD:s Arkiv 1920 ARS, HP/517/LXX, Assarasson to FM on conversations with Aktay, 19 Feb. 1941.

97. FO 371 29497 N159/88/38, telegram from Cripps, 11 Jan.; Cripps papers, letter to daughter Diane, 10 Jan., and letter to wife Isobel, 1 Feb. 1941.

98. FO 371 29777 R616/113/67, Cripps to the FO and minutes, 27 Jan. 1941.

99. See for example FO 371 29500 N262/122/38, Eden to Cripps, 21 Jan., and 29463 N29/3/38, telegram from Mallet, 16 Jan.; State Dept. 740.0011 EW 39/79809, telegram from Sterling (Sweden), 25 Jan. 1941.

100. See below, pp. 155–8.

101. FO 371 29778 R1476/113/67, Cripps to Eden on meeting the Turkish ambassador and Vyshinsky, 21 Feb., and minute by Sargent, 25 Feb. 1941.

102. FO 371 29463 N675 and N733/3/38, exchange of telegrams between Cripps and the FO, and minutes, 24 Feb. 1941.

103. PREM 3/395/16, 22 Feb., and Cripps papers, diary, 8 Mar. 1941.

104. Gorodetsky, *Cripps' Mission to Moscow*, chs 6–8.

105. FO 371 24891 R7849/5/67, FO note for Cabinet, 9 Dec. 1940.

106. AVP RF, f.017a, Maisky's diary, l.37, 25 Feb. 1941; AVP RF, f.07 op.2 p.9 d.20 l.1–2, record of Vyshinsky's meeting with Cripps, 24 Feb., and Politburo Archives, f.3 op.64 d.341 l.108–9, records of meetings between Vyshinsky and Cripps, 24

and 25 Feb. See also UD:s Arkiv
1920 ARS, HP/517/LXX, Assarasson to FM, 28 Feb. 1941.
107. The only detailed account is in
Cripps papers, entries in his diary
of 26 and 27 Feb. and travel diary, 8
Mar., and letters to his daughter
Diane, 26 Feb. and 8 Mar. There
is also a summary of the talks in
FO 371 29500 N1164/122/38, 9 Mar.
1941. Eden gives only a passing
and perfunctory reference to the
episode in *The Eden Memoirs: The
Reckoning* (London, 1965), p. 208.
108. See, for instance, B. Rubin, *Istanbul
Intrigues* (New York, 1989).
109. AVP RF, f.0132 op.24a p.236 d.7
l.165–73, Vinogradov on meeting
Eden; see also *DGFP*, XII, pp.
211–12, Papen to Ribbentrop, 28
Feb. 1941.
110. See Chapter 8, 'Churchill's Warning
to Stalin'.
111. AVP RF, f.0132 op.24 p.236 d.3
l.19–24, Vinogradov on meeting
Cripps, 2 Mar., and FO 371
30067 R1897/112/44, Knatchbull-
Hugessen to FO, 2 Mar. 1941.
112. AVP RF, f.069 op.25 p.71 d.6 l.41–6,
Maisky on meeting Butler, 5 Mar.
1941.
113. AVP RF, f. 017a, Maisky's diary,
l.56–7, 6 Mar. 1941.
114. M. Gilbert, *Finest Hour: Winston
S. Churchill, 1939–1941* (London,
1983), chs 52–4.
115. FO 371 29779 R2117/113/67,
Knatchbull-Hugessen to FO, 5
Mar., and CAB 69/2 DO (41)9, 5
Mar. 1941.
116. FO 371 30067 R2129/112/44, and
AVP RF, f.07 op.2 p.9 d.20 l.5–12,
record of Vyshinsky's meeting with
Cripps, 6 Mar., and FO minutes and
reply to Cripps, 7 and 11 Mar. See
also UD:s Arkiv 1920 ARS, HP/
517/LXX, Assarasson to FM, 7 Mar.
1941.
117. UD:s Arkiv 1920 ARS, HP/1554/
XLIX, Assarasson to FM, Mar. 1941.
118. AVP RF, f.07 op.2 p.9 d.24 l.3–5,
Vyshinsky on meeting Aktay, 9
Mar. 1941.
119. FO 371 29500 N1164/122/38, and
AVP RF, f.07 op.2 p.9 d.20 l.13–14,
records of Vyshinsky's meeting
with Cripps, 9 Mar., and FO
minutes, 13 Mar. 1941.
120. FO 371 30067 R2248/112/44,
minute by Cadogan, 13 Mar. 1941.
121. *DGFP*, XII, pp. 201–2, 246 and
285–6, exchange of letters between
Hitler and Inönü, 1 and 12 Mar.,
and Papen to FM, 8 Mar. 1941.
122. AVP RF, f.0132 op.242 p.236 d.7
l.199–201, and FO 371 29780
R2459/113/67, reports of Vinogradov's meeting with Knatchbull-
Hugessen, 14 Mar. 1941.
123. FO 371 30067 R2587/112/44,
Knatchbull-Hugessen to FM, 17
Mar. 1941.
124. *DGFP*, XII, pp. 308–12 and 384,
memorandum on Hitler's meeting
with Gerde, 18 Mar. Krigsarkivet,
Fo..rsvarsstaben, Ser. E/II/15/1,
military attaché's report, no. 27, 24
Mar. 1941.
125. FO 371 30124 R2836/1934/44,
Knatchbull-Hugessen to FO, 21
Mar. 1941.
126. FSB, *Organy Gosudarstvennoi Bezopasnosti SSSR*, I(2), pp. 60–1, report
by Merkulov, head of the NKGB, 22
Mar. 1941.
127. *Izvestiia*, 25 Mar. 1941.
128. See pp. 137–9.
129. AMVnR, d.51 p.45 op.1sh pop.333
l.61, Stamenov to FM, 26 Mar. 1941.

6. The Red Army on Alert

1. Volkogonov, *Stalin: Triumph and
Tragedy*, p. 368.
2. By far the best and most original
description of the novelty of the
doctrine is in Naveh, *In Pursuit
of Military Excellence*; on the forging
of the doctrine see D. Glantz, *The
Soviet Conduct of Tactical Manoeuvre:
Spearhead of the Offensive* (London,
1991), pp. 76–7.
3. Glantz, *Soviet Conduct of Tactical
Manoeuvre*, pp. 80–1.
4. See V. K. Triandafillov, *Kharakter*

operatsii sovremennykh armii (Moscow, 1929), pp. 125–37, and G. S. Isserson, *Evoliutsiia operativnogo iskusstva* (Moscow, 1937), pp. 11–18. Y. M. Zhigur's work *Budushchaia voina i zadach oborony SSSR* (Moscow, 1938) was devoted entirely to defence. The most authoritative account of the theoretical revolution is in J. Schneider, *The Structure of Strategic Revolution: Total War and the Roots of the Soviet Warfare State* (Novato, Calif., 1994).

5. The doctrine was clearly expounded in Narodnyi Komissariat Oborony, *Vremennyi polevoi ustav RKKA 1936* (Moscow, 1937). On the legacy of Tukhachevsky's contribution to this strategy see R. Savushkin, 'K voprosu o zarozhdenii teorii posledovael'nykh nastupatel'nykh operatsii', *VIZh*, 5 (1983), pp. 78–82, and Shimon Naveh, 'Tukhachevsky', in Shukman (ed.), *Stalin's Generals*.

6. Glantz, *Soviet Conduct of Tactical Manoeuvre*, pp. 80–2. See a discussion of the supposedly aggressive disposition of these forces below, pp. 209, 238–40.

7. On this aspect see below, p. 237f.

8. V. A. Anfilov, *Proval 'blitskriga'* (Moscow, 1974), pp. 162 and 178–89, and A. G. Khor'kov, 'Nekotorye voprosy strategicheskogo razvertyvaniia sovetskikh vooruzhennykh sil v nachale Velikoi Otechestvennoi voiny', *VIZh*, 1 (1986), pp. 9–11.

9. Dimitrov's diary, 28 Mar. 1940.

10. *Izvestiia TsK KPSS*, 1 (1990), pp. 193–6. See also Timoshenko's 'Smena rukovodstva Narkomata oborony SSSR v sviazi s urokami sovetsko-finliandskoi voiny 1939–1940 gg.', in *ibid.*, pp. 210–15.

11. Reproduced in *VIZh*, 3 (1991), pp. 5–8.

12. N. S. Khrushchev, *Khrushchev Remembers* (Boston, 1970), pp. 176–7, and E. Harrison Salisbury, *The Siege of Leningrad* (London, 1969), pp. 67–81.

13. See H. Hanak, 'The Implications of the Soviet–German Pacts for the Western European Democracies' (unpublished paper, 1989), pp. 13–17.

14. National Archives, Department of State, 740.0011 EW 1939/3446, 1 June 1940.

15. See pp. 23–4. On the strategic constraints see for example Leach, *German Strategy against Russia*, chs 3 and 4; V. A. Anfilov, *Bessmertny podvig* (Moscow, 1971), pp. 149–60; M. V. Zakharov, 'Stranitsy istorii sovetskikh vooruzhennykh sil nakanune Velikoi Otechestvennoi voiny 1939–1941 gg', *Voprosy istorii*, 5 (1970).

16. *DGFP*, IX, p. 566; Churchill, *Second World War*, II, pp. 118–19.

17. On the defensive nature of the deployment before the war see *Istoriia Velikoi Otechestvennoi voiny Sovetskogv Soiuza, 1941–1945* (Moscow, 1961), I, pp. 477–8, and G. K. Zhukov, *Vospominaniia i razmyshleniia* (Moscow, 1995), I, pp. 112–14. See a remarkable analysis of the issue in C. A. Roberts, 'Planning for War: The Red Army and the Catastrophe of 1941', *Europe-Asia Studies*, 47/8 (1995). In 'Tragediia krasnoi armii', *Moskovsky Novosti*, 7 May 1989, Lieutenant-General Nikolai Pavlenko, a leading Soviet military historian, presented a revealing and frank review of the performance of the Red Army in the opening stages of the war. An insightful discussion of the shortcomings is in B. M. Gerard, 'Mistakes in Force Structure and Strategy on the Eve of the Great Patriotic War', *Journal of Soviet Military Studies*, 4/3 (1991).

18. D. Glantz, *Soviet Military Strategy in the 1990s: Alternative Futures* (Carlisle, Pa., 1991), p. 75. See below, pp. 241–2.

19. See on this a fair judgment by Volkogonov, *Stalin: Triumph and Tragedy*, pp. 362–3.

20. 'Komitet Oborony pri SNK SSSR:

"Ob organizatsii i chislennosti Krasnoi Armii"'. SNK SSSR i TsK VKP(b), 'O proizvodstve tankov T-34 v 1940 godu', *Izvestiia TsK KPSS*, 2 (1990), pp. 181–3. See also 'Postanovleniia SNK i TsK, 5 June 1940', in *ibid.*, pp. 180–1.

21. Timoshenko's speech produced in *VIZh*, 3 (1991), p. 38.

22. Erickson, *Road to Stalingrad*, pp. 20–4.

23. M. V. Zakharov, *General'nyi shtab v predvoennye gody* (Moscow, 1989), p. 125. See also Glantz, *Soviet Military Strategy*, pp. 69–74.

24. *Izvestiia TsK KPSS*, 2 (1990), p. 182.

25. GRU GSh RF, f.16a op.2951 d.239 l.1–37, 19 Aug. 1940. See also 'Vpered byla voina', *VIZh*, 5 (1991), p. 6, and 'Pribaltiiskii voennyi okrug', in *VIZh*, 6 (1989), pp. 17–22.

26. See pp. 52–7.

27. *Der Prozess gegen die Hauptkriegsverbrecher*, I, p. 163, statement by General Jödl in Nuremberg, 6 Sept. 1940.

28. Volkogonov papers, Special 'Razvedyvatel'naia svodka po zapadu', No. 6, 25 Aug. 1940.

29. TsA SVR RF, d.21616 t.1 l.89–90, a report by the 5th Dept of the Ukrainian NKGD, 15 Aug. 1940.

30. GRU GSh RF, op.24119 d.4 l.65–6, 'Sophocles' in Belgrade to GRU, 27 Jan., and AVP RF, f.0125 op.27 p.122 d.5 l.50–3, record of Mikhailov's meeting with Spitsmuller, the French chargé d'affaires in Bucharest, 1 Feb. 1941.

31. The directive is AGSh RF, f.16 op.2951 d.237 l.138–56, 18 Aug. 1940. See also Zakharov, *General'nyi shtab*, pp. 219–20.

32. See pp. 310–11.

33. See pp. 39–43.

34. AGSh RF, f.16 op.2951 d.242 l.84–90, Timoshenko and Meretskov to Stalin, not later than 5 Oct. 1941.

35. AGSh RF, f.16 op.2951 d.239 l.245–77, report by Pukaev, head of the Kiev Military District, on the deployment plan, Dec. 1940.

36. Leach, *German Strategy against Russia*, p. 163.

37. Zhukov, *Vospominaniia i razmyshleniia*, I, pp. 332–3. See also B. Gugate, *Operation Barbarossa* (Novato, Calif., 1984), challenged by L. Rotundo, 'War Plans and the 1941 Kremlin War Games', *Journal of Strategic Studies*, 10/1 (1987), pp. 84–97.

38. Dekanozov to Molotov, 7 Dec. 1940, reproduced in *Izvestiia TsK KPSS*, 3 (1990).

39. AVP RF, f.059 op.1 p.325 d.2237 l.272–4, Maisky to FM on information received from Colonel Moravec of the Czech mission in London, 18 Dec. 1940.

40. The speech is in *DGFP*, XI, pp. 980–1, and Stalin's acquaintance with its content is attested by Anfilov.

41. GRU GSh RF, op.24119 d.3 l.7, 4 Jan. 1941.

42. FSB, *Organy Gosudarstvennoi Bezopasnosti SSSR*, I(2), p. 286, 'Corsicanets', 7 Jan. 1941.

43. *Ibid.*, pp. 5–7 and 19–21, 16 and 20 Jan. 1941.

44. *Ibid.*, p. 280, 20 Jan. 1941.

45. *Ibid.*, I(1), pp. 287–97, memorandum by Timoshenko and Voroshilov, 7 Dec. 1940, and I(2), pp. 3–4, report by Merkulov to Zhukov, 2 Jan. 1941.

46. p. 126.

47. See on this Zhukov, *Vospominaniia i razmyshleniia*, I, pp. 304–6. See also D. Glantz's insightful book, *The Stumbling Colossus: The Red Army in June 1941* (1998).

48. The verbatim proceedings of the conference were published by the Russian Institute of Military History under the title *Nakanune Voiny: Materialy soveshchaniia vysshego rukovodiashchego sostava RKKA, 23–31 dekabria 1940 g.* (Moscow, 1993).

49. On this see also Zakharov, *General'nyi shtab*, pp. 195–211.

50. See also a still very remarkable analysis of the conference in Erickson, *Road to Stalingrad*, pp. 40–6.

51. Zhukov, *Vospominaniia i razmysh-leniia*, I, pp. 306–7.
52. Interview with Anfilov, May 1994.
53. The following is based mostly on Zakharov, *General'nyi shtab*, pp. 239–51, which is the most revealing and authoritative description of the games.
54. *Ibid.*, p. 240.
55. E. Ziemke, 'Stalin as a Strategist, 1940–1941', *Military Affairs*, 47/4 (1983), pp. 174–80.
56. Zakharov, *General'nyi shtab*, pp. 247–54.
57. *Ibid.*, p. 247.
58. Presidential Archives, 'Special Collection', 'Postanovlenie Politburo TsK VKP(b)', 14 Jan. 1941; see also Zhukov, *Vospominaniia i razmysh-leniia*, I, pp. 308–11.
59. Erickson, *Road to Stalingrad*, pp. 53–4.
60. Zhukov, *Vospominaniia i razmysh-leniia*, I, p. 323. Glantz suggests that from the psychological point of view the legacy of the offensive strategy stifled discussion and implementation of the defensive measures, in *Military Strategy of the Soviet Union*, pp. 60–1.
61. Chuev, *Sto sorok besed s Molotovym*, p. 31.
62. TsA SVR RF, d.23078 t.1 l.199–201, Beria to Stalin and Molotov, 21 Jan. 1941.
63. Presidential Archives, t.8115 op.8 d.44 l.3, Stalin and Molotov to SNK and the CC of the CPSU, 21 Jan. 1941.
64. See pp. 52–6.
65. FSB, *Organy Gosudarstvennoi Bezopasnosti SSSR*, I(2), pp. 24–5, resolution of the Central Committee, 3 Feb. 1941.
66. TsA SVR RF, d.23078, t.1, l.205–9, report by Merkulov to Stalin and Molotov, 8 Feb. 1941.
67. GRU GSh RF, op.24119 d.1 l.394–5, 'Eshchenko', military attaché in Bucharest, to Golikov (transmitted to Stalin), 13 Mar. 1941.
68. FSB, *Organy Gosudarstvennoi Bezopasnosti SSSR*, I(2), pp. 45–6,

NKGB to the CC of the CPSU, 9 Mar. 1941.
69. TsA SVR RF, d.23078 t.1 l.202–4, Merkulov to Stalin, Molotov and Beria, 6 Mar. 1941.
70. Volkogonov papers, 'Razvedy-vatel'naia svodka po zapadu, No. 1', report for the period from 15 Nov. 1940 to 1 Feb. 1941.
71. GRU GSh RF, op.7237 d.2 l.15–20, special intelligence report by Golikov, 14 Feb. See also op.24122 d.1 l.49, a corroborating report from 'Dora', Zurich, 21 Feb. 1941.
72. *Ibid.*, op.24119 d.4 l.213–14, military attaché, Budapest, to Golikov, 15 Mar.; d.3, l.127, deputy military attaché, Paris, to Golikov, 15 Mar. 1941.
73. *Ibid.*, op.7237 d.2 l.21–50, special report by Golikov on the expansion and deployment of the German armed forces, 11 Mar. 1941.
74. On this see Chapter.
75. Reproduced in full in *Izvestiia TsK KPSS*, 4 (1990), pp. 205–6.
76. A report of 7 Feb. 1941 reproduced in *ibid.*
77. GRU GSh RF, op.24119 d.2 l.405–6, 'Sophocles' in Belgrade to Golikov, 9 Mar. 1941.
78. *Ibid.*, l.407–8, military attaché, Bucharest, to Golikov (transmitted to Stalin), 15 Mar., and l.195–6, Sorge to Golikov, 10 Mar. 1941.
79. NKGB to TsK and SNK in *Izvestiia TsK KPSS*, 4 (1990), p. 207.
80. GRU GSh RF, op.24119 d.4 l.213–14, military attaché, Budapest, to Golikov, 14 Mar. 1941.
81. NKGB to the CC of the CPSU and the government, reproduced in *Izvestiia TsK KPSS*, 4 (1990), p. 206, 9 and 14 Mar. 1941.
82. GRU GSh RF, op.24119 d.3 l.127, deputy military attaché, Paris, to Golikov, 15 Mar. 1941.
83. *Ibid.*, op.2421 d.3 l.138, military attaché, Paris, to Golikov, 22 Mar. 1941.
84. *Ibid.*, op.24119 d.1 l.452–5, military attaché, Bucharest, to Golikov, 24 Mar. 1941.

85. A report by 'Marsa', the GRU resident in Budapest, in GRU GSh RF, op.24119 d.4 l.160, and TsA SVR RF, d.23078 t.1 l.194, 'Lauren' from Berlin to the NKVD, 15 Jan. See also UD:s Arkiv 1920 ARS, HP/1554/L, Swedish ambassador in Berlin to FM, 4 Mar. 1941.

86. *DGFP*, XII, pp. 41–4, Hitler's 'Directive 23', 6 Feb. 1941.

87. GRU GSh RF, op.24119 d.4 l.210, military attaché in Budapest to Golikov, 13 Mar. 1941.

88. On this see pp. 180–6.

89. See pp. 157–8.

90. GRU GSh RF, op.14750 d.1 l.12–21, Golikov's report to the Soviet government and the CC of the CPSU, 20 Mar. 1941. Zhukov confirms the shattering impact of such evaluation in *Vospominaniia i razmyshleniia*, I, pp. 380–2.

7. At the Crossroads: The Yugoslav Coup d'Etat

1. *DGFP*, XII, pp. 111, Ribbentrop to legation in Belgrade, 16 Feb. 1941, and van Creveld, *Hitler's Strategy*, p. 65; and see his 'The German Attack on the USSR: The Destruction of a Legend', *European Studies Review*, 2/1 (1972).

2. Sudoplatov, *Special Tasks*, p. 119.

3. AVP RF, f.0144 op.20 p. 105 d.3 l.1–3 and 10, records of meetings of Lozovsky and Vyshinsky, both Deputy Foreign Ministers, with Gavriloviç, 9 July and 25 Oct. 1940.

4. AVP RF, f.059 op.1 p.328 d.2253 l.1020a–1026, Ivanov, first secretary, Soviet embassy, Paris, to Molotov, 13 Sept. 1940.

5. Based also on an enlightening unpublished paper on the coup by Gibiansky. See also A. L. Narochnitsky, 'Sovetsko-iugoslavskii dogovor 5 aprelia 1941 g. o druzhbe i nenapadenii (po arkhivnym materialam)', *Novaia i noveishaia istoriia*, 1 (1989), pp. 3–19.

6. AVP RF, f.059 op.1 p.317 d.2183 l.199, Plotnikov to FM, 17 Dec. 1940.

7. AVP RF, f.0132 op.23 p. 232 d.6 l.67–70, record of Vinogradov's meeting with Shumenkoviç, Yugoslav ambassador in Ankara, 19 Sept. 1940. A supportive account, based to a large degree on the papers of the Regent Paul at the Hoover Institute, is in Barros and Gregor, *Double Deception*, pp. 62–78.

8. *DGFP*, XI, pp. 728–35, record of the meeting, 28 Nov. 1940.

9. *Ibid.*, pp. 525 and 532–3, memorandum by the political division, 11 Nov. 1940.

10. *Ibid.*, pp. 927–8, Ribbentrop to legation in Belgrade, 21 Dec. 1940.

11. AVP RF, f.059 op.1 p.317 d.2183 l.63–4 and 2184 l.177–8, exchange of telegrams between Molotov and Plotnikov (Belgrade), 17 Oct. and 29 Nov. 1940.

12. AVP RF, f.07 op.2 p.10 d.32 l.1–3, Vyshinsky on meeting Gavriloviç, 4 Jan. 1941.

13. *DGFP*, XII, pp. 79–96, record of Hitler's and Ribbentrop's meetings with Cvetkoviç and Cincar-Markoviç, 15 Feb., and pp. 230–3 and 247, exchanges between Herren and Ribbentrop, 4 and 7 Mar. 1941.

14. FO 371 29777 R565/113/67, Eden to Knatchbull-Hugessen on meeting Maisky, 22 Jan. 1941; AVP RF, f.017a, Maisky's diary, p. 52, 2 Mar. 1941. On the fear of embroilment see pp. 85–94.

15. AVP RF, f.07 op.2 p.9 d.24 l.1–2, record of Vyshinsky's meeting with Aktay, 20 Feb., and f.059 op.1 p.342 d.2341 l.39, Lebedev, Soviet ambassador in Belgrade, to FM, 1 Mar. 1941.

16. AVP RF, f.07 op.2 d.32 l.4–6, Vyshinsky on meeting Gavriloviç, 8 Feb., and f.077 op.21 p.111 d.5 l.17–19, Sharonov on meeting Yaniç, former Minister and head of the Belgrade Radio Station, 10 Mar.; UD:s Arkiv 1920 ARS, HP/517/LXX, Assarasson to FM on meeting Schulenburg, 19 Feb. 1941.

17. Tupanjanin proved to be only of a partial value to the Russians as his party was also 'in receipt of a subsidy from His Majesty's Government', PREM 3/510/11 p. 448, minute, 2 Mar. 1941.

18. GRU GSh RF, op.24119 d.4 l.199, report by 'Sophocles' in Belgrade, 9 Mar. 1941.

19. FO 371 29779 R2357/113/67, 11 and 12 Mar. 1941.

20. *DGFP*, XII, pp. 269–73, Herren to FM, 11 Mar. 1941.

21. Archives of the Yugoslav Foreign Ministry (hereafter AJ), CK KPJ, 1941/9, resolution of the CC of the Yugoslav CP 'Against Capitulation – In Favour of a Pact of Mutual Assistance with the Soviet Union', 15 Mar. 1941. See also *Vestnik MID SSSR*, 15(49) (1989), p. 57.

22. *Komintern i vtoraia mirovaia voina*, I, p. 43, 22 Mar. 1941.

23. AJ, MIP, Politichko odeljenje, Gavriloviç to Cincar-Markoviç, 14 Mar. 1941.

24. FO 371 29780 R2446/113/67, Campbell to FO and minutes by Sargent, 12 and 15 Mar. 1941.

25. AJ, MIP, Politichko odeljenje, Cincar-Markoviç to Gavriloviç, 13 Mar. 1941.

26. AVP RF, f. 017a, Maisky's diary, p. 70, 1 Apr. 1941.

27. AVP RF, f.0132 op.24 p.236 d.3 l.19–24, Vinogradov on meeting Cripps, 2 Mar. 1941.

28. FO 371 29779 R2360/113/67, Cripps to Eden, 11 Mar. 1941.

29. FO 371 30228 R2878/394/92, Cripps to FO, 22 Mar. 1941.

30. AVP RF, f.07 op.2 p.9 d.20 l.15–24, record of Vyshinsky's meeting with Cripps, 22 Mar. The nature of the meeting is also confirmed in Cripps's talk with Steinhardt, see *FRUS*, I (1941), pp. 298–9, Steinhardt to the Secretary of State, 24 Mar. 1941.

31. AVP RF, f.07 op.2 p.10 d.32 l.7–8, Vyshinsky on meeting Gavriloviç, 22 Mar.; see also FO 371 30228

R2879/394/92, Cripps to FO, 23 Mar. 1941.

32. AVP RF, f.0132 op.24a p.236 d.7 l.223–6, record of Vinogradov's meeting with Papen, 25 Mar. 1941.

33. Such a claim is made by Sudoplatov, *Special Tasks*, p. 119. There is a more informative observation by Gafencu in *Misiune la Moscova*, tel. 1135, pp. 164–5, Gafencu to FM, 3 Apr. 1941. On the coup see E. Barker, *British Policy in South-East Europe in the Second World War* (London, 1976), pp. 78–108. On the British involvment see D. A. T., Stafford, 'SOE and British Involvement in the Belgrade Coup d'Etat of March 1941', *Slavic Review*, 36/3 (1977).

34. *DGFP*, XII, pp. 372–5, minutes concerning the situation in Yugoslavia, 27 Mar., and pp. 369–71, record of Hitler's meeting with Sztójay, 28 Mar. 1941.

35. Lebedev to MID, 28 Mar. 1941, is quoted in *Sovetsko-iugoslavskie otnosheniia, 1917–1941 gg.* (Moscow, 1992), p. 363.

36. AVP RF, f.144 op.23 p.107 d.1 l.14–15, Lebedev to FM (Political news from Yugoslavia), 31 Mar. 1941.

37. GRU GSh RF, op. 7237 d.2 l.79–81, special report by Golikov on the *coup d'état* in Yugoslavia, 28 Mar. 1941.

38. King Peter, *King's Heritage: The Memoirs of King Peter II of Yugoslavia* (London, 1955), p. 71; *DGFP*, XII, pp. 383–5 and 398–9, Herren to FM, 27 and 28 Mar. 1941.

39. Dimitrov's diary, 29 Mar., and *Komintern i vtoraia mirovaia voina*, I, p. 518–20, the Yugoslav CP to Dimitrov, 29 Mar. 1941.

40. AJ, CK KPJ 1941/10, resolution of the Yugoslav CP, 30 Mar. 1941.

41. FO 371 30228 R3254/394/92, Cripps to FO, 29 Mar. 1941, and Novikov, *Vospominaniia diplomata*, p. 75.

42. AVP RF, f.059 op.1 p.342 d.2341 l.80–1, 85 and 88–9, Lebedev to Molotov, 30 Mar. 1941.

43. See pp. 135–6.

44. Simoviç's diary, Archiv Vojeno-istorijskog instituta, R-16, II, reg.no.2/1, pp. 268–9.

45. AVP RF, f.059 op.1 p.342 d.2341 l.88–9, Lebedev to Molotov, 30–31 Mar.; f.0125 op.27 p.122 d.4 l.182–4, record of Lavrentev's meeting with Avakumoviç, Yugoslav ambassador in Bucharest, 31 Mar. 1941.

46. *Komintern i vtoraia mirovaia voina*, I, pp. 45–6, 5 Apr. 1941.

47. *FRUS*, I (1941), pp. 311–14, Steinhardt and Kelly (first secretary in Ankara) to Hull on Gavriloviç's talks with Stalin, 18 May 1941.

48. AVP RF, f.06 op.3 p.27 d.375 l.3, Vyshinsky on meeting Gavriloviç, 1 Apr. 1941; *ibid.*, f.059 op.1 p.342 d.2342 l.72–4, instructions by Molotov to Lebedev, 1 Apr. 1941.

49. Sobolev to Lebedev and Lebedev to Molotov, 1 Apr. 1940, reproduced in *Vestnik MID SSSR*, 15/49 (1989), p. 60.

50. AVP RF, f.06 op.3 p.27 d.375 l.7–10, record of Vyshinsky's meeting with the Yugoslav delegation, 3 Apr. 1941. On the proposals see S. Cvetkoviç, 'Sovjetska Prisutnost u Jugoslovenskoj Politici Na Pochetku Drugog Svetskog Rata', *Istorija 20. Veka*, 1 (1995), pp. 32–41.

51. AVP RF, f.059 op.1 p.342 d.2341 l.97, Lebedev to Molotov, 3 Apr. 1941.

52. TsA SVR RF, d.23078 t.1 l.240–1, Kobulov ('Zakhar') to Merkulov, and FSB, *Organy Gosudarstvennoi Bezopasnosti SSSR*, I(2), pp. 289–90.

53. GRU GSh RF, op.24119 d.74 l.279–82, 4 Apr. 1941.

54. *DGFP*, XII, pp. 426–7, Schulenburg to FM, 4 Apr. 1941.

55. AVP RF, f.06 op.3 p.1 d.4 l.75–81, Molotov on meeting Schulenburg, and *DGFP*, XII, pp. 451–2, Schulenburg to FM, 4 Apr. AMVnR, d.51 p.45 op.1sh pop.333 l.67, Stamenov to FM, 6 Apr. 1941.

56. On the Soviet theory of a split between the armed forces and Hitler see below, pp. 179–89.

57. UD:s Arkiv 1920 ARS, HP/1555/LIII, Assarasson to FM, 4 Apr.; see also FO 371 30228 R3405/394/92, Cripps to FO, 4 Apr. 1941.

58. *Vestnik MID SSSR*, 15/49 (1989), pp. 55–6, and AVP RF, f.017a, Maisky's diary, pp. 79–80, 6 Apr. 1941.

59. Presidential Archives, f.3 op.66 d.905 l.71–5, Vyshinsky on meeting Gavriloviç, 4 Apr. 1941; see also *FRUS*, I (1941), p. 300.

60. AVP RF, f.059 op.1 p.342 d.2342 l.80, Molotov to Lebedev, 4 Apr.; f.06 op.3 p.27 d.375 l.21, note by Molotov to the Politburo, 4 Apr. 1941.

61. Novikov, *Vospominaniia diplomata*, pp. 76–9.

62. AVP RF, f.06 op.3 p.27 d.375 l.25–7, Vyshinsky on meeting Simiç, 5 Apr. 1941.

63. AVP RF, f.059 op.1 p.342 d.2341 l.102, Lebedev to Molotov, 5 Apr. 1941.

64. *DGFP*, XII, p. 463, the German chargé d'affaires in Belgrade to FM, 5 Apr. 1941.

65. On this see UD:s Arkiv 1920 ARS, HP/1555/LIII, Assarasson to FM on conversations with Gavriloviç, 6 Apr. 1941.

66. Gafencu, *Misiune la Moscova*, tel. 1178, pp. 169–70, Gafencu to the FM, 7 Apr. 1941.

67. The following account of the events of the night of 5–6 April is based on AVP RF, f.144 op.3a p.4 d.4 l.3–6, report by Novikov, 6 Apr., and his *Vospominaniia diplomata*, pp. 76–9; *FRUS*, I (1941), pp. 300–1, Steinhardt to Hull on meeting Gavriloviç, and FO 371 29544 N1392/1392/38, Cripps to FO, 6 Apr. 1941.

68. The transcription of the call is in N. B. Popovich, *Jugoslovensko-sovjetski odnosi u drugom svetskom ratu (1941–1945)* (Belgrade, 1988), pp. 26–7. See also Simoviç's diary, Archiv Vojeno-istorijskog instituta, R-16, II, reg.no.2/1, pp. 268–9, and J. B. Hoptner, *Yugoslavia in Crisis, 1934–1941* (New York, 1962).

69. On this see Simoviç's diary, Archiv Vojeno-istorijskog instituta, R-16, II, reg.no.2/1, pp. 268–9.
70. Krigsarkivet, Fo..rsvarsstaben, Ser. E/II/15/1, military attaché's report, no. 59, 5 Apr. 1941.
71. Sudoplatov, *Special Tasks*, p. 119.
72. Novikov, *Vospominaniia diplomata*, pp. 79–82.
73. Gafencu, *Misiune la Moscova*, tel. 1161, pp. 165–6, Gafencu to FM, 6 Apr. 1941.
74. *Pravda* and *Izvestiia*, 6 Apr. 1941.
75. UD:s Arkiv 1920 ARS, HP/518/LXXII, Assarasson to FM, 5 Apr. 1941.
76. AJ, f. MIP, Poslanstvo Moskva, Shumenkoviç to Simoviç, 6 Apr. 1941.
77. AVP RF, f.059 op.1 p.342 d.2342 l.83, Vyshinsky to Lebedev, 6 Apr. 1941.
78. *DGFP*, XII, pp. 479–80 and 484, exchange of telegrams between Schulenburg and FM, 6 Apr. 1941.
79. By far the best account of the campaign is in van Creveld, *Hitler's Strategy*, pp. 160–5.
80. FSB, *Sekrety Gitlera*, pp. 25–8, a note by Merkulov to the CC of the CPSU, 10 Apr. 1941.
81. AVP RF, f. 017a, Maisky's diary, l.81–2, 7 Apr.; *DGFP*, XII, pp. 490–1, Weizsäcker on meeting Dekanozov, 8 Apr. 1941.
82. AVP RF, f.0125 op.27 p.122 d.4 l.199–201, record of Lavrentev's (Soviet ambassador in Bucharest) meeting with the Greek ambassador Kollas, 10 Apr. 1941.
83. AVP RF, f.07 op.2 p.10 d.32 l.10–12, Vyshinsky on meeting Gavriloviç, and f.0125 op.27 p.122 d.4 l.206–9, Lavrentev on meeting Avakumoviç, 11 and 12 Apr. 1941 respectively.
84. *Izvestiia*, 12 Apr. 1941.
85. UD:s Arkiv 1920 ARS, HP/518/ LXXII, Assarasson to FM, 27 May 1941.
86. *Vestnik MID SSSR*, 49 (1989), p. 55. See I. V. Bukharkin, 'No tut vmeshalas' Iugoslaviia', *Pravda*, 1 June 1991. A similar but far more critical

attitude in V. K. Volkov, 'Sovetsko-iugoslavskie otnosheniia v nachal'nyi period Vtoroi mirovoi voiny v kontekste mirovykh sobytii (1939–1941 gg)', *Sovetskoe slavianovedenier*, 6 (1990), pp. 3–17.

8. Churchill's Warning to Stalin

1. The present work is saturated with such reports.
2. Churchill, *Second World War*, III, pp. 316, 319–23.
3. See pp. 10–18. A more detailed discussion of controversy between Churchill and Cripps in Gorodetsky, *Cripps' Mission to Moscow*, chs 8–10.
4. FO 371 29464 N1526/3/38 and FO 837/1098, telegrams from Cripps, 23 and 29 Mar. 1941.
5. CAB 65/18 33(41)7, 31 Mar. 1941.
6. FO 371 29479 N1360/3/38, 2 Apr. 1941.
7. See Chapter 1, pp. 21–2ff for the role Orme Sargent played in developing the Foreign Office's political concept.
8. FO 371 26518–9 and 29479 are packed with such intelligence and appraisals.
9. J. Herndon, 'British Perceptions of Soviet Military Capability, 1935–9', an unpublished paper.
10. See the most revealing and authoritative study of F. H. Hinsley et al., *British Intelligence in the Second World War: Its Influence on Strategy and Operations* (London, 1979–90), I, pp. 237–41; FO 371 29479 N107, N255 and N286/78/38, minutes by Maclean, Collier, Cadogan and Eden, 10 and 18 Jan. 1941.
11. FO 371 29528 N648/648/38 20 Jan., and minutes by Maclean and Collier, 22 and 23 Feb. 1941.
12. FO 371 26518 C2222/19/18, telegrams from O'Malley, Halifax and Mallet, 6 and 7 Mar., and minutes by Cavendish-Bentinck, Strang, Cadogan and Collier, 9, 10, 11 and 12 Mar. 1941.

13. FO 371 29479 N1390/78/38, Mallet to FO and minutes, 4 Apr. 1941.
14. FO 371 29135 W2860/53/50, WIP, 12 Mar., and W3205/53/50, 19 Mar. See also FO 371 29479 N1132/78/38, Butler on conversation with Greek minister and FO minutes, 18 Mar. 1941.
15. See pp. 108–10.
16. FO 371 26518 C2924/19/18, Cripps to FO, 24 Mar. 1941.
17. For Cripps's views see State Department, 740.001 1 EW/39/8919, telegram from Steinhardt, 7 Mar. 1941; Assarasson, *I skuggan av Stalin*, p. 56; Gafencu, *Prelude to the Russian Campaign*, pp. 134–6. On the press conference see W. Duranty, *The Kremlin and the People* (New York, 1942), pp. 151–2; A. Werth, *Moscow 1941* (London, 1942), p. 133; H. Elvin, *A Cockney in Moscow* (London, 1958), p. 54.
18. On the accuracy of the information see B. Whaley, *Codeword Barbarossa* (Cambridge, Mass., 1973), pp. 50–1. As long as the Soviet archives remained closed, Whaley's work was considered to be the most authoritative and exhaustive work on the subject. It still is valuable, especially as far as the disinformation dimension is concerned. The Russians had obtained the same information from at least four independent sources, see note 43 below.
19. FO 371 26518 C2919/19/18, Cripps to FO and minutes, 24–28 Mar. 1941.
20. FO 371 29479 N1367/78/38, military attaché, Bern, 24 Mar., and minutes by Major Templin, the expert on Russian affairs in MI2 (Military Intelligence), 31 Mar. 1941.
21. Hinsley *et al.*, *British Intelligence*, I, pp. 446–50.
22. See below, p. 22.
23. Churchill, *Second World War*, III, p. 319.
24. On this see pp. 102–14.
25. Churchill, *Second World War*, III, p. 319, and Dilks (ed.), *Cadogan Diaries*, p. 367.
26. In December 1993 the British government opened the archives containing the raw intelligence prepared for Churchill. The present account is based on this material in PRO HW 1/3, 28 Mar. 1941.
27. PREM 3/510/11 pp. 363–4, Churchill to Eden, 30 Mar. 1941.
28. Dilks (ed.), *Cadogan Diaries*, p. 367.
29. Hinsley *et al.*, *British Intelligence*, I, p. 451.
30. FO 371 29479 N1354/78/38, Halifax to FO, 2 Apr. 1941.
31. FO 371 29479 N1316, N1324/78/38 Cripps, Campbell and Halifax to FO, and minutes, 2 and 3 Apr. 1941.
32. WO 190/983; FO 371 29135 W3859/53/50.
33. See for example his opposition to Eden's visit to Russia, PREM 3/395/16, telegram to Eden, 22 Feb. 1941.
34. *Ibid.*
35. Churchill, *Second World War*, III, pp. 320–1; PREM 3/403/7.
36. Churchill papers, 20/37, Churchill to Cripps, 30 Mar. 1941.
37. FO 371 29479 N366/78/38, telegram to Cripps and minute by Cadogan, 4 Apr. 1941.
38. Churchill, *Second World War*, III, p. 321.
39. See Chapter 7.
40. FO 371 29479 N1397/78/38, Cripps to Churchill, 5 Apr. 1941.
41. FO 371 29479 N1429/78/38 and 29479 N1429/78/38, Cripps to Churchill, 5 Apr. 1941.
42. FO 371 29479 N1364/78/38 and 29465 N1713/3/38, 12, 15 and 19 Apr. 1941.
43. AVP RF, f.06 op.3 p.27 d.375 l.4–6, record of Vyshinsky's meeting with Gavrilović, 2 Apr., and intercepted telegram of Aktay reproduced in *Izvestiia TsK KPSS*, 4 (1990), pp. 207–9, 26 Mar. and 7 Apr. See in particular a report which tallied with Churchill's own warning in GRU GSh RF, op.24119 d.3 l.138, military attaché, Vichy, to Golikov, 22 Mar. 1941.

44. FO 371 29479 N1510/78/38, exchange of telegrams between Churchill and Cripps, 8 Apr. 1941.
45. FO 371 29479 N1510/78/38 and N1534/78/38.
46. FO 371 29464 N1386/3/38, Cripps to Eden (in Athens), Eden to Cripps and minutes, 4–16 Apr. 1941.
47. FO 371 29479 N1510/78/38, 11 Apr. 1941.
48. Eden, *The Reckoning*, p. 262.
49. Monckton papers, Box 4, p. 201, 17 Apr.; Cripps papers, Isobel's diary, 16 and 20–4 Apr.; *ibid.*, Weaver papers, letter from Cripps, 18 Apr. 1941.
50. AVP RF, f.07 op.2 p.9 d.20 l.25–9, record of Vyshinsky's meeting with Cripps (not reported by Cripps to the FO), 10 Apr. 1941, and UD:s Arkiv 1920 ARS, HP/517/LXXI, Assarasson to FM, 9 Apr. 1941.
51. FO 371 29480 N1848/78/38, and AVP RF, f.06 op.3 d.89 p.8 l.1–6, Cripps to Vyshinsky, 11 Apr. 1941.
52. FO 371 29479 N1573/78/38, Cripps to FO and minutes by Eden and Churchill, 12–15 Apr. 1941. See also Churchill's quotations in *Second World War*, III, pp. 111 and 321, with the obvious omissions.
53. FO 371 29465 N1667/3/38, and 29473 N1889/22/38, FO minutes, 12 and 18 Apr. 1941.
54. CAB 65/18 42(41)3, 21 Apr. 1941.
55. PREM 3/395/16 p. 433, Churchill to Eden, 22 Apr. 1941.
56. Churchill Papers, 20/37, Churchill to Eden, 3 Apr. 1941. Much the best work on Churchill's strategy as far as the Balkan war is concerned and especially the decision to help Greece is Lawlor, *Churchill and the Politics of War*, ch. 10.
57. Churchill papers, 20/37, Churchill to Wavell, 4 Apr. 1941.
58. *Ibid.*, exchanges between Churchill, Eden and Wavell, 7 and 9 Apr.; see also Eden papers, diary, 11 April 1941.
59. Reported in *The Times*, 10 Apr., and commentary in *The Times*, 20 Apr. 1941.
60. Churchill papers, 20/37, Churchill to Dominion Prime Ministers, 15 Apr. 1941.
61. *Ibid.*, 20/36, Churchill's minute to Ismay, for COS, 20 Apr., and 20/38, Wavell to Churchill, 22 Apr. 1941.
62. *Ibid.*, Churchill's directive, 28 Apr. 1941.
63. See for instance AVP RF, f.017a, Maisky's diary, pp. 1–3, 62–5 and 69, 1 Jan. and 31 Mar. 1941.
64. Dimitrov's diary, 20 Feb. 1941.
65. AVP RF, f.017a, Maisky's diary, pp. 79–80, 4 Apr. 1941.
66. Reported in AVP RF, f.059 op.1 p.351 d.2401 l.130, Maisky to FM, and in Maisky's diary, pp. 83–4, 9 Apr. 1941.
67. AVP RF, f.069 op.25 p.71 d.6 l.58–9, Maisky to FM on meeting Brendan Bracken, 30 Apr.; f.017a, Maisky's diary, pp. 111–15, 30 Apr. 1941.
68. AVP RF, f.059 op.1 p.361 d.2401 l.133–4, Maisky to FM, 10 Apr.; f.017a, Maisky's diary, pp. 41–5 and 85–7, 1 Mar. and 10 Apr. 1941.
69. *Ibid.*, pp. 121–2, 5 May 1941.
70. See below, pp. 213–17.
71. FO 371 29465 N1999/3/38, Halifax to Eden, 5 May 1941. On the deliberate manifestation of confidence see below, pp. 207–8.
72. I am grateful to I. McDonald for this piece of information.
73. AVP RF, f.017a, Maisky's diary, pp. 152–3.
74. See pp. 202–4 below.
75. FO 371 29465 N1667/3/38, exchange of telegrams between Cripps and Eden, 17 and 19 Apr. See also Cripps papers, Isobel's diary, 28 Apr. 1941.
76. The following meetings are based on FO 371/29480 N1762/78/38, telegrams from Cripps, 23 Apr., and minutes by Sargent and Eden, 25 Apr. 1941.
77. FO 371 29465 N1828 and N1692/3/38, Cripps to FO, 18 Apr. AVP RF, f.06 op.3 d.75 p.7 l.11–16, Cripps to Vyshinsky, 18 Apr. See also State Department, 740.0011

EW39/8919, telegram from Stein-hardt, 7 Mar. 1941, on similar insinuations made earlier by Cripps to the American ambassador and which may well have reached the ears of the Soviet authorities.

78. On this see FSB, *Sekrety Gitlera*, pp. 25–8, Merkulov to the CC of the CPSU, SNK and NKVD, 10 Apr. 1941. See also Vyshinsky's conversations with Gavriloviç, on the same day in AVP RF, f.07 op.2 p. 10 d.32 l.10–12.

79. TsA FSB RF, f.'Zos' op.8 d.55 l.288–91, memorandum by Merkulov to Stalin on Cripps's secret press conference, 11 Mar. 1941.

80. State Department 740.0011 EW/39/8919, 7 Mar. 1941.

81. I am thankful to Sir Maurice Shock for his enlightening comments on Cripps and the *Blitzkrieg*.

82. PREM 3/395/2 fol. 29.

83. *DGFP*, XII, pp. 604–5, FM to Schulenburg, 22 Apr. 1941.

84. FO 371 29465 N1806/3/38.

85. AVP RF, f.017a, Maisky's diary, pp. 102–3, 22 and 23 Apr. 1941.

86. FO 371 29465 N1667/3/38, FO minutes, 17 and 19 Apr. 1941.

87. GRU GSh RF, op.24119 d.1 l.452–5, military attaché, Bucharest, to Golikov, 24 Mar. 1941.

88. FO 371 29480 N1725/78/38, telegram from Cripps, 22 Apr. 1941; P. A. Zhilin, *Kak fashistskaia Germaniya gotovila napadenie na Sovetskii Soyuz* (Moscow, 1966), p. 219; Zhukov, *Vospominaniia i razmyshleniia*, I, pp. 368, 371 and 373.

89. The meeting of 25 Apr. is covered in FO 371 29465 N1801/3/38 and in AVP RF, f.069 op.25 d.6 p.71 l.66–9 (and see also l.62–5 for earlier meeting on the 18th).

90. See p. 227.

91. Van Creveld, 'The German Attack on the USSR'.

92. Van Creveld, *Hitler's Strategy*, pp. 149 and 151.

93. Beaverbrook papers, D 93, Churchill to Eden and Beaverbrook, 1 Nov. 1941.

94. CAB 69/2 DO(41)69, 27 Oct.; CAB 79/55 COS(41)34 and minute by Churchill, 28 Oct. 1941.

95. PREM 3/403/7, Churchill to Beaverbrook, 14 Oct. 1941.

96. PREM 3/395/2, fol. 30, Eden to Churchill, 14 Oct. 1941; Werth, *Russia at War*, p. 270.

97. *FRUS*, I (1941), pp. 702, 712–13, 715.

9. Japan: The Avenue to Germany

1. TsA SVR RF, d.21616 t.2 l.36–41, Merkulov to Timoshenko, 31 Mar 1941.

2. *Ibid.*, l.11–12, Merkulov to Stalin, 31 Mar 1941.

3. Foreign Intelligence, NKVD, to GRU, reproduced in *Izvestiia TsK KPSS*, 4 (1990), p. 211.

4. GRU AGSh RF, op. 7237, report by Golikov, 16 Apr., and Volkogonov papers, 'Razvedyvatel'noi svodki po zapadu', No. 4, 20 Apr. 1941.

5. Sudoplatov, *Special Tasks*, p. 118.

6. On the hard military information which intrigued the armed forces in the first place see pp. 130–6.

7. AVP RF, f.059 op.1 p.315 d.2174 l.104, Shkvartsev to FM, 12 Feb. 1940.

8. See Chapter 8, 'Churchill's Warning to Stalin'.

9. Umansky to Molotov, 1 Mar. 1941, reproduced in *Vestnik MID SSSR*, 8/66, (1990), p. 78.

10. FSB, *Organy Gosudarstvennoi Bezopasnosti SSSR*, I(2), pp. 26–7, report from the 2nd Dept of the NKGB, 7 Feb. 1941.

11. TsA SVR RF, d.23078 t.1 l.210–14, Merkulov to Stalin and Molotov, 8 Mar. 1941.

12. GRU GSh RF, op.24127 d.2 l.195–6, Sorge to Golikov, 11 Mar. 1941. For a Soviet and a Western account of Sorge's activities see A. Egorov, 'Rikhard Zorge (K 90-letiiu so dnia rozhdeniia)', *VIZh*, 10 (1985), pp. 90–2, and G. W. Prange, *Target Tokyo: The Story of the Sorge Spy Ring* (New York, 1984).

13. GRU GSh RF, op.24127 d.2 l.340–1, Sorge to Golikov, 6 May 1941.

14. *Ibid.*, l.381, Sorge to Golikov, 21 May 1941.

15. *Ibid.*, l.422, two telegrams from Sorge to Golikov, 1 June 1941.

16. TsA FSB RF, f.'Zos' op.8 d.55 l.288–91, Merkulov to Stalin and Molotov, 11 March 1941.

17. UD:s Arkiv 1920 ARS, HP/1554/L and LVI, Swedish ambassador in Berlin to FM, 13 Mar. and 15 May; AVP RF, f.06 op.3 p.25 d.335 l.1–6, and Quai d'Orsay Archives, telegrams from Moscow, tel. 428–31, reports of Bogomolov's meeting with Bergery, 15 May. See also Gafencu, *Misiune la Moscova*, raport 1627, pp. 200–10, Gafencu to FM, 15 May 1941.

18. FO 371 29481 N2388/78/38, Halifax to FO, 23 May 1941.

19. See p. 135.

20. GRU GSh RF, op.14750 d.1 l.12–21, Golikov's report to the Soviet government and the CC of the CPSU, 20 Mar. 1941.

21. TsA SVR RF, d.23078 t.1 l.269–74, report by 'Stepanov' on information from 'Starshina', 17 Apr. Already in his report of mid-Mar. 'Corsicanets' pinpointed Göring as the leading spirit in the drive towards war, FSB, *Organy Gosudarstvennoi Bezopasnosti SSSR*, I(2), pp. 287–8, 'Corsicanets' to the Centre, 15 Mar. 1941.

22. TsA SVR RF, d.23078 t.1 l.291–5, Merkulov to Stalin, Molotov, Beria and Timoshenko, 24 Apr. 1941.

23. FSB, *Sekrety Gitlera*, p. 116, Merkulov to Stalin, Molotov and Beria, 19 May 1941; the original is in FO 371 29135 W5835/35/50, Soviet Union, 14 May 1941.

24. *Ibid.*, pp. 117–18, Merkulov to Stalin, Molotov and Beria, 19 May 1941.

25. Hitler's instructions of 12 May 1941, in *50 Let Velikoi Otechestvennoi voiny*, pp. 21–2.

26. TsA FSB RF, f.'Zos', op.8 d.57 l.1500–4, Merkulov to Stalin, Molotov and Beria, 25 May 1941.

27. TsA SVR RF, d.23078 t.1 l.331–2, and FSB, *Organy Gosudarstvennoi Bezopasnosti SSSR*, I(2), pp. 290–1, report on Kobulov's ('Zakhar') meeting with 'Corsicanets' and 'Starshina', 2 and 11 Apr., and Merkulov to Stalin, Beria and Molotov, 14 Apr. 1941; see L. Bezymensky, 'The Great Game', an unpublished paper.

28. Rosso quoted by Cripps in FO 371 29480 N1819/78/38, 26 Apr. 1941.

29. FSB, *Organy Gosudarstvennoi Bezopasnosti SSSR*, I(2), pp. 292–3, Berlin residency to NKGB, 1 May 1941, passed on to Stalin and Molotov on 5 May; see FSB, *Sekrety Gitlera*, pp. 65–7.

30. TsA SVR RF, d.23078 t.1 l.236–46, information transmitted through 'Zakhar' from 'Litseist', 16 Apr. 1941.

31. AVP RF, f.082 op.24 p.106 d.8 l.370–2, Bogdanov, first secretary in Berlin, 14 Apr. 1941.

32. TsA FSB RF, f.'Zos' op.8 d.56 l.792–5, Merkulov to the CC of the CPSU, SNK and NKVD, 22 Apr. 1941, and TsA SVR RF, d.23078 t.1 l.285–7, Merkulov to Molotov, 16 Apr. 1941.

33. See pp. 202–4

34. FSB, *Sekrety Gitlera*, pp. 31–2, a report from Berlin transmitted by Merkulov to the CC of the CPSU, 22 Apr. 1941.

35. TsA SVR RF, d.23078 t.1 l.388–90, report by 'Starshina', 9 May, and l.369–72, report by 'Zakhar' from Berlin, 10 May 1941.

36. AVP RF, f.0134 op.24a p.236 d.9 l.96–7, record of Zhegalov's (first secretary) meeting with Gruiç (Yugoslav), 5 May 1941.

37. TsA FSB RF, f.'Zos' op.8 d.56 l.1160–3, Merkulov transmits Cripps's telegrams 412 and 413 to Eden, of 30 Apr. and 5 May 1941.

38. AVP RF, f.094 op.26 p.331 d.5 l.5–8, record of Filomonov's (Soviet ambassador in Iran) meeting with Ishikava, Japanese ambassador in Iran, 21 Apr., AVP RF, f.0125 op.27

p.122 d.4 l.231–2, record of Lavrentev's meeting with Lon Liang, 6 May, d.5 l.108–110, record of Mikhailov's meeting with Nureldzhim, 7 May. See also GRU GSh RF, op.24119 d.1 l.762–3, 'Zevsa', Sofia, to Golikov, 9 May 1941.

39. *Ibid.*, op.24122 d.1 l.272, 'Dora', Zurich, to Golikov, 19 May 1941.

40. AVP RF, f.077 op.2 p.111 d.5 l.56–7, record of Sharonov's meeting with Unaidin, 21 May 1941.

41. TsA SVR RF, d.23078 t.1 l.349–51, Berlin residency to NKGB, 30 Apr. 1941.

42. *Ibid.*, l.352–5, Merkulov to Stalin, Molotov and Beria, 30 Apr. 1941.

43. See an enlightening insight in AVP RF, f.017a, Maisky's diary, pp. 106–7, 26 Apr. 1941.

44. Most of the works on intelligence, Whaley's *Codeword Barbarossa* in particular, dwell on the disinformation aspects of the episode.

45. *DGFP*, XII, pp. 490–1.

46. Quai d'Orsay Archives, 834/Z/312/1 pp. 127–8, report of conversations with Bogomolov, 9 Apr. 1941.

47. AVP RF, f.06 op.2 p.1 d.1 l.13–15, record of Molotov's meeting with Yan Tse, Chinese ambassador in Moscow, 8 Jan., and f.059 op.1 p.338 d.2312 l.8–9, Paniushkin, Soviet ambassador in China, to Molotov, 9 Jan. 1940.

48. AVP RF, f.06 op.2 p.2 d.11 l.64–7, record of Molotov's meeting with General Xe Iaotsu, 28 Apr. 1940. On the impact of the Soviet–Japanese war at Khalkin-Gol on the Soviet policy see A. D. Coox, *Nomonhan: Japan against Russia, 1939* (Stanford, 1986).

49. On his suspicions in 1940, see pp. 94–5. AVP RF, f.0100 op.24 p.196 d.8 l.6–10, Paniushkin on meeting Chinese Deputy Prime Minister and Minister of Finance Kun Siansi, War Minister Xe Intsin and Minister of Economics Ven Venkhao, 29 Feb. 1940.

50. AVP RF, f.0146 op.23 p.205 d.9 l.10–

16, report of Lozovsky's meeting with Togo, Japanese ambassador in Moscow, 21 Jan. 1940. J. Haslam's *The Soviet Union and the Threat from the East, 1933–1941* (London, 1992) should be considered the most exhaustive survey of Soviet policies in the Far East. However, Haslam overlooks Stalin's search for accommodation with Germany through the Japanese. He shows the fluctuations and strange fusion of Soviet Russia's imperial policies, *Realpolitik* and ideology in her foreign policy in the East.

51. AVP RF, f.06 op.2 p. 2 d.12 l.144–51, record of Molotov's meeting with Togo, 23 May 1940. The Japanese archives do attest to the correctness of that evaluation, see H. Chihiro, 'The Japanese–Soviet Neutrality Pact', in J. Morley (ed.), *The Fateful Choice: Japan's Advance into Southeast Asia, 1939–1941* (New York, 1980), pp. 28–31.

52. AVP RF, f.06 op.2 p. 2 d.13 l.3–9, 13–16 and 39–43, records of Molotov's meetings with Togo, 1, 3 and 7 June 1940.

53. AVP RF, f.06 op.2 p.2 d.13 l.68–71, record of Molotov's meeting with Chao Litse, Chinese ambassador, 9 June, and f.0100 op.24 p.196 d.6 l.54–5, record of Rezanov's (director of the Far Eastern Department of MID) meeting with Dzan Detinem, Chinese chargé d'affaires, 10 June 1940.

54. AVP RF, f.0146 op.23 p.206 d.14 l.69–75, Malik (Soviet embassy in Tokyo) to FM, 12 June. See a similar German appreciation of the change in *DGFP*, XI, pp. 19–20, FM minute, 4 Sept. 1940. See also Chihiro, 'The Japanese–Soviet Neutrality Pact', pp. 41–3.

55. *DGFP*, XI, pp. 206–7, Ott to Matsuoka, 27 Sept. 1940. Chihiro, 'The Japanese–Soviet Neutrality Pact', pp. 47 and 50.

56. AVP RF, f.06 op.2 p.3 d.17 l.1–3, record of Molotov's meeting with Togo, 1 Oct. The Swedish ambas-

sador, in close touch with the Axis powers, believed the way was paved for Russia's access to the pact, see UD:s Arkiv 1920 ARS, HP/516/LXVIII, Assarasson to FM, 12 Oct. 1940.

57. Presidential Archives, f.3 op.64 d.675 ll.13–15, Beria to Stalin, 24 Oct. 1940.
58. AVP RF, f.06 op.2 p.3 d.17 l.50–5, record of Molotov's meeting with Togo, 17 Oct. 1940.
59. UD:s Arkiv 1920 ARS, HP/517/LXIX, Assarasson to FM, 11 Nov. 1940.
60. AVP RF, f.059 op.1 p.335 d.2294 l.55–7, Molotov to Smetena, Russian ambassador in Tokyo, on conversations with Tatekawa, 1 Nov. 1940.
61. *DGFP*, XI, pp. 644–6, Ott to FM, 21 Nov., and AVP RF, f.0146 op.23 p.205 d.9 l.120–7, Lozovsky on meeting Tatekawa, 24 Dec, f.06 op.2 p.3 d.19 l.106–19, Molotov on meeting Tatekawa, 26 and 28 Dec., f.0146 op.23 p.205 d.9 l.131–49, record of Lozovsky's meeting with Tatekawa, 27 Dec. 1940, and f.06 op.3 p.1 d.3 l.2–8, Molotov on meeting Tatekawa, 17 Jan. 1941.
62. AVP RF, f.06 op.3 p.1 d.3 l.9–16 and 23–4, record of Molotov's meeting with Tatekawa, 27 and 29 Jan. 1941.
63. AVP RF, f.0146 op.24 p.224 d.7 l.111–13, Smetanin to Molotov, 11 Feb. 1940.
64. Chihiro, 'The Japanese–Soviet Neutrality Pact', p. 71.
65. *DGFP*, XII, pp. 100–1, Ott to FM on meeting Matsuoka, 15 Feb. The British recognized right away the priority attached to the Russian trip and the intention to sign a non-aggression pact, see FO 371 27956 F1125/421/23, Craigie to FO, 19 Feb. 1941.
66. AVP RF, f.06 op.3 p.1 d.3 l.37–40, record of Molotov's meeting with Tatekawa, 18 Feb. 1941.
67. UD:s Arkiv 1920 ARS, HP/517/

LXX, Assarasson to FM, 15 Mar. 1941.
68. *DGFP*, XII, pp. 139–51, memorandum on Ribbentrop's conversations with Oshima, 23 Feb. 1941.
69. AVP RF, f.06 op.3 p.1 d.4 l.67–9, Molotov on meeting Tatekawa, 18 Mar. 1941.
70. AVP RF, f.06 op.3 p.28 d.383 l.1–5, report on Molotov's meeting with Matsuoka, 24 Mar., and f.06 op.3 p.30 d.413 l.1, memorandum by Lozovsky, 22 Feb. See also UD:s Arkiv 1920 ARS, HP/517/LXX, Assarasson to FM, 24 Mar. 1941.
71. Presidential Archives, f.45 op.1 p.404 l.83–8, record of Stalin's meeting with Matsuoka, 24 Mar. Matsuoka was greatly impressed by Stalin's hostility towards England, see AMVnR, d.51 p.45 op.1sh pop.333 l.76, Stamenov to FM, 15 Apr. 1941.
72. UD:s Arkiv 1920 ARS, HP/517/LXX, Assarasson to FM, 25 Mar. 1941.
73. AVP RF, f.069, op.25 d.6 p.71 l.47–52, Maisky to FM on meeting Butler, 26 Mar. 1941.
74. *DGFP*, XII, pp. 386–94, 405–9 and 413–20, reports of Matsuoka's meetings in Berlin, 27–29 Mar. 1941.
75. *DGFP*, XII, pp. 386–94, record of Hitler's meeting with Matsuoka, 1 Apr. 1941.
76. TsDA MVR, f.176 op.8 a.e.995 l.2–4, Karadjov, Bulgarian ambassador in Rome, to FM, 4 Apr. 1941.
77. See pp. 152–3.
78. UD:s Arkiv 1920 ARS, HP/517/LXXI, Assarasson to FM, 7 Apr. 1941.
79. AVP RF, f.06 op.3 p.28 d.383 l.6–20, report of Molotov's meeting with Matsuoka, 7 Apr. 1941. See also G. Krebs, 'Japan and the German–Soviet War, 1941', in Wegner (ed.), *From Peace to War*, pp. 545–6.
80. AVP RF, f.06 op.3 p.28 d.383 l.19–35, report of Matsuoka's meeting with Molotov, 9 Apr. 1941.
81. AVP RF, f.06 op.3 p.28 d.383 l.36–46,

report by Molotov on meeting Matsuoka, 11 Apr. 1941; Zhukov, *Vospominaniia i razmyshleniia*, I, pp. 356–7, 13 Apr. 1941.

82. AVP RF, f.0125 op.27 p.122 d.4 l.199–201, record of Lavrentev's meeting with Kollas, Greek ambassador in Bucharest, 10 Apr. 1941.

83. FSB, *Organy Gosudarstvennoi Bezopasnosti SSSR*, I(2), pp. 93–4, Berlin residency to NKGB, 10 Apr. 1941.

84. Presidential Archives, f.45 op.1 d.404 l.91–101, record of Stalin's meeting with Matsuoka, 12 Apr. 1941.

85. The following description is based mostly on a detailed and lively report by Jack Scott, correspondent of the *News Chronicle*, in FO 37129480 N1829/78/38, corroborated by other reports quoted below.

86. FO 371 27956 F2960/421/23, Cripps to FO, 14 Apr. 1941.

87. A remarkable exception, recognizing the historiographical problem, is B. N. Slavinsky, *Pakt o neitralitete mezhdu SSSR i Iaponiei: diplomaticheskaia istoriia, 1941–1945* (Moscow, 1995), pp. 98–9.

88. Krigsarkivet, Fo..rsvarsstaben, Ser. E/II/15/1, military attaché's report on conversations with Krebs, no. 41, 13 Apr. 1941.

89. AMVnR, d.51 p.45 op.1sh pop.333 l.74, Stamenov to FM, 13 Apr. 1941.

90. Gafencu, *Prelude to the Russian Campaign*, pp. 158–9.

91. Slavinsky, *Pakt o neitralitete*, pp. 105–6 and 108.

92. A telegram by Aktay intercepted by the Germans in *DGFP*, XII, pp. 873–6, 1 May 1941.

93. *Ibid.*, pp. 723–4, Ott to FM, 12 Apr. 1941.

94. *Ibid.*, pp. 546–7, Boltze, German chargé d'affaires in Tokyo, to FM, 14 Apr. See similar observation by Craigie, Tokyo, to FO, in FO 371 27956 F3042 and F3046/421/23, 14 and 15 Apr. 1941.

95. See below, pp. 202–4.

96. *Komintern i vtoraia mirovaia voina*, I, pp. 525–6.

97. Quai d'Orsay Archives, 834/Z/312/1 pp. 132–3, report on conversation with Bogomolov, 11 Apr. 1941.

98. On the event see Cripps papers, Isobel's diary, 21 Apr. 1941.

99. Dimitrov's diary, 20 Apr. 1941.

100. *Ibid.*, 21 Apr. 1941.

101. Firsov, 'Arkhivy Kominterna', pp. 34–5.

102. Dimitrov's diary, 12 May 1941.

103. *Ibid.*, 22 June 1941.

10. 'Appeasement': A New German–Soviet Pact?

1. Gafencu, *Prelude to the Russian Campaign*, pp. 160–1, and AMVnR, p. 17 op.1b pop.13 l.50, Stamenov to FM, 14 Apr. 1941.

2. E. H. von Weizsäcker, *Memoirs* (London, 1951), p. 252.

3. *Ibid.*, p. 246.

4. Waddington, 'Ribbentrop and the Soviet Union', p. 22.

5. *DGFP*, XII, p. 802.

6. Weizsäcker, *Memoirs*, p. 248.

7. Hill (ed.), *Weizsäcker-Papiere*, pp. 565–6, n. 126.

8. UD:s Arkiv 1920 ARS, HP/517/LXX, Assarasson to FM, 4 Apr. 1941.

9. The essence of the memorandum, which has never been recovered (see *DGFP*, XII, p. 661, n. 2), is conveyed in Hilger and Meyer, *Incompatible Allies*, p. 328, and UD:s Arkiv 1920 ARS, HP/1554/L and LXX, Assarasson to FM, 25 Feb., 17 and 29 Mar. 1941.

10. Author's italics. *DGFP*, XII, pp. 536–7, Schulenburg to FM, 13 Apr. 1941. That he achieved this impact is attested by Hitler's interpreter P. Schmidt, *Hitler's Interpreter* (London, 1952) p. 232. The conversation between Stalin and Schulenburg is confirmed also by Assarasson in UD:s Arkiv 1920 ARS, Assarasson to FM, HP/517/

LXXI, 21 Apr. 1941, and in his *I skuggan av Stalin*, p. 57.

11. Telegram from Tippelskirch, 15 Apr., in *DGFP*, XII, pp. 560–1; AVP RF, f.082 op.24 p.105 d.3 l.95–6, Sobolev on meeting Tippelskirch, 15 Apr., and a second meeting on 24 Apr. 1941, in AVP RF, f.06 op.3 p.4 d.38 l.85–9.

12. AVP RF, f.07 op.2 p.10 d.31 l.32–3, Vyshinsky on meeting Gafencu, 15 Apr. 1941.

13. *DGFP*, XII, 15 Apr. 1941, pp. 563–5.

14. *Ibid.*, 25 Apr. 1941, pp. 623–4.

15. UD:s Arkiv 1920 ARS, HP/517/ LXXI, Assarasson to FM, 19 Apr., and AVP RF, f.07 op.2 p.10 d.32 l.13–14, record of Vyshinsky's meeting with Gavriloviç, 20 Apr. 1941.

16. *Pravda*, 19 Apr. 1941.

17. *DGFP*, XII, p. 602.

18. Fleischhauer, *Diplomatischer Widerstand gegen 'Unternehmen Barbarossa'*, p. 305.

19. Weizsäcker, *Memoirs*, p. 253, and Hill (ed.), *Weizsäcker-Papiere*, 21 Apr. 1941, p. 248. At his trial Weizsäcker stated: 'I know that I had been considered to be a defeatist for a long time with outdated views to whom no one listened. But I wanted, probably for the last time in my career, to convey my explicitly differing views to the knowledge of the leadership of the State': *ibid.*, p. 570, n. 156.

20. J. von Ribbentrop, *The Ribbentrop Memoirs* (London, 1954), p. 152.

21. *DGFP*, XII, p. 666, n. 1.

22. His full memorandum is reproduced in *ibid.*, pp. 661–2. See also Weizsäcker, *Memoirs*, pp. 247 and 253, and Hill (ed.), *Weizsäcker-Papiere*, 28 and 29 Apr. 1941, pp. 249–50.

23. Herwarth, *Against Two Evils*, pp. 190–1, 25 Apr. 1941.

24. Hilger and Meyer, *Incompatible Allies*, p. 328.

25. Weizsäcker, *Memoirs*, p. 257.

26. *DGFP*, XII, pp. 666–9. Hilger and Meyer, *Incompatible Allies*, p. 328.

27. Hilger and Meyer, *Incompatible Allies*, p. 328.

28. UD:s Arkiv 1920 ARS, HP/1556/ LV, Assarasson to FM on meeting Hilger, on 30 Apr., Schulenburg on 3 May, and Walter on 6 May. This was confirmed by Gafencu in *Misiune la Moscova*, raport 1405, pp. 183–94, 30 Apr., and by Cripps in FO 371 29481 N2172/78/38, 14 May 1941.

29. Dimitrov's diary, 9 Apr. 1941.

30. Sudoplatov, *Special Tasks*, p. 117.

31. AVP RF, f.0125 op.27 p.122 d.4 l.224–6, 22 Apr. 1941.

32. UD:s Arkiv 1920 ARS, HP/517/ LXXI, minute by the Swedish FM, 24 Apr., and Assarasson to FM, 5 May 1941.

33. AVP RF, f.0125 op.27 p.122 d.4 l.230, record of Lavrentev's meeting with Avakumoviç, 1 May 1941; almost a verbatim statement in Vinogradov's meeting with Knatchbull-Hugessen, on 3 May, in AVP RF, f.0134 op.24a p.236 d.7 l.288–92. See also the tone assumed by Maisky in all his conversations with Eden during May and June: below, p. 302.

34. FO 371 29465 N1999/3/38, Halifax to Eden, 5 May 1941.

35. AVP RF, f.07 op.2 p.9 d.21 l.6–11, record by Vyshinsky on meeting Steinhardt, 24 May 1941.

36. V. A. Nevezhin, 'Vystuplenie Stalina 5 maia 1941g. i povorot v propagande', in V. A. Nevezhin and G. A. Bordiugova (eds), *Gotovil li Stalin nastupatel'nuiu voinu protiv Gitlera?* (Moscow, 1995), pp. 147 ff., drives home effectively the message that the propaganda in the army was now geared towards preparing the soldiers for an 'offensive war'; it is a classic case however of an analysis overlooking the wider political, international and military context. Likewise J. Hoffman brings a similarly tendentious version in his 'The Soviet Union's Offensive Preparations in 1941', in Wegner (ed.), *From Peace to War*, pp. 365–9.

37. See for instance FO 371 29481 N2130/78/38, Cripps to FO, 5 May; Quai d'Orsay Archives, telegrams from Moscow, tels 409–13, Bergery to FM, 5 May; *DGFP*, XII, pp. 964–5, 5 May 1941; Erickson, *Road to Stalingrad*, p. 82, and Hilger and Meyer, *Incompatible Allies*, p. 330.

38. GRU GSh RF, op.24119 d.1 l.452–5, 'Eshchenko' to Golikov, 24 Mar. 1941.

39. Reproduced in *Izvestiia CC CPSU*, 5 (1990), pp. 191–6, head of indoctrination of the Red Army to Zhdanov, Jan. 1941.

40. Chuev, *Sto sorok besed s Molotovym*, p. 45.

41. The Russian Centre for the Preservation and Study of Contemporary History (hereafter RTsKhIDIN), f.88 op.1 d.898 l.14–22, directive by Shcherbakov, 5 May 1941.

42. Bezymensky papers, memo by General N. Liashchenko, 1954. I am grateful to Lev Bezymensky for this document.

43. RTsKhIDIN, f.558 op.1 d.3808 l.1–12, 5 May 1941.

44. *Pravda*, Timoshenko's speech, 1 May 1941.

45. FSB, *Organy Gosudarstvennoi Bezopasnosti SSSR*, I(2), pp. 128–9, Berlin residency to NKGB, Apr. 1941.

46. AVP RF, f.07 op.2 p.9 d.26 l.1, report by Vyshinsky on meeting Labonne, 5 Apr., and UD:s Arkiv 1920 ARS, HP/517/LXXI, Assarasson to FM, 25 Apr. 1941.

47. Quai d'Orsay Archives, 834/Z/312/1 pp. 131–3, Nemanov on conversation with Bogomolov, 11 Apr. 1941.

48. AVP RF, f.07 op.2 p.9 d.26 l.2–5, and Quai d'Orsay Archives, Moscow tels 369–75, reports of Vyshinsky's meetings with Bergery, 28 Apr. 1941.

49. AVP RF, f.06 op.3 p.25 d.335 l.1–6, and Quai d'Orsay Archives, telegrams from Moscow, tel. 428–31, Bergery to FM, 15 May; UD:s Arkiv 1920 ARS, HP/517/LXXI, Assaras-

son to FM, 22 May 1941. Earlier presentation of the appeasement is in M. Lisann, 'Stalin the Appeaser: Before 22 June, 1941', *Survey*, 76 (1970).

50. See a long report on the changes in Krigsarkivet, Fo..rsvarsstaben, Ser. E/I/15/3, military attaché's report, no. 30, 16 June 1941.

51. RTsKhIDIN, op.1 d.1a l.1–4, Protocol of the Plenum of the CC, 5 May, and Dimitrov's diary, 5 May 1941.

52. *DGFP*, XII, pp. 691–2. There are various indicators that Schulenburg had raised with Weizsäcker the possibility of exploiting Dekanozov's presence in Moscow to make an approach to the government. Weizsäcker had formed a positive impression of Dekanozov after his appointment in December 1940, as a 'man one could talk with in an objective way'. Weizsäcker, *Memoirs*, p. 246.

53. UD:s Arkiv 1920 ARS, HP/517/LXXI, Assarasson to FM, 7 May 1941.

54. Quoted in G. Kumanev, '22 June', *Pravda*, 22 June 1989. See for instance V. V. Sokolov's introduction of the document in *Vestnik Ministerstva innostranykh del SSSR*, 20 (1990), p. 58. This is borne out neither by the text nor by the next two meetings. See a critical review in S. Gorlov and V. Voyushin, 'Warnings Came Not Only from the German Ambassador', *New Times*, 2 (1991).

55. Hilger and Meyer, *Incompatible Allies*, p. 331.

56. Chuev, *Sto sorok besed s Molotovym*, p. 39.

57. See V. A. Voiushin and S. A. Gorlov, 'Fashistskaia agressia: o chem soobshchali diplomaty', *VIZh*, 6 (1991), pp. 22–3.

58. Presidential Archives, f.3 op.64 d.675 l.157–61, Dekanozov's report of a meeting with Schulenburg, 5 May 1941.

59. *DGFP*, XII, p. 446, Commander in Chief of the Wehrmacht to FM, 3

Apr., and pp. 698–9, Military Intelligence to military attaché in Moscow, 4 May 1941. Even before his return to Moscow, the German naval attaché informed the High Command of the Navy that he was 'endeavouring to counteract the rumours, which are manifestly absurd', *ibid.*, 24 Apr. 1941, p. 632. See also O. V. Vishlev, 'Pochemu zhe medlil I. V. Stalin v 1941 gg. (iz Germanskikh arkhivov)', *Novaia i noveishaia istoriia*, 2 (1992), pp. 93–4.
60. *DGFP*, XII, 4 May 1941, pp. 698–9.
61. FO 371 29481 N2418/78/38, Cripps to FO, 15 May 1941.
62. UD:s Arkiv 1920 ARS, HP/517/LXXI, Assarasson to FM, 12 May 1941.
63. *DGFP*, XII, pp. 730 and 734–5, Schulenburg to FM, 7 May 1941; Rosso's similar evaluation in AMVnR, d.51 p.45 op.1sh pop.333 l.89–90, Stamenov to FM, 8 May 1941.
64. *Pravda*, 9 May, and *DGFP*, XII, p. 792, Schulenburg to FM, 12 May 1941.
65. On this see p. 287f.
66. A memorandum by Dekanozov on his meeting with Schulenburg addressed personally to Molotov in only two copies is in Presidential Archives, f.3 op.64 d.675 l.162–8, record of Dekanozov's meeting with Schulenburg, 9 May 1941.
67. Presidential Archives, f.3 op.66 d.906 l.1–4, record of Vyshinsky's meeting with Gavriloviç, 8 May 1941. See also R. Douglas, *New Alliances 1940–41* (London, 1982), p. 60.
68. *DGFP*, XII, p. 66, n. 1.
69. *Ribbentrop Memoirs*, p. 152.
70. Hill (ed.), *Weizsäcker-Papiere*, 1 May 1941, pp. 252–3.
71. G. Ciano, *Ciano's Diplomatic Papers* (London, 1948), 15 June 1941, p. 358. Berezhkov formed a similar impression in his memoirs *History in the Making* (Moscow, 1982), pp. 70 ff.
72. Weizsäcker, *Memoirs*, pp. 253–4,

and Hill (ed.), *Weizsäcker-Papiere*, 1 May 1941, p. 252.
73. See below in this chapter.
74. With a view to securing the rear prior to the Russian campaign Hitler was in the midst of crucial negotiations with Marshal Pétain and Admiral Darlan about future relations between Vichy and Germany.
75. Hill (ed.), *Weizsäcker-Papiere*, 16 Feb. 1941, p. 238.
76. *DGFP*, XII, 7 May 1941, pp. 734–5.
77. Presidential Archives, f.3 op.64 d.675 l.174, note by Dekanozov on meeting Stalin and Molotov, 12 May 1941.
78. They were sent on 10 May but arrived by courier, as Schulenburg told Dekanozov without displaying their content, on the day of their meeting.
79. *DGFP*, XII, pp. 750–1.
80. Presidential Archives, f.3 op.64 d.675 l.169–73, record of Dekanozov's meeting with Schulenburg, 12 May 1941. Weizsäcker's short telegram to Schulenburg included a cryptic reference which may have led Schulenburg to this conclusion but it is unlikely to have referred to Hess. Weizsäcker wrote: 'The near future will again bring some meetings of important personalities which, however, will scarcely affect your particular province.' He was most probably referring to Ribbentrop's meeting with Mussolini two days later, *DGFP*, XII, p. 750. But the fact that both Schulenburg and Cripps had been alluding to the possibility of a separate peace surely alerted Stalin.
81. See p. 265.
82. See Hilger and Meyer, *Incompatible Allies*, p. 351.
83. Hill (ed.), *Weizsäcker-Papiere*, 2 May 1941, p. 253.
84. Herwarth, *Against Two Evils*, pp. 192–3.
85. *DGFP*, XII, pp. 791–3.
86. *Ibid.*, 22 May 1941, p. 870.

87. *Ibid.*, 4 June 1941, pp. 964–5.
88. AVP RF, f.059 op.1 p.361 d.2401 l.133–4, Maisky to FM, 10 Apr.; f.017a, Maisky's diary, pp. 41–5 and 85–7, 1 Mar. and 10 Apr.; and pp. 121–2, 5 May 1941.
89. Sudoplatov, *Special Tasks*, p. 123.
90. AMVnR, d.51 p.45 op.1sh pop.333 l.98, Stamenov to FM, 25 May 1941.
91. Bezymensky was told so by Zhukov in the 1960s.
92. Berezhkov, *History in the Making*, p. 59.
93. AVP RF, f.082 op.23 p.95 d.6 ll.141–2, report by Semenov, 19 Nov. 1940.
94. Barros and Gregor, *Double Deception*, pp. 150–9. Due to the unavailability of the Soviet records at the time of writing their book, the authors were unaware of the three crucial meetings held by Dekanozov and Schulenburg in the first half of May. Relying on Hilger's misleading account, they refer to only one meeting and wrongly date it to 19 May. They therefore attach undue significance to the meetings with Meisner, which aimed at reviving the talks. As they concede, Meisner never admitted to those meetings in his debriefings after the war; Cripps's report, which they rely on, spoke in general about rumours of talks. None of the reports are to be found either in the Presidential Archives or in the archives of the Security Services. The evidence therefore rests on the then extremely young Berezhkov, who had been serving in the embassy as an interpreter. However, as Meisner spoke fluent Russian Berezhkov's services would not have been needed at those particular meetings. The significance of the talks, therefore, is conjectural only; they were certainly secondary to those between Schulenburg and Dekanozov. And yet Barros and Gregor's intuition is certainly correct and therefore the episode, right or wrong, does not detract from their main argument about Stalin's self-deception, which is accepted by the present author.
95. See below, p. 303.
96. AVP RF, f.0132 op.24a p.236 d.8 l.42, report by Vinogradov of meeting Koskinen, 24 May 1941.
97. FSB, *Sekrety Gitlera*, pp. 131–2, Merkulov to Stalin, Molotov and Beria, 26 May 1941.
98. GRU GSh RF, op.24119 d.1 l.864–74, 'Eshchenko', Bucharest, to Golikov, 28 May 1941.
99. TsA SVR RF, d.21616 t.2 l.389–97, deputy director of the NKVD to Merkulov, 30 May 1941.
100. AVP RF, f.082 op.24 p.106 d.7 l.140–1, report by Dekanozov, 30 May; see also *ibid.*, l.142–3, record of Dekanozov's meeting with Gerde, 7 June 1941.
101. AVP RF, f.06 op.3 p.12 d.138 l.99–107, Dekanozov to Molotov, 4 June 1941.
102. Zhukov, *Vospominaniia i razmyshleniia*, I, pp. 346–7 and 373.
103. GRU GSh RF, op.7237 d.2 l.114–19, special report by Golikov, 31 May 1941.
104. TsA FSB RF, f.6894 l.238–9, 3 June 1941.

11. 'The Special Threatening Military Period'

1. Van Creveld, *Hitler's Strategy*, p. 150.
2. See 'The Gathering Clouds' section above in Chapter 6, and below, p. 237f.
3. Zhukov, *Vospominaniia i razmyshleniia*, I, pp. 362–3, an admission not printed before; the reference to the intelligence is debatable.
4. Erickson, *Road to Stalingrad*, p. 81; *Izvestiia TsK KPSS*, 2 (1990), pp. 202–3.
5. Zhukov, *Vospominaniia i razmyshleniia*, I, pp. 341–3 and 345. On Stalin's dacha and social life see Chuev, *Sto sorok besed s Molotovym*.

6. AGSh RF, f.8 op.2729 d.28 l.61–82, 214–26 and 262–3, Sokolovsky (CS) to the Commanders of the Western District, the Far East and the air force, 2–7 Mar. 1941.

7. See pp. 123–4.

8. AGSh RF, f.16 op.2951 d.241 l.1–15, Zhukov and Timoshenko to Stalin and Molotov, 11 Mar. 1941.

9. Zhukov, *Vospominaniia i razmyshleniia*, I, pp. 322–5.

10. See pp. 179–84.

11. TsA SVR RF, d.23078 t.1 l.302–6, report by 'Sidrov', 24 Mar. 1941.

12. *Ibid.*, d.21616 t.4 l.1–10, director of the Baltics NKGB to Merkulov, 27 Mar. 1941.

13. *Ibid.*, d.23078 t.1 d.21616 t.3 l.115–20, Savchenko, deputy-director Ukrainian NKGB, to Merkulov, 29 Apr. 1941.

14. GRU GSh RF, op.24119 d.4 l.346–7, 'Mars', Budapest, to Golikov, 30 Apr. 1941.

15. See pp. 180–6.

16. FSB, *Organy Gosudarstvennoi Bezopasnosti SSSR*, I(2), pp. 61–2 and 289, Berlin residency to NKGB, 24 Mar. 1941.

17. TsA SVR RF, d.23078 t.1 l.236–41, 'Zakhar' to NKGB, 2 Apr. 1941.

18. AGSh RF, f.16 op.2951 d.242 l.236–40, Merkulov to Timoshenko, 4 Apr. 1941.

19. GRU GSh RF, op.24119 d.1 l.468–9 and 472–3, 'Eshchenko' to Golikov from Bucharest, 26 Mar. 1941.

20. *Ibid.*, op.7237 d.2 l.84–6, special report by Golikov, 4 Apr. Corroborated a week later by Meshnik, head of the NKGB in the Ukraine, in TsA SVR RF, d.21616 t.3 l.53–9, 12 Apr. 1941.

21. AVP RF, f.082 op.24 p.105 d.3 l.103; *DGFP*, XII, pp. 602–3, records by Sobolev and Tippelskirch on their meetings, 21 Apr. 1941.

22. GRU GSh RF, op.7237 d.2 l.89–91, special periodical report by Golikov, 16 Apr. 1941.

23. *Ibid.*, op.24119 d.4 l.335–6, 'Mars', Budapest, to Golikov, 24 Apr. 1941.

24. Erickson, *Road to Stalingrad*, p. 84. L. S. Skvirski, 'V predvoennye gody', *Voprosy istorii*, 9 (1989), pp. 55–68.

25. See pp. 115–18.

26. AGSh RF, f.16 op.2951 d.237 l.48–64, directive by Timoshenko and Zhukov to Pavlov, 30 Apr. 1941.

27. See pp. 202–4.

28. Presidential Archives, Stalin's appointment diary, 23 Apr., and f.93, special collection, Stalin and Molotov to CC of the CPSU and the government, 23 Apr. 1941.

29. GRU GSh RF, op.38 d.1 l.161–6, directive by Timoshenko and Zhukov to the Western Military District, 29 Apr. 1941.

30. *Ibid.*, op.7277 d.1 l.140–52, Tupikov, Soviet military attaché in Berlin, to Golikov, 25 Apr. The following day Golikov transmitted to Stalin the gist of the report in a watered-down version. GRU GSh RF, op.7237 d.2 l.92–6, report by Golikov on the German deployment, 26 Apr. 1941. That the danger of war was well perceived can also be deduced from the hasty mobilization of the NKGB, placing the organization on a war alert. FSB, *Organy Gosudarstvennoi Bezopasnosti SSSR*, I(2), pp. 117–18, Kobulov's instructions on mobilization of NKGB, 26 Apr. 1941, and Sudoplatov, *Special Tasks*, p. 119.

31. AVP RF, f.0125 op.27 p.122 d.2 l.8, FM memorandum by Novikov on German intentions in Rumania, 29 Apr. See also GRU GSh RF, op.24119 d.1 l.737–45, 'Eshchenko' to Golikov, 5 May 1941.

32. TsA SVR RF, d.23078 t.1 l.391–2, report from Bucharest, 17 May 1941.

33. FSB, *Sekrety Gitlera*, pp. 40–5, Strokacha, Deputy Interior Minister, departmental memorandum, 30 Apr. 1941.

34. GRU GSh RF, op.7237 d.2 l.97–102, special report by Golikov, 5 May 1941. See also Zhukov, *Vospominaniia i razmyshleniia*, I, pp. 344–5.

35. TsA SVR RF, d.21616 t.2 l.269–71, Merkulov to Stalin, Molotov and Beria, 5 May. See a similar report in TsA SVR RF, d.21616 t.2 l.265–8, Fitin, director of the 1st Dept of the Ukrainian NKGB, to Golikov, 5 May 1941.

36. *Ibid.*, d.21616 t.3 l.156–60, Meshnik, commissar of the Ukrainian NKGB, to Merkulov, 15 May. See also intercepted telegram of the Japanese consul in Königsberg to Tokyo via Moscow, reproduced in FSB, *Organy Gosudarstvennoi Bezopasnosti SSSR*, I(2), p. 171 (intercepted telegram), 31 May 1941.

37. Zhukov, *Vospominaniia i razmyshleniia*, I, pp. 346–9, and in I. Bargamian, 'Zapiski nachal'nika operativnogo otdela', *VIZh*, 1 (1967).

38. See pp. 231–3.

39. AGSh RF, f.16 op.2951 d.259 l.1–17 and d.237 l.33–47 and 65–81, f.131 op.12507 d.1 l.71–5 and d.258 l.1–11, Zhukov and Timoshenko to the Commanders of the Odessa, Baltics, Kiev and Western Regions, 13 May 1941; Zakharov, *General'nyi shtab*, pp. 266–9. See also J. W. Kipp, 'Military Theory: Barbarossa, Soviet Covering Forces and the Initial Period of War: Military History and Airland Battle', *Journal of Soviet Military Studies*, 1/2 (1988), pp. 198–9. On the shortcomings of the deployment see Lieutenant-General N. Pavlenko, 'Tragediia krasnoi armii', *Moskovskii novosti*, 7 May 1989. M. M. Kiriia, 'Nchal'nyi period Velikoi Otechestvennoi voiny', *VIZh*, 6 (1988), G. P. Pastukhovsky, 'Razvertyvanie operativnogo tyla v nachal'nyi period voiny', and Iu. G. Perechnev, 'O nekotorykh problemakh podgotovki strany i Vooruzhennyx Sil k otrazhneniia fashistskoi agressii', *VIZh*, 4 (1988).

40. AGSh RF, f.16 op.2951 d.248 l.36–54, directive by Pavlov to the Commander of the 3rd Army, 14 May 1941.

41. Presidential Archives, Stalin's appointment diary.

42. Chuev, *Sto sorok besed s Molotovym*, p. 31.

43. AGSh RF, f.16 op.2951 d.237 l.1–15.

44. Iu. A. Gor'kov, 'Nakanune 22 iiunia 1941', *Novaia i noveishaia istoriia*, 6 (1992), p. 4. Presidential Archives, Stalin's appointment diary.

45. Zhukov, *Vospominaniia i razmyshleniia*, I, p. 342; V. Karpov, 'Zhukov', *Kommunist vooruzhennykh sil*, 5 (1990), pp. 62–8, and interview with Anfilov, May 1995.

46. 'Neopublikovannoe interv'iu marshala sovestskogo soiuza A. M. Vasilevskogo', *Novaia i noveishaia istoriia*, 6 (1992). See also Chuev, *Sto sorok besed s Molotovym*, p. 33.

47. Reproduced in an enlightening volume of documents on the preparations for war, *Skrytaia pravda voiny: 1941 god. Neizvestnye dokumenty* (Moscow, 1992), pp. 23–4, 25, 29 and 30–3.

48. Volkogonov papers, instructions by Timoshenko, Zhdanov and Zhukov, to the Commanders of the Military Districts.

49. Zhukov, *Vospominaniia i razmyshleniia*, I, pp. 348–51. See also A. G. Khor'kov, 'Ukreplennie raiony na zapadnykh granitsakh SSSR', *VIZh*, 12 (1987), pp. 47–54.

50. Glantz, *Military Strategy of the Soviet Union*, p. 75.

51. RTsKhIDIN, f.17 op.3 d.273 l.27–8, Politburo decree of 8 Mar. 1941.

52. Zhukov, *Vospominaniia i razmyshleniia*, I, pp. 349–52, and R. E. Tarleton, 'What Really Happened to the Stalin Line?', *Journal of Soviet Military Studies*, 2 (1992), pp. 187–219.

53. Quoted in *Izvestiia TsK KPSS*, 2 (1990), p. 207. On the intensive efforts invested in the construction of the URs see also V. I. Beliaev, 'Usilenie okhrany zapadnoi granitsy SSSR nakanune Vekiloi Otechestvennoi voiny', *VIZh*, 5 (1988), pp. 51–5, and A. D. Borshchev, 'Otrazhenie fashistskoi agressii:

uroki i vyvody', *Voennaia mysl'*, 3 (1990), p. 19.

54. Zhukov, *Vospominaniia i razmyshleniia*, I, p. 333.
55. *Ibid.*, pp. 336–7.
56. Presidential Archives, f.93, special collection, Molotov and Stalin to the SNK and Politburo, 15 Mar. and 12 Apr., and instructions by the government and the CC, 5 May 1941. See also D. T. Iazov, 'Vperedi byla voina', *VIZh*, 5 (1991), p. 13.
57. RTsKhIDIN, f.17 op.3 d.1037 l.33–4, protocol of the Politburo meeting, 9 Apr. 1941.
58. AGSh RF, f.8044 op.1 d.652 l.89–92, Zhigarev, Commander of the Air Force, to Stalin, 27 May 1941.
59. Zhukov, *Vospominaniia i razmyshleniia*, I, p. 346, previously unpublished.
60. *Ibid.*
61. *Ibid.*, pp. 368–9.
62. GRU GSh RF, op.7237 d.2 l.109–13, special report by Golikov, 15 May 1941. See corroborating information in *ibid.*, op.24119 d.1 l.814–15, 'Kosta', Sofia, to Golikov, 19 May 1941.
63. *Ibid.*, op. 7237 d.2 l.114–15, 31 May 1941.
64. UD:s Arkiv 1920 ARS, HP/1557/LVII, Assarasson to FM, 28 May. See also AVP RF, f.06 op.3 p.4 d.36 l.36–49, report by Lozovsky on meeting Steinhardt, 5 June 1941.

12. The Flight of Rudolf Hess to England

1. Stalin to Maisky, 19 October 1942, MID, *Sovetsko-angliiskie otnosheniia vo vremia Velikoi Otechestvennoi voiny, 1941–1945* (Moscow, 1983), 1, p. 294.
2. FO 371 30920 C10635/61/18, 2 Nov. 1942.
3. PREM 3/434/7, notes on Churchill's conference with Stalin, October 1944, 10 May 1945, and FO 800/414 fol. 21, 18 Oct. 1944. On the persisting views see the most recent

example in L. Schwartzchild, 'Neozhidanyi zakhvat Gessa v lovushku, podstroenuiu angliiskoi "Sikret servis"', *VIZh*, 5 (1991), pp. 37–41, and V. I. Chukreev, 'Zagadka 22 iunia 1941 goda', *VIZh*, 6 (1989), p. 39. The Americans formed a similar impression: see National Archives, Washington, RG 319, Box 83, B8026020, report on Hess by Raymond Lee, US military attaché in London, 10 May 1941.
4. H. Thomas, *The Murder of Rudolf Hess* (London, 1979). C. Andrew presented and dismissed the various conspiracy theories in 'Hess: An Edge of Conspiracy', in *Timewatch*, BBC2, 17 Jan. 1990.
5. One of the rare cases when Churchill's account is essentially accurate though not full, *Second World War*, III, pp. 43–9.
6. G. Gorodetsky, 'The Hess Mission and Anglo-Soviet Relations on the Eve of "Barbarossa"', *English Historical Review*, 101/399 (1986).
7. P. Padfield, *Rudolf Hess: The Führer's Disciple* (London, 1993), p. 353. See below, pp. 250, 253–4. See Cripps's report summing up the affair in FO 371 30920 C10635/61/18, 2 Nov. 1942.
8. This was admitted by Padfield in *Rudolf Hess*, pp. 334–5 and 355–6, after inspecting the relevant files in depth. See also J. Douglas-Hamilton, *The Truth about Rudolf Hess* (London, 1993), pp. 140–1, and introduction by Roy Conyers Nesbit, who had carried out a thorough research into the RAF records.
9. For this see WO 199/3288, Scottish Command: The Capture of Hess, 13 May 1941.
10. WO 199/3288/A, report by the Officer in Charge of the 3rd Battalion Renfrewshire Home Guard, 11 May 1941, and FO 1093/11 fols 152–5, interrogation of Hess by Battaglia, and comments by 'C', 10 May 1941.
11. Douglas-Hamilton, *The Truth about Hess*, pp. 142–3. Padfield, *Rudolf*

Hess, still raises some doubts at p. 354.

12. WO 199/3288, intelligence report, 10 May 1941.

13. See FO 371 30920 C10635/61/18 DEFE 1/134, collation of letters on Hess by the Postal Censorship, 23 May 1941.

14. FO 1093/9 p.15, FO minutes on Hamilton libel case against the CPGB, 17 June 1941.

15. FO 1093/7, fol. 26, memorandum by SO1.

16. FO 1093/1 pp.18–20, Duke of Hamilton's interview with Hess, 11 May 1941.

17. See interviews with Hess described below.

18. I. Maisky, *Memoirs of a Soviet Ambassador: The War, 1939–43* (London, 1967), p. 147.

19. Padfield, *Rudolf Hess*.

20. The newspaper articles and Foreign Office minutes which dismiss its essence are in FO 371 46780 C4725/44/18.

21. Padfield, *Rudolf Hess*, pp. 368–71.

22. See below, p. 261.

23. WO 3288/A f.4.

24. Padfield, *Rudolf Hess*, p. 364.

25. FO 371 26945 C4038, C4140, C4147, C4613/306/41, C4245/306, 20 and 25 April 1941. Padfield's comment that 'from a diplomat of Hoare's subtlety, this was hardly a disclaimer' is by no means convincing.

26. UD:s Arkiv 1920 ARS, HP/1555/ LIV, Swedish ambassador in Berlin to FM, 23 Apr. 1941.

27. FO 371 1093/14 fol. 101, 10 May 1942.

28. FO 1093/3 p. 92, letter to Professor Haushofer, 20 June 1942.

29. *News Chronicle*, 26 July 1945.

30. FO 1093/3 pp. 33 and 142–3, Hess to his mother, 28 Mar. and 9 Sept. 1942.

31. *DGFP*, XII, pp. 783–7, Albrecht Haushofer to Hitler, 12 May 1941. See a thorough discussion of this in Douglas-Hamilton, *The Truth about Hess*.

32. FO 1093/1 pp. 18–20, Duke of

33. FO 1093/8 pp. 221–2, 22 May 1941.

34. FO 1093/8 p. 206, Hess to his wife, 3 June 1941.

35. FO 1093/2 p. 8, 14 Sept. 1941.

36. Dilks (ed.), *Cadogan Diaries*, 11 May 1941. J. Costello, *Ten Days to Destiny: The Secret Story of the Hess Peace Initiative and British Efforts to Strike a Deal with Hitler* (London, 1991), pp. 415–16, concocts on the basis of this paragraph a whole story in an attempt to prove that Churchill was eager to fetch Hamilton because he already knew that he was carrying with him the German proposals.

37. Cadogan papers, diary, 1/10, 15 May 1941.

38. Douglas-Hamilton, *The Truth about Hess*, pp. 149–150.

39. PREM 3/219/7 p. 167, Churchill to Eden, 13 May 1941.

40. Cadogan papers, diary, 1/10, 14 May 1941.

41. PREM 3/219/7 pp. 146 and 165, minute by Churchill, 16 May 1941.

42. FO 1093/10 fols 54–5, Churchill to Roosevelt, 17 May 1941.

43. FO 1093/1 fols 20–30, Kirkpatrick interview, 12 May 1941.

44. FO 1093/11 fol. 93.

45. In *The Truth about Hess*, pp. 185–92, Douglas-Hamilton cites sufficient evidence to prove Hitler's tremendous shock when the news of Hess's flight was brought to him.

46. Eden papers, diary, 12 May 1941.

47. FO 1093/11 fol. 149, 13 May 1941.

48. PREM 3/219/4 fol. 18, Churchill's undelivered statement, 12 May 1941.

49. PREM 3/219/4 fols 14–19, 11 May 1941.

50. Minute by Morton, FO 1093/10 fols 82–3.

51. Dilks (ed.), *Cadogan Diaries*, pp. 175–80. Making a hero of Hess, which Bevin indeed complained was happening, only increased Russian suspicions, see Eden papers, diary, 15 May 1941.

52. FO 371 26565 C5301/5188/18, Halifax to FO, 17 May, and PREM 3/219/7 p. 147, Roosevelt to Churchill, 15 May 1941.
53. Eden papers, diary, 14 May 1941.
54. FO 1093/11 fols 132 and 140–1, minutes of FO, 14 May 1941.
55. Eden papers, diary, 19 May 1941.
56. PREM 3/219/7, Duff Cooper to Churchill, 15 May 1941, and Douglas-Hamilton, *The Truth about Hess*, p. 161.
57. FO 1093/11 fols 110–15, Churchill to Roosevelt, 16 May 1941.
58. FO 1093/11 fol. 121, Churchill to Cadogan, 16 May 1941.
59. FO 1093/11 fol. 123, Butler to Eden, 16 May 1941.
60. FO 1093/1 fols 20–30, Kirkpatrick interview, 12 May 1941.
61. FO 1093/10 fols 139–41, Major D. Morton to 'C' and report by Cadogan on Hess, 6 June 1941.
62. FO 1093/11 fols 51–4, Simon to Eden, 27 May; Dilks (ed.), *Cadogan Diaries*, p. 380, 19 May 1941.
63. PREM 3/219/7 pp. 113–15, Major Morton to Churchill, 9 June 1941.
64. *Ibid.*, pp. 117–18, Cadogan to Churchill, 6 June 1941.
65. FO 1093/10 fols 91–4, note by Kirkpatrick, 29 May 1941.
66. FO 1093/10 fol. 170, statement by Hess, and 11 fol. 85, SIS report no. 16 by phone, 30 May 1941.
67. FO 1093/10 fol. 129 and 146, 'C' to Foreign Office, 4 June, and report by SIS officer, 6 June 1941.
68. PREM 3/219/7 pp. 144–5, comments by Major Sheppard, MI6, 21 May 1941.
69. The written proposals are in FO 1093/1 pp. 154–6, 10 June 1941.
70. FO 1093/10 fols 95–6, preliminary report by 'C' to Eden, FO 1093/1 fols 1–13, Simon's own report on his interview with Hess, 9 June, and fols 70–147, verbatim report of the meeting, 10 June 1941.
71. Douglas-Hamilton, *The Truth about Hess*, p. 135.
72. FO 1093/10 fols 86–90, Cadogan to Eden, 12 June 1941.
73. FO 1093/7 fols 19–29 and 33–7, memorandum on the publicity of the affair by SO1, and FO minutes, 23 June 1941.
74. FO 1093/10 fols 58–63 and 82, 13 June 1941.
75. PREM 3/219/5 p. 3, Churchill to Eden, 14 June 1941.
76. FO 1093/10 fols 157–60, report by Colonel J. R. Rees, Consultant in Psychological Medicine to the Army at Home, 30 June 1941.
77. PREM 3/219/6 pp. 32–6, Clark Kerr to Churchill, 25 Oct. 1942.
78. FO 371 30941 C9971 and C10433/1299/18, 33036 C5566/5272/38 and PREM 3/219/6 fols 32–3.
79. Cripps papers, diary, 13 May; FO 371 29481 N2171/78/38, FO minutes, 14 May; FO 371 26565 C5301/5188/18, Halifax to FO, 17 May 1941.
80. FO 371 26565 C5251/5188/18, minute by Sargent, 14 May. On the earlier decision to adopt that method see PREM 3/219/7, Duff Cooper to Churchill, 15 May 1941.
81. Dilks (ed.), *Cadogan Diaries*, p. 382.
82. *Ibid.*, p. 387.
83. FO 1093/11 fols 125–6, FO minutes on Russia and propaganda, 16 May 1941.
84. FO 1093/11 fols 90 and 93, FO minutes on information re Russia, 22 May 1941.
85. FO 1093/6 pp. 2–10, SIS instructions. FO Directive to Stockholm, New York and Istanbul. Minutes by Cadogan, 23 May 1941.
86. FO 1093/11 fols 24–35, 27 May 1941.
87. *The Times*, 27 May 1941.
88. AVP RF, f.059 op.1 p.352 d.2402 l.174.
89. FO 371 29481 N2466/78/38, Cripps to FO and minutes, 27 May 1941.
90. FO 371 29482 N2787/78/38, FO to Cripps, 9 June 1941.
91. FO 1093/10 fols 142–5, minutes of FO committee on German propaganda, 5 June 1941, and fols 133–4, FO instructions to Military Intelligence, 6 June 1941.
92. FO 1093/10 fol. 132, MI to FO, and

fols 106–8, Major D. Morton to FO, 7 June 1941.

93. Khrushchev, *Khrushchev Remembers*, p. 137.

94. On the 'negotiations' see pp. 215–27.

95. TsA FSB RF, f.338 d.20566 l.71, 80 and 82–3, press summaries with departmental markings, 13 May 1941.

96. On this see pp. 67–75.

97. TsA FSB RF, f.338 d.20566 l.232–4, NKVD memorandum on Hess, 12 Dec. 1940.

98. *Ibid.*, l.101–2, information from 'Litseist', 14 May 1941.

99. *Ibid.*, l.60 and 65, 'Zakhar' to NKVD, 16 May 1941.

100. TsA FSB RF, f.338 d.20566 l.62–4 and 66, report from 'Zakhar', 16 May 1941.

101. FO 371 24844 N6072/30/38, 30 July 1940.

102. NKVD to GRU, 9 July 1940 in *Izvestiia TsK KPSS*, 4 (1990), p. 199.

103. Monckton papers, Box 5, p. 49.

104. FO 371/29465 N1801/3/38; Webb papers, diary, p. 7079; Monckton papers, Box 5, p. 49, memorandum, 28 May 1941. An insightful interpretation of these events is in Kitchen, *British Policy towards the Soviet Union during the Second World War*, pp. 52–5. See also S. M. Miner, *Between Churchill and Stalin: The Soviet Union, Great Britain, and the Origins of the Grand Alliance* (Chapel Hill, NC, 1988), pp. 130–7.

105. Maisky in conversation with the Webbs in their unpublished diary, pp. 6921–2, of 3 July; for similar views see his conversations with A. V. Alexander, the First Lord of the Admiralty, in his papers, AVAR 5/4/31, of 28 June; Halifax papers, A.7.8.4, diary, 10 July; and Dalton papers, diary, 26 July 1940.

106. AVP RF, f.017a, Maisky's diary, l.118–19 and 123–7, 2 and 10 May 1941.

107. AVP RF, f.059 op.1 p.351 d.2401 l.283, Maisky to FM, 13 May 1941.

108. AVP RF, f.069, op.25 d.6 p.71 l.72–4, Maisky to Molotov, 14 May 1941.

109. AVP RF, f.059 op.1 d.352 p.2402 l.12–14.

110. AVP RF, f.069 op.25 d.6 p.71 l.75–7, Maisky to Molotov, 16 and 21 May 1941.

111. TsA FSB RF, f.376 d.28889 t.1 l.47, 'Vadim', pseudonym of Ivan Chichaiev, NKVD residency in London, to the Centre, 14 May 1941.

112. *Ibid.*, f.338 d.20566 l.67–8., 'Vadim' to NKVD, 22 May 1941.

113. *Ibid.*, l.163, minute of the 1st Dept of the NKVD, 3 June; see also l.169–70, Schiller from Shanghai, 11 June 1941.

114. Maisky, *Memoirs of a Soviet Ambassador*, p. 145.

115. Webb papers, diary, pp. 7079–80. See also AVP RF, f.017a, Maisky's diary, pp. 130–3, 22 May 1941.

116. AVP RF, f.017a, Maisky's diary, pp. 138–40.

117. AVP RF, f.059 op.1 p.352 d.2402 l.149–52, Maisky to FM, 5 June 1941.

118. AVP RF, f.017a, Maisky's diary, pp. 146–7, 10 June 1941 (handwritten entry).

119. Webb papers, diary, pp. 7103–7, 14 June 1941; *FRUS* I (1941), p. 173.

120. AVP RF, f.059 op.415 d.3727 l.319, Maisky to Molotov, 27 June 1941. See also AVP RF, f.048 'z' op.1'b' d.1 p.11 l.8, 'Sovetsko-Angliiskie otnosheniia v 1941–1945 gg.'.

13. On the Eve of War

1. TsA FSB RF, f.'Zos', op.8 por.9 l.52–3, Beria to Stalin, 2 June 1941.

2. FSB, *Organy Gosudarstvennoi Bezopasnosti SSSR*, I(2), pp. 224–7, report by Major Tkachenko, head of the Lvov District of the Ukrainian NKGB, 12 June 1941.

3. *Ibid.*, pp. 206–7, Golikov to Beria, 3 June 1941.

4. TsA SVR RF, d.21616 t.4 l.184–98, director of the Baltic Region to

Merkulov, 6 June; FSB, *Organy Gosudarstvennoi Bezopasnosti SSSR*, I(2), pp. 209–11, Strokach, deputy commissar for interior affairs of the Ukraine, to NKGB, 6 June 1941.

5. GRU GSh RF, op.24210 d.3 l.319–20, 'Ostwald', Helsinki, to Golikov, 15 June 1941.

6. TsA SVR RF, d.21616 t.2 l.372–5, Kobulov to Timoshenko, 9 June 1941.

7. FSB, *Organy Gosudarstvennoi Bezopasnosti SSSR*, I(2), pp. 221–4, NKGB report to the CC on German warlike measures, 12 June 1941.

8. TsA FSB RF, f.'ZOS', op.8 por.9 l.87–9, Beria to Stalin and Molotov, 12 June 1941.

9. FSB, *Organy Gosudarstvennoi Bezopasnosti SSSR*, I(2), p. 217, intercepted telegram from the Japanese consul in Königsberg to Tekawawa, 10 June 1941.

10. GRU GSh RF, op. 24119 d.4 l.497, military attaché, Budapest, to Golikov, 14 June 1941.

11. GRU GSh RF, op.7237 d.2 l.120–1, report by Golikov, 7 June 1941.

12. TsA SVR RF, d.21616 t.2 l.421–6, 'Zakhar' to the Centre, 10 June 1941.

13. AGSh RF, f.48 op.3408 d.14 l.425 and 432, Zhukov to Kirponos, 10 and 11 June 1941.

14. AGSh RF, f.16 op.2951 d.261 l.22–3, Kirponos to Timoshenko, 11 June 1941.

15. AGSh RF, f.16 op.2951 d.265 l.26–30, Kirponos to the commanders of the 5th, 6th, 12th and 26th Armies, 11 June 1941.

16. AGSh RF, f.164 op.2951 d.236 l.65–9, report by Vatutin, 13 June 1941.

17. See below, p. 287f.

18. Zhukov, *Vospominaniia i razmyshleniia*, pp. 383–4. Similar evidence is provided by N. S. Khrushchev, 'Vospominaniia', *Voprosy istorii*, 2/8 (1990), p. 59. On the abortive attempts of the navy to bring about the mobilization see A. G. Golovko, *Vmeste s flotom* (Moscow,

1960), pp. 14–20; N. M. Kharlamov, *Trudnaia missiia* (Moscow, 1983), ch. 3; N. B. Kuznetsov, *Nakanune* (Moscow, 1989), pp. 324–40; Iu. A. Panteleiev, *Morskoi front* (Moscow, 1965), pp. 31–42; B. Vainer, *Severnyi flot v Velikoi Otechestvennoi voine* (Moscow, 1964), pp. 21–5.

19. Volkogonov papers, 'The plan for the covering of the Baltic Special Military District during mobilization, transfer and deployment of the troops'.

20. AGSh RF, f.16 op.2951 d.256 l.2–3, Timoshenko and Zhukov to Pavlov, 12 June 1941.

21. AGSh RF, f.16 op.2951 d.261 l.37–40, Timoshenko and Zhukov to Kirponos, 12 June 1941.

22. *Ibid.*, l.20–1, Zhukov and Timoshenko to the KOVO Military Council, 13 June 1941.

23. AGSh RF, f.140 op.680086c d.7 l.128, Sokolovsky to the commander of the Baltic District, 14 June 1941.

24. Presidential Archives, f.93, 'special collection of documents', directive by Zhukov and Timoshenko, 19 June 1941.

25. WO 193/644, note by Military Intelligence on 'The Possible Effect of a German–Soviet War', 11 June 1941. See also the illuminating work of W. K. Wark, 'British Intelligence and Operation Barbarossa, 1941: The Failure of Foes', in H. B. Peake and S. Halpern (eds), *The Name of Intelligence: Essays in Honour of Walter Pforzheimer* (Washington, DC, 1994).

26. See pp. 157–8.

27. FO 371 26518 C2919/19/18, Cripps to FO and minutes, 24 Mar. 1941. See also the debate concerning the information obtained from Hess, pp. 262–4.

28. FO 371 26520 C4791/19/18, Kelly (Berne) to FO, 6 May; 29480 N1957, N2200/78/38 and 2260N/78/38, Craigie to FO, 1, 16 and 19 May 1941 respectively.

29. FO 371 29481 N2234 and N2466/

78/38, memoranda by Brigadier Skaife and Professor Postan of the MEW, 12 May, and minute by Warner, 29 May; WO 190/893, report by MI14, 12 May 1941. See also similar analysis in FO 371 29481 N2392/78/38, Mallet to FO, 23 May 1941, and minutes by Sargent, Cadogan and Eden, 25 and 26 May.

30. FO 371 29481 N2500/78/38, 2 June 1941.
31. Note by the Secretary, 3 June, Churchill papers, 20/38, Churchill to Smuts, 16 May; 20/36, Churchill's minute to Ismay, 3 June; and CAB 80/28 COS(41)350, 3 June 1941.
32. FO 371 29482 N2673 and N2678/78/38, Mallet to FO, and Cripps to FO, 7 June, 30 May 1941.
33. FO 954/24 Su/41/13, Sargent on intelligence and German intentions, 1 June 1941.
34. FO 371 30068 R4882/112/44 and 29480 N1978/78/38, Cripps to FO, 1 and 3 May respectively, and UD:s Arkiv 1920 ARS, HP/1557/LVII, Assarasson to FM, 2 May; FO 371 29135 W5536/53/50, 8 May 1941, weekly intelligence reports.
35. FO 371 29480 N2020/78/38, Cripps to FO, 5 May 1941.
36. FO 371 30068 R4832/112/44, Cripps to FO, 3 May, and 29480 N1989/78/38, Halifax to FO, 4 May 1941.
37. FO 371 30125 R2366, R5368 and R5369/1934/44, Knatchbull-Hugessen, 18 and 20 May 1941.
38. FO 371 29481 N2380/78/38, Cripps to FO, 22 May 1941.
39. WO 208/1761, JIC(41)218, German intentions, 23 May 1941.
40. WO 190/893, report by MI14, 26 May 1941.
41. FO 371 30068 R5558/112/44, Knatchbull-Hugessen to FO, 23 May 1941.
42. *DGFP*, XII, pp. 828–9, 836–7, 839–40, 849–50, 866–7, 910–15, 937–40 and 985–7, exchange of telegrams between Ribbentrop and Papen, 16–29 May, and 1 and 6 June 1941. See also H. Knatchbull-Hugessen, *Diplomat in Peace and War* (London, 1949), pp. 168–9.
43. FO 371 30068 R6061/112/44, Knatchbull-Hugessen to FO, 9 June 1941.
44. *DGFP*, XII, pp. 1036–40, exchanges between Ribbentrop and Papen, 16 and 18 June; AVP RF, f.0134 op.24a p.236 d.9 l.125–6, memorandum by Zhegalov (first secretary Soviet embassy in Ankara), 20 June 1941.
45. *DGFP*, XII, p. 1080, Papen to Hitler, 22 June 1941.
46. AVP RF, f.069 op. 25 d.6 p.71 l.72–4, Maisky to Molotov, 14 May 1941.
47. *Ibid.*, l.79–82, and FO 371 29501 N2471/122/38, reports of Eden's meeting with Maisky, 27 May 1941.
48. FO 371 29481 N2466/78/38, Cripps to FO, 27 May. See also similar views in Krigsarkivet, Fo..rsvarsstaben, Ser. E/II/15/1, military attaché's report, no. 57, 2 June 1941.
49. FO 954/24 fols 304–9, Cripps's private letter to Eden, 27 May 1941.
50. WO 208/1761, JIC(41)234 (1st draft), 31 May 1941, and comment by MI14. WO 193/644, note by Military Intelligence on 'The Possible Effect of a German–Soviet War', 11 June 1941.
51. Eden papers, diary, 5 June 1941.
52. FO 954/24 Su/41/12 and 13, minutes by Warner, Sargent and Cadogan on intelligence and German intentions, 31 May and 1 June. CAB 79/86 COS(41)197, including War Office to C-in-C ME and India, 31 May 1941.
53. Gilbert, *Finest Hour: Winston S. Churchill, 1939–1941*, ch. 57, and M. Howard, *The Mediterranean Strategy in the Second World War* (London, 1968), ch. 2.
54. The meeting of 2 June 1941 is reported in AVP RF, f.059 op.1 p.352 d.2402 l.120–2, and FO 371 29465 N2570/2/38.
55. CAB 65/18 56(41), 2 June 1941. See also Eden, *The Reckoning*, p. 266.

56. FO 800/279 Su/41/1, minutes of 26, 29 and 30 Apr. 1941.

57. FO 371 29466 N2674/3/38, the press reaction to Cripps's recall, 9 June 1941.

58. On the Moscow meeting see AVP RF, f.07 op.2 p.9 d.20 l.35–6, record of Vyshinsky's meeting with Cripps, 4 June 1941; see also Quai d'Orsay Archives, 835/Z/312/2, pp. 264–5, Nemanov on meeting General Sousloparov, 5 June 1941.

59. AVP RF, f.059 op.1 p.352 d.2402 l.149–52, and FO 371 29466 N2628/3/38, reports of Eden's meeting with Maisky, 5 June 1941. See also FO 371 29483 N2982/78/38, Baggallay to FO, 20 June 1941.

60. Monckton papers, Box 5, p. 96.

61. J. G. Winant, *A Letter from Grosvenor Square: An Account of a Stewardship* (London, 1947), pp. 143–4.

62. J. P. Lash, *Roosevelt and Churchill, 1939–1941: The Partnership that Saved the West* (New York, 1976). Harper papers, H22.f.21, Harper to Henderson, 22 June 1941. See also R. H. Dawson, *The Decision to Aid Russia, 1941: Foreign Policy and Domestic Politics* (Chapel Hill, NC, 1959), pp. 60–1.

63. Maisky, *Memoirs of a Soviet Ambassador*, pp. 148–50, 165. A hint of a connection between Cripps's threats, the Hess episode and the communiqué is in F. D. Volkov, *SSSR-Angliia 1929–1945gg.* (Moscow, 1964), pp. 343–4. FO 371 29466 N2628/3/38, Eden to Cripps on meeting Maisky, 5 June, and N2674/3/38, FO minute, 9 June 1941.

64. Chuev, *Sto sorok besed s Molotovym*, p. 43.

65. Maisky, *Memoirs of a Soviet Ambassador*, p. 149. This episode, so central to the understanding of the events on the eve of the Soviet–German war, has been omitted from his later Russian version, I. M. Maisky, *Vospominaniia sovetskogo diplomata* (Moscow, 1987). Just as misleading

66. Maisky, *Memoirs of a Soviet Ambassador*, pp. 150 ff.

67. AVP RF, f.07 op.2 p.9 d.20 l.37–8, record of Vyshinsky's meeting with Baggallay, 16 June 1941.

68. 'Cripps Visit Sets Berlin Wondering', *News Chronicle*, 9 June 1941.

69. 9 and 8 June 1941.

70. FO 371 29483 N2862/78/38. On the attitude of the paper see also I. McDonald (ed.), *The History of the Times*, V: *Struggle in War and Peace: 1939–1966* (London, 1984), p. 84. I profited much from numerous conversations with Iverach McDonald on this and other aspects of British policy at the time during my stay at St Antony's and he made some detailed and useful comments on an earlier version of this manuscript.

71. FO 371 29483 N2992/78/38, Maisky to Eden, 13 June 1941.

72. AVP RF, f.017a, Maisky's diary, pp. 150–3, 12 June 1941.

73. AVP RF, f.069 op.24 p.68 d.7 l.88–94, FM memorandum, 2 June 1941.

74. FO 371 N2887/78/38, Warner's minute, 13 June 1941.

75. FO 418/87, Eden to Baggallay, 13 June 1941.

76. FO 371 29483 N2887/78/38, minutes by Cadogan and Sargent, 13 and 14 June; 29315 W7499/53/50, PIS, 18 June 1941.

77. Dilks (ed.), *Cadogan Diaries*, p. 382.

78. WO 208/1761, JIC(41)234 (1st draft), and comment by MI14; final draft in FO 371 29483 N/2906/78/38, and comment by Cavendish-Bentinck, 15 June, in N3047/78/38, see also JIC(41)218, 23 May, in FO 371 29483 N/2893/78/38, 31 May. For the wavering nature of MI appreciation see WO 190/893, 2 June 1941.

79. FO 371 29482 N2832/78/38, Mallet to FO, 14 June 1941.

80. *Izvestiia*, 14 June 1941.

81. *50 Let Velikoi Otechestvennoi voiny,*

p. 26, 'Starshina' to NKGB, 16 June 1941.

82. AVP RF, f.082 op.24 p.105 d.3 l.177–82, record of Vyshinsky's meeting with Schulenburg, 14 June 1941. See also Herwarth, *Against Two Evils*, pp. 194–5.

83. FO 371 29483 N2891/78/38, Eden to Maisky, 14 June 1941.

14. *Calamity*

1. Reproduced in *Vestnik MID SSSR*, 8 66 (1990), p. 76.
2. Reproduced in Vishlev, 'Pochemu Medlil Stalin v 1941', p. 82.
3. *Ibid.*, pp. 94–5.
4. *Ibid.*, p. 96.
5. *Ibid.*, pp. 82–3, 11 June 1941.
6. FSB, *Sekrety Gitlera*, pp. 148–50, Kobulov to Stalin, Molotov and Beria, 9 June 1941.
7. TsA SVR RF, d.23078 t.1 l.430–1, 'Starshina' to NKGB, 11 June 1941.
8. *Ibid.*, l.432–3, Kobulov to Stalin, Molotov and Beria, 12 June 1941.
9. Merkulov to Stalin reproduced in *Izvestiia TsK KPSS*, 4 (1990), p. 221, 16 June 1941. See also Sudoplatov, *Special Tasks*, pp. 120–1.
10. G. Kumanev, '22-go' na rassvete', *Pravda*, 22 June 1989.
11. Sudoplatov, *Special Tasks*, p. 122.
12. Zhukov, *Vospominaniia i razmyshleniia*, p. 324.
13. *Ibid.*, pp. 362–3.
14. FSB, *Organy Gosudarstvennoi Bezopasnosti SSSR*, I(2), p. 212, intercepted telegram from Tatekawa to the Japanese ambassador in Sofia, 9 June 1941.
15. TsA FSB RF, f.'Zos', op.8 d.58 l.1945–8, Merkulov to Stalin, Molotov and Beria, 18 June; see also Krigsarkivet, Fo..rsvarsstaben, Ser. E/II/15/1, military attaché's report, no. 58, 19 June, and UD:s Arkiv 1920 ARS, HP/1557/LVII, Assarasson to FM, 20 June 1941.
16. FSB, *Sekrety Gitlera*, pp. 168–9,

Kobulov to Stalin, Molotov and Beria, 19 June 1941.

17. TsA FSB RF, f.'Zos', op.8 d.58 l.1978–80, Kobulov to Stalin, Molotov and Beria, 20 June 1941.
18. Reproduced in *Izvestiia TsK KPSS*, 4 (1990), p. 217, 19 June 1941, and confirmed by the NKVD resident in Rome, in FSB, *Organy Gosudarstvennoi Bezopasnosti SSSR*, I(2), p. 269, 19 June 1941.
19. GRU GSh RF, op.24127 d.2 l.454, Sorge to Golikov, 15 June 1941.
20. *Ibid.*, l.463, Sorge to GRU, 20 June 1941.
21. FSB, *Organy Gosudarstvennoi Bezopasnosti SSSR*, I(2), pp. 254–64, special report by the NKGB, 19 June 1941.
22. I am indebted to Dr Lev Bezymensky for a signed statement by General N. Liashchenko, to whom Timoshenko volunteered the information.
23. TsA SVR RF, d.21616 t.3 l.68–73, special report by the deputy director of the Ukrainian NKGB, 16 Apr. 1941.
24. *Ibid.*, l.569–72, special report by the deputy director of the Ukrainian NKVD, 27 Feb. 1941, and also FSB, *Organy Gosudarstvennoi Bezopasnosti SSSR*, I(2), pp. 82–5, report by Pavel Meshik, the head of the Ukrainian NKGB, 9 Apr. 1941.
25. TsA FSB RF, f.3 op.8 por.373 l.367–9, Meshnik, head of the NKVD in the Ukraine, to Merkulov, 20 Apr. 1941.
26. TsA SVR RF, d.21616 t.2 l.366, 29 May 1941.
27. FSB, *Organy Gosudarstvennoi Bezopasnosti SSSR*, I/2, pp. 240–7, report by the 3rd Dept of the NKGB, 16 June 1941.
28. See pp. 213–17.
29. FSB, *Organy Gosudarstvennoi Bezopasnosti SSSR*, I/2, pp. 142–50, instructions by Merkulov to the Ukrainian and Baltic NKGB, 16 and 17 May 1941.
30. *Ibid.*, pp. 152–3, 154–6, 162–3, 165–6,

directive of the 3rd Dept of the NKVD and reports by Merkulov to the CC of the CPSU as well as reports by the heads of the local NKGB, 22 May 1941.

31. *Ibid.*, pp. 172–87, memorandum by the deputy director of the 3rd Dept of the NKGB, 31 May 1941.

32. *Ibid.*, pp. 218–19, report by Borshchev, deputy director of the 2nd Dept of the NKGB, 11 June, and pp. 247–8, Merkulov to the CC of the CPSU, 17 June 1941; Sudaplatov, *Special Tasks*, p. 122.

33. FO 954/24 Su/41/15, 9 June; CAB 65/22 58(41)2, 9 June 1941.

34. FO 371 29482 N2744/78/38, Mallet to FO, 11 June 1941.

35. FO 371 29482 C6668/19/18, minutes, 9–11 June 1941.

36. FO 954/24 Su/41/16, Eden to Baggallay (Moscow) on meeting Maisky, 10 June 1941.

37. AVP RF, f.059 op.1 p.352 d.2402 l.203–6, and FO 371 29482 N2793/78/38, reports of the meeting between Eden and Maisky.

38. FO 371 29483 N3047/78/38, minute by Cadogan and Cavendish-Bentinck on intelligence transmitted to Maisky, 15 June 1941.

39. FO 371/29466 N3047/78/38, minute by Cadogan; Dilks (ed.), *Cadogan Diaries*, p. 388; Maisky, *Memoirs of a Soviet Ambassador*, pp. 149, 165–71. As a central piece of evidence on the warnings to the Russians, Maisky's version has led most historians to a faulty and condemnatory interpretation of the Tass communiqué, among them Whaley, *Codeword Barbarossa*, pp. 107–8 and 114.

40. AVP RF, f.059 op.1 p.352 d.2402 l.214–15, Maisky to Molotov, 16 June 1941.

41. FO 371 29483 N2898/78/38, Baggallay to FO, 16 June 1941.

42. FO 371 29483 N2898/78/38.

43. FO 371 29466 N3099/3/38. For a similar erroneous British interpretation see FO 371 29482 N2842

and 29483 N2891/78/38, telegram from Baggallay and minute by Cadogan, 14 and 15 June 1941.

44. FO 371 29482 N2680/78/38, Mallet to FO, 8 June, and CAB 65/22 59(41)2, 12 June 1941; Boheman, *På Vakt*, pp. 154–5.

45. Eden papers, diary, 16 June 1941.

46. FO 371 30126 R6170/1934/44, minutes by Sargent and Cadogan, 16 June 1941.

47. Churchill papers, 20/40, Churchill to Smuts, 18 June 1941.

48. AVP RF, f.059 op.1 p.352 d.2402 l.246–7, Maisky to Molotov, 20 June 1941.

49. *Ibid.*, l.235–6, Maisky to Molotov, and f.017a, Maisky's diary, pp. 153–7, 18 June 1941.

50. FO 371 29466 N3099/3/38, memorandum by Cripps, 19 June 1941.

51. *The Times* archives, Dawson to Halifax, 22 June 1941. On 24 June Gallacher, Communist Member of Parliament, revealed that a change in appreciation had occurred on 19 June, *Parl. Deb. HC*, vol. 372, col. 986.

52. UD:s Arkiv 1920 ARS, HP/1557/LVIII, Swedish ambassador in Berlin, 21 June 1941.

53. Khrushchev, 'Vospominaniia', pp. 59 and 71–3.

54. UD:s Arkiv 1920 ARS, HP/1557/LVIII, Boheman minute, 21 June 1941.

55. *Ibid.*, Assarasson to FM, 21 June 1941.

56. Gafencu, *Misiune la Moscova*, tel. 45698, pp. 225, Gafencu to FM, 16 June 1941.

57. UD:s Arkiv 1920 ARS, HP/1557/LVII, Assarasson to FM, 16 June 1941.

58. Quai d'Orsay Archives, 834/Z/312/1 pp. 145–9, Nemanov to FM on meeting Bogomolov, 5 June 1941.

59. Quai d'Orsay Archives, 835/Z 312/2, pp. 261–4, Nemanov on meeting General Sousloparov, 18 June 1941.

60. AVP RF, f.059 op.1 p.352 d.2402 l.254–7, Maisky to Molotov, 21 June

1941, and a report by Cripps in FO 371 29484 N3047/78/38.

61. Dimitrov's diary, 21 June 1941.
62. AVP RF, f.06 op.3 p.1 d.5 l.6–7, report by Molotov on meeting Aktay, 19 June 1941.
63. AVP RF, f.082 op.24 p.106 d.7 l.94–7, report by Dekanozov on meeting Weizsäcker, 18 June 1941.
64. AVP RF, f.06 op.3 p.1 d.5 l.8–11, and *DGFP*, XII, pp. 1070–1, records of Molotov's meeting with Schulenburg, 21 June 1941.
65. *Ibid.*, pp. 1061–2, Weizsäcker on meeting Dekanozov, 21 June 1941.
66. AGSh RF, f.208 op.2513 d.71 l.69, Timoshenko and Zhukov, 22 June 1941; see also Zhukov, *Vospominaniia i razmyshleniia*, p. 387.
67. Presidential Archives, f.3 op.50 d.125 l.75–6, handwritten Politburo resolutions by Malenkov on the organization of the southern front, 21 June 1941.
68. Zhukov, *Vospominaniia i razmyshleniia*, I, pp. 386–9; Presidential Archives, Stalin's appointment diary. See also a confirmation in Zakharov, *General'nyi shtab*, pp. 276–7.
69. Chuev, *Sto sorok besed s Molotovym*, p. 47.
70. *DGFP*, XII, pp. 1063–5, Ribbentrop to Schulenburg, 21 June 1941.
71. Berezhkov, *Gody diplomaticheskoi sluzhby*, pp. 60–4; R. J. Sontag and J. S. Beddie, *Nazi–Soviet Relations, 1939–1941: Documents from the Archives of the German Foreign Office* (Washington, DC, 1975), pp. 353–6. Hilger and Meyer, *Incompatible Allies*, pp. 336 and 339. *DGFP*, XII, pp. 1071–5, Schulenburg to FM, and memorandum of the FM, 21 June 1941.
72. AVP RF, f.06 op.3 p.1 d.5 l.12–15, record of Molotov's meeting with Schulenburg, 22 June 1941. See also Hilger and Meyer, *Incompatible Allies*, pp. 334–6, and Gafencu, *Misiune la Moscova*, pp. 228–33, report by Gafencu to Antonescu, 1 Aug. 1941.

73. Zhukov, *Vospominaniia i razmyshleniia*, II, pp. 7–9; the full new version of the memoirs is vital for this episode as the older one was heavily censored.
74. Timoshenko, Zhukov and Malenkov to the Military Councils of the various fronts, 22 June 1941, in *50 Let Velikoi Otechestvennoi voiny*, p. 30.
75. FO 371 29466 N3232/3/38.
76. Dimitrov's diary, 22 June 1941.
77. FO 371/29466 N3018/3/38; Maisky, *Memoirs of a Soviet Ambassador*, pp. 156–7.
78. *Ibid.*
79. Churchill papers, 20/40, Churchill to Roosevelt, 20 June 1941.
80. *Ibid.*, 20/36, Churchill minute to Ismay for COS, 21 June 1941.
81. FO 371 29484 N3212/78/38.
82. AVP RF, f.17a, Maisky's diary, pp. 160–6, 23 June 1941.
83. *Daily Express*, 23 June 1941.
84. FO 371/29466 N3180 and N3489/3/38, minutes 23 and 28 June 1941.
85. Cripps papers, diary, 9 July. For Molotov's obsession see the Soviet records of his first meeting with Cripps on 27 June 1941 in MID, *Sovetsko-angliiskie otnosheniia*, I, pp. 47–50.
86. The Library of Congress, Ambassador Davies Papers, Box 11. See also Halifax papers, A.7.8.9, diary, 11 December 1941. Gromyko witnessed later on in New York a fierce row between Molotov and Litvinov in the back of a car he was driving, when Molotov continued to maintain that Britain and France had pushed Hitler into attacking the Soviet Union in 1941. See A. Gromyko, *Pamiatnoe* (Moscow, 1990), II, p. 423. In negotiating with the British in the early stages of the war, Stalin did not seek a second front but singlemindedly sought an agreement which would pledge both sides not to negotiate a separate peace.

Conclusion

1. Cripps papers, diary, 9 Mar. 1941. A most convincing argument in this direction is advanced by G. Roberts, 'Military Disaster as a Function of Rational Political Calculation: Stalin and 22 June 1941', *Diplomacy and Statecraft*, 4/2 (1993). See also R. Suny, 'Making Sense of Stalin – Some Recent and Not-So-Recent Biographies', *Russian History/Histoire Russe*, 16/2–4 (1989).

2. H. Kissinger, *Diplomacy* (London, 1995), pp. 335 and 103–4. One cannot but approve Kissinger's acute judgments that 'Stalin was indeed a monster; but in the conduct of international relations, he was the supreme realist – patient, shrewd, and implacable, the Richelieu of his period' (p. 333), or 'common geopolitical interest is a powerful bond, and it was pushing the old enemies, Hitler and Stalin, inexorably together' (p. 332). A similar conclusion is drawn in Paul Kennedy's classic study, *The Rise and Fall of the Great Powers* (London, 1988).

3. See p. 309.

4. Chuev, *Sto sorok besed s Molotovym*, p. 31.

Bibliography

Primary Sources:

Archives

Archives of the Russian Foreign Ministry (AVP RF).
Russian Military Archives: General Staff and GRU papers (AGSh RF and GRU GSh RF).
The Presidential Archives, Moscow: selected papers.
Archives of the Russian Security Services: Reports related to German intentions against Russia (TsA SVR RF and FsA FSB RF).
The Russian Centre for the Preservation and Study of Contemporary History (RsKhIDIN).
The Yugoslav Archive of Military History (Archiv Vojeno-istorijskog instituta).
Archives of the Yugoslav Foreign Ministry (AJ).
The Archives of the Quai d'Orsay (the Russian Files).
The Archives of the Bulgarian Foreign Ministry (AMVnR).
Bulgarian Central National Archives: Records of the Foreign Ministry (TsDA MVR).
Public Record Office, London: Archives of the Foreign Office (FO), Prime Minister's Office (PREM), Joint Intelligence Committee (JIC), Chiefs of Staff (COS), Joint Planning Staff (JP), Ministry of Economic Warfare (MEW), War Office (WO).
Archives of the Swedish Foreign Ministry (UD:s Arkiv 1920 ARS).
Swedish Military Archives (Krigsarkivet).
National Archives, Washington, DC: State Department papers.

Private Papers

Ivan Maisky's diary, Archive of the Russian Foreign Ministry.
Alexander Cadogan's papers, Churchill College, Cambridge University.
Neville Chamberlain's papers, Birmingham University.

Winston Churchill's papers, Churchill College, Cambridge.
Stafford Cripps's diary and papers, with Sir Maurice Shock.
Hugh Dalton's papers, London School of Economics.
Anthony Eden's papers, Birmingham University.
Lord Halifax's papers, York University.
Walter Monckton's papers, Bodleian Library, Oxford University.
Beatrice Webb's papers, London School of Economics.
Georgy Dimitrov's diary, National Library, Sofia, Bulgaria.
Dimitry Volkogonov's papers, Library of Congress, Washington, DC.

Printed Collections of Documents

E. L. Woodward (ed.), *Documents on British Foreign Policy, 1919–1939,* 3rd ser.,
  vol. V (London, 1952).
Documents on German Foreign Policy (DGFP), series D, vols I–XII (Göttingen,
  1966–1978).
*Der Prozess gegen die Hauptkriegsverbrecher vor dem Internationalen Militär-
  gerichtshoe: Nüremberg, 14. November 1945–1. October 1946* (Nuremberg, 1947).
Foreign Relations of the United States (FRUS), vol. I (1941).
Italian Foreign Ministry, Documenti Diplomatici Italiani, 8th ser., vol. 2 (Rome,
  1952).
Sontag, R., and J. S. Beddie (eds), *Nazi–Soviet Relations, 1939–1941: Documents
  from the Archives of the German Foreign Office* (Washington, DC, 1948).
Kimball, W. F., *Churchill and Roosevelt; The Complete Correspondence,* 3 vols
  (Princeton, 1984).
Kimball, W. F., *The Juggler: Franklin Roosevelt as Wartime Statesman* (Princeton,
  1991).
Gafencu, G., *Misiune la Moscova, 1940–41: Culegere de dokumente* (Bucharest,
  1995).
MID, *Dokumenty vneshnei politiki, 1939 god (DVP, 1939),* 2 vols (Moscow, 1992).
MID, *Dokumenty vneshnei politiki, 1940–22 iiunia 1941,* vol. I (Moscow, 1995).
MID, *Sovetsko-angliiskie otnosheniia vo vremiia Velikoi Otechestvennoi voiny,
  1941–1945,* 2 vols (Moscow, 1983).
FSB, *Sekrety Gitlera ha stole u Stalina: razvedka i kontrrazvedka o podgotovke ger-
  manskoi agressii protiv SSSR, mart-iiun' 1941 g.* (Moscow, 1995).
FSB, *Organy Gosudarstvennoi Bezopasnosti SSSR v Velikoi Otechestvennoi Voine.
  Sbornik dokumentov,* 2 vols (Moscow, 1995).
Kirpichenko, V., *Iz arkhiva razvedchika* (Moscow, 1992).
Komintern i vtoraia mirovaia voina (Moscow, 1994).
Skrytaia pravda voiny: 1941 god (Moscow, 1992).
Sovetsko-Bolgarskie otnosheniia i sviazi 1917–1944 gg. (Moscow, 1976).
Sovetsko-iugoslavskie otnosheniia, 1917–1941 gg. (Moscow, 1992).
Zolotarev, V. A. (ed.), *Russkii Arkhiv: Velikaia Otechestvennaia. Nakanune voiny:
  materialy soveshchaniia vysshego rukovodiashchego sostava RKKA, 23–31
  dekabriia 1940g.* (Moscow, 1993).
Zolotarev, V. A. (ed.), *Russkii Arkhiv: Velikaia Otechestvennaia. Prikazy narodnogo
  komissara oborony SSSR, 1937–21 iiunia 1941g.* (Moscow, 1994).

Collections of Documents Published in Journals

Besymensky, L., 'Die Rede Stalins am 5.Mai 1941. Dokumentiert und inter-
pretiert', *Osteuropa*, 3 (1992).
Bezymensky, L., and S. Gorlov, 'Nakanune: Peregovory V. M. Molotova v
Berline v noiabre 1940 goda', *Mezhdunarodnaia Zhizn'*, 6 and 8 (1991).
Gorchakov, O., 'Nakanune, ili tragediia Kassandry: povest' v dokumentakh',
Nedelia, 42–4 (1988).
Latysheva, A., 'Rech' v Bol'shom Kremlevskom dvortse, 5 Maia 1941 goda',
Iskusstvo kino, 5 (1990).
Leonidov, 'Voennaia razvedka o podgotovke k napadeniiu Germanii na
SSSR', *Voenno-istoricheskii zhurnal*, 3 (1995).
'O podgotovke Germanii k napadeniiu na SSSR', *Izvestiia TsK KPSS*, 4 (1990).
Petrov, Iu., 'Velikaia Otechestvennaia: neizvestnye dokumenty', *Krasnaia
zvezda*, 15 Feb. 1992.
Sandalov, L. M. (ed.), 'Nakanune voiny (1940–1941gg.)', *Izvestiia Tsk KPSS*, 4
(1990).
Sipols, V. Ia., 'Tainye dokumenty "strannoi voiny" ', *Novaia i noveishaia istoriia*,
2 (1993).
'Sovetsko–germanskie dokumenty 1939–1941 gg.: iz arkhiva TsK KPSS',
Novaia i noveishaia istoriia, 1 (1993).
Vishlev, O. V., 'Pochemu zhe medlil I. V. Stalin v 1941 gg. (iz Germanskikh
arkhivov)', *Novaia i noveishaia istoriia*, 1 and 2 (1992), pp. 86–100 and 70–96
respectively.
'Zapiski i informatsiia v TsK VKP(b) i SNK SSSR', *Izvestiia TsK KPSS*, 5 (1990).

Further and Secondary Sources:

Biographies, Autobiographies and Diaries

Assarasson, A., *I skuggan av Stalin* (Stockholm, 1963).
Berezhkov, V., *History in the Making* (Moscow, 1983).
Berezhkov, V., 'Stalin's Error of Judgement', *International Affairs*, September
1989.
Bullock, A., *Hitler and Stalin: Parallel Lives* (London, 1991).
Carlton, D., *Anthony Eden: A Biography* (London, 1981).
Chuev, F. I., *Sto sorok besed s Molotovym: iz dnevnika F. Chueva* (Moscow, 1991).
Chukreev, V. I., 'Zagadka 22 iunia 1941 goda', *Voenno-istoricheskii zhurnal*, 6
(1989).
Churchill, W., *The Second World War*, vols I–IV (London, 1948–50).
Ciano, G., *Ciano's Diplomatic Papers* (London, 1948).
Dilks, D. (ed.), *The Diaries of Sir Alexander Cadogan, 1938–1945* (London, 1971).
Eden, A., *The Eden Memoirs: The Reckoning* (London, 1965).
Egorov, A., 'Rikhard Zorge (K 90-letiiu so dnia rozhdeniia)', *Voenno-
istoricheskii zhurnal*, 10 (1985).
Elvin, H., *A Cockney in Moscow* (London, 1958).
Filov, B., *Dnevnik* (Sofia, 1986).

Fröhlich, E. (ed.), *Die Tagebücher von Joseph Goebbels: Sämtliche Fragmente*, vol. I: *Aufzeichnungen, 1924–1941* (Munich, 1987).
Gilbert, M., *Finest Hour: Winston S. Churchill, 1939–1941* (London, 1983).
Golovko, A. G., *Vmeste s flotom* (Moscow, 1960).
Gromyko, A., *Pamiatnoe*, 2 vols (Moscow, 1990).
Halder, Franz, *Kriegstagebuch* (Stuttgart, 1963).
Harvey, John (ed.), *The Diplomatic Diaries of Oliver Harvey, 1937–40* (London, 1970).
Herwarth, H. von, *Against Two Evils: Memoirs of a Diplomat–Soldier during the Third Reich* (London, 1981).
Hilger, G., and A. G. Meyer, *The Incompatible Allies: A Memoir-History of German–Soviet Relations, 1918–1941* (New York, 1971).
Hill, L. E. (ed.), *Die Weizsäcker-Papiere, 1933–1950* (Frankfurt, 1974).
Irving, D., *Hess: The Missing Years, 1941–1945* (London, 1989).
Karpov, V., 'Zhukov', *Kommunist vooruzhennykh sil*, 5 (1990).
Karpov, V., *Marshal Zhukov. Opala* (Moscow, 1994).
Kharlamov, M. M., *Trudnaia missiia* (Moscow, 1983).
Khrushchev, N. S., *Khrushchev Remembers* (Boston, 1970).
Khrushchev, N. S., 'Memuary Nikity Sergeevicha Khrushcheva', *Voprosy istorii*, 6, 7, 8, 9 and 10 (1990).
Kirkpatrick, I., *The Inner Circle* (London, 1959).
Knatchbull-Hugessen, H., *Diplomat in Peace and War* (London, 1949).
Knox, M., *Mussolini Unleashed, 1939–1941: Politics and Strategy in Fascist Italy's Last War* (Cambridge, 1982).
Kolesnikov, M., *Zhizn' i bessmertie Rikharda Zorge: Povest'* (Moscow, 1985).
Kuznetsov, H. G., *Nakanune* (Moscow, 1989).
Maisky, I., *Memoirs of a Soviet Ambassador: The War, 1939–43* (London, 1967).
Muggeridge, M. (ed.), *Ciano's Diaries, 1939–43* (London, 1948).
Novikov, N. V., *Vospominaniia diplomata: zapiski 1938–1947* (Moscow, 1989).
Novobranets, V. A., 'Vospominaniia', *Znamia*, 6 (1990).
Padfield, P., *Rudolf Hess: The Führer's Disciple* (London, 1993).
Papen, F. von, *Memoirs* (London, 1952).
Peter, King, *King's Heritage: The Memoirs of King Peter II of Yugoslavia* (London, 1955).
Radzinsky, E., *Stalin: The First In-Depth Biography Based on Explosive New Documents from Russia's Secret Archives* (New York, 1997).
Rendell, G., *The Sword and the Olive: Recollections of Diplomacy and the Foreign Service* (London, 1957).
Reuth, R. G. (ed.), *Goebbels Tagebücher. 1924–1945* (Munich and Zurich, 1992).
Ribbentrop, J. von, *The Ribbentrop Memoirs* (London, 1954).
Rokossovsky, K. K., *Soldatskii dolg* (Moscow, 1984).
Rokossovsky, K. K., 'Soldatskii dolg', *Voenno-istoricheskii zhurnal*, 7 (1991), pp. 4–11.
Sandalov, L. M., *Perezhitoe* (Moscow, 1966).
Sandalov, L. M., 'Stoiali nasmert', *Voenno-istoricheskii zhurnal*, 11 (1988).
Schacht, H., *Confessions of the Old Wizard* (Boston, 1956).
Schmidt, P., *Hitler's Interpreter* (London, 1952).
Speer, A., *Inside the Third Reich* (New York, 1970).

Sudoplatov, P., *Special Tasks: The Memoirs of an Unwanted Witness – a Soviet Spymaster* (London, 1993).
Thomas, H., *The Murder of Rudolf Hess* (London, 1979).
Trepper, Leopold, *Bol'shaia igra* (Moscow, 1990).
Vassilevsky, A. M., 'Nakanune voiny', *Novaia i noveiishaia istoriia*, 6 (1992).
Vassilevsky, A. M., *Delo vsei zhizni* (Moscow, 1975).
Weizsäcker, Ernst H., *Memoirs* (London, 1951).
Zakharov, M. V., *General'nyi shtab v predvoennye gody* (Moscow, 1989).
Zhukov, E. M., 'Proiskhozhdenie vtoroi mirovoi voiny', *Novaia i noveishaia istoriia*, 1 (1980).

Secondary Sources

Accoce, P., and P. Quet, *A Man Called Lucy, 1939–1945* (New York, 1967).
Andrew, C., 'Hess: An Edge of Conspiracy', *Timewatch*, BBC2 (17 Jan. 1990).
Andrew, C., and O. Gordievsky, *KGB: The Inside Story* (London, 1991).
Anfilov, V. A., *Nezabyvaemyi sorok pervyi* (Moscow, 1982).
Barker, E., *British Policy in South-East Europe in the Second World War* (London, 1976).
Barros, J., and R. Gregor, *Double Deception: Stalin, Hitler and the Invasion of Russia* (1995).
Beliaev, V. I., 'Usilenie okhrany zapadnoi granitsy SSSR nakanune Velikoi Otechestvennoi voiny', *Voenno-istoricheskii zhurnal*, 5 (1988).
Bell, P. M. H., *John Bull and the Bear: British Public Opinion, Foreign Policy and the Soviet Union, 1941–1945* (London, 1990).
Bezymensky, L., 'The Secret Protocols of 1939 as a Problem of Soviet Historiography', in G. Gorodetsky (ed.), *Soviet Foreign Policy, 1917–1991: A Retrospective* (London, 1994).
Bezymensky, L., 'Sovetskaia razvedka pered voinoy', *Voprosy istorii*, 9 (1996).
Bialer, S., *Stalin and his Generals: Soviet Military Memoirs of World War II* (New York, 1969).
Borshchov, A. D., 'Otrazhenie fashistskoi agressii: uroki i vyvody', *Voennaia mysl'*, 3 (1990).
Bukharkin, I. V., 'No tut vmeshalas' Iugoslaviia', *Pravda*, 1 June 1991.
Carley, M. J., 'End of the "Low, Dishonest Decade": Failure of the Anglo-Franco-Soviet Alliance in 1939', *Europe-Asia Studies*, 45/2 (1993).
Caulaincourt, General Armand de, *With Napoleon in Russia* (New York, 1935).
Chaney, O., 'Was It Surprise', *Military Review* 2 (1969).
Charmley, J., *Chamberlain and the Lost Peace* (London, 1989).
Chihiro, H., 'The Japanese–Soviet Neutrality Pact', in J. Morley (ed.), *The Fateful Choice: Japan's Advance into Southeast Asia, 1939–1941* (New York, 1980).
Chukreev, V. I., 'Zagadka 22 iunia 1941 goda', *Voenno-istoricheskii zhurnal*, 6 (1989).
Clarke, J. C., *Russia and Italy against Hitler: The Bolshevik–Fascist Rapprochement of the 1930s* (Westport, Conn., 1991).
Cliadakis, H., 'Neutrality and War in Italian Policy, 1939–1940', *Journal of Contemporary History*, 3 (1974).

Condren, P., 'Soviet Foreign Policy: Part Two, 1934–1941', *Modern History Review*, 1/4 (1990).

Conquest, R., *The Harvest of Sorrow* (New York, 1986).

Coox, A. D., *Nomonhan: Japan against Russia, 1939* (Stanford, 1986).

Costello, J., *Ten Days to Destiny: The Secret Story of the Hess Peace Initiative and British Efforts to Strike a Deal with Hitler* (London, 1991).

Creveld, M. van, 'The German Attack on the USSR: The Destruction of a Legend', *European Studies Review*, 2/1 (1972).

Creveld, M. van, *The Balkan Clue: Hitler's Strategy, 1940–41* (Cambridge, 1973).

Curtright, L. H., 'Great Britain, the Balkans, and Turkey in the Autumn of 1939', *International History Review*, 3 (1988).

Cvetkoviç, S., 'Sovjetska Prisutnost u Jugoslovenskoj Politici Na Pochetku Drugog Svetskog Rata', *Istorija 20. Veka*, 1 (1995).

Dallin, A., 'Hitler and Russia', *Canadian Slavonic Papers*, 16/3 (1974).

Dallin, A., 'Stalin and the German Invasion', *Soviet Union/Union Soviétique*, 1–3 (1991).

Dallin, D. J., *Soviet Russia's Foreign Policy, 1939–1942* (New Haven, 1942).

Deakin, F. W., and G. R. Storry, *The Case of Richard Sorge* (London, 1966).

Deringil, S., 'The Preservation of Turkey's Neutrality during the Second World War: 1940', *Middle Eastern Studies*, 18/1 (1982).

Deringil, S., *Turkish Foreign Policy during the Second World War: An 'Active' Neutrality* (Cambridge, 1989).

Desiatskov, S. G., 'Uitkholl i Miunkhenskaiia politika', *Novaia i noveishaia istoriia*, 3 (1979).

Douglas, R., *New Alliances, 1940–41* (London, 1982).

Douglas-Hamilton, J., *The Truth about Rudolf Hess* (London, 1993).

Erickson, J., *The Road to Stalingrad* (London, 1975).

Erickson, J., 'Threat Identification and Strategic Appraisal by the Soviet Union, 1930–41', in E. R. May (ed.), *Knowing One's Enemies* (Princeton, 1984).

Firsov, F. I., 'Arkhivy Kominterna i vneshniaia politika SSSR 1939–1941 gg.', *Novaia i noveishaia istoriia*, 6 (1992).

Fleischhauer, I., *Der Pakt: Hitler, Stalin und die Initiative der deutschen Diplomatie 1938–1939* (Berlin, 1990).

Fleischhauer, I., *Diplomatischer Widerstand gegen 'Unternehmen Barbarossa'* (Berlin, 1991).

Förster, J., 'Barbarossa Revisited: Strategy and Ideology in the East', *Jewish Social Studies*, 50/1–2 (1992).

Förster, J., 'Das Unternehmen "Barbarossa" als Eroberungs und Vernichtungskrieg', *DRuZW*.

Förster, J., 'Hitler Turns East – German War Policy in 1940 and 1941', in B. Wegner (ed.), *From Peace to War: Germany, Soviet Russia and the World, 1939–1941* (Oxford, 1997).

Fugate, B. I., *Operation Barbarossa: Strategy and Tactics on the Eastern Front, 1941* (Novato, Calif., 1984).

Gafencu, G., *Prelude to the Russian Campaign* (London, 1945).

Gareev, M. A., '1941-i god – nachalo voiny', *Muzhestvo*, 5 (1991).

Gareev, M. A., 'Eshche raz k voprosu: gotovil li Stalin preventivnyi udar in 1941', *Novaia i noveishaia istoriia*, 2 (1994).

Gerard, B. M., 'Mistakes in Force Structure and Strategy on the Eve of the Great Patriotic War', *Journal of Soviet Military Studies*, 4/3 (1991).

Gibbons, R., 'Opposition gegen Barbarossa im Herbst 1940: Eine Denkschrift aus der deutschen Botschaft in Moskau', *Vierteljahrshefte für Zeitgeschichte*, 23/3 (1975).

Gillessen, G., 'Der Krieg der Diktatoren: ein erstes Resümee der Debatte über Hitlers Angriff im Osten', *Frankfurter Allgemeine Zeitung*, 25 Feb. 1987.

Gladkov, T., and N. Zaitsev, *I ia emu ne mogu ne verit . . .* (Moscow, 1983).

Glantz, D., *Soviet Military Operational Art: In Pursuit of Deep Battle* (London, 1990).

Glantz, D., *The Soviet Conduct of Tactical Maneuver: Spearhead of the Offensive* (London, 1991).

Glantz, D., *The Military Strategy of the Soviet Union: A History* (London, 1993).

Glantz, D., *The Stumbling Colossus: The Red Army in June 1941* (1998).

Gor'kov, Iu. A., 'Gotovil li Stalin uprezhdaiushchii udar protiv Gitlera v 1941 g.', *Novaia i noveishaia istoriia*, 3 (1993).

Gorlov, S., and V. Voiushin, 'Warnings Came Not Only from the German Ambassador', *New Times*, 2 (1991).

Gorodetsky, G., *Stafford Cripps' Mission to Moscow* (Cambridge, 1984).

Gorodetsky, G., 'Was Stalin Planning to Attack Hitler in June 1941?', *Journal of the Royal United Services Institution*, 3 (1986).

Gorodetsky, G., '"Unternehmen Barbarossa": Eine Auseinandersetzung mit der Legende vom deutschen Präventivschlag', *Vierteljahrshefte für Zeitgeschichte*, 4 (1989).

Gorodetsky, G., 'The Impact of the Ribbentrop–Molotov Pact on the Course of Soviet Foreign Policy', *Cahiers du Monde Russe et Soviétique*, 31/1 (1990).

Gorodetsky, G. (ed.), *Soviet Foreign Policy, 1917–1991: A Retrospective* (London, 1994).

Gorodetsky, G., *Mif 'Ledokola': nakanune voiny* (Moscow, 1995).

Hanak, H., 'Sir Stafford Cripps as British Ambassador in Moscow, June 1941–January 1942', *English Historical Review*, 370 (1979) and 383 (1982).

Harrison, M., *Soviet Planning in Peace and War, 1938–1945* (Cambridge, 1985).

Haslam, J., *The Soviet Union and the Struggle for Collective Security, 1933–39* (London, 1984).

Haslam, J., 'Soviet Foreign Policy 1939–1941', *Soviet Union/Union Soviétique*, 1–3 (1991).

Haslam, J., *The Soviet Union and the Threat from the East, 1933–1941* (London, 1992).

Haslam, J., 'Stalin's Fears of a Separate Peace, 1942', *Intelligence and National Security*, 8/4 (1993).

Hauner, M., 'The Soviet Threat to Afghanistan and India, 1938–1940', *Modern Asian Studies*, 15/2 (1981).

Hidden, J., and T. Lane (eds), *The Baltic and the Outbreak of the Second World War* (Cambridge, 1992).

Higgins, T., *Hitler and Russia: The Third Reich in a Two-Front War, 1937–1943* (New York, 1966).

Hillgruber, A., *Germany and the Two World Wars* (Cambridge, 1981).

Hillgruber, A., 'Noch einnmal: Hitlers Wendung gegen die Sowjetunion 1940', *Geschichte in Wissenschaft und Unterricht*, 33 (1982).

Hinsley, F. H. *et al.*, *British Intelligence in the Second World War: Its Influence on Strategy and Operations*, 4 vols (London, 1979–90).

'Historikerstreit': Die Dokumentation der Kontroverse um die Einzigartigkeit der nationalsozialistischen Judenvernichtung (Munich, 1987).

Hitchens, M. G., *Germany, Russia and the Balkans: Prelude to the Nazi–Soviet Non-Aggression Pact* (New York, 1983).

Hoptner, J. B., *Yugoslavia in Crisis, 1934–1941* (New York, 1962).

Iakushevsky, A. S., 'Faktor vnezapnosti v napadenii Germanii na SSSR', *Istoriia SSSR*, 3 (1991).

Istoriia Velikoi Otechestvennoi voiny Sovetskogo Soiuza, 1941–1945 (Moscow, 1961).

Ivanitsky, G. M., 'Sovetsko-germanskie torgovo-ekonomicheskie otnosheniia v 1939–1941 gg.', *Novaia i noveishaia istoriia*, 5 (1989).

Jukic, I., *The Fall of Yugoslavia* (New York, 1974).

Kaslas, B. J., 'The Lithuanian Strip in Soviet–German Secret Diplomacy', *Journal of Baltic Studies*, 4 (1973).

Kennedy, P., *The Rise and Fall of the Great Powers* (London, 1988).

Khor'kov, A. G., 'Ukreplennye raiony na zapadnykh granitsakh SSSR', *Voenno-istoricheskii zhurnal*, 12 (1987).

Khor'kov, A. G., 'Nakanune groznykh sobytii', *Voenno-istoricheskii zhurnal*, 5 (1988).

Kipp, J. P., 'Military Theory: Barbarossa, Soviet Covering Forces and the Initial Period of War: Military History and Airland Battle', *Journal of Soviet Military Studies*, 1/2 (1988).

Kissinger, H., *Diplomacy* (London, 1995).

Kitchen, M., *British Policy towards the Soviet Union during the Second World War* (New York, 1986).

Koch, H. W., 'Hitler's Programme and the Genesis of Operation "Barbarossa"', *Historical Journal*, 26/4 (1983).

Kolasky, J., *Partners in Tyranny: The Nazi–Soviet Nonaggression Pact, August 23, 1939* (Toronto, 1990).

Koshkin, A. A., 'Predystoriia zakliucheniia pakta Molotova-Matsuoka (1941 g.)', *Voprosy istorii*, 6 (1993).

Krebs, G., 'Japan and the German–Soviet War, 1941', in B. Wegner (ed.), *From Peace to War: Germany, Soviet Russia and the World, 1939–1941* (Oxford, 1997).

Kuniholm, B. R., *The Origins of the Cold War in the Near East: Great Power Conflict and Diplomacy in Iran, Turkey, and Greece* (Princeton, 1994).

Laqueur, W., 'Disinformation', *New Republic* (1991).

Lavrova, T. V., *Chernomorskie prolivy* (Rostov, 1997).

Lawlor, S., *Churchill and the Politics of War* (Cambridge, 1994).

Leach, B. A., *German Strategy against Russia, 1939–1941* (Oxford, 1973).

Lensen, A., *The Strange Neutrality: Soviet–Japanese Relations during the Second World War, 1941–1945* (Tallahasse, Fla., 1972).

Leonhard, W., *Betrayal: The Hitler–Stalin Pact of 1939* (New York, 1989).

Lisann, M., 'Stalin the Appeaser: Before 22 June, 1941', *Survey*, 76 (1970).

Lukacs, J., *The Great Powers and Eastern Europe* (New York, 1953).

Macfie, A. L., 'The Turkish Straits in the Second World War, 1939–45', *Middle Eastern Studies*, 25/2 (1989).

Marzari, F., 'Prospects for an Italian-led Balkan Bloc of Neutrals', *Historical Journal*, 4 (1970).

Marzari, F., 'Western–Soviet Rivalry in Turkey, 1939', *Middle Eastern Studies*, 7 (1971).

Maser, W., *Der Wortbruch, Hitler, Stalin und der Zweite Weltkrieg* (Munich, 1994).

Medvedev, R., 'Diplomaticheskie i voennye proschety Stalina v 1939–1941 gg.', *Novaia i noveishaia istoriia*, 4 (1989).

Mel'tiukhov, M. I., 'Predystoriia Velikoi Otechestvennoi voiny v sovremennykh diskussiiakh', in G. A. Bordiugov (ed.), *Istoricheskie issledovaniia v Rossii: Tendentsii poslednikh let* (Moscow, 1996).

'Mezhdunarodnye otnosheniia i strany tsentral'noi i Iugo-Vostochnoi evropy nakanune napadeniia Germanii na SSSR (sentiabr' 1940–iiun' 1941 gg.)', *Sovetskoe slavianovedenie*, 4 (1991).

MID, *Sovetsko-iugoslavskie otnosheniia 1917–1941 gg. Sbornik dokumentov i materialov* (Moscow, 1992).

Miller, M. L., *Bulgaria during the Second World War* (Stanford, 1975).

Milstein, M., 'According to Intelligence Reports . . .', *New Times*, 26 (1990).

Miner, S. M., *Between Churchill and Stalin: The Soviet Union, Great Britain, and the Origins of the Grand Alliance* (Chapel Hill, NC, 1988).

Moravec, F., *Master of Spies* (London, 1975).

Murray, W., 'Barbarossa', *Quarterly Journal of Military History*, 4/3 (1992).

Narochnitski, A. L., 'Sovetsko-iugoslavskii dogovor 5 aprelia 1941 g. o druzhbe i nenapadenii (po arkhivnym materialam)', *Novaia i noveishaia istoriia*, 1 (1989).

Naveh, S., *In Pursuit of Military Excellence: The Evolution of Operational Theory* (London, 1997).

Nekrich, A. M., *Pariahs, Partners, Predators: German–Soviet Relations, 1922–1941* (New York, 1997).

Nevezhin, V. A., *Sindrom nastupatel'noi voiny* (Moscow, 1997).

Nevezhin, V. A., and G. A. Bordiugova (eds), *Gotovil li Stalin nastupatel'nuiu voinu protiv Gitlera?* (Moscow, 1995).

Orlov, A. S., 'SSSR – Germaniia: voenno-politicheskiie otnosheniia nakanune agressii', *Voenno-istoricheskii zhurnal*, 10 (1991).

Peshchersky, V. L., 'Gitler vodil za nos Stalina', *Novoe vremiia*, 47 (1994).

Peshchersky, V. L., ' "Bol'shaia igra", kotoruiu proigral Stalin', *Novoe vremiia*, 18 (1995).

Pietrow, B., 'Deutschland im Juni 1941 – ein Opfer sowjetischer Aggression?', *Geschichte und Gesellschaft*, 14 (1988).

Pons, S., *Stalin e la guerra inevitabile, 1936–1941* (Turin, 1995).

Popovich, N. B., *Jugoslovensko-sovjetski odnosi u drugom svetskom ratu (1941–1945)* (Belgrade, 1988).

Posen, B. R., 'Competing Images of the Soviet Union', *World Politics*, July 1987.

Post, W., *Unternehmen Barbarossa: Deutsche und sowjetische Angriffspläne 1940–1* (Berlin, 1996).

Prange, G. W., *Target Tokyo: The Story of the Sorge Spy Ring* (New York, 1984).

Prazmowska, A., *Britain, Poland and the Eastern Front, 1939* (Cambridge, 1987).

Presseisen, E., 'Prelude to "Barbarossa": Germany and the Balkans, 1940–1941', *Journal of Modern History*, 4 (1960).

Raack, R. C., 'Stalin Plans for World-War-II', *Journal of Contemporary History*, 26/2 (1991).

Raack, R. C., *Stalin's Drive to the West, 1938–1945: The Origins of the Cold War* (Stanford, 1995).

Read, A., and D. Fisher, *Operation Lucy* (London, 1980).

Read, A., and D. Fisher, *The Deadly Embrace: Hitler, Stalin and the Nazi–Soviet Pact, 1939–1941* (London, 1988).

Reese, R., 'The Impact of the Great Purge on the Red Army', *The Soviet and Post-Soviet Review*, 19/1–3 (1992).

Reshetnikova, O. N., *Mezhdunarodnye otnosheniia i strany Tsentral'noi i Iugo-Vostochnoi Evropy v period fashistskoi agressii na Balkanakh i podgotovki napadeniia na SSSR* (Moscow, 1992).

Richardson, C., 'French Plans for Allied Attacks on the Caucasus Oil Fields January–April 1940', *French Historical Studies*, 8/1 (1973).

Roberts, C. A., 'Planning for War: The Red Army and the Catastrophe of 1941', *Europe-Asia Studies*, 47/8 (1995).

Roberts, G., *The Unholy Alliance: Stalin's Pact with Hitler* (London, 1989).

Roberts, G., 'Military Disaster as a Function of Rational Political Calculation: Stalin and 22 June 1941', *Diplomacy and Statecraft*, 4/2 (1993).

Roberts, G., *The Soviet Union and the Origins of the Second World War: Russo-German Relations and the Road to War, 1933–1941* (London, 1995).

Robertson, E. M., 'Hitler Turns from the West to Russia, May–December 1940', in R. Boys and E. M. Robertson (eds), *Paths to War: New Essays on the Origins of the Second World War* (New York, 1989).

Rose, N., *Churchill: An Unruly Life* (London, 1994).

Rossi, A., *The Russo-German Alliance, August, 1939–June 1941* (London, 1959).

Rotundo, L., 'War Plans and the 1941 Kremlin War Games', *Journal of Strategic Studies*, 10/1 (1987).

Rotundo, L., 'Stalin and the Outbreak of War in 1941', *Journal of Contemporary History*, 24/2 (1989).

Rozanov, G. L., *Stalin Gitler: Dokumental'nyi ocherk Sovetsko-germanskikh diplomaticheskikh otnoshenii, 1939–1941 gg.* (Moscow, 1991).

Rubin, B., *Istanbul Intrigues* (New York, 1989).

Savushkin, R. A., *Razvitie Sovetskikh vooruzhennykh sil i voennogo iskusstva v mezhvoenny period (1921–1941)* (Moscow, 1989).

Savushkin, R. A., 'Military Strategy: In the Tracks of a Tragedy. On the 50th Anniversary of the Start of the Great Patriotic War', *Journal of Soviet Military Studies*, 2 (1991).

Schmidt, P. O., *Statist auf diplomatischer Bühne 1923–1945: Erlebnisse des Chef dolmetschers im Auswärtigen Amt mit den Staatsmännern Euopas* (Bonn, 1949).

Schmidt, R. F., 'Der Hess-Flug und das Kabinett Churchill. Hitlers Stellvertreter im Kalkül der britischen Kriegsdiplomatie Mai–Juni 1941', *Vierteljahrshefte für Zeitgeschichte*, 42/1 (1994).

Schneider, J., *The Structure of Strategic Revolution: Total War and the Roots of the Soviet Warfare State* (Novato, Calif., 1994).

Schwartzchild, L., 'Neozhidanyi zakhvat Gessa v lovushku, podstroenuiu angliiskoi "Sikret servis"', *Voenno-istoricheskii zhurnal*, 5 (1991).

Schwendemann, H., 'German–Soviet Economic Relations at the Time of the Hitler–Stalin Pact 1939–1941', *Cahiers du Monde Russe*, 1995.

Semiriaga, M. I., 'Sovetskii Soiuz i predvoennyi politicheskii krizis', *Voprosy istorii*, 9 (1990), pp. 49–64.

Semiriaga, M. I., *Tainy stalinskoi diplomatii, 1939–1941* (Moscow, 1992).

Sevostianov, P., 'Nakanune velikoi bitvy', *Novaia i noveishaia istoriia*, 4 (1981), pp. 99–128.

Sevostianov, P., *Before the Nazi Invasion* (Moscow, 1984).

Shukman, H. (ed.), *Stalin's Generals* (London, 1993).

Simonov, K. M., 'Zametki k biografii G. K. Zhukova', *Voenno-istoricheskii zhurnal*, 10 (1987).

Sipols, V. Ia., *Diplomatic Battles before World War II* (Moscow, 1982).

Sipols, V. Ia., 'Missiia Krippsa v 1940 g. beseda so stalinym', *Novaia i noveishaia istoriia*, 5 (1992).

Sipols, V. Ia., 'Eshche raz o diplomaticheskoi dueli v Berline v noiabre 1940g.', *Novaia i noveishaia istoriia*, 3 (1996).

Sipols, V. Ia, 'Torgovo-ekonomicheskie otnosheniia mezhdu SSSR i Germaniei v 1939–1941 gg. v svete novykh arkhivnykh dokumentov', *Novaia i noveishaia istoriia*, 1 (1997).

Sirkov, D., *V'nshnata politika na B'lgariia, 1938–1941* (Sofia, 1979).

Skvirski, L. S., 'V predvoennye gody', *Voprosy istorii*, 9 (1989).

Slavinsky, B. N., *Pakt o neitralitete mezhdu SSSR i Iaponiei: diplomaticheskaia istoriia, 1941–1945* (Moscow, 1995).

Sonnleithner, F. von, *Als Diplomat im 'Führerhauptquartier': Aus dem Nachlass* (Munich, 1989).

Stafford, D. A. T., 'SOE and British Involvement in the Belgrade Coup d'Etat of March 1941', *Slavic Review*, 36/3 (1977).

Stefanidis, X., 'Greece, Bulgaria and the Approaching Tragedy, 1938–1941', *Balkan Studies*, 2 (1991).

Stolfi, R. H. S., 'Barbarossa: German Grand Deception and the Achievement of Strategic and Tactical Surprise against the Soviet Union, 1940–1941', in D. C. Daniel and K. L. Herbig (eds), *Strategic Military Deception* (1981).

Suny, R., 'Making Sense of Stalin – Some Recent and Not-So-Recent Biographies', *Russian History/Histoire Russe*, 16/2–4 (1989).

Suvorov, V., *Icebreaker: Who Started the Second World War* (London, 1990).

Tarleton, R. E., 'What Really Happened to the Stalin Line?', *Journal of Soviet Military Studies*, 2 (1992), pp. 187–219.

Thielenhaus, M., *Zwischen Anpassung und Widerstand. Deutsche Diplomaten 1938–1941: Die politischen Aktivitäten der Beamtengruppe um Ernst von Weizsäcker im Auswärtigen Amt* (Paderborn, 1984).

Togo, S., *Vospominanuiia Iaponskogo diplomata* (Moscow, 1996).

Topitsch, E., *Stalin's War: A Radical New Theory of the Origins of the Second World War* (New York, 1987).

Toscano, M., *Designs in Diplomacy* (London, 1970).

Trepper, L., *The Great Game* (London, 1977).

Tsukertort, I., 'Germanskii militarism i legenda o "preventivnoi voine" gitlerovskoi Germanii protiv SSSR', *Voenno-istoricheskii zhurnal*, 5 (1991).

Tucker, R., *Stalin in Power: The Revolution from Above, 1928–1941* (New York, 1990).

Tumarkin, N., *The Living and the Dead: The Rise and Fall of the Cult of World War II in Russia* (New York, 1994).

Uldricks, T., 'Russia and Europe: Diplomacy, Revolution, and Economic Development in the 1920s', *International History Review*, 1 (1979).

Uldricks, T., 'Evolving Soviet Views of the Nazi–Soviet Pact', in R. Frucht (ed.), *Labyrinth of Nationalism: Complexities of Diplomacy* (Columbus, Ohio, 1992).

Uldricks, T., 'Soviet Security Policy in the 1930s', in G. Gorodetsky (ed.), *Soviet Foreign Policy, 1917–1991: A Retrospective* (London, 1994).

Vishlev, O. V., 'Pochemu zhe medlil I. V. Stalin v 1941 gg. (iz Germanskikh arkhivov)', *Novaia i noveishaia istoriia*, 1–2 (1992).

Vishlev, O. V., 'Byla li v SSSR oppozitsiia "germanskoi politike" Stalina nakanune 22 iiunia 1941 g.', *Novaia i noveishaia istoriia*, 4–5 (1994).

Volkogonov, D., '22 iunia 1941 goda', *Znamia*, 6 (1991).

Volkogonov, D., *Stalin: Triumph and Tragedy* (London, 1992).

Volkov, V. K., 'Sovetsko-iugoslavskie otnosheniia v nachal'nyi period vtoroi mirovoi voiny v kontekste mirovykh sobytii (1939–1941 gg.)', *Sovetskoe slavianovedenie*, 6 (1990).

Vorontsov, M., 'Pered voinoi: zapiski byvshego voennogo diplomata', *Morskoi sbornik*, 6 (1985).

Waddington, G. T., 'Ribbentrop and the Soviet Union 1937–1941', in J. Erickson and D. Dilks (eds), *Barbarossa: The Axis and the Allies* (Edinburgh, 1994).

Wark, W. K., 'British Intelligence and Operation Barbarossa, 1941: The Failure of Foes', in H. B. Peake and S. Halpern (eds), *The Name of Intelligence: Essays in Honor of Walter Pforzheimer* (Washington, DC, 1994).

Watt, D. C., *How War Came: The Immediate Origins of the Second World War, 1938–1939* (London, 1989).

Weber, F. G., *Evasive Neutral: Germany, Britain and the Quest for a Turkish Alliance in the Second World War* (Columbia, Montana, 1979).

Wegner, B. (ed.), *From Peace to War: Germany, Soviet Russia and the World, 1939–1941* (Oxford, 1997).

Weinberg, G. L., *Germany and the Soviet Union, 1939–1941* (Leiden, 1951).

Weinberg, G. L., *The Foreign Policy of Hitler's Germany*, 2 vols (Chicago, 1980).

Weinberg, G. L., *A World at Arms: A Global History of World War II* (Cambridge, 1994).

Whaley, B., *Codeword Barbarossa* (Cambridge, Mass., 1973).

Zhukov, G. K., 'Iz neopublikovannykh vospominanii', *Kommunist*, 9 (1988).

Zhukov, G. K., *Vospominaniia i razmyshleniia*, 3 vols (Moscow, 1995).

Ziemke, E., 'Stalin as a Strategist, 1940–1941', *Military Affairs*, 47/4 (1983), pp. 174–80.

Ziuzin, E. I. (ed.), 'Gotovil li SSSR preventivnyi udar?', *Voenno-istoricheskii zhurnal*, 1 (1992).

Zverev, B. I., and G. A. Kumanev, 'O voenno-ekonomicheskoi gotovnosti SSSR k otrazheniiu fashistskoi agressii', *Voprosy istorii KPSS*, 9 (1991).

Index

DATE DUE
